KU-534-099

FARMHOUSE COOKERY

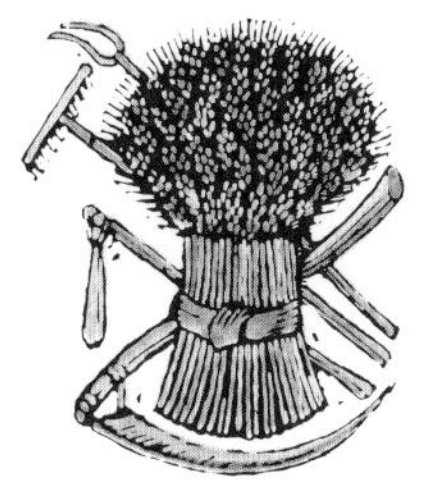

FARMHOUSE COOKERY

Recipes from the Country Kitchen

PUBLISHED BY THE READER'S DIGEST ASSOCIATION LIMITED LONDON NEW YORK MONTREAL SYDNEY CAPE TOWN

Eggs

The Government has warned that in some outbreaks of salmonella food poisoning, eggs have been the source of infection. Most infections have caused only a mild stomach upset, but the effects can be more serious in the very young or old, in those already weakened by poor health, and among pregnant women. They should eat only eggs cooked until hard. To other people there is very little risk in cooked eggs; but everyone should avoid raw egg and recipes containing it. Commercial products made with pasteurised egg have not been implicated.

FARMHOUSE COOKERY
Edited and designed by The Reader's Digest Association Limited, London

Printed in Great Britain

ISBN 0 276 42086 1

ACKNOWLEDGMENTS

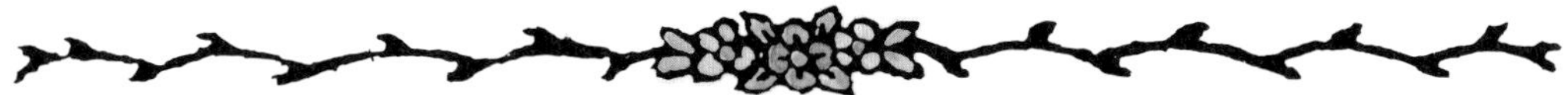

EDITOR Heather Maisner ART EDITOR Judy White

CONTRIBUTORS AND ADVISERS

Elisabeth Ayrton
Philippa Back
Michael Bateman
Brian Binns
Trudy Blacker
Lizzie Boyd
Dorothy Brown
Caroline Conran
Sheena Davis
Theodora Fitzgibbon
Jane Grigson
Molly Harrison
Moira Hodgson
Babs Honey
Margaret Leach
Margaret Mackenzie
Moya Maynard
Mary Norwak
Olive Odell
Jean Robertson
Simone Sekers
Marika Hanbury Tenison
Judy Urquhart
C. Anne Wilson

PHOTOGRAPHERS

Philip Dowell
Christine Hanscomb
Tessa Traeger

HOME ECONOMISTS FOR PHOTOGRAPHY

Alex Dufort
Caroline Ellwood
Dinah Morrison

STYLISTS

Antonia Gaunt
Carolyn Russell

ILLUSTRATORS

Peter Bailey
Frederick Bayliss
Richard Bonson
Leonora Box
Barbara Brown
Eric Fraser
Robin Jacques
Jeffery Matthews
Frederick Middlehurst

THOMAS BEWICK
(1753 – 1828)
The black and white illustrations to Farmhouse Recipes are reproductions of engravings by Thomas Bewick. These have been taken from the Memorial Edition of *Thomas Bewick's Works* (1855 – 7) and Thomas Hugo's *Bewick's Woodcuts* (1870).

The publishers are grateful for the help given by the following people and organisations:

Research Department, Allied Bakeries
Vanessa Binns
P. S. Birrel, Property Hire
The British Library
The British Sugar Bureau
Maryanne Charles
Eileen Crabtree, The Women's Institute, Upper Nidderdale, North Yorkshire
Gilly Cubitt
Ian Dewhirst, Keighley Area Library, Bradford
English Tourist Board
Cathy Gallop
Valerie Hall
Irish Embassy
Jersey State Tourism
Christine Lambert, French Embassy, London
Diana Lewis
Judy Lister
Ivan Massey, Maltby and Coates, Grimsby
Gil Niblock, Flour Advisory Bureau
Northern Ireland Tourist Board
Ruth Orme
Kathy Roche
Laura Rowe, Radio Merseyside
Research Department of Sunblest, Aberdeen
S. Minwel Tibbott, Welsh Folk Museum
Ulster Folk and Transport Museum
Wales Tourist Board
Rosamund Wallinger
Lynne White

The publishers acknowledge their indebtedness to the following books and journals, consulted for reference or as sources of illustrations:

The Art of Cookery Made Plain and Easy by Hannah Glasse (1747)
The Book of Household Management by Mrs Isabella Beeton (1861)
Britain in the Roman Empire by Joan Liversidge (Routledge & Kegan Paul 1968)
Cottage Economy by William Cobbett (1821)
The Country Housewife by Richard Bradley (1753)
The Diary of a Country Parson by James Woodford (Oxford University Press 1963)
Elizabethan England by A. H. Dodd (B. T. Batsford 1961)
Every One a Witness by A. F. Scott (White Lion Publishers 1975)
The Experienced English Housekeeper by Elizabeth Raffald (1769)
Food and Drink in Britain by C. Anne Wilson (Constable 1973)
Food in England by Dorothy Hartley (Macdonald & Jane's 1975)
From Domesday Book to Magna Carta by A. L. Poole (Oxford University Press 1955)
Glimpses of Welsh Life & Character by Marie Trevelyan (John Gogg 1893)
Good Things in England by Florence White (Jonathan Cape 1932)
Lark Rise to Candleford by Flora Thomson (Oxford University Press 1939)
Life in Norman England by O. G. Tomkeieff (B. T. Batsford 1966)
Medieval and Tudor Britain by A. J. Patrick (Penguin 1967)
Modern Cookery in all its Branches: Reduced to an Easy Practice by Eliza Acton (1845)
My Grandmother's Cookery Book by Suzanne Woolley (Shearwater Press 1975)—recipe for Baked Tanrogans with Cheese Sauce
Old English Household Life by Gertrude Jekyll (Batsford 1975)
Victorian England by W. J. Reader (B. T. Batsford 1973)

The publishers acknowledge their indebtedness to the following for the use of photographs or material used in photographic compositions:

Page 11 (top) By permission of the Board of British Library, Ms. Roy 2 B VII. (bottom right) By permission of the British Library, Add. Ms. 42130 f.166v
Page 13 (centre right) Mansell Collection
Page 18 Mary Evans Picture Library
Page 36 Charter Trustees, Penzance; Dowrick Design & Print, St Ives
Page 50 Mansell Collection
Page 116 Mansell Collection
Page 166 Bodleian Library, Oxford
Page 260 Mary Evans Picture Library
Page 302 Victoria and Albert Museum, Crown Copyright
Page 318 Mary Evans Picture Library
Pages 370–1 Victoria and Albert Museum, Crown Copyright
Page 243 Tessa Traeger

Most of the illustrations appearing in the pages of Notes, Advice and Directions are from Mary Evans Picture Library.

CONT

ENTS

PART THE FIRST~THE

HERE is the place of much Warmth and Comfort, for long the Heart of the Home; where Plain but Wholesome dishes of Homegrown produce and Dairy Foods are Cooked with Diligence by the Housewife; where Nourishing meals make a splendid Welcome for her Husband and his Helpers at the end of a long and hard day's Labouring

Written by Molly Harrison

FOR the Noble Lord in Medieval days, the huge hall and Kitchen were Twin symbols of his great wealth and Munificence.

The poor, of whom there were many thousands, Cooked over fires in the open air, or in the Small huts where they lived.

COUNTRY KITCHEN

BEFORE the Reign of Our Sovereign Queen, Elizabeth I, the large Kitchens of Country Houses were run by a Male Steward.

During the Queen's Reign, the Mistress of the Household became responsible for Provisions and Good Cooking.

Kitchens had big hearths, baking ovens, and all kinds of Ingenious Devices to make Cooking easier, such as mechanically turned Spits for Roasting and Iron Cranes for holding Cauldrons over the fire.

THE Country Kitchen continued to be Improved through the Centuries, with Divers Inventions and Devices; by the Reign of Our Sovereign Queen, Victoria, it was on the way to being the Kitchen we know today.

The MEDIEVAL PEASANT'S KITCHEN

THE PRICE OF POVERTY During the winter months the one-roomed hut was where the peasant and

FOR THE MEDIEVAL PEASANT in his sparsely furnished, one-roomed timber-framed hut—walled with mud and wattle—a kitchen was an unthinkable luxury.

In fine weather, cooking was done outside in the open air; throughout the winter a fire was used in the centre of the hut. The fire was seldom allowed to go out, and smoke escaped through a hole in the thatched roof.

Cooking implements were few and simple. The major item was a large three-legged cast-iron pot that was used for boiling stews, soups and water. The pot stood beside the fire or was suspended above it, either from a roof beam on a rope made of green hazel sticks, or on a metal tripod with an iron hook and an adjustable hanger.

In most cases a simple spit was used to roast the occasional hare or a rabbit, with a pan beneath to catch dripping fat. After the Norman game laws had been repealed in 1217, villagers could hunt hares, coursing them with dogs, without running the risk of being punished as poachers. Later, there were sufficient rabbits that could be caught, too.

The basic diet of the peasants was 'white meats'—milk products such as cheese, whey, butter, buttermilk and eggs. In addition they had bread, peas, beans, herbs for pottage, plus fruits such as apples, cherries and wild berries. A small amount of bacon was added—now and then throughout the year—to stews and pottages.

Most peasant families kept only one or two pigs at a time. When one was killed, the offal was eaten forthwith or made into sausages, while the rest was salted for ham or bacon.

The curing of sausages and bacon was important. At pig-killing time, the carcase was salted and hung up to smoke. The blood and fat were pounded together—sometimes with a little of the meat from the underside of the animal—the mixture flavoured with herbs and spices, and packed into its own gut, well-cleaned and cut into convenient lengths. Smoking helped the sausages to keep longer, and gave both sausages and bacon an agreeable flavour.

his family slept, cooked and ate their meals.

FATTENING THE SWINE During the 14th and 15th centuries tenant farmers had the legal right of pannage—permission to drive their pigs on to the lord of the manor's land to feed on acorns and beech nuts. Villeins gave service on the land or paid for the privilege.

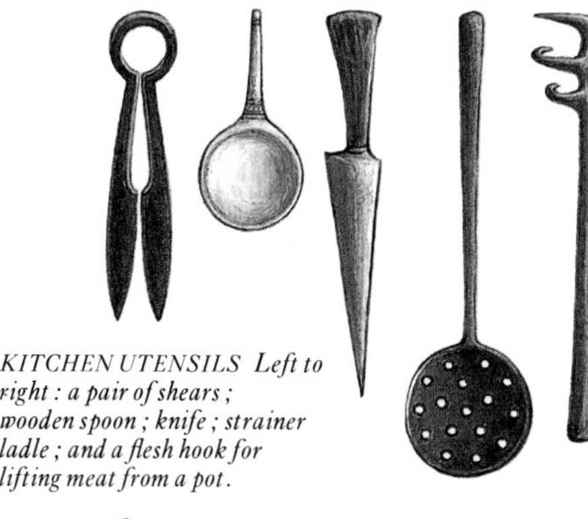

KITCHEN UTENSILS Left to right: a pair of shears; wooden spoon; knife; strainer ladle; and a flesh hook for lifting meat from a pot.

COOKING VESSELS In addition to a cooking pot, a peasant family sometimes had a metal skillet (left) and a boiler. Either could stand in the ashes of a fire.

BY HOOK OR BY CROOK Some peasants had the right to hook dead timber from trees on their employers' land for firewood. A shepherd's crook was often used—hence the expression 'by hook or by crook'.

PRECIOUS POULTRY Even the humblest families possessed a hen or two in medieval Britain. The woman depicted (c. 1340) has the hen tethered to a stick.

Not until the 16th century, when the hearth was moved to an outer wall, did homes have an oven. Before then, peasants and labourers baked their bread by the central fire. The dough was covered with an inverted clay pot or iron cauldron, over which were heaped hot ashes or peat.

Under feudal arrangements, the peasant was encouraged, and at some periods even forced, to take his dough to be baked at the manorial oven, giving up a proportion of his dough in exchange for the privilege. The dough thus donated went into loaves to feed the lord of the manor's personal servants and retainers.

In remote parts of the country, including the Highlands and islands of Scotland, peasants and labourers prepared their own corn with a quern. This was a small handmill, consisting of two stone discs—one fixed and one rotating above it—between which the corn was ground.

In lowland Britain, peasants took their corn to be ground at local watermills and, from the 13th century onwards, windmills. The miller usually rented the mill from the lord of the manor and kept a portion of the corn he ground as his fee.

Salt was an essential commodity that was usually kept in a box near the fire. Salt was collected from the coastline, where it evaporated, and used as a flavouring, as well as a preservative for any meat kept during the winter months. Inadequately salted meat was probably one of the contributory causes for some of the deficiency diseases then prevalent.

The ELIZABETHAN COUNTRY-HOUSE KITCHEN

FROM THE MIDDLE of the 16th century onwards a new and prosperous middle class began to emerge, composed of successful traders, merchants, craftsmen, yeoman farmers and professional men such as doctors and lawyers.

Many of them moved to the country, building small but comfortable houses and adopting the life-style of the squire.

The kitchen was built near to the staff's quarters, with separate rooms for the family and guests to dine in. As one of the largest rooms in the house, the kitchen became the hub of the home, for a country household during this period was practically self-supporting. There were candles and rush-lights to be made, hams to smoke or pickle, sides of bacon to cure, fruits to dry or conserve, and vegetables to salt or preserve.

Herbs were grown and dried for flavouring food, for medicinal purposes and for pomanders and scent bags.

The fire was still at floor level, as in peasants' homes, but was now built into an outer wall, with a brick-built chimney above the opening. The spit was supported on cast-iron fire dogs—so called because some of the early designs resembled animals. One type of fire dog was shaped with cups at the top, and these 'cup dogs' were used to hold candles or keep bowls of soup hot.

When meat was roasted on a spit the fat dripped into a long narrow trough standing underneath, in front of the fire. This 'dripping' was then run into a heavy three-legged greasepan and later used for making rush-lights and candles.

When spits were not in use, they were kept on a wooden rack, fixed to the wall above the fireplace opening.

To vary the heat needed in cooking it was necessary to raise or lower the pots. This was done by means of a chimney bar—an iron rod spanning the fireplace opening—with pots hung from it on adjustable metal ratchets.

In some kitchens there was also a small brick-built oven in the wall near the fire, used for baking. Burning wood from the fire was put in the oven and the iron door then closed. By the time the wood had burned, the oven was hot enough for baking. The ashes were then raked out and the bread, cakes and pies were put in with a flat, long-handled shovel. When the air inside the oven had cooled, the baking was complete.

In most country-house kitchens there were a great many cooking pots and pans, chiefly made of bronze; a selection of pewter plates and saucers—which were shallow dishes used for sauces and condiments; and usually a pair of pewter candlesticks. A pestle and mortar was an essential, used for grinding spices.

A salt box was kept in the kitchen, near the fireplace in order to keep the contents dry.

ELIZABETHAN PROSPERITY During the 16th and 17th centuries, the prosperous middle classes considered a spacious kitchen to be an essential in their country houses. There was a large household to cater for—including servants—in addition to entertaining guests.

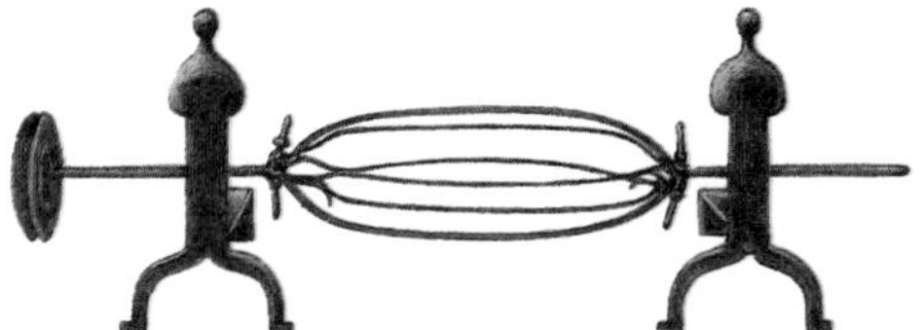

'DONE TO A TURN' The expression arose from the days when a spit was still one of the most useful ways of cooking at a floor-level hearth. The skewered roast was turned by a child or a servant — known as a turnspit — or by a mechanical system of ratchets and weights. Fat dripped into a tray.

ELIZABETHAN MARKET DAY Women selling fresh fish to a buyer, while a water carrier replenishes supplies at the pump. Many areas of the country depended upon these men for fresh water supplies.

CHIMNEY CRANE A crane was a cast-iron bracket — fixed to the wall beside the fireplace — that could be swung out to support a pot. Designs were often highly ornamental.

KITCHEN GADGETS As cooking became more sophisticated, so more kitchen gadgets were needed. The hour-glass (left) and nutmeg grater proved invaluable to Elizabethan cooks.

The VICTORIAN RURAL KITCHEN

AT THE TURN OF the 19th century George Bodley, a Devon ironfounder, patented the first cast-iron closed-top cooking range. It not only became the prototype of cooking ranges throughout the rest of the century, but was also a landmark in the development of the kitchen. The life of the open hearth was coming to an end.

The range had a raised open fire, flanked by an oven and a small water tank—all housed beneath a flat cast-iron top or hot plate. It was coal-burning, and a metal flue above the range took fumes and smoke to the chimney.

By the middle of the 19th century the 'kitchener', or closed-in range, had been developed and was being installed in the homes of those who were reasonably prosperous. Although these ranges led to more sophisticated methods of cooking, they burned fuel extravagantly and made a great deal of soot and smoke. They also had to be polished each day with black lead—or graphite powder.

By this time the Industrial Revolution had spawned the railways, enabling manufactured goods, which included many new domestic appliances, to be distributed to some of the principal towns.

But it was years before the small branch lines linking town and country were laid; and until then the rural housewife was in effect cut off by the high cost of transport from developments in the towns. She grew what food she could and made special journeys, perhaps once every three months, to buy supplies in the nearest market town.

The revolution in gas as a fuel—used first for lighting in town houses and later for cooking—occurred in the 1860s and 1870s, overtaken by electricity in the 1880s. But many country households—until well after the turn of the century—continued to use paraffin oil lamps and candles for artificial lighting.

The country kitchen often had a walk-in larder—with stone-slab shelving, where foodstuffs could be kept cool—as well as a scullery where washing up was done after meals. Sometimes the scullery was also used for washing clothes; but in the larger country house there would be a separate laundry room, as well as a pantry and wine cellar.

During the Victorian period, cast-iron cooking pots and pans became available, with lightweight handles and lids made of tin-plate. Although this ironware was no less heavy than the brass and copper utensils of the preceding century, it was easier to keep clean since it did not need polishing.

By the end of the 19th century, there was an abundance of gadgets and appliances being manufactured—labour-saving devices of many kinds that helped to make it easier to prepare and cook meals. A well-stocked kitchen had a battery of equipment, that ranged from jelly moulds and colanders to coffee-grinders, percolators, knife-polishers, mincers and can-openers.

In the homes of the better off, members of the family could summon staff from most parts of the house by means of a mechanical alarm system, linked to an indicator board on the wall above the kitchen door.

WEIGHTS AND SCALES Mrs Beeton considered 'a good set of weights and scales is absolutely necessary to every cook'. The set illustrated (right) was manufactured during the 1880s.

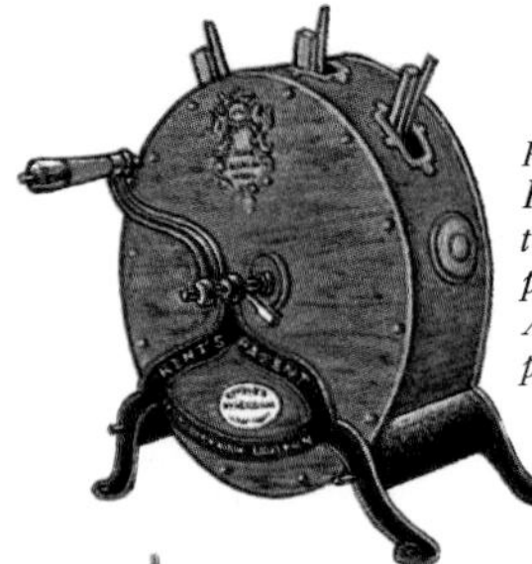

ROTARY KNIFE POLISHER Knife blades were inserted in the polisher with abrasive powder poured in at the top. As the handle was turned, felt pads inside polished the blades.

DUTCH OVEN A device used during the 18th and 19th centuries for roasting meat. The oven was set before an open fire and the joint hung on a hook that was turned by a clockwork mechanism until the meat was cooked. The surface helped to reflect heat.

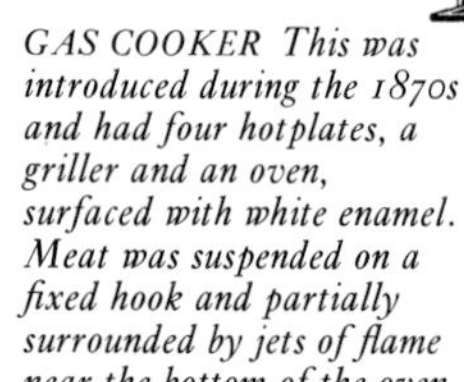

GAS COOKER This was introduced during the 1870s and had four hotplates, a griller and an oven, surfaced with white enamel. Meat was suspended on a fixed hook and partially surrounded by jets of flame near the bottom of the oven.

VICTORIAN COMFORT AND CONVENIENCE A typical country-house kitchen of the 1890s, built by those who settled in the country and were making their living from the land. The large cast-iron range, with its open fire flanked by ovens, and cast-iron cooking pots and pans were the most useful culinary inventions of the century.

PART THE SECOND ~

THE RECIPES are presented in Fourteen Sections, each including a selection of Recipes from Other Lands. Every section concludes with Notes, Advice and Directions, written by the Cookery Adviser Olive Odell.

With each recipe there is an Account of its origins, prepared by the Reader's Digest team of Researchers and Writers and verified by the Historian C. Anne Wilson.

The majority of Recipes in each Section have been Assembled by a Main contributor, as listed below.

FARMHOUSE RECIPES

METRIC MEASUREMENTS

Measurements are given in imperial units with metric units in brackets. Precise conversions are impracticable. To avoid error never mix the two; use either imperial or metric measurements for each recipe.

Of

WINTER AND SUMMER SOUPS AND BROTHS

CONTAINING

NUMEROUS *Useful* FAMILY RECIPES

for CLEAR & CREAMY SOUPS, MEAT & VEGETABLE BROTHS

& all other NOURISHING DELIGHTES

PAGES 20–30

AND

A SELECTION of RECIPES from OTHER LANDS

PAGES 31–32

AND WITH

NOTES AND ADVICE

on all kinds of Preparing, Simmering, Thickening and Garnishing of Stocks and Soups to Perfection

PAGES 33–35

HAIRST BREE
Scotland

A SCOTTISH FARMWORKER returning home in the evening tired from the harvest fields would be restored by a hearty bowl of Hairst Bree (Harvest Broth). Hotch Potch is another name for this substantial broth, almost a meal in itself, which needs only newly baked bread and farmhouse cheese to complete a satisfying supper.

At one time, if the year was a bad one for vegetables, the farmer's wife would use nettle tops, herbs and wild roots instead of her own produce.

When you make the soup, ask the butcher to separate the meat into cutlets for you.

PREPARATION TIME: 30 MINUTES
COOKING TIME: $2\frac{1}{4}$ HOURS

INGREDIENTS FOR FOUR TO SIX

2 lb. (900 g.) middle neck of lamb, separated into cutlets
4 pints (2·3 litres) water or stock (see pp. 33–34)
Salt
Freshly ground black pepper
Bouquet garni
6 spring onions, trimmed and finely chopped
2 carrots, peeled and finely diced
2 small turnips, peeled and finely diced
6 oz. (175 g.) shelled young broad beans
8 oz. (225 g.) shelled fresh peas or frozen peas
1 small cauliflower, divided into sprigs
1 lettuce, washed, dried and cut in fine shreds
$\frac{1}{4}$ teaspoon sugar
2 teaspoons finely chopped mint
2 tablespoons finely chopped parsley

Hairst Bree—a substantial lamb and vegetable soup flavoured with fresh mint.

Trim excess fat from the lamb, and place the meat in a large, heavy-based saucepan. Add the water or stock and season with salt and pepper. Add the bouquet garni and bring slowly to the boil, skimming off any white scum that rises to the surface. Cover tightly and simmer gently for about 1 hour, or until the flesh is beginning to come away from the bones. Lift out the meat with a slotted spoon and strip it from the bones. Discard the bones and chop the meat finely.

Skim off any fat from the stock. Return the meat to the pan and add the onions, carrots, turnips, beans and half the fresh peas. Cover and simmer for 45 minutes and then add the cauliflower, lettuce, remaining fresh peas, sugar and mint. Continue to simmer for a further 20–30 minutes until the vegetables added last are just tender but not broken. If using frozen peas instead of fresh ones, add them 5 minutes before the end.

Discard the bouquet garni, check the seasoning, and serve the broth very hot garnished with parsley.

MUSSEL BROSE
Scotland

THE SCOTTISH WORD brose was used for a thick broth or pottage. Scotland's most common thickener was oatmeal, whether in soup, porridge or a mixture of whisky and cream, and it is this staple of the Scottish kitchen that gives the distinctive character to the traditional recipe for Mussel Brose.

Scotland has famous mussel beds, indeed those at the mouth of the Esk gave the nearby town of Musselburgh its name. The mussels and oatmeal are combined here to make a subtly flavoured broth with plenty of substance.

If you like, you can plump up the mussels and help to clean them by covering them with cold salted water, adding two handfuls of porridge oats and leaving them to stand in a cool place overnight.

PREPARATION TIME: ABOUT $1\frac{1}{4}$ HOURS
COOKING TIME: 30 MINUTES
PRE-HEAT THE OVEN TO 200°C (400°F)—GAS MARK 6 OR THE GRILL TO MEDIUM

INGREDIENTS FOR FOUR

4 pints (2·3 litres) mussels, washed and scraped

$\frac{1}{2}$ pint (275/300 ml.) water
$2\frac{1}{2}$ level tablespoons oatmeal
$\frac{1}{2}$ oz. (15 g.) butter
2 shallots, peeled and finely chopped
1 pint (575/600 ml.) milk
Salt and white pepper
2 tablespoons finely chopped parsley

Discard any mussels that are not tightly shut, or that do not shut when tapped. Put the sound mussels in a large, heavy-based saucepan. Add the water, cover the pan tightly and put it over a high heat for 6 minutes, shaking occasionally. By then the shells will be open. Strain off and reserve the juices from the pan, and leave the mussels until cool enough to handle. Meanwhile, bake the oatmeal on a baking sheet in the pre-heated oven until it is golden-brown. If it is more convenient, spread it on kitchen foil and toast it gently under a medium grill, taking great care not to let it burn.

Take the mussels from the shells, and pull out the wiry black strips known as beards. Heat the butter in a clean pan and cook the shallots in it over a low heat, stirring frequently to prevent sticking. When the shallots are soft and transparent and have absorbed all the butter, add the mussels and the milk and heat through without boiling.

Put the reserved mussel juice into a small pan, bring to the boil and stir in the browned oatmeal. Mix well and add to the soup off the heat; the soup must not boil or it will curdle. Season to taste with salt and white pepper, sprinkle on the parsley and serve piping hot.

If you like, you can enrich the soup by replacing $\frac{1}{2}$ pint (275/300 ml.) of the milk with the same quantity of single cream. You can vary the flavour by substituting dry white wine for half the water.

London Particular, a warming winter pea soup, owes its name to Dickens.

London Particular
London

The dense, greeny-brown vapour known as London's 'pea soup' fog was a winter hazard until as recently as the 1960s. In *Bleak House* (1852–3) Charles Dickens described it as a 'London Particular' and the two terms became interchangeable for both the fog and the soup.

The soup was done an injustice: the acrid taste and clammy chill of fog are the very opposite of the soup's warming smoothness.

This dish of dried peas and cured pork has existed since at least the Middle Ages, and was served at chop houses and from street barrows in the 19th century. Different versions of the soup exist in many parts of the British Isles. For example, Ireland adds a pig's trotter and calls it Crubeen Pea Soup. On farms throughout the country, wherever pigs are bred and salted, pea soup with bacon or ham appears on the table.

When preparing the soup, remember to prepare your stock and put the peas to soak the evening before.

Soaking Time: overnight
Preparation Time: 15 minutes
Cooking Time: $2\frac{1}{4}$ hours

Ingredients for Six

3 rashers streaky bacon with rinds removed, diced
1 large onion, peeled and chopped
2 carrots, peeled and chopped
1 lb. (450 g.) dried peas, soaked overnight in cold water to cover
4 pints (2·3 litres) vegetable or chicken stock (see pp. 33–34)
Salt
Pepper
1 teaspoon Worcestershire sauce
6 tablespoons croûtons (see p. 35)

Put the bacon in a large, heavy-based saucepan and cook over gentle heat until the fat runs out. Add the onion and carrot and cook gently until the fat has been absorbed.

Drain the soaked peas and add to the pan with the stock. Bring to the boil, season lightly with salt and pepper, cover and simmer for about 2 hours, or until the peas are mushy.

Pass through a sieve or food mill, taste and adjust the seasoning. Add the Worcestershire sauce and re-heat. Serve topped with croûtons.

OXTAIL SOUP
Countrywide

FOLLOWING THE TRUE COUNTRY tradition of using every scrap of the cow except its moo, cooks long ago discovered the nourishing value and satisfying flavour of oxtail.

It was classified as offal and given the somewhat disparaging name, ox, rather than the grander title, beef, which was reserved for the so-called better cuts. But it was, nonetheless, converted into an incomparable brown broth. During its long simmering the dish gives off an appetising aroma, a prelude to the final steaming bowlful, with its unique, richly concentrated beefy taste. When you buy the oxtail, ask the butcher to joint it.

SOAKING TIME: AT LEAST 4 HOURS
PREPARATION TIME: 30 MINUTES
COOLING TIME FOR STOCK: 5 HOURS
COOKING TIME: 3¾ HOURS

INGREDIENTS FOR FOUR TO SIX

1 meaty oxtail, divided into joints
1 teaspoon vinegar
2 tablespoons dripping
2 onions, peeled and chopped
2 large carrots, peeled and chopped
3 sticks celery, trimmed and chopped
1 rasher bacon, roughly chopped after the rind has been cut off
3 pints (1·7 litres) stock (see pp. 33–34)
Bouquet garni
3 bay leaves
Salt
Freshly ground black pepper
1 carrot, peeled and cut into rings
1 small onion, peeled and sliced
2 tablespoons plain flour
¼ teaspoon grated nutmeg
½ teaspoon lemon juice
4 tablespoons sherry or Madeira

Soak the chopped oxtail in enough cold water to cover, with 1 teaspoon of vinegar added, for at least 4 hours. Drain and wipe dry. Heat half the dripping in a large, heavy-based saucepan. Add the oxtail pieces and cook over a high heat, shaking the pan frequently, until browned on all sides. Remove the oxtail with a slotted spoon.

Add the chopped onions, carrots, celery and bacon to the juices in the pan and cook over a medium heat, stirring every now and then, until the onions are golden-brown. Return the oxtail to the pan, add the stock, bouquet garni and bay leaves, season with salt and pepper and bring to the boil. Skim off any white scum that rises to the top, then simmer the soup for 3 hours, or until the meat is falling off the bones.

Strain off the stock into a large bowl and discard the onions, carrots, celery, bacon, bouquet garni and bay leaves. Leave the stock to cool for 1 hour, and then put in the refrigerator for about 4 hours, until any fat has hardened on the surface. Remove and discard the fat.

Boil 1 pint (575/600 ml.) of the stock in a small pan, add the carrot and onion rings, and simmer for 15 minutes. Strain off and keep the stock, and reserve the rings for garnishing.

Remove the meat from the bones and chop finely. Heat the remaining dripping in the cleaned saucepan. Add the flour and stir over a medium heat until the flour turns the colour of a hazelnut. Gradually add all the stock, stirring continuously until the soup comes to the boil and is thick and smooth. Simmer for 3 minutes and then add the meat, nutmeg and lemon juice. Taste and adjust the seasoning if necessary, and stir in the sherry or Madeira. Garnish each serving with a portion of the cooked carrot and onion rings.

Simple ingredients simmered slowly create the satisfying aroma and flavour of Oxtail Soup.

LORRAINE SOUP
Scotland

THE AULD ALLIANCE of Scotland and France against their common enemy, England, left its indelible mark on the law and church in Scotland—and also on the more practical matter of food. Generations of Scottish kings married French brides, and these ladies brought their tastes to the table. Mary of Lorraine, wife of James V and mother of Mary, Queen of Scots, is said to have introduced this soup.

Although some may dispute the soup's source, very few will dispute its excellence. Creamy in appearance and texture, it is a rich combination of chicken and almonds.

If you have no pestle and mortar, you can reduce the chicken, almonds and eggs to a paste in a liquidiser. Give the soup a little colour, if you wish, by garnishing it with a few asparagus tips or cooked young peas, instead of the diced chicken.

PREPARATION TIME: 25 MINUTES
COOKING TIME: 25 MINUTES

INGREDIENTS FOR FOUR

1 thick slice white bread with crusts removed
¼ pint (150 ml.) milk
2 breasts from a cooked chicken, skinned and finely minced
4 oz. (100/125 g.) ground almonds
2 hard-boiled egg yolks
2 pints (1·1 litres) chicken stock (see pp. 33–34)
Salt and white pepper
¼ teaspoon grated nutmeg
2 teaspoons lemon juice
2 egg yolks
¼ pint (150 ml.) double cream
2 tablespoons finely diced, cooked chicken for garnishing

Put the bread in a small saucepan, cover with the milk, bring to the boil and set aside to cool a little.

Pound the minced chicken, ground almonds and hard-boiled egg yolks in a mortar until smooth. Put the mixture in a large bowl and gradually beat in the bread and milk. Stir in the stock, then pass the mixture through a sieve or food mill into a saucepan.

Bring to the boil, season with salt and pepper and add the nutmeg and lemon juice. Simmer for 10 minutes then remove from the heat.

Beat the egg yolks with the cream and blend in 3 tablespoons of the hot soup. Stir the mixture into the soup and heat gently for 2–3 minutes without boiling, stirring continually until it thickens.

Serve at once garnished with the diced chicken.

CARROT SOUP
Countrywide

THE CRAVING FOR SWEETNESS in food made the versatile carrot particularly popular before sugar was available.

The Romans brought the carrot to Britain, where it grew so well that they held a British carrot to be superior to any raised at home. All through the Middle Ages, and later, carrots were boiled and buttered as a vegetable, and simmered in soups. At the end of winter, when the last of the apples had wizened or rotted, they were used in place of fruit in pies, puddings and cakes.

A hint of curry gives an edge to the sweetness of this 17th-century soup.

PREPARATION TIME: 10 MINUTES
COOKING TIME: 1 HOUR

INGREDIENTS FOR SIX TO EIGHT

2 oz. (50 g.) butter
1 lb. (450 g.) onions, peeled and thinly sliced
1 tablespoon plain flour
1½ lb. (700 g.) carrots, peeled and thinly sliced
3 pints (1·7 litres) stock (see pp. 33–34)
Salt and pepper
2 teaspoons mild curry powder
2 tablespoons water
Cauliflower sprigs, blanched for garnishing
Croûtons for garnishing (see p. 35)

Heat the butter in a large, heavy-based saucepan. Dust the onion rings with the flour and cook them gently in the butter, stirring well, until they are soft and golden after 10–15 minutes.

Add the carrots and the stock, and season with salt and pepper. Bring to the boil and simmer with the pan uncovered for about 30 minutes, or until the carrots are soft.

Pass the soup through a sieve or food mill and return it to the pan. Mix the curry powder to a smooth paste with the water. Stir it into the soup and simmer gently for 15 minutes. Serve hot, garnished with cauliflower sprigs and croûtons.

ALEXANDRA SOUP
Countrywide

ACCORDING TO SOME AUTHORITIES, this soup dates from March 1863, when Alexandra, Princess of Schleswig-Holstein-Sonderburg-Glucksburg married Edward, Prince of Wales. Throughout her long life as Princess of Wales, Queen and Empress and Queen Mother, she retained her affection for her Danish homeland. Soon after she came to live in this country, this version of the traditional Danish split-pea soup, *Gale Aerter*, was developed as a gentle antidote for homesickness.

SOAKING TIME: OVERNIGHT
PREPARATION TIME: 10 MINUTES
COOKING TIME: 2 HOURS

INGREDIENTS FOR SIX

4 oz. (100/125 g.) dried, yellow split peas
2 oz. (50 g.) pearl barley
2 pints (1·1 litres) stock (see pp. 33–34)
1 oz. (25 g.) butter
1 small onion, peeled and finely chopped
Salt
Freshly ground black pepper
2 tablespoons tomato purée
¼ pint (150 ml.) single cream
2 tablespoons finely chopped parsley

Put the peas and barley together in a large basin, cover well with cold water and leave to soak overnight. Next day drain them, and blanch in boiling water for 2 minutes. Drain well.

Put the peas and barley in a large, heavy-based saucepan with the stock, butter and onion. Season with salt and pepper, bring to the boil and simmer for 1 hour.

Mix in the tomato purée and continue to simmer for another 30 minutes, or until the peas and barley are absolutely tender.

Pass the mixture through a fine sieve or food mill into a clean pan. Stir in the cream and heat through without boiling. If the soup is too thick, thin it with a little milk. Taste and adjust the seasoning if necessary, and serve with the chopped parsley sprinkled on top.

EEL AND PARSLEY SOUP
Home Counties

WHATEVER did the Abbot of Ely do with all the eels he received? Records show that at the time of the Norman Conquest it was common, particularly in East Anglia, for people to pay their rent in eels, or even in eel pies. The Abbot of Ely received many thousands of eels a year in rent from his various manors.

Even the poor could afford eels, since their abundance made them cheap. Such a taste for them developed among Londoners that cooked eel dishes were sold from street barrows and shops. Jellied eels, eel pie, and eel and mash were the traditional ways of serving them. Parsley was the usual flavouring. The delicious combination of eel and parsley is repeated in this soup.

If you can, buy your eels from a fishmonger who keeps live eels. Ask him to prepare and skin them for you, then hurry home and cook them immediately, for the delicate flesh quickly deteriorates.

PREPARATION TIME: 15 MINUTES
COOKING TIME: 50 MINUTES

INGREDIENTS FOR SIX

1 pint (575/600 ml.) fish or white stock (see pp. 33–34)
1 pint (575/600 ml.) water
¼ teaspoon ground mace
Small piece of lemon peel, free of pith
8 whole black peppercorns
Bouquet garni
Salt
1 lb. (450 g.) small eels
2 oz. (50 g.) butter
2 large onions, peeled and chopped
3 tablespoons plain flour

½ pint (275/300 ml.) milk
2 egg yolks, beaten
¼ teaspoon sugar
4 tablespoons finely chopped parsley

Put the stock, water, mace, lemon peel, peppercorns and bouquet garni in a large saucepan. Season with salt, bring to the boil and add the eels. Simmer for 20–30 minutes, or until the eels are tender with the flesh beginning to come away from the bone.

Strain off and set aside the cooking liquid. Discard the lemon peel, peppercorns and bouquet garni. Remove the eel flesh from the bones and cut it into pieces about 1½ in. (4 cm.) long.

Heat the butter in the cleaned saucepan and cook the chopped onion in it over a low heat for about 15 minutes, until it is soft and transparent. Stir in the flour and gradually blend in the cooking liquid and the milk, stirring continuously over a medium heat until the soup comes to the boil and is thickened and smooth. Add the pieces of eel and simmer for 3 minutes.

Blend 3 tablespoons of the soup into the beaten egg yolks. Add this mixture to the soup with the sugar and stir over a low heat for 2 minutes. Do not let the soup boil or it will curdle. Stir in the parsley, check the seasoning and serve at once.

SAXE-COBURG SOUP
Southern Counties

IN SPITE OF ITS GRAND TITLE this is a soup of quite humble ingredients—Brussels sprouts and a little ham. Perhaps the soup's name was bestowed with witty intention, since the Saxe-Coburgs ruled in Brussels. Even more likely, since the soup was so popular in Victorian times, are suggestions that it did honour to that paragon of the time, Queen Victoria's beloved Prince Albert of Saxe-Coburg-Gotha, or to her son who was later Edward VII.

At the end of the sprout season the soup was made with sprout tops rather than with the sprouts themselves. This hardy vegetable, raised in abundance, is nowadays an unusual base for a soup—surprisingly, for it gives an attractive colour, a good texture and a subtle flavour.

PREPARATION TIME: 30 MINUTES
COOKING TIME: 35 MINUTES

INGREDIENTS FOR FOUR TO SIX

4 oz. (100/125 g.) lean ham
2 oz. (50 g.) butter
1 small onion, peeled and finely chopped
12 oz. (350 g.) Brussels sprouts, trimmed, washed and thinly sliced
Salt and freshly ground black pepper
¼ teaspoon grated nutmeg
1 tablespoon plain flour
2 pints (1·1 litres) stock (see pp. 33–34)
¼ pint (150 ml.) double cream
Croûtons (see p. 35)

Chop half the ham very finely. Heat the butter in a heavy-based, medium saucepan and cook the onion in it over a low heat for 10–15 minutes, until soft and transparent. Add the sprouts and chopped ham and stir over a low heat until all the butter has been absorbed.

Season with salt, pepper and nutmeg and sprinkle on the flour. Mix it in well, then gradually add the stock, stirring well over a medium heat until the soup comes to the boil. Simmer for 6 minutes, then pass the soup through a fine sieve or food mill and return the purée to a clean pan.

Cut the remaining ham into very thin matchstick strips and add it to the soup. Stir in the cream. Heat through, adjust the seasoning, and add some extra stock or a little milk if the soup is too thick. Serve garnished with crisp croûtons.

To vary the flavour, add a pinch of dried savory, or toss the croûtons in ½ teaspoon of curry powder a minute or two before they are fully crisped, finish frying, and drain.

TOMATO AND CARROT SOUP
Midlands

THE LOVE APPLE, a fruit thought capable of arousing dangerous passions and therefore treated with suspicion, reached Britain in the 16th century, having left its native Central America as the blameless *tomatl*. In

Europe the Italians had christened it both *pomo d'oro* (golden apple) and *pomo dei Mori* (apple of the Moors). The French misconstrued this second name as *pomme d'amour*, and the British then perpetuated the error.

The name and reputation clung until the 1850s, and even when the fruit became known as the tomato the British feared that it might be the cause of gout or worse ills. Certainly they considered it safer to cook the tomato rather than risk it raw, and so it was in stews and soups that it made its way into the national diet.

Soup remains an excellent vehicle for it. To enjoy the true taste, ignore those tomatoes with pallidly perfect globes and only a faint astringency and search out the fruits ripened deep red in the sun, swollen and bursting with flavour. In this recipe the carrot and apple give substance to the tomatoes' moistness without impairing the sweetness.

PREPARATION TIME: 15 MINUTES
COOKING TIME: $1\frac{1}{4}$ HOURS

INGREDIENTS FOR FOUR

$\frac{1}{2}$ oz. (15 g.) butter
2 teaspoons vegetable oil
1 onion, peeled and finely chopped
2 cloves garlic, peeled and finely chopped
6 oz. (175 g.) carrots, peeled and finely chopped
1 lb. (450 g.) tomatoes, skinned (see p. 198) and roughly chopped
1 eating apple, peeled, cored and chopped
Bouquet garni of thyme, marjoram and 3 bay leaves
2 pints (1·1 litres) stock (see pp. 33–34)
Salt
Freshly ground black pepper
4 tablespoons double cream
4 tablespoons croûtons (see p. 35)

Warming cups of Tomato and Carrot Soup, flavoured with onion, apple and herbs.

Heat the butter with the oil in a large, heavy-based saucepan. Put in the onion and garlic and cook over a low heat for 10–15 minutes until the onion is soft and transparent. Add the carrot and stir over a low heat until all the fat has been absorbed. Add the tomatoes, apple, bouquet garni and stock, season with salt and pepper and bring to the boil. Cover and simmer for 45 minutes.

Remove and discard the bouquet garni and pass the soup through a fine sieve or a food mill. Return it to a clean pan, heat through and adjust the seasoning.

Pour the soup into warm bowls, and garnish with a spoonful of cream with croûtons round it.

A particularly attractive garnish for this soup is a spoonful of whipped cream on each bowl, with a sprinkling of marigold petals or very finely chopped chives over it.

PALESTINE SOUP
Midlands

As JERUSALEM was the main city of Palestine, so Jerusalem artichokes were the main ingredient of Palestine Soup. By such devious logic was the soup named, but no logic has yet explained convincingly how this artichoke got its name. Many believe that it is a corruption of *girasole* (sunflower), which the Italians joined with their word for artichoke to describe this plant whose top growth resembles the sunflower and whose knobbly root tastes rather like the globe artichoke.

Jerusalem artichokes were commonly grown in kitchen gardens of the 19th century; their long, tough stems were invaluable as a windbreak for less hardy plants, and they could be used to make this soup.

The larger the artichokes, the easier they are to peel. Blanching them also helps to soften the skins and make them quite easy to rub off.

PREPARATION TIME: 20 MINUTES
COOKING TIME: 50 MINUTES

INGREDIENTS FOR SIX

- *1 lb. (450 g.) large Jerusalem artichokes*
- *3 oz. (75 g.) butter*
- *1 small onion, peeled and chopped*
- *1 clove garlic, peeled and finely chopped*
- *1 stick celery, washed, trimmed and chopped*
- *2 pints (1·1 litres) white or chicken stock (see pp. 33–34)*
- *Salt and white pepper*
- *4 tablespoons double cream*
- *1 tablespoon finely chopped parsley*
- *Croûtons (see p. 35), or toasted flaked almonds*

Wash the artichokes, put them in a pan of fast-boiling water and boil for 5 minutes. Stand under cold running water until cool enough to handle, then rub off the skins.

Heat 2 oz. (50 g.) of the butter in a heavy-based, medium saucepan, add the onion, garlic and celery and cook over a low heat for 10–15 minutes, until the onion is soft and transparent.

Add the artichokes and stir over a low heat for 2 minutes. Add the stock, season with salt and pepper and bring to the boil. Simmer for about 30 minutes, or until the artichokes are completely tender. Drain, and reserve the stock.

Pass the vegetables through a fine sieve or food mill, and return the purée to a clean pan with the stock and remaining butter. Heat through, and stir in the cream and finely chopped parsley. Check the seasoning, and serve with a garnish of croûtons or toasted flaked almonds on each serving.

KETTLE BROTH
Cornwall

THE CORNISH FARM LABOURER could rarely have suffered from poor circulation, spotty skin or warts; the marigold petals sprinkled over his daily Kettle Broth were believed to make him proof against such ills.

This simple pottage was prepared in a kettle—an iron cauldron—and its ingredients varied according to the prosperity of the times. In the leanest days it consisted merely of the finely chopped green leaves from the tops of leeks; these were seasoned and left to stand in boiling water for a few minutes with slices of stale bread spread with bacon fat. When times were better, whole leeks and good stock were used—but the marigold petals were always sprinkled on top.

The soup remains inexpensive, and it is light, stimulating to the appetite and full of flavour.

Kettle Broth—a simple, light soup decorated with marigold petals.

PREPARATION TIME: 15 MINUTES
COOKING TIME: 50 MINUTES

INGREDIENTS FOR SIX

- *1½ oz. (40 g.) dripping or bacon fat*
- *2 onions, peeled and chopped*
- *8 oz. (225 g.) leeks, washed, trimmed and thinly sliced*
- *2½ oz. (65 g.) white bread, sliced, with crusts removed*
- *2 pints (1·1 litres) chicken stock (see pp. 33–34)*
- *Salt*
- *Freshly ground black pepper*
- *About ½ pint (275/300 ml.) milk*
- *4 marigold heads (optional)*

Melt the dripping or bacon fat in a large, heavy-based saucepan. Cook the onions and leeks in it over a low heat for 10–15 minutes, stirring occasionally, until they are soft and transparent. Add the bread and stock, and bring to the boil. Season with salt and pepper, cover and simmer for 30 minutes.

Pass the soup through a fine sieve or food mill and return the purée to a clean pan. Add enough milk to give the consistency of thin cream. Check the seasoning and heat through. Serve very hot with a garnish of marigold petals floating in each bowl.

CREAM OF LEEK SOUP
Wales

DURING THE TROUBLED 15th century, displaying the leek declared you a follower of Henry Tudor, the Welsh contender for the English throne. Others had used the leek as their emblem, but for him it was most apt. Green and white, colours on his coat of arms, were plain to see in the leek, and also in the daffodil stem.

These plants, which grow so well in Wales, became Welsh emblems.

Many varieties of this popular soup are made in Wales. The simplest—sliced leek simmered in stock—was made for supper in double quantity when money was short, so that some would be left over for the next day's breakfast.

This rather more elaborate creamed version is pale green, smooth to the tongue and full of light onion flavour.

PREPARATION TIME: 20 MINUTES
COOKING TIME: 50 MINUTES

INGREDIENTS FOR SIX

2 oz. (50 g.) butter
1¼ lb. (575 g.) leeks, washed and trimmed
2 large onions, peeled and finely chopped
3 sticks celery with leaves, washed and chopped
1 large potato, peeled and chopped
1 tablespoon chopped parsley
2½ pints (1·4 litres) white or chicken stock (see pp. 33–34)
Salt
White pepper
¼ pint (150 ml.) double cream

Heat the butter in a large, heavy-based saucepan. Put aside one small leek and roughly chop the rest. Add to the pan with the onion and celery and cook over a low heat for 10–15 minutes until soft and transparent. Add the potato and stir over a low heat until the butter has been absorbed. Add the parsley and gradually stir in the stock. Season with salt and pepper, and bring to the boil. Cover and simmer for about 30 minutes until the vegetables are soft.

Pass through a fine sieve or food mill and return the purée to a clean pan. Add the cream and heat through. Stir in the sliced raw leek just before serving.

SCOTCH BROTH
Scotland

DR JOHNSON SAID SCATHINGLY, 'the noblest prospect which a Scotch man ever sees, is the high road that leads him to England!' Yet in 1776 he may have changed his opinion, when he enjoyed 'veal in Edinburgh, roasted kid in Inverness, admirable venison and generous wine in the castle of Dunvegan'.

Scotland also introduced him to Scotch Broth. His companion, Boswell, reported that at Aberdeen Johnson downed several plates of it 'and seemed very fond of the dish. I said, "You never ate it before?"—Johnson, "No, sir; but I don't care how soon I eat it again".'

Like all good country soups, this can be made with whatever is in season. A little meat, barley and vegetables are the only essentials.

SOAKING TIME: OVERNIGHT
PREPARATION TIME: 20 MINUTES
COOKING TIME: 3½–4 HOURS

INGREDIENTS FOR SIX

2 lb. (900 g.) scrag-end of lamb or mutton, with all excess fat trimmed off
3½ pints (2 litres) water
4 oz. (100/125 g.) pearl barley
4 oz. (100/125 g.) dried peas, soaked in water overnight
Bouquet garni
Salt
Freshly ground black pepper
1 large leek, washed and sliced
1 medium onion, peeled and finely chopped
1 small turnip, peeled and diced
2 large carrots, peeled and diced
4 oz. (100/125 g.) cabbage, shredded
1 tablespoon finely chopped parsley

Place the meat in a large, heavy-based saucepan and add the water, barley, drained soaked peas and bouquet garni. Season with salt and freshly ground black pepper.

Bring the pan slowly to the boil, skim any white scum from the surface, cover and simmer for 2 hours.

Add the leek, onion, turnip and carrots to the soup and continue to simmer for 1 hour, occasionally skimming off any fat that rises to the surface.

Remove the meat from the soup with a slotted spoon and leave it to stand until it is cool enough to handle. Strip the meat from the bones and cut it into small pieces.

Return the meat to the soup and add the cabbage. Adjust the seasoning and continue to simmer for another 30 minutes. Garnish each serving with a sprinkling of parsley.

PEA SOUP WITH MINT
Shropshire

THE ROMAN LEGIONARIES who trudged across barbarous Britain might have been surprised to know that the green pea was to become one of the most widely appreciated of the benefits they brought. What made the pea so welcome to the population of Britain was its sweetness and usefulness—it could be eaten fresh or dried for winter. The bubbling mixture in the cauldron became a thicker, smoother broth when dried peas were simmered in it.

Fresh garden peas make an exquisite soup. In hard times, even their pods have been used—they give a thinner, less well-flavoured, but palatable dish. This Shropshire soup is a rich green velvet, thickened with cream and egg yolks and flavoured with summer mint.

PREPARATION TIME: 20 MINUTES
COOKING TIME: 35 MINUTES

INGREDIENTS FOR SIX

2 oz. (50 g.) butter
1 small onion, peeled and finely chopped
1½ lb. (700 g.) shelled fresh peas
2 pints (1·1 litres) stock (see pp. 33–34)
Salt
White pepper
¼ teaspoon caster sugar
2 sprigs of mint
2 egg yolks
¼ pint (150 ml.) double cream
4 oz. (100/125 g.) shelled and boiled young peas
1 tablespoon finely chopped mint

Heat the butter in a heavy-based medium saucepan, put in the onion and cook it over a low heat for 10–15 minutes until soft and transparent. Add the peas and continue to cook over a low heat until the butter has been absorbed.

Stir in the stock, season with salt and pepper and add the sugar and sprigs of mint. Bring to the boil, cover and simmer gently for about 10 minutes, or until the peas are tender. Pass the soup through a fine sieve or food mill and return the purée to a clean pan.

Beat the egg yolks with the cream until smooth, and add to the soup. Heat through, stirring all the time until the soup has thickened. Do not let it boil or it will curdle. Check the seasoning. Serve garnished with the boiled peas and mint.

CHICKEN GIBLET SOUP
Countrywide

For people who rear hens, ducks or geese and eat their eggs and flesh, it is natural to look for some way of using the giblets (the edible internal organs, such as the heart, liver and gizzard).

Soup is a ready answer, and therefore giblet soup has been an important part of winter fare in the country for hundreds of years. An outstanding soup it is, thick and smooth, with an exceptionally rich, full flavour and plenty of substance given by the strips of meat.

Chicken giblets can now be bought from large food supermarkets, or can still be found on country market stalls. They are usually included with a chicken bought fresh from the butcher.

You can use gizzards only, or gizzards combined with hearts or with both hearts and necks.

PREPARATION TIME: 15 MINUTES
COOKING TIME: ABOUT 2½ HOURS

INGREDIENTS FOR SIX

- *1 lb. (450 g.) chicken giblets*
- *2 onions, washed but not peeled*
- *2 carrots, washed but not peeled*
- *2 large sticks celery, washed and trimmed*
- *3 pints (1·7 litres) water*
- *Bouquet garni*
- *Salt*
- *Freshly ground black pepper*
- *½ oz. (15 g.) butter*
- *1 small onion, peeled and finely chopped*
- *2 tablespoons plain flour*
- *2 large carrots, peeled and coarsely grated*
- *½ teaspoon Worcestershire sauce*
- *1 tablespoon finely chopped parsley*

Wash the giblets thoroughly, cutting off any stained or yellowed skin. Slit and clean the gizzard if necessary. Roughly chop the unpeeled onions and carrots and the celery sticks, and put them in a large saucepan with the giblets. Cover with the water, add the bouquet garni and season well with salt and pepper. Bring to the boil and skim off any white scum that rises to the surface.

Cover the pan and simmer gently for about 2 hours or until the gizzards are really tender. Strain off and keep the stock, but discard the hearts and necks. Leave the gizzards until cool enough to handle and then cut them into thin strips.

Heat the butter in a large, clean, heavy-based saucepan, add the finely chopped onion and cook over medium heat for about 10 minutes, stirring occasionally, until the onion is golden-brown.

Sprinkle on the flour, mix well and continue stirring until the flour is light brown. Add the stock a little at a time, stirring continuously over medium heat until the soup comes to the boil and is thick and smooth.

Add the grated carrots, the strips of gizzard and the Worcestershire sauce, stir well and simmer for 15 minutes. Taste, and add more salt and pepper if necessary. Serve very hot with a sprinkling of parsley over each serving.

COCK-A-LEEKIE SOUP
West Country

Slivers of chicken and rings of leek in good stock—this is Cock-a-Leekie, a broth substantial enough to make a meal on its own.

Scotland is often thought to be its home, but the dish has been made with slight variations in all parts of the country, nowhere more frequently than in Wales and the West Country.

The cock of the title may have been the old farmyard rooster, or the loser in a vicious cock-fight. Such tough fowl needed long simmering—but the stock was all the better for this.

Nowadays a capon gives the best flavour, but a well-seasoned boiling fowl or a roasting bird simmered in prepared stock will make a good soup.

You can either put all the meat in the broth or, if you prefer, put in only the wing meat and serve the chicken separately with vegetables. In some parts of the country, a few prunes are simmered in the soup.

PREPARATION TIME: 30 MINUTES
COOKING TIME: 2½ HOURS
CHILLING TIME FOR STOCK: ABOUT 4 HOURS

INGREDIENTS FOR FOUR TO SIX

- *1 small chicken or boiling fowl, with giblets, cleaned*
- *1 onion, unpeeled, washed and quartered*
- *2 carrots, unpeeled, washed and chopped*
- *Bouquet garni*
- *8 peppercorns*
- *1 teaspoon salt*
- *3 pints (1·7 litres) water*
- *1 oz. (25 g.) butter*
- *6 leeks, trimmed and thinly sliced*
- *2 spring onions, trimmed and thinly sliced*
- *2 tablespoons finely chopped parsley*

Place the chicken with its giblets in a large, heavy-based saucepan. Add the onion, carrots, bouquet garni, peppercorns and salt to the pan and cover with the water.

Bring the pan very slowly to the boil, skim off any white scum and then simmer for about 1¼ hours until the chicken is tender. Strain off the stock into a large bowl, leave it to cool and then chill it in a refrigerator until the fat has hardened on the surface. Lift off the fat carefully with a slotted spoon.

Discard the vegetables, chicken neck and heart, bouquet garni and peppercorns. When the chicken is cool enough to handle, remove the skin from it and cut the flesh and the gizzard into thin strips.

Heat the butter in a large, heavy-based saucepan, add the leeks and spring onions and cook over a low heat for about 15 minutes until they are soft and transparent, and the butter has been absorbed. Add the stock, from which the fat has been removed, bring to the boil and add salt and pepper to taste.

Simmer the soup for about 15 minutes until the leeks and onions are tender. Add the chicken strips and simmer for a further 10 minutes. Mix in the parsley and serve.

MUSHROOM SOUP
Yorkshire

THIS QUICK, easy and delicious soup is well flavoured, with an interestingly grainy texture. It is rich enough for a special occasion, and looks very pretty with cream marbling its pinky-fawn surface and crescents of raw mushroom floating on it.

Young field mushrooms (*Agaricus campestris*), whose gills are still pale brown, are best for this soup. Older mushrooms with blackened gills give a good flavour, but make the soup extremely dark. If possible use plants picked fresh from the fields; wind, rain and sun have given them a tang that even the best cultivated mushrooms cannot match.

PREPARATION TIME: 10 MINUTES
COOKING TIME: 20–30 MINUTES

INGREDIENTS FOR FOUR

8 oz. (225 g.) mushrooms, wiped
2 oz. (50 g.) butter
About 12 fl. oz. (350 ml.) milk
1 tablespoon plain flour
Salt and pepper
3–4 tablespoons single cream

Keep two or three small mushrooms for garnishing. Slice or chop the rest and cook them gently with half the butter in a covered pan for about 10 minutes, or until they are tender.

Pass the mushrooms through a sieve or food mill, keeping them coarse rather than puréed; this gives the soup a more interesting texture.

Strain the juice from the mushrooms and make it up to ¾ pint (450 ml.) with the milk. Melt the remaining butter in a pan, stir in the flour and gradually add the liquid, stirring over medium heat until it is smooth and thick. Add the mushrooms. Season with salt and pepper and bring to the boil. Simmer for 2–3 minutes.

Just before serving, spoon in the cream and stir it round a little to give the soup a marbled appearance. Thinly slice the raw mushrooms saved for garnishing and float them on the soup.

SALCOMBE BAY CRAB SOUP
Devonshire

CRAB SOUP, which seems an expensive, sophisticated luxury to so many of us, has been a traditional dish of the West Country for generations. Crabs are the most common shellfish that live in the seas round the area, and they are sometimes caught in such large numbers that they are given away.

Devonshire crabs are extremely large; their rich meat is served to perfection in this aromatic soup, laced with sherry.

Crabs are still one of the less-expensive shellfish. A medium-sized crab will give enough meat to make a soup for four hungry people. If a fresh crab is not available, frozen crabmeat makes an extremely good substitute in this recipe.

The makings of a rich Salcombe Bay Crab Soup, laced with sherry.

PREPARATION TIME: 30 MINUTES FOR FRESH CRAB
5 MINUTES FOR FROZEN, THAWED CRABMEAT
COOKING TIME: 40 MINUTES

INGREDIENTS FOR FOUR TO SIX

½ oz. (15 g.) butter
1 small onion, peeled and finely chopped
1 stick celery, trimmed and chopped very finely
3 oz. (75 g.) long-grain rice
1 pint (575/600 ml.) milk
Meat of 1 cooked medium crab, or 8 oz. (225 g.) frozen, thawed crabmeat
1 pint (575/600 ml.) fish or chicken stock (see pp. 33–34)
Salt and white pepper
1–2 teaspoons anchovy essence
¼ teaspoon Cayenne pepper
2 tablespoons sherry
¼ pint (150 ml.) double cream

Melt the butter in a heavy-based saucepan. Add the onion and celery and cook over a low heat for about 10 minutes, or until the onion is soft and transparent. Add the rice and milk, bring to the boil and cook for about 15–20 minutes or until the rice is swollen and tender. Drain off and reserve any excess milk.

Reserve 2 tablespoons of the meat, from the claws if the crab is fresh. Pass the remaining crabmeat with the vegetables and rice through a fine sieve or food mill and return the purée to a clean saucepan with the reserved milk and the stock.

Season with salt and freshly ground white pepper, bring to the boil and simmer for 10 minutes. Flavour with the anchovy essence and Cayenne pepper, stir in the sherry and cream and add more milk if the soup seems too thick. Heat through without boiling, and serve at once garnished with the reserved crabmeat.

Cullen Skink
Scotland

Clinging to the coast of the Moray Firth are numerous little fishing villages, where people incorporate in their everyday cooking fine ingredients that are prized delicacies to many of us.

Finnan haddock, a smoked fish rivalled only by the Smokie from nearby Arbroath, is the traditional fish used by the villagers of Cullen for this broth or 'skink'.

Finnan haddock is such a rarity these days that, sadly, you may have to use ordinary smoked haddock. Several versions of the recipe exist, some purèed to a creamy liquid and some replacing part of the stock with dry white wine. The finished dish is the consistency of thick cream.

Preparation Time: 40 minutes
Cooking Time: 40 minutes

Ingredients for Four to Six

1 lb. (450 g.) Finnan haddock or smoked haddock
1 onion, peeled and roughly chopped
1 pint (575/600 ml.) fish or chicken stock (see pp. 33–34)
8 oz. (225 g.) young leeks, trimmed, washed and thinly sliced
8 oz. (225 g.) cooked and mashed potatoes
2 oz. (50 g.) butter
½ pint (275/300 ml.) single cream
1 egg yolk
Salt
White pepper
1 tablespoon finely chopped parsley

Put the haddock and chopped onion in a shallow saucepan and just cover with cold water. Bring slowly to the boil and simmer gently for about 10 minutes, or until the fish flesh is coming away from the bone. Strain and reserve the liquid, but discard the onion.

Remove the skin from the fish and flake the flesh from the bones. Return the skin and bones to the pan with the reserved liquid. Bring to the boil and simmer for a further 10 minutes. Strain again and discard the skin and bones. Mix this liquid with the stock in a large pan. Bring to the boil, add the leeks and boil for 10 minutes or until tender. Mix in the mashed potato and butter until smooth. Add the flaked fish and simmer for 5 minutes.

Beat the cream and egg yolk until smooth and add to the soup. Stir over a low heat until the soup is thoroughly heated, but do not let it boil or it will curdle. Season with salt and pepper, and serve with a sprinkling of parsley on each dish.

Mulligatawny
Home Counties

The British Raj, among others, must be thanked for this inimitable curried broth. The sahibs who spent years in India as army officers, civil servants or diplomats came to love the highly spiced food of the country and brought back recipes to use and adapt at home.

The name of the soup, a native of southern India, is a corruption of the Tamil words *milagu* (pepper) and *tannir* (water)—a fitting description of one of the soup's several variations, for it was sometimes strained to serve as a clear consommé. Some preferred a thick purée and others liked large pieces of chicken in their soup.

The most popular variation is given here. Each serving is topped with fluffy boiled rice.

Preparation Time: 25 minutes
Cooking Time: 45 minutes

Ingredients for Four

1 oz. (25 g.) butter
1 onion, peeled and finely chopped
1 carrot, peeled and finely diced
2 oz. (50 g.) turnip, peeled and finely diced
1 small eating apple, peeled, cored and finely diced
2 oz. (50 g.) runner beans, topped, tailed, strung and cut into thin diagonal slices
2 teaspoons hot curry paste
1 teaspoon tomato chutney
2 pints (1·1 litres) brown stock (see pp. 33–34)
2 oz. (50 g.) cooked ham or chicken, finely chopped
Bouquet garni
¼ teaspoon ground mace
¼ teaspoon grated nutmeg
¼ teaspoon ground cloves
Salt
Freshly ground black pepper
1½ oz. (40 g.) long-grain rice, freshly boiled and drained

Heat the butter in a large, heavy-based saucepan. Add the onion, carrot and turnip and cook over a low heat for 10–15 minutes, stirring to prevent sticking, until the onion is transparent. Add the apple and runner beans, curry paste and tomato chutney, mix well and cook over a low heat for a further 3 minutes.

Gradually blend in the stock, stirring continuously until the soup comes to the boil and is thick and smooth. Remove from the heat and add the ham or chicken, the bouquet garni and the mace, nutmeg and cloves. Season with salt and freshly ground pepper and simmer gently for about 20 minutes until the vegetables are tender, skimming off any scum.

Remove and discard the bouquet garni. Serve the soup at once in hot bowls, with 2 teaspoons of the boiled rice in each serving.

For a smooth soup, purée it when the vegetables are tender and re-heat in a clean saucepan. Stir in some single cream before serving.

RECIPES from OTHER LANDS

SPAIN
Gazpacho

THIS LIGHT, SUMMER VERSION of Gazpacho comes from Andalusia, a pale ochre province of sweet herbs and spring flowers, where, so it is said, a single carnation possesses more fragrance than all the roses from other parts of Spain. The dish is in many ways a liquid salad, a cool and refreshing antidote to the heat of summer.

Traditionally, Gazpacho is made in an earthenware pot that lends its own touch of earthiness to the ingredients. It is placed outside in a shady place, giving the flavours time to mingle and settle; as the sun moves, the pot is moved also, following the shifting shade. In modern homes it is kept in the refrigerator.

At one time, the ingredients were pounded together with pestle and mortar, but a liquidiser will ease this labour considerably. This modern Gazpacho retains the essential lightness of Andalusian cookery.

PREPARATION TIME: 30 MINUTES
CHILLING TIME: 1 HOUR

INGREDIENTS FOR SIX

1½ lb. (700 g.) ripe tomatoes
8 oz. (225 g.) fresh breadcrumbs
5 tablespoons olive oil
1 cucumber, peeled and chopped
2 green peppers, with cores and seeds removed, chopped
2 large cloves garlic, peeled
4 tablespoons red wine vinegar
1 pint (575/600 ml.) water
1 tablespoon tomato purée
Salt
Freshly ground black pepper
12 ice cubes

For the garnishes:

2 slices white bread, prepared as croûtons (see p. 35)
2 hard-boiled eggs, shelled and chopped
6 spring onions, trimmed and finely sliced
½ small cucumber, peeled and finely diced
1 small red pepper, finely chopped after core and seeds have been removed

Blanch and skin the tomatoes (see p. 198). Quarter them, take out the cores and seeds and chop the tomato flesh.

Put the breadcrumbs in a liquidiser, switch it on and gradually pour in the olive oil. Continue blending for about 1 minute, or until all the oil has been absorbed by the bread. Add the tomatoes and continue liquidising until the mixture is reduced to a smooth purée. Transfer this mixture to a bowl.

Put the cucumber, green pepper and garlic in the liquidiser and switch on for about 1 minute, or until they have been reduced to a smooth purée. Combine with the bowl of puréed tomatoes, stir in the vinegar, water and tomato purée.

Taste and add salt and pepper if necessary. Cover the bowl and chill the soup for at least 1 hour in a refrigerator.

Serve very cold in six shallow soup bowls, with two ice cubes added to each. Hand round the garnishes in separate bowls.

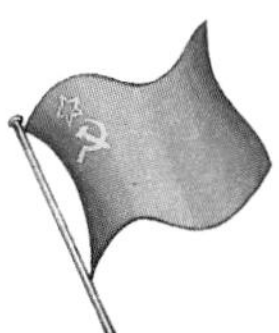

RUSSIA
Borshch

THOUGH NOW regarded as something of a delicacy, this thick soup was the staple diet of the pre-Revolutionary Russian peasantry, the basis of the daily main meal, which usually consisted of *kasha*—wheatmeal porridge—Borshch, and dark rye bread.

Strangely enough, since the soup is usually associated with beetroot, the word has nothing to do with beetroot, but comes instead from *borshchnevik*, an old Russian word signifying either parsnip, or the wild plant known as cow-parsnip or hogweed. Altogether, this would seem to indicate that the soup was originally made from whatever root vegetable was available.

Many other kinds of ingredient were added, varying according to local preference—even chopped sausage if the family was sufficiently prosperous. The dish was vital to survival: 'As long as we have this *borshchnevik*,' the old proverb runs, 'we can do without bread.'

Borshch without doubt ranks among the best of the classic soups of the world.

PREPARATION TIME: 25 MINUTES
COOKING TIME: 1 HOUR

INGREDIENTS FOR SIX

12 oz. (350 g.) whole, uncooked beetroot with leaves left on
2 large carrots, peeled
1 tablespoon vegetable oil
4 oz. (100/125 g.) streaky bacon, without rinds and cut into small pieces
1 large onion, peeled and finely chopped
3 sticks celery, trimmed and cut in matchstick strips
2½ pints (1·4 litres) stock (see pp. 33–34)
1 tablespoon vinegar
Salt
Freshly ground black pepper
8 oz. (225 g.) tomatoes
¼ pint (150 ml.) sour cream

Wash the beetroot and leaves well. Break off the leaves and separate them from their stalks and ribs. Cut the leaves into fine shreds and chop the stalks and ribs finely. Peel the beetroot and cut the flesh into thin strips. Slice the carrots thinly lengthwise, and cut the slices into fine strips.

Heat the oil in a large, heavy-based saucepan and cook the bacon in it over a low heat until the fat runs. Add the beetroot flesh, carrots, onion and celery to the pan and stir over a low heat until the fat has been absorbed. Add the stock and vinegar, stir well and season with salt and pepper. Bring to the boil, and simmer, covered, for 30 minutes.

Blanch and skin the tomatoes (see p. 198). Quarter them and remove the cores and seeds.

Pass the tomato flesh through a fine sieve or food mill to make a purée and add it to the soup with the beetroot leaves and stalks. Continue to simmer for a further 15 minutes, or until the beetroot is tender. Serve very hot with a swirl of sour cream in each serving.

The classic Borshch is always thick with vegetables, but if you prefer a less robust soup, strain it when the cooking is finished and serve as a clear liquid, hot or cold, with a spoonful of sour cream in each bowl.

Cucumber pickled in dill-flavoured vinegar can be chopped finely and added to either the soup or the sour cream, if liked.

FRANCE
Onion Soup

THE FRENCH, with their admirable ability to combine, or even confuse, what they fancy with what does them good, regard this superb soup as an infallible antidote to fatigue, chills, head colds and drunkenness. For one reason or the other, it was served in the small hours of the morning to porters and late partygoers at Les Halles, the Covent Garden of Paris, until the market was demolished a few years ago.

Use the big, mild Spanish onions to make the best soup; British onions are generally not sweet enough.

PREPARATION TIME: 20 MINUTES
COOKING TIME: 1¼ HOURS

INGREDIENTS FOR SIX

1½ oz. (40 g.) butter
2 tablespoons vegetable oil
1½ lb. (700 g.) onions, peeled, sliced and separated into rings
¼ teaspoon sugar
2½ pints (1·4 litres) stock (see pp. 33–34)
Salt and black pepper
6 slices French bread
2 teaspoons French mustard
3 oz. (75 g.) Gruyère cheese, grated
3 tablespoons brandy (optional)

Heat the butter and oil in a large, heavy-based saucepan. Put in the onion rings, sprinkle on the sugar and cook over a low heat, stirring every now and then, for about 15 minutes or until the onions are soft and golden-brown and all the fat has been absorbed. Gradually stir in the stock, season with salt and pepper, bring to the boil and simmer for 45 minutes.

Toast the slices of French bread and leave the grill on its highest setting for a final grilling of the soup. Spread the toast with the mustard and pile on the grated cheese, pressing it down firmly. Arrange six earthenware bowls on the grill pan and place a slice of the bread and cheese in each. Gently pour over the hot soup and, when the slices of bread rise to the surface, slide the pan under the hot grill until the cheese has melted and turned golden-brown. Serve at once.

If you like, add brandy to the soup just before pouring it into the bowls.

GREECE
Avgolemono

LEMON GROVES, startling in their cool, dark greenness, patch the hot, camel-coloured hills of the Greek islands. Visitors, grateful for the shade of the trees, climb the rocky paths to the taverna that some landowners provide in the heart of the groves. If the visitors are sensible, they will arrive at some time during the three-hour Greek lunch break, the traditional time to eat Avgolemono.

Avgolemono is a compound of the two Greek words for 'egg' and 'lemon', and is eaten not only as a soup, but also as a flavouring for other soups and as a sauce for vegetable dishes. It has played a vital role in the Greek cuisine for centuries, possibly since lemons were brought from Byzantium 1,000 years ago.

PREPARATION TIME: 20 MINUTES
COOKING TIME: 15 MINUTES

INGREDIENTS FOR SIX

2 oz. (50 g.) long-grain rice
Juice of 1 lemon
3 eggs, beaten
2½ pints (1·4 litres) hot chicken stock (see pp. 33–34)
2 oz. (50 g.) cooked chicken meat, finely chopped
Salt and white pepper
2 tablespoons finely chopped parsley

Cook the rice in boiling, salted water for 10–15 minutes and drain well.

Meanwhile, add the lemon juice to the beaten egg and mix well. Add about ¼ pint (150 ml.) of the hot stock a little at a time, beating well with a wire whisk after each addition.

Bring the remaining stock to the boil, remove from the heat and mix in the cooked chicken and rice. Season lightly with salt and pepper. Whisk in the egg mixture and return to a low heat. Stir continuously without boiling for about 5 minutes, until the soup is heated through and has a rich creamy texture. Adjust the seasoning and serve garnished with parsley.

NEW ENGLAND
Clam or Scallop Chowder

CLAM CHOWDER is as inseparable from New England as white clapboard houses. It is a speciality of big restaurants in towns like Marblehead and Salem that were old when the United States was young, and is prepared with equal reverence by Yankee housewives at home.

The basic raw material of this delicious soup is clams, but British chowder-makers may also use our native scallops. Both the dish and the term crossed the Atlantic with the Breton fishermen who, in the 16th and 17th centuries, sailed to the Newfoundland Grand Banks in search of cod. Their sole cooking utensil was a *chaudière* or cauldron, in which they prepared a daily hodge-podge of fish stew and biscuit—a process that they called 'making a *chaudière*'.

From this it would seem likely that the first American 'chowders' were made not from clams, but from cod.

PREPARATION TIME: 25 MINUTES
COOKING TIME: 40 MINUTES

INGREDIENTS FOR FOUR

1½ pints (850 ml.) shelled clams or 5 medium scallops
4 oz. (100/125 g.) rindless green streaky bacon, chopped
1 large onion, peeled and chopped
1 tablespoon plain flour
1 pint (575/600 ml.) fish stock (see pp. 33–34)
1 pint (575/600 ml.) milk
1 lb. (450 g.) potatoes, peeled and finely diced
¼ teaspoon sugar
Salt
Cayenne pepper
4 tablespoons double cream
2 tablespoons finely chopped parsley

If using scallops, remove and discard the black veins. Set aside the pink corals and slice the white bodies.

Put the chopped bacon into a heavy-based saucepan and cook over a low heat, stirring every now and then, until the fat has run out. Add the onion and continue to cook over a low heat until it is soft and transparent. Stir in the flour, raise the heat and gradually blend in the stock and milk, stirring continuously until the mixture thickens and comes to the boil.

Add the potatoes and the sugar, bring back to the boil and simmer for 10 minutes. Add the white parts of the scallops or the clams, and continue to simmer for 5 minutes, or until the potatoes are tender but not mushy. Add the corals and simmer for a further 3 minutes. Season with salt and Cayenne pepper and stir in the cream and parsley.

Notes and Advice on Preparing

All Kinds Of Soup

As soon as prehistoric farmers discovered how to make pottery, and later bronze and iron, cooking vessels, a new type of dish became possible. Different foods no longer had to be cooked separately in the fire or over it. They could be put together in the pot with some liquid, and 'seethed' to make a pottage new in texture as well as flavour.

Scraps of meat and bones left from a slaughtered domestic beast, fish bones, or some small animal or bird that had been caught would be put in the pot with the roots and leaves of wild plants, including seaweeds near the coast. The bitter taste of some of the plants was reduced in the pot, and the addition of aromatics such as the native onions and mints made them even more palatable. Handfuls of cereal would be put in the pot as well, and as they cooked their starchy content swelled and thickened the liquid to make a substantial, if rather stodgy, meal.

All over the world such broths have at some time formed the backbone of the peasant diet and made the most of whatever foodstuff was available locally. The liquid would be 'sopped' or soaked up by bread dipped in it; this is an explanation often given for the name soup.

Our main-course soups are a refinement of the early pottages and broths, and our first-course soups an even further refinement to stimulate the appetite for the courses to follow. The variety of soups we know today stems from a general rise in the living standard, perhaps more sophisticated tastes, and above all wider availability of ingredients.

Stocks

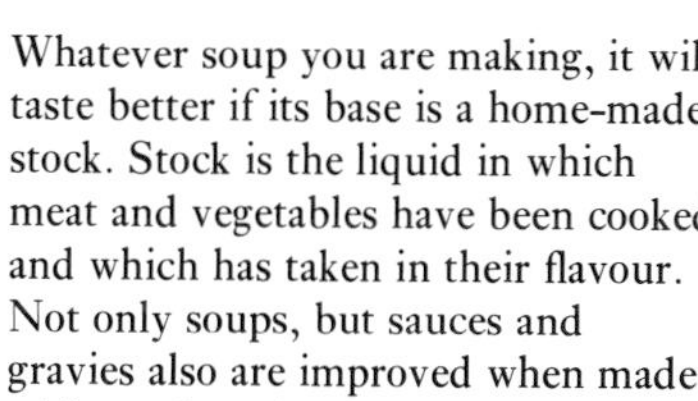

Whatever soup you are making, it will taste better if its base is a home-made stock. Stock is the liquid in which meat and vegetables have been cooked and which has taken in their flavour. Not only soups, but sauces and gravies also are improved when made with good stock.

It is simple and straightforward to make your own stock. Moreover, it makes use of scraps of meat, bones, poultry carcases, vegetable trimmings and leftovers that might otherwise be thrown away.

Cooking vessels
Most stock needs long simmering to produce the best flavour. Make it in a large, heavy-based saucepan with a well-fitting lid. A pressure cooker will reduce the amount of time and fuel needed to make the stock. An electric slow-cooking pot will reduce the amount of fuel used.

Main Types of Stock

Choose the stock that best suits the dish you are making. Many ingredients will give your stock flavour, but the greatest nutritional value it can have will come from gelatine. The best source of this is bones. There is eight times as much gelatine in bone as in meat. To extract the most goodness, break up bones with a hammer to expose as much of their surface as possible to the liquid. Simmer them until they are pitted with small holes. The bones will give an even better flavour if they are roasted before being simmered.

A cow heel or a sheep's head will produce well-flavoured and nourishing stock, and also give some meat to make broth. The heel or head must be plunged in boiling water for 2–3 minutes before going in the stockpot, to ensure thorough cleansing.

Household stock
For use as an economical all-round base in family soups and dishes. Use cooked and uncooked scraps of meat, bones and fowl carcases, giblets, meat juices, gravy and pieces of fresh vegetables or clean peelings.

Chicken, other poultry or game stock
For use in soups and casseroles. Use a raw or cooked carcase, the trimmings, giblets and feet. Cover the feet with boiling water for 5 minutes, and skin before use.

For making small amounts of stock you can use the giblets from your bird, barely covered with water, flavoured with onion and seasonings and simmered for 1 hour.

Vegetable stock
For use in vegetable soups and vegetarian dishes. Use large pieces of fresh vegetable, clean peelings and liquid in which rice or pasta has been cooked. Use within 48 hours unless deep-frozen.

Fish stock
For use in fish soups and sauces. Use fish heads, skins and trimmings, or cheap white fish such as coley. Do not use oily fish such as herring or mackerel. Instead of putting vegetables in the stock, add a little mace or a bay leaf, or a small piece of lemon rind free of all pith. Simmer the stock for only 30–45 minutes and use it within 24 hours unless it is stored in a deep-freezer.

First stock
For use as a clear soup. Use only fresh, uncooked meat and vegetables. Simmer the meat, such as shin of beef, or chicken, for 3 hours before adding the vegetables. It is essential to make this stock in advance so that every particle of fat can be removed when it has set.

White stock
For use as the basis of a white cream soup, or in chicken, rabbit or veal dishes. Use it also in galantines and in other dishes that require jellied stock. Use the knuckle and feet of veal and, if possible, some meat from a fowl.

Brown stock
For use in brown meat or vegetable soups and in casseroles and sauces. Use the same ingredients as you would for a basic, household, or vegetable stock, but fry the solid ingredients lightly in a little butter or dripping until golden-brown before adding to the liquid. Take care to have the fat hot before starting the frying, so that the surface of the meat or vegetables is sealed as soon as it touches the pan and does not absorb too much fat.

A basic stock
You can vary the first ingredient in the following recipe according to what you have available and the dish you are making. Keep the proportions of roughly 1 lb. (450 g.) of solid ingredients to 3½ pints (2 litres) of liquid. This will make about 2 pints (1·1 litres) of stock. For a larger amount, increase all the ingredients in proportion.

INGREDIENTS

1 lb. (450 g.) bones and meat (beef, poultry, fish and so on, see main types of stock above)
3½ pints (2 litres) cold water
1 teaspoon salt
2 large carrots, well scrubbed and cut in large pieces
1 large onion, peeled and halved
2 sticks celery, well washed, or ¼ teaspoon celery seeds

Break up the bones if they are large, using a hammer, and roast them if liked. Cut the meat into large cubes. Place the meat and bones in a large, heavy-based saucepan with the water and salt. Bring slowly to the boil and remove any white scum that forms on the surface. Cover with a well-fitting lid and simmer gently for 3 hours. Add the carrots, onion and celery, cover again and simmer for 2 more hours.

Strain through a nylon or hair sieve, taste, and if the stock lacks flavour boil it rapidly to reduce its volume and concentrate its flavour. Pour into a bowl, and leave to get quite cold. Remove any fat from the surface with a slotted spoon. Cover the bowl and store in a refrigerator. Use the stock within 1 week.

Storing stock
Nowadays, it is not usually necessary to boil up the stock every day to keep it fresh and wholesome, as had to be done in times gone by. Most stock can be kept covered in a refrigerator for up to 1 week. Cooks with a deep-freezer can prepare any kind of stock in bulk and divide it into suitable quantities for freezing. If it is not stored in a refrigerator or freezer, stock must still be boiled up every day. In any case it must be brought to the boil again before it is used.

Removing the fat
Even if you do not intend to store the stock in the refrigerator or freezer but want it for use the same day, try to make it a few hours in advance so that there is enough time for it to go cold and for any fat that has risen to the top to solidify. It is then easy to lift off the layer of fat. If speed is essential and there is no time for the fat to harden, let the stock stand for a few minutes so that the fat rises to the surface, then draw torn pieces of kitchen paper across the surface one after the other until they have absorbed the layer of fat. There are now available brushes made of fibres that attract fat and repel liquid. One of these drawn over stock that has stood for 5–10 minutes will remove the fat. Rinse it out with boiling water and draw it over the stock several times until all the fat has gone.

Meat glaze
Any brown meat stock can be made into a delicious glaze for cold meats. Measure out ½ pint (275/300 ml.) of stock from which all fat has been removed. Pour it into a saucepan and boil it briskly with no lid on. From time to time skim off any scum that has formed. Let the stock boil until it has greatly reduced in volume. Watch it carefully, and stir continuously at this stage because it can quickly burn. When it has become as thick as treacle, take it off the heat and let it cool before spooning it over cold meat or poultry. If it is not for immediate use, pour it into separate small containers, cover, and store in a refrigerator for up to 1 week.

Stock cubes
If you need stock quickly and have none prepared, stock cubes make a convenient standby, but they give a slightly synthetic flavour and leave a persistent after-taste, neither of which problems occur with home-made stock.

Meat extract or yeast extract as well as stock cubes are useful if you need to strengthen the flavour of a home-made stock that you have not had time to reduce and concentrate by boiling. The extracts and stock cubes are also among several additions you can make to a finished soup at the last minute if it lacks flavour.

Essential Points in Stock-making

1 All ingredients must be clean and sound.
2 Use a heavy-based saucepan with a well-fitting lid.
3 Cook bones and meat for 2–3 hours before adding vegetables. Once the vegetables are cooked they will start absorbing the flavour from the liquid, so do not leave them in the liquid too long either during or after cooking.
4 Do not cook fish stock for more than 45 minutes.
5 Use a balanced mixture of vegetables so that no one vegetable predominates.
6 Leave vegetables in large pieces.
7 Do not use too many green vegetables or the stock will have a bitter taste.
8 Use herbs and spices in very small amounts; too much will make the stock taste bitter.
9 Starchy ingredients, such as potato or thickened gravy, will make the stock cloudy and can give it a sour taste, so do not use too many of them.
10 The liquid in which bacon or salt beef has been cooked is not suitable for stock as it is much too salty.
11 Remove any white scum that rises during cooking, but do not remove brown scum; this is nourishing protein that has set in the hot liquid.
12 As soon as the stock is cooked, strain it into a clean china or plastic bowl. Leave it to cool and remove the fat before covering and storing in a refrigerator or deep-freezer.
13 Boil up the prepared stock every day if you are not able to store it in a refrigerator or freezer.
14 Never keep stock standing in a saucepan. The stock will develop a sour flavour and the saucepan will become stained.

Soups

Choose your soup to complement the rest of the meal. A hearty broth is welcome before a light main course but not before a substantial pie. Do not serve a fish soup before a main fish dish, or a tomato soup before a dish flavoured with tomatoes. Soups are usually classed as thin or thick.

Thin Soups

Among thin soups, some are absolutely clear liquids. Such a soup is now usually called a consommé. Chicken and beef are the ingredients most used. A clear soup should have a clean, sparkling quality, and be absolutely free of fat. Its clean, pure flavour and its lightness make it an excellent beginning to a rich or heavy meal.

Thin soups are not always clear. Even a consommé sometimes has added to it a few spoons of cooked peas or carrot. Others are broths in which the liquid is still unthickened but has pieces of vegetable or meat in it. Cock-a-leekie is a soup of this kind and Hairst Bree, a filling broth of lamb and vegetables, is unthickened. If you find this kind of soup is not thin enough when cooked, add some clear stock or a little wine to it.

Thick Soups

There is a larger variety of thick soups than of thin. Their satisfying and substantial nature makes them popular. Typical white soups include Palestine Soup, made from Jerusalem artichokes, Lorraine Soup, made from chicken and almonds, and Eel and Parsley Soup. Typical brown soups are Oxtail and Mulligatawny. Thickened broths, Chicken Giblet Soup and Scotch Broth, for example, have pieces of vegetable and meat in a liquid thickened with flour or a grain such as pearl barley. Among thick vegetable soups there are those based on fresh vegetables, for example Saxe Coburg Soup (made from Brussels sprouts), and those based on dried pulse vegetables, for example London Particular.

Most thick soups need a thickening or binding agent. Without it the solid ingredients will sink to the bottom.

The thickener is known as a liaison, from the French verb *lier* which means 'to bind'. Liaisons include:

Some form of starch, for example flour, cornflour, arrowroot, sago, pearl barley, semolina, oatmeal or potato.

Fat and flour in equal quantities heated gently together and mixed to a very thick, smooth paste called a roux.

Egg yolks mixed with cream, a little stock, or milk.

Double cream, which is usually added to smooth, rich or white soups.

If flour or cornflour is the liaison, mix it first to a smooth, thin cream with a little of the soup liquid or a little milk or water. Then stir it into the soup in the pan and stir while cooking gently for at least 5 minutes.

A liaison of egg yolks should be added to the soup just before serving. Beat the yolks well in a cup or small basin, and stir in several spoons of liquid from the soup. Draw the soup off the heat while you stir in the egg mixture. Return the soup to the heat to make sure that it is heated through well for serving, but stir it all the time and take great care not to let the soup boil again or it will curdle.

Texture

Although an even texture is what to aim for in thick soups other than broths, take care not to make the soup too smooth. An electric liquidiser will certainly save time in preparing the soup, but gives a rather bland, emulsified result. Rubbing through a sieve or passing through a food mill produces a more interesting, slightly grainy texture in the soup.

When you make a fish soup, take great care not to overcook it or the delicate texture of the fish will be spoiled and become rubbery.

Flavour

An appetising taste and aroma are a soup's most important features. The best guarantee of these is to start with a well-flavoured stock, but if your finished soup should be a little short of flavour you can add some reduced stock or meat glaze, small amounts of herbs or spices, a relish such as mushroom ketchup or tomato purée, or use a very old device—concentrated onion. Peel and slice an onion, dust it with flour and fry it in a little butter until it is well browned. Rub it through a sieve and then add it to the soup, a little at a time, until the flavour is as you want it.

If you over-salt a soup by mistake, put a peeled potato to cook in the soup until tender but not broken, then lift it out. It will have absorbed much of the salt. If you make a soup for freezing, do not season it. Salt and pepper increase their flavour while frozen, so add them when you heat the soup for serving.

Colour

Onion concentrate will enrich the colour as well as the taste of a brown soup or broth. Meat glaze and tomato purée also add colour. A pallid or muddy colour in a vegetable soup will not stimulate the appetite. Take care not to spoil green vegetables by overcooking them. If a green summer soup should look too pale, add a few drops of vegetable colouring to it.

Serving Soups

Serve a hot soup piping hot because as it cools, it loses flavour and any fat in it floats to the top. Pour the soup into heated bowls for serving.

A cold soup, such as Gazpacho, must be served really cold to achieve the refreshing effect it aims at. Chill the soup thoroughly in a refrigerator before serving, pour it into well-chilled bowls, and in hot weather add one or two ice-cubes before serving.

More seasoning is usually needed in a cold soup, as all cold foods tend to have less flavour than hot. Add a little lemon juice to sharpen the taste.

Croûtons and other garnishes

An attractive garnish will convert a humble soup into elegant fare. Use:

A tablespoon on each serving of croûtons; cut a crustless slice of bread into small cubes, fry in butter or oil until very crisp and add to the dish at the last minute.

Finely chopped parsley, chives or celery leaves.

A tablespoon of cream swirled on each serving and sprinkled with a pinch of Cayenne pepper or paprika.

Thinly sliced French bread toasted, covered with grated cheese and browned under the grill.

Thin slices of lemon or orange.

A few watercress leaves.

Marigold petals.

Of POTTED MEATS AND FISH

CONTAINING

NUMEROUS *Useful* FAMILY RECIPES

for MARBLED & MOULDED MEATS & FISH, BRAWNS & PASTES

& all other POTTED DELIGHTES

PAGES 38–45

AND

A SELECTION of RECIPES from OTHER LANDS

PAGES 46–47

AND WITH

DIRECTIONS *for* BASIC METHODS

for all kinds of Pounding, Pressing, Sealing and Storing of Potted Dishes to Perfection

PAGES 48–49

Potted Tongue and Chicken, served cold with Cumberland sauce, makes a spicy alternative to the Christmas turkey.

Potted Tongue and Chicken
Sussex

Country cooks sometimes boned several birds and stuffed them one inside the other to make an elaborate display at Christmas.

A legendary story relates how an epicure ordered an olive to be stuffed inside a boned lark, inside a pigeon, inside a chicken, inside a duck, inside a goose, inside a turkey, inside a bustard. When the complete dish was baked and set before him, the epicure ate—just the olive.

This dish merely wraps tongue in chicken, but needs some forethought as the tongue will have to be ordered from the butcher and put in brine for a week before cooking (see p. 49).

Preparation Time: 4 hours
Pre-cooking Time: 3 hours
Cooking Time: 1¾ hours
Pre-heat the Oven to 220°C (425°F)—gas mark 7

Ingredients for Eight to Twelve

- *1 salted ox tongue, about 3 lb. (1·4 kg.)*
- *1 onion, sliced*
- *1 carrot, sliced*
- *A bunch of bay leaves, parsley and celery leaves*
- *1 large chicken, about 4 lb. (1·8 kg.)*
- *2 teaspoons salt*
- *1 teaspoon white pepper*
- *1 teaspoon mixed spice*
- *2–2½ lb. (900 g.–1·1 kg.) butter, cut into cubes*
- *Flour and water paste (see p. 49)*
- *Bunches of parsley and watercress*

Put the tongue in a large saucepan, and add the onion, carrot and bunch of herbs. Cook slowly for about 3 hours, or until tender. Allow to cool, then remove the skin and any bones.

Bone the chicken (see p. 49). Season with salt, pepper and mixed spice. Lay the tongue on the boned chicken, and trim so that it can be enfolded by the chicken. Wrap the chicken round the tongue, and ease this parcel into a casserole which will hold it firmly. Cover with the cubed butter. Put on the lid, sealing with a strip of the flour and water paste. Place the casserole in the pre-heated oven for 30 minutes, then lower the temperature to 180°C (350°F)—gas mark 4 and cook for another $1\frac{1}{4}$ hours.

At the end of the cooking time, take the casserole out of the oven and leave to cool, without breaking the seal. When cool, place in a cold larder or at the bottom of the refrigerator.

To serve, break the seal and remove the chicken carefully. Scrape off the butter (which is excellent in sandwiches), and arrange the bird on a large dish. Decorate with generous bunches of parsley and watercress. Cumberland sauce (see p. 153) goes well with this dish.

COLLARED PORK
Shropshire

THIS OLD METHOD of preserving cooked meat in a wet pickle often used a whole pig. Indeed, one recipe by Elizabeth Raffald (1733–81), author of *The Experienced English Housekeeper*, begins with the instruction: 'Kill your pig...' Fortunately, there is no need to go to such lengths; this is an excellent way of cooking individual joints, particularly the relatively inexpensive hand of pork.

If you only want to preserve the meat for a few days, you can simply add a quantity of vinegar to the strained cooking stock, instead of using the salt and vinegar brine. But whichever method you use, pickled walnuts are served as the traditional accompaniment.

PREPARATION TIME: 30 MINUTES
COOKING TIME: $2\frac{1}{2}$ HOURS

INGREDIENTS FOR SIX

3 lb. (1·4 kg.) boned, but not rolled, hand of pork
1 egg yolk
2 oz. (50 g.) fresh white breadcrumbs
Grated rind of $\frac{1}{2}$ lemon
2 chopped anchovy fillets
1 tablespoon chopped parsley
2 sprigs chopped marjoram
$\frac{3}{4}$ teaspoon freshly grated nutmeg
Salt and freshly ground black pepper
1 carrot, sliced
1 onion, sliced
1 stick celery, sliced
10 peppercorns

For the brine:
$1\frac{1}{2}$ pints (850 ml.) water
6 oz. (175 g.) salt
$\frac{1}{2}$ pint (275/300 ml.) malt vinegar

Mix together the egg yolk, breadcrumbs, lemon rind, anchovies and chopped herbs. Add the nutmeg, salt, pepper, parsley, marjoram, and spread over the pork. Roll the pork into a sausage shape and tie firmly with string. Put into a pan with the carrot, onion and celery. Add the peppercorns, and cover with cold water. Bring to the boil, then simmer gently for $2\frac{1}{2}$ hours or until tender. Remove and drain. Leave until quite cold.

Boil the salt, water and vinegar together for 10 minutes, and leave to cool. Pour this brine into a deep bowl and immerse the pork in it, keeping the pork under the surface with a weighted plate. Leave for 5–7 days before serving.

PRESSED TURKEY
Norfolk

THIS RELATIVELY MODERN recipe comes, not surprisingly, from Norfolk, the home of the largest turkey farm in Europe.

East Anglia has always been associated with the raising of turkeys, both because it is a cereal-growing area and because it is within walking distance of London, the main market. In the days before road and rail transport, live flocks were herded to their destination on foot.

Pressed Turkey is an excellent dish for a cold buffet at Christmas, and is easy to carve.

PREPARATION TIME: 20 MINUTES
COOKING TIME: 2 HOURS, PLUS $1\frac{1}{2}$ HOURS
STANDING TIME: OVERNIGHT
PRE-HEAT THE OVEN TO 220°C (425°F)—GAS MARK 7

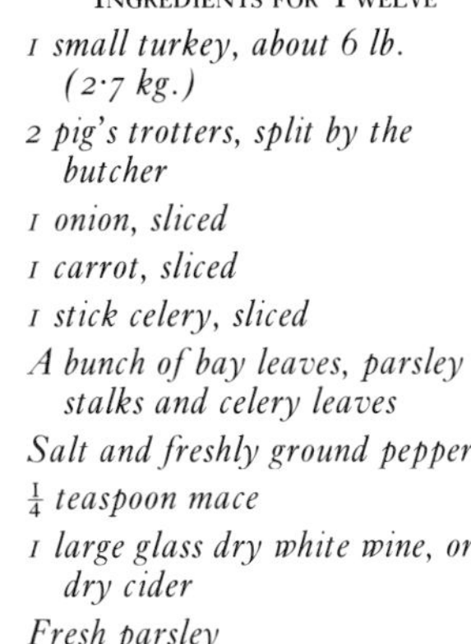

INGREDIENTS FOR TWELVE

1 small turkey, about 6 lb. (2·7 kg.)
2 pig's trotters, split by the butcher
1 onion, sliced
1 carrot, sliced
1 stick celery, sliced
A bunch of bay leaves, parsley stalks and celery leaves
Salt and freshly ground pepper
$\frac{1}{4}$ teaspoon mace
1 large glass dry white wine, or dry cider
Fresh parsley

Place the turkey in the pre-heated oven and roast for 15 minutes per pound (450 g.), plus 15 minutes. After 30 minutes, lower the heat to 190°C (375°F)—gas mark 5.

Baste the bird frequently with good dripping during cooking. When it is cooked, remove from the oven and allow to cool. Carve off all the meat.

Put the carcase into a pan, with the trotters, onion, carrot and celery. Add the bunch of bay leaves, parsley stalks and celery leaves and cover with cold water. Simmer for $1\frac{1}{2}$ hours. Strain off the stock into a clean pan and add the wine or cider. Boil fast to reduce the amount by half, and to concentrate the flavour. Season with salt, pepper and mace.

Line a 6 in. (15 cm.) cake tin (with a removable base) with waxed paper, and pack the turkey meat into this tin. Cover the meat with foil and put a light weight on top.

Allow the stock to cool, but before it becomes a jelly pour the stock over the turkey to just cover the meat. Press the turkey again, using a heavier weight. Leave overnight.

Next day, invert the tin on to a plate and ease the meat out by pressing on the base. Peel off the paper, and garnish the turkey with plenty of parsley.

PRESSED BEEF
Countrywide

THIS VICTORIAN DISH was served in farmhouses up and down the country. A simpler version was also prepared for use on early sailing ships. In both cases, it was prepared in enormous quantities. One recipe for 'a small household' called for '12 pounds of beef'.

The dish is just as good in the more manageable quantity suggested here. You will need to order the beef from the butcher in advance, as it needs to spend a week in brine before cooking. You can do this yourself (see p. 49).

Both pressed turkey (see p. 39) and pressed beef deteriorate quickly in hot weather, so they must be made only a day or so before you want to eat them. They do not freeze well.

PREPARATION TIME: 30 MINUTES
COOKING TIME: 2½ HOURS
STANDING TIME: OVERNIGHT

INGREDIENTS FOR SIX

3 lb. (1·4 kg.) salt brisket of beef, boned and rolled
2 pig's trotters, split by the butcher
1 large carrot, sliced
1 small turnip, sliced
2 large onions, stuck with 4 cloves (leave the skins on the onions, to colour the stock)
12 peppercorns
A bunch of celery leaves, parsley stalks and bay leaves

Cover the meat with cold water. Bring slowly to the boil, then throw away the water—this will get rid of excess salt.

Put the carrot, turnip, onions and trotters in the pan with the beef. Add the peppercorns, bunch of herbs and enough fresh cold water to cover. Bring slowly to the boil. Reduce the heat, and simmer very gently for 2½ hours, or until the meat is tender.

Take out the beef, and put it between two plates with a weight on top. Leave overnight.

Next day, remove the fat from the stock. Re-heat the stock, strain and check the seasoning. Put the meat on a dish and pour some of the stock round it, so that it sets into a pool of jelly. Let the rest of the stock set in a shallow dish, then chop roughly and pile on top of the beef.

Serve Pressed Beef with piccalilli (see p. 350) and baked potatoes.

MARBLED HAM
Yorkshire

THE GEORGIANS delighted in colour and design, not only in architecture but also in their food. They liked the look of 'marbled meats', contrived when preparing pressed or potted dishes by blending such contrasting ingredients and textures as veal, ham and tongue, sometimes with an additional pattern of herbs.

This Yorkshire recipe, which dates back to 1790, often appeared at country high teas and parties. It is an excellent way of using up cold ham and tongue.

PREPARATION TIME: 35 MINUTES
CHILLING TIME: OVERNIGHT

INGREDIENTS FOR SIX

1 lb. (450 g.) cold tongue
8 oz. (225 g.) softened butter
¼ teaspoon ground mace
Salt
Freshly ground black pepper
1 lb. (450 g.) cold ham
Clarified butter (see p. 49)

Mince the tongue finely and pound to a paste. Beat in half the butter, and season with mace, pepper and salt.

Mince the ham, pound to a paste, and beat in the rest of the butter. Season as for the tongue.

Put a thick layer of the ham paste over the bottom of a deep, 1 pint (575/600 ml.) soufflé dish, then dot lumps of tongue paste all over the top. Do not smooth these out. Put another layer of ham paste over the top, then another layer of lumps of tongue paste. Finish with a layer of ham. Cover with waxed paper, and weight the top with a heavy tin. Chill in the refrigerator overnight.

Remove the weight and paper, and seal with clarified butter. Leave in the refrigerator to get really cold before serving.

Serve cut in wedges so that the 'marbling' shows to advantage. A crisp salad is a good accompaniment.

DEVILLED CHICKEN-LIVER PASTE
Countrywide

'DEVILLING' is generally associated with chops and with pieces of poultry and game, which are treated with a hot mixture of pepper and spices.

This recipe gives similar treatment to a rich chicken-liver paste. It is good both cold on toast as a first course or hot as a savoury.

PREPARATION TIME: 2¼ HOURS
COOKING TIME: 15–20 MINUTES

INGREDIENTS FOR SIX

8 oz. (225 g.) chicken livers
Salt and freshly ground black pepper
½ teaspoon Cayenne pepper
¼ teaspoon freshly grated ginger
2 oz. (50 g.) butter
2 tablespoons dry sherry
1 teaspoon Tabasco sauce
Clarified butter (see p. 49)

Mix the salt, both peppers and ginger into the chicken livers, and leave them to stand for 2 hours.

Chop the livers roughly. Melt the butter in a heavy frying pan, and add the livers. Cook them over a medium heat until brown on the outside, but still pink inside. Tip them into a blender.

Blend the livers for 1 minute. Add the sherry and Tabasco sauce, and blend for a further minute. Taste, and add more seasoning, if you like.

Pot, and seal with clarified butter.

To serve hot as a savoury, spread slices of toast thickly with the paste and place under a hot grill until the surface bubbles. Put a generous teaspoon of cold clotted cream on top of each piece of toast, and serve at once on hot plates.

POTTED PIGEONS
Countrywide

THIS RECIPE comes from a book called *The Country Housewife*, written in the early 18th century by Richard Bradley, a Fellow of the Royal Society and Professor of Botany at Cambridge—although he is reputed to have faked a recommendation to obtain the latter appointment.

However dubious his ethics, his cookery was sound enough for this recipe to need little alteration over 250 years later: 'To Pot Pigeons—Season your Pigeons with savoury Spice, put them in a pot, cover them with Butter, and Bake them; then take them out and drain them; when they are cold, cover them with clarified Butter.'

Here is the modern detailed version. It has the added advantage of producing deliciously flavoured butter to spread on hot toast for tea.

PREPARATION TIME: 15 MINUTES
COOKING TIME: 3 HOURS
PRE-HEAT THE OVEN TO 150°C (300°F)—GAS MARK 2

INGREDIENTS FOR ONE SERVING

1 pigeon for each person, plucked and drawn (see p. 144)
Salt and freshly ground black pepper
¼ teaspoon freshly ground nutmeg
4 oz. (100/125 g.) butter per pigeon, cut into cubes
Flour and water paste (see p. 49)

Season each pigeon inside and out with salt, pepper and nutmeg. Put half the butter in the bottom of a heavy ovenproof pot which will hold the pigeons in one layer. Place the pigeons in the pot and cover with the rest of the butter. Put on the lid, sealing it with a strip of the flour and water paste. Bake at the bottom of the pre-heated oven for 3 hours. Remove the pigeons and drain in a colander. Allow to cool.

Leave the butter to solidify in the pot. Lift out the hard butter, leaving the juices in the casserole, and melt over a gentle heat.

Clean the cooking pot. Re-season the pigeons and replace them in the pot. Pour over the melted butter. If you want to keep them for more than 1 week, cover the pigeons completely with clarified butter (see p. 49).

Potted Pigeons make a delicious cold dish on their own, served with a watercress or tomato salad. They are also very good for picnics.

HARE PASTE
Staffordshire

THIS RECIPE comes from Staffordshire, but various forms of Hare Paste have been popular not only in the Midlands, but also in neighbouring Wales. George Borrow, on his walks through 'Wild Wales' in the 1850s, mentions that 'pots of hare' were served at an outstanding breakfast which also included potted trout and shrimps, sardines, beefsteak, eggs, muffins, bread and tea.

This recipe for Hare Paste is a good way of using up the remains of jugged or roast hare.

PREPARATION TIME: 20–30 MINUTES

INGREDIENTS FOR FOUR

8 oz. (225 g.) cold cooked hare, drained of all juices
3 oz. (75 g.) softened butter
1 teaspoon sherry
¼ teaspoon mixed spice
Salt and freshly ground black pepper
2–3 small bay leaves
Clarified butter (see p. 49)

Mince or finely chop the hare. Beat in the butter, sherry and mixed spice, and season with salt and pepper to taste.

Pack this paste into two or three small, very clean jars. Put a bay leaf on top of each, and pour on the clarified butter to seal.

Cover the pots with kitchen foil and keep the paste for at least 1 week before eating.

POTTED PHEASANT
Cumberland

THE PHEASANT has retained the flavour of wild game despite the fact that it is the only game-bird which is hand-reared, and almost hand-fed. This is probably because of its diet, which consists of a variety of berries, fruits, bulbs and grasses.

This rich flavour makes the bird particularly suitable for a simple recipe such as Potted Pheasant—and you will find that it is a good way of using up an old bird.

The pheasant should be hung for a week (longer if the weather is cold), or the flavour will not have fully developed (see p. 146).

Try serving Potted Pheasant for breakfast on a special occasion, as they did in large Victorian and Edwardian country households.

PREPARATION TIME: 15 MINUTES
COOKING TIME: 1–1½ HOURS

INGREDIENTS FOR FOUR TO SIX

1 large cock pheasant, plucked and drawn (see p. 144)
Salt and freshly ground black pepper
¼ teaspoon allspice
2 tablespoons Madeira or sherry
About 5–6 oz. (150–175 g.) butter
1 teaspoon lemon juice
Clarified butter (see p. 49)

Season the bird inside and out with salt, pepper and allspice, and place in a heavy pan with a well-fitting lid. Add the Madeira or sherry and 1 oz. (25 g.) of the butter. Braise the pheasant over a low heat for about 1–1½ hours, or until tender. Remove from the heat, and drain in a colander over a bowl.

When cold, strip off the flesh and weigh before mincing or chopping finely. Take about one-third of the weight of the meat in butter and beat it into the minced meat. Add the lemon juice and more seasoning if necessary.

Pack into small, decorative, scrupulously clean china pots. Seal with clarified butter and store for at least 1 week before eating.

The Potted Pheasant will keep for 1 month in a cool place, but once the butter seal is broken, eat within 2 days.

BRAWN
Countrywide

BRAWN WAS PART of the traditional Christmas fare in medieval times, when it was made from the head and shoulders of a wild boar. Wine and ale were often included in the old-time recipes.

Although wild boar are long extinct here, brawn is still popular—especially in the North of England. There, most towns have white-painted pork shops with gleaming, tiled shelves laden with cold pork meats, sausages, black puddings and pots of home-made brawn.

You can prepare brawn at home, but order the head and trotters in advance as they need to be kept in brine for 24 hours. The butcher may do this for you, or you can make up the brine yourself (see p. 49).

This recipe gives a savoury, delicate textured mould, which can be served at high tea, as a light supper, or even at breakfast time.

PREPARATION TIME: 20 MINUTES
COOKING TIME: 2–3 HOURS

INGREDIENTS FOR SIX

Half a pig's head, which has been in brine for 24 hours
2 pig's trotters, soaked in brine for 24 hours
1 onion, sliced
1 carrot, sliced
1 stick celery, sliced
½ pint (275/300 ml.) dry cider
A bunch of bay leaves, thyme, parsley and celery leaves
6 peppercorns
1 teaspoon salt
Freshly ground black pepper
¼ teaspoon freshly grated nutmeg
Fresh parsley

Brawn—a delicate savoury for any time of day.

Chop the head into manageable pieces. Put the pieces in a large pan with the trotters, carrot, onion and celery. Add the cider, herbs, peppercorns and 1 teaspoon salt. Cover with cold water. Bring to the boil, skimming frequently. Reduce the heat and simmer gently for 2–3 hours, or until the meat is very tender. Remove the pieces of head and, when cold, strip the meat from the bones.

Drain off the stock from the pan, and boil until reduced by half. Add the meat to the stock, season with salt and pepper, and add the nutmeg. Simmer for about 10 minutes.

Rinse a dish or mould with cold water. Pour in the meat and stock. Cover with a piece of foil and leave overnight to set.

Turn out and serve, decorated with fresh parsley.

POTTED BEEF
Wales

MEAT HAS BEEN POTTED, primarily to preserve it, since the days of Elizabeth I. In *The Housekeeper's Guide* (1834), Esther Copley scornfully described it as a method which would 'afford animal food to those who have not the means of chewing it'. How unfair this comment is will be seen from this delicious version.

As in many old recipes for potted meat, anchovies are included among the ingredients. Although they lose their identity in the cooking, they add great flavour and richness to the finished dish.

PREPARATION TIME: 20 MINUTES
COOKING TIME: 4–5 HOURS
PRE-HEAT THE OVEN TO 150°C (300°F)—GAS MARK 2

INGREDIENTS FOR SIX TO EIGHT

2 lb. (900 g.) topside of beef, in one piece
2 tins anchovy fillets, 1¾ oz. (45 g.) each
¼ teaspoon freshly grated nutmeg
Freshly ground black pepper
8 oz. (225 g.) unsalted butter, cut into cubes
2 bay leaves
Flour and water paste (see p. 49)
Clarified butter (see p. 49)

Using a larding needle (see p. 388), thread the anchovy fillets through the beef. Sprinkle the meat generously with nutmeg and pepper, and place in a casserole which will hold it comfortably without too much space to spare. Add the bay leaves, and the butter cut into cubes. Put on the lid, sealing it with a strip of the flour and water paste, or wrap the whole casserole in foil. Place the casserole on a low shelf in the pre-heated oven and leave absolutely untouched for the full cooking time—it can be left overnight in the low oven of an Aga.

When the meat is done (almost falling apart), remove and allow it to drain by putting it in a colander over a bowl. Leave the butter and meat juices in the casserole. When cold, put the meat through a mincer, or chop finely—you can leave on any fat, but remove the gristle.

The butter used in the cooking will solidify when cold, leaving the juices underneath. Lift out the hard butter and mix well with the minced beef. (The juices must *not* be included as they shorten the life of the finished dish.) Taste the beef and butter mixture and season. It should be spicy but not too salty—the anchovies will probably provide enough salt.

Pack the beef into china jars or pots which have been washed out with boiling water. Seal the pots with the clarified butter to a depth of about $\frac{1}{2}$ in. (1·5 cm.).

Potted Beef will keep for at least 1 month in a cold larder or refrigerator. Remove to room temperature about 1 hour before eating.

Serve with toast as a first course, or use in sandwiches.

Trout fillets, seasoned and potted, make a rich first course.

POTTED TROUT OR CHAR
Lake District

POTTED CHAR has been a Cumbrian delicacy for over 200 years. The once-plentiful char, which have a delicate pink, salmon-like flesh, are found in the deepest of the upland lakes of northern and western Britain. Celia Fiennes, a 17th-century traveller, said that 'their taste is very rich and fat'.

Large quantities were potted between Michaelmas and Christmas in seasoned butter, often in special pots: shallow circular dishes, sometimes decorated with a portrait of the fish.

This recipe makes a richly delicious first course for a winter dinner party, or the main course of a light summer menu.

As char are scarce these days, you can use trout instead.

PREPARATION TIME: 15 MINUTES
COOKING TIME: $1\frac{1}{2}$ HOURS
RESTING TIME: 2 DAYS
PRE-HEAT THE OVEN TO 150°C (300°F)—GAS MARK 2

INGREDIENTS FOR FOUR

4 trout
Salt
Freshly ground black pepper
$\frac{1}{2}$ teaspoon freshly grated nutmeg
8 oz. (225 g.) butter

Fillet the trout (see p. 75). Season each filleted trout, on both sides, with salt, pepper and nutmeg. Leave overnight.

Next day, wipe each fillet with a paper towel, and season each again with a little more salt. Melt 2 oz. (50 g.) of the butter and pour into an ovenproof dish. Sandwich the fillets together and place them in the dish. Cover them with the rest of the butter, then with a lid (make one out of foil if the dish does not have its own). Cook for $1\frac{1}{2}$ hours, or until a skewer pierces the fish easily.

With a plate over the dish, drain off the butter into a bowl. Put a plate over the trout in the cooking dish, and invert quickly to transfer the fish to the plate without breaking them. Allow to cool, and remove the skin.

Arrange in a shallow dish. Clarify the butter (see p. 49) in which the fish were cooked, and pour over the trout. Keep for 2 days before eating.

Serve with brown bread and butter and lemon quarters, or with a cucumber.

CAVEACHED FISH
London

THE NAME for this method of preserving fish comes from the Spanish word for the recipe—*escabeche*, originally meaning a pickle for fish. It came to England via the West Indies, where the Spanish and English colonists came into contact.

However, the actual practice of preserving fish in vinegar is much older; even the Romans were familiar with it.

Caveached Fish was particularly popular in England in the 18th century, when it was served as one of the selection of lighter dishes in the second part of the meal.

Nowadays this highly spiced dish can be served as a first course with brown bread and butter, or as a side dish with curry.

PREPARATION TIME: 6 HOURS
COOKING TIME: 10 MINUTES

INGREDIENTS FOR SIX

6 large herrings, or small mackerel
2 oz. (50 g.) block or sea salt
½ oz. (15 g.) freshly ground black pepper
1 teaspoon freshly grated nutmeg
½ teaspoon crushed cloves
½ teaspoon crushed allspice
Malt vinegar
Cooking oil

Ask your fishmonger to fillet the fish. Cut each fillet into 2 in. (5 cm.) squares. Mix together the salt, pepper, nutmeg, cloves and allspice. Rub each piece of fish, on both sides, with this mixture. Leave for 4 hours.

Fry the pieces of fish in a little hot oil until brown. This seals the spices into the fish. Leave to get quite cold.

Pack the fish into a clean bottling jar and cover them with vinegar to a depth of 1 in. (2·5 cm.). Pour a thin layer of cooking oil over the surface of the vinegar, and seal the jar.

Store in a cool place, and leave for at least a week before eating. The fish will keep up to 6 months.

POTTED HERRINGS
Lowestoft

WHEN LARGE CATCHES of herring were commonplace (in 1919, for example, 53,000 tons were landed at Lowestoft) they were often potted, as an alternative to the more usual methods of smoking and salting.

Today, they make an unusual addition to a mixed hors-d'oeuvre, or they can be served with salad for a light summer luncheon.

PREPARATION TIME: 20 MINUTES
COOKING TIME: OVERNIGHT
PRE-HEAT THE OVEN TO 110°C (225°F)—GAS MARK ¼

INGREDIENTS FOR SIX

12 herrings, scaled, gutted, heads and tails removed
¼ teaspoon crushed allspice
2 crumbled bay leaves
Salt and freshly ground black pepper
Cider vinegar
Cooking oil

Dry the herrings well, and arrange them in layers in a deep stoneware casserole. Sprinkle each layer with salt, pepper, allspice and bay leaves. Press them well down, and cover with vinegar to a depth of about ½ in. (1·5 cm.). Put a lid on the casserole and place in the pre-heated oven. Leave to cook overnight.

Next morning, take out the herrings and store them, in their casserole, in a cool place. The fish will keep for about a fortnight in winter, 7–10 days in summer. If you want to keep them longer, pour a film of cooking oil over the surface of the vinegar to exclude the air.

SMOKED FISH PASTES
Countrywide

THESE PASTES are often given a pseudo-French flavour by being called 'pâtés'. This title is inappropriate, as they are good in their own right as straightforward pastes.

Their excellence depends on the quality of fish used. Loch Fyne or Isle of Man kippers make a better paste than any packaged kipper fillets, and real Finnan Haddock a more delicate paste than dyed cod fillets. Smoked trout paste is bland, but is good served with grated, fresh horseradish.

PREPARATION TIME: 30 MINUTES
COOKING TIME: 15 MINUTES

INGREDIENTS FOR SIX

4 good-quality kippers, or 2 large Finnan Haddock, or 2 smoked trout
4 oz. (100/125 g.) soft butter
Freshly ground black pepper
Juice of 1 lemon
Salt
Clarified butter (see p. 49)

Cook kippers in water, the smoked haddock in milk and water, until the fish is tender—about 10–15 minutes. The trout need not be cooked further. Remove the skin and bones. Small kipper bones will be well broken up, so it is not necessary to spend time searching for every one.

Put the fish and butter in a blender with half the lemon juice and pepper. Blend until smooth. Check the seasoning and add salt (the trout will need most). Beat in the rest of the lemon juice if needed. Pot, and seal with clarified butter. Do not keep too long before eating.

CRAB PASTE
Yorkshire

OUR ANCESTORS must have had strong constitutions, for during the 1830s this deliciously rich Crab Paste was a popular late-night supper dish, particularly in Scarborough.

Today, it is probably more suitable as a first course, served with thin slices of cucumber, lemon quarters and wholemeal toast.

PREPARATION TIME: 45 MINUTES
COOKING TIME: 30 MINUTES

INGREDIENTS FOR SIX

1 large, cooked crab, about 2½ lb. (1·1 kg.)
2 oz. (50 g.) butter
Salt and freshly ground black pepper
2 egg yolks
3 tablespoons double cream
¼ teaspoon Cayenne pepper
Clarified butter (see p. 49)

Remove all the meat from the crab, and chop finely. Put in a heavy saucepan with the butter and seasoning. Heat gently, stirring often, for 10 minutes. Remove the pan from the heat.

Blend the egg yolks and cream together, and stir into the crab mixture. Stand the pan in another pan containing hot but not boiling water, and cook, stirring frequently, until thick. The water in the bottom pan must not boil, or the eggs may curdle. Allow the paste to cool a little, then add generous amounts of both peppers, and salt if necessary.

Pot in small jars, and seal with clarified butter. Chill in the refrigerator.

POTTED SHRIMPS
Lancashire

POTTED SHRIMPS have been popular in the North of England since the 18th century, and today shrimp teas are still very much in demand in Lancashire and Yorkshire.

In the original recipes most of the shrimps were pounded to a paste, although sometimes a few were left whole to give a contrast in texture.

Traditionally, the menu for a shrimp tea includes thin slices of brown or white bread, spread with butter and accompanied by a large plate of watercress. A pot of strong tea completes the picture.

PREPARATION TIME: 20 MINUTES

INGREDIENTS FOR FOUR

4 oz. (100/125 g.) butter
1 lb. (450 g.) peeled shrimps
¼ teaspoon powdered mace
¼ teaspoon Cayenne pepper
Salt and freshly ground black pepper
Clarified butter (see p. 49)

Melt the butter over a moderate heat. Add the shrimps, mace and Cayenne pepper. Season with salt and pepper. Heat thoroughly, but do not allow the shrimps to boil as this toughens them. Stir them as they cook.

Put into small pots, and seal with clarified butter. Leave to chill in the refrigerator.

Savoury Crab Paste and Potted Shrimps combine the tastes of York and Lancaster—old feuds buried at the tea-table.

RECIPES *from* OTHER LANDS

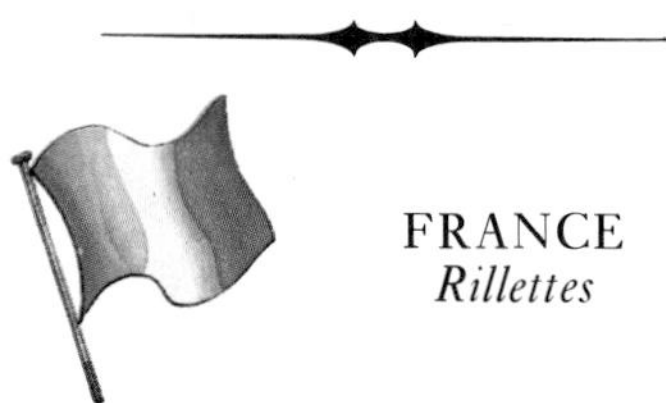

FRANCE
Rillettes

RILLETTES are said to have been served for the first time to that boisterous French gourmand, Rabelais, though there is evidence that they existed long before his time. However, he once visited a remote country inn to order a meal for a party of friends. The landlord, whose resources were limited, chopped up goose flesh and fat pork, which he simmered in a cauldron with a variety of herbs and seasonings. Served cold, the dish delighted Rabelais.

This version comes from the Touraine region of France. To ensure its characteristic coarse, meaty texture, chop the meat roughly by hand.

Use the pork rinds, which are not needed for the *rillettes*, to make a savoury snack of *rillons*.

PREPARATION TIME: 20 MINUTES
COOKING TIME: 4–5 HOURS
PRE-HEAT THE OVEN TO 150°C (300°F)—GAS MARK 2

INGREDIENTS FOR FOUR

2½ lb. (1·1 kg.) sliced belly pork, with as little bone as possible
3–4 large cloves garlic, crushed
1 tablespoon sea salt
Large sprig fresh rosemary, broken into two or three pieces
3 fl. oz. (90 ml.) water
Freshly ground black pepper

Remove the rinds from the pork slices and reserve. Cut the meat into small cubes, removing any pieces of bone.

Put the pork into a shallow ovenproof dish, and add the garlic, salt, rosemary and water. Grind plenty of pepper on top, then stir well. Cover the dish loosely with foil, and place on the bottom shelf of the preheated oven. Cook for 4–5 hours, stirring occasionally, until the pork is soft.

Stand a colander over a large bowl and tip in the pork. Leave to drain as it cools. Chop the drained meat, not too finely, and season with more salt and pepper. Pack tightly into very clean jars.

When the juices in the bowl have cooled, chill in a refrigerator until the pure fat can be lifted off. Melt it and use to seal the jars, adding more fresh lard if necessary. Cover the jars with their own lids, or ones made of foil. *Rillettes* can be stored for 1 month or more before eating, but once you start a jar, use it up quickly.

To make the *rillons*, score across the strips of pork rind at short intervals with a sharp knife, and cook them in a roasting tin on the top shelf of the oven in which the *rillettes* are cooking. Drain off the rendered fat from time to time. When the rinds are crisp and brown, drain on paper towels. Break into small pieces at the score marks and sprinkle with salt. Serve *rillons* with drinks, or as snacks for children.

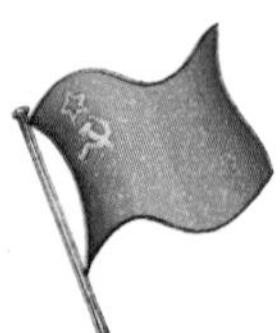

RUSSIA
Fish Pâté

IN RUSSIA, this pâté is served as a *zakuska* or hors-d'oeuvre.

Zakuski, almost a meal in themselves, were traditionally served in an annexe to the dining-room with large quantities of variously flavoured vodkas. In Tsarist days, it is said, so many toasts were drunk that some guests never reached the dining-room.

It is still appropriate to offer vodka if you are serving the pâté on its own as a first course. When you buy the fish, ask the fishmonger for some fish bones and trimmings to make the stock. If you do not use fish bones as well as fish pieces the stock will not set to a jelly.

PREPARATION TIME: 45 MINUTES
COOKING TIME: 45 MINUTES

INGREDIENTS FOR FOUR TO SIX

12 oz. (350 g.) whiting fillets
12 oz. (350 g.) coley fillets
8 oz. (225 g.) herring fillets
Fish bones and trimmings, about 1½ lb. (700 g.)
1 carrot, sliced
1 stick celery, sliced
10 peppercorns
A bunch of 2 bay leaves, some parsley stalks and celery leaves
Salt and freshly ground black pepper
3 thick slices stale white bread
1 onion
1 clove garlic
1 large egg, beaten
¼ teaspoon freshly grated nutmeg
Juice of ½ lemon
2 hard-boiled eggs, sliced
2 pickled cucumbers, sliced

Skin the fillets, and put this skin, with the bones and trimmings, in a large saucepan. Add the carrot, celery, peppercorns and the bunch of herbs. Season with salt. Cover with 2 pints (1·1 litres) of cold water and bring slowly to the boil. Lower the heat, and simmer while the pâté is prepared.

Soak the bread in water. Remove any bones from the fish, and mince the flesh finely. Put the onion and garlic through the mincer. Squeeze all the water from the bread. Put the bread, fish, onion, garlic and the egg in a large bowl, and beat well. Season and add the nutmeg and lemon juice.

Oil a large piece of foil and form the fish mixture into a roll on it. Fold the long edges of the foil tightly together, leaving room for the pâté to swell as it cooks. Twist the ends together, and lower the parcel into the simmering stock. Cook gently for 30 minutes. Allow the pâté to cool a little before lifting it out of the pan. Slide the pâté from the foil on to a long dish.

Strain the stock, and boil fast until reduced to one-third. Taste and add more lemon juice if required. When the stock is cold, but before it has begun to set, brush a little over the pâté. Leave the rest to set, then chop roughly and pile round the pâté. Decorate with egg and cucumber.

DENMARK
Salted Sprats

THIS DANISH VERSION of a typical Scandinavian dish is particularly good when served with sour cream and *blini* (see p. 294).

Set a dish of sprats, a plate piled with pancakes and a large bowl of sour cream on the table.

PREPARATION TIME: 30–40 MINUTES
STANDING TIME: ABOUT 1 WEEK
INGREDIENTS FOR SIX TO EIGHT

2 lb. (900 g.) sprats
10 black peppercorns
6 juniper berries
12 oz. (350 g.) sea or block salt
6 bay leaves
8 caraway seeds (optional)

Cut the heads and tails from the sprats, and remove the guts with the tip of a sharp knife. Crush the peppercorns and juniper berries with the salt, crumble the bay leaves, and mix all together. If you like the flavour, add the caraway seeds.

Put a layer of this salt mixture in the bottom of a stoneware storage jar, then a layer of fish. Repeat until all the ingredients are used up, ending with a salt layer.

Cover with a double thickness of waxed paper, and a weighted saucer to compress the contents so that the fish juices combine with the salt to make a preserving brine.

The sprats can be eaten after about 1 week or they can be kept for up to 1 month in the refrigerator.

FRANCE
Pâté de Foie de Porc

THIS PÂTÉ from the Perigord—a region of France famous for its rich cuisine—is often enhanced with the truffles found locally on the roots of stunted oaks. They grow about a foot beneath the surface; pigs and dogs are trained to smell them out.

The recipe incorporates a pig's trotter, which produces an aspic robe for the pâté as it cooks.

The pâté should not be stored in the freezer, or the aspic will liquefy.

PREPARATION TIME: 35 MINUTES
STANDING TIME: 1 HOUR
COOKING TIME: 4 HOURS
PRE-HEAT THE OVEN TO 150°C (300°F)—GAS MARK 2

INGREDIENTS FOR SIX

1 lb. (450 g.) fat belly pork, without bones or skin
1 lb. (450 g.) pig's liver
3 shallots, peeled and chopped
2 cloves garlic, crushed
¼ teaspoon grated nutmeg
¼ teaspoon ground cloves
2 teaspoons salt
Freshly ground black pepper
4–5 unsmoked streaky-bacon rashers, with rinds cut off
1 split pig's trotter
1 carrot, peeled and sliced
1 onion, peeled and sliced
1 bay leaf
1 sprig parsley and thyme
A strip of orange peel
4 tablespoons brandy
3 fl. oz. (90 ml.) dry white wine

Mince the pork and liver finely. Add the shallots, garlic, nutmeg and cloves. Season with salt and pepper. Mix very thoroughly and leave to stand for 1 hour at room temperature.

Take a small piece of the mixture and fry it. When cool, check the seasoning and add more salt if necessary, remembering that cold food needs to be more highly seasoned than hot food.

Line a 2½ pint (1·4 litre) terrine or stoneware dish with the bacon rashers, and fill with the minced meat. Arrange the split pig's trotter and the sliced carrot and onion on top. Add the bay leaf, parsley, thyme and orange peel. Sprinkle with a little extra salt and pepper and pour over the brandy and wine. Add just enough water to cover the meat.

Cover with the lid of the terrine, or with foil, and bake in a baking tin half full of hot water for 4 hours in the middle of the pre-heated oven.

Cool the pâté until lukewarm, then remove the trotter, vegetables and herbs. Smooth over the top with the side of a knife. Replace the lid and, when the pâté is quite cold, wrap the entire dish in foil and store in the refrigerator. Keep for at least 1 week before eating, restoring it to room temperature 1 hour before serving.

Pâté de Foie de Porc—minced liver with spices, herbs, brandy and wine.

GREECE
Taramasalata

PACKAGE HOLIDAYS in Greece and the Aegean, as well as the steady increase in the number of Greek restaurants in our towns and cities, have combined to make this first course much better known in this country than it was a few years ago.

The name simply means a salad of grey mullet's roe—if you cannot find this roe in your local shops, use smoked cod's roe instead.

Traditionally, this is served with hot *pitta*, the delicious unleavened Greek bread.

PREPARATION TIME: 30 MINUTES

INGREDIENTS FOR FOUR TO SIX

8 oz. (225 g.) smoked grey mullet or cod's roe
1 cold boiled potato, or a thick slice of white bread soaked in water and squeezed dry
2 cloves garlic, crushed
Juice of 1 lemon
6 tablespoons olive oil
Freshly ground black pepper
Parsley
Lemon quarters
Black olives

Split open and scrape the roe from its skin. Place in a bowl with the potato or bread and the garlic, and pound until smooth. An electric blender will do this quickly: add a little of the oil while blending to moisten the mixture.

Beat in the lemon juice and olive oil alternately, a little at a time. Season to taste with pepper. Pile into a shallow bowl and garnish with the parsley, lemon quarters and black olives. Eat within 24 hours.

POTTED MEATS AND FISH

DESCRIBING BREAKFAST AT AN INN in *Wild Wales,* an account of a walking tour, the 19th-century writer George Borrow said he found it delightful beyond his expectations. It included: 'Pot of hare: ditto of trout; pot of prepared shrimps.'

Borrow's delight echoed that of many British travellers since the 16th century, when cooks began to preserve meat and fish by potting it under an airtight covering of clarified mutton fat or butter. Two different meats could be combined during potting to give an attractive 'marbled' effect as well as a delicious dish for the cold table.

Brawns and pressed meats—preserved for a short while in their own jelly—also made a tasty cold dish. Brawn made from a boar's foreparts was traditionally served at Christmas.

Potted meat and fish could be bought generally until the 1920s. It is still available in northern England.

Potted and Pressed Meat and Potted Fish

Potted meat or fish is usually seasoned and cooked until tender, then either pounded to a paste, potted and covered with melted butter, or left whole in its cooking pot and covered with melted butter.

The butter solidifies to form an airtight seal, so that the contents can be kept in store. The butter is first clarified by heating and filtering to remove salt, buttermilk and impurities. Fat and dripping can also be clarified and used for sealing.

Potted meat and fish is a good way of making a tasty dish from cooked or uncooked leftovers or trimmings. You can also use bruised game unsuitable for roasting.

Store in a cool place, such as a larder or a refrigerator, for up to 1 month in winter. Once the seal is broken, eat the contents within 2 days.

The equipment you need

Mincer, liquidiser or pestle and mortar.

Baking dish. Ovenproof stoneware, porcelain or vitrified enamelware vessels are the most suitable. Earthenware cracks easily and may become unhygienic.

Large stainless-steel or heavy aluminium saucepan or fish kettle. Do not use enamel saucepans, which may have barely visible cracks in the enamel. The exposed metal can react with the cooking liquid.

Strainers.

Storage pots. Use straight-sided pottery jars or bottling jars. Wash in boiling water and drain before use.

Meat press. As an alternative, use a round cake tin (with a removable base if possible) large enough to hold the meat, a plate and 2–4 lb. (900 g.–1·8 kg.) weights.

A large stoneware or plastic jar with a lid, for brining meat.

PREPARING MEAT AND FISH FOR POTTING

Salted meat is required for some recipes. Soak the meat in brine (see right) for the length of time stated in the recipe.

Season the meat or fish well, particularly if you are using bland or tasteless leftovers. More seasoning is needed for food that is to be eaten cold rather than hot.

When preparing chicken livers, remove any discoloured parts.

If you want to test the seasoning of raw meat, fry a small portion before you begin cooking. Leave it to get cold before tasting.

To hold the meat or fish in shape, while it is cooking, make sure that the cooking vessel is not too large for the quantity to be cooked. Allow a capacity of $1\frac{1}{2}$ pint (850 ml.) for each $1\frac{1}{2}$ lb. (700 g.) of mixture.

Before mincing meat, remove the skin, gristle and bones to ensure a smooth texture.

Mince or chop the meat finely or coarsely as required to vary the texture. If possible, mix in some of the natural fats, particularly if you are using previously cooked leftovers. Failing this, mix in melted butter.

Boning chicken or game

1 If necessary, pluck and draw the bird and remove its feet and lower leg joints.

2 Lay the bird on its breast on a firm surface and cut off the lower part of each wing with a sharp-pointed knife.

3 Starting at the neck end, cut down the centre of the back to expose the backbone.

4 Working outwards from the backbone, cut away the flesh from one side of the bird. Cut between the bone and the flesh, but avoid slicing into the flesh or puncturing the skin.

5 Hold the cut-away flesh and pull it gently as you work. When you get to the wing joint, sever the sinews holding it to the carcase.

6 Hold the exposed carcase end of the wing bone in one hand and cut away the flesh along the bone. Pull out the bone as you work, so that the wing flesh is gradually turned inside out.

7 Cut through the sinews at the end of the bone and remove it.

8 Cut down the other side of the bird as far as the wing, and remove the wing bone in the same way.

9 Return to the first side of the bird and continue cutting until you reach the leg joint.

10 Sever the sinews between the leg

joint and thigh, and take hold of the carcase end of the leg bone.

11 Cut the flesh away from the leg bones, gradually turning the leg flesh inside out as you pull the bones through.

12 Cut through the sinews at the end of the second leg bone and remove the bones from the flesh.

13 Remove the flesh and leg bones from the other side of the bird in the same way.

14 Continue cutting away the flesh from the breastbone on each side. Take care not to puncture the skin, which is easily broken here.

15 Lift the rib-cage and carefully cut away the flesh from the tip of the breastbone.

Making flour-and-water paste

In the preparation of some potted-meat dishes, the meat is cooked slowly in a covered dish in melted butter or with very little liquid. To prevent steam escaping and keep the meat moist, the lid is sealed with a strip of dough round the rim.

1 Mix 4 heaped teaspoons of flour to a stiff dough with about 2 tablespoons of water.

2 Roll the dough to a thin strip. Damp the rim of the cooking vessel, press the dough strip round it and fit the lid. Also, seal any vent holes.

Potting and Storing

1 Fill pots to within $\frac{1}{2}$ in. (1·5 cm.) of the top and leave the contents to cool for about 30 minutes.

2 Pour on the clarified butter or other fat so that there is an overall covering of about $\frac{1}{8}$ in. (3 mm.).

3 Cover the pots with lids or tied-down covers. The covering need not be airtight.

4 Label the pots with the date of potting. Store in a cool place or on the bottom shelf of a refrigerator.

5 Leave pots to stand for 2 hours at room temperature before serving.

Clarified butter

1 Use 8 oz. (225 g.) of butter, which will produce about 5 oz. (150 g.) of clarified butter. Any that is left over can be stored.

2 Put the butter in a saucepan and place the saucepan over a low heat. Skim off the foam as the butter heats.

3 Sediment sinks to the bottom of the pan as the butter heats; 8 oz. (225 g.) of butter takes about 15 minutes to melt completely.

4 Remove the pan from the heat and leave to stand for up to 5 minutes, to make sure the sediment stays at the bottom. Then strain the butter through a double layer of scalded cheesecloth or fine cotton into a bowl.

5 Allow the butter to cool a little before pouring it over the surface of the potted meat or fish.

6 Store surplus butter in pots marked with the date of preparation. It will keep 3–4 weeks in a refrigerator or up to 6 months in a freezer.

Clarified fat or dripping

1 Add water to the fat or dripping—about one-third as much water as fat. For example, for 8 oz. (225 g.) of fat, use about $2\frac{1}{2}$ fl. oz. (75 ml.) of water.

2 Bring to the boil, then strain into a bowl and leave to cool.

3 When cold and set, remove the cake of clarified fat and scrape any scum from the bottom.

4 Store in a dry bowl or jar. It will keep up to 3 weeks in a freezer. Heat again to use for sealing.

Brining Meat

The cuts of meat most often salted in brine are brisket and silverside of beef, belly of pork and tongue.

This brine recipe includes saltpetre (a nitrate), usually obtainable from a chemist. If you cannot get it, or do not want to use it, you can make the brine without it, but the salted meat will be greyish in appearance.

Sugar is used to counteract the hardening action of the saltpetre, and need not be used if the saltpetre is omitted. But it does add flavour, especially dark, high-quality sugar.

INGREDIENTS

$3\frac{1}{2}$ pints (2 litres) of water
12 oz. (350 g.) cooking salt
1 oz. (25 g.) saltpetre
6 oz. (175 g.) brown sugar
1 bay leaf, 10 crushed juniper berries, 10 peppercorns, 10 all-spice berries and 1 sprig fresh or dried thyme, all tied in a muslin bag

Put the water, salt, saltpetre and sugar into a large saucepan, stir and bring to the boil. Add the herbs in the muslin bag and simmer for 10 minutes. Remove from the heat and leave until quite cold.

Soaking meat in brine

1 Sterilise a large, lidded stoneware or plastic jar with boiling water and leave to dry.

2 Place the meat in the sterilised jar and pour the cold brine over it.

3 Weight the meat with a sterilised plate to keep it below the surface.

4 Soak for the length of time stated in the recipe, usually about 1 week.

5 The brine can be used again, but first add another 4 oz. (100/125 g.) of salt and re-boil it.

Pressed Meat and Brawn

Pressed meat is seasoned and simmered for several hours, strained, then pressed under a weight. The cooking liquid can be boiled to concentrate it, then poured over the meat and left to set as a jelly round it.

Tongue and the cheaper cuts of beef, such as brisket, are often made into pressed meat. Coarse-fibred cuts can be carved in thinner slices when cold and pressed than when served hot.

Brawn is made from chopped meat placed in a pudding bowl or mould, covered with the liquid in which the meat was simmered, and left to set. It is not pressed. When cold it can be turned out and sliced.

Cow, sheep and pig heads and pigs' feet make good brawn because the bones produce a liquid with plenty of gelatine. If you make brawn with a selection of meats or meat scraps, cook some bones with the meat, otherwise gelatine will have to be added to the liquid to ensure setting.

Pressed meat and brawn will keep for about 1 week in a refrigerator. It is not advisable to freeze brawn or pressed meat with jelly, as it spoils the texture of the jellied stock.

Pressing Meat

1 Before cooking whole pieces of meat for pressing, tie them with fine string to keep them in shape while cooking. Remove the string after pressing.

2 Most brisket is bought boned and rolled. If it is not, remove the bones after cooking and before pressing.

3 Place the cooked meat, in whole pieces or chunks, in a meat press or cake tin. If using a meat press, follow the manufacturer's instructions.

4 If using a cake tin, cover the meat with a plate and place a 2–4 lb. (900 g.–1·8 kg.) weight on top. Leave until cool.

If the concentrated cooking liquid is to be poured over the meat during pressing and left to set, follow the instructions given in the recipe.

RIVER, SEA AND SHELLFISH

CONTAINING

NUMEROUS *Useful* FAMILY RECIPES

for FRESH & SMOKED FISH,

SHELLFISH & other FISHY DELIGHTES

PAGES 52–71

AND

A SELECTION of RECIPES from OTHER LANDS

PAGES 72–73

AND WITH

NOTES AND ADVICE

on all kinds of Cleaning, Preparing and Presenting of Fish to Perfection

PAGES 74–77

Suffolk Perch
Suffolk

THE PRAISE OF THE PERCH has been sung for centuries. The medieval monks of St Albans considered it a 'daynteuous fysshe, passynge holsom'; Izaak Walton thought it so 'wholesome that physicians allow him to be eaten by wounded men'; while the 19th-century writer, Kettner, also commenting on its wholesomeness, thought it was due to the fresh, clear waters in which it lives. 'They give it a flavour quite unlike that of the fish of muddy rivers.'

All in all, the consensus is that next to trout and salmon, it is the best of freshwater fish, a point perhaps better appreciated on the Continent than here. Poached perch is a delicacy of Northern France.

For this old Suffolk recipe, the dry cider that is produced around Stowmarket is recommended. But you can use any dry, vintage cider.

PREPARATION TIME: 20 MINUTES
COOKING TIME: 55 MINUTES
PRE-HEAT THE OVEN TO 180°C (350°F)—GAS MARK 4

INGREDIENTS FOR FOUR

4 perch, each about 8 oz. (225 g.)
2 tablespoons cooking oil
4 tomatoes, skinned and chopped
2 medium onions, chopped
A sprig of fresh thyme
Salt and pepper
4 oz. (100/125 g.) soft herring roes
2 oz. (50 g.) fresh brown breadcrumbs
¾ pint (450 ml.) dry cider
2 teaspoons chopped fresh parsley

Clean and gut the fish. Heat the oil in a flameproof casserole dish and add the tomatoes, onions, thyme, salt and pepper. Simmer over a low heat for 15 minutes.

Mix the soft roes and breadcrumbs in a bowl. Add 1 tablespoon of the tomato and onion mixture, mix well and season. Stuff the fish with the mixture.

Lay the fish on top of the remaining tomato and onion mixture and add the cider. Bake in the pre-heated oven for 40 minutes. Sprinkle with parsley and serve with mashed potatoes.

Elvers
Gloucestershire

SPAWNED IN THE SARGASSO SEA off Bermuda, untold millions of infant eels set forth each year to seek the rivers their parents came from—either westward to America, or east to Europe. They travel in miles-long, near-solid eel rivers, called 'eel-fares', from which the term 'elver' (young eel) is derived.

The Europe-bound elvers take three years to make the journey. Many never get there, since they are a major food source for everything that swims in the sea or flies above it. Nevertheless, the survivors press on to their ancestral rivers, such as the Severn. Here, sadly for them, they are hauled up by the bucket to be fried, put into pies or figure in elver-eating contests. An unhappy confirmation of the notion that to travel hopefully is better than to arrive.

For us, however, their arrival is welcome—they are delicious. Cook them the Gloucestershire way (being careful not to overcook) and provide a jug of dry cider to give them company.

PREPARATION TIME: 20 MINUTES
COOKING TIME: ABOUT 8 MINUTES

INGREDIENTS FOR FOUR

1 lb. (450 g.) whole elvers
2 tablespoons lard
8 long rashers streaky bacon, with rinds removed
3 large eggs, beaten
Salt and pepper

Thoroughly clean the elvers. Rinse them in a large bowl of cold water to which a handful of cooking salt has been added. You may need to repeat this rinsing three times to ensure cleanliness. Drain and dry.

Melt the lard in a frying pan and add the bacon. Fry until crisp, then remove with a slotted spoon and arrange round the edge of a warmed dish, leaving the fat in the pan.

Add the elvers to the pan and stir them about until they turn white—this takes just a few seconds. Pour on the beaten egg, season and cook briefly, stirring all the time, until the egg has just set. Tip into the middle of the bacon and serve at once.

Trout in Jelly
Countrywide

THIS RECIPE is an echo of late-medieval banquets, when fish jellies made from tench, pike, eels, turbot or plaice used to be served as part of the grand finale to the meal. The jelly, which consisted of fish stock, wine, and a dye such as saffron, was poured over the fish and left to set.

Cooked by almost any method, trout are the most perfect of freshwater fish, perhaps even including the salmon. Yet the Romans did not think much of their flavour.

When making this dish, bear in mind the advice of Izaak Walton, who, writing of the trout's fondness for the mayfly, said: 'These make the trout bold and lusty, and he is usually fatter and better meat at the end of May, than at any time of the year.'

PREPARATION TIME: 10 MINUTES
COOKING TIME: ABOUT 50 MINUTES
SETTING TIME: AT LEAST 6 HOURS

INGREDIENTS FOR SIX

¼ pint (150 ml.) dry white wine
1 tablespoon white wine vinegar
1 onion, sliced
1 small carrot, sliced
½ bay leaf
2 sprigs parsley
2 sprigs thyme
¼ teaspoon salt
6 peppercorns
6 trout, each about 8 oz. (225 g.), cleaned *(see p. 74)*

Pike, fresh and gleaming as the moment it was caught, will come to table with an anchovy-flavoured filling.

Put the wine, vinegar, onion, carrot, herbs and seasonings into a pan with $\frac{3}{4}$ pint (450 ml.) of water. Cover, bring to the boil and simmer for 30 minutes. Cool for about 10 minutes.

Put the trout into a pan in which they fit quite snugly. Strain the stock over them and bring it gently to the boil. Simmer the fish for 8 minutes, or until the flesh comes easily from the bone. Lift out, cool slightly, then skin the trout and remove the back-bones. Put the fillets into a serving dish 1 in. (2·5 cm.) deep.

Put the skins, bones and heads back into the cooking liquid and boil this down to $\frac{1}{2}$ pint (275/300 ml.). Taste the stock for seasoning—it should be quite strongly flavoured to offset the delicate taste of the trout.

Strain the liquid over the fish, and put the fish into the refrigerator overnight. The liquid will then set into a light, pale amber jelly.

Stuffed Pike
Countrywide

IZAAK WALTON, in *The Compleat Angler* (1653), describes the pike as '...a freshwater wolf...the Tyrant, as the salmon is the King, of the fresh waters'. No doubt he was embittered because the pike devours any other fish that enters the stretch of river it inhabits, leaving little for the fisherman.

When it came to stuffed pike, however, he relented. 'This dish of meat,' said he, 'is too good for any but anglers, or very honest men.'

The anchovy-flavoured stuffing makes the dish worthy of such high praise.

Preparation Time: 30 minutes
Cooking Time: 15–20 minutes
Pre-heat the Oven to
220°C (425°F)—gas mark 7

Ingredients for Four to Six

- *1 pike, weighing 3 lb. (1·4 kg.)*
- *2 oz. (50 g.) soft breadcrumbs, soaked in milk*
- *1 tablespoon chopped parsley*
- *4 oz. (100/125 g.) mushrooms, fried and chopped*
- *$\frac{1}{2}$ tin anchovy fillets*
- *4 oz. (100/125 g.) butter*
- *Juice of 1 lemon*

Clean the pike. Mix the breadcrumbs with the parsley, mushrooms, anchovies and half the butter. Fill the cavity with this mixture and lace it up, using small skewers and thread (see p. 76). Grease a baking dish and lay the fish carefully in it. Dot with the remaining butter. Measure the fish across the thickest part and bake in the pre-heated oven for 10 minutes per inch (2·5 cm.). When cooked, sprinkle with the lemon juice. Serve with plain boiled potatoes.

Trout with Bacon
Wales

Though not widely known to anglers, Welsh trout from the cold mountain lakes such as Llyn y Morynion are among the sweetest-tasting in Britain.

This recipe, with its subtle blending of flavours, closely resembles the Breton *Truite au lard*—a culinary link between two Celtic peoples. In Welsh it is known as *Brithyll a cig moch*.

Preparation Time: 5 minutes
Cooking Time: 20 minutes
Pre-heat the Oven to
180°C (350°F)—gas mark 4

Ingredients for Six

6 trout, each 6–8 oz. (175–225 g.)
Salt and pepper
12 thin rashers fat bacon, green or smoked
1 tablespoon chopped parsley

Clean the trout but keep them whole. Season them inside. Trim the rinds from the bacon rashers and place in a baking dish that will hold the fish snugly. Lay the fish head to tail on top of the layer of bacon. Season and scatter the top with parsley. If the ends of the rashers overlap, flip them over the fish. Cover with foil and bake for 20 minutes in the pre-heated oven.

Serve with creamed potatoes and a salad.

Baked Carp with Soft-Roe Stuffing
Countrywide

Because of its hardiness, its catholic feeding habits and obliging rapidity in fattening, the carp has been domesticated for a very long time indeed. Two-thousand years ago the Chinese kept carp in ponds, and at about the same period the Romans raised them in special enclosures called *vivaria*. Carp were introduced to Britain from Europe, probably in the 14th century.

For some time, the British, like other Europeans, have considered the roe to be the best part of the carp; the rest of this rather bony fish, according to Kettner in his *Book of the Table* (1877), requires 'all the rhetoric of the saucepan'.

The carp-roe stuffing is made in the same way as the soft-roe stuffing (see p. 59).

Preparation Time: 40 minutes
Cooking Time: about 20 minutes
Pre-heat the Oven to
200°C (400°F)—gas mark 6

Ingredients for Six

1 carp, about 2 lb. (900 g.)
Soft carp-roe stuffing, if available, or soft-roe stuffing using any kind of soft roe, such as herring roe (see p. 59)
1 oz. (25 g.) butter
2 large onions, chopped
2 tablespoons chopped parsley
Salt and pepper
½ pint (275/300 ml.) white wine

Clean the fish, removing the bitter gall sac at the back of the head. If the scales cannot be easily removed, pour a little boiling water over the fish and try again. To remove any muddy flavour, soak for 30 minutes in enough water to cover, adding 1 tablespoon of vinegar per pint (575/600 ml.).

Butter a baking dish. Line it with the onion and parsley, and season.

Measure the fish across its back at the thickest part. Fill the cavity with the prepared soft-roe stuffing, lace it up (see p. 76) and lay the carp in the dish. Pour the wine over and bake in the pre-heated oven for 10 minutes per inch (2·5 cm.).

Trout, fresh and sweet to the taste, served head to tail on a layer of crisp bacon.

MUSSEL RAGOO
Countrywide

EVERY NOW AND THEN, archaeologists working along the coastlines of Britain discover heaps of mussel and other shells. These are the remnants of meals eaten by our remote ancestors, the hunter-gatherers who eked out a precarious existence on shellfish and berries 6,000 and more years ago.

Their cooking arrangements were of the simplest. They dropped the mussels into the ashes of a fire and, when they opened, added some wild herbs and ate them. In fact, this is a delicious way of cooking them, especially if you add some small token of civilisation, such as garlic-flavoured butter.

The following recipe is medieval in origin. It is, in fact, the English version of the French mussel stews *mouclade* and *moules marinière*.

If you add water to the ragoo (from the French *ragoût*, meaning 'stew') as well as mussel liquid, you can turn the dish into a soup.

PREPARATION TIME: ABOUT 20 MINUTES
COOKING TIME: 20 MINUTES

INGREDIENTS FOR FOUR

4 lb. (1·8 kg.) mussels
3 oz. (75 g.) butter
6 oz. (175 g.) mushrooms, roughly chopped
1 rounded tablespoon flour
6–10 oz. (175–275 g.) whipping cream
Salt and pepper
A pinch of nutmeg
About 2 teaspoons lemon juice
1 tablespoon chopped parsley

Scrub, scrape and check the mussels (see p. 77). Discard any that are broken or already open. Put a double layer of mussels in a heavy pan and put on the lid. Cook for about 3 minutes over the highest possible heat, shaking the pan occasionally. Take the pan off the heat and leave the mussels in it for 3 minutes. Remove all the open mussels, leaving the shut ones a minute or two longer.

Repeat this process with the rest of the mussels. Cooking them in batches makes them more tender than cooking them all at once for a longer period of time.

Take the mussels from their shells, which can be thrown away. Strain the mussel juice carefully and reserve. Throw away any mussels which have refused to open.

Melt the butter in a frying pan and turn the mussels in it until they are lightly coated. Remove them with a slotted spoon. Add the mushrooms to the pan, cook for about 3 minutes and, when they are soft, stir in the flour. Cook for 2 minutes then add the mussel liquid and the cream.

A rich, thick sauce will take the full amount of cream stated in the ingredients, but if you prefer a lighter sauce, use only 6 oz. (175 g.).

Continue to cook the sauce for about 3 minutes, then stir in the salt, pepper, nutmeg and enough lemon juice to sharpen it slightly. Add the parsley and the mussels. Bring the mixture to just below boiling point to heat the mussels through, then divide between little pots and serve with wholemeal bread.

OYSTER LOAVES
Countrywide

IT IS SAID that the Romans invaded these islands for three reasons—oysters, slaves and hunting dogs. What satisfaction the last two afforded their new masters may be open to debate, but the native oysters of the Essex coast were and are the best in Europe, if not the world.

For centuries, they were the staple of the poor of South-east England. 'Poverty and oysters seem to go together,' says Sam Weller in *The Pickwick Papers*. Then, in the 1850s, something went wrong. Overfishing, to satisfy the demands of the new industrial towns, added to attacks by the sting winkle, turned the oyster into an expensive delicacy.

This recipe belongs to the oyster's golden days in the 18th century. When prices went up, oyster loaves moved to New Orleans. Sold hot on street corners, they became known as *les médiatrices* (mediators), and were taken home by tipsy husbands to placate their irate wives.

If oyster prices are prohibitive, use very large mussels instead. Open them (see p. 77), fry them in butter for no more than a few seconds, and add about half of the strained mussel liquid. More liquid can be added later, if the flavour requires it.

PREPARATION TIME: 30 MINUTES
COOKING TIME: 8 MINUTES
PRE-HEAT THE OVEN TO 220°C (425°F)—GAS MARK 7

INGREDIENTS FOR FOUR

16 oysters
4 baps, large bridge rolls or brioches
6 oz. (175 g.) butter
¼ pint (150 ml.) soured cream
¼ pint (150 ml.) double cream
Salt and pepper
A pinch of Cayenne pepper

Scrub and open the oysters (see p. 77). Put them into a sieve over a basin to drain.

Slice a lid from the rolls and scoop out most of the insides. Melt 5 oz. (150 g.) of the butter and brush the roll cases and lids inside and out. Crisp them in the pre-heated oven for about 7 minutes or until nicely browned. Check after 5 minutes to see if they need turning to colour evenly.

Meanwhile, fry the oysters in the remaining butter until opaque (about 45 seconds). Remove them, cut in half across and set them aside. Pour the oyster liquid and the two creams into the pan juices, stirring vigorously. Add the seasonings and raise the heat. Stir vigorously for a minute or two until you have a smooth, thick sauce. Taste and correct the seasoning.

When the cases are ready, re-heat the oysters in the sauce for a few seconds and divide them between the cases. Put the lids on top and serve.

BUTTERED PRAWNS, SHRIMPS OR CRAYFISH
Countrywide

ON PARTS OF THE SOUTH COAST it is still possible to roll up your trousers, or kilt up your skirt, and scoop a netful of shrimps out of the shallows. Few occupations are at once more contemplative and more rewarding on a seaside summer evening.

East Anglia and Morecambe are the other two great centres of shrimping and prawning; to the fishmonger, a prawn is a shrimp more than 3 in. (8 cm.) long. In these areas, where the men go out in boats to catch the fish in large fine-meshed nets, it is much easier to buy them than to attempt to catch them yourself.

Crayfish have never been really popular in this country. The great French chef Escoffier, in his *Guide to Modern Cookery* (1907), thought the reason was 'that ladies, dining in evening dress, find them difficult to manage'. This recipe dates back to at least 1760 and is a favourite in the Lake District.

PREPARATION TIME: 30 MINUTES
COOKING TIME: 25 MINUTES

INGREDIENTS FOR FOUR TO FIVE

2 pints (1·1 litres) boiled prawns, shrimps or freshwater crayfish
¼ pint (150 ml.) dry white wine
1 teaspoon white wine vinegar
Salt
¼ teaspoon grated nutmeg
2 oz. (50 g.) butter
1 level tablespoon plain flour
2 egg yolks
4–5 slices of bread

Prepare the shellfish (see p. 77). Simmer the shells and the discarded parts of the fish in a covered pan for 15 minutes with the wine, vinegar, salt, nutmeg and enough water to cover. Strain the liquid into a clean pan—there should be about ½ pint (275/300 ml.).

Add the shellfish meats and heat until the liquid is just under boiling point. Mash the butter and flour together and add to the pan in little pieces, stirring all the time.

Lightly beat the egg yolks in a small bowl. Add a little of the sauce to them, stir and return this mixture to the rest of the sauce. Stir and heat gently without boiling until the fish is just bound together with a thick, rich sauce. Add seasoning if necessary.

As it is important not to overcook shellfish, if possible prepare the toast during the last stages of making the sauce. Cut the crusts from the bread, toast it and cut it into fingers or triangles.

Divide the shellfish between four or five small pots, and tuck the toast shapes round the edges.

DUBLIN BAY PRAWNS
Countrywide

DUBLIN BAY PRAWNS are actually Norway lobsters *(Nephrops norvegicus)* that occur in all the colder waters of the European Continental Shelf. They are sometimes sold as scampi, which are larger relatives that live in the Adriatic.

The prawn's association with Dublin Bay dates from about 150 years ago. Then the fishing boats used to shelter in the bay, if there was a heavy sea running. The fishermen's wives often accompanied their men to sea and, by tradition, any prawns inadvertently caught in the nets became the automatic 'perk' of these hardy ladies. The prawns, no matter where they were caught, were boiled and sold in the streets of Dublin as Dublin Bay prawns. The money went to the women, who allegedly spent it on Irish stout and linen.

Use only fresh prawns for this recipe, and cook them by the simple method recommended. Frozen prawns are suitable only for prawn cocktails and deep-frying.

PREPARATION TIME: 40 MINUTES
COOKING TIME: ABOUT 3 MINUTES

INGREDIENTS FOR FOUR

2 lb. (900 g.) Dublin Bay prawns
3 heaped tablespoons butter
A pinch of salt
Juice of 1 lemon

Steam the prawns in a metal colander over boiling water for about 15–20 minutes. Leave them to cool for a few minutes, then shell them (see p. 77).

Melt the butter gently in a frying pan without letting it brown. Add the prawns to the pan and shake them gently in the butter. Sprinkle them lightly with salt and then add the lemon juice, stirring to mix it well together. Cook for just a few minutes until the butter is a faint pink.

BAKED TANROGANS
Isle of Man

'TANROGAN' WAS ORIGINALLY the Manx name for a scallop shell used in a simple lamp and consisting of a half shell filled with cod oil and a strip of rush for a wick. Later, the name was transferred to the scallops themselves, to distinguish them from the miniature scallops or 'queenies', which the island exports all over the world. There is a considerable difference between the two in size, if not in flavour—40 to 80 queenies to the pound (450 g.) as opposed to 8 to 12 tanrogans.

Try this Manx recipe for a novel and nourishing family supper.

PREPARATION TIME: 15 MINUTES
COOKING TIME: ABOUT 30 MINUTES
PRE-HEAT THE OVEN TO 180°C (350°F)—GAS MARK 4

INGREDIENTS FOR FOUR

8 scallops
¼ pint (150 ml.) fish stock
1 small onion, quartered
Salt and pepper
1 bay leaf
¼ pint (150 ml.) cheese sauce (see p. 150)
2 oz. (50 g.) grated Cheddar cheese

Remove the scallops from their shells and clean them (see p. 77). Keep the shells. Put the scallops in a small ovenproof dish with the stock, onion, seasoning and bay leaf. Cover the dish with a piece of buttered greaseproof paper, or a lid, and cook in the preheated oven for about 10 minutes.

Lift the scallops from the dish with a slotted spoon and put them back in their shells. Heat the cheese sauce and mix thoroughly with the cooking liquid. Pour a little over each scallop and sprinkle with the grated cheese. Brown under a hot grill until the sauce bubbles.

Serve with creamed potatoes and salad.

Stewed Scallops with Orange Sauce
Countrywide

The great scallop *(Pecten maximus)*, which occurs in large numbers off the Channel and Atlantic coasts of Britain, has the misfortune to possess the most delicate flesh of all our native shellfish, and is therefore in great demand both at home and overseas. The British use it to make the dish which we incorrectly term *Coquilles St Jacques*, but which the French know simply as scallops in Mornay sauce. *Coquilles St Jacques* is the French term for all scallops, whose shells were the emblem of St Jacques or James of Compostella.

The following recipe is based on an instruction given on how 'to stew scollops' in Hannah Glasse's *The Art of Cookery* (1760).

Preparation Time: 5 minutes
Cooking Time: 20–25 minutes

Ingredients for Six

18 scallops, off the shell
¼ pint (150 ml.) dry white wine
¼ pint (150 ml.) water
1 scant tablespoon white wine vinegar
½ teaspoon ground mace
2 cloves
1 tablespoon butter
1 tablespoon flour
Juice of 1 Seville orange, or of 1 sweet orange plus juice of ½ lemon
Salt, pepper and sugar

Remove the coral—the tongue-like roe—from the scallops, and slice the scallops in half.

Bring the following ingredients to the boil in a large saucepan: the wine, water, vinegar, mace and cloves. Cover and simmer for 10 minutes. Add salt and pepper to taste.

Lift the scallops and corals into the liquid and poach for 5 minutes, removing the corals as soon as they are firm—after about 3 minutes. Keep scallops and corals warm on a dish.

Strain the poaching liquid into a measuring jug. Reduce, if necessary, to obtain 8 fl. oz. (225 ml.). Mash the butter and flour together and add to the liquid in small pieces. Stir over a moderate heat without allowing the sauce to boil. Add the fruit juice and season to taste, adding a little sugar if necessary. Pour over the scallops and serve at once.

Orange Sauce adds zest to a dish of Stewed Scallops.

Partan Pie
Scotland

'Wha ca'ed ye partan-face, ma bonny lamb?' used to be a favourite insult of schoolchildren brought up on the windy coasts of Fife, and long familiar with the facial peculiarities of the partan, or crab. The luckier children were also familiar with this truly superb pie made in the shell of the crab.

'Crab is a slut to carve and a wrawde wight (or awkward cuss)', was the sour comment of the 15th-century author of the *Book of Nurture*. He was referring to the difficulty of extricating the meat from all the various sections of the crab's armour, a problem no less exasperating today. So before starting the operation, make sure to have skewers, nutcrackers and even a small hammer within reach.

Preparation Time: 15 minutes
Cooking Time: 5 minutes

Ingredients for Four

1 crab 2–3 lb. (900 g.–1·4 kg.) dressed *(see p. 77)*
Salt and white pepper
½ teaspoon nutmeg
3 tablespoons wine vinegar
2 tablespoons prepared mild mustard
3 tablespoons soft brown breadcrumbs
2 tablespoons butter

Mix all the crab meat together. Season with the salt, pepper and the nutmeg, and blend everything well together.

Heat the vinegar gently with the mustard, stirring well. Return the crab to its shell and pour the vinegar mixture over it. Cover with a layer of breadcrumbs and dot with the butter. Brown under a hot grill until heated through.

SUPPER HERRINGS
Wales

THIS RECIPE, known in Welsh as *Swper Sgadan*, reflects the simplicity of the old Welsh kitchen, whose equipment consisted of little more than a griddle, a bakestone and a great iron pot suspended by a chain over the fire. Consequently, boiling and stewing were the two most important methods of cooking. In England and Scotland, by contrast, herrings are almost always fried or grilled in breadcrumbs or oatmeal.

Sgadan Abergwaun, or Fishguard Herrings, is a very similar recipe; herrings caught by the Fishguard trawlers in the Irish Sea are reputed to be the best in Wales.

PREPARATION TIME: 10 MINUTES

COOKING TIME: 1 HOUR

PRE-HEAT THE OVEN TO 180°C (350°F)—GAS MARK 4

INGREDIENTS FOR FOUR

4 filleted herrings
1 tablespoon prepared mustard
Salt and pepper
1 oz. (25 g.) butter
1½ lb. (700 g.) potatoes, peeled and thinly sliced
1 large onion, peeled and sliced
1 large cooking apple, cored and sliced
¼ teaspoon dried sage
2 oz. (50 g.) butter, melted

Spread the cut side of the herrings with mustard and sprinkle them with salt and pepper. Roll them up, starting at the tail end. Spread the 1 oz. (25 g.) of butter over a pie or gratin dish large enough to accommodate all the ingredients.

Line the dish with a layer of the sliced potatoes and then a layer of onion and apple. Place the rolled herrings on top and cover them with the rest of the onion and apple, finishing with a layer of potato. Pour in enough boiling water to come halfway up the sides of the dish. Add the sage, season with salt and pepper, and pour the melted butter over the top.

Cover with foil and bake in the pre-heated oven for 30 minutes. Remove the foil and raise the temperature to 200°C (400°F)—gas mark 6. Taste the juices, and add more salt if necessary. Bake for another 20–30 minutes.

This is a complete meal, but a tomato salad is a delicious addition.

Supper Herrings, baked the Welsh way, on a bed of potatoes, onions and apples.

SOFT-ROE FRITTERS
Countrywide

MAKE THESE FRITTERS with large soft roes from either herring or mackerel. Make the sauce first, so that everything can be served piping hot when the last fritters are fried.

If you prefer the fritters without a sauce, serve them with quarters of lemon instead.

PREPARATION TIME: ABOUT 10 MINUTES

COOKING TIME: ABOUT 20 MINUTES

PRE-HEAT THE OVEN TO 140°C (275°F)—GAS MARK 1

INGREDIENTS FOR FOUR

12 pairs or 1 lb. (450 g.) of large soft roes
Salt and pepper
Cooking oil
½ pint (275–300 ml.) white sauce (see p. 162)
1 heaped teaspoon Dijon mustard

For the batter:

4 oz. (100/125 g.) flour
A pinch of salt
2 tablespoons oil
1 large egg yolk
About 6 fl. oz. (175 ml.) water or beer
1 large egg white

First make the white sauce and keep it warm over a pan of gently simmering water.

To make the batter, sift the flour and salt into a basin. Make a well in the centre and pour the oil and egg yolk into it, and a little water or beer. Using a wooden spoon, gradually mix this into the flour, adding more water or beer to make a smooth batter. Just before using the batter, whisk the egg white until stiff and fold it in.

Separate and season the roes. Dip them into the batter and fry them in hot, shallow oil, in batches, until crispy and golden-brown. Each batch will take about 3 minutes to cook.

Cover a baking sheet with crumpled kitchen foil. As each batch of roes is cooked, lift from the pan with a slotted spoon and spread on the baking sheet. Keep warm in the pre-heated oven.

While the fritters cook, heat the sauce to boiling point. Just before serving, slowly add enough mustard to taste, adding more if you like a stronger sauce. Do not add the mustard until the last minute, as it loses its flavour if cooked for any length of time.

Serve with rice and a green salad.

DEVILLED WHITEBAIT
Essex and Kent

WHITEBAIT—the infant stages of both herring and sprat—are a real Thames-side favourite. During the last century, shoals of these tiny creatures used to be caught each year between May and August in the estuary. They were served up at great feasts at Dagenham and Greenwich initially held, somewhat obscurely, to commemorate the draining of the Essex marshes. But perhaps the reason mattered less than the whitebait; deep-fried and married to brown bread and butter and lemon juice they were reason enough for celebration.

This traditional recipe 'devils' the whitebait by adding Cayenne pepper. If you prefer you can leave this out.

PREPARATION TIME: 10 MINUTES
COOKING TIME: ABOUT 10 MINUTES
PRE-HEAT THE OVEN TO 150°C (300°F)—GAS MARK 2

INGREDIENTS FOR FOUR

1 lb. (450 g.) whitebait
½ pint (275/300 ml.) milk
4 oz. (100/125 g.) flour
2 teaspoons salt
1 teaspoon black or Cayenne pepper
A little extra Cayenne
Lemon quarters
Parsley sprigs

If frozen, allow the whitebait to thaw, spreading them out as soon as you can to separate them without breaking the tiny fish.

When they are at room temperature, put the whitebait into a bowl of milk for about 4–5 minutes to help make the flour stick. Drain them in a sieve. Put the flour, salt and black or Cayenne pepper in a large plastic bag.

Fill a deep frying pan half-full of oil, and let it heat to between 180–190°C (350–375°F). While the oil is heating, put the whitebait in the bag and shake them about until they are coated with flour.

Put a quarter of the whitebait into the frying basket, shake off any surplus flour and deep-fry them for about 2 minutes or until they are crisp and golden. Lift them on to a baking tray lined with kitchen paper. Keep them warm in the pre-heated oven.

When all the whitebait are cooked, divide them between four hot plates, sprinkle them with Cayenne and garnish each plate with lemon quarters and parsley. Serve very hot with brown bread and butter.

MACKEREL WITH SOFT-ROE STUFFING
Countrywide

SOFT ROE IS THE SMOOTH, shiny substance that is part of the reproductive system of male fish. Hard roe, a mass of tiny eggs, is found only in the female fish.

Use only soft roes for the stuffing in this dish; their delicate taste and creamy texture turn a mackerel into a feast.

If you discover any hard roes in the fish you have bought, add them in the last 5 minutes of cooking.

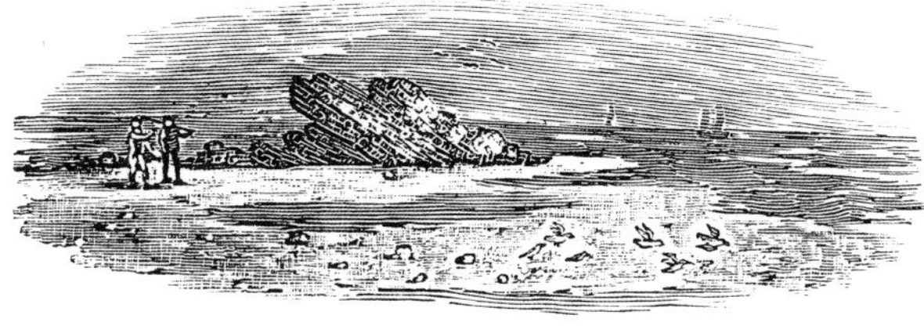

Mackerel stuffed with their own roes, flavoured with anchovies.

PREPARATION TIME: 20 MINUTES
COOKING TIME: ABOUT 25 MINUTES
PRE-HEAT THE OVEN TO 220°C (425°F)—GAS MARK 7

INGREDIENTS FOR FOUR

4 mackerel or herring, at least 2 with soft roes
2 oz. (50 g.) fresh white breadcrumbs
A little milk
2 oz. (50 g.) butter
1 medium onion, chopped
1 heaped tablespoon chopped green herbs (parsley, chives, chervil, tarragon)
Grated rind of ½ lemon
2 anchovy fillets, chopped, or 1 teaspoon anchovy essence
Salt and pepper
1 tablespoon lemon juice
1 oz. (25 g.) butter for greasing the dish

Clean the fish and remove the backbones (see pp. 74, 75). Season the fish and put them aside.

To make the stuffing, soften the breadcrumbs to a pasty consistency with a little milk. Melt the butter and cook the soft roes in it until they are barely stiff. This will only take a minute or two. Remove the roes from the pan. Add the onion to the pan and cover with a lid. Cook the onion over a low heat until soft and transparent.

Chop the roes roughly. When the onion is tender, mix in the roes, bread paste, herbs, lemon rind and the chopped anchovy or essence. Remove the stuffing from the heat and season with the salt, pepper and lemon juice. Fill the boned fish with the mixture.

Lay the fish closely together in a buttered ovenproof dish, making sure that the dish holds the fish snugly. Bake the fish for 10 minutes per inch (2·5 cm.) of thickness. Add any hard roes, sliced, in the last 5 minutes. Serve with new potatoes and vegetables.

TURBOT WITH CREAM
Countrywide

THE SPREAD of the railways in the 1850s and 1860s created both commuterdom and luncheon. As the distance between home and office increased, it became steadily more difficult for the breadwinner to return home for midday dinner. Instead, he partook of a steak or pie in a chop house, while his wife and children, with a true Victorian sense of their place in the scheme of things, made do with leftovers from the previous evening's meal.

Cookery books of the period abound with suggestions of how to make these scraps more palatable. This one comes from the practical pen of Mrs Beeton, and was described in her *Household Management* of 1861, though the sauce was imported from Normandy where it is still popular today. Halibut or any other firm white fish—or even salmon—can be used instead of turbot. Fresh, uncooked fish, too, is suggested here, since we are unlikely to have quite the same wealth of leftovers as ranged the shelves of middle-class Victorian larders.

PREPARATION TIME: 10 MINUTES
COOKING TIME: ABOUT 25 MINUTES

INGREDIENTS FOR FOUR

12 oz. (350 g.) turbot
2–3 slices bread with the crusts removed
4 oz. (100/125 g.) lightly salted butter
¼ pint (150 ml.) double cream
Salt and Cayenne pepper
¼ teaspoon ground mace or nutmeg
1 tablespoon chopped parsley

Poach the turbot gently for about 15 minutes in a large, heavy-based pan with just enough water or cooking liquid (see p. 76) to cover. The fish is cooked when the flesh parts easily from the bone. Drain, but keep the cooking liquid for another time.

Skin and bone the fish while it is still warm, and flake into small pieces. Set aside.

Toast the bread and cut it into triangles. Keep warm on a hot plate covered with a napkin. Cut the butter into cubes and melt in a wide sauté or frying pan over a moderate heat. When the butter starts to bubble, quickly stir in the cream. Keep stirring for a minute or so, until you have a smooth, rich sauce. If it looks oily, because it has been cooked too long or has overheated, quickly stir in 1 tablespoon of water, removing the pan from the heat. This should reduce the oiliness but, if not, add another tablespoon of water.

Remove from the heat and season to taste with salt, Cayenne, and the mace or nutmeg. Add the fish to the pan and heat through over a low flame, stirring gently all the time.

Divide the fish and sauce between four small serving dishes—ramekins are ideal. Garnish with the toast triangles and serve hot, sprinkled with parsley.

COD WITH MUSTARD SAUCE
Orkney

GUIDED BY THE LODESTONE, a scrap of magnetic iron ore suspended in a wooden box, 15th-century British fishermen sailed to the northern limits of the world in search of cod. They set forth each February, and returned, if they were lucky, in September with holds full of salted, dried cod, which they sold in inland markets as 'stockfish'.

Cod, both salted and fresh, was for centuries the most common fish on the market. This was especially true in coastal regions, where housewives constantly sought new methods of dealing with the glut. In this recipe from Orkney the mustard sauce reflects the strong Norse influence on the cooking of the area.

PREPARATION TIME: 10 MINUTES
COOKING TIME: ABOUT 15 MINUTES

INGREDIENTS FOR SIX

6 cod steaks
4 sprigs of parsley, with stalks
½ pint (275/300 ml.) milk
½ pint (275/300 ml.) water
Salt and pepper
2 oz. (50 g.) butter
1½ tablespoons flour
1 heaped teaspoon prepared English mustard

Line a large frying pan with the parsley—to stop the fish sticking—and place the cod steaks on top. Pour over enough milk and water to cover, and season with salt. Cover with a lid and simmer the fish gently, turning it once so that it cooks evenly. This will take about 10 minutes, depending on the thickness of the steaks. The fish is cooked when the flesh is opaque and easily comes away from the bone.

Remove the fish to a warmed dish and set it over a pan of simmering water. If you want to skin and bone the fish, do it now. Then cover it with a piece of buttered foil.

Melt the butter, stir in the flour and mustard and then add the warm fish liquid. Stir continually over a low heat until the sauce thickens and becomes creamy. Add pepper to taste. Pour the sauce over the fish and serve.

PENZANCE GREY MULLET
Cornwall

GREY MULLET are rare visitors both to our coasts and to our fishmongers' slabs, being more readily discovered in the waters off Greece and the Balkans, where the roes of the females are used as the basis of the justly famed Taramasalata (see p. 47). However, in warm summers, shoals do pay us an occasional visit when they obligingly swim into the ports and estuaries of the West Country.

One such visit occurred in Penzance in 1844, when ingenious local housewives took advantage of the bounty and married the mullet to clotted cream. The dish was noted by the minor poet and major cookery writer Eliza Acton, who published it in her *Modern Cookery* the following year.

If you can find a grey mullet, this is one of the most delicious ways of cooking it.

PREPARATION TIME: 10 MINUTES
COOKING TIME: ABOUT 40 MINUTES

INGREDIENTS FOR FOUR

1 large grey mullet, about 2 lb. (900 g.)
4–5 sprigs fresh parsley
Salt and pepper

For the sauce:

½ pint (275/300 ml.) clotted, double or whipping cream
1 heaped tablespoon chopped parsley
1 tablespoon lemon juice

Clean and scale the mullet under cold running water (see p. 74). Place on a chopping block and, using a sharp knife, cut across the fish to give two pieces of similar size.

Lightly grease a wide, shallow pan with vegetable oil or butter and put the fish pieces into the pan with the sprigs of parsley, salt and pepper to taste, and just enough water to cover.

Put the pan on the heat and bring to the boil. Simmer gently, covered, for about 5 minutes, or until the flesh flakes easily away from the backbone. Remove from the heat.

Using a fish slice, or two spoons, lift the mullet carefully out of the pan on to a warm serving dish.

Strain the cooking liquid into a jug, then return to the cleaned pan, bring to the boil and cook rapidly until it has reduced to about half the original volume and the flavour is well concentrated.

Gradually add the cream, whisking with a balloon whisk or fork. You may not need to use all the cream: add just enough to make a slightly thickened sauce. Season with salt and pepper to taste, and stir in the chopped parsley and lemon juice. Pour the sauce over the fish.

If you use double or whipping cream you may need to thicken the sauce with 1 tablespoon of arrowroot or cornflour, but do not allow it to get too thick—it should pour easily.

Mackerel with Gooseberry Sauce
Countrywide

Mackerel and gooseberries both come into season at about the same time—in May—and have been married on English tables since the 17th century at least. Characteristically, the French maintain that the notion was theirs, offering in confirmation that their very term for gooseberry is *groseille à maquereau*. Only one writer, Jules Breteuil, in his *Le Cuisinier Européen* (*c.* 1860), was prepared to admit that in his day the dish was much more current in England than in France, and threw chauvinism utterly to the winds by describing it as *Maquereau aux groseilles à l'anglaise*.

There is no doubt that the tartness of gooseberries offsets the oiliness of mackerel very well. An old Bristol recipe, in which the sauce for the mackerel is made by cooking rhubarb in dry cider with brown sugar, produced a similar effect. In either case, the tartness of the flavouring is all—so be careful not to overstate the sugar. This sauce is equally good with herring.

Preparation Time: 10 minutes
Cooking Time: 20 minutes

Ingredients for Six

6 mackerel or herring, cleaned
Salt and pepper

For the sauce:

1 oz. (25 g.) butter
12 oz. (350 g.) gooseberries, topped and tailed
Sugar to taste
½ teaspoon ground ginger or freshly grated nutmeg
1 egg, beaten, or 3 tablespoons white sauce (see p. 162)
1 tablespoon chopped fennel leaves (optional)

To prepare the sauce, melt the butter in a saucepan and add the gooseberries. Cover tightly, set over a low heat and cook gently. When the gooseberries are soft, after about 15 minutes, sieve them or put them through a food mill (an electric blender would make them too smooth and bland). Return the fruit purée to the rinsed pan, add sugar to taste and the ginger or nutmeg.

Set the grill as hot as possible. Season the fish inside with salt and pepper and lay them on a grilling rack. Season the outside of the fish, being quite generous with the pepper.

Measure the thickest part of the fish. If they are 1 in. (2·5 cm.) thick, grill at the highest heat for about 5 minutes on each side. Thinner fish will require proportionately less time.

When you turn the fish over, put the sauce on to re-heat. When the mackerel are cooked, place on a hot serving dish. When the sauce is almost boiling, remove from the heat and stir in the beaten egg or the white sauce. Heat through again, but if egg is used do not let the sauce boil or it will curdle. Add the fennel, if used. Serve the sauce separately.

Scotch Woodcock
Countrywide

Anchovies turn up in the most unexpected places, from the pungent sauces of ancient Greece and Rome to providing the glow in modern Thai cooking—and to Melton Mowbray, where they give a cheerful pink glow to the well-known pies.

They are also the chief ingredient in this Victorian savoury which, of course, has nothing to do with woodcock. The title is probably one of those perennial English witticisms about Scots parsimony—the woodcock being the most expensive of game birds. The Scots have the last laugh, however, for innocently or proudly they include the recipe in many of their cookery books.

Use the dish as a starter for a dinner party, or as a light but luxurious lunch by itself.

Preparation Time: 15 minutes
Cooking Time: about 7 minutes

Ingredients for Six

1 tin anchovies, 1¾ oz. (45 g.)
6 oz. (175 g.) butter
6 slices of bread, ½ in. (1·5 cm.) thick

For the sauce:

4 large egg yolks
½ pint (275/300 ml.) double cream
Pepper and Cayenne pepper
1 tablespoon chopped parsley

Drain the anchovies and mash them with one-third of the butter. (Or put the anchovies and butter in a blender to make anchovy paste.)

Cut two or three rounds from each bread slice, toast them and spread while still hot with the rest of the butter. Spread the anchovy paste on them and arrange on a hot serving dish.

To make the sauce, beat the egg yolks thoroughly with the cream. Add the seasonings, being generous with the Cayenne. Heat very gently in a small saucepan, without letting the mixture boil, until you have a thick creamy sauce. This will take about 3–4 minutes. Stir continuously with a wooden spoon while heating. Pour the sauce over the toast, sprinkle with the parsley and serve.

HERRINGS IN OATMEAL
Scotland

THIS IS A REMINDER of the days—some 200 years ago—when poor boys walked from the Highlands and Islands to the University of St Andrews, carrying the sack of oatmeal that had to sustain them through the coming term.

Wonderful were the deeds of scholarship they accomplished on this meagre diet—or so they said many years later in their autobiographies. The more honest, or the more adventurous, however, confessed to buying a few pence worth of herrings from the fishwives of Leith, using this recipe to enliven the endless menu of porridge and more porridge.

In fact, herrings and oatmeal were made for each other. If you do not have bacon fat to hand, buy a fatty end of bacon from a grocer, chop it roughly and melt it slowly in the pan before putting in the herrings. Brown bread and butter is the best companion for fried herrings.

PREPARATION TIME: 5 MINUTES
COOKING TIME: ABOUT 12 MINUTES

INGREDIENTS FOR SIX

6 herrings, filleted
Salt and pepper
3–4 oz. (75–125 g.) coarse oatmeal
4 oz. (100/125 g.) unsmoked bacon fat
1 tablespoon chopped parsley
Lemon quarters

Season the herrings well with salt and pepper. Spread the oatmeal on a plate, or on a piece of foil or greaseproof paper. Press both sides of the herrings well into the oatmeal. Since the fish is oily, the oatmeal will stick to it.

Heat the bacon fat until sizzling and fry the herrings in it for about 3 minutes on each side, or until brown and crisp. Arrange on a hot dish and serve lightly sprinkled with parsley, decorating the corners of the dish with the lemon quarters.

MARINATED OR SOUSED PILCHARDS
Cornwall

PILCHARDS USED TO BE A MAINSTAY of the Cornish fishing industry, the waters surrounding the southwest peninsula being the northernmost limit of the fish's range.

For centuries, 'between harvest and Allhallows' (October 31), small boats would lie offshore, seine nets ready and awaiting the command of the Huer or watchman, who stood on a clifftop or even on a specially built tower, such as the one at Newquay. Then like a great red stain spreading over the sea, the pilchards arrived in their millions. With whistles and signals, the Huer directed the speeding boats, the oarsmen beating the water to drive the fish ever closer inshore. Nets were stretched and dropped, and the ends thrown to the crowd on the beach, who hauled in the wriggling, tumbling harvest. At once, the pilchards were pressed, salted and barrelled for export to France or dispatch to London.

Then, about a century ago, the shoals changed their migratory habits, and though a few pilchards continued to arrive each year, the depletion in their numbers brought poverty to many Cornish families.

Even so, it could hardly be said that pilchards are a rarity, and many recipes exist for dealing with them. The following one, which can also be adapted to herring or mackerel, is given a Cornish touch by the addition of cold tea.

PREPARATION TIME: 10 MINUTES
COOKING TIME: 45 MINUTES
PRE-HEAT THE OVEN TO 180°C (350°F)—GAS MARK 4

INGREDIENTS FOR SIX

6 cleaned pilchards, herring or mackerel
Salt
3 bay leaves
2 heaped teaspoons black peppercorns
1 blade mace
¼ pint (150 ml.) white vinegar
¼ pint (150 ml.) strained cold tea
2 level tablespoons dark brown sugar

Split the fish and salt them lightly. Cut the bay leaves in half down the central rib and put one piece inside each fish. Close the fish and pack them, side by side and head to tail, in a lightly greased, ovenproof baking dish. The fit should be as close as possible.

Bruise the peppercorns lightly using a pestle and mortar. Scatter them over the fish. Tuck the blade of mace into the centre of the dish. Mix together the vinegar, tea and sugar, stirring well. Pour this liquid over the fish and cover with foil.

Bake in the pre-heated oven for 45 minutes or until the fish is tender. Remove from the oven and leave the fish to cool in the juices.

Serve chilled with brown bread or toast and butter.

FISHCAKES
Countrywide

FISHCAKES PROMOTE odd stirrings in the subconscious—visions of institutional crockery, bottles of brown sauce, echoing school cafeterias, or what HM Forces picturesquely term 'the tea-meal'. Somewhere in the middle is a ginger-coloured heavy disc of the consistency and flavour of damp blotting paper.

Yet if memory is stilled and a little care taken, the humble fishcake can be a revelation. Cease to regard it as a means of using up leftovers, and make it instead with freshly cooked salmon or other fish, and newly mashed potatoes. Eat it by the fire on a cold winter's evening, or with a salad in the height of summer.

PREPARATION TIME: ABOUT 20 MINUTES
COOKING TIME: ABOUT 25 MINUTES

INGREDIENTS FOR FOUR TO SIX

1 lb. (450 g.) any fresh or smoked fish, or a mixture of fish
8 oz. (225 g.) peeled and boiled potatoes
1 oz. (25 g.) butter
1 large egg, separated
1 tablespoon chopped parsley
Salt and pepper
1 teaspoon anchovy essence (optional)
A little flour
4 oz. (100/125 g.) fine white breadcrumbs
6 tablespoons clarified butter (see p. 49), or enough oil for deep-frying

Place the fish in a close-fitting pan and just cover with water. Poach over a gentle heat for about 10–15 minutes, or until the flesh comes easily away from the bone. Drain, remove the skin and bone and then measure out 12 oz. (350 g.) of the fish.

Pass the cooked potatoes through a sieve. Melt the butter in a pan, stir in the fish, potatoes, egg yolk and parsley. Add salt and pepper to taste. Keep over a gentle heat for a few minutes until thoroughly blended. Taste the mixture and add a little anchovy essence if it is on the dull side (this will depend on the type of fish chosen). Spread the mixture on a plate to cool.

With floured hands, form it into 12 even cakes. Break up the egg white with a fork, dip the cakes into it and then into the breadcrumbs. Fry the fishcakes in the clarified butter or the oil in a large frying pan until golden-brown all over. This should take about 2–3 minutes.

Serve with new potatoes and a tomato salad. Fishcakes are delicious with butter sauce or a home-made tomato sauce (see pp. 155, 160).

RED MULLET IN PAPER
Countrywide

THE ROMANS PRIZED the mullet so highly that, in the 2nd century BC, Cato the Censor felt it incumbent upon him to reproach his fellow citizens for paying more for mullet than they did for cows.

We have not quite reached that stage, though red mullet is fairly expensive and difficult to find. In Britain, it appears that the golden age of the mullet-eater was in the mid-1800s. Catches of 5,000 and more were taken from Weymouth Bay, where they turned the sea 'as red as sunset'.

Nowadays, cook the fish in foil rather than paper to keep all the juices inside the mullet, and serve with the following anchovy and port-flavoured sauce to counteract the blandness of the fish.

PREPARATION TIME: 25 MINUTES
COOKING TIME: 25 MINUTES
PRE-HEAT THE OVEN TO 220°C (425°F)—GAS MARK 7

INGREDIENTS FOR SIX

6 red mullet, each about 8 oz. (225 g.)
2 oz. (50 g.) butter
Salt and pepper
Butter sauce (see p. 155)
2 teaspoons anchovy essence
4 tablespoons port
A pinch of Cayenne pepper

First prepare the butter sauce using a double-boiler or a basin fitted over a saucepan of barely simmering water. Keep the sauce warm while you cook the fish.

Clean the mullet, but do not remove the livers—they are delicious. Cut six pieces of foil, each piece large enough to wrap around a mullet. Butter each piece generously. Season the mullet inside, lay them on the foil and season the outside.

Make six tightly closed but slightly baggy parcels. Put them on a baking sheet and cook in the pre-heated oven for 15 minutes. Test one of the fish after 10 minutes, as cooking time depends on thickness rather than weight. The fish will be cooked when the flesh moves easily away from the bone.

When the fish are cooked, remove them from their foil and put them on a hot serving dish. Pour the fish juices into a wide pan and boil to reduce the liquid to at least half the original amount. This concentrates the flavour to an essence to be used as a basis for the sauce.

Add this liquid to the butter sauce. Slowly add anchovy essence and port to taste. Check the seasoning and add a pinch of Cayenne. Serve the sauce separately and serve the fish with new potatoes.

Port-and-anchovy sauce brings out the best in Red Mullet—a dish prized by the Romans.

A whole Turbot, garnished with shrimps and served with shrimp sauce, makes an imposing dish for a dinner party.

Turbot with Shrimp Sauce
Countrywide

'How long,' said Ruskin, 'most people would look at the best book before they would give the price of a large turbot for it.' The price could be high indeed, for the turbot is one of the largest of flat fish, weighing as much as 60 lb. (27 kg.). This accounts for the gargantuan copper turbot kettles that can still be seen in the kitchens of the grander stately homes.

Turbot first became popular in the 18th century, shortly after the Dutch invented 'well-vessels', whose perforated holds permitted the great fish to be kept alive until they reached market. To palates long wearied with salted fish, fresh turbot with its firm, fine-flavoured flesh was a revelation.

Today we prepare this recipe with young (chicken) turbot, which are at their best between April and July.

Preparation Time: 25 minutes
Cooking Time: 50 minutes

Ingredients for Four to Six

- *1 large chicken turbot or 2 brill*
- *About 1 pint (575/600 ml.) milk with 1 pint (575/600 ml.) water to cover the fish*
- *1 slice of lemon*
- *Salt and pepper*
- *1 heaped tablespoon shelled shrimps (reserved from the amount below)*
- *1 tablespoon chopped parsley*

For the sauce:

- *½ pint (275/300 ml.) shrimps*
- *¾ pint (450 ml.) water*
- *2 teaspoons flour*
- *6 oz. (175 g.) butter*
- *Salt*
- *A pinch of ground mace*
- *A pinch of Cayenne pepper*

First prepare the sauce. Shell the shrimps and reserve a tablespoon of shrimps for decoration. Put the shells into a pan with the water, cover with a lid and boil for 20 minutes.

Strain into a measuring jug and either add more water or reduce the liquid by boiling to make ½ pint (275/300 ml.).

Gradually add this stock to the flour, stirring with a wooden spoon to make a smooth mixture. Pour this into a clean saucepan. Dice the butter and add it to the sauce. Continue to stir the sauce over a moderate heat so that it thickens without boiling while you cook the fish.

Score the cleaned fish through to the backbone on the dark-skinned side and place in a large pan. (Brill needs two pans.) Cover the fish with a mixture of half milk and half water. Add the lemon, and season to taste. Bring to the boil and then simmer until cooked (10–15 minutes for turbot, 7 minutes for brill). To test, pierce the thickest part with a pointed knife and see if the transparent flesh has become opaque to the bone. With a fish slice, lift the fish carefully on to a hot serving dish, preferably an old-fashioned one with a removable straining bag. Decorate with the reserved shrimps and parsley, and serve the sauce separately.

Keep the liquid the fish was cooked in for a fish soup, or to add to another fish sauce.

As an alternative to fresh shrimps, 4 oz. (100/125 g.) of potted shrimps (see p. 45) may be added to the sauce. First remove the layer of clarified butter from them and add less seasoning, since they are already spiced.

Grilled Sprats
Countrywide

SPRATS ARE CHEAP and plentiful—about 1½ million tons are landed annually, many of which are canned in oil and sold as 'brislings'. Brislings are delicious on toast, or as part of an hors-d'oeuvre, but the larger, fresh sprats should be grilled. They are oily fish, filling, and inclined to be indigestible to delicate constitutions. A few will go a long way, so do not overfill the family's plates.

PREPARATION TIME: 12 MINUTES
COOKING TIME: 6 MINUTES

INGREDIENTS FOR FOUR

1½ lb. (700 g.) sprats
Lemon quarters

Using a skewer, or large hairpin, clean the sprats through the gills, rather than risk tearing them with a knife.

Pre-heat the grill to as high a temperature as possible. Either line the grill pan with foil, or cover it with a generous layer of sea salt to stop the sprats from sticking.

Lay the sprats in one layer on the grill pan and cook them for 2–3 minutes on each side, turning them carefully. Serve with lemon quarters and brown bread and butter.

For a northern European alternative, sprats can be marinated in an oil and lemon dressing. First, place them in a lightly greased baking tray and put them in a hot oven, 220°C (425°F)—gas mark 7, for 5 minutes, or until cooked. Skin them carefully as soon as they can be handled. Prepare a dressing of 2 parts olive or vegetable oil to 1 part lemon juice. Add chopped herbs and spring onions and leave the sprats to marinate for several hours. Serve with brown bread and butter.

Baked White Fish, Bacon and Peas
Countrywide

THE VICTORIANS, who frequently sought for some moral content to excuse simple enjoyment, considered white fish 'wholesome', and liberally fed them to invalids. To be fair, they were probably right; white fish are often more digestible than oily fish.

This recipe, ideal for a light supper dish, carries a faint aura of the last century. It confirms Kettner's belief, put forward in his *Book of the Table* (1877), that baking was the ideal cooking method for the 'kitchen maid who is suddenly called upon for a nice hot supper when the fire has gone down'.

The dish has none of the dullness of the bland, white fish dishes fed to invalids. The bacon adds a pleasing saltiness and the green peas complete a charming combination of colours.

PREPARATION TIME: 5 MINUTES
COOKING TIME: 30–40 MINUTES
PRE-HEAT THE OVEN TO 190°C (375°F)—GAS MARK 5

INGREDIENTS FOR SIX

6 thick cod steaks, or other firm white fish
4 oz. (100/125 g.) seasoned flour (see p. 388)
16 rashers streaky bacon
1 oz. (25 g.) lard

Coat the fish well with the seasoned flour. Line a lightly greased baking dish with 6 bacon rashers. Lay the fish on top, cover with the remaining bacon rashers and dot with the lard. Cook in the pre-heated oven until the fish is opaque and flakes easily. Serve with young green peas tossed in butter and lemon juice.

Cream and Anchovy Savoury
Countrywide

THIS BRILLIANTLY SIMPLE RECIPE came over from France (where it was called *Canapés à la crème*) at the end of the 19th century, just in time to rescue country-house hostesses from offering the Prince of Wales and his circle yet another version of toasted cheese at the conclusion of dinner.

Its principal delight lies in the unique blending of piquancy, hot bread and icy Cornish cream—our native contribution to the recipe. Make the dish as a swift starter for a special occasion.

PREPARATION TIME: 2 MINUTES
COOKING TIME: 3 MINUTES

INGREDIENTS FOR SIX

6 slices of bread, ½ in. (1·5 cm.) thick
2 oz. (50 g.) butter
18 anchovy fillets from a 1¾ oz. (45 g.) tin
6 tablespoons chilled, clotted Cornish cream

Cut the bread into circles with a large scone-cutter, or trim into neat squares about 2½ in. (6·5 cm.) across. Heat the butter until frothy, and fry the bread until golden. Arrange the fried bread on a hot serving dish and quickly lay three anchovy fillets on each piece. Top with the chilled, clotted Cornish cream and serve.

Cod's Roe with Bacon
Countrywide

There are two kinds of roe—either 'hard', which is the mass of eggs in the ovarian membrane of the female, or 'soft', which is part of the reproductive system of the male. This last is also known as 'milt'.

Roe has been considered a delicacy since the earliest times; the most famous, of course, is caviare, which is obtained from the female sturgeon. Baked or fried pike roe was a great favourite in the Middle Ages, and only faded in popularity as cod's roe became more widely available.

The following recipe makes a good, cheap, quick meal for almost any time of the day. Roe is filling, so it is unnecessary to buy much more than 1 lb. (450 g.) to feed six people.

Preparation Time: 5 minutes
Cooking Time: 40 minutes

Ingredients for Six

1–1½ lb. (450–700 g.) cod's roe
Seasoned flour
12 rashers streaky bacon

Wrap the roe in a piece of cheesecloth and tie it tightly. Lower it into a saucepan containing enough very hot water to cover the roe, adding 2 teaspoons each of salt and vinegar to each 2 pints (1·1 litres) of water.

Simmer for 30 minutes without letting the water boil. Lift the roe from the pan, and let it drain and cool before untying the cloth.

Remove the skin and cut the roe into ½ in. (1·5 cm.) slices. Turn the slices in the seasoned flour.

Trim the rinds from the bacon and fry the rashers in a large frying pan. Put the bacon on a dish and keep warm.

Add the roe to the fat in the pan, adding more fat if necessary. Use butter rather than lard for this. Fry the roe on both sides.

Arrange the fried roe neatly on the serving dish, surrounded by the bacon slices.

Any leftover roe can be re-heated later in a buttered gratin dish. Cover it with a parsley or home-made tomato sauce (see pp. 150, 160), and place in a moderate oven for 20 minutes. Tuck triangles of fried bread around the edges of the dish, and serve.

Grilled Eel
Home Counties

Eel pie was so revered in London and the south-east, that an island in the Thames was named after it. Eel and mash, and jellied-eel shops proliferated when fish and chips were being experimented upon only by the most progressive of gourmets. Sadly, only a few of these establishments remain. Their interiors, all scrubbed wood, marble, burnished copper and stained glass, have remained unchanged for over 100 years, and their products—if you are an eel enthusiast—are as delicious as ever.

To this day, if you want one of these three traditional eel dishes, it is often easier to buy them from the shop. Grilled eels, however, are easily prepared at home. Make sure they are live when you buy them from the fishmonger, but get him to kill and clean them for you. For this dish, the skins may be kept on.

Preparation Time: 5 minutes
Cooking Time: 10 minutes

Ingredients for Two

1 lb. (450 g.) of eel
Salt
Bay leaves (optional)
3 tablespoons olive or vegetable oil
Lemon quarters

Pre-heat the grill. Salt the eel and cut it across into pieces 1 in. (2·5 cm.) long. Thread the pieces on to two skewers (one for each person), so that you can turn them easily. For additional flavour, place bay leaves between each piece. Brush the eel very lightly with oil.

Cook the eel under the hot grill for about 5 minutes on each side, depending on the thickness of the eel. It is cooked when the flesh begins to part easily from the bone. The heat of the grill will char the skin lightly and turn it an appetising brown. The skin is perfectly good to eat.

Serve the eel with lemon quarters and brown bread and butter.

Fish and Chips
Countrywide

Without recourse to civil war between North and South, it is unlikely that the date and place of the marriage between deep-fried fish and chipped potatoes will ever be settled. Prejudice abandoned, however, the story seems to go something like this.

By 1844 a number of shops in the poorer districts of London were selling fried potatoes, while at the same time, in the industrial towns of Lancashire and Yorkshire, enterprising piemen saw the possibilities in fried cod served with a slice of bread or a baked potato.

Chips as we know them were perhaps introduced by a Belgian who had a stall in Dundee market in the early 1860s; *pommes frites* had long been a favourite in his country. Within months, a pigs'-trotter salesman named Lees was selling fish and chips in Manchester, having gained the notion from an Oldham tripe-dresser. Malin's, in London's East End, had the delicacy on sale in 1868, and it is this establishment that the Fish Fryers' Federation acclaims as the first true fish and chip shop.

Salt, vinegar and pickled onions are common to the fried-fish establishments of both North and South, but there the resemblance ceases. To Northerners, fish and chips means haddock; Londoners, however, relish cod and a fish called rock salmon—actually dogfish.

Traditional fish and chips can be made quite easily at home. The secret is to make sure that the fat is hot enough, otherwise the chips will be soggy.

Preparation Time: 50 minutes
Cooking Time: about 25 minutes
Pre-heat the Oven to 140°C (275°F)—gas mark 1

Ingredients for Four

2¼ lb. (1 kg.) potatoes, peeled
About 1 pint (575/600 ml.) vegetable oil
4 cod or haddock fillets (with the skin left on, if liked)
Lemon slices

For the batter:

7 oz. (200 g.) self-raising flour
Water
½ teaspoon baking powder
1 teaspoon salt

Mix the flour, baking powder and salt in a bowl. Add the water, beating in a very little at a time, until the mixture is of pouring consistency. Leave the batter to stand for about 30 minutes before using it.

Cut the potatoes lengthways into chips. They should be about ½ in. (1·5 cm.) wide. Pat them dry with kitchen paper. Do not wash them, as this will make the chips too brittle.

Pour the oil into a deep pan. For a pan about 6 in. (15 cm.) deep you will need about 3 in. (8 cm.) of oil. Heat the oil to about 170°C (340°F). It will be at the right temperature when a cube of day-old bread turns golden-brown in 1¼ minutes.

Fry the chips in small batches so that they can move about in the pan freely. As soon as they start to brown, lift them out of the pan with a slotted spoon and drain on a thick layer of kitchen paper. A wire chip-basket makes draining easier.

For crisper chips, heat the oil up to 190°C (375°F)—a bread cube should brown in about 1 minute—and put the chips back in the pan for a minute.

Put the chips into the pre-heated oven in a dish lined with kitchen paper while you cook the fish. Keep the temperature of the oil at about 190°C (375°F). Dip the fish in the batter, turning it over so that it is well coated. Lower the fish into the oil, skin side down to stop it curling.

When the fish starts to turn golden (about 4 minutes), turn the pieces over and fry them for the same amount of time on the other side.

Serve with the chips, garnished with the lemon slices.

Soft Roes on Toast
Countrywide

In good King Edward's leisurely time—that is, around 1905 or thereabouts—the age-old custom of concluding formal dinners with light sweet and savoury dishes was refined to give brief precedence to a savoury course. This, it was felt, would serve better to clear the gentlemen's palates before embarking upon liqueurs and cigars. Such courses were spicy, and generally devoured in a few bites. *Croque monsieur*, a version of Welsh rarebit, was typical, and so was this spirited method of serving soft roes.

The savoury course is now but rarely observed. Use the following recipe for a light lunch, breakfast or supper instead.

Preparation Time: 7 minutes
Cooking Time: 13 minutes
Pre-heat the Oven to 140°C (275°F)—gas mark 1

Ingredients for Four

4 slices of white bread, ½ in. (1·5 cm.) thick
6 oz. (175 g.) butter
8–12 pairs large soft roes
2 oz. (50 g.) flour
1 level teaspoon Cayenne pepper
2 level teaspoons salt
4 sprigs parsley

Cut the crusts from the bread and toast the slices. Spread them with about half the butter and put them in the pre-heated oven to keep warm.

Spread out and separate the roes. Mix the flour, Cayenne pepper and salt in a bowl. Dip the roes in this mixture and turn to coat them well. Fry the roes in the rest of the butter. Do not overcook them—1–2 minutes a side is often enough, depending on the thickness of the roes. When cooked they should be a creamy colour inside.

Distribute the roes between the slices of buttered toast, tuck in the sprigs of parsley and serve.

There are several variations to this simple dish: roes may be seasoned, before dipping them in plain flour, with salt, pepper and lemon juice, rather than Cayenne; they may be spread on fried bread instead of toast, and the toast or fried bread may be spread with either Gentleman's Relish, Cheddar or Parmesan cheese.

Smoked Fish

Preserving fish by smoking, drying or salting has been a vital means of eking summer plenty through winter shortage for centuries. Iron Age fishermen on the River Bann smoked their catch over peat fires, while around the coasts stranded whales were cut up and preserved in the same way.

Smoked Trout
Countrywide

Smoked trout is an expensive way to start a meal, but few fish are more delicious. Surprisingly, since the fish are closely related, it tastes nothing like smoked salmon; the flesh is pink or white and firm, the taste subtle and completely lacking in the oiliness of the larger fish. Horseradish sauce, lemon, and brown bread and butter set the dish off to perfection.

Preparation Time: 5 minutes

Ingredients for Six

½ pint (275/300 ml.) double or whipping cream
Up to 2 oz. (50 g.) freshly grated horseradish root
2 teaspoons sugar
A pinch of salt
2 teaspoons lemon juice
6 smoked trout

Whip the cream. Stir in a little of the horseradish, 1 teaspoon of sugar, a little salt and 1 teaspoon of lemon juice. Taste and add more seasonings until the sauce is well flavoured—both tart and pungent.

Arrange each trout on a plate and serve with the cream piled in a bowl.

For a French variation, add 3 oz. (75 g.) shelled, skinned and chopped walnuts and 1 teaspoon of breadcrumbs to the cream.

Smoked Salmon
Countrywide

Smoked Scotch salmon is the prince of smoked fish, so serve it—generously—with finely cut slices of brown bread and butter. Season it, if you wish, with sprinklings of lemon juice and black or Cayenne pepper; further additions would be gilding the lily. The salmon's rosy-pink colour looks delicious served on tiny squares of dark rye bread as a party-time canapé.

Use the trimmings, pounded finely, as a filling for omelettes, little pastry cases and vol-au-vent. In the latter instance, bake them in the oven, then cover them with a velvety egg and cream custard to make a delicious starter.

A most luxurious notion, brought to Britain by Jewish immigrants from Eastern Europe at the turn of the century, is to serve smoked salmon with blini (see p. 294) or rolls and a covering of cream cheese or sour cream.

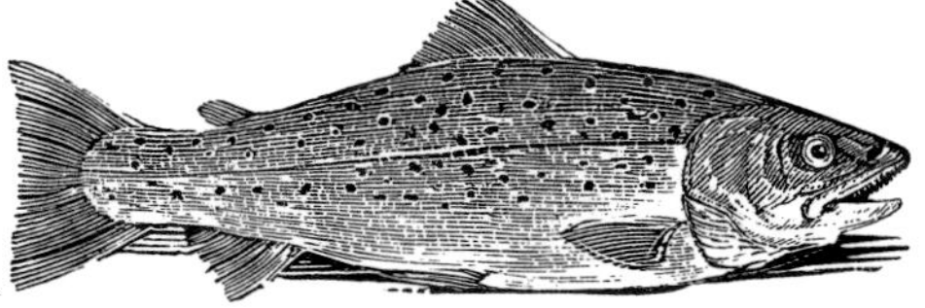

SMOKED EELS
Countrywide

FOR CENTURIES, eels were one of the few forms of fresh fish available to people in inland areas. So highly were they regarded that, in some districts, they came to be used as a form of currency. Thousands of eels were paid in annual rents to the Abbots of Ely in the 10th century, and later, under the feudal system, the tenants of many watermills paid their dues to their overlords in eels which were caught in wicker traps set in the mill-race above the water-wheel. Smoked eels are still looked upon as a delicacy, and make an excellent starter or a snack.

Allow a 3½–5 in. (9–13 cm.) piece of eel for each serving. Peel off the skin, raise the fillets and place them side by side, cut side down, on a plate. Serve with brown bread and butter and lemon quarters.

SMOKED CHICKEN HALIBUT
Countrywide

HALIBUT IS the largest flat fish found in northern waters, often attaining a length of 10 ft (3 m.) and a weight of 300 lb. (136 kg.). The young, or chicken, halibut, weighing up to 3 lb. (1·4 kg.), is perhaps better suited to the average kitchen, and it is fish of this weight, too, that are smoked. When preparing the halibut, skin it and cut away the fillets, serving them in pieces rather than in slices. They look especially attractive if served on thin rounds of buttered brown bread, and their flavour is brought out, and even enhanced, by a touch of strong, home-made horse-radish sauce (see p. 152).

SMOKED STURGEON
Countrywide

ALL STURGEON, whales and porpoises caught in British waters or found stranded on British beaches are the property of the Crown, and have been so since the 14th century. The sturgeon and porpoises were used to eke out royal banquets, while the whales supplied whalebone for the Queen Consort's gowns. The present Queen has waived these perquisites, just as the Queen Mother has waived her claim to whales. But gifts of sturgeon are still presented by loyal subjects unaware of Her Majesty's decision.

Sturgeon are fairly rare visitors to British seas and rivers, and it would be a shame indeed to eat these any other way but stuffed and roast. But smoked sturgeon, usually imported from Eastern Europe, is also superb, ranking with smoked salmon as the best of smoked fish.

Serve it in wafer-thin slices with lemon quarters and brown bread and butter.

BLOATERS
Norfolk

THE HARSH CURE of the red herring was invented at a time when the preservation of food was of much greater importance than flavour. The bloater is a much later creation—about 350 years ago—when ordinary people were for the first time able to regard eating as a source of pleasure rather than mere survival. The bloater's cure is gentler—a mere 12 hours in salt, followed by a similar period of smoking. This gives it a much subtler flavour than that of the red herring, though of course it does not keep nearly so long. Bloaters are at their peak only up to 36 hours after curing, and it is still best to shop for them personally in the towns of their source—Great Yarmouth especially—on the East Anglian coast.

In Britain, we generally re-heat bloaters or mash them to a paste to spread on tea-time buttered toast. To re-heat, either grill the fish quickly and serve them with butter, or fillet and serve them the Irish way. Spread the fillets out on a large ovenproof dish, just cover them with Irish whiskey and set it alight. When the flames die down, the bloaters are ready to eat.

Bloater fillets can also be baked the Swedish way under a layer of cream, seasoned with chopped leeks or dill-weed. But you can eat bloaters as they come, just as the French eat their very similar *harengs saurs*; or you can prepare them the German way, tossed in olive oil and served with a potato salad, or covered with soured cream and chopped chives. With a glass of cold schnapps to drink, this makes an unusual and excellent light supper on a warm summer evening.

KIPPERS
Countrywide

IN LESS-SOPHISTICATED DAYS, the mere mention of kippers, bagwash, mothers-in-law or Wigan was sufficient to send music-hall audiences into paroxysms. The British dearly love an old joke, and all the more if its significance is utterly beyond outsiders' comprehension.

They also love kippers—and especially their favourite brand of kipper—with the kind of devotion that Frenchmen reserve for a particular vineyard. Sadly, now that herring fishing is limited, the vintage kippers from Loch Fyne, the Isle of Man, Northumberland and East Anglia are in short supply. The only kind readily available is the ginger-dyed variety, which used to be disparagingly known as 'painted ladies'.

If you are fortunate enough to chance upon some true kippers, you should treat them like this. Slice the kipper flesh very thinly, using a sharp knife and cutting almost horizontally in the way that smoked salmon is sliced.

Serve with bread and butter and lemon quarters. Or make a Danish-style open sandwich with a nest of kipper slices arranged on a slice of buttered bread. Place a whole raw egg yolk in the middle, seasoned with freshly ground pepper. When you eat the sandwich, break the egg yolk with a fork and mix with the kipper.

All other varieties of kipper will need to be cooked. Buy them on the bone if you can, because the flavour is better than in fillets.

To jug kippers, put them tail up into a heavy stoneware jug and pour boiling water in to cover them. Leave them for 5–10 minutes according to size, then drain them and serve hot with bread and butter.

To grill kippers, arrange them skin side up on a rack in the grill pan. Cook them under a high heat until the skin begins to turn crisp, blisters and comes away from the flesh at the edges. This will take about 5 minutes. Serve at once—there is no need to grill the other side.

Another method is to arrange the kippers in pairs, skin side out, with plenty of butter between them, like a sandwich. Grill them for 5 minutes, then turn the pair over together to grill the other side for 5 minutes.

To fry kippers, grease a frying pan, heat it and put in the kippers, skin side down. Cook over medium heat for 2–3 minutes, then turn and fry the other side for 2–3 minutes.

To bake kippers, wrap them loosely in buttered foil, sealing the join and the ends well, and bake at 220°C (425°F)—gas mark 7. A single kipper will take about 5 minutes, and a pair sandwiched together with butter will take 10 minutes.

KEDGEREE
Countrywide

IN THE DAYS when country-house breakfasts were more leisurely affairs than they are now, the morning sideboards were laden with silver chafing dishes containing ham, bacon, eggs, devilled kidneys and kedgeree.

It is surprising that what now seems a very English dish should be Indian in origin. It was brought back by 18th-century nabobs of the East India Company, and installed, together with other mementoes of travel, in the country estates they purchased.

Kedgeree is no longer considered specifically as a breakfast dish. It makes an excellent light lunch, and is even better as a late-night supper.

PREPARATION TIME: 5 MINUTES
COOKING TIME: ABOUT 40 MINUTES

INGREDIENTS FOR FOUR

- *1 lb. (450 g.) piece Finnan Haddock*
- *6 tablespoons clarified butter (see p. 49)*
- *1 large onion, chopped*
- *6 oz. (175 g.) Patna or long-grain rice*
- *1 teaspoon curry paste*
- *3 tablespoons butter*
- *3 hard-boiled eggs*
- *1 tablespoon chopped parsley*

Place the haddock skin side up in a wide, shallow pan, over a low heat. Pour over it enough boiling water to barely cover the fish. Cook over a low heat for 10 minutes, without letting the water boil.

Remove the haddock and discard the skin and bone. Flake the fish; you should have about 12 oz. (350 g.), but if there is more it does not matter.

Meanwhile, in a large pan, heat the clarified butter. Add the onion and cook it gently until it begins to soften. Then raise the heat so that the onion browns slightly. Stir in the rice and, as it becomes transparent, add the curry paste. Cook for a minute or two, stirring all the time. Pour in 1 pint (575/600 ml.) of the water in which the haddock was cooked.

Cover, and leave the rice to cook until tender—about 20 minutes. Check every 5 minutes and add more haddock liquid or water, if necessary, to prevent the rice from drying out.

While the rice is cooking, shell and either slice or quarter the eggs. When the rice is tender, mix in the haddock and let it heat through, adding enough butter to keep the mixture moist (dry kedgeree is the sign of a mean cook).

Pile on to a hot serving dish, decorate with hard-boiled eggs and parsley, and serve.

Three hearty breakfast dishes: Cod's Roe with Bacon, Kippers and Kedgeree.

Finnan Haddie with Egg Sauce
Aberdeenshire

FINDON, a small fishing hamlet in the Mearns of Aberdeenshire, gave the world the Finnan Haddie to be revered wherever gourmets meet.

In the 18th century, the haddock were beheaded, split, and smoked and partly cooked over a slow fire of peat and sphagnum moss which, according to Sir Walter Scott, produced a 'relish of a very peculiar and delicate flavour'. The end product was then hard, dry and black; the present beautiful lemon colour dates from about 100 years ago when the peat ran out and oak chips were used to smoke the fish instead. Finnan Haddies still retain their individuality, differing from their near-neighbours, the Arbroath Smokies, in subtlety of flavour, colour, and in still being smoked split rather than whole.

PREPARATION TIME: 15 MINUTES
COOKING TIME: 40 MINUTES

INGREDIENTS FOR SIX

1 pint (575/600 ml.) milk
1 bouquet garni
1 small carrot, sliced
1 small onion, sliced
3 Finnan Haddock

For the sauce:

6 oz. (175 g.) butter
1 oz. (25 g.) flour
4 fl. oz. (100/125 ml.) whipping cream
2 large eggs
Salt and pepper
A pinch of nutmeg
1 tablespoon chopped parsley

Simmer the milk with the bouquet garni, carrot and onion in a half-covered pan for 20 minutes.

Cut the haddock into six pieces and place them, skin side up, in a wide pan. Pour the milk over them and enough boiling water to just cover. Cook over a moderate heat for about 10 minutes—but check after 5 minutes—the fish are cooked as soon as the flesh parts easily from the bone. Do not let the fish overcook.

Place the cooked fish on a serving dish. Cover with buttered greaseproof paper, and keep warm over a pan of warm water. Strain the liquid into a measuring jug, return to the saucepan and boil until it has reduced to ½ pint (275/300 ml.).

Now prepare the sauce. Melt one-third of the butter and stir in the flour. Cook for 2 minutes over a low heat, stir in the reduced fish liquid and the cream. Simmer until slightly thickened—this will take about 10 minutes—stirring occasionally.

Meanwhile, hard-boil and shell the eggs, and mash them with a fork. When the sauce is ready, stir in the remaining butter in small pieces, using a wooden spoon. Add the mashed eggs, seasonings and parsley. Stir well with a wooden spoon.

Pour a little sauce over the haddock and serve the rest separately. Boiled potatoes or home-made bread go well with this dish.

Finnan Haddie have been smoked over oak chips to give colour and flavour.

Smoked Mackerel
West Country

DESPITE its apparently inexhaustible abundance, the mackerel is notoriously prone to quick decay. For this reason, in the last century it was the only fish that was allowed to be hawked in city streets on Sundays. It was for this reason, too, that the great mackerel smokeries were set up in Devon and Cornwall, whose ports, Newlyn especially, are still centres of the mackerel-fishing trade.

Smoked mackerel are cheap, nourishing and with a flavour all their own. Before buying them, check that the inner flesh is not soft and squashy—a sign that the mackerel has been smoked for too long.

Half a mackerel is enough for most people, so serve each fillet on bread and butter as an open sandwich.

A light green salad goes perfectly with smoked mackerel; so does a bowl of mayonnaise sharpened with an equal amount of gooseberry purée.

Smoked Sprats
Suffolk

SMOKED, OR RED, SPRATS have been enjoyed by the English for many years. The Jacobean dramatists Beaumont and Fletcher commented sourly upon 'a plump Vintner kneeling, and offring incense to his deitie, which shall be only this, red sprats and pilchers'.

Dismissing such cheerless criticism,

Londoners continued to look forward to the annual smoked-sprat harvest which arrived in the City from Aldeburgh and Southwold each year. By a fortunate coincidence it often turned up about November 9, the day of the Lord Mayor's Show, which for many years was known irreverently as 'Sprat Day'.

Since sprats are salty, they are best served as part of mixed hors-d'oeuvre. Skin and fillet them, place on a serving dish and pour a little dry white wine over them. Turn them in the liquid as they chill in the refrigerator.

Serve with brown bread and butter and lemon quarters.

RED HERRINGS
Countrywide

THE PROVERBIAL USE for red herrings—to divert a speaker from the matter in hand—dates from the 17th century, when these strong-smelling fish were sometimes used to lay a false trail to break hounds off a scent.

The heavily salted and smoked red herrings were purely medieval in origin—a means of preserving fish for the longest possible period. To say they were a favourite with our ancestors would be an exaggeration; the rich disguised the strong flavour with sauces, but by the end of Lent the poor were heartily sick of them. For rich and poor alike, they were a major staple of their diet.

Properly prepared, and not too often repeated, they can be delicious. The most important thing is to rid them of the briny taste of the cure. To do this, pour boiling water over the fish and leave them for 30 minutes or more. Break off a tiny bit of the fish, and taste to make sure that you have soaked them for long enough.

When the herrings are ready, cut off the heads and tails, drain and split them down the back. Rub with butter, and either grill them or toast them on long forks in front of the fire.

Serve on or with buttered toast with a good sprinkling of Cayenne pepper.

Re-heated red, or golden, herrings, like other smoked fish, are delicious served with scrambled eggs on toast.

As a midwinter treat, serve with fluffy, buttered mashed potatoes.

ARBROATH SMOKIES
Angus

ARBROATH SMOKIES—small haddock or whiting—resemble Finnan Haddies in that they are 'hot-smoked', that is, partly cooked during the smoking process. Smokies, however, are smoked rather longer than the Haddies, giving the skin a deeper colour.

They originated in the early 19th century when a number of fishermen from Auchmithie migrated to nearby Arbroath, taking with them their ancient practice of curing fish by hanging them in the lums (chimneys) of their cottages. The astute folk of Arbroath quickly saw commercial possibilities in the notion, and extended it by sinking halved whisky barrels in the ground and filling them with smouldering oak and silver birch chips, over which they smoked the fish.

Smokies can be eaten cold, like smoked trout, but traditionally they are grilled with a knob of butter and served with brown bread.

Red Herrings, smeared with butter and grilled or toasted for a fireside meal.

RECIPES *from* OTHER LANDS

ITALY
Spaghetti Alle Vongole *(Spaghetti with clams)*

IN ROME *vongole*, *capperozzoli* in Venice, *arselle* in Genoa and *telline* in Florence—all mean the same thing, the small clams that are used throughout Italy to make soup and an accompanying sauce for pasta dishes. With a strong red wine, this dish will recall Italian sunshine even in winter.

If fresh clams are not available buy a small tin, but be sure the clams are not preserved in vinegar; this can ruin the fine flavour of the sauce. You can also make the dish with cockles.

PREPARATION TIME: 10 MINUTES
COOKING TIME: ABOUT 30 MINUTES

INGREDIENTS FOR FOUR

3 oz. (75 g.) butter
1 large onion, chopped
2 cloves garlic, crushed
1½ lb. (700 g.) tomatoes, skinned and de-seeded, or a 1 lb. (450 g.) tin of tomatoes
¼ teaspoon each basil and thyme
A good pinch of peperoncino (dried chilli pepper), or Cayenne pepper, or a few drops of Tabasco sauce
3 pints (1·7 litres) water
3 teaspoons salt
1 lb. (450 g.) spaghetti
½ pint (275/300 ml.) cooked, shelled clams or cockles, or an 8 oz. (225 g.) tin of clams

Melt 2 oz. (50 g.) of the butter in a large saucepan and fry the onion until soft (about 15 minutes). Lower the heat and stir in the garlic. Cook for 2 minutes then add the tomatoes with any juice, and the herbs. Cook for a further 10–15 minutes and then stir in the pepper or Tabasco. Keep the sauce on a low heat, stirring occasionally, while you cook the spaghetti.

To cook the spaghetti, bring the water and salt to a rolling boil in a large saucepan. Add the spaghetti, bring to the boil again, stir and reduce the heat. Cook until tender, but not mushy. After about 10 minutes lift a strand from the pan to test if it is ready—soft but firm to the bite.

When the spaghetti is almost ready, add the drained clams to the tomato sauce and heat them through gently.

To serve, drain the spaghetti in a colander and pile it into a serving bowl. Add the remaining butter and toss the spaghetti in it. Taste the sauce, add salt if necessary, and serve separately.

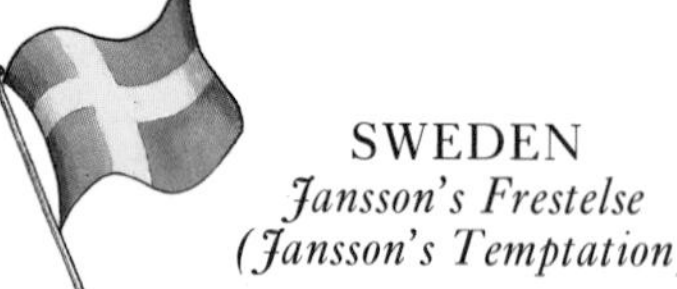

SWEDEN
Jansson's Frestelse *(Jansson's Temptation)*

ERIC JANSSON, a 19th-century religious reformer, was famed throughout Sweden and the USA for his asceticism. He abhorred all but the simplest foods. Then one day—horrors!—he was discovered tucking into this delicious anchovy casserole by one of his most zealous followers. Thenceforward the dish was known as 'Jansson's Temptation'.

The dish is very often a centrepiece of the famous Swedish *smörgåsbord*—the nearest equivalent in English would be a buffet lunch or supper. Guests take plates and help themselves to the smoked and pickled herrings, to the *gravalax*—salted salmon, pressed with dill and brandy—to the many hot dishes, rye bread and cheese, and Jansson's Temptation.

There is no need, of course, to create the entire *smörgåsbord*; the casserole will suit very well as the first course of a British meal. But if you want to give an authentic Swedish touch, serve it with iced aquavit.

PREPARATION TIME: 20 MINUTES
COOKING TIME: ABOUT 45 MINUTES
PRE-HEAT THE OVEN TO 220°C (425°F)—GAS MARK 7

INGREDIENTS FOR SIX

3 oz. (75 g.) unsalted butter
1 tablespoon vegetable oil
3 medium onions, thinly sliced
6 potatoes, peeled and cut into thin rounds
12 anchovy fillets, drained and chopped
White pepper
7 fl. oz. (200 ml.) thin cream
2 tablespoons chopped parsley

Heat 1 oz. (25 g.) of the butter in a frying pan with the oil. Fry the onion gently until soft and transparent.

Grease a fairly deep ovenproof dish. Place a layer of potato in the bottom, cover with a layer of onion and then a layer of anchovy. Sprinkle the layers as you go with white pepper. Repeat the layers, finishing with a layer of potato. Pour half the cream over the top and dot with the rest of the butter.

Bake in the pre-heated oven for about 15–20 minutes, until the potatoes are slightly brown on top. Add the rest of the cream and continue cooking for a further 25–30 minutes, until the potatoes are tender. If the top becomes too brown before the potatoes are cooked, cover with foil. Sprinkle with chopped parsley.

HUNGARY
Fish with Paprika Cream Sauce

HUNGARY HAS NO COASTLINE, so freshwater fish, particularly carp, sturgeon and wels, which is similar to the catfish, tend to figure prominently in its cuisine. In this Hungarian recipe, however, the usual and more readily obtainable ocean fish may be substituted without really altering the character of the dish.

It is the paprika that adds the true Magyar quality. This fine, subtle spice, made from the ground seeds of pimentoes, ranges from hot to sweet, and comes in several shades from rose to scarlet. Many Hungarians believe that brown is best, but do not ask them why unless you really want to know and have an afternoon to spare. Paprika, like football, seems to be a national passion.

PREPARATION TIME: 10 MINUTES
STANDING TIME: 30 MINUTES
COOKING TIME: ABOUT 45 MINUTES

INGREDIENTS FOR SIX

2 lb. (900 g.) firm, white fish fillets, such as cod, halibut or coley
Salt
2 oz. (50 g.) butter
1 large onion, peeled and finely chopped
2 teaspoons paprika
¼ pint (150 ml.) sour cream
1 red pepper, de-seeded and finely chopped
1 tomato, skinned and finely chopped

Cut the fish into cubes, about 1 in. (2·5 cm.) square, and sprinkle them with salt. Set aside for 30 minutes.

Melt the butter in a saucepan and fry the onion gently until transparent.

Remove from the heat, sprinkle on the paprika and stir in the sour cream. Return to the heat and add the fish pieces. Turn the fish gently in the pan and then add the chopped pepper and tomato. Cover, and cook over a very low heat for 25–30 minutes.

Serve with dumplings (see p. 159) or noodles.

CHINA
Whole Marinated Fish

CHINESE COOKING requires no exotic utensils, except sometimes the *wok*—a round-bottomed frying pan—and a few specialised ingredients such as soy sauce, which can be obtained from most delicatessens.

The special Chinese flavour often depends on seasoning and marinating, followed by short, fierce cooking.

This recipe is very easy to make, and can be used for mullet and sea-bass as well. Serve it with plain, boiled rice.

PREPARATION TIME: $1\frac{1}{4}$ HOURS
COOKING TIME: 20 MINUTES
PRE-HEAT THE OVEN TO
220°C (425°F)—GAS MARK 7

INGREDIENTS FOR FOUR TO SIX

1 red bream, about 2–3 lb. (900 g.–1·4 kg.)
3 carrots, cut in thin rounds
6 spring onions, finely chopped
$\frac{1}{2}$ pint (275/300 ml.) chicken stock

For the marinade:

A $\frac{1}{2}$ in. (1·5 cm.) piece of root ginger, peeled and chopped or 2 teaspoons powdered ginger
1 tablespoon soy sauce
2 teaspoons brown sugar
1 clove garlic, crushed
Juice of $\frac{1}{2}$ lemon

To make the marinade, combine the ginger, soy sauce, sugar, garlic and lemon juice in a large dish. Add the fish and leave for at least 1 hour, turning the fish from time to time to soak it completely.

Lightly grease a roasting dish and put in the sliced carrots and spring onions. Arrange the fish on top. In a small saucepan mix the marinade liquid with the chicken stock and quickly bring it to the boil. Pour the liquid over the fish and cover the dish closely with a double sheet of kitchen foil. Put the dish in the pre-heated oven.

After 5 minutes, reduce the heat to 190°C (375°F)—gas mark 5. Cook for another 8–10 minutes then transfer the fish to a warmed, deep-sided serving dish. Lift the vegetables from the dish with a slotted spoon and arrange them around the fish. Pour the liquid into a saucepan and boil it, stirring all the time until reduced and thickened. Pour it over the fish.

Red bream Chinese style—flavoured with ginger and soy sauce.

SPAIN
Baked Basque Fish

THE BASQUES know how to make the best of fish, as befits one of the great pioneer fishing peoples of Europe. As long ago as the mid-17th century they hunted whales across the Atlantic to the Grand Banks off Newfoundland where, in company with the Portuguese and the British, they found the finest cod-fishing in the world.

Fresh cod still holds its own in Basque cookery, but all other northern fish, they contend, lose their taste through 'rigidity', just as southern fish are insipid due to lack of exercise in the warm waters of the Mediterranean. The cod excepted, the only fish worth eating are those from the Bay of Biscay, where the warm and cold waters meet.

From this follows the Basque insistence upon natural flavours in fish cookery. In its original form this recipe suggested wrapping the fish in paper with a few herbs, so retaining the entire flavour for the table. But kitchen foil is even more successful.

PREPARATION TIME: 15 MINUTES
COOKING TIME: 30 MINUTES
PRE-HEAT THE OVEN TO
180°C (350°F)—GAS MARK 4

INGREDIENTS FOR FOUR

4 fillets white fish, such as cod, haddock or coley, skinned
2 oz. (50 g.) butter
1 small green pepper, de-seeded and chopped
1 medium onion, chopped
1 clove garlic, crushed
1 tomato, skinned, de-seeded and chopped
Salt and pepper
2 bay leaves
8 tablespoons white wine
Juice of $\frac{1}{2}$ lemon

Cut out four pieces of kitchen foil about 12 in. (30 cm.) square, and spread each piece of foil generously with the butter. Put one fish fillet on each piece of foil and divide the pepper, onion, garlic and tomato equally among the pieces of fish, covering each fish with the chopped vegetables. Put half a bay leaf on each piece of fish and sprinkle each with the wine and lemon juice. Season well and fold the edges of the foil together, making four firmly sealed but slightly baggy parcels.

Put the parcels on a baking sheet and cook in the pre-heated oven for 30 minutes. Undo one of the parcels after 20 minutes to check if the fish is cooked. It is ready when the flesh is opaque and flakes easily, and the vegetables are tender.

Serve with new potatoes or rice.

RIVER, SEA AND SHELLFISH

EATING FISH WAS ENCOURAGED by the early Christian Church as a form of abstinence, for fish flesh was thought to reduce passions whereas meat was thought to stimulate them. So, until about the 17th century, special 'Fyssche Days' were observed on which Christians were obliged to go without meat. For about half the year—every Wednesday (until the 15th century), Friday, Saturday, and during the 40 days of Lent—the poor endured a monotonous diet of salt fish. The rich avoided salt fish as much as possible and enjoyed the choicer kinds, such as sturgeon. Country estates generally had fish 'stews' or ponds stocked with pike, perch and other freshwater varieties.

Preserving fish by smoking over wood or peat fires, drying or salting—or a combination of all three—was known from prehistoric times. Salted, smoked Scotch salmon were sold in London from Tudor days; not until the 18th century were they packed in ice and sent fresh.

River and Sea Fish

Fish provides, pound for pound, slightly more protein than meat. Its price is no indication of dietary value; many cheaper varieties, herrings for example, are the most nutritious.

River fish, such as salmon and trout, are sometimes known as game fish. Salmon and trout are sold commercially, but most other types are caught by anglers. Rainbow trout reared on fish farms are the most widely sold trout.

Sea fish are generally classified as oily fish, such as herrings, or white fish, such as cod. In white fish, the oil is concentrated in the liver; some are flat (such as plaice) and some round (such as haddock).

Oily fish generally have more flavour, but white fish are less fatty and more easily digested. Both white fish and oily fish can be bought fresh, but are often frozen at sea.

Oily fish are often sold smoked—originally a method of preservation but now used mainly to vary the flavour. Some types of white fish are smoked—haddock for example.

Fish may be cold-smoked at a temperature below 29°C (84°F), so that the flesh is not cooked. Alternatively they may be hot-smoked at a temperature of 66–93°C (150–200°F). Hot-smoked fish are lightly cooked and have a smokier flavour than cold-smoked fish.

HINTS ON BUYING FISH

White fish are sold whole or filleted, large round ones in steaks or cutlets. Fresh oily fish are usually sold whole, smoked oily fish are often filleted.

When buying fresh river or oily sea fish, make sure they are as fresh as possible (see Choosing fresh fish), as they go off more quickly than other types. Whitebait must be absolutely fresh, as it is not gutted before cooking.

Smoked fish can go mouldy. Look at it closely when buying. The skin should be glossy, the flesh firm and there should not be an unpleasant smell. Hot-smoked fish does not keep well—eat on the day of buying.

If you buy fresh whole fish, the fishmonger will usually clean and gut it and remove the head on request. Alternatively, you can do it at home.

If you buy the fish filleted, ask the fishmonger for the skin and bones. Use them to make a liquid for fish sauce.

Unwrap the fish as soon as you get home, and put it in a covered container in a refrigerator or cool place until ready to cook it.

Choosing fresh fish

Fresh fish has a firm, stiff body with a shiny, smooth skin. Avoid fish that is flabby and limp with dry, dull skin that dents when you touch it.

Check that the eyes are bright and full, not sunken and opaque. The gills should be bright red, not pale.

Any skin colouring should be bright, not dulled. On plaice, for example, the spots should be orange, not dull brown.

There should be only a slightly fishy smell. Do not buy fish that smells strongly, with any scent similar to ammonia. This indicates decay.

PREPARING FISH

Clean all fish before cooking, and gut all except whitebait, which are tiny.

Cleaning a fresh fish

Some fish, such as pike, carp and tench, tend to have a muddy flavour. Soak them in salt water for up to 3 or 4 hours after cleaning.

1 Hold the fish in a sink and put a cloth beneath it to prevent slipping. Remove loose scales with the back of a knife, working from tail to head.

If you have difficulty in removing the scales (perch scales are often tricky), plunge the whole fish into boiling water for 2 minutes, then into cold water for 1 minute, then scale.

2 Use a good, sharp-pointed knife to gut the fish. Slit round fish (such as pilchards, mullet, perch, trout, pike and bream) along the belly. Lay flat fish (such as chicken turbot) with the dark-skinned side up and head towards you, and slit just behind the head from the right side to the centre.

3 Rinse the fish under the tap while you scrape out the entrails and any dark skin.

4 If you want the head removed, cut it off just below the gills. If you leave the head on, remove the eyes with a sharp-pointed knife.
5 Cut off the tails and fins with a sharp knife or scissors.

Cutting round fish into steaks
1 After scaling, gutting and beheading, cut round fish such as hake and cod into steaks.
2 Divide the body length into steaks each about $1\frac{1}{2}$ in. (4 cm.) thick, cutting through the flesh and backbone with a sharp knife.

Boning small round fish such as herring and mackerel
1 After scaling, gutting, beheading and trimming the fish, cut along the belly from head to tail and open out.
2 Lay it skin side up and press firmly with your thumbs down the back to loosen the bone.
3 Turn the fish over and, with thumb and forefinger, lift the backbone away from the flesh. It should lift easily, bringing most of the bones with it.
4 Fold back into shape or cut in two.

Filleting round fish such as herring and trout
1 Clean the fish and lay it on a firm surface.
2 Trim off the head and fins with a good, sharp-pointed knife, then cut along the length of the backbone.
3 Raise the first fillet (one side of the fish), easing it up with a sharp knife, and cut it off along the belly. Work from head to tail and sever the fillet at the tail end.
4 Lift the backbone from the remaining fillet, easing it out gently with the point of a knife.
5 Cut the tail off the second fillet.

Skinning a freshwater eel
1 Hold the head in a cloth.
2 Using a good, sharp-pointed knife, cut through the skin round the neck.
3 Grip the edge of the cut skin and turn it back a little. Then pull the head with one hand and the skin with the other. If you have difficulty, use pliers to grip the skin.

Filleting flat fish such as plaice and sole
1 Clean the fish and lay it on a firm surface, dark side up.
2 Using a good, sharp-pointed knife, trim off the fins and then make a slit down the backbone (the centre of the dark side).
3 Cut a semicircle behind the head, then raise the first fillet (half the upper side) by cutting the flesh from the bone with a sharp knife, working from the middle to the outside.
4 Cut off the raised fillet with sharp strokes of the knife, working from head to tail. Sever it at the tail end.
5 Turn the fish round, same side up, and remove the second fillet (the other half of the dark side), working from tail to head.
6 Turn the fish over and remove the other two fillets in the same way.

Skinning filleted fish
1 Partly thaw frozen fillets before attempting to skin them.
2 Place the fillet on a firm surface, skin side down. Put a small bowl of salt to hand.
3 Rub your fingers in the salt to prevent slipping, and hold the tail of the fillet with your left hand.
4 Using a good, sharp-pointed knife held at a slant, saw the flesh from the skin, taking care not to break the flesh.

Skinning the dark flesh from a sole
1 Lay the fish on a firm surface, dark side uppermost, with the head pointing away from you. Put a small bowl of salt to hand.
2 Using a good, sharp-pointed knife, cut the skin just above the tail.
3 Raise the end of the skin a little, then loosen the skin by running your thumb between skin and flesh, first along one side, then the other.
4 Hold the tail firmly with your left hand. Dip the fingers of your right hand in the salt to prevent slipping, grasp the tail end of the skin and draw it off quickly towards the head. If you have any difficulty, ease the skin off with a sharp knife.

Tips for Cooking Fish

To eat fish at its best, cook it the day you buy it. Before cooking filleted fresh fish, rinse it quickly and wipe all surfaces with a damp cloth.

Never overcook fish—it will toughen the flesh and destroy the flavour. Short, gentle cooking over a low heat gives the best results.

Test for readiness by inserting a skewer. The fish is cooked when the flesh separates easily from the bone, or, if boned, when a soft white liquid similar to curd oozes out.

If you need to re-heat fish that has already been cooked, it must be thoroughly heated through—to a temperature of 77°C (170°F). Finely slice, chop or mince the fish to allow the heat to penetrate. Do not re-heat more than once.

Line the grill pan with foil when grilling fish. This prevents fishy smells from clinging to the pan.

When grilling fish whole, make two or three deep cuts on each side to help the heat penetrate.

To prevent fish sticking to the grill rack, brush with melted fat, butter or oil on both sides before cooking.

Fish for frying should be crisp and dry and free from grease. To prevent the fat soaking into the fish, sprinkle it with a little salt or coat with seasoned flour, oatmeal, beaten egg and breadcrumbs or—for deep-frying—batter.

Do not overfill the pan when frying fish. The cold fish reduces the temperature of the cooking oil.

When baking fish without foil, use moderate heat and baste occasionally to prevent it drying out.

Roll stuffed fillets of flat fish from head to tail with the skin innermost before you bake them. This prevents the flesh from breaking.

Jugged kippers or kippers baked in foil are more digestible than when fried or grilled, and as a bonus the house does not reek of kippers.

Sprinkle a few drops of lemon juice on white fish before steaming. This prevents discoloration. Serve the fish with a colourful garnish, such as chopped parsley, fennel or watercress, or sieve hard-boiled egg yolk over it.

Simmer fish gently when poaching. Cooking too rapidly will break the skin before the flesh near the bone is properly cooked.

Preparing and Cooking a Whole Round Fish

1 Soak to remove the muddy flavour if necessary, then clean and gut the fish in the normal way (see Cleaning a fresh fish).
2 Fish can be cooked with the scales on, provided that you remove the skin after cooking and before serving.
3 Large, whole round fish, or large cuts, can be poached in a flavoured cooking liquid, cooked in foil, or baked and stuffed (see overleaf).
4 For poaching, use a fish kettle—an oval or oblong pan fitted with a draining plate to lift the fish out. If you do not have a fish kettle, use a large saucepan. Pin the fish diagonally in a white cloth, using safety pins, with two ends trailing so that it can be lifted out easily after cooking.

Making basic cooking liquid
This liquid, which is also known as court-bouillon, is used to poach fish.

PREPARATION TIME: 10 MINUTES
COOKING TIME: 20 MINUTES

INGREDIENTS

2 carrots
1 onion
2 sticks celery
2 shallots
1 bay leaf
3 parsley stalks
2 sprigs thyme
2 tablespoons lemon juice
½ pint (275/300 ml.) white or flavoured vinegar or dry white wine
Salt, black pepper

Peel and finely chop the vegetables. Place all the ingredients in a large saucepan with 1½ pints (850 ml.) of water and bring to the boil.
Cover with a lid and simmer over a low heat for 15 minutes.
Leave to cool slightly, strain, and pour over the fish to be poached.

Poaching in foil to serve cold
1 Season the cleaned inside of the fish.
2 Brush a piece of heavy foil with cooking oil and wrap the fish in it. Do not press the foil too closely against the fish—it should be loose enough to accommodate juices during cooking.
3 Seal the packet carefully.
4 Use a fish kettle or pan that will hold the fish easily but not surround it with too much water.
5 Cover the packaged fish with water. Weight it with a light weight, such as a plate, to keep it submerged.
6 Bring fully to the boil, and when the water is properly bubbling take the kettle or pan from the heat and put it in the larder to cool down.
7 When cool, remove the foil. The cooked fish will be surrounded by delicious juices set into a jelly.

Baking in foil to serve hot
1 Pre-heat the oven to 220°C (425°F)—gas mark 7.
2 Measure the width of the fish across its back at the widest part.
3 Prepare the fish in a package of greased foil as for poaching (above). Alternatively, for smaller fish, place in a buttered baking dish—for a fish 2–3 lb. (900 g.–1·4 kg.) put butter over the top.
4 Bake the fish in the pre-heated oven for 10 minutes for each 1 in. (2·5 cm.) of the measured width.

Lacing a baked stuffed fish
1 Avoid stuffing the fish too tightly; the stuffing will swell during cooking.
2 Hold the edges of the cavity as close together as possible and secure with small skewers stuck through from edge to edge at intervals.
3 Take a length of strong thread or string and loop the centre behind and under each end of the first skewer.
4 Working down the cavity, cross each end of the string from side to side and loop it under the skewers. Knot it at the last skewer.
5 After cooking, remove the skewers gently and the lacing will come away.

Boning large round fish such as salmon
1 Before cooking, clean the fish and trim off the fins and gills. Cut an inverted V shape around the tail to prevent the skin from shrinking.
2 After cooking, lay the fish on a firm surface and snip the skin below the head and above the tail.
3 Gently peel off the skin from each side; leave the head and tail intact.
4 Slit the fish along the backbone with a good, sharp-pointed knife.
5 Ease out the backbone through the slit without disturbing the flesh.

Shellfish

SHELLFISH have been a popular food since prehistoric times, when they were roasted in their shells.

Although oysters are today regarded as a luxury, they were for centuries a food for the poor. In medieval times, when shellfish were a welcome change from the monotonous diet of salt fish endured during the days of obligatory fish eating imposed by the Church, oysters were one of the few fresh fish the poor could afford. If pickled in vinegar, they could be kept for several weeks.

Even as recently as Victorian times, oysters were equated with poverty. In Charles Dickens's *Pickwick Papers*, first published in the 1830s, Sam Weller declares: 'Blessed if I don't think that ven a man's very poor, he rushes out of his lodgings and eats oysters in reg'lar desperation.'

But late in the 19th century, the British oyster beds became polluted. Oysters were harder to get and so became a food for the rich.

Facts about shellfish
Crustaceans (such as lobsters) have jointed shells that can be removed after cooking, and molluscs (such as oysters) have hinged shells that are opened by force or heat to remove the fish for eating. Live lobsters are dark blue, but turn bright red when boiled.

All shellfish must be eaten as fresh as possible. Clean and cook them on the day they are bought. Oysters are often eaten raw. All other shellfish are boiled before eating. Oysters and mussels can be bought smoked.

English oysters are considered best for eating raw. They are at their best from September to April (the months containing the letter R).

Overcooking can make the flesh of shellfish fibrous and indigestible. Always follow the recipe carefully.

BUYING SHELLFISH

Crustaceans
Lobsters Usually sold ready cooked. Sometimes sold live.
Prawns Sold boiled, shelled or unshelled.
Crayfish Usually sold cooked or deep-frozen and uncooked, rarely live.
Shrimps Fresh shrimps are sold cooked in their shells. Frozen shrimps are uncooked.
Crabs Usually sold ready boiled. The fishmonger will dress the crab (take the flesh from the shell) on request. Sometimes sold live.

Molluscs
Mussels Sold live in their shells.
Oysters Sold live in their shells.
Scallops Sold fresh in their opened shells, or shelled and frozen.
Cockles Sold shelled and cooked.
Whelks Sold shelled and cooked.

Choosing shellfish
The shells of live, fresh molluscs should be tightly closed or should shut when tapped. Do not buy any with open shells, they will be stale.

The largest oysters are best for eating raw, the smallest are usually sold as cooking or sauce oysters.

Always buy crabs and lobsters from

a reputable source. Choose crabs weighing 2–3 lb. (900 g.–1·4 kg.) that feel heavy for their size and have stiff claws, all attached. Shake them to make sure there is no sound of water inside the shell—if there is, do not buy them.

On a fresh lobster, the tail should spring back when pulled. Choose one weighing 1–2 lb. (450–900 g.) that feels heavy for its size.

Cooked prawns and shrimps should be pink and crisp when fresh. If pale, limp and smelly, they are stale.

PREPARING SHELLFISH

Cleaning and opening mussels

1 Discard mussels with slightly open or gaping shells, or any that do not close when lightly tapped.
2 With a stiff brush, thoroughly scrub and clean the shells under the cold tap.
3 Scrape away the black weed, or beard, from the outside of the shells.
4 Shells open during cooking. Follow the recipe, or place in a heavy-based pan with ½ in. (1·5 cm.) of water or white wine and chopped parsley and shallots or onions. Cook with the lid on for about 5 minutes over a low heat until the shells open. Discard any that remain closed.

Opening and serving raw oysters

1 The usual serving is six oysters for each person. Ask the fishmonger to let you have the seaweed packing.
2 Using a stiff brush, scrub all grit from the tightly closed shell.
3 To open a shell, hold it in your left hand and wrap a tea towel round your hand and most of the shell, just leaving the hinge showing. Hold the shell over a bowl to catch any juice that may be lost during opening.

Alternatively, hold the shell on a flat surface with your left hand.
4 Take a short, strong knife, or a special oyster knife, and insert the point in the crack between the upper and lower shells, near the hinge.
5 Once the knife is in, ease it about until you feel it cut the muscle attaching the oyster to the flat upper shell. At the same time, twist the knife so that it prises the shell apart. Keep the flat side uppermost.
6 Remove the flat top half of the shell to reveal the oyster and its juice held in the deeper half.
7 Make a bed of cracked ice on each plate. Strew on the rinsed seaweed.
8 Arrange the oysters in their deep shells on top, and serve with lemon quarters and brown bread and butter.
9 Serve also with Guinness, or wine— Chablis, Muscadet, Sancerre or its neighbouring Quincy.

Cleaning opened scallops

1 Scrape off the surrounding fringe, or beard, and the black intestinal thread. The white part is the flesh and the orange part, or coral, is the roe. Both are edible.
2 Ease the flesh and coral from the flat shell with a short, strong knife. Wash thoroughly and drain dry.

Shelling cooked shrimps, prawns and crayfish

1 Hold the head between the thumb and forefinger of your right hand.
2 Hold the tail with the fingers of your left hand and gently pinch and pull off the tail shell.
3 Hold the body while you gently pull off the head, the soft body shell and the small claws.
4 For crayfish, remove and discard the intestinal cord.

Cooking crabs and lobsters

1 Scrub a crab and rinse a lobster well under cold running water.
2 Put the live shellfish in an empty saucepan. Pour tepid water on it.
3 For a lobster, strongly salt the water (use seawater if available), and for a crab add seasoning, a strip of lemon rind and a few stalks of parsley.
4 Cover the saucepan with a lid and weight it.
5 Bring the water to the boil. The shellfish will quickly lose consciousness. This method is considered by many people to be more humane than plunging the shellfish into boiling water.
6 Simmer a crab for about 20 minutes, a lobster for about 20 minutes for each 1 lb. (450 g.).
7 Leave crabs of 3 lb. (1·4 kg.) and over, and all lobsters, to cool in the liquid before dressing.

Dressing a crab

1 Place the cooked, cooled crab shell upwards on a firm, stable surface.
2 Twist off the two large claws and the legs, then crack each claw open with a hammer, claw cracker or the handle of a knife.
3 Empty the white meat from the claws into a bowl, scraping round the insides of the claws with a skewer or knitting needle.
4 If the legs are large enough, crack them open also and scrape out the white meat. Otherwise use them to decorate the finished dish.
5 Turn the crab on its back and firmly pull the body from the shell.
6 Remove and discard the greyish stomach that lies behind the head, and also the grey, feathery-looking gills and the greenish intestines.
7 Scrape the soft brown meat from the shell; collect in a second bowl.
8 Cut the body in two, and scrape out any white meat left in the leg sockets into the first bowl.
9 Using a knife handle, tap off the irregular sharp edge of the shell. Trim to the dark line round the rim.
10 Scrub and rinse the shell inside and out under the cold tap.
11 Dry the shell and rub or brush it outside with a few drops of oil.
12 Chop the white meat and season it to taste with salt, black pepper, Cayenne pepper and a few drops of lemon juice or white wine vinegar.
13 Take the brown meat and add 1–2 tablespoons of fresh, fine white breadcrumbs. Mix well, and add seasoning in the same way as for the white meat. If you wish, add a little chopped parsley to give extra flavouring and colour.
14 Arrange the brown meat in the centre of the cleaned shell and pile the white meat on each side.
15 Garnish with tiny sprigs of parsley and small 'butterflies' of lemon.

Dressing a lobster

1 Lay the cooked lobster on a firm surface and twist off the claws and pincers.
2 Crack open the large claws with a hammer or claw cracker and scrape the meat into a bowl. Discard the membrane from the claw centre.
3 Lay the lobster with its back uppermost and, using a sharp knife, split it in two from head to tail.
4 Open out the two halves and remove and discard the gills, the small stomach behind the mouth and the dark vein running down the tail.
5 If desired, keep the greenish liver, which is considered a delicacy, and serve it as a garnish.
6 In a female lobster there may be orange spawn (eggs), known as coral, in the tail. Add it to the accompanying sauce, or mash with butter and sieve over the white meat as a garnish.
7 Take out the tail flesh and scrape the meat from the rear legs with a skewer or knitting needle.
8 Wash and dry the two halves of the shell and buff with a dry cloth.
9 Pile the meat back into the shell halves and garnish with the claws.

Of
ROASTS, STEWS AND OTHER MEATS

CONTAINING

NUMEROUS *Useful* FAMILY RECIPES

for LAMB, BEEF, VEAL & PORK

in DELIGHTEFUL MEATY DISHES

PAGES 80 – 107

AND

A SELECTION of RECIPES from OTHER LANDS

PAGES 108 – 109

AND WITH

GUIDANCE *on* BASIC METHODS

for all kinds of Choosing, Preparing, Stewing and Roasting of Meats to Perfection

PAGES 110 – 115

COLD BRISKET OF BEEF IN CIDER
West Country

CIDER CAME FROM NORMANDY with the Conquest, and for years after was the staple drink of the poor of Kent and Sussex, where water was the only—unthinkable—alternative. Water was avoided not through fear of contamination, but because the physicians regarded it as 'cold, slow and slack of digestion'. Not that cider was without its critics. In 1541 a doctor noted that people in cider-drinking districts 'had the skin of their visage rivelled, although that they be young'.

Cider-making did not spread to the West Country until the 13th century, but perhaps greater use was made of it there than in other regions. Cooking in cider is a speciality of the region, and this local beef recipe is no exception.

Served cold with salad, pickles and home-made bread, brisket of beef was traditional fare for Harvest Home, or for a special high tea.

To take into account the standing time, remember to order the meat from your butcher at least two days before you plan to eat it.

SOAKING TIME: OVERNIGHT
PREPARATION TIME: 20 MINUTES
COOKING TIME: 4 HOURS
STANDING TIME: 2 DAYS
PRE-HEAT THE OVEN TO 130°C (250°F)—GAS MARK ½

INGREDIENTS FOR SIX TO EIGHT

3–4 lb. (1·4–1·8 kg.) salted brisket of beef, soaked overnight in cold water and then drained
2 carrots, cut in thick rings
1 onion, peeled and quartered
Salt and pepper
A bundle of fresh, mixed herbs (parsley, thyme, sage, marjoram)
12 peppercorns
12 cloves
1 teaspoon ground allspice
1 teaspoon ground mace
1 pint (575/600 ml.) cider
1 pint (575/600 ml.) boiling water

Put the beef in a large casserole with the carrots and onion, and season with salt and pepper. Add the herbs and spices. Pour on the cider and boiling water. Cover tightly and cook in the pre-heated oven for 4 hours.

Remove from the oven and allow to cool in the liquid overnight. The next day remove the beef and place it in a deep basin.

Cover the meat with a plate that fits inside the rim of the basin and put a heavy weight on top. Leave in a cool place until next day.

Carve the beef in very thin slices to serve.

Cold Brisket of Beef in Cider—a Harvest Home treat to serve with pickled walnuts, salad and bread.

BRAISED BEEF
Countrywide

WITH THE INTRODUCTION of modern gas and electric cookers, true braising became a rarity because it depends on a supply of burning coals. In former days these coals were placed in the scooped-out lid of the braising pan, as it stood on the cooker. The stew, or braise, was thus sandwiched between two layers of heat.

Cooking in the oven gives a slightly different, but nevertheless satisfying, result, as you will find with this unusual recipe for braised beef. You can use any inexpensive cut of meat; the marinade helps to tenderise it and develop its flavour.

In Norfolk they maintain that braised beef is as good to eat as pheasant; and an old pheasant is excellent cooked in this way.

PREPARATION TIME: 30 MINUTES
STANDING TIME: 4 HOURS OR OVERNIGHT
COOKING TIME: 2 HOURS
PRE-HEAT THE OVEN TO
180°C (350°F)—GAS MARK 4

INGREDIENTS FOR SIX

- *2–2½ lb. (900 g.–1·1 kg.) topside of beef or brisket*
- *8 oz. (225 g.) carrots, chopped*
- *8 oz. (225 g.) leeks, cleaned and sliced*
- *2 onions, peeled and chopped*
- *2 oz. (50 g.) cooking fat or dripping*

For the marinade:

- *A bunch of fresh herbs such as parsley, thyme, marjoram and a bay leaf, or 1 teaspoon mixed dried herbs*
- *½ pint (275/300 ml.) red wine, or a mixture of red wine and water*
- *Salt and pepper*

Place the beef in a large bowl. Put the peeled and sliced vegetables over and around the beef.

For the marinade, tie the fresh herbs in a bunch and lay on the beef, or sprinkle the dried herbs over it. Stir 1 teaspoon of salt and ¼ teaspoon of pepper into the wine, or wine and water.

Pour this liquid over the meat, vegetables and herbs, and leave for at least 4 hours or, preferably, overnight. Spoon the liquid over the meat from time to time, and turn the beef in the marinade at least once to distribute the liquid evenly.

When you are ready to begin cooking, heat the dripping in a wide, deep casserole until it is very hot. Lift the joint from the marinade, draining the liquid from it back into the bowl. Fry the beef on all sides, briefly but at a high temperature, to seal in the juices.

Remove the vegetables from the marinade and put into a large, wide casserole. Place the beef on top and pour over the marinade. Add enough cold water to bring the level halfway up the joint.

Place the uncovered casserole in the pre-heated oven for 2 hours, basting frequently. If the top of the joint begins to look dry, baste well and cover with foil.

The gravy need only be skimmed and seasoned before serving, but it can be thickened with cornflour if you prefer.

Serve the braised beef in its casserole. If liked, serve it with savoury dumplings that you have made separately (see p. 159).

POT ROAST OF BEEF
Countrywide

POT ROASTING is an ancient cooking method dating back to prehistoric times. Pots of clay, and later of bronze or copper, were hung over a fire or placed on the hot stones of the hearth, partly surrounded by ashes. In these vessels fowl, or whole cuts of meat, were cooked with vegetables, herbs, a little fat and very little water.

Topside or fresh silverside are good joints to choose for pot roasting, because they require slow cooking and have little fat.

Pot Roast of Beef—one of the world's oldest cooking techniques.

PREPARATION TIME: 20 MINUTES
COOKING TIME: 1½ HOURS
PRE-HEAT THE OVEN TO
180°C (350°F)—GAS MARK 4

INGREDIENTS FOR FOUR TO SIX

- *2½–3 lb. (1·1–1·4 kg.) topside or fresh silverside of beef*
- *2 oz. (50 g.) butter, melted*
- *2 large onions, peeled and quartered*
- *8 oz. (225 g.) carrots, scraped and sliced*
- *1 medium turnip or swede, peeled and sliced*
- *1 teaspoon fresh thyme, or ¼ teaspoon dried thyme*
- *1 clove fresh garlic, crushed or ¼ teaspoon garlic salt*
- *Salt and pepper*
- *½ pint (275/300 ml.) stock (see pp. 33–34)*
- *¼ pint (150 ml.) red wine*
- *Mushrooms, peas or broad beans (optional)*

Fry the beef on all sides in the melted butter to brown it well, then set aside.

Lightly fry the onions, carrots and turnip or swede in the butter until they just begin to brown, then put them into a large, deep casserole.

If possible, place a small rack in the pot so that the beef stands above the vegetables. Otherwise, stand it on the bed of vegetables. Sprinkle the beef with thyme and the garlic and then season with salt and pepper. Pour in the stock and wine and cover the casserole with a lid or foil. Cook in the pre-heated oven for at least 1½ hours, or until tender, removing the lid for the last 20 minutes to brown the meat. If you like, add mushrooms, peas or broad beans for the last 20 minutes of cooking.

Serve the meat on a flat dish with the vegetables round it. Hand the unthickened gravy separately. Creamed potato and a green salad are good accompaniments.

SHEPHERD'S PIE
Countrywide

TO THE THRIFTY VICTORIANS, a Shepherd's Pie was a way of using up leftovers. But since their day it has developed into a satisfying meal in its own right, with many local variations.

Some shepherd's pies are bland, others are made fiery with Worcestershire sauce or Cayenne pepper. You can give this simple version extra table-appeal by following Mrs Beeton's advice and glazing the top with a beaten egg before baking.

PREPARATION TIME: 30–40 MINUTES
COOKING TIME: ABOUT 1 HOUR
PRE-HEAT THE OVEN TO 180°C (350°F)—GAS MARK 4

INGREDIENTS FOR FOUR

¾–1½ lb. (350–700 g.) potatoes, peeled
1 lb. (450 g.) minced lamb, mutton, beef or pork—either cooked or raw
3 oz. (75 g.) butter
1 medium onion, peeled and finely chopped
½ pint (275/300 ml.) stock (see pp. 33–34)
Salt and pepper
1 oz. (25 g.) cornflour
About ¼ pint (150 ml.) milk

Cut the potatoes in half and place them in a saucepan with salted water to cover. Cook until tender, and drain immediately. While the potatoes are cooking, prepare the mince.

If the mince is raw, use the following method. Melt 1 oz. (25 g.) of butter in a frying pan and fry the onion lightly in it. Add the mince and stir until lightly browned. Add the stock and simmer gently for 30 minutes. Allow to stand for a few minutes then skim off as much fat as possible. Season highly with the salt and pepper.

Thicken the liquid a little by stirring in the cornflour, mixed to a paste with a little water. Boil for 3 minutes, stirring constantly to prevent sticking. Turn into an ovenproof dish in which the pie will be served. The meat must cool enough to form a skin before the potato is put on to it.

If you use meat already cooked, fry the onion as above and stir it into the mince. Season well and add a little thickened stock until the meat has a soft, moist consistency. Set aside to form a skin.

Mash the cooked potatoes with at least 1 oz. (25 g.) of butter and enough milk to make it creamy. Season well. When the mince has a skin, spread the mashed potato on top carefully, so that it does not sink into the mince. The potato layer should be about 1–1½ in. (2·5–4 cm.) thick. Mark the top with a fork, and dot with the remaining butter. Bake for 30 minutes near the top of the oven so that the potato is well browned.

To vary this traditional recipe, add 1 tablespoon of tomato purée to the mince with the stock, or sprinkle the top with grated Cheddar cheese before baking.

CURRIED MEATS
Countrywide

EIGHTEENTH-CENTURY clerks and officers of the Honourable East India Company used to vie with each other in eating the most savage curries their servants could devise. Such curries were made from prepared powder to disguise the poor-quality meat foisted on to their masters, and in any case the servants considered the British palate too brash to appreciate the subtleties of true Indian cookery. They may have been right, for as early as 1780 curry powder—usually stale by the time it reached this country—was being recommended in English recipe books. This was several years before better-informed travellers began to teach us how to blend spices the Indian way.

The curries of India vary enormously from one area to another; generally speaking, the further south, the hotter they become. Various meats are banned in different parts of the subcontinent for religious reasons; but we may apply this traditional recipe to almost any meat.

It is best to prepare the blend of spices given in the recipe, but you can, if you prefer, use 1 level tablespoon of good-quality, ready-made curry powder instead.

The suggested accompaniments give the essential cool contrast to the hot spices in this recipe.

PREPARATION TIME: 1 HOUR
COOKING TIME: 1½ HOURS

INGREDIENTS FOR FOUR TO SIX

1½–2 lb. (700–900 g.) lean pork, lamb or beef
2–3 tablespoons seasoned flour
3 oz. (75 g.) butter
1 large onion, very finely sliced
1½ pints (850 ml.) stock (see pp. 33–34)
2 bay leaves
Salt
2 tablespoons raisins or sultanas
8 oz. (225 g.) long-grain Patna rice

For the blended spices:

1 teaspoon coriander seeds
2 teaspoons turmeric
½ teaspoon cumin seeds
A pinch of fenugreek
½ teaspoon mustard powder
1 teaspoon powdered ginger
½ teaspoon freshly ground black pepper or 12 peppercorns
½ teaspoon dried chillis
3–4 cardamom seeds
¼ teaspoon powdered cinnamon
12 cloves
½ teaspoon Cayenne pepper

For the accompaniments:

1 banana, peeled and sliced
1 large eating apple, peeled and finely sliced
2 tomatoes, blanched and quartered
1 small melon, cut into cubes or balls
2 tablespoons mango chutney
2 tablespoons any other sweet chutney
Bombay duck (if available)
Poppadoms (if available)

Remove all skin and fat from the meat and cut it into $\frac{1}{2}$ in. (1·5 cm.) cubes. Coat the meat with seasoned flour and set aside.

Melt the butter in a frying pan. Add the sliced onion and fry until it is soft but not brown. Transfer the onion to a saucepan large enough to hold the remainder of the ingredients for the curry.

Fry the meat in the butter in which the onion cooked, browning it well on all sides. Add the meat to the onion in the saucepan and pour over the stock. Put in the bay leaves and simmer gently for 1 hour.

While the meat is cooking, blend the spices for the curry. Put all the ingredients together through a coffee grinder. Alternatively, you can pound the ingredients in a mortar, but they must be ground as fine as medium-coarse black pepper and well mixed together.

When the meat has cooked for 1 hour, stir in the spices or ready-made curry powder. Put in half the quantity, taste, and add more spices or powder as required.

If you are using the blended spices, heat a small, heavy frying pan just before you add the mixture to the meat. Put the spices in it without fat. Stir with a wooden spoon for about half a minute, until the spices are smoking, then quickly scrape the desired amount into the meat.

Add salt, if necessary, to the meat and spice mixture and 2 tablespoons of seedless raisins or sultanas. Simmer the curry very gently for another 30 minutes.

Meanwhile, cook the rice (see p. 199) and prepare the accompaniments for the curry.

Serve the curry separately, and the rice in a snowy pile on a shallow dish. Arrange the accompaniments, each in a separate little dish or saucer, around the curry and the rice.

Crushed spices give the taste and aroma of the East to Curried Meats.

BUBBLE AND SQUEAK
Countrywide

WHAT MOST OF US THINK of as Bubble and Squeak was a 19th-century dish of warmed leftovers, popular with the poor of London and the south-east. The title is a somewhat poetic interpretation of the noise the mingled potato, cabbage and onion makes while sizzling in the pan.

The following recipe is an older and grander version that incorporates pieces of cold roast beef; these may either be laid on top, or layered between slabs of the vegetables.

PREPARATION TIME: 10 MINUTES
COOKING TIME: 20 MINUTES

INGREDIENTS FOR FOUR

12 oz. (350 g.) cold roast beef
3 oz. (75 g.) beef dripping or butter
2 onions, peeled and chopped
Salt
Freshly ground black pepper
1 lb. (450 g.) potatoes, cooked and mashed
6 oz. (175 g.) cooked green cabbage, well drained and chopped

Cut the roast beef into slices about 2 in. (5 cm.) by 1 in. (2·5 cm.). Heat 1 oz. (25 g.) of the dripping or butter in a large, heavy-based frying pan and fry the onions in it over a gentle heat until light golden-brown. Remove from the pan and keep hot. In the same fat, fry the pieces of beef for 4–5 minutes, stirring or turning them over so that they brown on all sides. Sprinkle with salt and pepper, remove from the pan, cover and keep hot.

Melt half the remaining dripping or butter in the pan and put in the potatoes. Mix in the cabbage, season with salt and pepper, and spread out over the base of the pan to make a cake about 1 in. (2·5 cm.) thick. Cook for 4 minutes, or until golden-brown underneath, shaking the pan to prevent sticking. Put a large plate over the pan and turn the pan upside-down, so that the Bubble and Squeak is on the plate.

Heat the remaining dripping or butter in the frying pan and slide the cake back into the pan, so that the underside will brown. Cook the cake for another 4 minutes. Turn on to a plate as before, and slide on to a warm serving dish. Arrange the onions and beef on half of the cake and fold the other half over it. Serve very hot with good brown sauce (see p. 163) or gravy.

BEEF STEW WITH PARSLEY DUMPLINGS
Devonshire

DUMPLINGS OR POT-BALLS, boiled with beef and eaten with butter, were invented in Norfolk in the 16th century, though it seems strange that so simple an idea had not occurred to anyone before that time. Nevertheless, by the end of Elizabeth I's reign, the notion, with variations, had spread through almost every English shire, immortalising the Norfolk Dumpling as one of the bastions of our national cuisine.

Parsley Dumplings set off a cider-flavoured Beef Stew from Devon.

Some people made them with bread dough, others with pancake batter. Occasionally, dumplings were sprinkled with currants or seasoned with herbs.

Parsley seasoning is Devon's contribution to the dumpling galaxy; few better companions could be found to set off this cider-flavoured stew.

PREPARATION TIME: 20 MINUTES
COOKING TIME: $2\frac{1}{2}$ HOURS

INGREDIENTS FOR SIX

2 lb. (900 g.) shin beef
$1\frac{1}{2}$ oz. (40 g.) well-seasoned flour
2 oz. (50 g.) beef dripping
8 oz. (225 g.) onions, peeled and sliced
1 pint (575/600 ml.) stock (see pp. 33–34)
$\frac{1}{2}$ pint (275/300 ml.) cider
Salt
Freshly ground pepper
8 oz. (225 g.) carrots, peeled and diced
8 oz. (225 g.) turnips, peeled and diced
2 sticks celery, cleaned and diced
12 parsley dumplings (see p. 159)

Cut the meat into 1 in. (2·5 cm.) cubes and toss in the seasoned flour. Heat the dripping in a heavy-based, 4 pint (2·3 litre) pan or flameproof casserole and cook the onions in it gently until transparent. Add the meat and fry until brown.

Stir in the stock and cider, scraping up any bits sticking to the pan, and season with salt and pepper. Bring the contents to the boil, and remove any white scum from the surface. Add the carrots, turnips and celery. Reduce the heat, cover the pan with a lid, and simmer the stew for about $2\frac{1}{2}$ hours or until the meat is tender.

Make the dumplings and place them on top of the stew for the last 15–20 minutes of cooking.

Ladle the stew and vegetables into a deep dish and surround with the dumplings. Serve immediately with hunks of crusty bread.

ROAST BEEF AND YORKSHIRE PUDDING
Yorkshire

'IN OLD ENGLAND our cheer is Roast Beef and Beer,' says John Gay in his *Beggar's Opera* (1728). But Gay was from the south and probably unaware that in Yorkshire a 'dripping pudding' had been invented that was to oust even beer as beef's traditional companion—though, in fact, it was originally thought of as an accompaniment to mutton. Not until 1747 was it called 'Yorkshire Pudding', and then by Hannah Glasse, in her *Art of Cookery*. She says: 'It is an excellent good pudding; the gravy of the meat eats well with it.' No one has ever described it better.

In Yorkshire it was, and in some places still is, the custom to serve the pudding with gravy as a first course to blunt hearty appetites before they encroach on the beef. Other Yorkshire cooks serve it with the meat.

PREPARATION TIME: 20 MINUTES

COOKING TIME: 1¾–2¼ HOURS

PRE-HEAT THE OVEN TO 220°C (425°F)—GAS MARK 7

INGREDIENTS FOR SIX TO EIGHT

- *3½–4 lb. (1·6–1·8 kg.) joint of roasting beef*
- *2 tablespoons dripping*

For the Yorkshire Pudding:

- *4 oz. (100/125 g.) plain flour*
- *½ teaspoon salt*
- *1 large egg*
- *½ pint (275/300 ml.) milk*
- *2 tablespoons cold water*

For the gravy:

- *1 tablespoon plain flour*
- *½ pint (275/300 ml.) stock from boiled vegetables*

Wipe the joint and put it in a roasting tin with the dripping. Place in the pre-heated oven for 15 minutes, then reduce the oven temperature to 190°C (375°F)—gas mark 5. Continue roasting the meat for a further 15 minutes per pound (450 g.) for rare beef, and 20 minutes per pound (450 g.) if you do not like it rare.

To make the Yorkshire Pudding, sieve the flour and salt into a large basin and make a well in the centre. Break the egg into the well and add a little of the milk. With a wooden spoon gradually draw in the flour, and mix the ingredients together, adding milk a little at a time until you have a thick batter. Beat with a wooden spoon until the batter is smooth, then stir in the remaining milk. Leave the mixture to stand for about 1 hour, or until the meat is cooked. Remove the joint from the oven and keep it hot. Increase the oven temperature to 230°C (450°F)—gas mark 8.

Cover the bottom of a baking tin with a thin layer of fat from the roast, and put it in the oven until the fat is smoking hot. Quickly stir the batter, mix in the cold water and pour it into the tin. Bake on the top shelf of the pre-heated oven for 25 minutes, until risen, crisp and golden-brown.

If you like, you can make small puddings in a bun tray instead of one large pudding. Put 1 teaspoon of fat from the roasting tin into each bun tin and put the tray in the top of the oven until the fat is smoking hot. Put 2 tablespoons of batter into each tin and bake for 15 minutes.

While the Yorkshire Pudding is cooking, make the gravy in the roasting tin. Pour off almost all the fat from the tin, but retain the brown juices. Mix the flour into the juices until smooth, then gradually add ½ pint (275/300 ml.) of stock, taking it from the vegetables you have boiled to accompany the beef, if possible. Stir continuously while you add the stock, then put the tin over a gentle heat and continue stirring until the gravy thickens and comes to the boil.

As soon as the Yorkshire Pudding is cooked, cut it into squares and serve it with the gravy, either as a first course on its own in the traditional way, or with the beef. Roast potatoes and a green vegetable are admirable accompaniments for the dish.

HASHED BEEF OR LAMB WITH TOMATOES
Gloucestershire

THE INCLUSION of tomatoes in this recipe from a Gloucestershire farmhouse indicates that it is comparatively recent. The tomato was grown as a decorative plant from the 17th century, but it was not accepted as a food for a century or more.

This dish is typical of many created in the 19th century to make an interesting and filling meal for a large household, using leftover cold meat.

SOAKING TIME: OVERNIGHT FOR THE BEANS

PREPARATION TIME: 35 MINUTES

COOKING TIME: 30–40 MINUTES

PRE-HEAT THE OVEN TO 180°C (350°F)—GAS MARK 4

INGREDIENTS FOR FOUR

- *8 oz. (225 g.) dried beans: haricot, butter, red beans or others as available*
- *2 oz. (50 g.) butter*
- *2 large onions, peeled and quartered*
- *4 oz. (100/125 g.) mushrooms, wiped and sliced*
- *8–12 slices cooked beef or lamb, trimmed of fat*
- *Salt and freshly ground black pepper*
- *1 oz. (25 g.) flour*
- *1 pint (575/600 ml.) brown stock (see pp. 33–34)*
- *1 teaspoon dried thyme*
- *¼ teaspoon dried basil*
- *12 oz. (350 g.) ripe tomatoes, blanched, skinned and quartered (see p. 198)*
- *1 teaspoon sugar*

Pour cold water over the beans, and leave to soak overnight. Next day, drain and put them in a saucepan with fresh water. Boil gently for about 35 minutes, until tender but not mushy, while preparing the other vegetables.

Melt half the butter and fry the onions in it gently until soft and transparent, but not brown. Lift them out with a slotted spoon and put into a shallow casserole. Use the butter in the pan again to fry the mushrooms lightly. Place them on the onions and lay the slices of meat on top. Season with salt and pepper.

Melt the remaining butter in the pan in which the vegetables were cooked, and stir in the flour. Add the stock a little at a time, stirring continuously over medium heat until a thin, smooth sauce is formed.

Drain the cooked beans and put them in a layer over the meat. Sprinkle with the chopped thyme and basil. Pour in the sauce and put the tomatoes on top. Season with salt and pepper, and sprinkle the sugar over the tomatoes. Cook the casserole, uncovered, in the centre of the pre-heated oven for 30–40 minutes. Serve the hash with plain boiled rice (see p. 199), a green salad and crusty white bread (see p. 265) and butter.

COLLOPS
Scotland and the North of England

THE MONDAY falling before Ash Wednesday used to be known in the North of England as Collop Monday. It was on this day that the devout took their leave of flesh for Lent. Their last meat meal consisted of collops—the dish also traditionally served on Burns' Night, January 25—slices of meat or bacon lightly fried and then gently stewed in gravy.

In the south, collops are generally cut from bacon or ham. In the north and in Scotland venison is sometimes used, but steak or lamb are a more likely choice.

PREPARATION TIME: 20 MINUTES
COOKING TIME: 45 MINUTES
PRE-HEAT THE OVEN TO 180°C (350°F)—GAS MARK 4

INGREDIENTS FOR FOUR

1½ lb. (700 g.) frying steak, leg of lamb or leg of pork, cut into 8 collops about 2 in. (5 cm.) by 4 in. (10 cm.) by ½ in. (1·5 cm.) thick
1 oz. (25 g.) seasoned flour
Salt and freshly ground black pepper
2 oz. (50 g.) butter
12 oz. (350 g.) mushrooms, sliced
2 teaspoons cornflour
1 pint (575/600 ml.) brown stock (see pp. 33–34)

Dip both sides of each collop in the seasoned flour. Melt the butter in a frying pan and lightly fry the sliced mushrooms. Put them in a casserole. In the same butter, fry the collops for 2 minutes on each side. Lay them on top of the mushrooms and season.

Mix the cornflour to a smooth paste with 2 tablespoons of the stock. Heat the remaining stock, stir in the cornflour paste, and continue to stir over medium heat until the mixture thickens. Pour into the casserole, cover closely and cook in the pre-heated oven for 45 minutes.

Serve with creamed potatoes, and leeks or cabbage. Rowan or redcurrant jelly (see pp. 343 and 340) makes a good accompaniment.

BOILED BEEF IN ALE
North Country

ROBERT HERRICK (1591–1674) in *Harvest Home* expounded the delights of beef: 'Well on, brave boyes to your Lord's Hearth Glittering with fire; where for your mirth Ye shall see first, the large and cheefe Foundation of your Feast, Fat Beefe.'

Beef was the foundation of many a good meal, and often the centrepiece at harvest and other festivals.

Most farmers brewed their own ale, and this formed the natural ingredient in many meat dishes.

PREPARATION TIME: 20 MINUTES
STANDING TIME: 8 HOURS
COOKING TIME: 3 HOURS

INGREDIENTS FOR EIGHT

4 lb. (1·8 kg.) piece of lean beef (flank, skirt, brisket or other slow-cooking cut) tied in one piece
2 lb. (900 g.) onions, peeled and sliced
2 pints (1·1 litre) light ale

For the marinade:

¼ pint (150 ml.) wine vinegar
4 oz. (100/125 g.) black treacle
A large bundle of fresh herbs, or 1 teaspoon each dried thyme, sage, rosemary and oregano, and a sprig of parsley
3 or more cloves
1 teaspoon ground mace
1 teaspoon turmeric
12 peppercorns
Salt

Make the marinade by combining the vinegar, treacle, herbs, spices and salt in a large bowl or pan. Place the beef in the marinade and pile the onions on top. Leave in a cool place for 8 hours, spooning the liquid over the meat from time to time to keep it moist.

To cook the meat, place it in a very large saucepan with the onions and the marinade. Pour on the ale, cover, heat almost to boiling, then simmer very gently for 3 hours. Check the seasoning and serve sliced with the sauce poured over. Boiled potatoes, red or white cabbage and a sweet chutney go well with this dish.

LOBSCOUSE
Lancashire

THE ORIGINS of this dish are curiously mixed. As described here, it must have begun with the Irish smallholders who settled in Lancashire towards the end of the 17th century and introduced the potato to the area. Within 50 years their meat and potato stew, known as 'lobscouse', was famed throughout the north.

But it was also the name of a seaman's dish, consisting of salt beef boiled with ship's biscuit, dried peas and whatever root vegetables were to be found in the galley at the time. 'Lob' means a lump of meat, or a bumpkin; 'scouse' is of uncertain beginnings, but in Nelson's navy it was the invariable nickname for any Liverpool-Irish sailor. Later, by extension, 'scouse' came to mean all things Liverpudlian, especially the dialect. Whatever its derivations, this casserole is a warming and filling meal for a winter's night.

SOAKING TIME: OVERNIGHT
PREPARATION TIME: 20 MINUTES
COOKING TIME: 4 HOURS
PRE-HEAT THE OVEN TO 150°C (300°F)—GAS MARK 2

INGREDIENTS FOR SIX

1½ lb. (700 g.) salted silverside of beef, soaked overnight
2 oz. (50 g.) butter or dripping
3 lb. (1·4 kg.) potatoes, peeled and halved
1 carrot, scraped and sliced
1 large onion, skinned and quartered
8 oz. (225 g.) dried peas, soaked overnight in cold water to cover
¼ teaspoon chopped thyme
¼ teaspoon chopped mint
1 teaspoon freshly ground pepper
2 pints (1·1 litres) heated brown unsalted stock (see pp. 33–34)

Trim any skin and fat off the beef and cut the meat into ½ in (1·5 cm.) cubes. Melt the butter or dripping in the bottom of a deep casserole. Put in the potatoes, carrots and onion and lay the cubes of beef on top. Drain the peas and put them on top of the meat. Add the thyme, mint and pepper. Pour on the warmed stock, adding a little water if there is not enough to cover the peas. Cover closely with the lid, or with foil, and cook in the pre-heated oven for 3–4 hours.

Serve straight from the pot, making sure that each person gets some meat and peas as well as potato.

Ragoût of Beef
Countrywide

Ragoût or ragoo—the word was anglicised in this way in the 17th century—both stem from the French verb *ragoûter* (to restore the taste). In its land of origin a ragoût is simply a stew, but in England the term implies slow braising with the addition of a highly seasoned sauce.

Though consumed by the better-travelled for a long time, it was not until the 19th century that ragoûts began to overcome the average Englishman's deep aversion to 'made' meat dishes.

Preparation Time: 30 minutes
Cooking Time: 2 hours

Ingredients for Four to Six

2 lb. (900 g.) best stewing steak, divided into portions with all fat, skin and gristle removed
8 oz. (225 g.) ox kidney, skinned, cored and cut up finely
A little flour
2 oz. (50 g.) butter
2 onions, peeled and chopped
2 bay leaves
Bouquet garni
Salt and pepper
8 oz. (225 g.) tomatoes, skinned and quartered (see p. 198)
4 oz. (100/125 g.) mushrooms
12 forcemeat balls (see Country Forcemeat p. 157), optional

Dip the steak and the kidney in the flour. Melt the butter in a large, heavy-based pan or casserole in which the meat will be stewed. First fry the steak in the butter, browning it on all sides. Then add the onions and the floured kidney and fry lightly. Add the bay leaves, bouquet garni, salt, pepper and enough water to cover the meat. Cover the casserole with a lid and leave to stew gently for 1½ hours.

Add the tomatoes and mushrooms, cover and stew for a further 20 minutes. At the same time, heat the forcemeat balls for 15–20 minutes in a covered dish in the oven, pre-heated to 180°C (350°F)—gas mark 4.

Take the meat out of the stock and place in a warm serving dish. Remove the bouquet garni and bay leaves and season the stock highly. It should be the consistency of thin cream. If it is too thin, thicken it with 2 teaspoons of cornflour, stirred into a little cold water and added to the boiling stock. Pour over the beef and put the forcemeat balls around it.

Beef or Veal Olives
Countrywide

Beef or veal olives made their earliest appearances in English cookery in the Middle Ages, alongside such delicacies as pudding of porpoise and morsels of whale.

The olives consisted then, as now, of meat slices wrapped round herb stuffing and baked.

Preparation Time: 30 minutes
Cooking Time: 30–35 minutes
Pre-heat the Oven to 170°C (325°F)—gas mark 3

Veal Olives—thinly sliced meat rolled round a savoury herb filling.

Ingredients for Four

6 large escalopes of veal or 6 thin frying beef steaks
1 pint (575/600 ml.) stock (see pp. 33–34)
1 oz. (25 g.) butter
1 oz. (25 g.) flour
3 tablespoons of sherry

For the stuffing:

4 oz. (100/125 g.) fine white breadcrumbs
2 anchovy fillets, mashed and pounded in a mortar or with a wooden spoon in a small bowl
1 teaspoon dried thyme
½ teaspoon dried sage
1 small onion, peeled and very finely chopped
1 egg, well beaten
Salt and pepper

Make the stuffing first by mixing all the ingredients in a bowl. Form the mixture into 12 small balls.

Pound the steaks or veal escalopes with the back of a heavy knife to flatten them. Trim off any fat and cut each piece in two lengthwise. You should have 12 pieces about 2½ by 5 in. (6·5 by 13 cm.). Place a ball of stuffing on each, and roll the meat tightly around it. Tie each olive round the middle with thread or string.

Lightly grease a shallow fireproof dish and lay the olives in it so that they touch each other. This helps them to stay in shape. Pour the stock over the olives. Cover the dish closely with foil and cook in the pre-heated oven for 40 minutes.

Lift the olives very carefully on to a warm serving dish, snip the strings with scissors and pull them away. Keep the olives warm and covered while you prepare the gravy. Make a roux with the butter and flour, stir in the stock and bring to the boil. Add the sherry and check the seasoning. Pour the gravy over the olives and serve immediately.

BEEF LOAF
Countrywide

MEDIEVAL TRENCHERMEN kept hunger at bay with 'mortrews', a pottage of pounded pork or chicken, flavoured with minced onion and stiffened with egg yolks and breadcrumbs sufficiently 'that it be standing'. This was certainly the ancestor of the recipe described here, although, like so many of our older country dishes, it crossed the Atlantic with the Pilgrim Fathers or their successor settlers and, considerably altered and adapted, returned to Britain in the last 50 years or so as an American innovation.

Buy lean stewing beef or topside, and mince it finely; the ready-minced beef usually on sale is too coarse and fatty for this recipe.

PREPARATION TIME: 20 MINUTES
COOKING TIME: 1½ HOURS
PRE-HEAT THE OVEN TO 150°C (300°F)—GAS MARK 2

INGREDIENTS FOR FOUR TO SIX

- *1½ lb. (700 g.) stewing steak or topside of beef, finely minced*
- *1 onion, peeled and minced*
- *2 oz. (50 g.) fine white breadcrumbs*
- *½ teaspoon dried thyme*
- *½ teaspoon dried oregano or marjoram*
- *1 clove garlic, crushed or ¼ teaspoon garlic salt*
- *½ teaspoon salt*
- *¼ teaspoon freshly ground black pepper*
- *2 eggs, beaten*
- *¾ pint (450 ml.) stock (see pp. 33–34), reduced to ¼ pint (150 ml.) by fast boiling*
- *½ oz. (15 g.) soft butter*

Mix all the ingredients very well together and mould into a roughly oblong shape. Butter an oblong loaf tin, 8 in. (20 cm.) long, and press the mixture into it until almost full.

Stand it in a shallow roasting tin with enough boiling water to come halfway up the side of the loaf tin. This prevents the loaf from sticking at the base. Bake uncovered in the centre of the pre-heated oven for 1½ hours. If necessary, add more boiling water to maintain the level.

Turn out the loaf on to a warmed serving plate, and serve hot with fresh tomato sauce (see p. 160).

VEAL CUTLETS IN WHITE WINE
Dorset

THE TRUE English countryman's traditional aversion to veal probably dates back to Saxon indignation at being forced to kill calves, and so wastefully deplete herds, to satisfy Norman demands for the meat. For centuries, veal was considered suitable only for invalids and the effete, and when it was eaten it was as a kind of pudding rather than as a sturdy main course. Blancmange was originally white meat—veal or chicken stewed in milk.

It was not until about 150 years ago that Continental influences and imports began to erode our long-held prejudices about meat. Veal is still not as widely available as other meats, but you can substitute pork cutlets in this recipe from Dorset, which dates from the adventurous era of the Edwardian ladies' luncheon parties.

PREPARATION TIME: 20 MINUTES
COOKING TIME: 35–45 MINUTES
PRE-HEAT THE OVEN TO 190°C (375°F)—GAS MARK 5

INGREDIENTS FOR FOUR

- *4 veal or pork cutlets*
- *2 oz. (50 g.) butter*
- *8 oz. (225 g.) onions, finely chopped*
- *¼ pint (150 ml.) white wine*
- *¼ pint (150 ml.) brown stock (see pp. 33–34)*
- *1 oz. (25 g.) breadcrumbs*
- *1 oz. (25 g.) Parmesan cheese*

Trim any excess fat off the cutlets. Melt the butter in a frying pan, add the onions and fry them gently until they are soft and golden. Stir in the wine and the stock, and set aside.

Combine the breadcrumbs and the Parmesan cheese. Coat the cutlets with the mixture, and place flat in an ovenproof dish large enough to hold them without overlapping. Carefully pour the onions and stock around the cutlets and cook uncovered in the pre-heated oven for 30 minutes or until the meat begins to come away from the bone very slightly. If the liquid should reduce too much, add more wine and stock in equal quantities.

Serve the cutlets straight from the dish, with creamed potatoes and a fresh green vegetable or a green salad.

SCALLOPS OF VEAL WITH CUCUMBERS
Countrywide

THAT OUR SEVENTEENTH-CENTURY ancestors had more time for the preparation and digestion of food than we have, is apparent in many of their recipes. One example suggests assuaging the pangs of appetite with a supper pie of veal, 'cowcumbers', cocks' combs, oysters, artichoke hearts, spices, herbs and a quart of cream.

Nowadays, such a dish would be a passport to insomnia at least. Nevertheless, the basic idea of blending the subtle flavours of veal, cucumber and cream is a good one.

PREPARATION TIME: 20 MINUTES
COOKING TIME: ABOUT 30 MINUTES
PRE-HEAT THE OVEN TO 220°C (425°F)—GAS MARK 7

INGREDIENTS FOR FOUR

- *6 oz. (175 g.) puff pastry, optional (see p. 219)*
- *1 cucumber*
- *1½ lb (700 g.) veal, cut into 8 very thin slices and flattened by the butcher (scallops)*
- *2 tablespoons seasoned flour*
- *4 oz. (100/125 g.) butter*
- *½ pint (275/300 ml.) double cream*
- *Salt and pepper*
- *¼ teaspoon paprika*

Roll out the puff pastry thinly. Cut it into triangular pieces, each side about 1½ in. (4 cm.) long, and bake in the pre-heated oven for 5–10 minutes. These can be made in advance and re-heated in a cool oven.

Peel the cucumber, cut it in rings ½ in. (1·5 cm.) thick, and cut each ring in half. There should be about four pieces of cucumber for each scallop. Cover the cucumber with boiling salted water and boil for about 10 minutes until tender. Drain, and cover to keep warm.

Coat the veal scallops with the seasoned flour, reserving 1 teaspoon for the sauce. Heat the butter in a large frying pan and fry the scallops for about 3 minutes on each side, until nicely brown. Remove and keep warm in a covered dish.

Stir 1 teaspoon of flour into the juices in the pan and cook for 1 minute. Then stir in the cream, mix well and boil fiercely for a minute or two to reduce and thicken. Unless it boils, the cream will not thicken to the right consistency. Season, as the sauce boils, with salt, pepper and paprika.

Arrange the veal fillets on a flat serving dish with the cucumber pieces among them. Pour the sauce over and serve, garnished with the pastry triangles if used.

RAGOÛT OF VEAL OR LAMB
Countrywide

RAGOÛTS occur in several European cuisines; the only trouble is that no two countries agree exactly what the word means. *Kettner's Book of the Table* (1877) says severely: 'The proper English word for what the French understand by a ragoût is a relish . . . a ragoût in English means no more than a good stew.'

The book goes on to say that the French were equally perplexed. At one time they called a mutton stew a ragoût, but due to the Germanic accents of Alsace, where it was a favourite dish, it became known as a 'haricot' instead. Since this was also the name of the kidney bean, the stew had to be re-christened again, this time, obscurely, as a 'navarin'.

Whatever is meant by it, this ragoût is an excellent supper or party dish, whose flavour and succulence comes from being kept standing overnight.

PREPARATION TIME: 1 HOUR 10 MINUTES
COOKING TIME: 1 HOUR 50 MINUTES
STANDING TIME: OVERNIGHT

INGREDIENTS FOR SIX

3 lb. (1·4 kg.) breast of veal or lamb, boned
Seasoned flour
2 oz. (50 g.) butter
1 medium onion, peeled and stuck with 2 cloves
2–3 sprigs of parsley
2–3 sprigs of thyme
1 sprig of rosemary
2 bay leaves
1½ pints (850 ml.) stock (see pp. 33–34)
3 medium carrots, peeled and diced
4 oz. (100/125 g.) mushrooms, lightly fried
8 oz. (225 g.) cooked peas or broad beans

For the thickening:
1 oz. (25 g.) butter
1 oz. (25 g.) plain flour
8 fl. oz. (225 ml.) stock from the ragoût
¼ pint (150 ml.) red wine
Salt and pepper
A few drops of lemon juice

Cut the meat into 1 in. (2·5 cm.) pieces, removing the skin, gristle and as much fat as possible. Dip the pieces in seasoned flour and fry on all sides in the butter until lightly browned.

Put the clove-stuck onion, with the parsley, thyme, rosemary and bay leaves, in a large saucepan with the stock and bring to the boil. Add the meat, cover closely and simmer for 1½ hours, stirring from time to time to prevent the meat sticking to the pan.

Brown the diced carrots in the pan in which the meat was fried, and add them to the ragoût after 1 hour. At the end of 1½ hours, the meat should be tender and the gravy brown and fairly thick. Remove from the heat and leave to stand overnight with the lid on.

Next day, remove the layer of fat and discard the herbs, onion and bay leaves. To make the final thickening, melt the butter, stir in the flour and cook for 2 minutes. Slowly add the stock and then the wine, stirring continuously over medium heat until smooth and well thickened. Season well with the salt and pepper and squeeze in the few drops of lemon juice.

Stir this thick sauce into the ragoût and add the mushrooms and the peas or beans. Bring to the boil then simmer for about 20 minutes, stirring to combine the stock with the sauce. Serve with plain boiled rice.

IRISH STEW
Ireland

THE ORIGINAL IRISH STEW, unlike the one served today, was made with male kid, an animal that had little value apart from its skin.

It was cooked, suspended over a peat fire, in the bastable oven, the all-purpose iron pot that was used for boiling, roasting and even for baking bread. Further slabs of red-hot peat were piled on the lid to increase the heat. Those who have tasted Irish Stew ladled straight from the bastable say that no modern cookery method can compare with it.

It used to be the practice, too, to seal the pot with a paste of flour and water to keep in the fragrance. When the stew was ready, the paste was thrown to the hens and the family settled down to supper.

PREPARATION TIME: 20 MINUTES
COOKING TIME: 2 HOURS

INGREDIENTS FOR FOUR TO SIX

2 lb. (900 g.) best end of neck of lamb, divided into cutlets, trimmed of skin and fat
1 teaspoon salt
½ teaspoon freshly ground pepper
3 lb. (1·4 kg.) potatoes, peeled and thickly sliced
1 lb. (450 g.) onions, peeled and quartered
1½ pints (850 ml.) cold water

Lay half the cutlets in the bottom of a large, flameproof casserole and season with a little salt and pepper. Cover with half of the onions, season, cover with potatoes and season again. Repeat the layers, ending with a layer of potatoes.

Pour in the water and bring to the boil. Remove any white scum, lower the heat, cover and simmer very gently for 2 hours.

A few minutes before serving, remove the lid and place the pan under a hot grill or in a hot oven, to brown the top layer of potatoes.

Irish Stew can also be cooked in a moderate oven at 180°C (350°F)—gas mark 4 for 2 hours.

DEVILLED SHOULDER OF LAMB
Yorkshire

IN GEORGIAN TIMES, devilling was a popular method of treating joints, pieces of poultry and game, and even leftovers.

There were 'wet' devils and 'dry' devils. In both cases, the meat was treated with a mixture of hot spices. For a dry devil, the spiced meat was broiled under a grill or roasted, as in this 18th-century recipe. In a wet devil, the meat was cooked or heated in a sauce.

PREPARATION TIME: 10 MINUTES
COOKING TIME: 1½ HOURS
PRE-HEAT THE OVEN TO 200°C (400°F)—GAS MARK 6

INGREDIENTS FOR SIX

4–4½ lb. (1·8–2 kg.) shoulder of lamb
2 tablespoons seasoned flour

For the devil mixture:

3 teaspoons mild (French) mustard
½ teaspoon paprika
¼ teaspoon Cayenne pepper
¼ teaspoon white pepper
¼ teaspoon salt
½ teaspoon turmeric
½ teaspoon powdered mace
3 oz. (75 g.) butter or cooking fat
2 teaspoons lemon juice

Rub the shoulder of lamb with half the seasoned flour and roast in a baking tin for 40 minutes.

While the lamb is roasting, make the devil mixture. Beginning with the mustard, combine all the ingredients in a small bowl. Put in the lemon juice last, and mix well.

After 40 minutes remove the joint from the oven and make four deep crosswise slashes in it. Spread the prepared devil mixture in the slashes. Baste with the juices which have run out from the slashes. Sprinkle again with the remaining seasoned flour and return to the oven for 40 minutes.

Keep the lamb hot on a serving dish while you make gravy in the pan (see p. 115). Check the seasoning of the gravy and add a pinch of Cayenne pepper if you want it hotter. Serve with rice or creamed potatoes, accompanied by crab-apple or redcurrant jelly (see p. 340).

A treat from Georgian times—Shoulder of Lamb with a hot spicy 'devil' rubbed into the meat.

HARICOT OF MUTTON
North Country

ACCORDING TO the *Oxford English Dictionary*, the word haricot at first meant a stew, which contained 'mutton sod (boiled) with little turneps, some wine and tosts of bred crumbled among'. The beans were not included until a later date. This is possibly as a result of some confusion over their name, which is derived from the same Norman word *halicot* (chopped up).

PREPARATION TIME: 30 MINUTES
SOAKING TIME: OVERNIGHT FOR THE BEANS
COOKING TIME: 2 HOURS
PRE-HEAT THE OVEN TO 180°C (350°F)—GAS MARK 4

INGREDIENTS FOR FOUR

6 oz. (175 g.) dried haricot beans
1 lb. (450 g.) lean lamb from the leg, cut into 1 in. (2·5 cm.) cubes
1 oz. (25 g.) seasoned flour
3 oz. (75 g.) butter
2 medium onions, peeled and sliced
8 oz. (225 g.) carrots, scraped and cut in rings
1 turnip, peeled and cut in ½ in. (1·5 cm.) cubes
1 leek, cleaned and cut in 1 in. (2·5 cm.) lengths
1 clove garlic, crushed or ¼ teaspoon garlic salt

1 teaspoon dried thyme
Salt and pepper
1½ pints (850 ml.) stock (see pp. 33–34)
1 tablespoon finely chopped parsley

Wash and drain the beans. Pour cold water over them and soak overnight.

Dip the pieces of lamb in seasoned flour. Melt 2 oz. (50 g.) of the butter in a large frying pan and lightly fry the lamb. Turn the pieces two or three times to brown evenly. Lift the lamb on to a plate, and keep warm.

In the same pan, fry the onions, carrots, turnip and leek until they begin to brown. Turn the vegetables into the bottom of a deep casserole and place the meat on top. Add the thyme, the garlic, pepper and salt. Pour in the stock and add the drained haricot beans, which should be just covered by the stock.

Place the casserole in the pre-heated oven and allow to cook, uncovered, for 2 hours. As the beans soften they will form a crust over the meat and vegetables. After 1 hour remove the casserole from the oven, dot the beans with the remaining butter and return to the oven.

When the dish is ready to serve, sprinkle the top thickly with parsley and serve from the casserole.

LANCASHIRE HOTPOT
Lancashire

LANCASHIRE HOTPOT was traditionally cooked in the farmhouse bread oven at the end of a busy baking day. This oven in the wall beside the hearth was heated with faggots of brushwood. Then the larger cordwood was set alight inside it. When all had burned to ash and embers, it was raked out, the oven brushed and wiped over with a wet cloth, and the bread inserted. When the bread was done and the oven was beginning to cool down the hotpot was put in and left to cook until the evening meal.

Some hotpots use beef or chicken, but a true Lancashire hotpot should be made with mutton or lamb. At one time it was the custom to put a dozen or so oysters under the potatoes. Today, these, like mutton, have become scarce, and this recipe uses lamb and mushrooms instead.

PREPARATION TIME: 30 MINUTES
COOKING TIME: 3 HOURS
PRE-HEAT THE OVEN TO 180°C (350°F)—GAS MARK 4

INGREDIENTS FOR SIX

3 lb. (1·4 kg.) best end of the neck of lamb, divided into cutlets
Salt and pepper
1 lb. (450 g.) onions, peeled and sliced
1½ pints (850 ml.) stock (see pp. 33–34)
8 oz. (225 g.) mushrooms, wiped
2 lb. (900 g.) potatoes, peeled and thickly sliced
1 oz. (25 g.) butter, in small pieces

Put a layer of cutlets, lying head to tail, into a 4 pint (2·3 litre) casserole with a lid or into a large, deep pie dish. Sprinkle with salt and pepper. Cover with a layer of onions and season again. Repeat with the rest of the cutlets, covering each layer with sliced onions and seasoning with salt and pepper. Pour in the stock, which should almost cover the meat.

Place the mushrooms over the cutlets and onions and cover thickly with overlapping potato slices. Dot with half the butter pieces, cover tightly and cook in the pre-heated oven for 2 hours. Remove the cover, dot with the remaining butter and cook for a further hour to brown the potatoes. Serve with a well-buttered and seasoned mixture of finely chopped carrots and swede.

Piping hot, well-seasoned layers of cutlets and onions with mushrooms and potatoes make a Lancashire Hotpot.

CROWN ROAST OF LAMB
Countrywide

IN EDWARDIAN TIMES the elegant 'Crown Roast' of lamb was particularly fashionable at small country-house dinners.

Although most country butchers have been preparing lamb in this way since the 1920s, you will still need to order the crown from your butcher in advance.

PREPARATION TIME: 30 MINUTES
COOKING TIME: 1½ HOURS
PRE-HEAT THE OVEN TO 200°C (400°F)—GAS MARK 6

INGREDIENTS FOR FOUR

Crown of 12 best-end-of-neck lamb cutlets

3 oz. (75 g.) butter

For the filling:

1 lb. (450 g.) forcemeat of your choice, or 1 lb. (450 g.) hot creamed potato, highly seasoned, or 1 lb. (450 g.) hot mixed vegetables—green peas, broad beans, diced carrots and turnips and tiny new potatoes, simmered together in salted water until tender

For the sauce:

½ pint (275/300 ml.) brown gravy (see p. 115)

2 teaspoons redcurrant jelly

2 tablespoons sherry

Place the butter in small pieces in a roasting tin and stand the crown upright in the tin. If using forcemeat for the filling, spoon the mixture into the centre of the crown before roasting. Otherwise, cook without the filling.

Place the roast in the pre-heated oven for 15 minutes. Then reduce the heat to 180°C (350°F)—gas mark 4 and roast for another 1¼ hours. While the crown is cooking, baste the top of the forcemeat repeatedly with the dripping from the pan, or prepare one of the alternative fillings.

To make the sauce, heat the gravy thoroughly in a small pan and stir in the redcurrant jelly and sherry.

Lift the cooked crown carefully on to a hot serving dish and, if not filled with forcemeat, spoon the very hot potato or mixed-vegetable filling into the centre.

If the crown is filled with forcemeat or potato, you can put small heaps of peas, carrots, cauliflower, small onions or green beans round it. For a dinner party, top each bone of the crown with a paper frill.

Serve the sauce separately.

STUFFED LOIN OF LAMB
Yorkshire

THIS IS A MODERN version of a very old and much-loved recipe, the modern aspect being the use of lamb rather than mutton. But whether of lamb or mutton, the loin has always been considered the noblest cut. Mrs Beeton, in her *Household Management* (1861), having debated at some length whether sheep were eaten before the Flood, gives a recipe for 'Rolled Loin of Mutton (Very Excellent)'. She says 'with Scriptural authority' that the 'tail and adjacent part is the most exquisite morsel in the whole body'. The adjacent part is, of course, the loin.

This stuffed version, which comes from Yorkshire, is equally good hot or cold. If hot, serve it with onion sauce, or with quince or medlar jelly; or on a summer evening, produce it cold with salad. As well as being delicious, loin, pound for pound, is an economical cut of lamb.

PREPARATION TIME: 10 MINUTES
COOKING TIME: 1–1½ HOURS
PRE-HEAT THE OVEN TO 190°C (375°F)—GAS MARK 5

Elegance combined with flavour—Crown Roast of Lamb, trimmed with paper frills and surrounded by vegetables.

INGREDIENTS FOR SIX

4 lb. (1·8 kg.) loin of lamb, boned

6 oz. (175 g.) fresh white breadcrumbs

3 oz. (75 g.) shredded suet

1 tablespoon chopped parsley

1 teaspoon chopped, fresh mixed herbs or ½ teaspoon mixed dried herbs

Grated rind of 1 lemon

2 eggs, beaten

Salt

Freshly ground pepper

To prepare the stuffing, mix together the breadcrumbs, suet, parsley, mixed herbs and grated lemon rind. Season with salt and pepper and stir in beaten egg to bind the mixture.

Spread the stuffing on the meat where the bone has been removed. Roll up the meat with the stuffing inside and tie securely with string at several points along the roll. Roast in the pre-heated oven, allowing approximately 20 minutes per pound (450 g.) of lamb.

Serve with potatoes, green peas and gravy made from the pan juices (see p. 115).

BREADED LAMB CHOPS WITH MAYONNAISE
Home Counties

BREADED LAMB or pork chops and cutlets were a popular main course 70 years ago in town and country. They could be served with a variety of different sauces, including onion and tomato.

According to Lady Blanche Hozier, whose daughter Clementine married Winston Churchill, pork cutlets with mayonnaise, an even richer partnership than the following lamb and mayonnaise, were a particular favourite of Edward VII. He enjoyed dishes such as this at late-night suppers. Today, it makes a good main course for a dinner party.

PREPARATION TIME: 10 MINUTES
COOKING TIME: ABOUT 10 MINUTES
PRE-HEAT THE GRILL TO VERY HOT

INGREDIENTS FOR TWO

2 large loin lamb chops, trimmed of all fat

3 oz. (75 g.) fine white breadcrumbs, seasoned with salt and pepper

1 egg, well beaten

2 oz. (50 g.) butter, melted

2 large potatoes, baked in their jackets

4 tablespoons home-made mayonnaise (see p. 161), well chilled

Dip the chops in the seasoned breadcrumbs, pressing the crumbs well on to both sides. Then dip the chops in the egg, and again in the breadcrumbs.

Place them on the heated grill rack and pour half the melted butter over them. Grill at the highest setting for 3–5 minutes, then turn over and pour the rest of the butter over the chops. Grill for a further 4–7 minutes. The crisp, golden coating should show the darker marks of the grill, and the chops should be pink and juicy inside. Serve immediately with the iced mayonnaise and jacket potatoes.

STUFFED BREAST OF LAMB WITH BACON
Sussex

RICH GRAZING on the Sussex Downs gives the celebrated local lamb its superb flavour. Roast leg or saddle of Sussex lamb is always a delight, but other cuts should not be overlooked. Breast of lamb, in particular, is such a good and inexpensive joint that it deserves a better reputation than it possesses today.

The Victorians braised and boned the breast, cut it into strips to be served as 'epigrams'—coated with egg and breadcrumbs, crisply fried.

Stuffed breast of lamb is another long-standing favourite. Ask your butcher to bone and trim the lamb, but make sure he includes the bones and trimmings for the stock.

PREPARATION TIME: 20 MINUTES
COOKING TIME: 1½–2 HOURS
PRE-HEAT THE OVEN TO 200°C (400°F)—GAS MARK 6

INGREDIENTS FOR FOUR TO SIX

2–3 lb. (900 g.–1·4 kg.) breast of lamb, with bones and trimmings reserved

1 pint (575/600 ml.) water

1 medium onion, peeled and quartered

3 oz. (75 g.) butter

6 rashers streaky bacon, without rinds

1 oz. (25 g.) plain flour

For the stuffing:

3 oz. (75 g.) fresh breadcrumbs

1½ oz. (40 g.) shredded suet

4 oz. (100/125 g.) bacon without rinds, finely chopped

1½ teaspoons chopped parsley

½ teaspoon grated lemon rind

½ teaspoon mixed dried herbs

Salt

Freshly ground black pepper

1 egg, beaten

Milk

Place the lamb bones and trimmings in a pan with the water and onion. Bring to the boil, then simmer for 1 hour to make a stock.

To make the stuffing, mix together the breadcrumbs, suet, chopped bacon, parsley, lemon rind and herbs. Season with salt and pepper, stir in the egg and add enough milk to bind the mixture.

Flatten out the lamb and spread the stuffing on it. Roll up and tie firmly with string at about 2 in. (5 cm.) intervals. Place the roll in a roasting tin, spread the butter over it and cook in the upper third of the pre-heated oven. Allow 30 minutes' cooking for each 1 lb. (450 g.), plus 15 minutes. Baste several times during the cooking.

Flatten out each bacon rasher with the back of a knife and roll up tightly. Thread the rolls close together on a skewer, and place with the lamb in the roasting tin 15 minutes before the cooking is finished.

When the stock has simmered for about 1 hour, remove from the heat and strain. Discard the bones, trimmings and onion. Return the stock to the pan and boil rapidly until reduced to about ½ pint (275/300 ml.).

When the meat is cooked, lift from the oven and remove the string. Put the meat on a hot plate, slide the bacon rolls off the skewer and arrange round the meat. Keep warm while making the gravy.

Pour off the fat from the roasting tin, keeping back any brown juices and sediment. Stir the flour into the sediment and stir in the strained stock a little at a time. Bring to the boil, stirring all the time until smooth and thickened. Season as necessary.

Serve the lamb in thick slices, with a bacon roll on each serving, and hand the gravy separately. Potatoes and green peas or broad beans go well with this dish.

RISSOLES OF LAMB
Countrywide

THE ROMANS, having won an empire, were defeated at last by roast peacock. The bird was so tough that they were forced to mince it and turn it into rissoles.

In medieval English society, rissoles, or risshewes, helped to overcome the difficulties of eating with knife and spoon. On preparing the meat for the dish, the 14th-century cookbook *The Forme of Cury* instructs: 'Hewe it small, and grounde it alle to douste.' It was then rolled in breadcrumbs and fried. Rissoles of dried fruit encased in batter were also made for Lent.

The poor public image achieved by the rissole in wartime Britain was due to the curiosity of its contents—whalemeat or flavoured bread were among the least offensive. With peace, however, there returned rissoles such as these—creamy within, crisp golden-brown without.

PREPARATION TIME: 25 MINUTES
COOKING TIME: 5–15 MINUTES
PRE-HEAT THE OVEN TO
180°C (350°F)—GAS MARK 4

INGREDIENTS FOR 18 RISSOLES

1 lb. (450 g.) cooked lamb, minced
Salt
Freshly ground pepper
¼ pint (150 ml.) well seasoned white binding sauce (see p. 163)
2 tablespoons plain flour
2 eggs, beaten
8 oz. (225 g.) dried breadcrumbs
Cooking oil for frying

Season the lamb with plenty of salt and pepper and mix the white sauce into it to bind it together.

Sprinkle the flour over a working surface and put small pieces of the mixture on to it; there should be 18 pieces. Roll them in the flour so that they are shaped like thick sausages. Dip each in the beaten egg, then roll in breadcrumbs.

Shallow-fry gently in oil for 5–7 minutes to brown on all sides, then put into the pre-heated oven in a roasting tin for 10 minutes before serving.

As an alternative to shallow-frying and roasting, deep fry the rissoles in oil heated to 200°C (400°F)—a cube of white bread dropped in should turn golden-brown in about 45 seconds—and fry for 5 minutes or until golden-brown. Serve immediately.

Brown sauce (see p. 163) and redcurrant jelly (see p. 340) go well with the rissoles. They can also be served with a home-made tomato sauce (see p. 160).

BRAISED EBERNOE LAMB
Sussex

THIS UNUSUAL METHOD of cooking lamb recalls Ebernoe Horn Fair, held each year on July 25—the Feast Day of St James—in the little West Sussex village of Ebernoe. The traditional festivities—suspended only temporarily by the Second World War—include a cricket match and the roasting of a whole ram on the village green. A horn from the head of the ram is presented to the batsman who has made the highest score in the match, in recognition of his achievement. After victory is celebrated, and defeat consoled, in beer, both teams queue with the remainder of the village and the spectators for their share of the sizzling, roasted ram.

The name of the Ebernoe Horn Fair is commemorated in this delightful recipe.

PREPARATION TIME: 40 MINUTES
COOKING TIME: 2½ HOURS
PRE-HEAT THE OVEN TO
220°C (425°F)—GAS MARK 7

INGREDIENTS FOR SIX

4 lb. (1·8 kg.) shoulder of lamb
1 oz. (25 g.) dripping
3 rashers rindless streaky bacon, chopped
8 oz. (225 g.) onions, peeled and sliced
8 oz. (225 g.) carrots, sliced
4 oz. (100/125 g.) turnip or swede, diced
2 sticks celery, diced
½ pint (275/300 ml.) stock (see p. 33)
¼ teaspoon each of freshly chopped parsley, basil, thyme, rosemary
1 teaspoon salt

Remove all the fat from the lamb shoulder and heat the dripping in a large flameproof dish. Fry the bacon in it, taking care not to let it brown, then add the onions, carrots, turnip or swede and the celery, and fry for 10 minutes, stirring frequently until all the fat is absorbed.

Pour in the stock, add the herbs and salt, and bring to the boil. Place the lamb on top of the vegetables and cover with a well-fitting lid. Reduce the heat, and simmer very gently for 2 hours. Take the dish off the heat, remove the lid, and cook in the centre of the pre-heated oven for 30 minutes or until the top of the meat is crisp and brown.

Transfer the meat and vegetables to a warmed serving dish and keep warm.

Strain the stock from the casserole into a saucepan and skim off the fat. Boil the stock until it is reduced by half.

Serve the lamb surrounded by the vegetables and with the reduced stock poured over the meat.

BOILED MUTTON WITH CAPER SAUCE
Countrywide

'MY WIFE HAD got ready a very fine dinner,' noted Samuel Pepys in January 1660, 'viz., a dish of marrow-bones; a leg of mutton; a loin of veal; a dish of fowl, three pullets and a dozen of larks all in a dish; a great tart; a neat's tongue; a dish of anchovies; a dish of prawns and cheese.'

A fine dinner indeed, though it is to be hoped that he had some help with it. One or two of the dishes he mentions have long passed from our national repertoire, but the others are still very much with us. The neat's tongue, for example, is simply ox tongue, and while the mutton may have been roasted, in Pepys's day it was more likely to have been boiled. Capers, too, would have appealed to him; they were a novelty recently imported from southern Europe. If he could not obtain them, he would have made do with pickled broom buds instead. Today we can use 'English' capers—pickled nasturtium seeds.

Mutton is not so easy to find now as it was, though some butchers are selling it as a 'novelty'. If your local shop does not have it, use a lean leg of lamb instead.

PREPARATION TIME: 10 MINUTES
COOKING TIME: $2\frac{1}{2}$ HOURS

INGREDIENTS FOR SIX TO EIGHT

- *4 lb. (1·8 kg.) leg of mutton or lamb*
- *2 onions, peeled and left whole*
- *2 carrots, peeled and quartered*
- *1 turnip, peeled and quartered*
- *Bouquet garni*
- *Salt*
- *Freshly ground pepper*

For the Caper Sauce:

- *1 oz. (25 g.) butter*
- *1 oz. (25 g.) plain flour*
- *$\frac{3}{4}$ pint (450 ml.) hot stock from the mutton*
- *1 tablespoon capers*
- *2 teaspoons finely chopped parsley*
- *2 teaspoons lemon juice*
- *Salt and pepper*
- *1 tablespoon single cream*

Boiled Mutton or lamb with tangy Caper Sauce—a dish that would have tempted Samuel Pepys.

Trim off any excess fat, and put the meat in a large pan with the onions, carrots, turnip and bouquet garni. Cover with warm water and bring to the boil for about 5 minutes. Remove the scum as it rises to the surface. Reduce the heat, add a generous seasoning of salt and pepper, and simmer the mutton, covered, allowing 25–30 minutes per lb. (450 g.), plus 25–30 minutes. If using lamb, allow 20 minutes per lb. (450 g.), plus 20 minutes. From time to time during the cooking, skim off the fat from the surface. When the meat is cooked, take it out of the pan and keep hot. Measure out $\frac{3}{4}$ pint (450 ml.) of the stock and keep the rest to use in a soup.

To make the sauce, melt the butter in a pan over gentle heat. Mix in the flour, and cook for 2–3 minutes, stirring continuously. Remove the pan from the heat and gradually add the measured hot stock, stirring until smooth and creamy. Put back on the heat and bring to the boil, stirring continuously, then simmer for a further 5 minutes, stirring from time to time. Add the capers, parsley and lemon juice. Season to taste and stir in the cream.

Place the mutton on a serving dish, and fix a paper ruffle round the bone. Serve the sauce separately. Potatoes, carrots, and boiled turnips mashed with cream and butter, are the traditional accompaniments.

The bounty of sea, farm and garden go into spicy, hot Pepper Pot.

PEPPER POT
West Country

ALTHOUGH Pepper Pot became popular in the West Country in the 18th century, it was not of British origin. Traders brought it to the great port of Bristol as part of their exciting and exotic cargoes from the New World.

In 1760, the satirical writer, Thomas Brown, tasted the dish and called it, 'That most delicate, palate-scorching soup called pepper-pot, a kind of devil's broth much eaten in the West Indies'.

Pepper Pot, with its combination of meat and shellfish, is a cross between a stew and a soup. It is best served in bowls or soup plates.

PREPARATION TIME: 1 HOUR
COOKING TIME: 2 HOURS

INGREDIENTS FOR TEN

- *2½ lb. (1·1 kg.) leg of lamb, fat and bone removed, diced*
- *8 oz. (225 g.) gammon rashers, without rinds, diced*
- *3 onions, peeled and finely chopped*
- *2 or 3 fresh chilli peppers, de-seeded, or dried ones, crushed*
- *2 green peppers, de-seeded and finely sliced*
- *1 tablespoon finely chopped thyme*
- *1 teaspoon Cayenne pepper*
- *1 teaspoon paprika*
- *12 peppercorns*
- *Salt*
- *8 oz. (225 g.) cabbage, finely shredded*
- *1 small lettuce, finely shredded*
- *A handful of chopped spinach or sorrel*
- *1 small lobster or crab (cooked, taken from the shell and diced, see p. 77), or 4 oz. (100/125 g.) shelled prawns, chopped*
- *20 very small suet dumplings (see p. 159)*
- *1 tablespoon lemon juice (or fresh lime juice if available)*
- *1 banana per person*

Put the lamb, gammon and onions in a large pan containing 3½ pints (2 litres) of cold water. Add the chilli peppers, green peppers, thyme, Cayenne, paprika and peppercorns. Season with salt. Bring to the boil, cover and simmer for 1½ hours.

Add the cabbage, the lettuce and the spinach or sorrel, and cook 20 more minutes. Gently stir in the shellfish, then add the dumplings. Cover again and cook for 10 minutes. Stir in the lemon or lime juice and check the seasoning, adding more Cayenne if the dish is not hot enough.

The Pepper Pot should have a great deal of almost clear, very hot (in both senses of the word) gravy, and the meat and vegetables should not be mushy.

Serve in large soup bowls with plain boiled rice (see p. 199), served separately and spooned into each dish by the diners. Give each person, as a side dish, a peeled and sliced banana in a small plate or saucer. A little lemon juice squeezed over the bananas will prevent discoloration.

HONEYED LAMB
Western Wales

WELSH MOUNTAIN LAMB is arguably the best in the world; at least, most Welshmen argue that it is. What makes it special is first, its compact leanness—a leg weighs little more than 4 lb. (1·8 kg.)—and second, its aromatic succulence, derived from the wild thyme, rosemary and other herbs of the Welsh hills.

It is these same herbs, and the tiny mountain flowers, that give Welsh honey the inimitable flavour that has been valued since the Celts made their honey mead.

The marriage of lamb and honey, known in Wales as *Cig oen a mel,* is a particularly happy one, especially with a few herbs added to point up the subtle flavour of the dish.

PREPARATION TIME: 10 MINUTES

COOKING TIME: $1\frac{3}{4}$ HOURS

PRE-HEAT THE OVEN TO
230°C (450°F)—GAS MARK 8

INGREDIENTS FOR SIX

4 lb. (1·8 kg.) shoulder of lamb
1 clove garlic
Sea salt
Freshly ground pepper
4 oz. (100/125 g.) honey
$\frac{3}{4}$ pint (450 ml.) dry cider
1 teaspoon chopped mint
$1\frac{1}{2}$ teaspoons chopped thyme
1 oz. (25 g.) plain flour
1 teaspoon lemon juice

Line a roasting tin with a piece of foil large enough to wrap over the top of the joint. Rub the meat all over with the clove of garlic. Place the joint in the tin and season well with salt and pepper.

Mix the honey with $\frac{1}{2}$ pint (275/300 ml.) of the cider, and pour over the joint. Sprinkle the top with the chopped mint and thyme. Fold the foil loosely over the joint and cook in the pre-heated oven for 30 minutes. Open the foil and baste with the remaining $\frac{1}{4}$ pint (150 ml.) of cider.

Close up the foil again, reduce the oven temperature to 180°C (350°F)—gas mark 4, and cook for a further hour, folding back the foil to brown the meat after 30 minutes.

Remove the meat from the oven, place on a serving dish, and keep hot.

To make the gravy, pour off the juices from the roasting tin into a small saucepan, leave to stand for 5 minutes and then skim off the fat from the surface. Blend the flour in a basin with 4 tablespoons of the juices then stir back into the saucepan. Bring to the boil, stirring constantly until smooth and thickened. Season with salt and pepper and stir in the lemon juice. Serve piping hot with the joint.

Baked onions (see p. 182) and boiled new potatoes sprinkled with mint are excellent accompaniments for honeyed lamb.

PORTMANTEAU'D LAMB CHOPS
Home Counties

THE PORTMANTEAU was a rather heavy leather case, which Victorian ladies and gentlemen favoured for train travel. It opened along the top and part of the way down each end. Clothes and toilet articles could be stuffed into it and shut safely away. In just this way, the filling of chicken livers and mushrooms is sewn into these Portmanteau'd Lamb Chops.

Portmanteau'd Chops—stuffed with liver and mushrooms and coated in breadcrumbs.

The 'carpet bag' or 'carpet bagger', on the other hand, is the more usual beef stuffed with onions.

Savoury butter (see p. 164), new potatoes and peas with mint turn this recipe into a dish for a dinner-party.

PREPARATION TIME: 30 MINUTES

COOKING TIME: 15–25 MINUTES

PRE-HEAT THE OVEN TO
200°C (400°F)—GAS MARK 6

INGREDIENTS FOR SIX

6 large loin lamb chops, $1\frac{1}{2}$–2 in. (4–5 cm.) thick
4 chicken livers, about 2 oz. (50 g.)
8 medium mushrooms, wiped
Salt and pepper
4 oz. (100/125 g.) butter
2 eggs, beaten
8 oz. (225 g.) white breadcrumbs

Remove the skin and trim off some of the fat from each chop. With a very sharp knife, slit the lean eye of the chop, cutting inwards to the bone.

Finely chop the livers and mushrooms and season with salt and pepper. Melt 2 oz. (50 g.) of the butter in a small frying pan, add the mushrooms and liver and cook gently for about 5 minutes without browning. Allow to cool, then stuff the mixture into the incisions in the chops. Sew up, using a darning needle and heavy cotton thread.

Dip the stuffed chops in the beaten egg and coat generously with breadcrumbs. Place the chops in a roasting tray. Melt the remaining 2 oz. (50 g.) of the butter and pour a little over each chop.

Bake in the pre-heated oven for 6 minutes, then turn and bake for another 6 minutes. Cook the chops longer if you like them well done. If you prefer, you can shallow-fry the chops in $\frac{1}{2}$ oz. (15 g.) butter and 1 tablespoon cooking oil. Be sure to remove the stitches before serving.

PAPERED FILLETS OF PORK
Countrywide

THE 'PAPERING' of spit-roasted meat, as a means of preventing the outside from becoming too hard, succeeded the earlier method of dredging the meat with herb-flavoured breadcrumbs about the beginning of the last century.

This present suggestion of 'parcelling', primarily designed to seal in the flavours, belongs to the kitchen-range-and-oven era of 100 years later.

You can wrap the fillets in foil instead of paper, but allow 10 minutes extra cooking time, since foil acts as a barrier to heat.

PREPARATION TIME: 20 MINUTES
COOKING TIME: 35 MINUTES
PRE-HEAT THE OVEN TO
180°C (350°F)—GAS MARK 4

INGREDIENTS FOR FOUR

- *2 pork tenderloins*
- *½ oz. (15 g.) butter*
- *1 tablespoon finely chopped onion*
- *3 oz. (75 g.) fresh breadcrumbs*
- *1 tablespoon finely chopped parsley*
- *1 teaspoon dried, or very finely chopped fresh, rosemary*
- *Salt and pepper*
- *4 oz. (100/125 g.) softened butter*
- *¼ teaspoon ground mace*
- *1 tablespoon plain flour*

Cut each tenderloin in half and make a slit lengthwise in each half without cutting right through, as the back should still be joined. Set the four fillets aside while you prepare the forcemeat and the papers.

Heat the butter in a small saucepan and cook the onion in it very gently until just soft but not coloured. Mix the breadcrumbs, parsley and rosemary into it and season lightly.

Fillets of Pork with fine herb filling keep all their flavour when cooked in paper.

Cut four ovals of greaseproof paper about 10 in. (25 cm.) long and 6 in. (15 cm.) wide. Spread the softened butter thickly over the centre of each paper. Sprinkle with salt, pepper and a very little mace.

Fill the slit in each fillet with a quarter of the forcemeat mixture, spreading and firming in place with the blade of a knife. Rub the stuffed fillets with flour.

Place each fillet on a prepared piece of greaseproof paper. Fold the longer sides loosely over the meat, leaving some space round the fillet, and twist the ends tightly. Place in a large baking dish, and cook in the centre of the pre-heated oven for 35 minutes.

Serve in their parcels so that each person can unwrap their own and enjoy the full aroma.

GALANTINE OF PORK AND HAM
Countrywide

ACCORDING TO *Kettner's Book of the Table* (1877), Galantines should only be entrusted to those who 'can make a romance out of the breast of a turkey, and a scene out of the merry-thought of a chicken, raise a pheasant into a personage, put wit into a pistachio and endue a truffle with the soul of poetry'.

Presumably such persons are born rather than made, but provided you are moved by at least one of the qualifications, then this recipe is well worth attempting. Galantine, a dish of meat served cold in its own jelly, is, according to the French, a Gallic creation, though the Italians also claim it, pointing out that *gelatina* is Italian for 'jelly'.

Whatever the case, early Galantines—as can be gathered from Kettner's lyricism—involved game or poultry. This version, using two pig-meats, is entirely British.

PREPARATION TIME: 40 MINUTES
STANDING TIME: OVERNIGHT
COOKING TIME: 2 HOURS
PRE-HEAT THE OVEN TO
150°C (300°F)—GAS MARK 2

INGREDIENTS FOR SIX TO EIGHT

- *8 oz. (225 g.) home-cooked ham or boiled gammon*
- *2 lb. (900 g.) lean, cooked pork*
- *2 onions, peeled and par-boiled*
- *Salt and pepper*
- *½ teaspoon ground mixed spice*

3 fl. oz. (90 ml.) sherry
¾ pint (450 ml.) warmed white stock (see pp. 33–34)
2 bay leaves
6 rashers streaky bacon with rinds removed

Cut the ham into ¼ in. (5 mm.) strips and set aside. Mince the pork and onions together and place in a large bowl. Add salt and pepper to taste, and the mixed spice. Stir in the warmed stock and the sherry.

Put the bay leaves in the bottom of a 1½ pint (850 ml.) pudding basin and then line the basin completely with bacon rashers. Add a layer of the minced pork mixture. Lay eight strips of ham across the pork, pressing them down into it. Continue alternating minced pork and ham strips until all are used up, about five layers of each. Finish with a layer of ham.

Cover the top of the galantine with foil. Stand the basin in a shallow baking tray and pour boiling water around the basin. This will prevent the dish from becoming too dry while cooking. Place in the pre-heated oven and cook for 2 hours, renewing the water in the baking tin if necessary.

Remove from the oven, and rest a flat plate just smaller than the top of the basin on top of the meat. Stand a weight on it and leave overnight.

To serve, gently ease the galantine away from the sides of the basin with a knife and turn out on to a plate.

Potato salad and a crisp lettuce salad go well with the galantine.

HOME-MADE SAUSAGES
Gloucestershire

MOST INHABITANTS of these islands have a favourite brand of sausage which, first tasted in extreme youth, remains fixed in the mind as the finest ever created. A typical attitude to the sausages of long ago was that of the writer James Joyce who, when he was exiled in Paris, used to beseech visiting pilgrims to bring a pound of Dublin sausages and a bottle of Irish whiskey.

Sausage skins are not always easy to find, though many butchers will order them for you. The same mixture can, of course, be made skinless. Simply roll it, cut it to length, flour the sausages lightly and fry them.

PREPARATION TIME: 30 MINUTES

INGREDIENTS FOR ABOUT 20 FULL-SIZE OR 40 CHIPOLATA SAUSAGES

2 lb. (900 g.) very lean pork, finely minced
12 oz. (350 g.) shredded suet
8 oz. (225 g.) fresh white breadcrumbs
¼ teaspoon grated nutmeg
1 teaspoon powdered sage
½ teaspoon powdered thyme
½ teaspoon powdered marjoram
1½ teaspoons salt
½ teaspoon freshly ground black pepper
Sausage skins

To make the sausages, mix all the ingredients very thoroughly together, making sure that the herbs, spices and seasoning are evenly distributed. To put the mixture into the skins, use a forcing bag with a long, wide nozzle. Knot one end of a length of skin about 3 ft (90 cm.) long. Place the other end over the nozzle and push the rest of the length on until the knot is as near the nozzle as possible.

Force the meat in, drawing the filled skin back from the nozzle. Do not overstuff. Knot the open end and twist the filled skin at 3 in. (8 cm.) intervals. Let the twisted sausages lie in a cool place for up to an hour to set before cooking or storing.

Home-made Sausages, flavoured with sage, thyme, marjoram and nutmeg.

PORK AND PEASE PUDDING
Countrywide

PEASE PUDDING—or pease pottage until the 17th century—has been a British winter standby ever since the Romans introduced the pea in the first or second century AD. Possibly this was the most important of their vegetable gifts to us. Not only were the fresh peas a source of sugar; they could also be dried, and kept for use in winter months.

This recipe dates back to Stuart times at least. Cooked together, the pork and peas take up each other's flavours, making a tasty supper dish. Remember to order the pickled pork in advance from your butcher.

SOAKING TIME: OVERNIGHT FOR PEAS
PREPARATION TIME: 15 MINUTES
COOKING TIME: 2 HOURS

INGREDIENTS FOR SIX

4 lb. (1·8 kg.) pickled hand and spring of pork
1 onion, peeled and sliced
2 carrots, peeled and sliced
2 turnips, peeled and sliced
4 sticks celery, trimmed and chopped
6 peppercorns
1 small cabbage, trimmed and quartered (optional)

For the Pease Pudding:

6 oz. (175 g.) split, dried peas soaked overnight in cold water
1 sprig each of parsley, mint and thyme
¼ teaspoon sugar
Freshly ground pepper
1 oz. (25 g.) butter
1 egg yolk

The making of Pork and Pease Pudding—with a hint of parsley, mint and thyme.

Drain the soaked peas and tie them in a floured pudding cloth with the herbs, sugar and pepper. Leave plenty of space in the cloth for the peas to swell. Place the bag of peas in a very large saucepan and tie it to the handle.

Put the pork in the pan on top of the peas with enough water to cover. Bring to the boil and remove any scum. Add the onion, carrots, turnips, celery and peppercorns. Reduce the heat, and simmer, covered, allowing 25 minutes per lb. (450 g.) of pork. If using the cabbage, add it for the last 20 minutes of cooking.

When the pork is cooked, remove it from the pan, slice and keep warm. Allow the peas to cook for another 10 minutes, then lift out the pudding cloth, and drain the peas in a colander, removing the herbs. Mash the peas to a purée or rub them through a sieve. Put the purée in a clean pan, and beat in the butter and egg yolk. Taste, adjust the seasoning, and heat the pease pudding through.

Serve the sliced pork on a warm

serving dish, handing the pease pudding in a separate dish and using the pork broth as gravy.

Glazed carrots (see p. 182) and braised celery (see p. 184) are good accompaniments to the dish.

TOAD-IN-THE-HOLE
Countrywide

TOAD-IN-THE-HOLE, also known in Norfolk as Pudding-pye-doll, has changed its ingredients over the centuries. According to one theory, toad-in-the-hole began when 18th-century cooks first wrapped a small piece of mutton in a large piece of suet crust to make the meat go further. This dish was thought to resemble a toad in a hole. But for the majority of the population then, as now, a 'toad' is a sausage and the batter a Yorkshire pudding.

PREPARATION TIME: 15 MINUTES
COOKING TIME: 25–30 MINUTES
PRE-HEAT THE OVEN TO 220°C (425°F)—GAS MARK 7

INGREDIENTS FOR SIX

1 lb. (450 g.) pork sausages
2 tablespoons dripping

For the batter:

6 oz. (175 g.) plain flour
½ teaspoon salt
2 eggs
1¼ pints (725 ml.) milk

To make the batter, sift together the flour and the salt in a mixing bowl, and break the eggs into the middle. Stir well with a wooden spoon and add the milk, a little at a time, beating hard until the batter is smooth and has the consistency of thin cream. Leave it to stand while you prepare the sausages.

Cut the sausages in two. Put half the dripping in a frying pan and fry the sausages gently until golden-brown.

Put the rest of the dripping in a baking tin or shallow, ovenproof dish. Place in the pre-heated oven for a few minutes to get very hot. Then arrange the sausages in the dish so that they stand on their ends, if possible, and pour the batter gently around them. Return to the oven for 25–30 minutes, until the batter has set and risen around the sausages whose crisp, browned tops should be just visible. Serve with a good brown sauce (see p. 163) and vegetables.

PORK AND BAKED BEANS
Countrywide

LONG BEFORE the economical version of this recipe saw the inside of the famous can, pork and baked beans were a poor man's staple all over Britain. The Pilgrim Fathers took the dish with them to the New World in 1620. Within a few years it gave rise to the American delicacy of Boston baked beans and brown bread.

More than a century later, George III sampled a dish of pork and beans that was being cooked over an open fire by the men who were building Woolwich Arsenal; he thereafter demanded that the dish should be served to him 'as often as possible'.

Cooked in large quantities, this recipe makes an inexpensive dish.

SOAKING TIME: OVERNIGHT
PREPARATION TIME: 20 MINUTES
COOKING TIME: AT LEAST 4 HOURS
PRE-HEAT THE OVEN TO 150°C (300°F)—GAS MARK 2

INGREDIENTS FOR SIX TO EIGHT

2 oz. (50 g.) butter
1 lb. (450 g.) lean fresh pork, cut into ½ in. (1·5 cm.) cubes
2 rashers rindless streaky bacon, cut into strips
1 lb. (450 g.) dried haricot beans, soaked overnight and par-boiled for 10 minutes
12 oz. (350 g.) tomatoes, blanched and skinned (see p. 198)
1 teaspoon salt
½ teaspoon freshly ground pepper
¼ teaspoon dried basil
¼ teaspoon dried thyme
2 teaspoons sugar
1 pint (575/600 ml.) stock (see pp. 33–34), heated through

Heat 1½ oz. (40 g.) of the butter in a heavy frying pan and fry the pork cubes, turning until lightly browned all over.

Grease a deep casserole with the remaining butter and put the strips of bacon at the bottom. Drain the par-boiled beans and put half of them in the casserole. Put the pork on top and cover with the rest of the beans.

Pass the tomatoes through a sieve or food mill, season with salt and pepper and add the basil, thyme and sugar. Add the stock to the purée, stir well and pour over the beans and meat. Cover the casserole closely with a lid or foil and cook in the pre-heated oven for at least 4 hours. The dish can be made in advance but should then be reheated thoroughly before serving.

PORK TENDERLOIN WITH MUSHROOMS
Countrywide

UNTIL THE FIRST WORLD WAR the pig was still the countryman's mainstay, just as it had been since Saxon times.

Every part of the pig was used except the squeak, as the old saying goes. Sausages, puddings, hams, fatty bacon for mid-day dinners, dumplings, dripping—even the head was roasted for Christmas. But the most prized part of this remarkable animal was the tenderloin; this was generally claimed by the pig's owner and therefore seldom appeared on the market. Nowadays, however, most butchers carry tenderloins in quantity; they are called fillets in the north. Mushrooms set them off admirably, and creamed potatoes and French beans are fine accompaniments.

PREPARATION TIME: 30 MINUTES
COOKING TIME: 15 MINUTES

INGREDIENTS FOR FOUR

2 lb. (900 g.) pork tenderloin
Salt and pepper
½ teaspoon chopped fresh thyme
3 oz. (75 g.) fine white breadcrumbs
2 large eggs, well beaten
4–5 oz. (100–150 g.) butter
8 oz. (225 g.) mushrooms, wiped and finely chopped
1 tablespoon finely chopped parsley

Cut the tenderloin into at least 12 slanted slices, ¾ in. (2 cm.) thick.

Rub each slice of pork with salt and pepper. Mix together the thyme and the breadcrumbs. Dip the pork slices in the egg, then in the breadcrumb mixture, pressing the breadcrumbs as firmly as possible on to the slices.

Melt about half the butter in a large frying pan over a low heat until hot but not brown. Fry the slices of pork very gently for 3–4 minutes on each side, adding more butter as necessary. When the slices are golden-brown, remove and keep hot.

Add the remaining butter to the pan in which the pork was cooked and fry the mushrooms for 2 minutes, shaking and turning. Pour the mushrooms and butter from the pan over the pork. Sprinkle with parsley and serve immediately.

BRAISED COOKED HAM
Wiltshire

THERE ARE FEW country recipes for cooked ham. The meat was generally served cold as a packed lunch with a chunk of freshly baked bread, or simply fried in pork fat.

But occasionally a slightly more elaborate recipe was produced, such as this one from Wiltshire. It uses a piece of gammon, boiled a day in advance, and the gravy is based on good home-made brown stock. The gravy is enriched with sherry, but wine-makers can substitute their own raisin wine.

PREPARATION TIME: 15 MINUTES
COOKING TIME: 20–25 MINUTES
PRE-HEAT THE OVEN TO 180°C (350°F)—GAS MARK 4

INGREDIENTS FOR FOUR TO SIX

2–2½ lb. (900 g.–1·1 kg.) piece of cold home-cooked ham or gammon
12 oz. (350 g.) mushrooms, sliced
¾ pint (450 ml.) well-seasoned brown stock (see pp. 33–34)
2 teaspoons cornflour
4 fl. oz. (100/125 ml.) medium-sweet sherry
1 tablespoon finely chopped parsley
Salt and freshly ground black pepper

Cut the meat into eight slices about 3 in. (8 cm.) square and ¼ in. (5 mm.) thick. Trim off any fat.

Butter a large, fireproof casserole, and arrange the slices of ham so that they overlap. Fry the sliced mushrooms lightly in butter for about 3 minutes and sprinkle them over the meat. Closely cover the dish with foil, and stand it in a baking tray containing ¾ in. (2 cm.) warm water. Bake in the pre-heated oven for 20 minutes. Drain away the cooking liquid.

Boil the stock in a pan. Mix the cornflour with a little cold water, and pour into the stock. Stir rapidly until the sauce is smooth and semi-transparent, and as thick as heavy cream. Check the seasoning and add the sherry.

Pour over the meat and mushrooms so that the slices are well covered. Sprinkle with parsley.

Serve with creamed potatoes and broad beans.

HAM SPREAD TOASTS
Countrywide

SPREAD TOASTS had their origins in the medieval custom of serving food on thick slices of bread or trenchers—a habit that also gave rise to the phrase 'a good trencherman' for somebody with a hearty appetite. Meat juices soaked into these trenchers, turning them into delicious morsels. When wooden and pewter plates became popular, the trenchers were missed so much that diners insisted on having sauces poured on to slices of bread—on plates of course.

By the 16th century, these 'sops' had evolved into spread toasts. At first they had spiced and sweetened meat toppings but, later, savouries such as this spread came to be preferred.

PREPARATION TIME: 10 MINUTES
COOKING TIME: 5–10 MINUTES

INGREDIENTS FOR FOUR

8 oz. (225 g.) cooked ham, minced
1 oz. (25 g.) butter, melted
4 eggs, beaten
Freshly ground black pepper
4 slices fresh, hot buttered toast
1 tablespoon freshly chopped parsley

In a heavy saucepan, combine the minced ham, melted butter, beaten eggs and pepper. Hold the pan just off the heat, and stir well until there is no liquid egg visible. The consistency should be thick but still creamy.

Pile the ham and egg mixture on to the rounds of hot buttered toast. Sprinkle with parsley and serve at once.

SWEET-CURED HAM
Suffolk

THE PIG WAS ESSENTIAL to cottage and farm economy from Saxon days until recent years.

Countrymen depended so much on the pig that every area developed its own recipes for preserving the meat. In Scotland, unsmoked hams were pickled in ale and brown sugar; treacle was used for York hams, and vinegar for Ayrshire bacon. The following is a traditional Suffolk method.

Nowadays hams are generally factory-cured but, as with all home cooking, it tastes that much better if you cure your own. Your butcher will get a fresh one for you if you give him enough notice. After curing, you can store the uncooked ham in a refrigerator for about a week. Two cooking methods are given below: either simmer it in cider and water, or bake it in a crust.

PREPARATION TIME: 30 MINUTES
SALTING TIME: 1½ DAYS
PICKLING TIME: 10½ DAYS
SOAKING TIME: 2–3 HOURS
COOKING TIME: 3–4 HOURS

INGREDIENTS FOR 30–40

A 14 lb. (6·4 kg.) fresh ham for curing
3½ lb. (1·6 kg.) table salt

For the pickling brine:

1 lb. (450 g.) sea-salt crystals
1½ oz. (40 g.) allspice
3 oz. (75 g.) ground black peppercorns
12 oz. (350 g.) golden syrup
8 oz. (225 g.) clear honey
8 pints (4·5 litres) cold water

For cooking the cured ham in cider:

½ pint (275/300 ml.) cider
8 oz. (225 g.) brown sugar
4 oz. (100/125 g.) fine bread-crumbs, or 4 oz. (100/125 g.) brown sugar and 24 cloves

For baking in a crust:

3 lb. (1·4 kg.) plain flour

Lay the ham on a very large, flat dish or a marble slab and rub 2 lb. (900 g.) of the table salt into it. Cover with another 1 lb. (450 g.) of the salt and leave to stand for 24 hours. A good deal of salty liquid will run from the ham. Rub this back into the ham twice during the 24 hours.

To prepare the pickling brine, put the rough sea-salt crystals, allspice, pepper, syrup and honey in a large fish kettle or preserving pan and add 8 pints (4·5 litres) of cold water. Bring to the boil remove from the heat, cover and leave to get cold.

When the ham has been salted for 24 hours, place it in the pickling brine, cover and leave in a cool place for 12 hours. Remove the ham from the brine and cover with the remaining 8 oz. (225 g.) of table salt. Leave to stand for 12 hours.

Boil up the brine and allow it to become cold, then put the ham back into it. Leave in a cool place for 10 days, turning the ham from time to time.

Before cooking cured ham, soak it in cold water for 2–3 hours. Put the soaked ham into a very large fish kettle or preserving pan and cover with fresh water. Add the cider and brown sugar. Bring to the boil, cover, and simmer for 3–4 hours. Leave, covered, in the liquid until cold.

Pre-heat the oven to 230°C (450°F)—gas mark 8. Lift out the ham, wipe dry and trim off all the skin. Cover with the breadcrumbs and brown in the oven for 10 minutes. Instead of coating the ham with crumbs, you can stick cloves in it at 1½ in. (4 cm.) intervals and sprinkle thickly with brown sugar. Put in the pre-heated oven for 5–10 minutes to set and crisp the sugar.

Instead of simmering the ham, you can, if you prefer, bake it in a sealed crust—a method that preserves all the ham's flavour and moisture. Mix 3 lb. (1·4 kg.) of plain flour to a stiff dough with cold water. Roll out to ¼ in. (5 mm.) thick, and use to encase the soaked and wiped ham completely. Damp the edges of the dough to seal them. Bake for 3 hours in the oven, pre-heated to 180°C (350°F)—gas mark 4, then break off and discard the crust. Increase the oven temperature and finish cooking the ham by trimming off the skin, coating with crumbs or brown sugar and cloves, and crisping in the oven for 5–10 minutes, according to the directions given above for simmered ham.

Sweet-Cured Ham, baked in a sealed crust, keeps all its taste and moisture. Sugar and cloves make a final coating.

SKUETS OF PORK, VEAL OR LAMB
Home Counties

THE FIRST KEBABS were cooked by prehistoric man, squatting in front of a fire and holding over it pieces of meat speared on thin, straight sticks. This method, still popular in various primitive areas of the world, was in general use in Britain until the Middle Ages. Then a touch of elegance was bestowed on the process at the flamboyant court of Richard II. Here, one of his 300 cooks produced tiny silver skewers, on which were served dainty titbits of meat.

Stainless-steel skewers have since replaced the silver ones, but this early recipe still retains much of its old-time attractiveness.

PREPARATION TIME: 30 MINUTES
COOKING TIME: 12 MINUTES
PRE-HEAT THE GRILL TO VERY HOT

INGREDIENTS FOR SIX

- *3 large onions, peeled*
- *1½–2 lb. (700–900 g.) lean veal, lamb or pork from the fillet or top of the leg*
- *8 rashers streaky bacon, in rolls*
- *8 oz. (225 g.) button mushrooms*
- *Salt and pepper*
- *¼ teaspoon powdered mace*
- *¼ teaspoon garlic salt*
- *¼ teaspoon ground cloves or ginger*
- *3 oz. (75 g.) melted butter*

A gift from Richard II's cook—tender pork pieces on a skewer.

Partially boil the whole onions in salted water for 10 minutes, then cut them into quarters. Cut the meat into neat 1 in. (2·5 cm.) cubes. Cut each rasher of bacon into thirds.

Mix the salt and spices together and rub them into the meat. Thread the meat on six skewers, putting a piece of bacon, a mushroom and a quarter of onion between each cube. Pack the skewers closely with the meat and vegetables.

Dip each filled skewer in the melted butter so that it is coated all over, and spoon a little butter over the skewers twice while cooking.

If possible, cook on a spit-grill. Otherwise, lay the skewers on a grid in a shallow pan and grill for 6 minutes on each side, turning each skewer once.

Serve with brown sauce (see p. 163) or fresh tomato sauce (see p. 160), plain boiled rice and green beans, or peas cooked with mint.

KIDNEYS IN POTATOES
Countrywide

THE ROMANO-BRITISH considered lamb's kidneys a dish fit for an Imperial Governor at least; they cooked them in a *clibanus*, a double-walled portable oven that was also used for cooking dormice.

By the 1500s, however, and despite the undoubted popularity of a number of specialised dishes, kidneys were thought of as nourishment principally for the poor. Even as late as 1849, E. Copley, in *Cottage Cookery*, obviously had misgivings in advocating a food 'sold at a very low rate for dogs and cats', though 'no person need . . . think it any degradation to eat that which has hitherto been put to an inferior purpose'.

Then, during the next 20 years or so, insular suspicions gradually yielded to French adventurousness, so that by the end of Victoria's reign devilled kidneys were a common feature of the breakfast sideboard, and even dukes went to bed sustained by light snacks such as these 'surprise potatoes'.

PREPARATION TIME: 10 MINUTES
COOKING TIME: 2 HOURS
PRE-HEAT THE OVEN TO 180°C (350°F)—GAS MARK 4

INGREDIENTS FOR FOUR

- *4 large, well-scrubbed potatoes, pricked to prevent bursting*
- *4 lamb's kidneys*
- *Salt and pepper*
- *5 oz. (150 g.) butter*
- *2 tablespoons milk*

Rub the potatoes all over with ½ oz. (15 g.) of the butter, slightly softened. Bake them in the pre-heated oven for 1½ hours.

Meanwhile, skin and core the kidneys, being careful to keep each whole. Put a little salt and pepper on each, and set aside until the potatoes are soft.

Remove the potatoes and cut off a small lid from a long side of each. Reserve the lids and scoop out the contents of the potatoes, making certain you do not tear the skin. Mix the potato with 2 tablespoons of milk, three-quarters of the remaining butter and plenty of salt and pepper, and beat well.

Re-fill the potatoes, putting a kidney into each when the bottom of the shell is half filled. Pile the potato on top to make a neat, mounded shape and gently press a lid on each. Put back in the oven for 30 minutes to cook the kidneys.

To serve, divide the remaining butter into four pieces and put a piece under the lid of each potato. The kidneys should be perfectly cooked, and will have flavoured part of the potato.

Serve with mild French mustard—Dijon or Pommery—and a mixed salad.

TRIPE AND ONIONS
Lancashire

TRIPE ROASTED OR CURRIED, stuffed, pied, fried or fricasseed is revered in traditional dishes in places as far apart as London, Kilkenny, Derbyshire and East Anglia. But tripe and onions belongs wholly and completely to Lancashire. There, the tripe-dresser's trade—basically that of cleaning and parboiling the stomach-linings of cattle—includes many skills, best admired in the stalls of the towns and cities of the county that sell not only tripe, but also cowheel, pig's trotters and elder (pressed cow's udder).

These are the delicacies of a society long accustomed to making every penny count, and using the resources of ingenuity rather than cash to feed the family.

Tripe and Onions is the delicious result of generations of experiment in homely cooking.

PREPARATION TIME: 30 MINUTES
COOKING TIME: $3\frac{1}{4}$ HOURS

INGREDIENTS FOR FOUR

$1\frac{1}{2}$ lb. (700 g.) tripe, dressed by the butcher
$1\frac{1}{4}$ pint (725 ml.) milk
$\frac{1}{2}$ pint (275/300 ml.) water
3 large onions, peeled and finely sliced
Salt and pepper
1 tablespoon flour
2 fl. oz. (50 ml.) milk
$\frac{1}{2}$ oz. (15 g.) butter
4 slices of toast, crusts removed and each cut in two triangles

Cut the dressed tripe into 3 in. (8 cm.) squares. Place the pieces in a saucepan and cover with cold water. Bring to the boil over high heat and then throw away the water, leaving the tripe in the saucepan.

Add the milk, water, onions, salt and pepper to the tripe and simmer for 3 hours.

To make the sauce, mix the flour and milk, and strain into the saucepan away from the heat. Return to the heat, add the butter and stir until the liquid boils and thickens. Add salt and pepper to taste. Serve the tripe and its sauce very hot with slices of dry toast or mashed potatoes.

HAGGIS
Scotland

ROBERT BURNS paid the homage due to Scotland's national dish in his *Address to a Haggis,* which begins:

'Fair fa' your honest sonsie face,
Great chieftain o' the puddin'-race!
Aboon them a' ye tak your place.'

This large mutton sausage, which is what a Haggis really is, was devised on Scottish sheep farms as a way of using up the lights of the sheep together with the heart and liver. Haggis can usually be bought outside Scotland for such occasions as New Year's Day, St Andrew's Day and Burns Night, but it is not difficult to make at home.

If you do make your own Haggis, just remember to order the liver, heart and lights (if liked)—or buy them all together as the pluck— and the paunch from your butcher a few days before you plan to make it.

SOAKING TIME: AT LEAST 3 HOURS FOR THE PAUNCH
PREPARATION TIME: $1\frac{1}{2}$ HOURS
COOKING TIME: $4\frac{1}{2}$ HOURS

INGREDIENTS FOR 12–14

1 lamb's paunch
1 lamb's heart
Lights of a lamb (optional)
1 lamb's liver
12 oz. (350 g.) coarse oatmeal
12 oz. (350 g.) beef suet, shredded
2 large onions, peeled and finely chopped
Juice of 1 lemon
$1\frac{1}{2}$ pints (850 ml.) stock (see pp. 33–34)
2 teaspoons grated nutmeg
1 oz. (25 g.) salt
1 teaspoon freshly ground black pepper
2 tablespoons whisky (optional)

Prepare the paunch by stirring 3 tablespoons of salt into 4 pints (2·3 litres) of cold water and soaking the paunch in it for at least 3 hours, or overnight if more convenient. Turn the soaked paunch inside out and rinse under running cold water for several minutes. Set aside while you prepare the filling.

If you are using the lights, wash, place in a large saucepan with the windpipe trailing over the side, cover with cold, salted water, bring to the boil and cook for 45 minutes. Then wash the heart and add to the pan and continue boiling for another 45 minutes before draining well.

If you are not using the lights, wash the heart and place in boiling, salted water, cook for 45 minutes, then drain.

Cut half the liver into $\frac{1}{2}$ in. (1·5 cm.) cubes. Chop very finely, or coarsely mince, the other half of the liver, along with the cooked heart and lights. Put in a large mixing bowl and stir in the oatmeal, suet, onions, lemon juice, stock, nutmeg, salt and pepper, and whisky if used.

Put the mixture into the prepared paunch and sew up the opening with linen thread or string. The paunch must not be too tightly packed or it will burst as the oatmeal swells during cooking.

Put the Haggis in a large saucepan of boiling water and simmer gently for 3 hours. Prick once or twice during the first hour to allow steam to escape and prevent the Haggis from bursting.

If any of the filling will not fit in the paunch, it can be pressed into a basin, covered and steamed for 2 hours, then served immediately.

Serve the Haggis turned out of the paunch on to a large dish with slices of freshly made brown toast. The traditional Scottish accompaniment is mashed swede.

FARMHOUSE FRY
Countrywide

LONG BEFORE the term 'mixed grill' was concocted, the better-off yeomen farmers used to celebrate the Michaelmas killing of surplus beasts with a fry-up of offal, which could not be preserved. Kidneys, liver and brains, together with chops and bacon, were dropped into the great black frying pan; in the north, black and white puddings were also added.

There is still no better meal to anticipate or enjoy at the end of a long country walk on a darkening winter's afternoon. Add fried potatoes if you wish, and serve the whole feast with home-made chutney.

PREPARATION TIME: 15 MINUTES
COOKING TIME: ABOUT 25 MINUTES

INGREDIENTS FOR FOUR

4 rashers streaky bacon, without rinds
2 oz. (50 g.) butter
4 medium onions, peeled and sliced
2 pig's kidneys or 4 lamb's kidneys, skinned and cored
4 small pork chops or lamb cutlets
8 oz. (225 g.) pig's liver or lamb's liver, cut in 4 thin slices
1 oz. (25 g.) seasoned flour
4 tomatoes, blanched, skinned and halved (see p. 198)
8 oz. (225 g.) mushrooms, sliced
2 large slices white bread, with crusts removed

Heat two large frying pans. Put the bacon rashers to fry in one and melt the butter in the other. Fry the onions gently in the butter.

As soon as the bacon rashers begin to crisp, lift them from the pan and keep hot in a large flat dish.

If you are using pig's kidneys, cut each one in half. Dip the chops or cutlets, the liver slices and the kidneys in seasoned flour. Fry them all gently in the bacon pan until cooked through, turning once to brown both sides. (If the pan is not large enough, fry the chops first and the liver and kidneys afterwards.)

Turn the onions from time to time, and push them together to make room in the pan to fry the tomatoes and mushrooms.

When the meat and vegetables are cooked, arrange them on the warm dish with the bacon and keep hot. Pour any fat and juice from the vegetable pan into the bacon pan. Cut each bread slice in half and quickly fry until crisp and golden-brown on both sides. Arrange round the dish and serve immediately.

STUFFED SHEEP'S HEART
Yorkshire

A WEALTH OF OFFAL was available to country people after the autumn slaughter of surplus beasts. They invented not only ways of making it more palatable, but also names that disguised its humble origins. One recipe for stuffed heart was known in Tudor times as 'Love-in-disguise'; another, a Yorkshire dish similar to this one, was known as 'Mock Goose', and really did resemble goose in flavour.

This present recipe makes a cheap and nourishing family supper dish, well worth the preparation time.

SOAKING TIME: ABOUT 1 HOUR FOR THE HEARTS
PREPARATION TIME: 30 MINUTES
COOKING TIME: 2–2½ HOURS
PRE-HEAT THE OVEN TO 170°C (325°F)—GAS MARK 3

INGREDIENTS FOR FOUR

2–4 sheep's hearts
8 oz. (225 g.) pork sausagemeat
2 oz. (50 g.) breadcrumbs
1 teaspoon dried thyme
1 teaspoon dried sage
2 teaspoons finely chopped parsley
1 small onion, peeled and finely chopped
1 egg, well beaten
Salt and pepper
1 tablespoon seasoned flour
2 oz. (50 g.) butter or dripping

For the gravy:

1 level tablespoon plain flour
½ pint (275/300 ml.) stock (see pp. 33–34)
Salt and pepper

Soak the hearts for 1 hour in cold water with a little salt added. Meanwhile, mix thoroughly the sausagemeat, breadcrumbs, herbs, onion and egg. Season the mixture well with salt and pepper.

Drain the hearts, wash under cold running water and dry well with kitchen paper. Fill each heart with the stuffing, fold over the flaps at the top and secure with a skewer. Dust all over with the seasoned flour.

Heat the butter or dripping in a roasting tin and place the hearts in it. Roast in the pre-heated oven for 2 hours or until tender, basting several times.

Lift on to a hot dish and make gravy in the roasting tin by stirring the flour into the pan juices over a high heat and blending well. Gradually add the stock and bring to the boil, stirring constantly. Taste and adjust the seasoning.

Pour the gravy round the hearts. Serve with redcurrant jelly.

BRAISED OXTAIL
Countrywide

OXEN, castrated male cattle, hauled the heavy ploughs of the ancient Celts, and continued to be used for this purpose, in Sussex at least, until the beginning of the Second World War. Slower but stronger than horses, they possessed, in the farmer's eyes, one enormous additional advantage; after their working life was over, they could be eaten.

Tough and sinewy, the meat from an old ox was not to everyone's taste. But the offal was much relished by the country poor; this is why the terms oxtail and ox liver have survived, transferred to beef cattle, long after the last ox yielded to the tractor.

Oxtail still requires a deal of cooking, but the end result is well worth it. This long-despised dish of the working classes has even been said to rival turtle soup for flavour.

PREPARATION TIME: 25 MINUTES
COOKING TIME: 3–4 HOURS
PRE-HEAT THE OVEN TO 150°C (300°F)—GAS MARK 2

INGREDIENTS FOR FOUR

- *2–2½ lb. (900 g.–1·1 kg.) oxtail, jointed*
- *2 medium onions, peeled and finely sliced*
- *2 leeks, trimmed and sliced*
- *1 lb. (450 g.) carrots, cut in rings*
- *2 sticks of celery, sliced*
- *1 oz. (25 g.) seasoned flour*
- *2 bay leaves*
- *½ teaspoon thyme*
- *6 cloves*
- *12 peppercorns*
- *1 clove garlic, crushed, or ½ teaspoon garlic salt*
- *2 pints (1·1 litres) boiling water, or half water and half red wine or cider*
- *8 oz. (225 g.) tomatoes, skinned and quartered (see p. 198)*
- *1 tablespoon finely chopped parsley*

Fry the oxtail in a heavy-based frying pan for 5 minutes, turning frequently. Lift the pieces on to a dish.

Fry the onions, leeks, carrots and celery in the fat until they begin to brown. Then place them in a large, deep casserole. Rub the cooled oxtail pieces with the seasoned flour and put them in the casserole. Add the bay leaves, thyme, cloves, peppercorns and garlic and cover with the liquid.

Cover the casserole tightly and place in the pre-heated oven for 2½–3½ hours until the meat is tender. Add the tomatoes and cook for a further 30 minutes.

Check the seasoning. If the gravy seems too thin, thicken it by the following method: mix 1 tablespoon of cornflour with a little water and pour a cup of the hot gravy on to it, stirring all the time. Stir the mixture back into the casserole and place in the oven for a further 5 minutes.

Serve in soup bowls, garnished with the parsley. Add one or two boiled potatoes to each serving.

OX TONGUE
Countrywide

OX TONGUES were the neats' tongues of our medieval ancestors—almost the only form of offal considered fit for a gentleman's table.

At first, ox tongue was roasted with cloves, gilliflowers and yolks of eggs; later, tongues were chopped, pressed and preserved in melted butter and, in the last 100 years or so, pickled ox tongues have often been added to the festivities of Harvest Home or Christmas.

Tongue is delicious whether served hot or cold. Mustard sauce (see p. 153) is the traditional accompaniment, but this recipe gives some equally delicious alternatives.

SOAKING TIME: 1–2 HOURS
PREPARATION TIME: 20 MINUTES
COOKING TIME: 3¼ HOURS

INGREDIENTS FOR 10–12

- *1 ox tongue weighing about 4 lb. (1·8 kg.)*
- *2 carrots, scraped*
- *2 medium onions, peeled and quartered*
- *1 medium turnip, peeled and quartered*
- *12 peppercorns*
- *Bouquet garni*

For cold tongue:

- *1 pint (575/600 ml.) first or chicken stock (see pp. 33–34)*
- *½ oz. (15 g.) gelatine*

Wash the tongue thoroughly and put to soak in cold water for 1–2 hours. Drain, put into a very large saucepan and cover with water heated until tepid. Bring slowly to the boil and remove the scum. Add the carrots, onions, turnip, peppercorns and the bouquet garni. Cover and boil gently for 3 hours.

Lift the tongue on to a board and carefully remove the skin and small bones. Discard the stock, which tends to be greasy and tasteless. If the tongue is to be served hot, place in its natural shape on a large serving dish and serve with a home-made Cumberland, or tomato sauce (see pp. 153 and 160) or with cider or Madeira sauce. Pour a little of the sauce over the meat and serve the rest separately.

If it is to be served cold, curl the boned and skinned tongue in a large, round cake tin or soufflé dish. Dissolve the gelatine in the first or chicken stock and pour into the tin or dish until it is just level with the top of the tongue. Cover with foil and place a heavy weight on the meat. Leave in the refrigerator overnight. Next day, turn out and carve horizontally in thin, round slices. Serve cold ox tongue with salads.

BLACK PUDDING ON TOAST
Shropshire

SUET, pig's blood, oatmeal, liver and herbs were among the ingredients when black pudding was first prepared many centuries ago. Now only the pig's blood, suet and oatmeal remain, but it is still a filling, nourishing food.

Continental cooks often simmer black pudding in stock and serve it in stews. The British prefer it either boiled or fried, as in this Shropshire recipe.

Sweet chutney or crab-apple jelly accompany the dish when it is served at high tea or as a light supper dish.

PREPARATION TIME: 10 MINUTES
COOKING TIME: 15 MINUTES

INGREDIENTS FOR FOUR

- *12 oz. (350 g.) black pudding*
- *1 oz. (25 g.) butter*
- *1 large onion, peeled and finely chopped*
- *3 oz. (75 g.) oatmeal*
- *½ teaspoon salt*
- *½ teaspoon freshly ground black pepper*
- *4 large rounds of hot toast, crustless and well buttered*
- *1 tablespoon finely chopped parsley*

Remove the skin from the black pudding and mash it well.

Melt the butter in a large, heavy pan, add the onion and cook gently for 5 minutes. Stir in the oatmeal and continue cooking for 2–3 minutes. Add the mashed black pudding and blend well. Season with salt and pepper. Stir for a further 3–4 minutes and check the seasoning.

Pile the mixture on to the rounds of toast, sprinkle with parsley and serve immediately.

RECIPES *from* OTHER LANDS

MOROCCO
Couscous

COUSCOUS IS THE STAPLE of North Africa, as bread is to us or as rice is to the Chinese. The word has two meanings—the completed dish, and the granules from which it is made, which is usually semolina, but might also be barley, wheat, millet or even crushed acorns. The grain becomes part of the whole dish when it is steamed in the upper, colander-like part of the *couscousière*—a two-decker steamer, from whose lower vessel the thick stew bubbles its fragrance into the upper.

All kinds of customs govern the serving and eating of couscous. It is the worst of bad manners to leave any on your plate; at some tribal weddings the bride divides the grains between the two families to symbolise the sharing of happiness; at Moroccan parties it is served at the end of the meal to calm any still-yearning appetites and fulfil the first tenet of Arab hospitality—that no guest should depart less than satiated.

There are literally hundreds of different types of couscous. The one that is described here is an adaptation of the traditional Berber variety, made with lamb, chicken, turnips and creamy milk. It is served on the day after the Festival of the Sacrifice of the Lamb that comes at the end of the long fast of Ramadan.

You are probably unlikely to have a *couscousière* among your battery of kitchen implements; however, two saucepans will do almost as well.

SOAKING TIME: OVERNIGHT
PREPARATION TIME: 1 HOUR
COOKING TIME: $1\frac{3}{4}$ HOURS

INGREDIENTS FOR TEN

- *1 lb. (450 g.) cracked wheat or millet (soaked overnight)*
- *8 oz. (225 g.) haricot beans (soaked overnight)*
- *8 oz. (225 g.) chick peas (soaked overnight)*
- *A chicken, weighing about $2\frac{1}{2}$ lb. (1·1 kg.)*
- *2 lb. (900 g.) fillet end of leg of lamb*
- *2 large onions, peeled and cut in rings*
- *Salt*
- *24 black peppercorns*
- *2 oz. (50 g.) butter*
- *1 teaspoon freshly ground black pepper*
- *4 carrots, scraped and diced*
- *8 oz. (225 g.) courgettes, sliced*
- *8 oz. (225 g.) tomatoes, blanched, skinned and quartered*
- *1 large green pepper, de-seeded and finely chopped*
- *1 teaspoon celery salt*
- *1 teaspoon Cayenne pepper*
- *1 teaspoon chopped thyme*
- *1 teaspoon chopped parsley*

Place the cracked wheat or millet, the haricot beans and the chick peas in separate basins, cover with cold water and leave to soak overnight.

Next day, drain the beans and place in a very large saucepan with the chicken, lamb, onions, salt and peppercorns. Cover with water, bring to the boil and remove the scum. Lower the heat and stew gently for 1 hour.

Meanwhile, drain the wheat or millet and pour it into a separate saucepan containing 2 pints (1·1 litres) of salted boiling water. Stir the grain frequently as it boils to stop lumps from forming; it will absorb almost all the liquid. After 15 minutes reduce the heat to very low and stir in the butter and freshly ground pepper. Cover closely with a lid, or with foil, and leave it over the heat to soften and swell while you continue preparing the stew.

When the chicken and lamb have cooked for 1 hour, lift them from the pan and slice off all the meat, discarding the skin, fat and bones. Return the meat to the pan. Drain the chick peas and add to the meat with the carrots, courgettes, tomatoes and chopped green pepper. Add the celery salt, Cayenne pepper, thyme and parsley. Boil gently for a further 35 minutes. Taste and adjust the seasoning.

Just before serving, increase the heat under the wheat or millet and stir until it is very hot.

Serve the couscous and the stew in separate dishes, and let each person take first a helping of couscous and then several spoonfuls of the stew to put on top. Traditionally, couscous is accompanied by a hot chilli sauce called *harissa*.

ITALY
Scaloppine di Vitello Alla Bolognese (Veal Escalopes)

BOLOGNA, and the surrounding province of Emilia-Romagna, is known to other Italians as *Bologna la grassa* (Fat Bologna), both from the richness of its cuisine and from the effect it has on the inhabitants of the region. The Bolognese believe in hearty eating and hearty living. They enjoy good things such as sausages singing with garlic, stuffed pasta, *tortellini*, the best pork in Italy, sweet cherries, fat eels and delicate asparagus.

This recipe combines three of the most famous products of the region—milk-fed veal, Parma ham and Parmesan cheese.

Serve the escalopes round a mound of the well-buttered pasta, cooked *al dente*, to make a dish true to the taste of Northern Italy.

PREPARATION TIME: 10 MINUTES
COOKING TIME: 10 MINUTES

INGREDIENTS FOR FOUR

- *4 small slices of veal, about 6 in. (15 cm.) square and $\frac{1}{4}$ in. (1 cm.) thick when beaten flat*
- *2 eggs, beaten*
- *4 oz. (100/125 g.) white breadcrumbs*
- *2 oz. (50 g.) butter*
- *1 tablespoon cooking oil*
- *4 very thin slices Parma ham or cooked ham*
- *2 oz. (50 g.) grated Parmesan cheese*
- *4 slices of lemon*

Dip the veal slices first in the egg and then in the breadcrumbs, pressing the crumbs well into the meat.

Heat the butter and oil together in a heavy frying pan until very hot. Fry the veal for 2 minutes on each side until light golden-brown. Lift on to a board and lay a slice of ham on each piece of veal. Cover with grated cheese, piling on as much as possible and pressing it on with a knife.

Re-heat the fat in the pan until hot but not smoking. Return the meat, cheese uppermost, and spoon over a little of the fat. Cover with a lid or with foil and fry gently for 3 minutes, or until the cheese has melted. Serve immediately, garnished with the lemon slices and accompanied by spaghetti and a green salad.

GREECE
Moussaka

MOUSSAKA, IT SEEMS, was an Arab invention that Turkish invaders carried through the Balkans and the eastern Mediterranean. But Greece, with its aubergines, its olive groves and its sun-drenched hills, warm-scented with thyme and rosemary, has made the dish especially its own.

Recipes vary considerably throughout the mainland and islands. Some cooks will cover the moussaka with batter, others with a cheese or yoghurt sauce. All diners agree, however, that it is best set off by the raw, pine flavour of *retsina* wine.

SOAKING TIME: 30 MINUTES FOR THE SLICED AUBERGINES

PREPARATION TIME: 45 MINUTES

COOKING TIME: 1 HOUR

PRE-HEAT THE OVEN TO 150°C (300°F)—GAS MARK 2

INGREDIENTS FOR SIX

2 lb. (900 g.) aubergines
4 tablespoons olive oil
1 oz. (25 g.) butter
1 large onion, peeled and finely chopped
2 cloves of garlic, crushed, or 1 teaspoon garlic salt
1½ lb. (700 g.) lean raw lamb, minced
1½ lb. (700 g.) tomatoes, blanched, skinned and quartered
1 teaspoon dried thyme
1 teaspoon dried rosemary
Salt and pepper
¾ pint (450 ml.) cheese sauce *(see p. 150)*
2 egg yolks, well beaten
2 oz. (50 g.) Parmesan cheese, grated

Slice the unpeeled aubergines thinly and soak them in salted water for 30 minutes. Drain well.

Heat 2 tablespoons of the oil in a large frying pan, and put in a single layer of aubergine slices. Fry gently for 1 minute, then turn over and fry on the other side for 2 minutes. Turn again and fry the first side for another minute. Transfer to a plate and fry the rest of the slices, adding more oil if needed. Set the slices aside.

Heat the butter in a large saucepan and fry the chopped onion in it. After 3–4 minutes, add the garlic or garlic salt and the minced lamb. Fry, stirring all the time for about 5 minutes, to brown the mince a little. Stir in the tomatoes, thyme and rosemary, and season well with salt and pepper. Simmer very gently for 15–20 minutes, stirring occasionally.

Meanwhile, make the cheese sauce. Allow it to cool for 5 minutes and stir in the beaten egg yolks.

Butter a deep, oblong, ovenproof dish or a bread tin and place a layer of aubergine slices in the bottom. Cover with a layer of mince about ¾ in. (2 cm.) deep. Put in another layer of aubergines and another layer of mince, and finish with a layer of aubergines. Cover with the cheese sauce and sprinkle the Parmesan cheese over the top. Bake in the pre-heated oven for 1 hour, or until the top is very crisp and well browned. Serve the moussaka in its dish.

FRANCE
Cassoulet

THE LANGUEDOC REGION of southern France gave the world the troubador and the cassoulet. The name of the dish comes from the casserole in which it is traditionally made, *cassol d'Issel*, a simple, earthenware pot constructed from the clay deposits near the village of Issel. The origin of the recipe itself, one of the chief glories of French country cooking, is claimed by three places, Castelnaudary, Toulouse and Carcassonne, all of which have different versions. Toulouse includes a pig's trotter or preserved goose, for example, while Carcassonne insists upon a boned leg of lamb studded with garlic.

All of them take the cassoulet very seriously, especially the long, slow cooking that is the secret of its success. It is no unusual occurrence, it is said, to find a shop with its shutters up and a notice on the door saying 'Closed to make a cassoulet'.

Enthusiasts say it should be eaten at mid-day on Sunday or a holiday when there is plenty of time to relax afterwards.

SOAKING TIME: OVERNIGHT FOR THE BEANS

PREPARATION TIME: 1¼ HOURS

COOKING TIME: 4½–5 HOURS

PRE-HEAT THE OVEN TO 190°C (375°F)—GAS MARK 5

INGREDIENTS FOR TEN

2 lb. (900 g.) haricot beans
2–2½ lb. (900 g.–1·1 kg.) spare rib of pork (rind removed and kept)
8 oz. (225 g.) salt pork or streaky bacon in one piece (rind removed and kept)
1 large onion, peeled and chopped
2 cloves garlic, crushed
1 sprig each thyme, rosemary and marjoram tied together, or a bouquet garni
24 black peppercorns
1 teaspoon salt
2½–3 lb. (1·1–1·4 kg.) shoulder of lamb, boned
1 lb. (450 g.) coarse-textured pork sausages
8 oz. (225 g.) freshly made white breadcrumbs

Pour cold water over the beans to cover them; leave to soak overnight.

Next day, cut the rinds of the fresh and salt pork or bacon into ¼ in. (5 mm.) squares. Place in the bottom of a large, deep saucepan. Drain the beans and add them to the pan with the onion, garlic, herbs, peppercorns and salt. Cover with water and boil gently with the lid on for 1½ hours.

Meanwhile, roast the lamb and both kinds of pork in the pre-heated oven for 45 minutes. Add the sausages to the meat for the last 20 minutes of the roasting time. When the meats are cooked, remove from the oven and reduce the oven temperature to 150°C (300°F)—gas mark 2. The meats will receive further cooking later, when the cassoulet is assembled.

Cut the lamb into 1½ in. (4 cm.) cubes and remove as much fat as possible. Remove the meat from the pork spare rib and cut the sausages into 1 in. (2·5 cm.) lengths. Mix the meats and sausages together.

When the beans and squares of rind are ready, drain them but reserve the liquid. Remove from it the herbs, and as many peppercorns as you can.

Put a layer of the beans and rind into a large, deep, fireproof casserole. Put the mixed meats on top of the beans, cover with the rest of the beans and pour in the reserved liquid to almost, but not quite, cover them. Sprinkle with half the breadcrumbs.

Cook in the pre-heated oven for a good 2–3 hours until the meat is tender. Remove from the oven and gently stir the now golden crumbs down among the beans. Cover with the remaining breadcrumbs and put back in the oven until a second golden crust has formed, after 30 minutes or more.

Serve from the pot, making sure that each person gets some of the crust and all the different ingredients. Serve with green salad and red wine.

ALL KINDS OF MEAT

THE LABOURER IN HIS COTTAGE, the baron in his hall, even the king in his castle, in all probability never tasted meat so tender as comes to our table today. Until about 300 years ago, farm animals were small and sinewy, with less meat on their bones than modern breeds—and that tending to be stringy. Fodder was scarce in winter, so many animals were slaughtered and the meat salted down for use mainly between Easter and midsummer, before young stock was ready.

Rich spices and sauces were used to hide the salty taste, and sometimes also the taint that developed after long storage. The use of spices became habitual even when the meat was fresh.

Not until the late 17th century, when new farming methods and fodder crops were introduced, could more animals be kept throughout the winter. Larger, fatter animals with more tender, juicier meat began to be bred, and the 18th century was a great age of meat eating.

Facts about meat

Lean meat is muscle fibre and tissue, and is a good source of protein—body-building food. Fat is high in energy value. Offal (the internal organs), particularly liver, is richest in vitamins essential to health.

Cheap cuts of meat, which have long, coarse fibres, are from the tougher, most worked parts of the animal, such as the leg and shin. The choice, most expensive, cuts are the tender, more protected and less fatty or bony parts, such as the loin.

There is no nutritional difference between cheap and expensive cuts, but cheaper cuts need more preparation and longer cooking. Meat from older animals generally has more flavour, but is likely to be tougher.

Fat forms a protective layer around lean meat, and in mature animals is also distributed among the muscle fibres, giving a flecked appearance known as marbling. Fat gives meat its juiciness and much of its flavour.

Carcases are hung by the butcher for several days after slaughter. During hanging, acids develop that soften the muscle fibres, and this helps to make the meat tender and improve the flavour. Another method is to vacuum pack meat, which has a similar effect to hanging.

Beef, Veal, Lamb and Mutton

IN PAST centuries, Britain's roast beef—from young, tender animals—was mainly the food of the rich. Peasants and labourers had to make do with the flesh of worn-out draught oxen, which needed long stewing to make it digestible. Veal, too, was food for the wealthy, who could enjoy such dishes as veal olives—seasoned veal slices, rolled and spit-roasted or grilled.

Until the 18th century, sheep were bred for their wool, but weaker animals from the wool herds were eaten. Mutton, although often four years old or more, was still roasted—it was not as tough as draught ox.

BEEF

The best beef is the meat from bullocks and heifers (cows that have not calved) at least 18 months old. Barley beef is from younger animals.

If you buy beef on the bone, allow 8–12 oz. (225–350 g.) per person. For boned joints, allow 6–8 oz. (175–225 g.) per person, and for steaks 5–6 oz. (150–175 g.) per person.

The lean flesh should be red and marbled with fat, firm and slightly moist. The fat should be cream or slightly yellow, and firm but not hard.

Dark red meat with gristle under a layer of yellow fat is from an old animal and will be tough. Very red meat may also be tough, because it has not been hung long enough.

THE BEST WAYS TO USE CUTS OF BEEF

Choice cuts

Sirloin (back). Roast, preferably with the fillet still attached. Roasting on the bone gives the best flavour.

Fillet or undercut (tender, boneless lean meat from the sirloin). Roast on its own (larded, see p. 145) or in a pastry case.

Wing rib and fore rib Roast on the bone, or boned and rolled.

Medium-price cuts

Middle rib (top rib and back rib). Roast on the bone, or boned and rolled.

Chuck and blade (from the shoulder, with little fat. Very good stewing or braising steak). Stew or braise after removing gristle.

Topside (hindquarters). Most tender when braised, but it can be roasted. For roasting, ask the butcher to tie a piece of fat round it to keep it moist.

Silverside (hindquarters). Pot-roast or boil, or salt (see p. 49) and boil.

Top rump or thick flank Pot-roast or braise.

Cheaper cuts

Brisket (forequarters). Boil, bone and press (see p. 49). It is sometimes salted (see p. 49) before cooking. Or pot-roast, boned and rolled.

Flank (belly). Braise or stew or use in pies.

Skirt (lower rump). Use in stews.

Clod or sticking-piece (neck). Stew or use in soups.

Shin and leg (fore and hind legs). Stew or use in soups.

Hints on Buying and Storing Meat

When you buy fresh meat, make sure the flesh is firm and there is no unpleasant smell. Choose meat with a moderate amount of fat that is firm and free from bloodstains.

Meat may be sold on the bone or boned and rolled, depending on the cut. If you want it boned and rolled, ask the butcher to do it for you. Give him a few days' notice to prepare special joints such as crown roast of lamb. Very large roasting joints such as baron of beef (the undivided sirloin) or saddle of lamb (the undivided loin) are rarely seen, except at banquets.

Imported meats and some home-produced meats are chilled or frozen, but usually thawed before sale. Do not buy thawed or partly thawed meat for the freezer. Buy frozen meat or fresh meat to freeze at home.

All meat must be labelled with the country of origin and the weight and cost per pound. But the part of the animal is not always labelled.

The method of cutting up carcases and the names of the cuts vary in different parts of the country, but a general guide to the best uses of the common cuts is given below.

After buying meat, remove the wrapping and dry if necessary. Wrap loosely in a polythene bag so that air can circulate, and put the meat at the bottom of the refrigerator.

Fresh meat will keep for 2–3 days in a refrigerator. If you have to keep it outside a refrigerator for 1 or 2 days, dust it lightly with flour and pepper, cover loosely with muslin and hang in a well-ventilated larder.

Minced meat and offal do not keep well, and should be used on the day of purchase. Store them in a refrigerator until ready to use.

Steaks

Steaks are small portions from choice cuts of beef. They are expensive, but tender enough to grill or fry.

Fillet Slices from the fillet or undercut of the sirloin.

Chateaubriand A cut about $1\frac{1}{4}$ in. (3 cm.) thick from the centre of the fillet. Usually enough for two.

Sirloin or entrecote A cut about 1 in. (2·5 cm.) thick from the upper part of the sirloin.

Porterhouse A cut about $\frac{3}{4}$–1 in. (2–2·5 cm.) thick from the sirloin, containing part of the fillet.

Rump A cut up to $1\frac{1}{4}$ in. (3 cm.) thick from the rump, generally thought to have the most flavour. Avoid a steak with gristle between skin and meat.

T-bone A thick cut from the fillet end of the sirloin, containing some bone. It usually serves two.

Minute steak Thin cuts of steak, about the size of the palm of the hand, for quick frying or grilling.

VEAL

Veal is the meat from calves 4–5 months old, although some is from 'bobby' calves under 3 weeks old. Because the animals are immature, there is little fat and the bones are large in proportion to the meat, which has a lot of gelatinous tissue.

The meat generally needs long cooking to make it tender, and has a rather bland flavour. Veal from milk-fed calves (usually imported) is the most tender, but is very expensive and sold mainly to restaurants. Veal from grass-fed calves usually has more flavour.

Because veal does not keep well, it needs to be sold and cooked within 2–3 days of slaughter. Butchers do not stock it unless there is a regular demand. Buy about 8 oz. (225 g.) of veal on the bone for each person, or 6 oz. (175 g.) if boned. The flesh from grass-fed calves is pale pink, from milk-fed calves, off-white. Both types should be moist and fine-grained and have firm, white fat. Avoid veal with a bluish tinge or soft, white fat.

THE BEST WAYS TO USE CUTS OF VEAL

Choice cuts

Fillet or cushion (top of hind leg). This weighs 8–12 oz. (225–350 g.). Roast on the bone or boned, stuffed and rolled.

Escalope (thin slices cut from the fillet or loin). Beat until very thin and fry in seasoned flour or egg and breadcrumbs.

Loin (back). Roast whole or boned, stuffed and rolled.

Loin chops Grill or fry.

Leg (hind leg). Roast on the bone.

Medium-price cuts

Breast Roast or braise, boned, stuffed and rolled.

Shoulder, bladebone or oyster (shoulder and forehock, known as the oyster when boned and rolled). Roast or stew.

Best end of neck (loin end). Roast or braise. It can be boned and rolled.

Cheaper cuts

Scrag end of neck (head end). Stew or braise.

Middle neck Stew, braise, use in pies.

Foreknuckle and hind knuckle or hock Stew or use them for making soup or stock.

LAMB AND MUTTON

Lamb is the meat from sheep 3–12 months old, mutton the meat from sheep 18 months to 2 years old. Mutton is cheaper than lamb, but not as easy to get. Although not as tender, it has more flavour. Good young mutton is worth searching for.

If buying lamb or mutton on the bone, allow 12 oz. (350 g.) per person. If buying boned, allow 6–8 oz. (175–225 g.) per person.

Lamb and mutton flesh varies from pale pink to dark red, according to the age of the animal. Mutton is darker red than beef and has more fat. The flesh of home-produced lamb, cheapest from September to November, is slightly paler than that of imported lamb. Both lamb and mutton fat should be hard and white, although fat on imported lambs sometimes looks crumbly.

THE BEST WAYS TO USE CUTS OF LAMB

Choice cuts

Loin (back). The best end (neck end) has less bone than the chump end (tail end). Roast whole, or boned, stuffed and rolled.

Loin chops Grill or braise.

Leg or gigot (hindquarters). Roast. A useful joint for a family, as there is little waste except for the central bone. Choose a short, thick leg.

Medium-price cuts

Best end of neck (loin end). Roast, braise or boil. It can be boned and rolled. If you want to roast the cut whole, ask the butcher to chine it—saw through the backbone in a number of places. Crown roast is shaped from two best ends of neck.

Shoulder (sometimes divided into

blade and knuckle). Roast, braise or boil. Fattier but sweeter than the leg, this is the cheapest roasting joint.

Cheaper cuts
Scrag end of neck (head end). Stew or braise.
Middle neck Stew, or bone, slice and fry.
Breast or flank Roast or braise, boned, skinned, stuffed and rolled.

Pork, Bacon, Ham and Offal

PIGS WERE the main meat animals of British farmworkers for centuries. They were cheap to feed, for they could forage in the woods. After slaughter they needed less salting than other meat and stayed juicy longer. Cured hams and sides of bacon were hung in the rafters, where the rising wood smoke from the fire helped to preserve them and add to their flavour.

No part of a pig was wasted, for one carcase might have to feed a family for six months. Ears were boiled, sliced and fried, trotters pickled, lard used for cooking, and blood made into black puddings. At Christmas there was souse—the pickled hindquarters, ears, cheeks, snout and trotters of a hog or boar.

Umbles, or offal, included more of the internal organs than is common today—entrails, lungs, gut, all went into pottages or pies.

PORK

Pork is the meat of young pigs whose carcase weight is 90–120 lb. (45–54 kg.). It has more fat to lean than other meats, and does not keep well.

Fresh pork should have firm, close-grained, pale pink flesh without too much marbling. The fat should be white, not grey or oily, and the rind smooth and thin. Dark meat with a brownish tinge and thick, rough rind is from an older animal.

Most pork is tender and suitable for roasting. It has more flavour if cooked on the bone. When buying, allow 8–12 oz. (225–350 g.) per person for pork on the bone, or 6 oz. (175 g.) per person for boned pork.

Ask the butcher to score the rind—make close cuts that penetrate it—so that the heat will reach the meat during cooking. Pork needs thorough cooking—undercooked pork is dangerous to health.

THE BEST WAYS TO USE CUTS OF PORK

Choice cuts
Loin (middle back). Roast.
Loin chops (chump chops are from the leg end of the loin). Grill or fry.
Leg or gigot (hind leg; it is often divided into the upper part, or fillet half, and the lower part, called the knuckle or shank). Roast or boil.
Leg fillet (a slice cut from the fillet half). Roast, or cut into steaks and grill or fry.
Tenderloin or fillet (lean meat from beneath the backbone in the hind loin of a bacon pig, taken before curing). Stuff, roll and roast, or braise, grill or fry.
Suckling or sucking pig (a whole pig, 4–8 weeks old). Spit-roast.

Medium-price cuts
Spare rib (from the shoulder). Roast, grill or bake spare-rib chops.
Blade (top of foreleg). Roast on the bone, or boned and rolled.
Hand and spring (upper part of foreleg—sold whole or in two parts). Roast (whole joint only), or braise or boil. Can be salted (see p. 49) to vary the flavour, especially if it is to be served cold.

Cheaper cuts
Belly Roast, boned, stuffed and rolled. Or salt, boil and use for pâtés, potted meat and galantines. (Chinese spare ribs are thin chops from the lean part of the belly. They are not the same as spare-rib chops.)

BACON AND HAM

Bacon pigs are larger than pork pigs and have a higher proportion of lean to fat. After slaughter, their flesh is cured—or preserved—by soaking the carcase in brine then leaving it to mature for a time. Gammons are the hindquarters of a bacon carcase. Hams are the hindquarters also, but are usually cut from the carcase before brining and cured separately.

Bacon sold after brining is known as green bacon. It does not keep as well as bacon that has also been dried and smoked over wood shavings. Smoked bacon also has a stronger flavour.

Most shop-bought bacon has been mild-cured in a weak brine for a short period. There are many different cures, particularly for hams, using brines of different strengths for varying periods. The stronger the brine, the longer the meat is likely to keep after curing. Most brines include salt and saltpetre (potassium nitrate).

Ham is usually sold with cooking instructions, as the cooking depends on the method of curing. Sometimes shoulder and collar cuts of bacon are cured in the same way as ham and sold as picnic ham. They are cheaper but do not have such a good flavour.

Whole hams may weigh about 16 lb. (7 kg.) and may be sold in one piece or divided. They are not often smoked. Cooked and smoked ham is usually sold ready-sliced.

What to look for when buying
Green bacon cuts and rashers should have moist, pale pink flesh, firm white or cream fat and thin, pale rind. Smoked bacon has darker flesh and golden-brown rind. Do not buy bacon that is brown and dry with green or yellow stains in the fat, or with soft, oily fat. Rashers are often sold in date-stamped vacuum packs. Store them in a refrigerator, and once the packet is opened use within about 3 days. If you buy loose rashers, lightly wrap them in foil or put them in a container with a lid. Green bacon will keep about 5 days in a refrigerator or 2 days in a cool larder, smoked bacon 7 days in a refrigerator and 3 days in a larder.

Choose cuts of bacon or ham that are short and thick without too much fat. Most need soaking before cooking (see p. 114). Cured uncooked hams will keep for up to 6 months in a freezer, about 14 days in a refrigerator or about 2 days in a cool larder.

THE BEST WAYS TO USE CUTS OF BACON

Choice cuts
Corner gammon Boil or roast to serve hot or cold.

Middle gammon Boil or roast to serve hot or cold.
Gammon rashers (cut from middle gammon). Grill or fry.
Back Boil, braise or roast.
Back rashers or chops (the choicest are short back). Grill or fry.

Medium-price cuts
Gammon hock or knuckle (the cheapest gammon joint). Boil on the bone, or boned and rolled to serve hot or cold. Use the knuckle for mince.
Prime collar (nearest the back). Parboil and roast, or boil. Grill or fry collar rashers.
Middle collar Boil or roast.
Butt (shoulder end of foreleg). Roast, boil or braise.
Middle cut (Middle back, collar end). Roast, boned and rolled.
Middle rashers Grill or fry lean rashers. Use streaky rashers for bacon rolls, larding (see p. 145) or stews.
Oyster cut (Middle back, gammon end). Boil or braise. Grill or fry rashers.

Cheaper cuts
Small hock (knuckle end of foreleg). Boil, cut the flesh from the bone and use for mince.
Belly, flank or streaky Roast, boned and rolled, or boil or slice and use for barding. Grill or fry rashers.

SAUSAGES

Most sausages are made from minced pork mixed with cereal, herbs and flavourings and encased in cleaned pigs' intestines or synthetic material.

Commercially sold sausages must contain 50% meat or, if the meat is named, at least 65%. They will keep 4–5 days in a refrigerator.

You can sometimes buy lengths of skin from the butcher to make sausages at home—wash thoroughly before using. Or make the mixture into small cakes or rolls without a skin.

For good home-made pork sausage meat, use 1 lb. (450 g.) fat pork to 2 lb. (900 g.) lean pork, and up to one-third of the total weight in breadcrumbs, herbs and seasoning.

OFFAL

Offal is the edible internal organs from animals—the liver and kidneys, for example. It is generally cheap in comparison with other meats, but is very nutritious. Delicacies such as brains and sweetbread are more expensive. Offal from beef is usually termed ox.

When buying offal, make sure it is very fresh and has no discoloration. It does not keep well, so use it on the day of purchase or freeze it until you are ready to use it. Frozen offal must be completely thawed before cooking.

Parts such as the head, tail and feet of a meat animal, although not offal, are often sold as offal. They are not always stocked but can usually be ordered, giving a few days' notice.

THE BEST WAYS TO USE OFFAL

Liver (calf liver, which is in short supply, is the most expensive, followed by lamb, pig and strong-flavoured ox liver). Buy 4–6 oz. (100–175 g.) per person. Fry. Alternatively, braise or stew ox liver, and use pig liver in pâtés.
Kidney Buy two per person, except for ox kidney, which weighs about 1½ lb. (700 g.). Lamb kidney is best for frying and grilling. Grill, fry or stew calf and pig kidney. Stew ox kidney or use in pies and puddings.
Heart (lamb heart is the most tender, ox heart the cheapest). Buy one per person, except for calf (1½ lb., 700 g.) and ox (4½ lb., 2 kg.). Stuff and pot-roast lamb or pig heart. Stew or braise ox or calf heart.
Sweetbreads (throat and chest glands from lamb or calf. Lamb has the most flavour and is the dearest). Buy 1 lb. (450 g.) to serve three to four. Break into pieces the size of a teaspoon, poach (cook gently in water or stock just under boiling point) then braise or fry.
Brain (lamb or calf). Buy one lamb brain per person, two calf brains between three. Poach gently in stock, or boil, cool and gently fry.
Tripe (ox stomach lining). Buy 1 lb. (450 g.) to serve four. Sold blanched and partly cooked. Ask the butcher how much more cooking is needed. It should be firm and white—if slimy and greyish it is stale. There are several kinds, the commonest being blanket (from the first stomach) and honeycomb (from the second).

Boil, with onions and serve, or boil with onions, cut into strips and fry.
Lamb fry and pig fry (a mixture of liver, sweetbreads, heart—lamb fry only—and fat). Buy 8 oz. (225 g.) per person. Fry gently.
Sheep pluck (sheep heart and liver and sometimes part of the 'lights' or lungs). Usually made into haggis or faggots.
Head (pig and sometimes sheep and calf heads can be bought fresh—calf is sometimes salted).

If you buy a whole head, ask the butcher to split it and remove the eyes. Pig head includes the tongue.

Boil pig head and make into brawn (see p. 42). Boil calf head and serve hot with sauce, or bone and press to serve cold, or make into brawn or potted meat. Boil or stew sheep head and use for broths or pies.
Cheek Ox cheeks are sometimes available. Pig cheeks may be cured separately and sold as Bath chaps. Use ox cheek for stews or brawn. Boil Bath chaps to serve hot or cold.
Feet or trotters (usually pig). Buy one pair per person. Boil, stew or use in pies. Cow heel or calf foot is good for jellied stock or savoury jellies.
Oxtail Usually sold ready skinned in 2 in. (5 cm.) portions. One tail serves three or four. Braise or stew or make into soup.
Tongue Sold salted or fresh. One ox tongue serves six, two lamb tongues serve three. Boil and skin, and serve hot with sauce. Or press and serve cold in slices.

Preparing and Cooking Meat

ROASTING ON A SPIT and stewing in a pot over the fire were the main methods of cooking meat until about 150 years ago, although in ancient times beef was boiled in hides slung over stakes, with red-hot stones dropped in to heat the water.

Braising was known by the 15th century, when meat was steamed in a pot suspended in a cauldron of boiling water. In the 18th century, poor people took small joints to be roasted in a baker's oven. Oven-roasting in the home became usual only after the development of the kitchen range in the 19th century.

PREPARING MEAT

The methods of preparing meat vary according to the type and recipe, but wipe all fresh meat with a damp cloth before cooking. If you have to trim off any fat, render it down for dripping.

Pork, bacon and ham

Pork chops Snip the rind and fat edge of loin chops with scissors in several places. This prevents them from curling during cooking.

Bacon, gammon and ham Soak cuts in cold water for 1–2 hours before cooking to remove excess salt. Soak a whole ham for 12–24 hours, changing the water twice. A quicker method is to cover the meat with cold water and bring to the boil, then remove from the heat, drain and replace the water before cooking.

Offal

Liver Cut away fat, gristle and tubes. Clean with a damp cloth and dry. If you want to tenderise ox liver and reduce the strong flavour, soak in milk for 20–30 minutes before cooking.

Kidneys Remove the layer of white fat surrounding lamb kidneys.

For all kidneys, peel off the transparent outer skin. Cut the kidney in half lengthways and remove the white core. Drop the two halves in hot water for 2 minutes, then remove and drop in cold water for 30 seconds. This stops the kidneys from curling during cooking. If desired, soak ox and calf kidneys in milk or water for 2 hours before preparing to reduce the strong flavour.

Heart Wash thoroughly under cold water to remove all blood. Cut away gristle, fat and membranes from the cavity with a sharp knife. Trim away the ends of arteries and tendons with scissors. Soak in cold water for 30–60 minutes before cooking.

Brains Soak in cold water for 2 hours before cooking to remove any blood. Snip off fibres and any pieces of bone.

Sweetbreads Soak in warm salt water for 30 minutes to remove any blood. Remove and drop into fast-boiling salted water for 2 minutes. Rinse under cold running water and remove the thin covering membrane and the black veins running through.

Tongue Soak 1–2 hours in cold water; soak salted ox tongue overnight. To remove the skin after cooking, plunge the tongue into cold water then slit the skin at the tip with a sharp knife and peel. Remove any bones or gristle at the root, and trim.

Heads Wash both halves thoroughly; soak in cold salted water for 1 hour.

Tenderising steaks

Veal escalopes and sometimes beef steaks can be made tender by beating before grilling. Put between sheets of waxed paper, and beat for about 1 minute each side with a wooden hammer to break down the tissues.

For beef steaks, another method is to brush with lemon juice or vinegar. The acid converts the tissues to gelatine. Alternatively, marinate the steaks before cooking.

Marinating meat

Meat can be made more tender and given a variety of flavours by marinating for 4 hours or longer before cooking.

A marinade is generally composed of red or white wine with herbs and seasoning added, and the meat is steeped in it. Do not use too much salt or Soy sauce in the seasoning, as they tend to make the meat dry.

If time is short, lightly score the surface of the meat to allow the liquid to penetrate, and soak for 30 minutes.

After use, the marinating liquid can be heated and served with the meat as a sauce, thickened or unthickened.

COOKING MEAT

Roasting and grilling are methods of cooking by radiant heat. As the meat shrinks, the juices rise to the surface and dry, so concentrating the flavour.

Because meat fibres and tissues toughen at high temperatures, roasting and grilling are suitable only for tender cuts. Tough meat cooked in this way will become tougher.

Pot-roasting, boiling, braising and stewing—cooking with low, moist heat—softens fibres and tissues and is the best way of cooking tougher cuts.

Meat that is pot-roasted or braised is cooked mainly in steam in a covered pot after browning in hot fat to seal in the juices. Evaporation is slight and much of the flavour is retained.

In pot-roasting, the base of the pan is covered with water and the meat raised above it on a rack. In braising, the meat rests on a bed of diced, lightly fried vegetables with just enough water or stock to cover them. It can be removed and roasted in the oven for the last 30 minutes of cooking to crisp the surface.

Boiled and stewed meat are cooked in water or stock, and much of the flavour passes into the liquid.

Frying—fast cooking in hot fat—is suitable only for small, tender cuts as the high heat seals in the juices.

How to tell when meat is roasted

To test whether roasted meat is ready, stick a skewer into it, near the bone if there is one, and check the colour of the juice that comes out.

If you want it slightly underdone, it is ready when the juice is pink. If you want it more thoroughly cooked, wait until the juice is clear.

Re-heating meat

Meat that has been cooked once can be re-heated, provided that it is thoroughly heated right through. If it is not, there is a danger to health.

Cook at a temperature of at least 77°C (170°F), or if the meat is covered by a sauce, cook until the sauce bubbles.

A General Guide to Cooking Times

Method	Meat	Time in minutes
Roasting 180–190°C (350–375°F)	Beef and lamb	20 per lb. (450 g.) + 20
	Mutton	25 per lb. (450 g.) + 20
	Pork and veal	30 per lb. (450 g.) + 30
Boiling 82°C (180°F)	Unsalted meat	20 per lb. (450 g.) + 20
	Salted meat	25 per lb. (450 g.) + 25
Grilling and frying (see Tips for cooking meat)	Beef steak (1 in., 2·5 cm.)	Each side: 4 rare; 6 medium 8 well done
	Minute steak	1 each side
	Pork chop	8–10 each side
	Lamb and veal chops	6–8 each side
	Veal escalope	2 each side
	Sausages	5–8 each side
	Gammon steaks	5–8 each side
	Bacon rashers	3–5 each side
	Kidneys	3–5 each side
	Liver (½ in., 1·5 cm.)	2–4 each side

TIPS FOR COOKING MEAT

Roasting

When roasting boned and rolled meat, put the removed bones in the roasting tin to add flavour to the juices and gravy. Afterwards, boil the bones to make stock (see p. 33). If roasting in foil, which reflects heat, raise the oven temperature slightly.

Cover veal for roasting with strips of pork or similar fat during cooking (this is known as barding). Otherwise it may be rather dry.

Always roast pork with the rind uppermost. This produces crisp crackling. Cooking with the rind underneath the joint makes it soggy and tough. Another way to ensure crisp crackling is to rub the rind with olive oil or vegetable oil and coarse salt before roasting.

Do not sprinkle meat for roasting with salt before cooking. The salt draws out the juices, and some may be lost before the meat is heated enough to dry them on the surface.

When cooking crown roast, tie a piece of foil round the tip of each upright rib to prevent burning. You can buy paper cutlet frills for decorating the ribs when serving. Alternatively, spear a glazed onion or grilled tomato on each rib.

Grilling and frying

Before grilling meat, brush the rack or pan with oil or melted butter to prevent the meat sticking to it. Make sure the grill is red hot before you place the meat under it, otherwise some of the juices may be lost before browning. Turn the heat down a little once the surface is browned, and keep careful watch during cooking.

Use vegetable oil for frying. It has a high 'smoking' temperature—that is, it will reach a high heat without burning. With other fats there is a risk of burning. Do not put too much meat in the pan at once. The meat lowers the temperature of the fat and the cooked meat will be greasy.

Fry liver slices rapidly to prevent toughening. Test for readiness with a skewer—the juice should be slightly pink in colour.

Braising, pot-roasting and boiling

When braising or pot-roasting meat, make sure the pan is large enough to allow a gap between the side and the meat, or the meat may scorch.

When pot-roasting, braising, boiling or stewing meat, make sure the cooking vessel has a closely fitting lid to minimise evaporation.

Parboiling ham before roasting helps to keep it moist. Boil for half the cooking time, then roast in the oven for the remainder.

When boiling meat, bring the water just to the boil, then reduce the heat to keep it simmering. The heat needed to keep the water constantly on the boil would toughen the meat.

Making good gravy

The best gravy is made from the concentrated meat juices left in the pan after roasting. It can be left thin, or thickened with flour, according to taste. If gravy recipes include wine or sherry in place of or as well as stock or water, follow the directions given.

1 To make thin gravy, pour or spoon the fat from the roasting tin, leaving only the meat juices.

To make thick gravy, leave 1 tablespoon of fat in the pan with the juices and add 1 level tablespoon of flour—or cornflour for a smoother texture. Blend the flour and juices together over a gentle heat until golden-brown, stirring to give a smooth texture and avoid burning.

2 For both types, remove the pan from the heat and add about ½ pint (275/300 ml.) of hot stock of a suitable flavour, or boiling water.

3 Scrape the base of the pan with a spatula or metal spoon to mix in all the meaty sediment. For thin gravy, boil for 2–3 minutes. For thick gravy, boil for 3–4 minutes, stirring well to remove lumps.

4 Season to taste and skim off any fat with a piece of kitchen paper drawn across the surface of the gravy.

5 If thick gravy is lumpy, sieve it or beat it with a balloon whisk for a few seconds.

6 If gravy is pale, stir in a drop or two of gravy browning or meat extract to improve the colour.

7 If the gravy lacks flavour, stir in a little yeast or meat extract.

STEWS AND HOTPOTS

Stews are made from small pieces of meat cooked slowly in a liquid—stock or water—that is served as part of the dish. The liquid is usually flavoured with onions and diced root vegetables, and is often thickened with flour or pearl barley. Traditional hotpots are similar but with a topping of potatoes.

Brown stews are generally made with beef, mutton, lamb or rabbit; white stews with veal, chicken or rabbit. Cook stews and hotpots in a covered flameproof pan or dish on top of the stove or in the oven. Any kind of meat can be stewed, but the long, slow cooking is particularly suitable for softening coarse, tough, gelatinous meats such as shin of beef.

Very coarse, tough meat may need up to 4 hours' stewing, but generally beef needs 2½–3 hours, mutton about 2 hours and lamb and veal 1–1½ hours. For a hotpot, remove the lid for the last 30 minutes of cooking to crisp and brown the potatoes.

Stews are even better in flavour the day after cooking—all you need do is re-heat just to boiling point.

A guide to making stew

1 Remove the fat from the meat. If you want to make it a little more tender or add extra flavour, marinate the meat for 4–12 hours (see p. 114).

2 Cut the meat into bite-size pieces. This exposes more of the surface to the action of the liquid.

3 To improve the colour and concentrate the flavour, fry better-quality meat, such as chuck steak, a little on both sides before stewing. But do not fry tough, coarse-fibred meat, as the liquid will penetrate better if the fibres are not sealed.

4 Make sure the dish or pan has a close-fitting lid so that the stewing liquid will be reduced as little as possible by evaporation.

5 Use 12–15 fl. oz. (350–450 ml.) of water or stock to every 1 lb. (450 g.) of meat to give a good, full flavour.

6 If thickening the stew with flour, use 1 oz. (25 g.) to each 1 lb. (450 g.) of meat.

7 For brown stews, fry the diced root vegetables to improve the colour. Remove the vegetables from the frying pan, add the flour and cook gently until the flour is light chestnut brown in colour.

8 Always add cold liquid to the meat, increase the heat gently to boiling point, then reduce the heat until the stew is barely simmering.

Do not bring the stew to the boil too quickly at too high a temperature, the meat will be tasteless and stringy.

9 Add the vegetables and any other flavourings (unfried in white stews) to the stew as directed in the recipe.

10 While the stew is simmering, remove the lid occasionally and skim off any fat.

11 For a white stew, drain off the stock after the meat is cooked and use it, with a little butter, milk and flour, to make a white sauce (see p. 162). Pour the sauce back on to the meat and re-heat.

POULTRY AND GAME

CONTAINING

NUMEROUS *Useful* FAMILY RECIPES

for PARTRIDGE & CHICKEN, HARE, GROUSE & GUINEA FOWL

& other CREATURES of FARM & FIELD

PAGES 118–141

AND

A SELECTION of RECIPES from OTHER LANDS

PAGES 142–143

AND WITH

NOTES AND ADVICE

on all kinds of Plucking, Preparing, Roasting and Carving of Poultry and Game to Perfection

PAGES 144–147

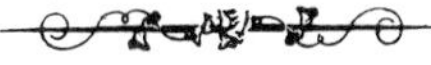

Egged, Breaded and Roasted Chicken
Countrywide

The notion of dredging spit-roast meat with fine white breadcrumbs or oatmeal to prevent it drying out in the heat of the fire probably goes back to the early medieval period, when thrifty housewives used to gather up and store crumbs for a number of purposes. That the suggestion did not appear in print until 1615 is perhaps because it was simply too obvious to mention. At any rate, it is known that the practice continued until well into the 18th century, and chicken was cooked in this way in the 19th century.

This recipe has been adapted for oven use. It is a delicious method of sealing in all the succulence and flavour of a roasting chicken.

Preparation Time: 30 minutes without stuffing; 50 minutes with

Cooking Time: about 1½ hours

Pre-heat the Oven to 200°C (400°F)—gas mark 6

Ingredients for Four to Six

1 good roasting chicken, about 4 lb. (1·8 kg.)
4 oz. (100/125 g.) butter
6 oz. (175 g.) fresh breadcrumbs
Salt and pepper
1 egg, separated
Finely grated rind of 1 lemon
½ teaspoon ground cinnamon
1 tablespoon chopped tarragon, parsley (and lemon thyme, if available)

For the stuffing (optional):
Country Forcemeat (see p. 157)

Wipe the chicken clean and remove the giblets. If using a stuffing, fill the bird loosely from the neck cavity. (Allow an extra 30–45 minutes cooking.) Secure with a skewer, or use a trussing needle and string (see p. 145).

Rub 2 oz. (50 g.) of the butter over the breast and legs of the chicken, put it in a roasting pan and cook in the centre of the pre-heated oven for 35 minutes.

Meanwhile, gently melt the rest of the butter. Season half the breadcrumbs with salt and pepper, and stir the yolk from the separated egg into them. After 35 minutes, take the bird out of the oven and spoon about half of the melted butter over it, then sprinkle on the egged breadcrumbs, pressing them down slightly.

Put the chicken back in the oven to cook for another 20 minutes.

Meanwhile, add the grated lemon rind, cinnamon and herbs to the remaining crumbs, season and mix well together. Whisk the egg white lightly and fold it gently into the breadcrumb mixture using a metal spoon.

Remove the chicken from the oven after 20 minutes, and spread the second mixture of breadcrumbs over the first. Dribble the remaining butter over the top. Baste, but take care not to dislodge the crust.

Cook for a further 30 minutes. If liked, serve with lemon sauce (see Hindle Wakes, p. 120).

The succulence of roast chicken, sealed with a covering of egg and breadcrumbs.

Farmhouse Chicken
Kent

'Well-fattened and tender, a fowl is to the cook what the canvas is to the painter; for do we not see it served boiled, roasted, fried, fricasseed, hashed, hot, cold, whole, dismembered, boned, broiled, stuffed, on dishes and in pies—always handy and ever acceptable?' Thus said Mrs Beeton, in a rare mood of exaltation, in the 1861 edition of her famous *Household Management*.

Indeed, chicken, well prepared and cooked, can be a delight, and the changes rung upon it almost infinite. This particular recipe is said to have been taken to Kent by followers of William of Orange in the 17th century. In fact, a closely related dish appears in *Forme of Cury*, the feast book of Richard II, written about 1390. It is not always easy to obtain boiling fowl these days, but most butchers will order one for you if you ask them and allow time for delivery.

Preparation Time: 20 minutes

Cooking Time: 4½ hours

Pre-heat the Oven to 130°C (250°F)—gas mark ½

Ingredients for Four

1 boiling fowl, about 3½ lb. (1·6 kg.)
8 oz. (225 g.) long-grain brown rice
¼ teaspoon ground mace
¼ teaspoon ground sage
Salt and pepper
4 small onions, peeled
1 pint (575/600 ml.) warmed milk

Wipe the chicken clean and remove the giblets. (Set aside for use in a soup or stock.) Place in the middle of a heavy-based casserole. Put the rice in a strainer and rinse several times under cold running water. Spread it round the chicken.

Sprinkle on the ground mace and sage and season with salt and pepper. Put a whole, peeled onion in each corner, and pour over the warmed milk. Cover tightly and cook in the centre of the pre-heated oven for 2 hours. If the casserole is drying up, add a little more warmed milk. Continue to cook, covered, for another 2 hours. Turn the oven heat up to 200°C (400°F)—gas mark 6, and cook for a further 30 minutes. If liked, pour on a little cream.

Serve with a fresh, green vegetable such as leaf spinach or broccoli.

Roast Stuffed Chicken
Countrywide

FROM THE EARLY MEDIEVAL PERIOD to Chicken 'n' Chips, roast chicken has met with universal approval. Apart from a lengthy period of shortage in the 16th and 17th centuries, when poultry prices rose, the dish was within the reach of almost everyone: even the poorest peasant kept a few chickens for eggs. At the other end of the scale, John, 5th Duke of Portland (1800–79), constructed a labyrinth of tunnels beneath his house at Welbeck, Nottinghamshire. In these he wandered musing by the hour, emerging only to demand fresh supplies of roast chicken, a large number of which were kept constantly turning on a spit. One of the tunnels connected the kitchen with the dining-room, and through this a heated railway wagon ran, thus ensuring that his Grace's chicken always arrived on time and at the very peak of condition.

This time-honoured recipe produces a meal that would enchant even the most exacting duke.

PREPARATION TIME: 20–30 MINUTES
COOKING TIME: 1½ HOURS
PRE-HEAT THE OVEN TO 200°C (400°F)—GAS MARK 6

INGREDIENTS FOR FOUR TO SIX

1 large roasting chicken, about 4 lb. (1·8 kg.)
1 oz. (25 g.) butter or chicken dripping

For the stuffing:

4 slices stale bread with crusts removed, or 4 oz. (100/125 g.) fresh breadcrumbs
¼ pint (150 ml.) milk
Chicken liver
1 tablespoon fresh parsley, thyme and chives, mixed and chopped, or ½ tablespoon dried mixed herbs
Grated rind and juice of 1 lemon
1 small onion or shallot, chopped
1 tablespoon shredded suet, or 1 oz. (25 g.) butter
1 tablespoon ground almonds
Salt and pepper

For the gravy:

½ pint (275/300 ml.) poultry stock (see pp. 33–34), or cider

Wipe the chicken, remove the giblets and set aside the liver. To make the stuffing, soak the bread in the milk. If using breadcrumbs, add the milk gradually and do not over-saturate. Leave for 20 minutes, until all the moisture has been absorbed.

Add the chopped chicken liver, herbs, lemon rind and juice, onion or shallot, suet or butter and the ground almonds. Mix together well; season with salt and pepper to taste.

Spoon the stuffing into the crop (neck) cavity of the chicken until the breast is plump, but do not pack too tightly: the stuffing will swell a little during the cooking.

Secure with a skewer or with a trussing needle and string (see p. 145).

Use the remainder to stuff the body of the bird from the tail end or shape into small forcemeat balls, to be added to the pan juices for the last 30 minutes of cooking.

Lightly grease a roasting tin. Rub the breast and legs of the chicken with the butter or dripping, and sprinkle with salt and pepper. Put in the roasting tin and cover loosely with greaseproof paper or aluminium foil. Roast in the centre of the pre-heated oven for 1 hour. Then reduce the oven temperature to 180°C (350°F)—gas mark 4, remove the greaseproof paper or foil, baste well and cook for a further 30 minutes, or until golden-brown on top. Keep warm.

To make the gravy, pour off the fat from the roasting pan. Add the strained poultry stock or cider. Stir well and boil rapidly on top of the stove for a few minutes. Season to taste. To make a thicker gravy, add 1 dessertspoon of cornflour to the cold poultry stock and stir continuously as you bring it to the boil.

Country Captain
Countrywide

THE SIMPLE ADDITION of curry powder to a stew does not make a curry; all the same, the English once thought it did, and a recipe very similar to this one appears in Hannah Glasse's *Art of Cookery* (1747), under the title of 'How to make a Curry, the Indian Way'. Whatever purists may think, this is an excellent and relatively inexpensive dish for a small dinner party. If your guests should cast doubts upon its origins, you could tell them either that 'Captain' is a corruption of 'capon', or that the dish may derive from the many professional soldiers, from Major-General downwards, who spent happy retirements testing and writing about Indian cookery.

PREPARATION TIME: 30 MINUTES
COOKING TIME: 1 HOUR

INGREDIENTS FOR FOUR TO SIX

1 capon or roasting chicken, about 3½ lb. (1·6 kg.), jointed (see p. 145)
Juice of 1 lemon
1 tablespoon seasoned flour
3 tablespoons vegetable oil
3 medium onions, peeled and sliced
Salt and pepper
2 eating apples, peeled, cored and chopped
2 tablespoons sultanas
1 tablespoon curry powder
2 teaspoons turmeric
¾ pint (450 ml.) warmed poultry stock (see pp. 33–34)

Skin the chicken joints, and rub the lemon juice into each piece. Coat the joints evenly in seasoned flour.

Heat the oil in a heavy-based pan and fry the onions very gently until soft but not coloured. Season, and add the apples and sultanas. Cook for about 5 minutes, stirring from time to time. Add the curry powder and turmeric, then the chicken joints.

Add the warmed chicken stock, stir well and simmer gently, covered, for 30 minutes or until the chicken is tender. Turn the joints from time to time. If it seems to be getting too dry, add a little more stock or water.

Serve with plain boiled rice.

BOILED CHICKEN WITH PARSLEY SAUCE
Countrywide

PARSLEY was the essential ingredient of the early medieval 'green sauce', the herb-based sauce that also contained sage and was considered to be a suitable accompaniment to any kind of fish. Boiled fowl at the same period was served with a blander companion—a sauce of ground almonds.

White fish and boiled fowl are wholesome and easily digestible, virtues that commended both dishes to those who ministered to Victorian sick-rooms. Parsley sauce added palatability to both dishes, and though chicken served in this way is still considered ideal fare for invalids, it also makes a sound light supper for the hale and hearty.

PREPARATION TIME: 40 MINUTES WITH STUFFING; 15 MINUTES WITHOUT
COOKING TIME: 2–3 HOURS

INGREDIENTS FOR FOUR TO SIX

1 boiling fowl or large roasting chicken, about 4 lb. (1·8 kg.)
1 large onion, peeled and sliced
3 medium carrots, scrubbed and chopped
1 large leek, washed and sliced
¼ teaspoon mixed chopped herbs
¼ teaspoon ground mixed spice
Grated rind and juice of ½ lemon
Salt and pepper

For the stuffing (optional):
Skirlie or Country Forcemeat (see pp. 156, 157)

For the sauce:
1½ oz. (40 g.) butter
1½ oz. (40 g.) plain flour
½ pint (275/300 ml.) chicken stock
½ pint (275/300 ml.) milk
3 tablespoons chopped, fresh parsley

Wipe the chicken clean and remove the giblets. If using a stuffing, spoon it into the neck cavity of the bird. Secure well with a poultry skewer or sew up with a trussing needle and string (see p. 145).

Put the onion, carrots and leek in the bottom of a large, heavy-based pan and place the chicken on top. Add the herbs, mixed spice, lemon rind and juice, and season with salt and pepper.

Pour in enough cold water just to cover the chicken and bring to the boil. Skim off any scum which rises to the surface, being careful not to take out the lemon rind and herbs. Reduce the heat to keep the pan at a steady simmer. Cover tightly. Remove the scum from time to time. After 2 hours, test for tenderness with the tip of a sharp-bladed knife in the thickest part of the thigh.

When the chicken is cooked, skin it and strain off ½ pint (275/300 ml.) hot chicken stock.

Put the lid back on the pan and keep the chicken warm.

Melt the butter in a saucepan over a gentle heat, add the flour and cook for 2–3 minutes, stirring continuously. Remove from the heat and gradually add the hot stock, stirring all the time until it is smooth, then stir in the milk. Put back on the heat, and cook for a few minutes more, stirring continuously until the sauce thickens.

Remove from the heat, add the parsley and check the seasoning. Do not cook again: the fresh, raw flavour of parsley gives the sauce its very distinctive taste.

Serve the chicken with the sauce. Plain boiled rice (see p. 199) and glazed carrots (see p. 182) are good accompaniments. Use the chicken stock and vegetables left in the pan as a base for making soup another time.

As an alternative, use 3 tablespoons of chopped fresh tarragon instead of the parsley.

As a variation, joint the chicken first (see p. 145) and cook it with the vegetables for 30 minutes. Make the white sauce and finish cooking the chicken joints in it for a further ¾–1 hour. Test for tenderness after 30 minutes' cooking in the sauce.

HINDLE WAKES
Lancashire

WAKES WEEK is the traditional annual holiday in the cotton and wool-manufacturing towns of the north; the term and the custom are derived from the Vigils or Wake-nights that were once held in every parish on the eve of the festival of its church's patron saint.

There is no such place as Hindle, though until the last century the name was applied to a locality between Burnley and Accrington. The word was borrowed by Stanley Houghton for the title of his highly successful play *Hindle Wakes* (1912), which portrays life in an imaginary Lancashire town during Wakes Week.

Hindle Wakes may long pre-date both Houghton and his play. It has been suggested that the name comes from 'Hen of the Wake', a medieval poultry dish for festive occasions. Like this version, in which the dark prunes and the green of the herbs make a brilliant contrast against the white chicken flesh, the original Hen of the Wake lent a colourful touch to any celebration.

PREPARATION TIME: ABOUT 40 MINUTES
SOAKING TIME: 4 HOURS
COOKING TIME: ABOUT 4½ HOURS
STANDING TIME: OVERNIGHT

INGREDIENTS FOR SIX

1 large boiling chicken, about 4 lb. (1·8 kg.)
¼ pint (150 ml.) malt vinegar
2 tablespoons soft brown sugar

For the stuffing:
1 lb. (450 g.) prunes, soaked for 4 hours
8 oz. (225 g.) fresh white breadcrumbs
2 oz. (50 g.) almonds, blanched and chopped
1 teaspoon each chopped fresh sage, parsley, marjoram and thyme, or 2 teaspoons mixed dried herbs
2 oz. (50 g.) shredded suet
1–2 tablespoons vinegar
Salt and pepper

For the lemon sauce:
1 oz. (25 g.) butter
1 oz. (25 g.) plain flour
¾ pint (450 ml.) chicken stock
2 eggs, beaten
Grated rinds and juice of 2 lemons

For the garnish:
Parsley sprigs, lemon slices

First make the stuffing: drain the soaked prunes and set six aside. Stone and chop the remainder and mix with the breadcrumbs, almonds, herbs, suet and vinegar. Season well with salt and pepper.

Clean the chicken and remove the giblets. Spoon the stuffing loosely into the neck cavity and secure with a skewer or by sewing up with a trussing needle and string (see p. 145).

Put the chicken in a large, heavy-based saucepan. Cover with cold water, ¼ pint (150 ml.) vinegar and the sugar. Bring to the boil, then reduce to a simmer. Cover and cook for about 4 hours or until the bird is tender. Remove the pan from the heat and leave the chicken to cool in the broth overnight.

Remove the chicken, skin it and place it on a large serving dish. Skim the fat from the cold broth. Strain ¾ pint (450 ml.) of the stock into a saucepan and heat through.

To make the sauce, melt the butter, stir in the flour and cook gently for 2–3 minutes. Add the warm chicken stock and simmer, stirring continuously, until the sauce is smooth and creamy. Blend a few tablespoons into the beaten eggs and strain this mixture back into the sauce. Heat through until thickened, stirring all the time and taking care not to let the sauce boil or it will curdle. Then remove from the heat, season to taste and blend in the lemon juice and half of the grated rinds. Set aside to become cold.

Coat the chicken with the sauce. Sprinkle the remaining lemon rind on top and decorate with the six reserved prunes, stoned and cut in half, parsley sprigs and lemon slices.

To make a good soup, mix any sauce left over with some of the cooking liquid and heat gently: do not boil. Add a little cream.

Hindle Wakes—chicken with prune and almond stuffing, coated with lemon sauce.

DEVILLED CHICKEN
Countrywide

DR KITCHINER, in his *Cook's Oracle* (1817), introduces Devil Sauces with fine Regency aplomb: 'Every man must have experienced that when he has got deep into his third bottle... his stomach is seized with a certain craving which seems to demand a stimulant. The provocatives used on such an occasion an ungrateful world has combined to term devils.'

Throughout the 19th century, devilling—flavouring to give a hot, sharp taste—was a popular and lively means of returning the remains of the previous day's joint or fowl to the table.

That devilling was particularly esteemed in officers' messes is apparent in Alexis Soyer's *Culinary Campaign in the Crimea* (1857), which suggests treating turkey remnants to a dose of 'Mephistophelian Sauce'. 'Do not be afraid of the title,' reassures the author, 'for it has nothing diabolical about it.' It will not make the chicken too savage, either.

PREPARATION TIME: 20 MINUTES
COOKING TIME: 10–15 MINUTES

INGREDIENTS FOR FOUR

6–8 meaty poultry joints, such as chicken or turkey, cooked or freshly part-cooked

For the sauce:

4 oz. (100/125 g.) butter
1 tablespoon mustard powder
2 tablespoons stale breadcrumbs
1 tablespoon Worcestershire sauce
1 tablespoon sweet mango chutney or home-made chutney (see pp. 344–7)
Salt
Cayenne pepper

Place the chicken joints in a grill pan lined with a sheet of foil and lightly greased with butter or vegetable oil.

To make the sauce, put the butter, mustard, breadcrumbs, Worcestershire sauce and chutney in a bowl and blend with a fork or the back of a spoon. Break up any pieces of fruit or vegetable in the chutney. Season with salt and Cayenne pepper.

Spread the sauce over the chicken joints and grill gently so that the meat heats through or completes cooking as the sauce browns. Serve on warmed plates and mop up with hot, crusty bread.

If you have any sauce left, add it to a little giblet or game stock. Heat thoroughly and pour around the devilled joints.

As an alternative to chutney, use 3 teaspoons of mushroom ketchup blended with 1 teaspoon of curry powder.

This is an excellent party dish. Serve with a variety of salads such as potato, coleslaw and Chinese Watercress Salad (see p. 195).

A smothering of hot, sharp sauce adds a new dimension to grilled chicken joints in Devilled Chicken.

TURKEY STUFFED WITH CHESTNUTS AND OYSTERS
Countrywide

AN OLD SCHOOL JINGLE, which dates from the 17th century at least, informs pupils that:

'Turkeys, heresy, hops and beer,
Came into England, all in one year.'

Although this statement is not absolutely correct, it is not so far wrong either. The Dissolution of the Monasteries, the growing southern-English preference for Flemish hop-flavoured beer over the ale of their ancestors, and the introduction of a new species of domestic fowl from the Americas, were all in full swing in the latter part of the 1530s and early 1540s.

Turkeys have nothing to do with the country of the same name in Asia Minor. They are indigenous to North and Central America, and were first imported from Mexico to southern Europe by the Spaniards in the 1520s. From Europe the birds were very soon brought to England by East Mediterranean spice merchants, known to the English as 'Turkey Merchants'. Hence the name of the bird.

They were swiftly recognised as a dish for special occasions, demanding the most luxurious stuffings and accompaniments.

This version of roast, stuffed turkey well interprets the spirit of those 16th-century recipes.

PREPARATION TIME: 1 HOUR
COOKING TIME: ABOUT 2½–3 HOURS
PRE-HEAT THE OVEN TO 200°C (400°F)—GAS MARK 6

INGREDIENTS FOR 12–15

1 hen turkey, about 10 lb. (4·5 kg.)
2 oz. (50 g.) melted butter

For the body stuffing:

12 large chestnuts, slit along one side
6 oz. (175 g.) fresh breadcrumbs
¼–½ pint (150–300 ml.) milk
6 large oysters, fresh or canned, drained
1 small shallot or onion, chopped
Turkey liver, chopped
1 tablespoon chopped parsley
Salt and pepper

For the neck stuffing:

8 oz. (225 g.) sausagemeat

For the gravy:

1 pint (575/600 ml.) hot poultry stock (see pp. 33–34)
2 tablespoons redcurrant jelly

Wipe the turkey clean and remove the giblets. Set aside the turkey liver for the stuffing and prepare stock from the rest.

Cover the chestnuts with water and boil for about 30 minutes, or until tender. Remove the shells and skins while still warm. Meanwhile, soak the breadcrumbs in the milk. If the oysters are very large, chop them in half. Mix the chestnuts with the breadcrumbs, oysters, shallot or onion, turkey liver, parsley and salt and pepper to taste.

Put the stuffing into the body of the turkey and secure well with a skewer or a trussing needle and string. Then spoon all the sausagemeat, seasoned with salt and pepper, and 1 oz. (25 g.) of the butter, into the neck cavity and secure.

Place the bird into a large roasting pan and rub the rest of the butter into the breast. Cover loosely with foil or greaseproof paper and cook in the centre of the pre-heated oven for 2½–3 hours, or for 15 minutes for each pound (450 g.) and then 15 minutes extra.

After 30 minutes pour in half the strained poultry stock, turn the oven heat down to 180°C (350°F)—gas mark 4, and continue cooking. Baste about every 30 minutes with the remaining stock. Twenty minutes before the turkey is ready, remove the foil or greaseproof paper and dust the breast with salt and pepper.

When ready, transfer to a warmed serving dish. Reduce the stock on top of the stove by boiling rapidly and add the redcurrant jelly, mixing in well. Taste for seasoning and strain into a gravy boat.

Serve with about 1½ lb. (700 g.) grilled small sausages and bread sauce (see p. 152).

For alternative stuffings, see pp. 156–8. If you use dried chestnuts, soak for 2–3 hours until they swell, then drain.

Chestnuts, oysters and shallots—ingredients that go to make a rich stuffing for Roast Turkey.

BRAISED TURKEY COUNTRY STYLE
Countrywide

THE FIRST MENTION of turkeys in England is contained in a stiff reprimand issued by Archbishop Cranmer in 1541 against the gluttonous habits of the clergy. Henceforward, he tells them, they must eat no more than a single 'greater fowl'—crane, swan or turkey cock—at any one meal.

By the beginning of the 17th century the turkey was widely domesticated in this country and, for both the rich and the common folk, was rapidly ousting the other, more traditional 'greater fowl' as the most popular bird for celebratory occasions. When the Pilgrim Fathers ate turkey at the first Thanksgiving in 1621, they were no strangers to the dish—though the wild turkeys of New England must have seemed a special bonus.

This turkey and vegetable recipe makes a fine one-dish meal.

PREPARATION TIME: 30–45 MINUTES
SOAKING TIME: OVERNIGHT
COOKING TIME: ABOUT 2–2½ HOURS
PRE-HEAT THE OVEN TO 180°C (350°F)—GAS MARK 4

INGREDIENTS FOR EIGHT TO TEN

1 small turkey, about 6 lb. (2·7 kg.)
2 lb. (900 g.) collar bacon or gammon, soaked overnight
2 fl. oz. (50 ml.) oil, or 2 oz. (50 g.) dripping
2 large onions, peeled and sliced
4 carrots, scrubbed and sliced
1 turnip, peeled and sliced
Bouquet garni
Salt and pepper
About 2 pints (1·1 litres) poultry stock (see pp. 33–34)

Wipe the turkey clean and remove the giblets. Drain the bacon or gammon, pat dry and remove the rinds and fat. Cut into cubes about 1 in. (2·5 cm.) in size.

Truss the turkey (see p. 145). Heat the fat in a heavy-based casserole and brown the turkey in it. Add the bacon cubes, vegetables and herbs. Season with salt and pepper. Pour on the hot, strained poultry stock. Bring to the boil and remove any scum that rises to the surface. Cover tightly and cook in the pre-heated oven for about 2–2½ hours or until tender.

Serve the turkey with some of the bacon and vegetables.

SALT DUCK
Countrywide

THIS RECIPE calls for the use of sea salt in the preliminaries, and it may be that salted duck was a progression from the salt-curing of fish that has been carried out round our coasts since time immemorial.

The superiority of sea salt over rock salt as a curing agent for meat was recognised as long ago as the 17th century. Despite the fact that it was much more costly, it was imported from workings on the Atlantic coasts of France and Spain.

Salt Duck—sprinkled generously with crystals of sea salt before simmering in cider.

PREPARATION TIME: 20–30 MINUTES
STANDING TIME: 2–3 DAYS
COOKING TIME: 2 HOURS
PRE-HEAT THE OVEN TO 180°C (350°F)—GAS MARK 4

INGREDIENTS FOR FOUR

1 duck, about 4 lb. (1·8 kg), or 2 smaller duck
8 oz. (225 g.) sea salt
1 large onion, peeled and sliced
Pepper
1 pint (575/600 ml.) hot poultry stock (see pp. 33–34)
½ pint (275/300 ml.) still cider

Wipe the duck clean and remove the giblets.

Put the duck in a deep dish and rub it all over with the sea salt. Cover with a cloth and leave in a cool place or larder for 2–3 days. Turn the duck over and rub the salt into its skin again over this period.

Pre-heat the oven to 180°C (350°F)—gas mark 4. Rinse the duck thoroughly, pat dry and put it into a large casserole with the onion. Season with pepper. Strain the stock, return it to the saucepan, add the cider and boil rapidly to reduce to about 1 pint (575/600 ml.). Pour into the casserole, cover and cook for about 2 hours.

Serve hot with an onion sauce (see p. 152), made with half duck stock and half milk.

DUCK WITH TURNIPS
Countrywide

THE ASSOCIATION of duck and turnips is one of those quiet, long-standing marriages that has stood the test of time. The idea probably came over with the Romans, who served the bird with a separate turnip sauce. From the Middle Ages to the 17th century, Duck with

Turnips made regular appearances in one English cookery book after another. After that the dish was served less and less here—and when it made a rare appearance it was described as a French dish.

The combination works well as the turnips offset the duck's fattiness.

PREPARATION TIME: 40 MINUTES
COOKING TIME: ABOUT 2 HOURS
PRE-HEAT THE OVEN TO
180°C (350°F)—GAS MARK 4

INGREDIENTS FOR THREE TO FOUR

1 duck, about 4½ lb. (1·8 kg.)
1 pint (575/600 ml.) poultry stock (see pp. 33–34)
Salt and pepper
1 medium onion, peeled and sliced
1 bay leaf
1 teaspoon chopped, fresh mixed herbs or ½ teaspoon mixed, dried herbs
3 tablespoons sherry
3 rashers bacon, with rinds removed
1 lb. (450 g.) white turnips

Wipe the duck clean and remove the giblets. Prick the skin all over with a fork and rub salt and pepper into it.

Place in a large casserole with the onion, bay leaf and mixed herbs. Add 1 tablespoon of the sherry and the strained stock. Lay the bacon rashers over the top and bring to the boil. Cover with greaseproof paper or foil, then the lid, and cook in the pre-heated oven for 30 minutes. Reduce the heat to 170°C (325°F)—gas mark 3, and cook for a further hour.

Meanwhile, peel and thickly slice the turnips. (If they are small, peel and leave whole.) Take about 1 cup of stock from the duck and add it to the turnips with the remaining sherry. Bring to the boil and simmer until almost tender.

Add the turnips with their stock to the casserole, increase the heat to 190°C (375°F)—gas mark 5, and cook it, uncovered, for about 30 minutes more, or until the duck has crisped up a little. Place the duck in the centre of a warmed serving dish surrounded by the turnips. Strain the stock, skimming off the fat, and serve separately.

DUCK BRAISED WITH PEAS
Countrywide

As DUCK WITH TURNIPS FADED from the English culinary scene in the 17th century, it was gradually replaced by Duck Braised with Green Peas—described at the time as being 'in the French manner', just as Duck with Turnip was to be labelled a century later.

PREPARATION TIME: ABOUT 20 MINUTES
COOKING TIME: ABOUT 2½ HOURS
PRE-HEAT THE OVEN TO
190°C (375°F)—GAS MARK 5

INGREDIENTS FOR THREE TO FOUR

1 duck, about 4 lb. (1·8 kg.)
2 oz. (50 g.) butter or oil
1 tablespoon seasoned flour
1 pint (575/600 ml.) poultry stock (see pp. 33–34)
1 lb. (450 g.) shelled, fresh green peas
1 tablespoon chopped mixed mint and marjoram
¼ teaspoon ground mace
1 small lettuce, chopped
½ oz. (15 g.) kneaded butter (see p. 163)

Wipe the duck clean and remove the giblets. Then prick the duck all over with a fork.

Heat up the butter or oil in a heavy-based casserole on the top of the stove, and brown the duck all over. Shake over the seasoned flour, rub it into the crisped duck skin and cook for 1 minute more.

Remove from the heat and skim off any excess fat. Then pour on the strained stock, bring to the boil, cover and transfer to the pre-heated oven and cook for 30 minutes. Reduce the oven temperature to 180°C (350°F)—gas mark 4. Take the casserole out of the oven and add the peas, herbs, mace and lettuce. Taste for seasoning, cover and cook for a further 1½ hours.

Stir in the ½ oz. (15 g.) of kneaded butter, in small pieces, remove the cover and continue cooking until the duck is tender and the stock and kneaded butter have thickened into a creamy sauce.

ROAST DUCK WITH GOOSEBERRY SAUCE
Countrywide

THROUGH the centuries few dishes have remained as popular as this, though in 1861, Mrs Beeton, in her *Household Management*, felt it her duty to point out a more regrettable aspect of the bird's character. 'In the wild state, (the duck) is a faithful husband, but no sooner is he domesticated, than he makes nothing of owning 10 or a dozen wives ...'

PREPARATION TIME: 30–45 MINUTES
COOKING TIME: ABOUT 1½ HOURS
PRE-HEAT THE OVEN TO
200°C (400°F)—GAS MARK 6

INGREDIENTS FOR TWO TO THREE

1 duckling, about 3½ lb. (1·6 kg.)
1 lemon, cut in half
2 tablespoons oil or butter
½ pint (275/300 ml.) poultry stock (see pp. 33–34)
2 teaspoons seasoned flour
½ pint (275/300 ml.) dry cider

For the stuffing:

Sage and onion stuffing (see p. 156)

For the sauce:

8 oz. (225 g.) green gooseberries, washed, topped and tailed
¼ pint (150 ml.) dry cider or white wine
2 tablespoons sugar
¼ teaspoon ground mace
1 oz. (25 g.) butter, cut in small pieces

First make the sage and onion stuffing. Wipe the duck clean and remove the giblets.

Prick the duck all over with a fork, and rub inside and out with the cut lemon. Squeeze some of the juice inside and over the top. Spoon in the stuffing from the tail end and secure well. Put the duck on a rack in a roasting tin and rub the oil or butter into the breast and legs.

Roast in the pre-heated oven for about 1½–2 hours, or 20 minutes to each 1 lb. (450 g.) including the weight of the stuffing, and 20 minutes extra. Baste from time to time. About halfway through cooking, dust the breast with seasoned flour and baste.

Meanwhile, make the sauce. Simmer the gooseberries in the cider or wine with the sugar and mace until quite soft. Pass through a sieve or liquidiser and return to the cleaned pan. Add the butter and stir well.

When the duck is cooked, put it on a warmed serving dish and keep warm. Skim off the excess fat from the pan juices, add the warm strained stock and pour on the cider. Season and boil up rapidly on top of the stove to reduce until syrupy. Serve the duck with the gooseberry sauce and the gravy served separately. Traditional accompaniments are plain boiled new potatoes and green peas.

Stuffing for the goose—apples soaked in dark, rich-flavoured rum, with mace and sage.

ROAST GOOSE WITH RUM-SOAKED APPLES
Countrywide

At some time in the late 18th century it was finally settled that onion, sage and apples make the ideal stuffing for roast goose. The ingredients and the principal complement one another, while the apple also does much to counteract any greasiness.

Despite this sound precept, there were always a few people who looked back to far more adventurous days—to 1390, for example, when Richard II's master chef suggested stuffing a goose with quinces, pears and grapes and 'put thereinne wyne, if it be to thyk'.

The alcohol theme lingers on in this recipe, although it cannot be older than the 17th century, when rum was first imported from Barbados.

PREPARATION TIME: 30 MINUTES
SOAKING TIME: 4 HOURS
COOKING TIME: ABOUT 4 HOURS
PRE-HEAT THE OVEN TO 180°C (350°F)—GAS MARK 4

INGREDIENTS FOR SIX TO EIGHT

1 goose, about 10 lb. (4·5 kg.)
Salt and pepper
3 tablespoons oil or dripping
1½ pints (850 ml.) poultry stock (see pp. 33–34)
4 fl. oz. (100/125 ml.) dark rum

For the stuffing:

6 large eating apples, peeled, cored, chopped and soaked in rum for 4 hours
3 finely chopped sage leaves or ¼ teaspoon ground sage
¼ teaspoon ground mace
12 oz. (350 g.) freshly made breadcrumbs

Remove the giblets and wipe the goose clean inside and out.

Mix the stuffing ingredients together and spoon into the body of the bird. If there is any left, put into the neck cavity.

Rub salt and pepper into the skin and then prick it all over. Place the goose on a rack in a baking tin and spread the legs and wings with the oil or dripping. Cover the breast with a large piece of aluminium foil or greaseproof paper. Place in the centre of the pre-heated oven.

Roast for 30 minutes then spoon off any excess fat and baste well with the warm, strained poultry stock. Do this every 30 minutes. After 2½ hours, remove the foil or greaseproof paper so the breast can crisp up and brown.

Place the goose on a warmed serving dish and keep warm. Strain off excess fat from the pan juices and boil rapidly to reduce and make gravy.

Heat the rum in a ladle or small pan and pour over the bird, then set it alight. Serve immediately with mashed celeriac and potatoes (see p. 193) or a purée of turnips, parsnips or Jerusalem artichokes, and a salad.

ROAST GOOSE STUFFED WITH POTATO
Countrywide

'IF ANY GOOSE be eaten above four months old,' said Thomas Moufet, the 16th-century author of *Health's Improvement*, 'it is badly digested without garlic sauce, exercise and strong drink.' The situation is not quite so disastrous as that, however; while it is true that a young goose requires little more than an inner dusting with pepper and salt, a mature bird is much improved by more robust accompaniments.

A stuffing of breadcrumbs and herbs is traditional, but potatoes serve just as well, while offering the added advantage of novelty. Possibly the idea dates from the latter half of the 18th century, when the wider cultivation of potatoes coincided with a long succession of poor grain harvests. Certainly, the high corn prices of the period did much to popularise the potato in general; in particular, it is interesting that the first published mention of potato stuffing occurs at this period—in the quaint *Adam's Luxury and Eve's Cookery* of 1744.

Serve with the gravy and apple or gooseberry sauce (see p. 154). The stuffing is especially good served cold next day with leftover goose and pickles.

PREPARATION TIME: 45 MINUTES–1 HOUR

COOKING TIME: ABOUT 4 HOURS

PRE-HEAT THE OVEN TO 190°C (375°F)—GAS MARK 5

INGREDIENTS FOR SIX TO EIGHT

1 goose, about 10 lb. (4·5 kg.)
Salt and pepper
1 pint (575/600 ml.) dry cider or poultry stock (see pp. 33–34)

For the stuffing:

Potato Stuffing (see p. 158)

Wipe the goose clean and remove the giblets.

Prick the bird all over with a fork. Put the stuffing into both the body and neck cavities and rub salt and pepper into the skin.

Place on a rack in a roasting tin. Bring the cider or strained stock to the boil and pour all but 2 tablespoons over the goose. Put in the centre of the pre-heated oven and roast for about 4 hours, or 20 minutes per lb. (450 g.) plus 50 minutes. Baste from time to time and, if it gets too brown on top, cover with a piece of foil or greaseproof paper.

When ready, transfer the goose to a warmed serving dish and keep warm. Spoon off excess fat from the pan drippings, add the remainder of the hot cider or stock, check seasoning and boil rapidly on top of the stove.

YORKSHIRE STUFFED GOOSE
Yorkshire

UNTIL the 16th century at least, swans and peacocks were the fowls chiefly eaten by great men. With aristocratic stoicism they put up with the near inedibility of the birds' flesh in exchange for their richly ornamented appearance on the table.

Goose was the fare of poorer people; though it was much better eating than the choice of their betters, it could be afforded only on special occasions, such as at Michaelmas and Christmas. Then, of course, the dish would be made as festive as possible, using the finest stuffings available. Although goose was eventually displaced by turkey, many farmers still keep the old tradition of having a few geese in the farmyard. In addition to being a good source of food, they are useful 'watch dogs'.

Prunes have been imported from southern Europe since the 15th century but, until about 100 years ago, they were never cheap. So this would probably have been a very special recipe indeed, and one that has fortunately survived to our own day.

PREPARATION TIME: ABOUT 30 MINUTES

SOAKING TIME: OVERNIGHT FOR THE PRUNES

COOKING TIME: ABOUT 4 HOURS

PRE-HEAT THE OVEN TO 190°C (375°F)—GAS MARK 5

INGREDIENTS FOR EIGHT

1 goose, about 10 lb. (4·5 kg.)
Salt and pepper
1 lb. (450 g.) prunes, soaked overnight, stoned and chopped
2 oz. (50 g.) soft brown sugar
1 lb. (450 g.) apples, peeled, cored and chopped
½ pint (275/300 ml.) poultry stock (see pp. 33–34)
1 pint (575/600 ml.) dry cider
2 tablespoons redcurrant jelly

Wipe the goose clean, remove the giblets and prick the skin all over. Rub the bird inside and out with salt and pepper.

Mix the chopped prunes, apples and sugar together. Spoon into the body of the goose and secure well with a skewer, or with a trussing needle and string.

Stand the bird on a rack in a roasting tin and cook in the centre of the pre-heated oven for about 3½ hours. (Allow 20 minutes for each lb. (450 g.) plus 50 minutes.)

Strain the stock into a saucepan, add the cider and bring to the boil.

After the goose has been roasting for 30 minutes, reduce the heat to 170°C (325°F)—gas mark 3. Baste generously with the mixed stock and cider about every 20 minutes, until all the liquid is used up. To see if the bird is ready, after it has been cooking for almost 4 hours, prick one of the legs with the blade of a sharp-pointed knife. If pink juices run out, it needs further cooking; if they are clear, it should be done and you can prepare the bird for serving.

Put the goose on to a warmed serving dish. Strain the fat from the surface of the liquid in the pan, and stir in the redcurrant jelly. Boil rapidly on top of the stove to reduce, and if more gravy is needed add a little extra cider.

Serve with the strained gravy, apple or gooseberry sauce (see p. 154) and bread sauce (see p. 152).

As alternatives, try bread and herb stuffing (p.156); country forcemeat—including herbs and bacon (p. 157); or chestnut stuffing (p. 158).

Roast Guinea Fowl with Stuffing
Countrywide

When guinea fowl were introduced into Britain from West Africa in the 16th century they were considered something of a wonder, yet they had been domesticated here to some extent during the four centuries of Roman occupation.

Guinea fowl did not long survive the departure of their protectors; the trusting habits they had developed during their period of domestication made them an easy catch for the hungry peasantry.

Since their reintroduction, guinea fowl have lived totally in domestication, though they are still sufficiently wild to wander if not securely penned. Despite this, they used to be regarded as game birds, though their position was sufficiently confused for them to be eaten between March and July, the months when other varieties of game are out of season.

Preparation Time: 1 hour
Cooking Time: 1–1½ hours
Pre-heat the Oven to
180°C (350°F)—gas mark 4

Ingredients for Three to Four

1 guinea fowl, about 2½ lb. (1·1 kg.), with giblets
4 rashers streaky bacon, with rinds removed
½ pint (275/300 ml.) hot stock (see pp. 33–34)
½ pint (275/300 ml.) hot dry cider

For the stuffing:

8 oz. (225 g.) sausagemeat
Guinea-fowl liver, chopped
¼ teaspoon ground mixed spice
2 celery stalks or 1 large lovage leaf, chopped
Salt and pepper

Clean the guinea fowl and remove the giblets. Set the liver aside for the stuffing and prepare the stock from the remaining giblets.

Mix all the stuffing ingredients together and spoon into the body of the bird. Secure well. Put into the roasting tin, cover the breast with the bacon rashers and add the hot stock and cider.

Roast the fowl in the centre of the pre-heated oven for 1–1½ hours, depending on size. Baste it at least twice during the cooking.

Put the bird on to a warmed serving dish and keep warm. To make the gravy, reduce the pan juices by fast boiling on top of the stove. Taste for seasoning.

Serve with redcurrant jelly (see p. 340) and bread sauce (see p. 152). Game chips (see p. 185) and Brussels sprouts with chestnuts (see p. 189) go well with this dish.

Casseroled Guinea Fowl
Countrywide

Casseroling, the process of sealing meat or poultry in a pot with herbs and vegetables, and permitting it to cook slowly in the natural juices strengthened perhaps by a little wine, or other liquid, was introduced into England from France towards the end of the 17th century.

It is a process particularly well suited to fowl or game birds that have passed the first flush of youth. The older and tougher they are, the longer they should be cooked. Indeed, to re-heat the pot after allowing it to stand and cool overnight, will add even greater distinction to both the flavour and the texture.

Guinea fowl is particularly good cooked in this way. Produce the casserole at a spring dinner party when the season for true game birds has come to an end.

Preparation Time: 30 minutes
Cooking Time: 1½ hours
Pre-heat the Oven to
180°C (350°F)—gas mark 4

Ingredients for Four

1 guinea fowl, about 2½ lb. (1·1 kg.), with giblets
1 large onion, peeled and sliced
2 carrots, scrubbed and sliced
2 leeks, trimmed, washed and sliced
Bunch of mixed fresh herbs or 1 teaspoon dried mixed herbs
Salt and pepper
8 thin rashers streaky bacon, with rinds removed

For the sauce:

½ pint (275/300 ml.) giblet stock (see pp. 33–34)
1 tablespoon butter
1 tablespoon flour
4 tablespoons single cream
1 tablespoon chopped parsley

Clean the bird and remove the giblets. Truss it (see p. 145) and put in a deep casserole with the vegetables, herbs, salt and pepper to taste and just enough water to cover. Bring to the boil then put in the pre-heated oven, tightly covered, for 1 hour or until the bird is tender.

During this hour prepare the giblet stock.

Take the casserole from the oven and strain off ½ pint (275/300 ml.) of cooking liquid. Lower the oven heat to 130°C (250°F)—gas mark ½ and put the casserole back. Strain the prepared stock into the cooking liquid and boil rapidly to reduce to about ½ pint (275/300 ml.).

Roll up the bacon rashers and thread on skewers. Grill for about 5 minutes, turning, until they are crisp. Keep warm.

To make the sauce, heat the butter, stir in the flour and cook gently for 2–3 minutes. Pour on the hot stock, stirring all the time until smooth and thickened. Taste for seasoning, then add the cream and parsley. Heat the sauce through well but do not allow it to come to the boil.

To serve, take the bird from the dish and carve into serving portions. Place on a warmed serving dish, pour on the sauce and arrange the bacon rolls round it.

Serve the casserole with plain boiled new or creamed potatoes and a crisp green salad; or with glazed carrots (see p. 182), boiled rice and a watercress salad.

Pupton of Pigeon
Countrywide

Despite interbreeding with all kinds of visitors, our two native types of pigeon still predominate. These are the rock pigeons that nest as happily on the buildings surrounding Trafalgar Square as on their ancestral cliffs, and the wood pigeons that with contemptuous skill, rise a lazy foot or two above the range of the guns of the farmers whose fields they have plundered.

All pigeons, except the city-dwellers, make good eating, and have been considered a delicacy since the time of the Romans, who encouraged them to nest in tall towers called *columbaria*, or in earthenware turrets perched on top of their houses. In medieval winters, pigeons were one of the few forms of fresh meat available;

most great houses had dovecots, some large enough to house as many as 1,000 pairs of birds.

The name of the following deliciously traditional dish is derived from *pulpeta*, a Spanish delicacy made from rabbits and fowls encased in a crust of forcemeat. Somewhere through the years, jelly replaced the forcemeat, until by the end of the 18th century our ancestors were enjoying a pupton very similar to the one given here.

PREPARATION TIME: 1 HOUR
COOKING TIME: 1 HOUR
CHILLING TIME: OVERNIGHT

INGREDIENTS FOR FOUR

3–4 wood pigeons

3 oz. (75 g.) fat bacon, diced

2 shallots, peeled, or the whites of 4 medium spring onions, finely chopped

2 oz. (50 g.) mushrooms, finely sliced

A bouquet of herbs including fresh thyme, parsley, bay leaf, and the outside leaves of a leek

3 fl. oz. (90 ml.) dry white wine

¾ pint (450 ml.) well-reduced, lightly seasoned white stock (see pp. 33–34), or ¾ pint (450 ml.) clear first stock (see pp. 33–34) with ¾ oz. (20 g.) gelatine dissolved in it (see p. 257)

For the decoration:

2 hard-boiled eggs, sliced in ¼ in. (5 mm.) thick rings

5 stoned green olives, or stuffed green olives, halved

1 large carrot, peeled, cooked whole, and cut in rings

2 oz. (50 g.) small mushrooms, washed, sliced, and poached 2 minutes in 2 fl. oz. (50 ml.) dry white wine and 1 oz. (25 g.) butter

Cut the pigeons into joints, and set aside only the breasts and the thighs for the pupton. The other parts can be used to make stock.

Heat the diced bacon in a frying pan until the fat runs. Toss the pigeon pieces in the fat, adding the chopped shallots or onions and the mushrooms. Cook for 5 minutes. Then transfer the pigeon pieces, shallots and mushrooms into a saucepan with a close-fitting lid. Add the bouquet of herbs and the wine. Bring to the boil and simmer over a low heat for 1 hour. If the liquid begins to dry up, add a little more wine.

Meanwhile, decorate a 1½ pint (850 ml.) mould. Warm the stock slightly to liquefy it, then let it cool. Lightly coat the base of the mould with 3–4 tablespoons of the almost-cold jellied stock. Put in the refrigerator for 10–15 minutes to set. Then arrange the slices of egg, olive, carrot and mushrooms decoratively on top of the layer of jelly in the bottom of the mould. Cover with another layer of jellied stock and chill for a further 10–15 minutes until set. When the pupton is turned out, this arrangement will be visible on top.

When the pigeon has cooked for 1 hour, lift the pieces out of the saucepan and take all of the meat off the bones. Pound the flesh with a pestle in a mortar, or with a mallet. Place the pounded meat on top of the jellied stock in the mould. Pour on the remainder of the stock. Return the mould to the refrigerator to chill overnight.

To turn out the jelly, stand the mould for 15–30 seconds in a bowl of boiling water; or, with a cloth carefully wrapped round your hand, hold the mould over steam from a boiling kettle for 15–20 seconds. Then turn it on to a plate.

Serve cut in portions as a first course, garnished with lettuce, sliced tomato and sliced gherkin.

Pupton of Pigeon—first simmered in wine and herbs, then decorated and given shape by a jelly mould.

STEW OF VENISON
Countrywide

SELLARS AND YEATMAN, in their *1066 and All That* (1930), say that any medieval peasant caught poaching the King's deer had his hands and feet chopped off, and was then permitted to flee the country. The real penalties were almost as dire but, even so, many poor men did poach deer and turn them into pottages, the ancestors of this present recipe.

By the 17th century, venison pottage had achieved respectability. A recipe of 1673 suggests the addition of spicy red beetroot, while 70-odd years later, Hannah Glasse speaks of adding 'as much red wine as will make it of the thickness of a ragoo'.

This recipe can be prepared with stewing venison, in which case, the cooking time should be increased.

PREPARATION TIME: 20 MINUTES
COOKING TIME: 1½–2 HOURS
PRE-HEAT THE OVEN TO
180°C (350°F)—GAS MARK 4

INGREDIENTS FOR FOUR

2 lb. (900 g.) venison meat from the shoulder or haunch
Seasoned flour
1 oz. (25 g.) butter
2 tablespoons cooking oil
1 pint (575/600 ml.) red wine or stock (see pp. 33–34), or a mixture of both
¼ teaspoon grated nutmeg
1 blade of mace
4 whole cloves
1 stick of cinnamon
¼ teaspoon Cayenne pepper
Salt

Cut the venison into 1 in. (2·5 cm.) cubes, and dust with seasoned flour.

Heat the butter and oil in a frying pan, and quickly brown the venison cubes all over in it. Put them in a casserole with a well-fitting lid.

Pour the wine or stock into the frying pan. Stir well to take up all the browned juices from the pan, and pour the liquid into the casserole. Add the spices, season with salt, cover, and place in the pre-heated oven. Cook gently for 1½–2 hours, until the meat is tender. Remove the cinnamon before serving. Creamed potatoes and braised celery (see p. 184) or a green vegetable go well with this dish.

ROAST SADDLE OF VENISON
Countrywide

VENISON has a long and emotive history, arising partly out of the fearful punishments meted out to those who dared to defy the law and kill animals intended for the sport of their betters. Andrew Boorde, in his *Compendyous Regyment or Dyetary of Helth* (1542), said that venison was 'a meat for great men. And great men do not set so much by the meat, as they do by the pastime of killing it'.

By common consent, the saddle is the finest cut, and it was dressed in different ways at different periods. The Romans served it with fruit sauces, dates and damsons, while the English, throughout Tudor times ate it flavoured with cloves or rosemary and a cinnamon and butter sauce. This recipe is soundly Edwardian.

PREPARATION TIME: 30 MINUTES
MARINATING TIME: 2 DAYS
COOKING TIME: 1½ HOURS
PRE-HEAT THE OVEN TO
200°C (400°F)—GAS MARK 6

INGREDIENTS FOR 12

1 saddle of venison
8 rashers streaky bacon
4 fl. oz. (100/125 ml.) port wine (optional)
Kneaded butter (see p. 163) for thickening (optional)

For the marinade:

½ pint (275/300 ml.) red wine
½ pint (275/300 ml.) red wine vinegar
½ pint (275/300 ml.) water
1 sprig of thyme
6 juniper berries, crushed
2 bay leaves, crumbled
1 blade of mace, crumbled
1 piece of orange peel, dried or fresh with pith removed, about 1 in. (2·5 cm.) square

Using a very sharp knife, trim any hard skin off the meat. Take care not to tear the flesh. Put the meat in a dish that almost completely encloses it.

Combine all the ingredients for the marinade, and pour the mixture over the meat. Add more water, if necessary, to cover the saddle. Leave in a cool place for 2 days. Do not put a lid on the dish, but cover it with a net or a piece of loosely woven material to keep off flies or dust. Turn the meat from time to time.

At the end of the marinating time, drain the joint and pat it dry with absorbent paper. Lay the bacon rashers across the top of the saddle and tie them on with string. Place the saddle in a roasting tin, cover with a sheet of aluminium foil and cook in the pre-heated oven for 30 minutes.

Reduce the temperature to 180°C (350°F)—gas mark 4, and continue cooking for another ¾–1 hour. During this time, lift the foil and baste the saddle with the marinade every 15 minutes, or as often as necessary to keep it from drying out. If desired, pour some port wine into the roasting tin when you reduce the oven temperature, and incorporate it with the basting mixture.

Ten minutes before the meat is done, remove the foil and take off the bacon rashers, reserving them for garnish, if liked. Raise the oven temperature to 200°C (400°F)—gas mark 6, and return the saddle to the oven for 10 minutes to brown the outside of the meat.

Remove the venison from the oven and keep warm. Add enough boiling water to the meat juices in the roasting tin to make ½ pint (275/300 ml.) of liquid. Stir over a high heat to blend and, if you like, thicken with kneaded butter.

Strain the sauce and hand separately. Serve with redcurrant jelly and game chips.

Roast Saddle of Venison, marinated in wine and the wild flavours of juniper and thyme and served with redcurrant jelly.

RABBIT WITH MUSTARD
Countrywide

THE ROMANS were exceedingly fond of rabbit and established colonies of the creatures in most of the Empire, including Britain. The animal's proverbial fecundity gave rise to the usual problems when introducing it to a new area, and in some places the army had to be called in to deal with its overwhelming numbers. In Britain, however, the rabbit died out in the Dark Ages, and was not re-established until the 12th century. The first colonies were on Lundy and the Scillies and, to this day, Lundy rabbits are darker than their mainland cousins.

During the Middle Ages, rabbit was esteemed above hare by both cottage and castle. It was not subject to the savage game laws of the period, and to the medieval palate its flavour was more delicate than that of hare.

Consequently, rabbit recipes tended to be the more imaginative, making plentiful use of herbs. The Dijon mustard that distinguishes the recipe given here is, of course, a more recent and delicious addition.

PREPARATION TIME: 15 MINUTES
COOKING TIME: 1½ HOURS

INGREDIENTS FOR FOUR

1 oz. (25 g.) butter
2 tablespoons cooking oil
2 rashers rindless streaky bacon, diced
1 large rabbit, jointed
2 large onions, peeled and roughly chopped
3–4 tablespoons Dijon mustard
¼ teaspoon thyme
6 fl. oz. (175 ml.) dry white wine
Salt and freshly ground black pepper

Heat the butter and oil together in a frying pan, and gently fry the bacon in it until the fat runs. Remove the bacon pieces to a large, heavy-based saucepan with a well-fitting lid. Put the pieces of rabbit in the frying pan and cook them over a high heat until browned on all sides. Add them to the bacon and keep warm.

Cook the onions gently in fat that is left in the frying pan for about 10 minutes, then lift out with a slotted spoon, letting as much fat as possible drain off, and put in the saucepan with the rabbit and bacon. Add the mustard, thyme and wine. Season with salt and pepper, cover and bring to the boil. Turn down to the lowest heat and simmer for 1 hour.

Alternatively, you can cook the rabbit in an oven, pre-heated to 240°C (475°F)—gas mark 9. In this case, transfer the browned ingredients to a casserole and bring the wine almost to the boil before adding it. After 10 minutes, reduce the oven temperature to 190°C (375°F)—gas mark 5, and cook, covered, for 1½ hours or until tender.

Serve the rabbit with glazed carrots (see p. 182) or braised leeks (see p. 183) and creamed or boiled potatoes followed by a green salad.

FRICASSEE OF RABBIT
Countrywide

FROM the Middle Ages to the land enclosures of the early 1800s, landowners whose acres encompassed sandy heath and bracken-covered hill actively encouraged rabbits to breed there. Rabbits were more profitable than sheep on such inhospitable soil. Rabbit skins were sold to tailors, glovers and hatters, while the carcases could either be marketed or distributed among the estate workers, for whom rabbit provided a rare taste of fresh meat during the winter months.

The animal also made frequent appearances on manor-house tables, plain stewed, roasted or served in a fricassee, as in this recipe, which probably dates from the 18th century.

PREPARATION TIME: 20 MINUTES
COOKING TIME: 1¼–1½ HOURS

INGREDIENTS FOR FOUR

1 large rabbit, whole or halved
1 large carrot, washed and roughly chopped
1 large turnip, washed and roughly chopped
1 large onion, roughly chopped
1 bay leaf
½ teaspoon chopped fresh thyme or a sprig of parsley
Salt and pepper
2 thick slices dry bread, crusts removed
Butter for frying
1 tablespoon finely chopped parsley

For the sauce:

About ¼ pint (150 ml.) stock from the rabbit
1 oz. (25 g.) butter
1 oz. (25 g.) plain flour
1 tablespoon dry sherry
2 tablespoons double cream
Salt and pepper

Put the rabbit into a large saucepan, cover with cold water and bring to the boil. Rinse away this water and the scum that forms with it. Cover the rabbit a second time with water, adding the carrot, turnip, onion, bay leaf, thyme or sprig of parsley, salt and pepper. Bring to the boil, reduce the heat and simmer for 30–40 minutes or until the rabbit is tender. Remove the rabbit from the liquid, and leave it to cool. Strain the stock, discarding the vegetables and herbs and keeping the clear liquid for making the sauce.

When the rabbit is cool enough to handle, strip the flesh from the bones, taking care to remove the tiny bones. Put the meat on a covered plate and keep warm.

To make the sauce, melt the butter in a saucepan, and stir in the flour with a wooden spoon. When it is well blended, gradually add the hot stock, stirring continuously over a medium heat until the sauce is smooth. Keep cooking and stirring for at least 10 minutes to rid the sauce of any floury taste. Stir in the sherry and cream and correct the seasoning. Put the rabbit back in the sauce and simmer very gently for 5–10 minutes until the meat is heated thoroughly. Meanwhile, cut the thick slices of dry bread into cubes and fry them quickly in the butter until crisp. Pour the fricassee on to a hot, shallow serving dish, arrange the fried bread cubes round it and garnish with a sprinkling of chopped parsley.

YOUNG RABBIT FRIED
Countrywide

HISTORICALLY, the term 'young rabbit' is something of a misnomer. Until the 18th century at least, the word 'rabbit' meant the animal up to a year old; after that age it was called a 'coney'. The difference was quite distinct in our forbears' minds. Andrew Boorde's *Dyetary of Helth*, published in 1542, says 'Coneys' flesh is good, but rabbits' flesh is best of all wild beasts, for it is temperate and doth nourish, and is singularly praised in physic...' Baby rabbits were much relished by the Romans, and rabbits up to a few months old by the monks of the Middle Ages, who conveniently decided that they did not count as meat, and could therefore be eaten on fast days.

The stamp of history's approval gives this best of rabbit recipes an extra glow. Try it for a family supper or small, informal dinner party.

PREPARATION TIME: 1¼ HOURS (INCLUDING MAKING THE STOCK)

COOKING TIME: 30 MINUTES

INGREDIENTS FOR FOUR

2 young rabbits, jointed
1 oz. (25 g.) butter
2 tablespoons cooking oil
8 oz. (225 g.) spinach, washed and drained, or young cabbage leaves, finely chopped
1–2 oz. (25–50 g.) butter, in small pieces
Salt and pepper

For the stock:

Trimmings from the 2 jointed rabbits
1 carrot, roughly cut
1 turnip, roughly cut
1 onion, peeled and roughly chopped
Salt and pepper

Ask the butcher to joint the rabbits, or do it yourself (see p. 147). Use only the back and thighs for the dish.

To make the stock, place the rabbit trimmings in a saucepan with the carrot, turnip, onion and seasoning. Add just enough water to cover, then simmer, covered, for 1 hour. Strain and set aside the stock.

Heat the butter and oil together in a large frying pan with a well-fitting lid, and fry the rabbit pieces on both sides over a medium heat for 5 minutes, turning occasionally. Remove the back pieces and put them to keep warm in a covered dish, leaving the thighs to continue cooking for a further 5 minutes.

Return the back pieces to the pan, with the spinach or cabbage, ¼ pint (150 ml.) of the stock, and salt and pepper. Cover with the lid, and simmer for 10 minutes. Remove the spinach or cabbage from the pan and put it on a hot serving dish. Arrange the rabbit pieces over the vegetable and keep warm.

Quickly make a sauce by stirring the butter pieces into the remaining liquid in the pan. Season to taste with salt and pepper and pour the sauce over the rabbit.

Young rabbit, lightly fried, mingles its flavours with spinach.

JUGGED HARE
Countrywide

HARES have been eaten in Britain for at least 5,000 years. Generally, they were hunted with dogs, and the trained hounds used for the purpose were famed throughout Europe long before the Roman invasion. Indeed, one of the reasons for the invasion is said to have been to ensure the regular supply of hunting dogs.

For most of our history, hare was poor man's meat. At various times, Acts of Parliament were passed to prevent the creatures being wiped out; and in 1723 the 'Black Act' made poaching an offence punishable by death—if the poacher were armed or masked.

Curiously, this seems to have elevated the hare to respectability, for within the next few years a range of hare recipes was published, including one for Jugged Hare.

PREPARATION TIME: 30 MINUTES
COOKING TIME: 4 HOURS

INGREDIENTS FOR FOUR

- *1 medium-size hare, prepared and jointed by the butcher, with blood if possible*
- *Salt and pepper*
- *4 oz. (100/125 g.) rindless streaky bacon, chopped*
- *4 oz. (100/125 g.) smoked ham, chopped*
- *6 shallots, peeled and finely chopped*
- *2 medium onions, peeled and coarsely chopped*
- *¼ pint (150 ml.) dry red wine*
- *¼ pint (150 ml.) game, poultry or brown stock (see pp. 33–34)*
- *Juice of 1 Seville orange, or juice of ½ lemon and ½ sweet orange*
- *1–2 teaspoons each chopped fresh herbs, such as parsley, marjoram and thyme, or ½–1 teaspoon each if dried*
- *¼ teaspoon ground mace*
- *4 cloves*
- *¼ teaspoon grated nutmeg*
- *¼ teaspoon grated lemon peel*
- *4 heaped tablespoons plain flour*
- *Kneaded butter (see p. 163) for thickening*
- *½–¾ pint (275/450 ml.) hare's blood (optional)*

Season the jointed hare well with salt and pepper and place in a tall jug with a lid, or place the joints in a large pudding basin.

Mix together in a bowl the bacon, ham, shallots and onions. Add the wine, stock and orange juice, the herbs and spices and the lemon peel.

Cover the hare with the mixture and place the lid on the jug.

Mix the 4 heaped tablespoons of flour to a thick paste with a little water and use it to seal the lid on the jug.

If you are using a pudding basin, tie on securely a greased and floured pudding cloth, or seal with foil.

Stand the jug or basin in a large saucepan and pour in enough boiling water to reach two-thirds of the way up the side. Simmer on a low heat for 4 hours, adding more boiling water as necessary to maintain the level as it evaporates.

Remove the pieces of hare and keep them warm on a serving dish. Allow the stock to cool a little and strain off the fat from the juices. Thicken, if necessary, with the kneaded butter.

If you want to follow the traditional method of serving Jugged Hare, the sauce can be thickened with the hare's blood.

Ask your butcher to preserve the blood when he prepares the hare, and bring it home in a separate container. Mix it with 1 rounded teaspoon of flour to prevent it curdling. Stir the

Jugged Hare, stewed in its own rich juices, fortified with wine, herbs and spices, and served with lemon slices.

blood into the juices instead of the kneaded butter. Heat gently, but be very careful not to let the blood boil as it will curdle.

Pour the sauce over the joints of hare and garnish with lemon slices and redcurrant jelly (see p. 340).

HARE HODGE-PODGE
Countrywide

WELL-BORN PEOPLE in the Middle Ages did not eat hare—an aversion that may have been due to the Biblical edict upon it—'an unclean beast'—but more likely it was simple snobbery; the animal was eaten by the poor. But by the 17th century, attitudes were changing.

H. Butler, in his *Diet's Dry Dinner* (1599), says 'that use of a Hare's flesh procureth beautie . . . insomuch as the Italians speaketh thus of a faire man, He hath devoured an Hare'.

While their betters were debating the point, country people continued to enjoy hare. A favourite recipe was this simple version of jugged hare. 'Hodge-podge' is an old term for a stew of chopped meat and vegetables.

PREPARATION TIME: 10 MINUTES

COOKING TIME: 4–5 HOURS

INGREDIENTS FOR FOUR

1 medium hare, prepared by the butcher and jointed
4 medium onions, peeled
2 sticks celery, chopped
Bouquet garni
Salt and pepper
3 oz. (75 g.) butter
½ pint (275/300 ml.) boiling stock (see pp. 33–34) or water

Put the pieces of hare in a tall jug, deep stewpot or basin just large enough to hold all the ingredients. Add the whole onions, celery and bouquet garni. Season with salt and pepper, put the butter on top and pour in the boiling stock or water. Cover the top tightly with foil or a lid sealed with a flour and water paste as for Jugged Hare (see opposite page).

Stand the container in a large saucepan and pour in enough boiling water to reach two-thirds of the way up the side. Simmer gently for 4 hours, or for 5 hours if the hare is an old one. Add more boiling water as necessary to maintain the level.

Serve the hare and its juices with creamed potatoes and sprouts.

ROAST SADDLE OF HARE
Countrywide

THE FIRST MENTION of the hare in British history occurs in AD 60, when, so it is said, Queen Boudicca released one from beneath her robe as a means of determining which route her armies should take.

In 1662, Isobel Gowdie of Fife was hanged after confessing to running about the countryside in the guise of the animal.

Understandably, many countrymen eyed the the hare askance. However, there were always a few hardy souls who defied superstition and appreciated it for its flavour—especially the saddle, without doubt the best cut. By the 18th century, the Age of Reason, Roast Saddle of Hare was firmly established as a delicious dish.

Order your hare in advance from the butcher, and ask him to prepare it.

PREPARATION TIME: 20 MINUTES

COOKING TIME: 1¼ HOURS

PRE-HEAT THE OVEN TO 180°C (350°F)—GAS MARK 4

INGREDIENTS FOR FOUR

Saddle and rear legs of a young hare
¼ pint (150 ml.) milk, or mild or brown ale
2 oz. (50 g.) butter, melted
2 oz. (50 g.) plain flour

For the stuffing:

6 oz. (175 g.) dry white bread, crusts removed
1 egg, beaten
2 oz (50 g.) rindless streaky bacon, chopped and gently fried
2 oz. (50 g.) mushrooms, wiped and finely chopped
1 tablespoon finely chopped parsley
½ teaspoon chopped fresh thyme or ¼ teaspoon dried
4 whole cloves
¼ teaspoon ground mace
¼ teaspoon grated nutmeg
Salt and freshly ground pepper
1 oz. (25 g.) softened butter
About 4 fl. oz. (100/125 ml.) red wine or port

Ask your butcher to prepare the meat by removing the tough membrane from the back, but leaving the loose flaps of thin flesh on the belly of the hare to wrap round the stuffing.

To make the stuffing, soak the bread in water and then squeeze out the liquid. Mix the bread with the beaten egg, the bacon, mushrooms, herbs and spices. Season with salt and pepper. Work in the butter and just enough wine or port to moisten the mixture without making it too wet.

Fill the hollow inside the saddle with the stuffing and wrap the thin flaps of flesh round it.

Cut a piece of aluminium foil, large enough to enclose the saddle, and lay the hare on it belly side down. Fold the foil loosely over the hare and seal the edges firmly. This prevents the meat from drying out during roasting. Place the hare in a roasting tin.

Roast in the pre-heated oven for 20 minutes, by which time the juices will have started to run. Open the foil and baste well with the milk or ale.

Cover with foil again and continue roasting for another 20 minutes. Then baste again, this time with the melted butter, and again cover with the foil. Raise the oven temperature to 200°C (400°F)—gas mark 6, and cook the hare for a further 25 minutes.

Remove from the oven and sprinkle the hare evenly with flour. Baste again with the surrounding juices and continue cooking, uncovered, for 10 minutes more to brown the saddle.

Serve the saddle with the juices poured over it. Roast onions and sautéed or creamed potatoes are excellent accompaniments for this dish.

ROAST GROUSE
Scotland

ON AUGUST 12, known to shooting men as The Glorious Twelfth, grouse shooting opens, the beaters turn out, and the startled birds explode from the heather, coming fast and low like bullets over the butts.

The grouse family, which includes capercaillie, ptarmigan and blackcock, is native to the chillier regions of the Northern Hemisphere. But the best of them, at least from the gourmet's point of view, is the red grouse, of which a few adventurous representatives have settled in northern England. The remainder live on the Scottish moors.

There is only one way to cook young grouse, and that is to roast it.

PREPARATION TIME: 10 MINUTES
COOKING TIME: 20–30 MINUTES
PRE-HEAT THE OVEN TO 200°C (400°F)—GAS MARK 6

INGREDIENTS FOR FOUR

- *4 young grouse, plucked and drawn, with livers*
- *4 rashers fat bacon*
- *2 oz. (50 g.) butter, softened, or bacon fat*
- *Salt and pepper*
- *Juice of 1 or 2 lemons*
- *8 oz. (225 g.) red currants, rowan berries or cranberries, or jelly made from these*
- *Flour for sprinkling*

For the garnish:

- *4 grouse livers*
- *1 oz. (25 g.) butter*
- *Salt and pepper*
- *4 slices of buttered toast*

Wipe the insides of the birds and rub each inside with the butter or bacon fat. Sprinkle in salt, pepper and lemon juice and fill each with a share of red currants, berries or jelly. Truss the birds (see p. 145) and tie a rasher of bacon over each breast.

Cut four pieces of aluminium foil, each large enough to enclose a grouse. Wrap each bird in foil and place, breast down, in a roasting tin. Roast in the pre-heated oven for 20–30 minutes, depending on the size of the birds.

Meanwhile, place the grouse livers in a saucepan with just enough water to cover. Poach them for 2 minutes, then remove and mash with a fork, adding the butter, salt and pepper. Spread the liver on the slices of toast.

Roast Grouse filled with red currants and presented the traditional way.

Ten minutes before the grouse are cooked, remove the foil and bacon, turn the birds breast up and dredge with flour. Put a slice of the prepared toast under each bird to absorb the juices. Roast the birds for 10 minutes more to brown them.

Make a gravy by adding 2–3 tablespoons of boiling water to the juices in the pan, and stirring over a high heat for 2–3 minutes.

Serve the grouse with its traditional accompaniments—bread sauce (see p. 152), hot game chips (see p. 185), fried breadcrumbs, and redcurrant or rowan jelly (see pp. 340 and 343).

GROUSE IN CASSEROLE
Countrywide

A GOOD GAME DEALER will sell grouse either as 'young' or 'casserole' birds. The former have downy feathers on the breast, rounded spurs on the legs and are ideal for roasting. Older grouse are delicious cooked more slowly.

PREPARATION TIME: 15 MINUTES
COOKING TIME: 1¾ HOURS
PRE-HEAT THE OVEN TO 180°C (350°F)—GAS MARK 4

INGREDIENTS FOR FOUR

- *4 old grouse, plucked and drawn by the butcher, but not trussed*
- *2 tablespoons well-seasoned flour*
- *2 oz. (50 g.) butter*
- *2 tablespoons Cognac or Armagnac*
- *2½ fl. oz. (75 ml.) game or poultry stock (see pp. 33–34)*
- *4 fl. oz. (100/125 ml.) dry red wine or sherry*

Joint the grouse and use only the breasts and legs for the casserole. The remaining parts of the birds will make excellent stock for another dish.

Roll the pieces of grouse in seasoned flour. Heat the butter in a frying pan, and quickly fry the pieces for a few minutes until the meat stiffens. Warm the Cognac or Armagnac in a ladle or very small pan over a low heat, set light to it and, while it is flaming, pour it into the pan, shaking to spread the flames over all the meat. Remove the grouse pieces, and place in a casserole or oven dish with a tightly fitting lid. Pour the stock and wine into the frying pan, stir well to take up all the browned juices, and add to the grouse.

Cover and cook in the pre-heated oven for 1½ hours, or until tender. Adjust the seasoning and serve with roast or creamed potatoes, redcurrant jelly, and fried breadcrumbs.

WILD DUCK OVEN-GRILLED
Countrywide

WILDFOWLING—the art of shooting wild duck and geese—calls for an odd range of preferences. Chief among these is a desire to crouch up to your waist in East Anglian estuary mud on a freezing February pre-dawn, waiting for the heart-lifting beat of wings that denotes the morning flight coming in. Those who practise the art say that it promotes fortitude and a love of wildlife.

But there is no doubt at all about the eating qualities of roast wild duck, and particularly that of mallard. Small and lean, its special flavour exceeds that of farmyard duck.

PREPARATION TIME: 20 MINUTES
STANDING TIME: 2 HOURS
COOKING TIME: 20–30 MINUTES
PRE-HEAT THE OVEN TO 220°C (425°F)—GAS MARK 7

INGREDIENTS FOR FOUR

- *2 young wild duck, prepared by the butcher*
- *2 oz. (50 g.) plain flour for dredging*
- *1–2 oz. (25–50 g.) softened butter*
- *Salt and pepper*
- *Kneaded butter (see p. 163) for thickening (optional)*
- *1 teaspoon redcurrant jelly or honey (optional)*

For the marinade:

- *8 juniper berries, crushed, or 2 tablespoons gin*
- *12 black peppercorns, lightly crushed*
- *4 fl. oz. (100/125 ml.) dry red wine*
- *Juice of ½ lemon*
- *2 tablespoons olive oil*

Split each duck in half down the middle to make four pieces. Using a sharp knife, or boning knife, cut away the backbone and breastbone. Trim off the ends of the wings and legs, and use to make stock for another dish.

To make the marinade, mix together the juniper berries or gin, peppercorns, wine, lemon juice and olive oil. Turn the four pieces of duck in the marinade to coat them well, then leave them in it, uncovered, for 2 hours to absorb the flavours. Turn the pieces frequently.

After 2 hours, remove the duck, and strain and reserve the marinade. Wipe the duck dry, dredge with flour, and rub with the softened butter, salt and pepper. Put the duck pieces on an oven rack on the top level of the oven. Put a roasting tin on the next level to catch the drippings.

Roast in the pre-heated oven for 20–30 minutes, basting two or three times with the juices from the roasting tin.

A few minutes before the duck is cooked, boil up the strained marinade and add it to the juices in the roasting tin, stirring well. Taste the sauce. If it is too sharp for your liking, add the teaspoon of redcurrant jelly or honey. If you like a thick sauce, place the tin over a medium heat and thicken the juices with a little kneaded butter.

Serve the wild duck garnished with watercress and accompanied by roast potatoes and braised celery (see p. 184). Hand the sauce separately.

PARTRIDGE IN PAPER
Countrywide

THE ASSOCIATION of partridge with mushrooms is an old one. Eliza Acton, in her *Modern Cookery for Private Families* (1845), gives two recipes for partridge stuffed with mushrooms. 'Nothing,' she observes, 'can be finer than the game flavour imbibed by the mushrooms with which the birds are filled.' It would be difficult to quarrel with her.

The Edwardians, rather grandly, called this dish 'Partridge en papillote', from the culinary term meaning to cook in buttered paper.

PREPARATION TIME: 30 MINUTES
COOKING TIME: 35–40 MINUTES

INGREDIENTS FOR FOUR

- *4 very young partridges, prepared by the butcher*
- *2 oz. (50 g.) butter*
- *4 fl. oz. (100/125 ml.) dry white wine*
- *About 2 tablespoons cooking oil*
- *4 rashers rindless streaky bacon, finely chopped*
- *Watercress to garnish*

For the mushroom sauce:

- *2 oz. (50 g.) butter*
- *8 oz. (225 g.) mushrooms, finely chopped*
- *¼ pint (150 ml.) game or poultry stock (see pp. 33–34), heated*
- *2½ fl. oz. (75 ml.) double cream*
- *Salt and pepper*

Use only the eight breasts of the birds for this dish.

Melt the butter in a frying pan and gently fry the partridge breasts for 5–10 minutes. Remove and drain on kitchen paper. Add the white wine to the pan, stir well and put to one side for the sauce.

Cut eight pieces of aluminium foil in 8 in. (20 cm.) squares. Fold each square into four and trim off the corners to make circles. Brush the circles with oil.

Place a partridge breast on each circle and sprinkle with bacon. Fold the foil tightly round each breast, crimping the edges. Put the foil parcels under a hot grill and cook for 15–20 minutes, turning over several times.

Meanwhile, to make the mushroom sauce, melt the butter in a second frying pan, add the mushrooms, cover and fry gently for about 5–10 minutes. Reduce the mushrooms to a purée in a liquidiser or by passing them through a food mill, adding a very little stock if necessary. Return the purée to the frying pan, and stir in the heated stock and then the cream. Season well.

When the partridge is nearly done, open the foil packets for the last 3 minutes of cooking time to crisp the bacon. At the same time, add the mushroom sauce to the frying pan with the wine and butter mixture. Stir over a moderate heat for 3–4 minutes.

Remove the partridges from the foil, garnish with watercress, and serve the sauce separately.

Cold Partridge in Vine Leaves
Countrywide

THE USE OF VINE LEAVES in British cookery is not so recent an innovation as it sounds. Mrs Blencowe, a Northamptonshire housewife, wrote down a recipe for dolmades—stuffed vine leaves—in 1694. In the Tudor and Stuart periods they were used to enhance the colour of stewed apples, while in the 1796 edition of *The Art of Cookery*, Hannah Glasse suggests a dish of vine-leaf fritters.

However, the notion of wrapping small birds—partridges, quail or thrushes—in vine leaves before cooking them, seems to have originated in France, though there they are eaten hot rather than cold. Either way, it is one of the simplest methods of cooking a partridge, and one that best retains the delicate flavour of the bird.

PREPARATION TIME: 10 MINUTES
COOKING TIME: 45 MINUTES

INGREDIENTS FOR FOUR

4 young partridges, prepared by the butcher and trussed
4 rashers streaky bacon
Salt and pepper
8–12 vine leaves, tinned or fresh, or cabbage leaves

Wrapping partridge in bacon and vine or cabbage leaves preserves the delicate flavour of the bird.

Season the partridges with salt and pepper and tie one rasher of bacon over the breast of each. Rinse any brine off the vine leaves and simmer them in a little water for 5 minutes. Wrap each bird closely with two or three leaves, and tie securely with string.

If vine leaves are not available, use cabbage leaves that have been blanched, then refreshed in cold water.

Place the wrapped partridges in a large saucepan, standing the birds on end, in a circle. Cover with water and bring to the boil. Then reduce the heat and simmer, covered, for 35 minutes on a low heat.

Have ready a bowl full of ice-cold water, straight from the refrigerator. When the partridges are cooked, remove them from the saucepan and plunge them immediately into the cold water, so that they cool quickly. Leave them for 5–10 minutes, when they will be ready to eat.

Unfold the leaves and remove the bacon. Serve the birds whole, with apple sauce (see p. 154), game chips and a watercress salad.

SALMI OF SNIPE
Countrywide

QUIET RIVER BANKS, marshes and dark and lonely pools are the haunts of the snipe, a darting, jinking little bird that more often than not manages to avoid the gun and lives to fly another day. It is not by chance that a crack shot, picking off his targets from concealment, is known as a sniper.

The snipe is one of the best-tasting of small game birds. Since there is only a mouthful or two of meat on it, it is perhaps famed more as a grand first course than as a main one; this salmi is a case in point. The origin of the word is obscure, though it is derived from the Latin *salmagundi*, which in the 17th century meant 'a mixed salad'. Over the years, the word became abbreviated, and was applied to concoctions of game birds instead. This salmi, which is also an excellent way to cook partridge, is delicious as an appetiser, or as a light supper dish for a special occasion.

PREPARATION TIME: 10 MINUTES
COOKING TIME: 25 MINUTES
PRE-HEAT THE OVEN TO 220°C (425°F)—GAS MARK 7

INGREDIENTS FOR FOUR

4 snipe, prepared by the butcher for roasting
4 rashers streaky bacon
2 shallots, peeled and finely chopped
¼ pint (150 ml.) stock, preferably game or white stock (see pp. 33–34)
8 tablespoons dry red wine
¼ teaspoon salt
¼ teaspoon Cayenne pepper
Juice of ½ lemon
4 slices bread fried in butter
Slices of lemon for garnishing

Tie one bacon rasher round each snipe. Place the four birds in an ovenproof dish and roast in the pre-heated oven for 15 minutes. The snipe should still be underdone.

Remove the bacon and cut each snipe into four pieces—two breasts and two legs. Put the pieces into a saucepan with the shallots, stock, wine, salt, Cayenne pepper and lemon juice. Simmer over a low heat for 10 minutes.

Serve the snipe with their sauce on pieces of crisply fried bread, and garnish with slices of lemon.

ROAST WOODCOCK
Countrywide

THE WOODCOCK is a relative of the snipe, but tends to live in open woodland rather than in the marshes and river banks favoured by its cousin. It also has the misfortune to be regarded, by gourmets, as the most desirable of all game birds. Be careful not to overcook it; if it is roasted over an open fire, a touch of flame helps to bring out the flavour.

Unlike most game birds, woodcock is not drawn before cooking, since its insides, or 'trail', possess a particularly delicate flavour; only the gizzard must be removed. It is usually hung for about 3 days.

PREPARATION TIME: 10 MINUTES
COOKING TIME: 20 MINUTES
PRE-HEAT THE OVEN TO 200°C (400°F)—GAS MARK 6

INGREDIENTS FOR FOUR

4 woodcock, plucked and trussed, but not drawn
4 rashers fat bacon
4 slices of dry white bread, with crusts removed, lightly toasted
1 teaspoon brandy
½ teaspoon lemon juice
Salt and pepper

Tie one rasher of bacon round each woodcock. Place the rounds of toast in a roasting tin and set one bird on each. The toast will absorb the juices as the birds cook. Roast in the pre-heated oven for 15–20 minutes, as woodcock is usually preferred underdone.

Before serving, spoon out the insides of the birds, mash with the brandy and spread on the toast rounds. Make a gravy from the pan juices by adding the lemon juice and enough boiling water to make about 6 fl. oz. (175 ml.) of sauce. Stir the sauce well, and season to taste with salt and pepper.

Serve the woodcock on the toast rounds, and hand the gravy separately. Game chips and an orange or green salad make good accompaniments for this dish.

PHEASANT POT ROAST
Countrywide

THOUGH THEY HAVE LIVED in this country since before the Norman Conquest, and perhaps as long ago as the Roman occupation, pheasants, the males at least, still strike a florid and foreign note in our sober countryside. The bird came originally from China and the Caucasus, and the male can be any colour from black to brown shot with gold.

The hens, however, are uniformly brown and cream and, by common consent, make the better eating. Both sexes should be hung for about 3–10 days before roasting or stewing, according to the bird's age. Young birds should be roasted, but the following is ideal for second-year birds.

PREPARATION TIME: 10 MINUTES
COOKING TIME: ABOUT 2 HOURS
PRE-HEAT THE OVEN TO 180°C (350°F)—GAS MARK 4

INGREDIENTS FOR FOUR

4 rashers streaky bacon
2 pheasants, prepared by the butcher and trussed
3 oz. (75 g.) butter
2 tablespoons cooking oil
2 tablespoons Cognac or Armagnac
Salt and pepper
¼ pint (150 ml.) game or poultry stock (see pp. 33–34)

Tie two rashers of bacon across the breast of each pheasant. Heat one-third of the butter with the oil in a frying pan. Put the remaining butter in a warm place to soften. Fry the birds until lightly browned on all sides. Warm the Cognac or Armagnac in a ladle or small saucepan, set it alight and pour it, flaming, over the pheasants. Transfer the birds to an ovenproof dish with a closely fitting lid.

Spread the softened butter over the birds and season with salt and pepper. Pour in the juices from the frying pan and cover the dish. Seal the lid tightly with foil, if necessary, or with a paste of flour and water (see Jugged Hare, p. 134). Bake in the pre-heated oven for 1½ hours or until tender.

Remove and discard the bacon, and transfer the pheasants to a warm serving dish. Heat the stock and stir it into the juices in the casserole in which the birds were cooked. Simmer for 1 minute to blend to a thin sauce. If you prefer a thicker sauce, stir in a little kneaded butter (see p. 163). Taste, and season with salt and pepper, if necessary.

Serve the pheasants with creamed potatoes and a green salad, and serve the sauce separately.

Ingredients for Stewed Pheasant with chestnut and artichoke sauce.

STEWED PHEASANT WITH CHESTNUTS
Countrywide

THIS IS THE BEST, and perhaps the only, way of cooking old pheasants, the tough, wily veterans that have survived, astonishingly, into their third shooting season. Battle scars apart, it is easy to tell cock birds of this age by their long, sharp spurs; second-year cocks have short, sharp spurs, while the spurs of those in their first season are short and rounded. The age of hens is more difficult to assess beyond the first year, when they have soft feet and light plumage. But the difference here is not so significant, since the hens are always more tender than the males.

Sound stewing rids them of their toughness, yet does nothing to diminish the flavour. Chestnuts, classic companions of pheasant, are here mingled with artichoke hearts in a rich and unusual sauce.

PREPARATION TIME: 20 MINUTES
COOKING TIME: 1 HOUR

INGREDIENTS FOR FOUR

2 pheasants, prepared by the butcher

1 pint (575/600 ml.) white, game or poultry stock (see pp. 33–34)

For the sauce:

1 lb. (450 g.) chestnuts

2 oz. (50 g.) butter

1 tablespoon double cream

Salt and pepper

2 or 3 artichoke hearts simmered until soft in boiling, salted water

4 fl. oz. (100/125 ml.) dry white wine

¼ teaspoon powdered mace

Kneaded butter (see p. 163) to thicken (optional)

Cut each pheasant in half, lengthwise, and place the pieces in a large saucepan. Cover with the stock and simmer over a low heat for ¾–1 hour, until the meat is tender. Older birds will require a longer cooking time.

Meanwhile, prepare the sauce. Slit the chestnuts at the narrow end and simmer in a little water for 15 minutes, until the skins split. Drain and peel. Reduce the chestnuts to a purée in a liquidiser, or by passing through a food mill or sieve. Beat in the butter and cream, and season. Mash the artichoke hearts and mix into the chestnuts.

When the pheasant is tender, remove the pieces to a serving dish and keep them warm. Boil the cooking liquid quickly to reduce it to ½ pint (275/300 ml.). Add the chestnut and artichoke purée, the wine and mace. Season and stir until smooth. If necessary, thicken the sauce by adding the kneaded butter.

Pour the sauce over the pheasant, and serve garnished with small fried sausages and watercress.

RAGOÛT OF QUAIL
Countrywide

QUAIL, small migratory game birds from India and Africa, are very seldom seen here now in the wild, though 50 years ago fair numbers of them reached our shores, even though others were netted in their thousands on their long trek across Europe. In most countries, netting the birds is now illegal and, in any case, they seem to have changed their route, so avoiding many of the traditional netting areas, such as Capri. Most of the quail seen in shops or served in restaurants were born and bred on Kentish farms. An exception is the bobwhite quail, a much larger bird related to the partridge that was introduced as a game bird to East Anglia from North America a few years ago.

Elderly gourmets say that farm-bred quail cannot approach the wild birds for delicacy of flavour, but this may be a matter of distance lending enchantment. To modern palates, Kentish quail are very attractive indeed. Serve this ragoût as an elegant—if somewhat expensive—supper dish on special occasions.

PREPARATION TIME: 15–30 MINUTES
COOKING TIME: 25 MINUTES

INGREDIENTS FOR TWO TO FOUR

4 quail, prepared by the butcher
2 rashers of streaky bacon, diced
1 oz. (25 g.) butter
2 tablespoons cooking oil
Seasoned flour
2 tablespoons brandy (optional)
4 oz. (100/125 g.) mushrooms, sliced
¾ pint (450 ml.) chicken or white stock (see pp. 33–34)
A bouquet of herbs, such as fresh parsley, thyme, bay leaf, and the outside leaves of a leek
Salt and pepper
Juice of 1 orange
Kneaded butter (see p. 163) for thickening (optional)

Ask the butcher to cut the quail in two, or do it yourself with a heavy knife or cleaver. Dust over the halves with seasoned flour and set aside. Heat the butter and oil together in a frying pan, and gently cook the bacon until the fat runs. Remove from the pan and add the pieces of quail. Fry them, in batches if necessary, for about 5 minutes on each side until they are golden-brown.

When all the quail are browned, return them to the pan and, if you want to give the dish an aromatic character, flame the quail with the brandy. Warm the brandy in a ladle over a flame. Set it alight and pour it into the frying pan. Shake the flames around the pan. Turn the quail into a deep saucepan with a close-fitting lid. Add the mushrooms, stock, herbs and salt and pepper. Bring almost to the boil, cover and simmer very gently for 15–25 minutes until the birds are tender and juicy. Just before serving, stir in the juice of the orange. For a thicker sauce, add a little kneaded butter towards the end of the cooking time.

Serve with creamed potatoes and glazed carrots.

QUAIL CASSEROLE
Countrywide

THE ROMANS, who ate most things that moved and were more than partial to game birds, drew the line at quail, which they fancied lived on an unrelieved diet of that deadly plant, hemlock, and were therefore poisonous.

It took many years to overcome this prejudice, but by the Middle Ages cautious experiment had proved that quail caught in this country at least were perfectly wholesome. They were served with cameline, a very popular and highly spiced sauce of the period, made chiefly from ginger and cinnamon.

Quail Casserole is a rich and splendid dish, ideal for a small dinner party or a special occasion. Unlike many game birds, quail should not be hung, but eaten as fresh as possible, preferably the day after killing. Check this with your game dealer before buying the birds.

PREPARATION TIME: 15 MINUTES
COOKING TIME: 25–30 MINUTES
PRE-HEAT THE OVEN TO 220°C (425°F)—GAS MARK 7

INGREDIENTS FOR TWO TO FOUR

4 quail, prepared by the butcher
1 oz. (25 g.) butter
4 fl. oz. (100/125 ml.) port
½ pint (275/300 ml.) game or poultry stock (see pp. 33–34)
2 small pieces of dried orange peel or grated rind of ½ orange
2 oz. (50 g.) redcurrant jelly (see p. 340)
Salt and pepper
Juice of ½ lemon

Heat the butter in a frying pan and cook the quail for about 5 minutes, turning, to brown all over. Then transfer the birds to an ovenproof casserole.

Add the port to the juices in the frying pan and stir to blend. Then add the stock and orange peel. Bring to the boil and simmer for 5 minutes. Dissolve the redcurrant jelly in the liquid and pour this over the quail in the casserole. Season with salt and pepper, place in the pre-heated oven and cook for 10–15 minutes. Just before serving, stir in the lemon juice. Serve straight from the casserole with stewed red cabbage (see p. 190) and creamed potatoes. Any liquid left in the dish may be added to any leftover cabbage and reheated.

Quail, casseroled in a blend of port, orange and redcurrant jelly.

RECIPES *from* OTHER LANDS

INDIA
Murgh Mussallam Dahi (Chicken Curry)

FOR THOSE WHO REGARD CURRY powder as an unsatisfactory way of presenting curry, this spicy chicken dish is guaranteed to be the real thing. Instead of ready-made powder it uses a subtle combination of spices.

Gently heat the coriander and cumin seeds in a dry frying pan until brown, shaking the pan to prevent sticking. This process releases the full aroma of the seeds, which are then crushed; or use ground spices.

Serve with rice or chapatis (rounded, unleavened bread) and chutney.

PREPARATION TIME: 30 MINUTES
STANDING TIME: 30 MINUTES
COOKING TIME: 1½ HOURS

INGREDIENTS FOR FOUR

1 roasting chicken, about 3½ lb. (1·6 kg.)
4 oz. (100/125 g.) butter or ghee
1 lb. (450 g.) onions, sliced
10 fl. oz. (275/300 ml.) plain yoghurt
2 tablespoons milk
1 teaspoon coriander seeds, whole or ground
1 teaspoon cumin seeds, whole or ground
1 teaspoon poppy seeds
2 cardamoms, cracked and crushed
2 cloves
1 teaspoon chilli powder
1 teaspoon ground ginger
½ teaspoon turmeric
½ teaspoon freshly ground black pepper
1 teaspoon ground cinnamon
2 teaspoons salt

For the garnish:
2 oz. (50 g.) sultanas or raisins
2 oz. (50 g.) almonds
1 oz. (25 g.) butter

Skin the chicken and wipe clean with a damp cloth. Remove the giblets and set aside as a base for stock or soup (see pp. 33–34).

To make the curry paste, crush all the spices together in a mortar with a pestle, or use the back of a spoon. Stir 2 tablespoons of water into the crushed spices and add the salt. Rub the chicken all over with this paste and leave to stand for 30 minutes.

Meanwhile heat the butter in a heavy-based pan and gently fry the onions for about 15 minutes, until lightly browned. Remove from the pan with a slotted spoon.

Brown the chicken in the butter, turning until it is evenly coloured all over. Put the chicken in a large, heavy-based saucepan.

Put the yoghurt in a bowl and beat in the milk, then the fried, drained onions. Heat the mixture in a saucepan to simmering point and pour on to the chicken. Cover tightly and simmer gently for 1 hour or until tender.

To finish, put the chicken on a warmed serving dish and keep warm. Heat the cooking liquid in a saucepan, letting it boil rapidly to reduce by half. Test for seasoning, stir well and pour over the chicken.

Toast the almonds in a dry heavy-based pan over a high flame, shaking occasionally to prevent burning. Melt the butter and lightly fry the sultanas. Sprinkle both over the chicken.

As a variation, joint the chicken before rubbing with paste. If you prefer, cook the dish in a casserole in an oven pre-heated to 200°C (400°F)—gas mark 6 for 1½ hours.

PUERTO RICO
Arroz con Pollo (Chicken with Rice)

PUERTO RICO WAS ONE of the earliest Spanish settlements in the West Indies, discovered by Columbus in 1493. It is a beautiful island, rugged and hilly, with a tropical climate which favours palm trees, bamboos and mangroves. Birds and fish abound, and the landscape is splashed with the vivid colours of flowering plants.

Today Puerto Rico is a Commonwealth of the United States but the influence of Spain is still strong in language, customs—and cooking. *Arroz con Pollo* is a traditional Spanish dish but in this distinctly Caribbean version, a deliciously aromatic flavour is combined with a rich contrast of colours.

PREPARATION TIME: 10 MINUTES
COOKING TIME: 1 HOUR

INGREDIENTS FOR FOUR TO SIX

1 roasting chicken, about 3½ lb. (1·6 kg.), jointed (see p. 145)
2 oz. (50 g.) lard or 2 fl. oz. (50 ml.) vegetable oil
1 Spanish onion, sliced
½ sweet red pimento, de-seeded and sliced
4 tomatoes, skinned and quartered
12 black olives, stoned
1 tablespoon capers, drained
Salt and pepper
1 lb. (450 g.) long-grain rice, well washed
1½ pints (850 ml.) boiling water

For the garnish:
4 oz. (100/125 g.) cooked green peas

Wipe clean the chicken joints and pat dry. Heat the fat in a large, heavy-based pan and gently fry the onion for about 10 minutes, until soft. Add the pimento, tomatoes, olives and capers. Season with salt and pepper, add the chicken pieces, cover, and cook for 30 minutes.

Add the rice to the pan and pour on the boiling water. Cover tightly and cook gently for 12–20 minutes, until all the water is absorbed and the rice tender. Stir several times and add extra water if necessary.

Serve the chicken pieces on their bed of savoury rice. Lightly fry the cooked peas in a little melted butter to warm them through, and use as a garnish. Alternatively, add 4 oz. (100/125 g.) mushrooms, lightly fried in butter or oil.

CHINA
Deep-fried Pigeon

IN ONE FORM OR ANOTHER, pigeons have been eaten since the days of the ancient Egyptians. They were possibly the first birds to be tamed by man, and the Chinese believed that they helped people to overcome illness. They also believed them to be an aid to potency—a conviction they extended to many different kinds of food at one time or another. Serve Deep-fried Pigeon as an unusual first course and eat it with your fingers, if you like.

PREPARATION TIME: 10 MINUTES
STANDING TIME: 30 MINUTES
COOKING TIME: 10 MINUTES

INGREDIENTS FOR FOUR

2 pigeons, prepared by the butcher
2 fl. oz. (50 ml.) dry sherry
2 fl. oz. (50 ml.) soy sauce
Oil for deep-frying
1 teaspoon salt

Using a sharp knife, split each pigeon in half and divide each half in two.

Combine the sherry and the soy sauce in a bowl and turn the pigeon pieces in the mixture. Leave them in the bowl with the liquid for 30 minutes, then drain and pat dry with kitchen paper.

In order to ensure crisp, brown, well-cooked pigeon, cook each piece twice in the following way. Heat the oil in a heavy-based saucepan until it is very hot, 180°C (350°F). Fry the pigeon pieces a few at a time for 1 minute each. Remove from the oil and set aside. Increase the temperature of the oil to 200°C (400°F). Fry the pigeon pieces again a few at a time for 3–4 minutes or until they are crisp and brown. Drain well on kitchen paper. Sprinkle with the salt, and garnish with slices of lemon.

SPAIN
Perdices Escabechadas (Soused Partridges)

ONE OF THE MOST DISTINCTIVE features of rural Iberian cookery is the wide variety of game it employs. Partridges are plentiful, especially in the plains of Cuidad Real in New Castile; there the skills of the shooting man are as highly esteemed as those of the chef—reasonably so, since one could scarcely operate without the other in this particular branch of cookery.

Another area famed for its game—partridges included—is Catalonia where, as in parts of rural Britain, autumn is practically dedicated to the bird. It is said that in Barcelona you can tell the season simply by the gamey odour of partridge wafting on the air.

The following method of marinating the birds can also be used for marinating small, fresh fish such as sardines, whiting, anchovies and mullet.

PREPARATION TIME: 30 MINUTES
STANDING TIME: 2 DAYS
COOKING TIME: 45 MINUTES–1 HOUR

INGREDIENTS FOR FOUR

4 partridges, prepared by the butcher
2 tablespoons olive oil
1 medium onion, peeled and finely chopped
2 cloves of garlic, finely chopped
2 bay leaves, crushed
2 cloves
12 black peppercorns
2 tablespoons salt
7 fl. oz. (200 ml.) white wine vinegar
7 fl. oz. (200 ml.) dry white wine
7 fl. oz. (200 ml.) water

Wipe the inside of each partridge. Heat the olive oil in a frying pan and brown the partridges on all sides. Remove the birds and place them in a large saucepan.

In the same oil, lightly fry the onion and garlic until the onion is transparent, but do not let it brown. Add this to the partridges in the saucepan and put in the crushed bay leaves, cloves, peppercorns and salt.

Combine the vinegar, wine and water and pour it over the partridges. Set the saucepan over a high heat, bring the liquid to the boil, then reduce the heat, cover and simmer slowly for $\frac{3}{4}$–1 hour.

Remove the birds from the liquid and allow it to cool for about 1 hour. Skim off the fat and put the partridges back in the liquid. Refrigerate for 2 days before serving, turning the birds over twice a day. The escabeche sauce both pickles the birds and makes them moist and tender.

Serve the partridges cold. Using a slotted spoon, transfer them to a serving dish, sprinkle over some of the onion and discard the liquid. Serve with watercress salad, cold apple purée and chutney.

ITALY
Golden Fried Rabbit

RABBITS ORIGINALLY came from the Iberian Peninsula, and do not seem to have ventured very far from it until the end of the 1st century BC—after the Roman conquest. The Romans called the rabbit *cuniculus*, which was a Latin version of the old Iberian name for it; from this in turn came the Italian *coniglio* and the English term 'coney'.

The Romans imported rabbits from Spain and bred them in enclosures called 'hare-gardens'. The meat of rabbits was very much prized. Apicius, a famous gourmet of the first century AD, praised rabbit *isicia* (meat balls), which he regarded as second only to those made from pheasant.

Rabbit is, in fact, very popular in Italy today. There are many different methods of cooking it, ranging from the Sicilian *agrodolce* (sweet-sour) casserole, which includes sugar, vinegar, sultanas and pine nuts, to recipes from northern Italy which use red wine and rosemary or tomatoes.

This traditional 'golden-fried' version makes a good main course for lunch or supper.

PREPARATION TIME: 20 MINUTES
MARINATING TIME: 1 HOUR
COOKING TIME: 10 MINUTES

INGREDIENTS FOR FOUR

1 rabbit, prepared by the butcher
2 oz. (50 g.) plain flour
1 teaspoon salt
2 eggs, beaten
4 oz. (100/125 g.) dry, white breadcrumbs
2 oz. (50 g.) butter
2–3 fl. oz. (50–90 ml.) olive oil

For the marinade:

Juice of 1 lemon
2 tablespoons olive oil
1 small onion, peeled and finely chopped
Salt and pepper

Joint the rabbit (see p. 147) and cut it into small serving pieces. Place them in a bowl.

Make the marinade by combining the lemon juice, olive oil and onion. Season the mixture well with salt and pepper and pour it over the rabbit. Allow the rabbit to marinate for 1 hour, turning the pieces over from time to time to distribute the liquid as evenly as possible.

Combine the flour and salt and spread the mixture over a plate. Place the beaten egg in a bowl and spread the breadcrumbs over another plate. Dip each piece of marinated rabbit first in the flour, then in the egg and finally in the breadcrumbs.

Heat the butter and oil together in a frying pan. Fry the pieces of rabbit over a gentle heat, turning once, for about 8 minutes or until the crust is golden-brown. Remove and drain on kitchen paper. Garnish with parsley and lemon wedges.

Serve the Golden Fried Rabbit with a side dish of spaghetti, dressed with a savoury butter (see p. 164) and a green salad.

POULTRY AND GAME

THOUGH POULTRY and, to a lesser extent, game still figure highly in our cookery, they are no longer as important as they were even as late as the beginning of the 18th century. Then, for rich and poor alike, they were the principal forms of fresh meat available during the winter, and wide use was made of both wild creatures and domesticated fowl. Roasting on a spit was the favourite cooking method. For birds such as blackbirds, thrushes and the very popular lark, small bird spits were used and tied on to full-sized spits.

Poultry

WHEN Julius Caesar visited Britain in 55 BC, he observed that the natives kept both hens and geese, but that we appeared not to eat them. From this he assumed that the British had some sort of religious objection to eating the birds. So far as chickens were concerned, it may have been that the British were still overwhelmed by their novelty. Descended from the red jungle fowl of India that the Persians had domesticated long before, they arrived in this country, via Greece, Rome and Gaul, only a few years before Caesar.

However, they stayed much longer, to become, like geese, ducks and, at a later date, turkeys, a major part of our national diet. Turkeys had, during the 16th century, begun to take the place of such birds as peacocks and swans at the festive meals of the wealthy, and in the 18th century were common farmhouse Christmas fare.

Facts about poultry

Poultry is defined as birds bred especially for the table: chickens, turkeys, ducks, geese, and now guinea fowl—formerly regarded as game.

Methods of breeding and rearing have changed dramatically over the past 50 years, so that chicken, in particular, is cheap, plentiful and almost entirely intensively reared. Although freshly killed poultry is far superior in flavour and texture, frozen birds, properly thawed and cooked, can be very good.

CHOOSING POULTRY

When buying a bird in feather, see that the legs are smooth and the scales small and pliant. Spurs on the male should be small, scaly knobs.

The quills on the wings should be easy to pluck, and the feathers soft and full.

The eyes should be clear and the flesh firm, with no unpleasant smell. Young birds have short, sharp claws.

Fresh, oven-ready birds

Look for a soft, flexible breastbone and a plump breast in a roasting bird.

If the breastbone is rigid, the bird may be old and suitable only for casseroling, boiling or making soup.

Frozen poultry

Always buy birds from a reputable source.

Make sure that the bag covering the bird is unbroken and that there are no marks of 'freezer burn'—discoloured dried-up patches on the skin caused by faulty or damaged packaging. If this occurs the flavour will be poor.

It is absolutely essential that frozen poultry is completely thawed before cooking. Incomplete thawing can lead to the risk of salmonella poisoning. Leave overnight at room temperature. Remove the pre-packed giblets and make sure that the inside of the bird is thawed, as well as the outside.

PREPARING POULTRY

Almost all poultry is now sold oven-ready. If you are offered a bird in feather or rough-plucked, it will need to be hung, plucked and drawn before you prepare it for the oven.

Hanging

Poultry, like other meats, should be hung to tenderise it. If bought in feather, ask how long the bird has already been hanging.

With fresh poultry, hang chicken for 24 hours after killing; ducks or geese for up to 48 hours; turkeys for 3–5 days.

Hang the bird by the feet in a cool, dry, well-ventilated place, free from flies. Check its condition occasionally, as the hanging time will vary a little according to weather conditions. In hot, thundery weather, a bird will decompose more rapidly.

If flies are a nuisance, dredge the bird with pepper or enclose it in a loose muslin bag.

Plucking

1 Hold the bird firmly on a large sheet of paper, in a draught-free space. Have a large bag handy to hold the feathers as you pluck them.
2 Start with the legs and wings, drawing the feathers out with a slight, backward pull against the lie of the feathers.
3 Pluck the breast last. Do not try to pluck too many feathers at one time, and take care not to tear the skin.
4 After plucking, get rid of remaining down and hairs by singeing. Use a lighted taper, or pour a little methylated spirit into a dish, set alight and turn the bird over the flame. Be careful not to scorch the skin.
5 Wipe the bird with a clean cloth. If any long hairs or quills still need to be removed, pluck them out with a pair of tweezers.

Drawing

1 Cut off the head, leaving about 3 in. (8 cm.) of neck. Slit the skin on the underside of the neck and pull it towards the body. Cut the neck again close to the body. (Set the neck aside to use for giblet stock.)

2 Put your hand, knuckles upwards, into the neck cavity. Remove the crop, windpipe and any fat present. Keeping your hand high under the breastbone, gently loosen and dislodge the entrails.

3 Turn the bird on to its back. Make a slit with a sharp knife to enlarge the vent at the tail end. Loosen the fat and the skin, then, holding the bird firmly with one hand, put the other hand inside and gently draw out the entrails.

4 Clean the giblets and cut the bitter, green gall bladder away from the liver. Put the liver, heart, gizzard (the bird's second stomach) with the neck to make stock.

5 Wipe the bird thoroughly, inside and out, with a damp, clean cloth.

6 Break the legs at the lower joint, at the base of each drumstick, to expose the tendons. Use a skewer to pull out one tendon at a time, taking care not to tear the flesh. Bend the joint backwards, then twist and break the bone. Cut through the skin. Scald and scrub the feet and remove the scales. Put the feet with the giblets to make stock.

Stuffing

See Using forcemeat (p. 164).

Trussing

1 Place the bird, breast down, on a table or chopping block. Close the neck cavity by folding the loose skin over the back, folding back the wings, and hold in place with a poultry skewer or with a trussing needle and fine string.

2 Turn the bird over. Make a horizontal slit in the skin above the tail vent, and push the parson's nose (tail) through it.

3 Draw the thighs close to the body and cross the legs over the tail end. Loop the string around the legs and parson's nose, and tie securely.

Boning

See Boning chicken or game (p. 49).

Jointing

1 Pull the bird's leg away from the body and, using a sharp knife, slice down to the thigh joint. Break at the joint and cut away the whole leg. Repeat with the other leg.

2 Slice through the outer breast meat towards the wing joint. Sever the wing from the body. Fold the breast meat over the wing joint. Repeat with the other wing.

3 There is a natural division in the rib cage. Slice along it to separate the breast from the lower carcase.

4 Cut the breast meat into serving portions. If jointing a large bird, separate the drumstick (the lower leg joint) from the thigh.

5 Use what is left of the carcase to make poultry stock (see pp. 33–34).

Larding

Larding is a method of adding fat to poultry, game and meat which has no fat and would be dry when cooked. It is done by threading strips of fat (lardons) through the flesh.

To make lardons, take a piece of firm, fat bacon and place it, rind down, on a chopping block. Using a sharp knife, cut the bacon into lardons about 2 in. (5 cm.) long and $\frac{1}{4}$ in. (5 mm.) thick. Put the lardons in a refrigerator for about 30 minutes to cool and become firm.

Place a lardon in the split end of a larding needle and draw through the bird or meat, leaving roughly equal projecting ends. Arrange lardons roughly $\frac{3}{4}$ in. (2 cm.) apart. Insert them on either side of the breastbone and at right-angles to it.

Cooking Poultry

Poussin A chicken 4–8 weeks old weighing up to $1\frac{1}{4}$ lb. (575 g.). Roast, spit-roast or grill. If roasting, place a nut of butter inside the bird. In spit-roasting, first brush all over with melted fat or oil.

Double poussin A chicken between 2 and $2\frac{1}{4}$ lb. (900 g.–1 kg.) in weight. Roast, spit-roast or grill.

Spring chicken A 12–14 week old chicken, averaging $2\frac{1}{2}$ lb. (1·1 kg.) in weight. Roast, spit-roast, grill or fry.

Roasting chicken or broiler The most widely sold bird, 4–9 months old weighing 3–4 lb. (1·4–1·8 kg.). Roast, spit-roast, grill or fry.

Boiling fowl Usually 12 months old or more. It can weigh up to 7 lb. (3·2 kg.) and is well flavoured and meaty, but tougher than a roasting bird. Boil, casserole or steam it—or use it to make soup. A pressure cooker speeds up the cooking process.

Capon A neutered cockerel, specially bred to produce a good, meaty roast. The usual weight is 5–8 lb. (2·3–3·6 kg.).

Turkey Choose a turkey of medium size—about 10–12 lb. (4·5–5·4 kg.). The best choice is a hen bird 6–8 months old. Turkey is usually dry, so bard it with bacon rashers or lard it and cover with foil or greaseproof paper for most of the cooking time.

Duck Oven-ready ducks on sale usually weigh between 4 and 6 lb. (1·8–2·7 kg.). The proportion of meat to bone is less generous than in chicken—a 4 lb. (1·8 kg.) duck will serve no more than four people.

A duck is fatty: always prick the skin a little before cooking to allow some of the fat to escape.

Duckling A young duck between 3 and 4 lb. (1·4–1·8 kg.) in weight. Ducklings are at their best from late March to August. Always roast.

Goose A fresh bird, at its best from October to February, will have yellow, soft, pliable feet. Roast or braise. Goose can be bought all the year round, but it is sensible to order well in advance of requirements. The average weight is 6–12 lb. (2·7–5·4 kg.), but the proportion of meat per pound weight is less than for chicken.

Guinea fowl Available all the year round, they are sold as squabs, about $1\frac{1}{4}$ lb. (575 g.); chicks, $1\frac{1}{4}$–$2\frac{1}{4}$ lb. (575 g.–1 kg.); or fowl, weighing up to 4 lb. (1·8 kg.). Roast, braise or casserole. Because the bird is inclined to dryness, if roasting make sure the breast is securely covered with rashers of bacon or pork fat.

Testing whether poultry is cooked

Never serve poultry undercooked. To see if a roast bird is ready, push a skewer into the thickest part of the thigh.

If clear juices run out, the bird is ready; if the juices are pink, it needs longer cooking.

A bird which is being boiled or casseroled will be ready when a skewer penetrates the thigh easily.

Carving poultry

1 First, cut off both legs. Hold the leg in position with a fork while you use a sharp knife to sever the thigh joint.

2 Remove the wings on both sides of the breast.

3 Carve the meat from the breast downwards, in thin or thick slices, according to your preference.

4 Very small chickens, called poussins or double poussins, serve 1–2 people. Cut in half with a knife or poultry shears before serving. This applies also to small game birds.

5 When carving a turkey, make sure you serve a mixture of white meat, from the breast, and dark meat, from the body and legs.

WILD BIRDS and animals, hunted and killed for their flesh, are termed game. They may be hunted only at certain times; out of season, they are protected by law.

From the dawn of recorded history, the hunting, at least of larger game, has been the prerogative of the rich. In Norman England, penalties of fearful savagery were inflicted on those who stole the king's deer, and well into the 19th century, poachers faced man-traps and even the death sentence in pursuit of their craft.

However, for much of our history, there were always a number of creatures that the peasantry were permitted to hunt and eat. Hare, bustard, heron and, later, rabbit were all poor man's fare, while the gentry preferred the more showy swan, peacock, venison, pheasant and partridge.

Nowadays, many big shoots are owned by syndicates whose members pay huge subscriptions, and even private shoots must sell their 'bag' to defray expenses. The result is that more game is available in shops than ever before. Prices vary from season to season according to scarcity but, generally speaking, in mid-season, game can be cheaper than other meat.

Feathered Game

Frozen birds are generally available all year. Fresh birds, which have a far better flavour, are available only in season. Common British game birds and the dates when they are in season are given below.

Choosing game birds

Look for smooth, pliant legs, with rounded or short spurs on the male.

If unplucked, turn the feathers back to see if the breast is plump and firm.

The plumage of a young bird will not be as bright as that of an older bird.

Avoid a bird that shows signs of having been badly shot (its skin will be 'peppered' with shot marks). Some parts will be decomposing before the rest is tender.

If buying game, use a reputable poulterer whose advice you can rely on. He will certainly pluck and draw game and, given enough notice, will order game especially for you.

Game birds

Red grouse In season: August 12–December 10.
Look for: pointed flight feathers; downy breast feathers; soft, pliant feet.
Hang: for 3–4 days.
Cooking: roast or grill young birds; braise or casserole older birds. If roasting, bard with bacon and take care not to overcook.

Other varieties of grouse are capercaillie, black grouse and ptarmigan.

Partridge In season: September 1–January 31.
Look for: rounded tips on feathers and yellow-brown, pliable feet.
Hang: for 3–4 days.
Cooking: roast or casserole. Baste well during roasting.

Pheasant In season: October 1–January 31 in England; October 1–December 10 in Scotland.
Look for: in young birds, pointed flight feathers and downy breast feathers; older birds have round-tipped feathers.
Hang: 3–10 days.
Cooking: roast or casserole. Often sold as a brace, a cock and a hen. The hen has a more delicate flavour and is usually more tender.

Pigeon In season: throughout the year, but at its best from August to October.
Look for: pink legs in a young bird, which darken as the bird gets older.
Hang: for 24 hours.
Cooking: braise, casserole, pot-roast or use in a pie. Pigeon is a dry bird and needs plenty of liquid in cooking and some fat, such as bacon rashers.

Quail In season: all the year round. Most are imported because it is illegal to kill wild quail. At their best from June to September.
Look for: pointed flight feathers; soft feet with rounded spurs.
Do not hang: they must be eaten fresh. Do not draw.
Cooking: roast, grill or casserole.

Snipe In season: August 12–January 31.
Look for: plump breast, pliable feet.
Hang: for 3–4 days. Do not draw.
Cooking: these are very small birds, best roasted, lightly and quickly.

Snipe are usually trussed complete with the head, and the long beak is pushed through the wings and legs, from one side to the other, to act as a skewer.

Wild duck In season: September 1–30.
Look for: in a mallard (one of the largest of the wild duck), plump breast; brightly coloured feet; soft, pliable breastbone; brittle beak. In a teal (a small, wild duck), there is a blue-green strip around the eyes.
Hang: mallard, 24 hours. Do not hang teal.
Cooking: both mallard and teal are good roasted. The mallard will serve 2–3 people, the teal 1 person. Teal is regarded as the best of all wild duck; the duck (female) mallard is better in flavour than the drake.

Woodcock In season: October 1–January 31.
Look for: a plump, firm breast; pliable feet.
Hang: about 3 days. Do not draw.
Cooking: roast or braise.

Hanging

Hang by the neck, unplucked and undrawn, in an airy, cool larder or pantry. Do not hang two or three together: there should be a free circulation of air around each bird.

If flies are a nuisance, dredge the birds with pepper or enclose in a loose muslin bag.

Hang, in general, for the length of time listed (above) for the particular bird. But hanging time depends on age and condition, and the weather. If the weather is warm and humid the bird will decompose faster.

Pheasant, grouse, snipe and partridge are hung for longer than most birds to develop the flavour, but keep personal preferences in mind; although some people like a really 'high' flavour from longer hanging, others do not.

Plucking and drawing

Follow the instructions for plucking and drawing poultry (see pp. 144–5).

Roast game is often served with the feet still on the bird. If you decide to do this, after plucking scald the feet in boiling water and scrub clean.

Cooking
Young birds are best roasted. If you have an older, tougher bird, braise or casserole it.

In general, small birds such as quail, snipe and woodcock provide a meal for 1 person. After roasting, they are often served on a slice of crustless fried bread or hot buttered toast.

Even if you do not make a forcemeat to stuff a game bird, if roasting you can put one or two small pieces of butter in the body, a few pieces of juicy steak, a peeled, cored apple or a whole, skinned onion to give moisture.

About 10 minutes before a roast bird is served, remove the strips of bacon covering the breast. Baste well with butter and pan juices, dredge with seasoned flour, baste again and return to the oven. This gives a good, golden-brown, crispy finish.

To give a distinctive flavour to game and counteract any fattiness, flame it with brandy when almost cooked. Heat 1–2 tablespoons in a ladle, set it alight and pour over the bird.

VENISON

Venison is the meat of the deer. The buck is in season from June 1 to September 30, the doe from October 1 to December 31. Venison is usually bought in joints—the haunch (leg) and the saddle (back) are regarded as best for roasting. Chops from the saddle, loin and neck should be used for braising. Venison is dry and inclined to be tough, so after it is hung for at least 7 days (2 weeks if the weather is cold and dry), you can put it in a marinade to tenderise it.

If roasting, cover with rashers of bacon. Baste frequently.

If casseroling or braising, cook with red wine, onions and root vegetables. You can also cook venison in a pie, with a little fat pork to give moisture.

Serve with a redcurrant or rowan jelly (see pp. 340, 343); gravy enriched with soured cream; potatoes; and a purée of Brussels sprouts and chestnuts.

FURRED GAME

Wild rabbits and hares are in season from September to March. In a young animal, look for smooth, sharp claws, soft, delicate ears and small, white teeth. If the animal has dry, ragged ears and blunt claws, it is older and suitable for casseroling, not roasting.

Rabbits must be fresh, with firm, plump, flesh. Wild rabbits are smaller than domesticated animals, but have a better flavour. Young hares (leverets) are good for roasting.

If possible, have the animal prepared by your poulterer. Most are sold already hung, whole or jointed. If you have a whole, unprepared animal, hang in a cool place by the feet, a hare for 7–10 days, a rabbit for up to 24 hours.

For a hare, place a bowl under the head to collect the blood. It can be used to thicken the gravy, and it is often an ingredient in jugged hare. Add a little vinegar or flour so that it does not coagulate.

Skinning
1 Put the animal on several sheets of paper on a table. Using a sharp knife, cut off the feet.
2 With a sharp pair of scissors, cut the skin along the belly and ease the skin away from the flesh.
3 Pull the skin over the back legs. Holding the back legs firmly in one hand, pull the skin towards the head, easing it off the forelegs and head. Cut off the head.

Paunching
Paunching rabbits or hares must be done soon after skinning.
1 Using a pair of sharp scissors, cut open the belly, up to the breastbone.
2 Draw out and remove all the internal organs. Keep the kidneys, liver and heart for stock or as a base for a sauce, and discard the others.
3 Wipe clean inside and out.

Jointing
Rabbits and hares are usually jointed, if they are to be casseroled or braised.
1 With a sharp knife, cut away the skin flaps below the rib cage. Discard.
2 Slice the carcase in half lengthways, cutting down the backbone.
3 Cut off the hind legs at the thigh, slicing through the joint.
4 Remove the forelegs, cutting through the shoulder joints.
5 Divide the carcase in half along the backbone and cut each half into two serving portions.
6 If you intend to use the saddle for roasting, joint as above but leave the backbone complete.

Cooking
Roast a young hare whole, stuffed with a forcemeat (see pp. 156–7), or roast the saddle; otherwise cook it in a casserole.

Roast a young rabbit, or use it in a fricassée, stew or pie.

An old hare is better for being marinated overnight before cooking.

A general guide to roasting poultry and game birds

Type of bird	Weight	Time	Temperature
Chicken	1–8 lb. (450 g.–3·6 kg.)	15–20 minutes per lb. (450 g.) + 20 minutes	180°C (350°F)—gas mark 4
Duck	3–6 lb. (1·4–2·7 kg.)	20 minutes per lb. (450 g.) + 20 minutes	190°C (375°F)—gas mark 5
Goose	6–10 lb. (2·7–4·5 kg.)	20 minutes per lb. (450 g.) + 20 minutes	190°C (375°F)—gas mark 5
Guinea Fowl	1¼–4 lb. (575 g.–1·8 kg.)	20 minutes per lb. (450 g.) + 20 minutes	180°C (350°F)—gas mark 4
Turkey	6–10 lb. (2·7–4·5 kg.)	20 minutes per lb. (450 g.) + 20 minutes	180°C (350°F)—gas mark 4
	10–18 lb. (4·5–8·1 kg.)	15 minutes per lb. (450 g.) + 15 minutes	180°C (350°F)—gas mark 4
Grouse		30–40 minutes	190°C (375°F)—gas mark 5
Partridge		30–45 minutes	190°C (375°F)—gas mark 5
Pheasant (hen)		45 minutes–1 hour	190°C (375°F)—gas mark 5
Pheasant (cock)		1–1½ hours	190°C (375°F)—gas mark 5
Quail, Snipe and Woodcock		20 minutes	200°C (400°F)—gas mark 6

For poultry and game stuffed with a forcemeat, allow an extra 15–20 minutes for a bird weighing up to 3½ lb. (1·6 kg.); 30–45 minutes for birds weighing 4–10 lb. (1·8–4·5 kg.).

These are general guidelines only: see individual recipes for specific cooking times.

OATMEAL
EGGS
ANJOU
CREAM

Of

SAUCES, FORCEMEATS, DUMPLINGS, HERBS AND SPICES

CONTAINING

NUMEROUS *Useful* FAMILY RECIPES

for SIMPLE & ELABORATE SAUCES, SUSTAINING FORCEMEATS, ENRICHING DUMPLINGS & other SAVOURY ADDITIONS

PAGES 150 – 159

AND

A SELECTION of RECIPES from OTHER LANDS

PAGES 160 – 161

AND WITH

DIRECTIONS *for* BASIC METHODS

for all kinds of Preparing, Flavouring, Cooking and Use of Savoury Accompaniments to Perfection

PAGES 162 – 165

PARSLEY SAUCE
Countrywide

'THE EXCELLENCY of this Hearbe accordeth with the frequent use thereof', wrote Henry Buttes, Fellow of Corpus Christi College, Cambridge. Almost 400 years later parsley remains the best known and most used of all herbs, although it is no longer true to assert, as Henry Buttes did, that 'there is almost no meate or sauce which will not have parsley either in it or about it'.

It is recorded that Henry VIII liked rabbit served with a sauce of parsley, boiled butter and verjuice (made from crab apples), seasoned with salt and pepper and thickened with breadcrumbs. This was clearly an early version of the melted-butter parsley sauce recommended by Mrs Beeton in the 19th century.

Parsley sauce is the classic complement to broad beans and carrots. Serve it also with boiled bacon, ham, poultry and all white fish.

PREPARATION TIME: 10 MINUTES
COOKING TIME: 15–20 MINUTES

INGREDIENTS FOR FOUR

1 pint (575/600 ml.) milk
1½ oz. (40 g.) butter
1½ oz. (40 g.) plain flour
4 tablespoons finely chopped parsley
Salt and white pepper

Heat the milk gently in a pan, remove from the heat, cover and set aside.

Melt the butter gently in a small saucepan. Add the flour, mixing with a wooden spoon until smooth, and continue to cook for 2–3 minutes, stirring all the time.

Remove from the heat and add the warm milk, stirring continuously. Return the pan to the heat and bring to the boil, still stirring, then simmer for about 5 minutes more, stirring from time to time.

When the sauce is smooth and creamy, add the finely chopped parsley and season to taste. Do not cook further because the taste of the fresh parsley may be lost. Serve hot with poached fish, boiled meats, poultry or vegetables. Chives, tarragon or a mixture of fresh herbs can be used in place of parsley. To make shrimp sauce, add 2 oz. (50 g.) peeled shrimps to the basic sauce, with a pinch of Cayenne pepper and a tablespoon of sherry.

Parsley—the sauce fit for King Henry VIII—with broad beans and chicken.

CHEESE SAUCE
Somerset and Cheshire

ENGLISH CHEESE SAUCES are best made with Cheddar or Cheshire. Cheddar gives a sharper tang to the sauce, but Cheshire is more appropriate with recipes from farmhouses in the north of England. Experiment with other strong cheeses, if you like. The character of the sauce will change, sometimes subtly, sometimes dramatically.

PREPARATION TIME: 15 MINUTES
COOKING TIME: 15 MINUTES

INGREDIENTS FOR FOUR

1 pint (575/600 ml.) milk
1½ oz. (40 g.) butter
1½ oz. (40 g.) plain flour
1 teaspoon mustard powder
4 oz. (100/125 g.) Cheddar or Cheshire cheese, grated
A pinch of Cayenne pepper or ¼ teaspoon ground nutmeg

Heat the milk through gently in a saucepan. Remove when warm, cover with the lid and set aside. Melt the butter over the same gentle heat in another pan. Mix in the flour, using a wooden spoon, and continue to cook gently for 2–3 minutes, stirring all the time. Add the mustard powder.

Remove from the heat and add the warm milk, stirring continuously. Return the pan to the heat and bring the sauce up to the boil, still stirring, then simmer for about 5 minutes, stirring from time to time.

When the sauce is creamy, add the grated cheese, a little at a time, stirring it in as it melts. If the sauce is too thick, thin it with a little extra milk. Season to taste.

This sauce is an excellent accompaniment to fish, eggs, and broccoli as well as the more usual cauliflower.

Wow-wow Sauce: Dr Kitchiner's spicy relish of mustard, port and pickled walnuts.

WOW-WOW SAUCE
Home Counties

WHEN DR WILLIAM KITCHINER, scientist and enjoyer of the good things of life, died in 1827, a friend wrote of him that 'to invent odd things and give them odd names was his special hobby'. This is probably as close as we shall ever get to knowing why the doctor, who created the sauce, should have called it 'Wow-wow'. The name may be derived from an exclamation at the sauce's spiciness, or more fancifully, since it was thought to go rather well with venison, from the warning bark of a deer. Only Kitchiner knew the truth, and he took his secret with him.

The recipe first appeared in his *Cook's Oracle* (1817). It is easy to prepare, and excellent for serving with grills at barbecues; the name alone should provide a useful conversational gambit.

PREPARATION TIME: 10 MINUTES
COOKING TIME: 20 MINUTES

INGREDIENTS FOR FOUR TO SIX

- *2 oz. (50 g.) butter*
- *1 oz. (25 g.) plain flour*
- *½ pint (275/300 ml.) stock (see pp. 33–34)*
- *1 tablespoon vinegar*
- *1 teaspoon prepared English mustard*
- *1 tablespoon mushroom ketchup or port*
- *1 tablespoon finely chopped parsley*
- *6 pickled walnuts, diced*

Melt the butter in a pan over a low heat. Stir in the flour and cook gently for 2–3 minutes, stirring all the time. Gradually add the stock, stirring well to avoid lumps.

When the sauce is smooth and creamy, add the vinegar, mustard and ketchup or port. Simmer, stirring from time to time, until it has the consistency you want.

Stir in the chopped parsley and the diced pickled walnuts. Let the sauce heat through for another minute or so, and serve hot with boiled beef or lamb chops.

CHESTNUT SAUCE
Countrywide

EARLY COOKS BELIEVED that chestnuts 'doo noursysshe the bodye strongely'. They were often roasted in the embers of the kitchen fire and used as a basic accompaniment to meat in the days before potatoes were generally available.

Even after this they remained popular. In *The Art of Cookery* (1747), Hannah Glasse gives an early description of chestnut sauce. She tells her readers to take some roasted chestnuts and 'put them into some good gravy with a little white wine, and thicken it with a piece of butter rolled in flour'. The recipe that follows is a modern version.

PREPARATION TIME: 1 HOUR
COOKING TIME: 30 MINUTES

INGREDIENTS FOR FOUR

- *20 chestnuts, slit along one side*
- *1 oz. (25 g.) butter*
- *6 button mushrooms, wiped and finely chopped*
- *½ pint (275/300 ml.) consommé, stock or milk*
- *Salt and pepper*

Put the chestnuts in a large pan with a little water. Bring to the boil, then simmer for 30 minutes or until tender. Drain, and remove the shells and skins while they are still warm. Pound the chestnuts in a mortar with a pestle, or rub them through a sieve.

Place the chestnuts in the cleaned pan with the butter, chopped mushrooms and consommé, stock or milk. Stir well with a wooden spoon and bring slowly to the boil, still stirring. Season to taste. If the sauce is too thick, add a little more liquid. Serve hot.

You can also make chestnut sauce in a liquidiser. Reduce the shelled, skinned chestnuts and other ingredients to a purée, then heat through in a saucepan. As a variation, replace the mushrooms with two small, finely chopped shallots.

Serve chestnut sauce with ham, game or turkey.

HORSERADISH SAUCE
Countrywide

FOR CENTURIES THE MAIN USES of horseradish were medicinal, and it is possible that the practice of serving grated horseradish with roast beef was introduced to aid digestion.

By the 17th century, however, horseradish sauce had assumed a recognisable form. Sir Kenelm Digby, the Stuart author, naval commander, cook and student of philosophy and chemistry, gives a recipe that could be followed today. He advises adding vinegar to the grated horseradish and 'very little sugar, not so much as to be tasted but to quicken (by contrariety) the taste of the other'.

PREPARATION TIME: 30 MINUTES

INGREDIENTS FOR SIX

1 large horseradish root, to give 4 tablespoons when grated
1 tablespoon caster sugar
½ teaspoon mustard powder
About 2 tablespoons white wine vinegar
¼ pint (150 ml.) double cream, lightly whipped

Wash and peel the horseradish root, then grate it finely into a bowl. Stir in the sugar, mustard and vinegar, and add the lightly whipped cream. Chill in the refrigerator before serving with roast beef, smoked fish and salads.

Horseradish gives out fumes even more pungent than those of onions, so a more comfortable method of preparing the clean, peeled root is to chop it roughly and place it in the mincer or shredder attachment of an electric food mixer with a little water. Drain, then add the other ingredients.

To make hot horseradish sauce, grate about 3 tablespoons of the root into ½ pint (275/300 ml.) white sauce (see p. 162). Simmer, stirring from time to time, for about 10 minutes. Hot horseradish sauce goes well with boiled salt beef and fish.

ONION SAUCE
Countrywide

SIR THOMAS ELYOT, diplomat and author, wrote in the *Castel of Health* (1539) that 'onyons beying eaten in great abundance with meate, they cause one to sleape soundly'. Maybe this belief lingering on led to lamb cutlets with onion sauce being such a popular Edwardian supper dish. Today, however, it is gourmets and not insomniacs who look on the combination with favour.

PREPARATION TIME: 15 MINUTES
COOKING TIME: 30–40 MINUTES

INGREDIENTS FOR FOUR TO SIX

1 lb. (450 g.) onions, peeled and thinly sliced
2 oz. (50 g.) butter
1 pint (575/600 ml.) milk or stock (see pp. 33–34)
A pinch of ground mace
A pinch of ground nutmeg
Salt
Freshly ground black pepper
1 oz. (25 g.) plain flour

Melt 1 oz. (25 g.) of butter in a large pan and slowly fry the sliced onions, stirring from time to time, until they are soft but not brown. Meanwhile, heat the milk or stock in another pan. Remove from the heat when hot.

Add the milk or stock to the onions. Season with the mace and nutmeg and add salt and pepper to taste. Simmer for 10–15 minutes, then strain; reserve liquid and onion.

Melt the remaining 1 oz. (25 g.) of butter in the cleaned pan. Add the flour, stirring with a wooden spoon, and cook gently for 2–3 minutes. Remove from the heat and gradually add the onion liquid, stirring all the time to avoid lumps.

Chop all the drained onions very finely, or rub them through a sieve and add them to the sauce, stirring well. Heat through again and serve hot with mutton, lamb, or rabbit.

CRANBERRY SAUCE
Countrywide

DIFFERENT VARIETIES of cranberry, all with acid-tasting crimson berries, occur in peat bogs in many of the chillier parts of the northern hemisphere. The name comes from 17th-century German settlers in New England, who, having recognised the fruits, gave them their own name of 'craneberries'. Eventually the word came into use here, where hitherto the berries had been known as 'marshworts'. But whatever the name, they make an excellent sauce for game.

PREPARATION TIME: 10 MINUTES
COOKING TIME: 20 MINUTES

INGREDIENTS FOR SIX TO EIGHT

1 lb. (450 g.) fresh cranberries
½ pint (275/300 ml.) water
12 oz. (350 g.) sugar
Juice of ½ orange (optional)

Wash and pick over the cranberries, removing the stalks and discarding any damaged fruit.

Heat the water and sugar gently in a saucepan until the sugar dissolves. Add the cranberries and bring to the boil. Remove from the heat and strain in the orange juice, if used. Return to the heat and simmer for about 10 minutes or until the cranberries are tender. Stir occasionally to prevent the fruit from sticking, but do not crush the fruit. Skim. Serve with poultry, game, pork or ham.

BREAD SAUCE
Scotland

BREAD SAUCE is one of the last medieval sauces remaining in general use.

In the days before kitchen ranges provided hobs for simmering, almost all sauces had to be thickened with breadcrumbs. Occasionally an early recipe suggested that 'for a lord, it shall be thickened with yolks of eggs well beaten'.

This milk-based sauce, first recorded in Scotland, is occasionally maligned because of the unfortunate practice of boiling the breadcrumbs for too long. To avoid this, serve the sauce immediately and do not re-boil.

PREPARATION TIME: 25 MINUTES
COOKING TIME: 45 MINUTES

INGREDIENTS FOR FOUR

1 medium onion, peeled
4 cloves
¼ teaspoon ground mace
4 peppercorns
¾ pint (450 ml.) milk
8 rounded tablespoons fresh white breadcrumbs
1 rounded teaspoon butter
2 tablespoons single cream
Salt and pepper

Stick the onion with the cloves and put it in a pan with the mace, peppercorns and the milk. Bring it to the boil, then remove it from the heat immediately and leave it to infuse, covered, for about 30 minutes.

Strain the milk into another pan and stir in the breadcrumbs. Return to the heat, stirring continuously until the mixture boils and becomes quite thick.

Season to taste, and stir in the butter and the cream. Serve warm but do not re-boil.

Serve the sauce with roast chicken, turkey and game.

Mustard Sauce
North-east England & Orkney

The Romans thought that many things tasted better with mustard, and so took the seeds with them to the outermost parts of the empire, such as Britain, where the plants have flourished ever since. This was an especial boon in the Middle Ages, when imported spices were beyond the means of most people in northern Europe, and great play was made with the few home-grown spices available, such as mustard and horseradish.

This sauce is Scandinavian in origin, and is therefore most widely used in those parts of the country settled by the Danes and Norsemen during the Dark Ages. In Yorkshire it is frequently eaten with pork, and in the Northern Isles with herring or cod.

Preparation Time: 5 minutes
Cooking Time: 15 minutes

Ingredients for Four

1 pint (575/600 ml.) milk
1½ oz. (40 g.) butter
1 oz. (25 g.) plain flour
1 tablespoon mustard powder
1 tablespoon vinegar
1 teaspoon sugar
Salt

Put the milk in a pan over a gentle heat. Remove when warm, put the lid on the pan and set aside. Melt the butter over the same gentle heat in another pan. Mix in the flour with a wooden spoon until smooth, and continue to cook gently for 2–3 minutes, stirring all the time.

Remove from the heat and add the warm milk, stirring continuously. Return to the heat and bring the sauce up to the boil, stirring. Simmer for 5 minutes, stirring from time to time.

When the sauce is smooth and creamy remove from the heat and stir in the mustard, vinegar, sugar and salt.

Serve hot with grilled herrings or mackerel, cold with cold meats. If serving cold, cover the surface of the warm sauce with a circle of greaseproof paper dipped in cold water and place wet side down. Cover with a lid. This prevents a skin from forming.

Cumberland Sauce
Countrywide

Queen Victoria's uncle, the Duke of Cumberland, is said to be honoured in the name of this sauce, although no one seems to know how or when the Cumberland label became attached. During the last year of Victoria's reign, and under various names, the sauce became an almost inseparable companion to any game dish. It was an especial favourite as an accompaniment to pheasant and partridge at hunt breakfasts in High Leicestershire, even though its colour did not complement hunting pink quite so well as the more traditional redcurrant jelly.

Preparation Time: 20 minutes
Cooking Time: 1 hour

Ingredients for Eight to Ten

1 lb. (450 g.) redcurrant jelly
½ bottle port
Grated rind and juice of 1 orange and 1 lemon
¼ teaspoon Cayenne pepper
2 tablespoons Worcestershire sauce

Place the redcurrant jelly in a small saucepan. Add the port and bring to the boil, stirring from time to time. Cook over a gentle heat until the liquid is reduced by about one-third and just runny. Leave to cool.

Stir in the grated orange and lemon rinds and strain in the orange and lemon juice. Add the Cayenne pepper and the Worcestershire sauce, and mix well.

Serve Cumberland Sauce cold as an excellent complement to all cold meats and game and even to hot dishes of ham or tongue. It will keep for about two months in a screw-top jar under refrigeration.

Laver Sauce
Wales

Laver, sometimes known as sea spinach, is a highly nutritious seaweed found along parts of Britain's west coast. In South Wales and parts of the West Country, it is regularly collected and eaten.

Prepared laver—washed and boiled to a pulp—is often called laver bread, and can be bought in some Health Food shops in Britain. Store it in a freezer, or in a sterilised screw-top jar in a cool place for about 1 week, for use as needed.

Addicts maintain that nothing is finer than Laver Sauce with roast mutton, lamb or even shellfish. You can also eat laver for breakfast, made into flat cakes with oatmeal.

Preparation Time: 5 minutes
Cooking Time: 10 minutes

Ingredients for Four to Six

8 oz. (225 g.) prepared laver
1 oz. (25 g.) butter
Juice of 1 Seville (bitter) orange
2–3 tablespoons gravy
Pepper

Put the prepared laver in a heavy-based aluminium pan with the butter, orange juice, gravy and pepper to taste. Heat gently, stirring with a wooden spoon, until the ingredients are thoroughly blended. Serve hot with roast lamb or mutton.

To make a sauce for fish or shellfish, replace the gravy with 2–3 tablespoons of single cream.

For a breakfast dish, season the prepared laver with salt, pepper and a dash of lemon juice or wine vinegar. Shape into flat cakes, coat with medium-ground oatmeal and fry in bacon fat for 6–8 minutes. Serve with eggs and bacon.

CELERY SAUCE
Countrywide

IT WAS NOT UNTIL the 17th century that celery was developed in its present form. Italian gardeners were mainly responsible, using as a prototype the wild celery known in England as smallage.

Smallage and, to a certain extent, the aromatic herbs lovage and alexanders had been used since early days both for medicinal purposes and to provide a celery-like flavour. But smallage has a bitter, 'ungrateful' taste when raw, so the new vegetable was welcomed in Europe. It did not, however, come into general use in England and America until the 19th century. It was then that country housewives discovered its suitability as an accompaniment for poultry and ham, particularly in a sauce such as the one that follows.

PREPARATION TIME: 20 MINUTES
COOKING TIME: 45 MINUTES

INGREDIENTS FOR SIX

- *1 large head of celery or 2 celery hearts, washed, drained and finely chopped*
- *1 pint (575/600 ml.) water, or chicken stock (see pp. 33–34)*
- *Salt*
- *Pepper*
- *¼ teaspoon ground nutmeg*
- *1½ oz. (40 g.) butter*
- *1½ oz. (40 g.) plain flour*
- *¾ pint (450 ml.) milk*
- *2 tablespoons single cream (optional)*

Put the chopped celery in a pan with the water or stock. Bring it to the boil, then simmer, covered, until tender—about 20 minutes. Drain, reserving the cooking liquid, and rub the celery through a sieve or liquidise it. Season with salt, pepper and nutmeg.

Melt 1 oz. (25 g.) of the butter and stir in 1 oz. (25 g.) of the flour. Cook gently, stirring continuously with a wooden spoon, for 2–3 minutes.

Add the milk and ¼ pint (150 ml.) of the celery stock, stirring well to avoid lumps. Bring to the boil, then simmer for about 5 minutes. Stir in the puréed celery.

Blend the remaining ½ oz. (15 g.) of butter with the ½ oz. (15 g.) of flour, and add to the sauce in small pieces, stirring well until the sauce appears smooth and thick. You can add 2 tablespoons of cream, if liked. Serve hot.

Celery sauce goes well with ham, roast or boiled poultry, veal and partridge.

REFORM SAUCE
Home Counties

VICTORIAN COUNTRY GENTLEMEN, who came up to London and dined at the Reform Club, found when they got back home that they could not forget the tangy taste of the sauce that had been served with their grilled mutton chops. It was the creation of the club's chef, Alexis Soyer.

There are some who believe that it should have been named after the chef who created it. He was certainly a remarkable man, always ready to sacrifice personal profit for public benefit. At one stage he helped the government to fight famine in Ireland by establishing special kitchens in Dublin. Later he went to the Crimea to reorganise the victualling of the military hospitals. His good deeds are of the past, but his recipes live on.

Some purists insist that the sauce should include anchovy essence and Harvey's sauce, but this recipe will appeal to the modern taste for a smooth, rich sauce.

PREPARATION TIME: 20 MINUTES
COOKING TIME: 30 MINUTES

INGREDIENTS FOR FOUR TO SIX

- *2 tablespoons wine vinegar*
- *2 tablespoons caster sugar*
- *1 tablespoon black peppercorns, crushed*
- *1 small onion, peeled and finely chopped*
- *½ pint (275/300 ml.) brown gravy or stock (see pp. 115, 33–34)*
- *1 tablespoon redcurrant jelly*
- *2 oz. (50 g.) ham or tongue, sliced matchstick thin and chopped*
- *2 tablespoons finely chopped beetroot*
- *2 small gherkins, sliced very thin*
- *1 hard-boiled egg white, sliced very thin*

Put the vinegar, sugar, crushed peppercorns and finely chopped onion in a pan. Bring to the boil, then simmer for about 20 minutes, stirring occasionally, until the onions are soft. Add the gravy or stock and the redcurrant jelly, stir well and simmer for a further 5 minutes. Strain, and return to the cleaned pan.

Add the sliced ham or tongue, the beetroot, gherkins and hard-boiled egg white. Stir and bring quickly to the boil.

Serve hot with grilled mutton or lamb chops, or cutlets coated with egg and breadcrumbs and then fried. Spoon a little over the chops and serve the rest in a gravy boat.

APPLE SAUCE
Kent

IN THE MIDDLE AGES, a sweet pottage known as 'appulmos' was popular at castle banquets. It was more elaborate than apple sauce, since it contained almond-milk and honey as well as boiled apples. Nonetheless, it probably accompanied a number of dishes, and in Caxton's *The Governal of Health* (1489), it is claimed that: 'Salt and sour meats (foods) can be amended with sweet Apples.'

The modern form of apple sauce was already in existence by the 17th century and was being served then as it is today, with pork and goose. It was particularly popular in apple-growing areas; such as Kent.

PREPARATION TIME: 15 MINUTES
COOKING TIME: 20–25 MINUTES

INGREDIENTS FOR SIX

- *1 lb. (450 g.) cooking apples, peeled, cored and sliced*
- *4–6 tablespoons water*
- *2 oz. (50 g.) butter*
- *2 tablespoons sugar*
- *¼ teaspoon ground nutmeg*
- *¼ teaspoon salt*

Put the sliced apples in a pan with the water. Bring to the boil, then simmer for 15–20 minutes, stirring from time to time with a wooden spoon, until they are soft. Rub the pulp through a sieve or liquidise it.

Melt the butter in the cleaned pan and add the apple purée, sugar, nutmeg and salt. Beat well and taste, adjusting the seasoning if necessary.

The sharpness of apple sauce acts as a foil to the richness of pork, duck, game and mackerel. Serve hot or cold. Gooseberry sauce is made in the same way: use 1 lb. (450 g.) of the fruit, topped and tailed.

BUTTER SAUCE
Countrywide

DURING the Stuart and Georgian periods, butter sauce seems to have been the only form of sauce the British recognised. But what we lacked in variety, we made up in quantity. M. Misson, a Frenchman visiting London in the 1690s, was awed by the English habit of dousing everything—boiled beef, vegetables, mutton, rabbit, pigeon, tongue, ox-tripe and fowls—with liberal libations of butter.

Fortunately for the national cholesterol level, the custom faded somewhat. Even so, if used sparingly, butter sauce still makes an excellent change from the now more usual white sauce. Serve this recipe either as it is, or married to other ingredients such as parsley or anchovy.

PREPARATION TIME: 5 MINUTES
COOKING TIME: 20–30 MINUTES

INGREDIENTS FOR FOUR TO SIX

1 oz. (25 g.) plain flour
¼ teaspoon ground nutmeg
¼ teaspoon freshly ground black pepper
½ pint (275/300 ml.) water
6 oz. (175 g.) butter, cut in small pieces
Salt

Half fill the bottom of a double boiler or a large pan with water. Bring to the boil and remove from the heat. Place the top of the double boiler or a large bowl in position over the water. Put in the flour, nutmeg and pepper and mix in the ½ pint (275/300 ml.) of cold water. Return to the heat but do not allow to boil; stir with a wooden spoon until it makes a smooth paste.

When it is hot, add the butter, either stirring vigorously or whisking until all the ingredients are blended. The sauce will be smooth and creamy, just slightly thickened. Season with salt just before serving.

The sauce will keep for about 30 minutes away from the heat but over hot water. Do not leave it over boiling water or the butter will become oily. Beat well before serving hot.

Serve with poached and grilled fish, asparagus and broccoli. Stir in the juice of half a lemon if you want a sharper flavour, or add 1 tablespoon of anchovy essence.

TO MAKE CRAB SAUCE

Add 4 oz. (100/125 g.) diced crabmeat to the sauce with the juice of half a lemon. Blend well together.

TO MAKE CUCUMBER SAUCE

Peel and de-seed a 3 in. (8 cm.) length of cucumber. Chop finely and add to a pan containing about ½ oz. (15 g.) butter. Heat gently for a few minutes, stirring with a wooden spatula, but do not let it fry. Stir into the sauce with the juice of half a lemon and 1 tablespoon of chopped, fresh herbs such as mint or savory.

TO MAKE SHRIMP OR PRAWN SAUCE

Add 4 oz. (100/125 g.) of peeled shrimps or prawns. Heat through and add 1 tablespoon of chopped parsley and a squeeze of lemon juice.

EGG SAUCE
Scotland

MARY, QUEEN OF SCOTS is reputed to have been fond of this fine Scottish sauce. It combines readily available eggs and milk to make a fine accompaniment to white fish such as cod or haddock, and is a refreshing change from the more usual parsley sauce.

PREPARATION TIME: 20 MINUTES
COOKING TIME: 20 MINUTES

INGREDIENTS FOR FOUR TO SIX

2 eggs
1 pint (575/600 ml.) milk
1 bay leaf
4 white peppercorns
2 sprigs parsley
2 oz. (50 g.) butter
2 oz. (50 g.) plain flour
¼ teaspoon grated nutmeg
Salt and pepper

Put the eggs in a small pan and cover with cold water. Bring to the boil, then lower the heat and boil gently, to prevent cracking, for 10 minutes. Plunge the eggs into cold water and shell immediately. Separate the whites from the yolks and chop them separately into small pieces.

Put the milk with the bay leaf, peppercorns and parsley in a pan over a gentle heat. Remove when warm, put the lid on the pan, set aside to infuse for 15 minutes, then strain. Melt the butter over the same gentle heat in a clean pan. Add the flour and nutmeg to the butter and stir with a wooden spoon until smooth. Continue to cook gently for 2–3 minutes, stirring all the time.

Remove from the heat and add the strained, warm milk, stirring continuously. Return the pan to the heat and bring the sauce up to the boil, still stirring, then simmer for about 5 minutes, stirring from time to time.

When smooth, add the chopped egg whites, season generously with salt and pepper and stir in half the chopped yolks. Use the sauce to coat poached fish, or boiled cauliflower.

A taste of Scotland—creamy Egg Sauce coats cod cutlets and potatoes.

BREAD AND HERB STUFFING
Countrywide

SIMPLE MIXTURES of bread and herbs are amongst the earliest recorded stuffings, dating back to the Middle Ages. This particular recipe, however, cannot have been in common use before the end of the 16th century, as tarragon was not introduced into Britain as a seasoning before 1520.

The chives that go with the tarragon are a native plant. Both are believed to stimulate the appetite. This stuffing would be used when the country wife noticed members of her family lacking interest in food, perhaps when they were recovering from mild illnesses. Even if your appetite requires no stimulation, you will find it a savoury addition to roast poultry.

PREPARATION TIME: 20–30 MINUTES

INGREDIENTS TO STUFF A 3½ LB. (1·6 KG.) CHICKEN

3 thick slices stale white bread, with crusts removed

About ¼ pint (150 ml.) milk

1 chicken liver, chopped

1 tablespoon chopped parsley

1 tablespoon chopped, mixed chives and tarragon

Grated rind and juice of ½ lemon

1 small onion or shallot, peeled and chopped

Salt

Pepper

Put the slices of stale bread in a shallow bowl and add just enough milk to cover. Leave to soak for about 20 minutes, until the bread has absorbed the milk but is not sloppy.

Squeeze out any excess moisture and roughly chop the bread. Place the pieces in a bowl and mix in the chopped chicken liver, herbs, grated lemon rind and juice, and chopped onion or shallot. Season well with salt and pepper.

As a variation, add two stalks of celery, finely chopped. To stuff a turkey, use double quantities of the ingredients.

SKIRLIE
Scotland

IT HAS BEEN SAID that just as beef and beer have made Englishmen, so oatcakes and oatmeal have made the Scots. Oats will flourish in a poor soil and a minimum of sunshine that wheat could not tolerate; consequently, oatmeal has always been vital to the Scots cuisine, taking the place of wheat flour and bread in England, and even of meat in some poor areas.

Skirlie is a case in point, since at one time it was served in place of meat. But in these better-off days, it is probably more often used as a poultry stuffing.

The name, incidentally, comes from the noise the suet makes while cooking in the pan, which to the fanciful ear might suggest the skirling of the bagpipes.

PREPARATION TIME: 15 MINUTES

INGREDIENTS TO STUFF A 3½ LB. (1·6 KG.) CHICKEN

4 oz. (100/125 g.) medium or coarse oatmeal

1 medium onion, peeled and chopped

2 oz. (50 g.) shredded suet, or dripping or butter, melted

¼ teaspoon grated nutmeg

½ teaspoon mixed dried herbs

3 tablespoons stock (see pp. 33–34), or whisky

Salt

Pepper

Make sure the oatmeal is completely dry. Put it in a heavy-based pan and shake it over a medium heat for 1–2 minutes.

Place in a mixing bowl and add the chopped onion, fat, nutmeg, herbs and stock or whisky. Blend together well with a fork or wooden spoon and season to taste with salt and pepper.

An alternative method is to heat the suet, dripping or butter in a heavy-based pan and quickly fry the onion in it before mixing in the oatmeal and other ingredients.

Oatmeal stuffing can be cooked like dumplings. Take small spoonfuls and roll into balls, then simmer for 5–10 minutes in stews or soups such as Scotch Broth (see p. 27). It is a good stuffing for all poultry, boiled as well as roast, and fish.

SAGE AND ONION STUFFING
Countrywide

SIR KENELM DIGBY, seaman, philosopher, diplomat and amateur man of science, found time lying somewhat heavily on his hands when he fell into royal disfavour and was banished from the court of Charles II. Casting around for ways of using his many-faceted intellect, he embarked on scientific and literary projects—and also pondered on the more everyday subject of stuffings for birds.

He considered that the wild duck of the time were given over-elaborate and over-rich stuffings, and proposed the simple use of sage and onion. He recommended that the combination be buttered and then worked into a mass before roasting. His invention proved so successful that before long it was used in the preparation of domestic duck, geese and also with pork—as it still is today.

PREPARATION TIME: 20 MINUTES

INGREDIENTS TO STUFF A 4 LB. (1·8 KG.) DUCK

8 oz. (225 g.) onions, peeled and roughly chopped

8 sage leaves or 1 teaspoon dried and rubbed sage

4 oz. (100/125 g.) fresh white breadcrumbs

2 oz. (50 g.) melted butter

1 egg, beaten

Salt and pepper

Put the roughly chopped onions in a small pan with about 4 tablespoons of water. Bring to the boil, then simmer, covered, for about 10 minutes before draining. If using fresh sage, blanch the leaves in boiling water for 1 minute, then drain and chop finely.

Chop the parboiled onions finely and put in a mixing bowl. Add the sage, breadcrumbs, melted butter and beaten egg. Season with salt and pepper, and stir well together so that all the ingredients are thoroughly mixed.

You may also use this stuffing for a goose or for pork. As a variation, peel, core and chop 2 medium cooking apples and cook them with the onion. Or add the finely grated rind of ½ a lemon or orange and 2 teaspoons of soft brown sugar.

VEAL FORCEMEAT
Countrywide

'FORCE HIM with praises, pour in, pour in, his ambition is dry,' wrote William Shakespeare in *Troilus and Cressida*. Although there is no evidence that the great dramatist was ever a cook, it is plain that he understood the role a good forcemeat plays in keeping moist the flesh of a joint or bird.

The recipe that follows came long after his day; it was a favourite of Mrs Beeton and other leading 19th-century cookery writers.

Veal Forcemeat is good in raised pies; try it mixed with ham for an unusual veal and ham pie, or use to stuff veal or turkey.

PREPARATION TIME: 20 MINUTES

INGREDIENTS FOR FOUR TO SIX

8 oz. (225 g.) pie veal
2 oz. (50 g.) raw ham or bacon
4 oz. (100/125 g.) fresh white breadcrumbs
2 oz. (50 g.) suet, shredded, or butter
1 tablespoon chopped parsley
½ teaspoon chopped tarragon
Grated rind of ½ lemon
¼ teaspoon grated nutmeg
1 egg, beaten
Salt and pepper

Pass the veal and ham, or bacon, through the fine blade of a mincer into a mixing bowl. Blend in the breadcrumbs, suet or butter, parsley and tarragon, lemon rind, nutmeg and beaten egg. Finally season well with salt and pepper.

To make a very smooth paste to complement veal or fish, chop the veal and bacon roughly and blend in a liquidiser with the other ingredients. Add the juice of the ½ lemon.

COUNTRY FORCEMEAT
Countrywide

IT IS SOMETIMES DIFFICULT to tell whether our ancestors included particular herbs and spices in their food as flavourings or for their medicinal value.

In bygone days, forcemeat, for example, might well have included herbs such as bitter rue or tansy—neither of which is particularly pleasing to the palate.

This modern version of a country herb stuffing, however, can be enjoyed simply for its flavour. If the herbs also act as an aid to digestion, as herbalists have for centuries declared, so much the better.

PREPARATION TIME: 20 MINUTES

INGREDIENTS FOR FOUR

6 oz. (175 g.) fine white breadcrumbs
4 oz. (100/125 g.) shredded suet
2 oz. (50 g.) lean bacon, diced
Grated rind of ½ lemon
1 tablespoon chopped, mixed parsley, thyme and marjoram
¼ teaspoon grated nutmeg
Salt and pepper
1 egg, beaten

Combine the breadcrumbs with the shredded suet and diced bacon in a large bowl. Stir in the lemon rind, herbs and nutmeg, then season well with salt and pepper. Finally, work in the beaten egg to bind the mixture.

Use this stuffing for all kinds of poultry and meat. For pork, substitute sage for the thyme; use chopped tarragon instead of thyme in veal dishes.

For a very smooth stuffing, blend all the ingredients in a liquidiser. Make small forcemeat balls out of any leftover stuffing, and place round roasting poultry or meat for the last 30 minutes of cooking.

The delicate blending of herbs in Country Forcemeat balls offsets the sweetness of roast pork.

Sausagemeat and Prune Stuffing
Warwickshire

Forcemeats combining fruit, herbs, minced meat and spices were popular from the Middle Ages right up to the 17th century. Prunes were a favourite ingredient in such stuffings, at least in wealthier kitchens, almost from the time they were first imported from the Middle East in the late 1300s. This recipe, still a favourite in Warwickshire, is a lingering echo of those far-off days.

Use it to stuff a goose or a hare.

Soaking Time: overnight
Preparation Time: 40 minutes

Ingredients for Four

6 oz. (175 g.) prunes
About ½ pint (275/300 ml.) wine, red or white
8 oz. (225 g.) sausagemeat
¼ teaspoon ground cinnamon
¼ teaspoon ground ginger
¼ teaspoon grated nutmeg
1 tablespoon chopped parsley
Salt and pepper
1 egg yolk

Wash the prunes and add them to the wine to soak overnight.

Next day, put the soaked prunes and their wine in a large pan. Add more wine if necessary to cover the prunes. Bring to the boil, then simmer for about 20 minutes or until the prunes are soft. Drain, reserving the cooking liquid.

Stone the prunes and chop them finely. Put them in a mixing bowl with the sausagemeat, spices and parsley. Season well with salt and pepper. Stir in enough of the cooking liquid to make a soft mixture. Add the egg yolk and stir well again to blend the ingredients thoroughly.

Chestnut Stuffing
Countrywide

Many of the best English recipes were taken to America by early settlers, and remained popular there even when they became unfashionable at home. Chestnut Stuffing is one of these. By the early part of this century it had dropped out of favour, but 150 years earlier it was much in demand. The 18th-century cookery writer Hannah Glasse, for instance, gives two versions in *The Art of Cookery* (1747). The recipe which follows is one adaptation.

Preparation Time: 40–50 minutes

Ingredients to Stuff a 15 lb. (6·8 kg.) Turkey

1½ lb. (700 g.) chestnuts
1 turkey liver, chopped
4 oz. (100/125 g.) melted butter
Salt
Pepper

Make a slit along the side of each chestnut, place in a large pan and cover with water. Bring to the boil, then simmer, covered, for about 20 minutes or until tender. Remove from the heat, take the lid off the pan but do not drain.

Take the chestnuts out of the hot cooking water one at a time and remove the shells and skins. Mash or chop about half, but leave the remainder whole. Put them all in a mixing bowl and stir in the chopped liver, melted butter, and salt and pepper to taste.

For a variation, use 12 oz. (350 g.) of chestnuts and 12 oz. (350 g.) of sausagemeat, adding 2 tablespoons of chopped parsley and 1 beaten egg.

The medieval way of preparing a goose—with Prune and Sausagemeat Stuffing.

Potato Stuffing
Countrywide

Like many of the more practical and economical country recipes, Potato Stuffing went largely unrecorded in cookery books published in the 18th and 19th centuries. These were intended for town households, not for farms where tradition was valued above the printed word.

It is clear, however, that this stuffing is much later in origin than most stuffings, which date back in some form to the Middle Ages. Potatoes in fact were not brought to England before the end of the 16th century, and did not gain wide acceptance until a hundred years later, when they were grown in large numbers by Irish settlers in Lancashire.

This is a delicious, smooth stuffing, as good eaten cold as hot.

Preparation Time: 40 minutes

Ingredients to Stuff a 10 lb. (4·5 kg.) Goose

1 lb. (450 g.) potatoes, peeled
2 oz. (50 g.) salt pork or smoked bacon, diced
1 medium onion, peeled and chopped
1 teaspoon chopped mixed herbs
8 oz. (225 g.) sausagemeat
Salt and pepper

Boil the peeled potatoes in a large pan for 15–20 minutes or until tender. Drain and mash. Set aside, covered with a cloth to absorb the moisture, and keep warm.

Put the salt pork or bacon in a pan over a low heat until the fat begins to run, then fry the chopped onion with it until soft but not coloured. Add the mashed potatoes, herbs and sausage-meat, mixing well. Season to taste with salt and pepper.

SUET DUMPLINGS
Norfolk

IN THE DAYS before the potato was introduced into the nation's diet, country people would put a ball of flour and fat to boil in the pot containing broth, vegetables and perhaps a bit of rabbit or bacon.

The first dumplings were made in Norfolk, and they became famous. The 17th-century playwright Robert Arnim tells in *The Nest of Ninnies* of a character who 'lookt like a Norfolk Dumpling, thicke and short'. A century later, the essayist Sir Richard Steele wrote in *The Tatler* of 1706 about a Norfolk squire who was reputed to eat 'two pounds' of dumplings at every meal.

Modern appetites will not cope with that quantity, but these dumplings, plain or flavoured with a little horseradish, will disappear fast on a cold day.

PREPARATION TIME: 10 MINUTES
COOKING TIME: 15 MINUTES

INGREDIENTS FOR FOUR

4 oz. (100/125 g.) self-raising flour
2 oz. (50 g.) shredded suet
Salt and pepper
Water to mix

Sieve the flour into a mixing bowl. Stir in the suet and a generous seasoning of salt and pepper. Carefully mix in just enough water to make a soft dough.

Turn on to a floured surface and, with lightly floured hands, shape into balls about the size of large walnuts.

If serving the dumplings with a meat dish such as boiled beef, remove the meat when it is cooked and keep it warm. Bring the cooking liquid up to the boil in a very large pan which will allow enough room for the dumplings to swell during cooking. Put in the dumplings and poach at a gentle boil, turning them over once. They will rise to the surface when they are cooked, after about 15 minutes.

Dumplings can also be cooked with a stew in a very large pan. Add them for the last 15–20 minutes. They will lie on top and cook through in the steam without being turned over.

If the dumplings are to accompany a dish which is not cooked in its own stock, poach them in a large pan of boiling, salted water.

TO MAKE HORSERADISH DUMPLINGS
Have ready about 2 teaspoons of grated horseradish. Carefully roll the dough into walnut-sized balls, then make a hollow in each by pushing a finger into it. Put a portion of the horseradish into each hollow and squeeze the dough over it to seal it in tightly. Horseradish Dumplings are very good with salt beef and carrots.

BREADCRUMB DUMPLINGS
Countrywide

BEFORE modern baking powders became available, breadcrumbs were frequently used in puddings to give a light texture. They improve many suet recipes; dumplings made with them are deliciously fluffy.

For extra flavour, add parsley, chives, sage, or your own choice of herb. Serve the dumplings with beef or chicken stew or poached fish.

PREPARATION TIME: 20 MINUTES
COOKING TIME: 15 MINUTES

INGREDIENTS FOR FOUR

2 oz. (50 g.) fresh white breadcrumbs
2 oz. (50 g.) shredded suet
2 oz. (50 g.) plain flour
½ teaspoon baking powder
1 tablespoon finely chopped parsley, chives, sage or other fresh herb (optional)
Salt and pepper
1 egg, beaten

Put the breadcrumbs, suet, flour, baking powder, and herbs if used, in a large mixing bowl. Season well with salt and pepper, mix together well, then stir in the beaten egg to make a fairly stiff dough. If too stiff, add a teaspoon or so of water.

Turn on to a floured board and, with lightly floured hands, shape them into balls the size of large walnuts.

Poach the dumplings in the same way as Suet Dumplings (see previous recipe).

PARSLEY DUMPLINGS
Countrywide

THE PLIABLE SUET PASTE of dumplings offered a wealth of opportunities to the medieval farmhouse cook. She stuffed them with small birds such as pigeons and even sparrows, buttered them and spiced them, and mixed them with finely chopped onions and pieces of bacon. Above all she added herbs, according to her taste. Occasionally she coloured these herb dumplings with spinach water.

Without the spinach water, the green of the chopped parsley contrasts attractively with the white of the basic dumpling in this recipe.

PREPARATION TIME: 15 MINUTES
COOKING TIME: 15–20 MINUTES

INGREDIENTS FOR FOUR TO SIX

2 oz. (50 g.) self-raising flour
2 oz. (50 g.) fresh breadcrumbs
2 tablespoons shredded suet
1 tablespoon finely chopped parsley
2 teaspoons finely grated lemon rind
Salt
Pepper
1 egg, beaten

Put the flour, breadcrumbs, suet, parsley and grated lemon rind in a large bowl. Mix together well with a fork or wooden spoon. Season with salt and pepper and blend in the beaten egg.

Use lightly floured hands to shape into balls the size of large walnuts. Poach in the same way as Suet Dumplings (see left).

Recipes *from* Other Lands

EGYPT
Stuffing for Vegetables

An Egyptian tradition tells of poor orphan girl, Samia, who worked all day in a vineyard to keep her younger brothers and sisters. One of her tasks was to thin out the leaves that shaded the young grapes. She was so poor that instead of throwing the leaves away she took them home and cooked them, wrapping them round handfuls of seasoned rice.

One day the vineyard owner promised a fine dowry to any girl who could produce a dish to tempt his favourite wife. Needless to say, Samia won the prize with her stuffed vine leaves. And so was born one of the world's great dishes.

Preparation Time: 20 minutes
Cooking Time: about 10 minutes

Ingredients for Four to Six

2 tablespoons olive or vegetable oil
1 medium onion, finely chopped
1 clove garlic, peeled and crushed
2 oz. (50 g.) long-grain rice
6 oz. (175 g.) beef or lamb, minced
2 large tomatoes, skinned and chopped
1 tablespoon sultanas, currants or seedless raisins
2 oz. (50 g.) pine nuts or chopped walnuts (optional)
¼ teaspoon ground cinnamon or allspice
Rind of ¼ orange or lemon, finely grated
5 leaves fresh mint, chopped, or ½ teaspoon dried mint
1½ tablespoons chopped parsley
Salt and ground black pepper

Heat the oil in a heavy-based pan and gently fry the chopped onion for a few minutes, stirring from time to time. When it is soft, but not brown, add the crushed garlic and the rice. Cook over a low heat for 2 minutes, until the rice begins to look translucent. Stir in the minced meat and cook for 2–3 minutes more.

Remove from the heat and place in a mixing bowl. Add the tomatoes, dried fruit and nuts. Stir well. Add the spice, orange or lemon rind, herbs, salt and pepper to taste. Stir again.

Use this stuffing for vine leaves, sweet peppers, cabbage or marrow, and cook the stuffed vegetable for up to an hour. Leave room for the rice to swell as it cooks.

Dried apricots, soaked overnight and chopped finely, make a good substitute for the sultanas, currants or raisins. You can make the mixture without the meat and use it for stuffing breast of lamb.

Vary the herbs and spices as you like: basil, oregano, ground mace, ginger or saffron are all good. About 2 teaspoons of fresh orange or lemon juice or a little rosewater will give another change of flavour.

ITALY
Fresh Tomato Sauce

It is difficult to imagine Italian cookery without tomato sauce. Certainly Italy was the first European country to adopt the *pomodoro* or 'golden apple' without reservations. The claim is even made that a monk, Brother Serenio, brought tomato seeds to Italy from China in the 15th century, although generally it is accepted that the tomato did not reach Europe until the 16th century—and then from the New World.

The tomato and the many dishes based on it thrive in the hot southern districts of Italy. There are few more simple and satisfying summer dishes than this sauce served over a plate of pasta with a little grated cheese.

Preparation Time: 15 minutes
Cooking Time: 35–45 minutes

Ingredients for Four

1½ oz. (40 g.) butter or 1 tablespoon olive oil
1 small onion, peeled and finely chopped
*2 lb. (900 g.) ripe tomatoes, skinned (**see p. 198**) and quartered, or a large tin of tomatoes*
1 bay leaf
1 sprig thyme
2 tablespoons red wine (optional)
1 clove garlic, peeled and crushed
¼ teaspoon salt
¼ teaspoon sugar
¼ teaspoon freshly ground black pepper
2 teaspoons lemon juice
½ teaspoon each finely chopped fresh basil and marjoram, or ¼ teaspoon each dried

Heat the butter or oil in a large, heavy-based pan. Add the onion and cook gently, stirring occasionally, until it is soft but not brown. Put the tomatoes in the pan with the bay leaf, thyme, wine, garlic and salt. Stir, cover and simmer until tender.

Rub through a sieve and return to the cleaned pan. Bring to the boil and cook for about 20 minutes until reduced to a purée. Season with sugar, pepper, lemon juice and the herbs. Taste, and adjust the seasoning.

Fresh tomatoes, herbs, red wine and lemon make the traditional sauce for pasta.

FRANCE
Mayonnaise

THE SECRET of making perfect mayonnaise lies in the 'unremitting beating of the olive oil into the egg yolks'. That was the pronouncement of Antonin Carême (1784–1833), the master chef generally regarded as the founder of classic French cookery. He called the sauce 'magnonaise', although the spelling 'mayonnaise' was current at the same time. No one knows quite how the name originated, but it may have come from the Minorcan town, Mahon.

Whatever its origins, it does not take a great deal of skill and patience to make this classic sauce, a rich and subtle complement to many cold dishes and salads. You can even whisk it up in an electric mixer or a liquidiser. Make sure all the ingredients are at room temperature before you start. If the mayonnaise curdles, beat another egg yolk in a clean bowl, then beat the curdled mixture into it, drop by drop.

PREPARATION TIME: 20 MINUTES

INGREDIENTS FOR FOUR TO SIX

2 egg yolks
1 tablespoon lemon juice or wine vinegar
¼ teaspoon salt
¼ teaspoon mustard powder
½ pint (275/300 ml.) olive or vegetable oil
Water
¼ teaspoon freshly ground black pepper

Put the egg yolks in a mixing bowl and whisk well for 1 minute. Add the lemon juice or vinegar, the salt and the mustard powder and beat the mixture for 1 minute more.

Add the oil, drop by drop, whisking continuously. After about a quarter of the oil has been added, the mayonnaise takes on the consistency of thin cream. The rest of the oil can be added more rapidly; beat well after each addition.

Put a little water on to boil. When all the oil has been absorbed, whisk in 1 tablespoon of boiling water. This helps to ensure that the mayonnaise will not curdle and will keep better. Taste, add a little more lemon juice and salt if necessary, and stir in the freshly ground black pepper.

You may flavour the mayonnaise with finely chopped fresh herbs, garlic, onions or tomato purée.

FRANCE
Hollandaise Sauce

THE RENOWNED French chef Auguste Escoffier (1846–1935) listed Hollandaise Sauce as one of five basic sauces which no cook—in town or country—should be without. This classic French sauce is, as its name suggests, of Dutch origin, and was originally made with best butter on Dutch farms.

It made its debut in France in the 18th century and soon crossed to England, where it quickly became popular. Later, in the 1860s, Mrs Beeton recommended it to her readers as a valuable accompaniment to fish and vegetables.

Hollandaise Sauce should be served warm with fish, or with vegetables such as asparagus, broccoli, courgettes or artichokes.

PREPARATION TIME: 5 MINUTES
COOKING TIME: 10–15 MINUTES

INGREDIENTS FOR FOUR TO SIX

8 oz. (225 g.) butter
3 egg yolks
1 tablespoon water
1 tablespoon lemon juice
Salt and pepper

Cut the butter into pieces and place all but about 1 oz. (25 g.) in a small, heavy-based pan. Put the pan over a very gentle heat and remove as soon as the butter has melted.

Half fill the bottom of a double boiler or a large pan with water. Bring to the boil, then remove from the heat. Put the egg yolks with the tablespoon of water in the top of the boiler, or in a bowl over the pan, and whisk for 1–2 minutes.

Put the pan back over a low heat and add half the reserved cold butter. Whisk again for 1 minute. Whisk in the other half of the reserved butter, remove from the heat, but keep the bowl over the hot water. The mixture should look smooth and creamy.

Gradually add the melted butter, whisking it in until the sauce is thick. Then beat in the lemon juice and season with salt and pepper to taste.

If the sauce curdles during the cooking, remove it from the heat immediately. Put another egg yolk in a bowl and gradually beat the sauce into it. Then resume the cooking. If the sauce is too thick, add 1–2 teaspoons of hot water.

For a variation, flavour the cooked sauce with tomato purée, orange juice, fresh herbs or horseradish to taste.

GERMANY
Liver Dumplings

IN BAVARIA, where the variety of dumplings exceeds even that of sausages, Liver Dumplings are, according to 19th-century guidebooks, 'eaten at every opportunity'. In other parts of Germany the populace is more restrained, but even there the dish is highly esteemed.

If you are feeling adventurous, this recipe is ideal for giving body to a soup. In Germany, the soup may well contain a strong local beer.

PREPARATION TIME: 25 MINUTES
COOKING TIME: 10–15 MINUTES

INGREDIENTS FOR FOUR

8 oz. (225 g.) calf or chicken liver, minced
3 oz. (75 g.) fresh white breadcrumbs
½ pint (275/300 ml.) stock (see pp. 33–34)
½ small onion, peeled and grated
1 egg, beaten
Salt
Freshly ground black pepper

Pass the liver through the fine blade of a mincer twice. Place in a large bowl. Put the breadcrumbs into a small pan, add the stock and leave to soak for 10 minutes.

Put the pan over a gentle heat and with a wooden spoon, or a pestle, pound the breadcrumbs and stock to a fine paste. Add more stock only if the mixture is too dry.

Remove from the heat and add the paste to the liver with the onion and beaten egg. Season well with salt and pepper and blend together.

Roll into small balls, about 1½ in. (4 cm.) in diameter.

Put the liver dumplings into a chicken or vegetable broth or a consommé for about the last 10 minutes of its cooking, keeping the pan covered.

The dumplings can be made very quickly and easily in a liquidiser. Use only ¼ pint (150 ml.) stock or the dumplings may not hold.

Sauces, Forcemeats, Dumplings, Herbs and Spices

Good plain cooking, plainly presented, is central to the tradition of British cooking, yet there is room within that tradition for the use of simple sauces, herbs and spices that bring out and complement the flavour of the main dish. Country housewives know the value of such flavourings—just as they know the value of extras, such as forcemeats and dumplings, to make a meal go further.

Some of the early sauces were extremely simple, mostly consisting of the pressed juice of crab apples and salt. But, with the coming of the Normans, more elaborate sauces were introduced. The Normans were also responsible for our forcemeats, which are used to flavour meat, poultry and fish, and add bulk to other dishes. The word 'forcemeat'—or 'farcemeat' as it was originally—comes from the French *farcer* (to stuff). Herbs and spices play an essential part in our sauces, forcemeats and dumplings. They—and the various juices, oils, perfumes and powders extracted from them—have long been used both for medicinal and culinary purposes.

Savoury Sauces

Sauces have been used in British cooking at least since Roman days—although the reasons for their use have changed through the ages. In Tudor times, for example, rich sauces were often employed to disguise any off flavours of meat or fish that was less than fresh. Initially influenced by French cooks, sauces soon became an integral part of many dishes. The flour and butter thickening, later called a roux, was introduced in the 17th century; and by the 18th century there was a proliferation of sauces—thin, thick, simple, complex—many of which are modified and used today.

Facts about Savoury Sauces

Some sauces are traditionally served with certain dishes because it has been discovered by the best of all methods—the test of how a dish tastes—that the interaction of flavours and textures is hard to improve.

A sauce can act as a foil and a contrast to a dish: apple sauce cuts the sweetness of pork; gooseberry sauce counters the oiliness of mackerel; bread sauce gives moisture to a turkey. For some dishes, a sauce is a foundation; it binds croquettes and rissoles, for example.

The most common sauces in Britain are those thickened with a roux—a blend of fat and flour. The word 'roux' is derived from the French for 'reddish brown', and has been an English cookery term since the 19th century. Roux-based sauces can be given many flavourings. Some sauces are thickened in other ways—with other starches such as cornflour, or with eggs, butter, oil, or by reduction.

Sauces should be carefully flavoured so they do not overpower the individual taste of the dish and at the same time do not lose their own distinctive taste. They should be smooth, light—without being liquid—and attractively glossy to the eye.

Contrary to what is often supposed, sauces are easy to make and mistakes can be remedied; but do follow the instructions carefully.

The equipment you need

Heavy-based saucepan.
Double saucepan or a large, heavy-based saucepan with a bowl to fit over it.
Wooden spoon or spatula.
Balloon whisk.
Sieve.
Sharp knife.
Liquidiser (optional).
Greaseproof paper.

Sauces Thickened with a Roux

A roux consists of equal quantities of fat and plain flour blended together and cooked for a few minutes over a gentle heat. The length of cooking depends on whether you want a white or brown sauce. The proportion of fat and flour to liquid varies according to the consistency required—thin enough for pouring or thicker for coating and binding. The following recipes are for pouring sauces.

A basic white sauce

This basic recipe can be used with various flavourings to make sauces for vegetables, poultry, fish and egg dishes.

Ingredients to Yield about 1 pint (575/600 ml.)

1½ oz. (40 g.) butter
1½ oz. (40 g.) flour
1 pint (575/600 ml.) warm milk or white or poultry stock (see pp. 33–34)

1 Melt the butter in a heavy-based saucepan, then draw the pan off the heat and mix in the flour smoothly with a wooden spoon or spatula.
2 Stir continuously over a gentle heat for 2–3 minutes until you

have a thick paste. Do not allow the roux to develop any colour.

3 Remove the pan from the heat again and add the warm, strained liquid, stirring all the time.

4 When the mixture is thoroughly blended, return the saucepan to the heat and bring to boiling point, stirring continuously. Cook gently for 5–7 minutes, stirring from time to time, until the sauce is smooth and creamy.

A flavoured white sauce

When making the basic sauce, put a small, peeled onion, a bay leaf, 2–3 cloves, peppercorns and a blade of mace in the saucepan with the milk or other cooking liquid. Heat gently, put the lid on the pan and leave to infuse for 5–10 minutes. Strain before using.

Alternatively, add a little cream, an egg yolk or a few drops of lemon juice to a white sauce. Always add these ingredients off the heat, just before serving, so the sauce will not curdle. Soured cream curdles very easily.

Another method is to add up to 1 teaspoon of Dijon mustard. (Despite the French name, recipes for Dijon mustard have appeared in English cookery books since 1660.)

Whisk in a nut of butter to give a glossy finish.

A basic brown sauce

A basic brown sauce is used to accompany many dishes. Gravy can also be made in this way.

INGREDIENTS TO YIELD ABOUT 1 PINT (575/600 ML.)

1½ oz. (40 g.) butter
1½ oz. (40 g.) flour
1 pint (575/600 ml.) brown stock (see pp. 33–34)

1 Melt the butter in a heavy-based saucepan, then draw the pan off the heat and mix in the flour smoothly with a wooden spoon or spatula.

2 Stir continuously over a gentle heat for 2–3 minutes until you have a thick paste. Cook for a further 3–4 minutes to a light chestnut brown.

3 Remove the pan from the heat again and add the warm, strained liquid, stirring all the time.

4 When the mixture is thoroughly blended, return the saucepan to the heat and bring to boiling point, stirring continuously. Cook gently for 5–7 minutes, stirring from time to time, until the sauce is smooth.

A rich brown sauce

This sauce, also known as Espagnole sauce, is the basis of many other sauces to accompany meat. Different versions can include mushrooms, onions, red wine, Madeira, tomatoes, brandy or jellied veal stock.

INGREDIENTS TO YIELD ABOUT ¾ PINT (450 ML.)

1 rasher bacon, diced
1 tablespoon vegetable oil
1 small onion, finely chopped
1 carrot, diced
1 stick of celery, diced
2 teaspoons flour
1 teaspoon tomato purée
¾ pint (450 ml.) brown stock (see pp. 33–34)
1 bouquet garni or ½ teaspoon dried mixed herbs
Salt and pepper

1 Gently fry the diced bacon in the oil. Add the onion, carrot and celery.

2 Stir in the flour and cook the mixture for 6–8 minutes, until golden-brown.

3 Remove from the heat and stir in the tomato purée and stock.

4 Bring to the boil and add the bouquet garni. Season to taste.

5 Reduce heat to a simmer and cook, covered, for 15–20 minutes.

6 Strain and skim off any fat.

Coating and binding sauces

To make a coating sauce for dishes such as cauliflower cheese, use 2 oz. (50 g.) fat and 2 oz. (50 g.) flour to 1 pint (575/600 ml.) milk, or white or poultry stock. To coat cold poultry, game or fish, add a little aspic jelly made from gelatine dissolved in water. Use the proportions given on the packet.

A binding sauce, also called a panada, is used to bind meat, fish and poultry into croquettes. It is also the basis of many hot soufflés. Use 4 oz. (100/125 g.) fat and 4 oz. (100/125 g.) plain flour to 1 pint (575/600 ml.) milk, or white or poultry stock.

How to rescue a roux-based sauce that has gone wrong

Too thick Dilute with a little milk, water or stock. Bring to the boil, stirring or whisking continuously, then remove from the heat.

Too thin Reduce by cooking rapidly, uncovered, for a few minutes. Stir or whisk continuously until the consistency is correct, then remove the pan from the heat.

Lumpy Remove the pan from the heat and beat the sauce vigorously with a whisk for a few seconds. Alternatively rub the sauce through a sieve or liquidise it.

Keeping and re-heating roux-based sauces

If you want to make a sauce for use a little later, remove it from the heat as soon as it is cooked. If the sauce includes herbs, do not add them until it is re-heated, or their distinctive flavour will be lost. To prevent skin forming on top, cover the surface with a circle of greaseproof paper dipped in cold water and placed wet side down. Cover the pan with a lid.

To re-heat, remove the paper and put the pan over a gentle heat, or put the sauce in the top of a double saucepan, or in a bowl over simmering water. Stir or whisk continuously as the sauce heats through, so that lumps do not form.

OTHER THICKENING FOR SAUCES

Sauces thickened with cornflour

Like flour, this is a reliable thickener. Use in small quantities and cook well so that the sauce is not dominated by a starchy taste. Add 1 good teaspoon to 2 tablespoons of cold water for ½ pint (275/300 ml.) of liquid. Blend into a smooth paste and stir into the hot cooking liquid. Boil for 2–3 minutes, stirring all the time. Follow the directions in individual recipes for quantities different from those above.

Sauces thickened with arrowroot

Arrowroot gives a clear thickness to a sauce. Use in the same way as cornflour but after you bring the sauce to the boil, simmer for 2–3 minutes, remove from the heat and serve immediately. Arrowroot liquefies easily and sauces and glazes incorporating it cannot be re-heated.

Sauces thickened with kneaded butter (Beurre Manié)

This is a quick and easy way to thicken a sauce or soup. Use equal quantities of butter and flour—about ½ oz. (15 g.) of each to each ½ pint (275/300 ml.) of liquid. Soften the butter, blend with the flour and, just before serving, add in small pieces to the cooking liquid whisking continuously.

Sauces thickened with eggs, butter or oil

Eggs, butter or oil are used as thickeners for hot sauces such as Hollandaise and cold sauces such as Mayonnaise. The ingredients are blended by whisking and beating.

Have all the ingredients at room temperature before you start, or the sauce may curdle. It will also curdle if the eggs are overheated.

Salad Dressing

This sauce, called a vinaigrette, is the classic dressing for a salad and is excellent with cooked vegetables.

Ingredients to Yield
7 fl. oz. (200 ml.)

1 teaspoon dry or made mustard
1 teaspoon sugar
½ teaspoon salt
¼ pint (150 ml.) olive oil or good vegetable oil
4 tablespoons wine or cider vinegar (or 2 tablespoons vinegar and 2 tablespoons lemon juice)
Freshly ground black pepper

1 Blend together the mustard, sugar and salt.
2 Whisk in the oil.
3 Stir in the vinegar or vinegar and oil.
4 Add freshly ground black pepper. Taste and adjust seasoning as desired.

Vary the proportion of oil to vinegar to suit your taste. If liked, blend in 1 clove of garlic, crushed with the dry ingredients. If available, add chopped, fresh herbs such as tarragon, parsley and chives.

Savoury Butters

Savoury butters provide an instant sauce or garnish for many meat and fish dishes. They can also be added to white sauces or spread on plain biscuits.

To each 4 oz. (100/125 g.) of unsalted or lightly salted butter, add ½–1 teaspoon of lemon juice. Using a fork or the back of a spoon, blend in 1 oz. (25 g.) of any chopped fresh herb such as basil, chervil, dill, fennel, marjoram, mint, parsley, tarragon or thyme. Use rosemary and sage in smaller quantities, adding and tasting until the flavour is to your liking.

As an alternative to herbs, blend in 4 cloves of garlic, crushed in a little salt; or 6–8 tinned anchovy fillets, drained; or 3–4 teaspoons of dry or made mustard; or the juice of ½ orange and 1–2 teaspoons of paprika.

Forcemeats and Dumplings

The Romans used forcemeats as flavouring and to keep poultry moist, and the technique descended through the Goths and Franks in France to the Normans.

Over the centuries forcemeats have ranged from the simple to the highly exotic. In the 17th century, for example, they were often richly coloured and flavoured with dried fruit, minced meat, herbs and spices. But in the same century, Sir Kenelm Digby, diplomat and writer, suggested a plain sage and onion stuffing for duck, which is the ancestor of the one we commonly use today.

Dumplings, or pot-balls, have been used for centuries by thrifty cooks to add bulk to soups and stews.

The Victorian novelist Mrs Gaskell (1810–65) writes in *Cranford* of a host who disliked 'new-fangled ways' in which meat was eaten without first partaking of broth and 'balls' or suet dumplings. He states that his father's inflexible rule was, 'No broth no ball; no ball no beef.' He adds that the beef came last of all, and only to those who had done justice to broth and ball.

Forcemeats

A forcemeat, or stuffing, consists of a base to which fat, seasoning and flavouring are added. The base may be breadcrumbs, sausagemeat, potatoes, rice, oatmeal or a similar bulk ingredient. The flavouring can include herbs, fruit, nuts or any ingredients which complement the food with which it is to be served.

Forcemeats are used to flavour and add bulk to meat, poultry and fish. They also keep the flesh moist as they steam during cooking. All stuffed dishes need slightly longer cooking, as the heat does not easily penetrate.

Forcemeats can be made ahead of time and kept in the refrigerator or deep-freeze. However, never put the stuffing inside the food and then freeze it, as it can easily turn sour.

Making forcemeats

If the recipe calls for breadcrumbs, make them yourself from slightly stale (2-day-old) bread. Cut the crusts off the bread and rub through a grater or wire sieve or use a liquidiser. Commercially dried breadcrumbs are not a suitable base for forcemeat.

If you use the liver of the bird, brown it lightly in fat before chopping it finely and adding it.

If you cannot buy good sausagemeat, skin well-flavoured sausages. Those flavoured with herbs are especially good.

Use chopped, fresh herbs if you can. For dried herbs, halve the quantity.

Always taste the forcemeat before you use it, to make sure the balance of flavours is right.

Make sure the texture is crumbly. If too wet, it will be sodden and heavy when cooked; if too dry, it will fall apart. Too much egg used in binding the mixture will make the forcemeat hard and close-textured.

Using forcemeat

As a general rule, use 4 oz. (100/125 g.) forcemeat to each 1 lb. (450 g.) of bird or meat.

Most poultry and game birds are stuffed from the crop (neck) cavity. Do not fill too tightly: the forcemeat needs room to expand. Ducks and geese are commonly stuffed from the body (tail) end. Turkeys traditionally have two stuffings: a bread-and-herb based one spooned into the neck; and sausagemeat filling for the body.

If any forcemeat is left over, use it to make forcemeat balls to add to soups or stews.

Dumplings

Dumplings are small balls of dough, forcemeat or potato mixture that are steamed or poached to serve with soups and stews.

Make sure the dumpling dough is moist, and the dumplings quite small—the size of a large walnut. They will swell during cooking, so allow room for them to expand in stocks and broths. If there are too many, cook half at a time, take them out with a ladle or slotted spoon and keep warm while cooking the rest.

Cook dumplings gently, at simmering point or a gentle boil. Too vigorous cooking will make them crumble and break up.

When making potato dumplings, choose a floury potato. It will bind better than a waxy potato.

Herbs and Spices

HERBS have been in continuous use for flavouring food and for medication since prehistoric times. When the Romans settled in Britain in AD 43, they brought in many new varieties of herbs from the Mediterranean and established them here. During the Middle Ages, herbs were being cultivated by all classes—even the poorest grew a few beside their homes.

Spices, too, have been prized in this country for some 2,000 years, and the history of the spice trade in Europe reflects the rise and fall of civilisations.

The great revival of interest in traditional British recipes has been accompanied by a renewed interest in the use of herbs and spices in the kitchen.

HERBS IN COOKING

The essential oils contained in herbs give them distinctive flavours that enhance the taste of many foods.

Use fresh herbs whenever possible. If you do not have a herb garden, you can grow basic herbs such as parsley, mint, chives and thyme in pots on the window-sill.

If you have to use dried herbs, buy them from a shop which has a rapid turnover. Store in opaque, airtight jars and label with the date of purchase. Never keep longer than 6 months, as they will get stale and lose their flavour.

As an average measure, use twice the quantity of fresh herbs to dried.

Balm The leaves have a strong lemon scent when bruised. Use in omelettes, stuffings, sauces and fruit drinks.

Basil The flavour is strong and clove-like, and keeps its pungency when the herb is dried. Use in tomato dishes, soups, sausages, and herb mixtures.

Bay Use to flavour fish, stews, sauces, milk puddings and custards.

Chervil Add to soups, eggs and fish. It has a delicate flavour and scent.

Chives A member of the onion family. The finely chopped leaves flavour salads, egg and cheese dishes, baked potatoes and 'dips'.

Dill The mild aniseed flavour complements fish, salads and sauces. It goes well with cucumber.

Fennel Also has an aniseed flavour. Especially good with an oily fish.

Garlic Use sparingly, as it has a powerful and lingering taste. An essential ingredient of many stews, salads and soups.

Marjoram Use for its spicy flavour in soups, stews, forcemeats, omelettes, tomato and mushroom dishes.

Mint One of the most widely grown herbs, with many different varieties. Use to flavour peas, carrots and potatoes; in sauces and jellies.

Parsley Use generously, raw and cooked: it is rich in vitamin C. Add to sauces, Mayonnaise, and egg dishes.

Rosemary Use sparingly: it is aromatic and pungent. Complements lamb, veal, pork and poultry.

Sage Has a strong, slightly bitter flavour, so use cautiously. Add to forcemeats and in sausages.

Savory There are two varieties, summer and winter, both with a subtle, peppery taste. Use with beans, in omelettes and tomato sauces.

Tarragon There are two kinds of tarragon, French and Russian. French has the better flavour. Use it in Hollandaise and Tartare sauces, and in chicken and veal dishes.

Thyme A strong, aromatic and versatile herb, with many varieties. Use it to flavour forcemeats, stews, soups and jugged hare. Add a little to courgettes, aubergines and onions.

SPICES IN COOKING

Spices are vegetable substances that are used as flavourings because of their sharp or fragrant flavours that stimulate appetite.

Buy in small quantities to avoid using spices that have lost most of their flavour.

Store in small, airtight containers in a cool, dry place.

Keep whole spices wherever possible. Cinnamon sticks, whole cloves, nutmeg and peppercorns give a far better flavour than powdered varieties.

Allspice The fruit of the tropical allspice tree, with a flavour of cinnamon, clove and nutmeg.

Caraway seed The seed-like fruits of a plant similar to parsley. Use to flavour bread and cakes, in cheeses, with pork dishes and stews.

Cayenne This is derived from a fiery, hot pepper pod. Use it sparingly with eggs, cheese and in chutneys.

Cinnamon A pungent, sweet spice, sold in sticks, curled from the dried bark of the cinnamon tree, or in powdered form. Use to flavour sugar, cakes, beef stews and stewed fruit.

Cloves The dried, unopened flower buds of a tropical tree, with a pungent, aromatic flavour. Use whole or powdered with apples, bread sauce, soused herrings and ham.

Cumin The small, aromatic seed-like fruit of an Indian and North African plant. Available whole or ground. Use in curries or meat, poultry, rice, egg and cheese dishes.

Ginger A spice from the rhizome of a tropical plant. The end near the stem is preserved in syrup or crystallised. The root end is dried or powdered. Use in cakes, biscuits, puddings and preserves.

Mustard Prepared from the seeds of the mustard plant. Use whole seeds in pickles, soused herrings and salted meat. Mustard adds zest to a large range of dishes.

Nutmeg and mace Mace is the amber, fibrous network surrounding the brown nutmeg, the fruit of a tropical tree. Both have a sweet, delicate taste. Use mace for savoury food; nutmeg for sweet or savoury.

Paprika A member of the capsicum family, like Cayenne. It is bright red, sweet and mild. Use to flavour egg, cheese, rice, chicken, meat and fish.

Pepper The dried berries from a tropical vine, which we know as black or white peppercorns, provide the most widely used spice of all. Black peppercorns are aromatic; white have a hotter flavour. Both retain their flavour better when whole.

Saffron The dried stigmas of the purple-flowering saffron crocus, with a musky aroma and golden colouring. Saffron is also sold powdered. Use to flavour soups, cakes and savoury rice dishes.

Turmeric A dried, ground root of a plant of the ginger family. It is aromatic and mild. Use to flavour and colour curries and pickles.

EGG AND CHEESE DISHES

CONTAINING

NUMEROUS *Useful* FAMILY RECIPES

for OMELETTES & PANCAKES, SOUFFLÉS & MOUSSES

& other DAIRY DISHES

PAGES 168–175

AND

A SELECTION of RECIPES from OTHER LANDS

PAGES 176–177

AND WITH

NOTES AND ADVICE

on all kinds of Boiling, Poaching, Baking and Mixing of Egg and Cheese Dishes to Perfection

PAGES 178–179

SHRIMP OMELET
Countrywide

THE PRETTILY NAMED 'herbolace' of medieval times was a baked egg dish flavoured with herbs and cheese. In France, the method of frying this egg and herb mixture over a strong flame was popular for a long time before the English finally adopted it in the 17th century. The confusion over whether the result was an amulet or an omelet, and whether it should be cooked on both sides or only on one, persisted even longer.

The English are often derided for their omelet-making, but this is unjust. A 19th-century connoisseur declared: 'The best I ever tasted—a perfect one—was made at Stoodleigh Rectory in the 1890s and served for luncheon. It was not what is known as a French *omelette*, nor exactly American, but a cross between the two—light and puffy, but creamy in the middle.' And that is just the result you should achieve with this recipe.

PREPARATION TIME: 10 MINUTES
COOKING TIME: 2–3 MINUTES

INGREDIENTS FOR TWO TO THREE

6 eggs
Salt and freshly ground pepper
1 tablespoon fresh parsley and chives, finely chopped
4 oz. (100/125 g) shelled shrimps or prawns, coarsely chopped
1 spring onion, finely chopped
1 teaspoon plain flour
3 oz. (75 g.) butter, cut into pieces

Place a serving dish under the grill at a low heat to warm.

Whisk the eggs in a bowl with the chopped herbs and seasonings until they are very light. Stir in the chopped shrimps or prawns and the finely chopped spring onion. Sprinkle on the flour, and drop in 1 oz. (25 g.) of the butter, cut into small pieces.

Melt the remaining butter in a large 8 in. (20 cm.) omelet pan. When the butter starts to brown, pour in the mixture and cook quickly for 2–3 minutes, stirring it round a little and lifting the edges with a spatula to allow the butter to run underneath.

Place the heated serving dish beside the cooker. Slide the omelet on to the dish, folding it in half as you do so. Serve it very hot. The butter will run out round the omelet in a golden pool—spoon it over each piece of omelet as you serve it.

EGGS IN OVERCOATS
Countrywide

BEATEN EGG WHITES, 'bird's milk' as the ancient Greeks once called it, is what makes this combination of eggs and potatoes so surprisingly light-textured. The recipe was collected in the 1930s by Mrs Leyel, a famous herbalist and author of several delightful recipes. Served with salad it makes an excellent light supper.

PREPARATION TIME: 30 MINUTES
COOKING TIME: $1\frac{1}{4}$ HOURS
PRE-HEAT THE OVEN TO 200°C (400°F)—GAS MARK 6

INGREDIENTS FOR SIX

6 large potatoes
$2\frac{1}{2}$ fl. oz. (75 ml.) hot milk
3 tablespoons chopped cooked ham
2 tablespoons chopped parsley
2 oz. (50 g.) butter, softened
2 tablespoons double cream
Salt and freshly ground pepper
6 eggs, and the whites of 2 more
1 tablespoon malt vinegar
2 tablespoons grated Cheddar cheese

Scrub the potatoes and prick them. Bake them in the pre-heated oven for about 55 minutes, depending on their size. Remove from the oven and allow to cool.

Lay the potatoes flat, and slice the top off each with a sharp knife. Scoop out the insides, and place in a bowl. Put the potato skins on one side.

Mash the potato with the hot milk until smooth. Mix in the ham, parsley, butter and cream, and season with salt and pepper.

Beat the egg whites until stiff, in a separate bowl, and stir into the potato mixture. Check the seasoning, and keep the mixture hot.

Lightly poach the whole eggs by sliding them into simmering water to which you have added 1 tablespoon of vinegar, but *no* salt. Lift out the eggs using a slotted spoon and drain them very carefully.

Half fill the potato skins with a layer of the mashed-potato mixture. Place a poached egg in each, cover with the remaining mixture and sprinkle the tops with grated cheese. Brown quickly in the top of the pre-heated oven or under a hot grill.

BAKED EGGS IN SAUCERS
Countrywide

THIS SIMPLE, NOURISHING snack is a descendant of the old French *ramequin*. Both the dish and the word crossed the Channel about 1700, when they meant a concoction of bread, eggs and cheese baked together in a mould. By the end of the 19th century, however, the 'ramekin' was cooked and served in a little china container, which by transference came itself to be known as a ramekin.

Replacing the cheese with mushrooms, as in this recipe, makes an interesting variation on the original theme. Saucers are used in place of the traditional ramekins.

PREPARATION TIME: 10 MINUTES
COOKING TIME: 20 MINUTES
PRE-HEAT THE OVEN TO 180°C (350°F)—GAS MARK 4

INGREDIENTS FOR FOUR

3 oz. (75 g.) butter
4 thin slices white bread, with crusts removed
8 eggs
Salt and freshly ground pepper
4 oz. (100/125 g.) mushrooms, washed

Use four old saucers to make this dish. Grease them lightly, using a very little of the butter.

Melt 2 oz. (50 g.) of the butter in a small saucepan. Remove from the heat and dip the slices of bread quickly into the pan, coating both sides lightly with the butter. Allow any excess butter to run off. Press the bread into the saucers, sprinkle with salt and pepper, and bake in the pre-heated oven for 5 minutes.

Take the saucers out of the oven, and break two eggs into each one. Season with salt and pepper, and return the saucers to the oven for 8–10 minutes.

Meanwhile, slice the mushrooms and fry them in the remaining butter in a small saucepan.

Serve the eggs in the saucers, with the mushrooms on top.

Minted Egg Pie
Somerset

'ECONOMY IS ONE THING, skimping, odious skimping is another,' said Osbert Sitwell in his preface to *Lady Sysonby's Cook Book* (1935), a selection of recipes from her family.

This recipe, which is extremely economical, is also perfectly delicious. It comes from the section on luncheons, which the author prefaces with the declaration that 'nowadays all self-respecting households start the midday meal with a dish of eggs in some form or other, and a very pleasant beginning I think it is'.

PREPARATION TIME: 15 MINUTES
COOKING TIME: 40 MINUTES
PRE-HEAT THE OVEN TO 220°C (425°F)—GAS MARK 7

INGREDIENTS FOR FOUR

8 oz. (225 g.) shortcrust pastry (see p. 217)
8 oz. (225 g.) cream cheese
2 oz. (50 g.) Cheddar cheese, finely grated
¼ teaspoon grated nutmeg
Salt and freshly ground pepper
4 eggs
1 heaped tablespoon chopped, fresh mint

For the salad:

3 heads chicory, coarsely sliced
2 lettuces
½ small onion, finely chopped
¼ pint (150 ml.) home-made mayonnaise (see p. 161)

Place a baking sheet in the middle of the pre-heated oven to get really hot.

Butter a deep 7½ in. (19 cm.) pie plate and line with half the shortcrust pastry. Mix the grated Cheddar, nutmeg and seasoning into the cream cheese thoroughly and spread the mixture over the pastry.

A classic combination of eggs and cheese, blended with mint and sealed in a pie.

Make little nests and break the eggs into these hollows. Sprinkle thickly with the mint, and season again lightly. Cover with the rest of the pastry. Stand the plate on the baking sheet so that the bottom crust cooks, and bake in the pre-heated oven for about 40 minutes. After 25 minutes cover lightly with greaseproof to prevent over-browning. Remove and cool before serving with a chicory salad.

Make the salad by mixing together the coarsely sliced chicory with the inner hearts of the lettuce and the finely chopped onion. Serve with the home-made mayonnaise.

Eliza Acton's Forced Eggs
Suffolk

DURING the 18th and 19th centuries the sharp and pungent flavour of anchovies was immensely popular, especially when used as a seasoning for egg and cheese dishes.

Eliza Acton, the author of this recipe, was a Suffolk lady who could be called the Mrs Beeton of the early 19th century. Her cookery book *Modern Cookery for Private Families* was first published in 1845, and it stayed in print for the next 50 years.

PREPARATION TIME: 20 MINUTES
COOKING TIME: 10–12 MINUTES

INGREDIENTS FOR THREE

6 eggs
8 anchovy fillets, drained from a 1¾ oz. (45 g.) tin
2 oz. (50 g.) unsalted butter, softened
¼ teaspoon ground mace
¼ teaspoon Cayenne pepper

Boil the eggs for 10–12 minutes, then cool under cold running water. Shell carefully, slice in half lengthways and take out the yolks. Put the egg whites on one side.

Pound the anchovy fillets to a paste. In a separate bowl, mash the egg yolks with the butter, working them together well with a fork. Season with mace and Cayenne pepper. Add the anchovies, and beat together thoroughly or put through a liquidiser. Check the seasoning and spoon the mixture into the egg whites.

Serve with a salad of young lettuces mixed with a variety of chopped, fresh herbs, such as chives, mustard and cress and tarragon.

For a variation, substitute pounded ham for the anchovies.

Scotch Eggs
Scottish Lowlands

In the land of their origin, Scotch Eggs are part of the traditional and, to foreigners, staggering Scots breakfast, which also includes porridge, bacon, fried eggs, flat sausage, black, white and fruit puddings and hot baps and jam *ad lib*. But Scotch Eggs are also sufficiently versatile to be served hot with gravy at high tea, or cold as a snack.

It is in this last role that the English know them best, since they often figure as bar food in pubs. Whatever the Scots say, cold Scotch Eggs, piccalilli or pickled walnuts and beer were made for each other.

Preparation Time: 20 minutes
Cooking Time: 10 minutes

Ingredients for Six

6 eggs
12 oz. (350 g.) sausagemeat
1 dessertspoon parsley or sage, finely chopped
Finely grated rind of 1 lemon
¼ teaspoon grated nutmeg
¼ teaspoon sweet marjoram, basil or savory
Salt
Freshly ground pepper
1 egg, beaten
4 oz. (100/125 g.) dried breadcrumbs
Refined peanut or vegetable oil for deep-frying

Boil the eggs for 10–12 minutes, then cool under cold running water. Peel off the shells carefully, and put the whole eggs on one side.

Put the sausagemeat into a bowl with the finely chopped parsley or sage, lemon rind and nutmeg. Add the marjoram, basil or savory—these herbs greatly improve the flavour. Season with salt and pepper, and work all the ingredients well into the sausagemeat with your hands.

Make a coating for each hard-boiled egg out of the sausagemeat, working it round the eggs with wet hands to form an even layer.

Roll the covered eggs in beaten egg, and then in dried breadcrumbs.

Heat the oil in a deep frying pan—use refined peanut oil for the best results. When the oil has just started to smoke—at 180–190°C (350–375°F)—carefully put in 3 eggs and fry for 4–5 minutes, until they turn deep golden. Turn them as they cook so that they brown evenly. Remove with a slotted spoon, drain on kitchen paper, and repeat with the remaining 3 eggs.

Eat cold, halved lengthwise, with a green salad.

Eggs and Asparagus
Countrywide

June, the season when 'asparagus is plentiful', was considered the best time for serving this dish, according to its originator Meg Dods in *The Cook and Housewife's Manual* (1826).

Now, over 150 years later, when fresh asparagus cannot be so easily obtained, fresh green peas can be used as a replacement for it.

Scrambled, rumbled or buttered eggs, as they were originally called, made their first appearance in cookery books in the 17th century. In those days fashionable cooks garnished them with musk, and flavoured them with bitter orange juice and spices.

This simpler version, garnished with coarsely ground black pepper, makes a delicious light lunch, or it can be served as a supper dish.

Preparation Time: 5–10 minutes
Cooking Time: 20–30 minutes

Ingredients for Two

12 stalks asparagus
4 eggs, beaten
Salt and freshly ground pepper
2 slices bread for the toast
1½ oz. (40 g.) butter

Wash the asparagus in cold water and cut off the woody parts from the base of the stalks. Using a sharp knife, scrape the white part of the stalks downwards. Tie in a bundle that will stand upright.

Put salted water on to boil in a deep pan. Plunge the stalks upright into the water, making sure the level comes just below the heads. Cover the pan and boil for 18–20 minutes, or until tender when pierced at the stalk end with the tip of a sharp knife.

Drain, refresh briefly under cold running water and drain again.

Cut the tender parts of the asparagus into short lengths, about ½ in. (1·5 cm.). Discard the tougher parts of the stems, or keep aside for use in soups or stocks later. Stir the asparagus pieces into the beaten eggs in a bowl, and season to taste.

Toast the bread and spread it with ½ oz. (15 g.) of the butter. Keep hot under the grill. Melt the remainder of the butter in a small, heavy-based saucepan. Pour in the egg and asparagus mixture and stir constantly with a wooden spoon over a moderate heat until it thickens to a creamy consistency.

Divide the mixture between the two slices of buttered toast and serve immediately, very hot.

This dish can be made with frozen asparagus. Simmer the asparagus in a very little salted water, covered, for about 5–10 minutes or until tender. Drain and chop into small lengths, then cook with the beaten eggs.

Egg Mousse
Countrywide

The essence of a good mousse is lightness. The name comes from the French word for 'moss', and it is an apt derivation. Mousses became popular in England in the 19th century and continue to be popular.

The following dish was originated by the excellent cook and prolific writer Mrs Philip Martineau in her book *Caviare to Candy—Recipes for small households from all parts of the world* (1927). As a savoury it makes a good first course for a dinner. It can also be served as the main dish for a light summer luncheon.

Preparation Time: 1 hour
Chilling Time: 50 minutes

Ingredients for Four to Six

6 eggs
4 oz. (100/125 g.) button mushrooms, chopped
Juice of ½ lemon
2 oz. (50 g.) butter
¼ pint (150 ml.) tinned consommé
½ oz. (15 g.) gelatine
1 tablespoon Worcestershire sauce, or 2 tablespoons sherry
Salt and freshly ground pepper
½ pint (275/300 ml.) double cream, chilled
6 leaves fresh tarragon, or 3 sprigs flat parsley
Mayonnaise, made green with finely chopped parsley (optional)

Boil the eggs for 10–12 minutes, then cool them under cold running water to prevent a black ring forming around the yolks. Then shell the eggs carefully and chop them coarsely or cut them in slices.

Squeeze lemon juice over the mushrooms to prevent them discolouring. Melt the butter in a small frying pan and cook the mushrooms gently for 3–4 minutes. Transfer to a wire sieve to drain.

Heat the consommé, add the gelatine and, when it is dissolved, add the Worcestershire sauce or sherry, and salt and pepper. Remove from the heat and allow to cool.

Lightly whisk the chilled cream until thick but not stiff. Mix together the cream, consommé (reserving 4 tablespoons of it), chopped eggs and mushrooms. Check the seasoning and adjust as necessary. Then pour the mixture into a soufflé dish and chill it until it is set firm—this will take about 30 minutes.

Garnish the mousse with the tarragon leaves or parsley. Carefully pour the remaining consommé over the mousse (if the consommé has set, re-heat and allow to cool). Chill again until set firm.

Serve the mousse on its own or with the mayonnaise.

CURRIED EGGS
Countrywide

IN THE DAYS when the British Empire was spread over vast expanses of the globe, a number of colonial recipes came to be adopted by English households. Mrs Beeton devoted a whole chapter to the art of Indian cooking, and curry was so popular in the late Victorian age that it came to be regarded as something of a traditional English dish.

Eliza Acton, in *Modern Cookery for Private Families* (1845) gives this recipe for curry powder:

Mix together
3 level teaspoons ground turmeric
3 level teaspoons ground coriander
1 level teaspoon ground cumin
½ level teaspoon ground fenugreek
½ level teaspoon ground Cayenne pepper

and you can still use this recipe today.

PREPARATION TIME: 10 MINUTES
COOKING TIME: 45 MINUTES
PRE-HEAT THE OVEN TO 170°C (325°F)—GAS MARK 3

INGREDIENTS FOR FOUR TO SIX

8 eggs
2 oz. (50 g.) butter
1 large onion, finely chopped
1½ tablespoons curry powder
½ pint (275/300 ml.) chicken stock
Salt and freshly ground pepper
1 teaspoon arrowroot
¼ pint (150 ml.) single cream
3 tablespoons desiccated or fresh coconut, grated
Juice of ½ lemon

Boil the eggs for 10–12 minutes, then cool under cold running water. Shell carefully, and put on one side.

Melt the butter in a heavy-based pan over a low heat, and add the chopped onion and curry powder. Fry the onion gently, stirring until tender and transparent. Add the stock, season with salt and pepper and simmer for 10 minutes. Mix the arrowroot with the cream, and stir into the curry sauce. Simmer for 5 minutes.

Add 2½ fl. oz. (75 ml.) of boiling water to the coconut. When cool, pour through a fine wire sieve into the curry sauce. Add the lemon juice and check the seasoning.

Halve the eggs and place in an ovenproof dish. Pour in the sauce, cover loosely with foil, and heat in the pre-heated oven for 15 minutes.

Serve with boiled long-grain rice (see p. 199).

Sweet coconut counteracts the sharpness of the hot spices in Curried Eggs, a light and nourishing dish.

TOASTED CHEESE
Wales

'THIS academic, histrionic and poetical preparation ... has ever been a favourite morsel with those gentlemen who think a second supper fairly worth the other three regularly-administered meals of the day.'

Toasted cheese, often called Welsh Rabbit or Rarebit, was the subject of this tribute in Mistress Margaret Dod's *The Cook and Housewife's Manual*, a most entertaining book published in 1826. Early Welsh recipes for the dish place a layer of cold roast beef, spread with mustard and horseradish, beneath the cheese which is then soaked with ale and shallot vinegar.

The recipe given here uses Stilton, an unusual cheese for toasting, but you can use any other well-flavoured cheese that melts easily, such as Cheddar or Lancashire.

PREPARATION TIME: 15 MINUTES
COOKING TIME: ABOUT 5 MINUTES

INGREDIENTS FOR FOUR

- *4 thick slices of fresh white or brown bread, crusts removed*
- *½ oz. (15 g.) butter*
- *1 teaspoon English mustard*
- *Freshly ground black pepper*
- *8 oz. (225 g.) Stilton cheese*
- *2 teaspoons red wine or ale*

Make four rounds of toast and butter them well. Spread with mustard and season with black pepper. Place the toast in an ovenproof dish, making sure that the slices do not overlap.

Slice the cheese thinly and distribute it over the toast. Sprinkle the cheese with the red wine or ale and put the dish under a moderate grill. Heat the cheese until runny and piping hot. Serve at once.

Pastry Ramakins and Toasted Cheese—two savoury variations on a supper theme.

PASTRY RAMAKINS
Countrywide

IN GEORGIAN DAYS supper was a 'light, showy and exhilarating repast' among the well-to-do, and an ideal occasion for serving a number of delicate savoury dishes. The table would be set out with anchovy toasts; Welsh, English and Scottish rarebits; re-heated game or poultry in a hot devilled sauce; dried fruit; and an appetising mound of cheese straws, or Pastry Ramakins as they were called at that time.

PREPARATION TIME: 15 MINUTES
COOKING TIME: 15–20 MINUTES
PRE-HEAT THE OVEN TO 190°C (375°F)—GAS MARK 5

INGREDIENTS FOR ABOUT 20 RAMAKINS

- *4 oz. (100/125 g.) puff pastry (see p. 219), or any puff pastry left from the making of pies*
- *4 oz. (100/125 g.) Cheddar or other cheese, finely grated*
- *1 teaspoon curry powder*

Roll out the pastry fairly thinly—about ¼ in. (5 mm.). Sprinkle half of it lavishly with half the grated cheese, and season with half the curry powder. Fold the other half of the pastry over the cheese, and roll lightly. Sprinkle the surface of the pastry with the rest of the cheese and curry powder. Fold over and lightly roll again until about ¼ in. (5 mm.) thick.

Cut into 20 strips. Twist the strips, and bake on a lightly greased baking tray in the top of the pre-heated oven for 15–20 minutes. Serve hot.

WALNUT AND CHEDDAR PASTE
Somerset

FLORENCE WHITE, the moving spirit behind the English Folk Cookery Association in the 1930s, said of potted cheese: 'This probably is one of the most individual cookery preparations we have, as so much depends on the cook's palate.'

Ingredients vary with the cheese selected and can include sherry, port, mustard, curry powder and Cayenne.

In this recipe freshly chopped walnuts are combined with real farmhouse Cheddar—the sort with a rind and a full nutty flavour. It makes a good ploughman's lunch with crisp celery and home-made bread.

PREPARATION TIME: 15 MINUTES

INGREDIENTS FOR FOUR

8 oz. (225 g.) Cheddar cheese, grated

3 oz. (75 g.) unsalted butter, softened

2 oz. (50 g.) shelled walnuts, roughly chopped

A few drops Worcestershire sauce

Salt and freshly ground black pepper

Using a fork, blend the grated cheese with the butter and walnuts in a bowl. Season with salt and pepper, and add the Worcestershire sauce.

Place in a decorative jar, and seal with a disc of foil pressed firmly down over the surface. Use as required; keep in the refrigerator only if the weather is very warm.

HOT CHEDDAR PUFFS
West Country

IN GEORGE ELIOT'S charming evocation of 19th-century country life, *The Mill on the Floss*, Mrs Tulliver followed a related, though sweeter, recipe when she made little round cheese cakes, 'more exquisitely light than usual: a puff o' wind 'ud make 'em blow about like feathers'. Such is the ideal end result of these delicious little appetisers, which first became popular around the end of the last century. They can be served on their own or with a light cream sauce.

PREPARATION TIME: 15 MINUTES

COOKING TIME: ABOUT 20 MINUTES

PRE-HEAT THE OVEN TO 180°C (350°F)—GAS MARK 4

INGREDIENTS TO MAKE 15 PUFFS

3 oz. (75 g.) plain flour

3 oz. (75 g.) Cheddar cheese, grated

Salt

¼ teaspoon Cayenne pepper

2 oz. (50 g.) butter, cut into cubes

¼ pint (150 ml.) water

2 large eggs

1 egg, beaten, for glazing

Mix together the flour and cheese in a bowl, and season to taste with salt and Cayenne pepper.

Put the butter and water in a medium saucepan, and bring to the boil. Remove from the heat.

Tip the flour and cheese mixture into the pan. Return to the heat, stirring continually with a wooden spoon, for about 1 minute, until the mixture comes away from the sides of the pan cleanly.

Allow to cool for about 5 minutes, then break in the eggs one at a time. Beat them in to make a soft mixture that just drops from a spoon.

Butter a baking sheet very lightly. Place well-spaced, heaped teaspoons of the mixture on the tray—they will swell to three times their original size when they are cooked.

Brush the tops with beaten egg, and bake in the centre of the pre-heated oven (with the oven door open just a crack) for 15–20 minutes, until they are puffed and golden-brown all over. Serve hot.

MACARONI CHEESE
Countrywide

'MACROWS' was the rather daunting name given to the earliest prototype of our macaroni. It was first introduced to Britain in the 14th century, and became popular in the late 18th century when it used to be served with a sprinkling of hard, grated cheese.

Macaroni Cheese—always a good standby meal—reached its height of popularity as a supper dish in Victorian times. The secret of culinary success is simply to be lavish with the strongly flavoured cheese sauce.

PREPARATION TIME: 5 MINUTES

COOKING TIME: 45–50 MINUTES

PRE-HEAT THE OVEN TO 190°C (375°F)—GAS MARK 5

INGREDIENTS FOR FOUR

12 oz. (350 g.) macaroni

For the sauce:

1 oz. (25 g.) butter

1 oz. (25 g.) flour

¾ pint (450 ml.) creamy milk

Salt and freshly ground pepper

¼ teaspoon grated nutmeg

4 oz. (100/125 g.) grated Cheddar cheese

2 oz. (50 g.) lean cooked ham, chopped

1 oz. (25 g.) fine, home-made breadcrumbs

½ oz. (15 g.) butter, cut into pieces

Bring a large pan of well-salted water to the boil, and put in the macaroni. Cook it for 15–20 minutes, until just tender. Do not overcook, or it will not absorb the sauce. Drain well.

To make the strongly flavoured cheese sauce, melt the butter in a medium saucepan. Stir in the flour and let it cook for 2–3 minutes over a gentle heat. Gradually add the milk, stirring all the time with a wooden spoon to obtain a smooth, velvety sauce. Season, and add the nutmeg.

Let the sauce cook gently for 10–15 minutes, stirring from time to time, then add the cheese and ham. When the cheese has melted, stir in the cooked, drained macaroni. Check the seasoning, and pour the mixture into a pie dish. Sprinkle the top with breadcrumbs, dot all over with the ½ oz. (15 g.) butter, and bake in the pre-heated oven for 20 minutes until golden-brown.

CHEESE PUDDING
Lincolnshire and Huntingdonshire

CHEESE PUDDING has long been a popular dish with farmers in East Anglia and the Midlands. It was often eaten at sheep-shearing time, and was served with a bowl of steaming hot frumenty—a dish made of wheat and dried fruit boiled in milk and flavoured with brandy and grated nutmeg.

Variations of this dish have been prepared since the 17th century, some with the unexpected inclusion of grated green ginger. The simple version given here was in Esther Copley's *'The Housekeeper's Guide'*, first published in 1834.

PREPARATION TIME: 10 MINUTES

COOKING TIME: 30 MINUTES

PRE-HEAT THE OVEN TO 180°C (350°F)—GAS MARK 4

INGREDIENTS FOR FOUR

8 oz. (225 g.) Cheddar, Cheshire or Lancashire cheese, grated

4 eggs, beaten

¼ teaspoon Cayenne pepper

¼ teaspoon grated nutmeg

Salt

1 oz. (25 g.) butter

Put the grated cheese and the eggs in a bowl. Add the Cayenne pepper, nutmeg and a little salt. Add salt very sparingly since the cheese is already quite salty. Beat the ingredients together well.

Melt the butter in a small saucepan, let it cool, and beat it into the egg and cheese mixture. Pour into a buttered, oval ovenproof dish and bake in the pre-heated oven for 30 minutes.

Serve with spring onions and brown bread and butter.

SAVOURY PANCAKES
Countrywide

THE DISTINGUISHING MARK of English pancakes—savoury or otherwise—is that they are rolled up. On the Continent most pancakes are left open, with their contents exposed. Unlike their sweet counterparts, Savoury Pancakes are not associated with Shrove Tuesday, and can be eaten at any time of year. With their creamy, mushroom filling they make a delicious light lunch or supper dish.

PREPARATION TIME: 20 MINUTES
COOKING TIME: 25 MINUTES

INGREDIENTS FOR 12 PANCAKES

For the pancakes:

5 oz. (150 g.) flour
A pinch of salt
1 egg
¼ pint (150 ml.) milk and ¼ pint (150 ml.) water, mixed
1 oz. (25 g.) melted butter
A little butter for frying

For the filling:

1½ oz. (40 g.) butter
8 oz. (225 g.) mushrooms, washed and chopped
A squeeze of lemon juice
Salt and pepper
¼ teaspoon grated nutmeg
½ oz. (15 g.) flour
¼ pint (150 ml.) milk
2 tablespoons single cream

First make the pancake batter. Put the flour and salt in a large bowl, break in the egg and add about one-third of the milk and water mixture. Beat to a smooth paste, and then pour in the rest of the milk and water mixture. Add the melted butter and beat well, so that you have a smooth, creamy batter. Allow to rest.

Make the filling by melting 1 oz. (25 g.) butter in a pan. Add the mushrooms, lemon juice and a generous sprinkling of salt, pepper and nutmeg. Cover the pan and simmer gently for 7–8 minutes.

Meanwhile, make the sauce. Melt the remaining butter in a small saucepan and stir in the flour. Let it bubble for 1 minute and then add the milk, stirring it in gradually to keep the mixture smooth. Allow it to cook for 5 minutes over a low heat, stirring from time to time to prevent it sticking to the pan. Then add the mushrooms and their liquid, and the cream. Keep hot over a very low heat.

Use an 8 in. (20 cm.) frying pan to cook the pancakes, and for each pancake grease it lightly with butter and heat until it smokes. Pour 2–3 tablespoons of the batter into the centre of the pan and quickly tilt the pan to-and-fro to spread the mixture.

Cook over a high heat for just under 1 minute, until the batter has set and the underside is light brown. Slide the pancake out on to a hot plate. Place 1 dessertspoon of the filling in the centre and roll up the pancake. Put on a warmed serving dish and keep warm under a moderate grill while you make the rest of the pancakes. Serve with a cucumber or chicory salad.

POTTED STILTON
Leicestershire and Huntingdonshire

THE VILLAGE OF STILTON in Huntingdonshire gave its name to this most noble of English cheeses. There is still some dispute about the cheese's origin, but it was the landlord of the Bell Inn who first sold it towards the end of the 18th century. Passengers on the London to Edinburgh coach, that passed his door, swiftly spread its fame.

In the 18th century a number of cheeses were potted with spices and a

Stilton goes even further when it is potted. Serve this rich spread with crisp oatcakes.

'glass of sack' (sherry). Sack, which benefits a milder cheese, is not the best for Stilton; if it is very dry, add a little port. Serve with Scots oatcakes.

PREPARATION TIME: 10–15 MINUTES

INGREDIENTS TO YIELD ABOUT 10 OZ. (275 G.)

8 oz. (225 g.) mellow Stilton
2 oz. (50 g.) unsalted butter at room temperature
¼ teaspoon ground mace
½ teaspoon freshly made English mustard

Mash the cheese with the butter, add the mace and mustard and work to a cream. Pack into earthenware or china pots, making sure the cheese is well pressed down. To keep the cheese for any length of time, cover it with clarified butter (see p. 49).

You can make potted cheese in this way with any mixture of leftover cheeses. If it seems too dry, mix in 2 tablespoons of sherry. To vary the flavour, add ¼ teaspoon curry powder or Cayenne in place of the mace and mustard.

OMELETTE ARNOLD BENNETT
Home Counties

THIS PERFECT MARRIAGE of two deeply honoured and traditional ingredients—Finnan Haddie and Parmesan cheese—took place in no less hallowed a spot than London's Savoy Grill. The name is a salute from one great artist to another—from Jean Baptiste Virlogeux, then *Chef de cuisine*, to Arnold Bennett, the novelist who had immortalised Virlogeux as 'Roho', in his novel *Imperial Palace* (1930), based on life in the Savoy.

Finnan Haddie (see p. 70) has been part of our cooking heritage since the 18th century, and Parmesan cheese, oddly enough, since long before that. Though originating in Parma, it was well known here in the late 16th century.

Serve this dish as a light lunch or supper dish, or as a snack before an evening at the theatre.

PREPARATION TIME: 15 MINUTES
COOKING TIME: 5 MINUTES

INGREDIENTS FOR ONE SERVING

3 oz. (75 g.) cooked, flaked Finnan haddock
½ teaspoon grated Parmesan cheese
Salt and freshly ground black pepper
2 eggs
1 tablespoon water
½ tablespoon butter
1 tablespoon double cream

Mix together the haddock and cheese, season with salt and pepper and set aside. Break the eggs into a bowl, add 1 tablespoon of water and season with a little salt and pepper. Beat lightly with a fork.

Melt the butter in an omelette pan, and when it is frothy pour in the beaten eggs. Cook over a medium heat until the omelette is only just set and still liquid in the middle. Transfer, unfolded, to an ovenproof plate.

Spread the haddock and cheese mixture over the top of the omelette and pour on the cream. Slide under a very hot grill for a few minutes, until slightly browned and bubbling. Serve immediately.

STILTON SOUFFLÉ
Huntingdonshire

ALTHOUGH THE SOUFFLÉ is originally a French speciality, it made its impact on English cooking in the mid-19th century when cheese soufflé became a popular party piece. The use of blue-veined Stilton—the 'King of English Cheese'—together with peppery Cayenne creates a uniquely flavoured version of the dish.

PREPARATION TIME: 15–20 MINUTES
COOKING TIME: 35 MINUTES
PRE-HEAT THE OVEN TO 200°C (400°F)—GAS MARK 6

INGREDIENTS FOR FOUR

2 oz. (50 g.) butter
1½ oz. (40 g.) plain flour
½ pint (275/300 ml.) milk
5 oz. (150 g.) Stilton cheese, crumbled
Salt
½ teaspoon Cayenne pepper
5 eggs

Melt the butter in a medium saucepan. Stir in the flour and let it cook gently for a minute or two. Add the milk gradually, stirring after each addition to obtain a smooth, fairly thick sauce. Let it cook over a very low heat for several minutes, stirring quite frequently so that it does not stick to the bottom of the pan.

Add the crumbled Stilton and let it melt into the sauce. Stilton is often quite salty, so taste the sauce before adding salt. Season well with the Cayenne and allow to cool slightly.

Separate the eggs and beat four of the egg yolks into the sauce one at a time. Store the fifth yolk for later use. In a mixing bowl, whisk the five egg whites into stiff peaks. Stir 1 tablespoon of beaten egg white into the sauce to make it a little lighter, then fold the mixture thoroughly into the egg whites.

Grease a 3 pint (1·7 litre) soufflé dish with a little butter. Spoon the mixture lightly into the soufflé dish and cook in the pre-heated oven for about 25 minutes. Serve at once.

CORNISH CHEESE BREAD
Cornwall

TEA HAS ALWAYS been a most important meal in all Cornish households, and cheese bread was often a central feature on the table. In spite of their name, these little cakes are more like savoury scones than bread. They can also be made with chopped, cooked bacon added.

PREPARATION TIME: 35 MINUTES
COOKING TIME: 15 MINUTES
PRE-HEAT THE OVEN TO 180°C (350°F)—GAS MARK 4

INGREDIENTS TO MAKE 16–18 ROLLS

8 oz. (225 g.) self-raising flour
½ teaspoon salt
4 oz. (100/125 g.) butter or margarine
4 oz. (100/125 g.) mature Cheddar cheese, grated
4 oz. (100/125 g.) cooked potato, mashed and sieved
½ teaspoon dry mustard

Sieve the flour and salt together into a bowl. Rub in the fat with your fingertips until it resembles fine breadcrumbs. Add the grated cheese, the sieved potato and mustard. Work it lightly into a dough with fingertips or a wooden spoon.

Roll out the dough ½ in. (1·5 cm.) thick and cut it into rounds 2 in. (5 cm.) across. Arrange them on a greased baking tray and bake on the top shelf of the pre-heated oven for about 15 minutes.

Serve hot with butter.

RECIPES *from* OTHER LANDS

FRANCE
Oeufs en Cocotte à la Crème

THERE ARE MANY WAYS of serving *Oeufs en Cocotte*—eggs baked in small dishes. When *'à la Crème'* is added to the name, this indicates the classic version, which is simply eggs baked with cream. They can be varied by putting different things underneath the eggs—two or three cooked asparagus tips, some mushrooms cut in small cubes and lightly cooked in butter, shrimps, or small pieces of cooked chicken breast.

The classic dish makes a perfect light breakfast—while the more elaborate versions provide excellent first courses at lunch or dinner. *Cocotte* has several meanings, one of which is a child's name for a farmhouse hen or a chicken.

PREPARATION TIME: 5 MINUTES
COOKING TIME: 8 MINUTES
PRE-HEAT THE OVEN TO 200°C (400°F)—GAS MARK 6

INGREDIENTS FOR FOUR

½ oz. (15 g.) butter
Salt and freshly ground pepper
4 eggs
4 tablespoons double cream

Put a dab of butter and a tiny pinch of salt and pepper in the bottom of each of four small ovenproof *cocotte* dishes. Break an egg into each and season the tops with more salt and pepper. Pour 1 tablespoon of cream over each egg and add a further dab of butter.

Put the *cocottes* in a roasting tin, and pour round them enough boiling water to come halfway up the sides of the dishes. Place in the pre-heated oven and bake for 7–8 minutes, until the white has just set (shake a *cocotte* to see if the white is still liquid) and the yolks are still runny. Eat at once.

INDIA
Omelette Curry and Vegetables

OVER THE CENTURIES, the Hindus have evolved the world's greatest vegetarian cuisine. They base their dishes on vegetables, cereals and rice. Omelette Curry and Vegetables is one of their specialities, and it is a particular favourite on Hindu feast-days. The festivals—which include the Hindu New Year and the Rice Harvest Celebration—are marked by offerings of food to various gods and friends.

Even around Calcutta—noted as a lamb-eating area—vegetarian meals have come into favour. Omelette Curry and Vegetables is on the menu of the city's Spence's Hotel—the oldest hotel in Asia. It is recommended as the perfect lunchtime meal for couples who want to eat moderately and modestly.

PREPARATION TIME: 10 MINUTES
COOKING TIME: 20 MINUTES

INGREDIENTS FOR FOUR

1 green or red chilli, fresh or dried
2 pints (1·1 litres) cold water
2 teaspoons Madras curry powder
Salt
2 potatoes, peeled and diced
3 carrots, peeled and diced
8 oz. (225 g.) spinach, washed and coarsely chopped
1 oz. (25 g.) butter
1 onion, finely chopped

For the omelettes:

6 eggs
3 tablespoons water
Salt and freshly ground black pepper
2 oz. (50 g.) butter

Wash and chop the chilli, removing the seeds—take care not to put your fingers near your eyes while doing this; chillis can burn delicate skin.

Put 2 pints (1·1 litres) of water in a saucepan. Sprinkle in the curry powder and salt and bring to the boil. Add the potatoes, carrots and chilli to this spiced water and continue boiling for 5 minutes. Put in the chopped spinach and cook until the vegetables are just tender, about 10 minutes. Drain the vegetables well.

Melt 1 oz. (25 g.) of butter in a medium frying pan. Add the onions and cook for 5 minutes, until they are tender and transparent. Add the drained vegetables and fry them with the onion for a few minutes.

Break 3 eggs into a bowl, add 1½ tablespoons of water and season with a little salt and pepper. Beat lightly with a fork.

Melt 1 oz. (25 g.) of butter in an omelette pan, and when it is frothy pour in the beaten eggs. Cook over a medium heat until the omelette is just set.

Put half the curried vegetables into the middle of the omelette and fold both sides over to cover the filling.

Make another omelette in the same way. Each omelette is enough for two people. Serve any excess vegetables with the omelettes.

SWITZERLAND
Swiss Fondue

FONDUE is not just a delicious party dish, it is a whole performance. It usually consists of one or two kinds of melted Swiss cheese—flavoured with Kirsch—into which diners dip pieces of bread on the end of forks. If anyone is unfortunate enough to let their bread fall into the pot, they have to pay for the next bottle of wine or round of drinks.

Fondue has long been a favourite dish in Switzerland, where the finest farmhouse cheese and good local wine are used in its making.

It is extremely rich, and it helps the digestion if one drinks a tot of Kirsch with it, or some hot tea, or some chilled Neuchâtel—crisp Swiss white wine.

PREPARATION TIME: 15 MINUTES
COOKING TIME: 6 MINUTES

INGREDIENTS FOR SIX

2 cloves garlic
¼ pint (150 ml.) dry white wine
1¼ lb. (575 g.) grated Emmenthal cheese, or Emmenthal and Gruyère mixed
1 teaspoon flour, preferably potato flour
Freshly ground black pepper
¼ teaspoon grated nutmeg
1 small glass Kirsch with 1 drop of corn oil
Plenty of French bread cut into quarters lengthwise and then cut into 1 in. (2·5 cm.) thick pieces

Crush one clove of garlic and rub an ovenproof dish with it, using up the whole clove. Peel the second clove and place it whole in the dish. Pour in the wine, and place the dish over a low heat. When hot, stir in the grated cheese and potato flour with a wooden spoon. Cook for 5–6 minutes, stirring continuously, until the cheese has melted to a cream. Add a little more wine if the mixture seems too thick.

Remove from the heat and stir in the pepper, nutmeg and the Kirsch.

Place a spirit burner on the dining table, and light it. Carry the dish of fondue to the table and place over the heat. When the fondue is bubbling gently, the guests can start dipping the bread on the end of forks into the cheese. Twist the forks round to prevent the cheese dropping off in long strings. When the cheese at the bottom of the dish starts to form a crust, turn the heat down to prevent it from burning. Use spoons to scrape up the delicious crust.

HUNGARY
Liptauer Cheese

LIPTAUER is the German adjective derived from the old Hungarian region of Liptó, now part of Czechoslovakia. The delicately pink cheese is authentically made with sheep or goat's curd cheese, but a very fine version can be made with ordinary cottage cheese.

The dish is popular throughout the area of the old Austro-Hungarian Empire. Its unusually sharp flavour combines well with wholemeal or light rye bread, with radishes and a couple of spring onions, or even a slice or two of strong, raw onion. Washed down by a glass of the light Pilsener beer that can be found throughout most of its home range, it makes an excellent light lunch or appetiser.

Liptauer Cheese improves with keeping, as the caraway seeds expand and permeate it with their flavour.

PREPARATION TIME: 15–20 MINUTES

INGREDIENTS FOR SIX

1 lb. (450 g.) cottage cheese
½ teaspoon sweet paprika
1 teaspoon caraway seeds
1 teaspoon mustard powder
1 teaspoon chopped capers
1 teaspoon finely chopped chives or spring onions
2 tablespoons plain yoghurt
1 tablespoon beer, preferably Pilsener
Radishes and onion to garnish

Work the cottage cheese with a wooden spoon through a sieve into a large bowl. Mix in enough paprika to colour the cheese a faint pink. Blend in the caraway seeds, mustard, capers and chives or spring onions. Add the yoghurt and beer and mix all the ingredients together until thoroughly distributed.

Arrange the cheese in a mound on a dish, and surround with whole or cut radishes, a sliced raw onion and slices of home-made wholemeal or rye bread.

If you do not wish to eat the cheese at once, it will keep in the refrigerator for several days.

Serve sharp, aromatic Liptauer Cheese with rye bread, onions and radishes.

BELGIUM
Oeufs Meulemeester

THIS DISH, to which the Meulemeesters—a family of restaurant owners in Bruges—gave their name in the 19th century, is a traditional north Belgian method of serving eggs. It pre-dates the family's connection with it, and has long been a favourite with local farmers and their families.

PREPARATION TIME: 10 MINUTES
COOKING TIME: 20 MINUTES
PRE-HEAT THE OVEN TO 200°C (400°F)—GAS MARK 6

INGREDIENTS FOR FOUR

8 eggs
½ oz. (15 g.) butter
½ tablespoon chopped chervil
½ tablespoon chopped parsley
½ teaspoon Dijon mustard
4 oz. (100/125 g.) prawns, shelled
½ pint (275/300 ml.) single cream
Salt and freshly ground black pepper
2 tablespoons Cheddar cheese, grated

Boil the eggs for 10–12 minutes. Hold them under cold running water until cool. Shell them carefully, chop coarsely and set aside.

Put the butter, chopped chervil and parsley, mustard, prawns and cream into a medium saucepan. Season and stir well with a wooden spoon.

Stir in the chopped eggs and heat through, stirring.

Grease an ovenproof dish and pour in the mixture. Sprinkle with the grated cheese and bake in the top of the pre-heated oven for about 10 minutes until the top is golden-brown. Serve very hot.

EGG AND CHEESE DISHES

IN THE PAST, many types of egg were commonly eaten—plover, seagull, swan, goose, duck, peacock and turkey, as well as hens' eggs, which were generally smaller than those of today. Peacock eggs were a luxury kept for feasts. Until the 16th century, eggs were more often baked in the soft ashes of the wood fire than boiled.

Cheese-making has been known in Britain since ancient times. It may have started with the discovery of milk curd in the stomachs of young milk-fed animals slaughtered for meat. The natural rennet and acid in the stomach lining caused the warm milk to separate into curds and whey.

In large Tudor households, as much as 160 lb. of cheese might be eaten in a week. Until about 100 years ago, every farmhouse had its cheese-making secrets, so flavours and textures varied even within small areas. Popular colourants were marigold petals or saffron.

Eggs and Egg Cookery

Eggs are a good, cheap source of protein, and also contain Vitamins A and D and small amounts of some B vitamins. Although high in cholesterol, they contain a counter-balancing substance, lecithin, that breaks up fat.

The yolk of an egg is 33% fat, the white mainly water. The shell is porous and can be penetrated by air, water or smells. The air chamber between the shell and the inner lining at the larger end gets bigger with age.

On their own, eggs thicken and solidify at 60–68°C (140–154°F)—temperatures considerably lower than the boiling point of water. But when mixed with other ingredients they solidify at higher temperatures.

How eggs can be used in cooking

Eggs make a meal on their own or can be used in other dishes, both sweet and savoury, in the various ways listed below:

To bind the dry ingredients for stuffing, rissoles and meat loaves.

As raising agents in batters and cakes, particularly sponges. Eggs retain the air beaten into them (see Hints for beating eggs, p. 258).

To thicken custards, sauces, soups and fruit curds. One egg will thicken about ½ pint (275/300 ml.) of liquid.

Mixed with breadcrumbs or flour to make a crisp coating that protects fried foods from very hot fat.

As a garnish—chopped hard-boiled egg or sieved egg yolk adds colour and nutrients to many dishes.

To enrich cakes and puddings by adding food value and giving a moistening and melt-in-the-mouth effect.

Egg whites whisked to a foam are the main ingredient of meringues and soufflés.

Egg yolks act as emulsifiers—blending oil and other liquids, as in mayonnaise.

Current official advice on the use of eggs in cooking should be noted: see the page facing the Acknowledgments, at the front of this book.

CHOOSING AND STORING EGGS

Buy eggs as fresh as possible, ideally less than 1 week old, but certainly not more than 2 weeks old. Always check the packing date on the carton.

Eggs are graded according to quality and weight at packing stations. The quality is determined by 'candling'—holding against a light to examine the interior. Class A eggs have excellent interior quality, Class B eggs fair.

Weights are given in seven grades, Grade 7, the smallest, being up to 45 g. (about 1¾ oz.). Grades rise in categories up to Grade 1, which weigh 70 g. (about 2½ oz.) or over.

Use fresh Class A eggs, Grades 1–5, for serving eggs whole or as the main ingredient in a dish. Grade B or small eggs can be used in cakes and puddings. Brown eggs are sometimes dearer than white eggs, but there is no difference in food value. Free-range eggs are usually considerably dearer, but may have a stronger flavour.

Storing eggs

Store eggs in a clean, cool place with the pointed end down. Do not wash unless absolutely necessary, and keep away from strong-smelling foods whose flavour might permeate the porous shell.

Eggs up to 1 week old when bought will keep for 2 weeks at normal room temperature—about 18°C (65°F)—or up to 5 weeks in a refrigerator.

Store separated whites and yolks in a refrigerator in separate containers. Pour a thin layer of milk or water over the yolks to prevent them hardening.

Yolks are best used within 2 days, whites can be kept up to 4 days.

Take eggs out of the refrigerator and leave them at room temperature for 45 minutes before using. Very cold eggs will crack when boiled, and chilled whites cannot be whisked easily.

How to tell a fresh egg

A fresh egg feels heavy. If you put it in a solution of salt and water (10% salt), it will sink to the bottom. If it floats, it is stale.

When broken into a bowl, a fresh egg has a rounded yolk and a firm white. A stale egg has a flat yolk and a runny white.

Tips for Cooking Eggs

Never overcook eggs. Cooking for too long at too high a temperature makes them hard and rubbery.

To soft-boil eggs, slide them into a pan of boiling water full enough to just cover them. Time from the moment the water re-boils and cook for 3–4½ minutes, depending on size.

Hard-boil eggs for 10–12 minutes, according to size. Move them gently around the pan during boiling to centralise the yolks. As soon as you take them from the pan, plunge them into cold water to stop a grey-black line forming between white and yolk.

If an egg cracks during boiling, add 1 teaspoon of vinegar or salt to stop the white coming out.

Break eggs into a cup one at a time before putting into a pan or cooking mixture, to make sure they are fresh.

When scrambling eggs, use a heavy-based pan to ensure even cooking. Take the pan off the heat just before the eggs set, while still creamy, to prevent them being too dry. They will finish cooking in the heat from the pan.

When poaching eggs, salt and boil the water then lower the heat so that it is simmering before you break the eggs and slide them in. The whites will keep their shape better.

For frying eggs, the fat should be hot but not smoking. When you slip the egg in, the white should solidify at once but not bubble and burn at the edges. If it does, lower the heat. Baste with fat from the pan during frying.

For omelettes, use a pan with a rounded side and of a suitable size to allow about ¼ in. (5 mm.) depth of egg. For two or three eggs, this means a pan 6 in. (15 cm.) across.

Use unsalted or clarified butter (see p. 49) for omelettes if possible; salted butter can cause the omelette to stick to the pan. Warm the pan before you put the butter in—it should be hot enough to make the butter sizzle.

To add eggs to a hot mixture, first beat in a bowl and stir in a little of the hot mixture with them. Do not add them directly—they will solidify at once and the dish will have threads or lumps of cooked egg in it.

Cheese and Cheese Dishes

Cheese is made from curds—the solid part of milk after it has been separated by heat and acid or rennet (a natural substance from the stomach lining of young mammals) from the liquid whey. After processing, it is left to mature for periods varying from 1 to 16 months. The wide range of types and flavours results from differences in the quality and type of milk used, the method of processing and the conditions of maturing.

Hard cheeses, such as Cheddar, Cheshire and Leicester, are firmly pressed during processing. Semi-hard cheeses, such as Lancashire and Caerphilly, are only lightly pressed and contain more water and less fat. Soft cheeses, such as Crowdie and cream cheese, are not pressed but slowly drained. Blue cheeses, such as Stilton, are injected with moulds to give blue-veined marking.

Cheese is rich in calcium, essential for strong bones and teeth, and is a good source of protein. It also contains some riboflavin, a B vitamin.

Buying and storing cheese

If possible, buy pieces of hard and semi-hard cheese cut fresh from the whole cheese in the shop. Ready-cut pieces are likely to go stale quicker.

Do not buy cheese that has cracks running from the edges or is darker in colour in the middle. It is stale and drying out. Avoid cheese that is 'sweating', because it has been stored at too high a temperature and the flavour may be impaired.

Foil-wrapped soft cheese should feel soft, not rubbery, when the wrapping is gently pressed.

Cheese is best bought in small quantities for quick use, but it can be stored. Wrap it in cling film or foil to keep it moist, and store in a refrigerator or cool place. Light destroys the B vitamin, so keep it in the dark.

Hard or semi-hard cheese will keep 5–7 days in a larder or up to 2 weeks in a refrigerator. Soft or cream cheese keeps 2–3 days in a larder or 5–7 days in a refrigerator. Always remove cheese from the refrigerator 1 hour before it is to be used, to allow the full flavour to develop.

If you have any odds and ends of cheese left over, grate them for use in cooking and store in a covered jar.

Cooking with Cheese

Most cheeses can be used for cooking, but hard or semi-hard cheeses that grate easily are best. Cheddar, Leicester and Wensleydale are good.

Good cheeses for grilling are Cheshire, Dunlop and Leicester. For fondues, Gruyère and Emmenthal are traditionally used (although Cheddar and Stilton are also good).

When melting cheese in a pan, as for Welsh Rabbit, keep the heat low, or it will be tough and stringy.

If you use cheese as a topping for a cooked dish, do not add it until the last 5–10 minutes of cooking—long enough for it to melt.

How to make simple cottage cheese

Mild-flavoured cottage cheese can easily be made at home. Serve it with salad or jacket potatoes, or use as a sandwich filler.

Preparation Time: 15–20 minutes
Standing Time: 4–12 hours
Draining Time: about 4 hours

Ingredients for 4 oz. (100/125 g.)

1 pint (575/600 ml.) creamy milk (not sterilised), or goat's milk
1 tablespoon vinegar or lemon juice
1 tablespoon chopped chives
Salt and pepper to taste

1 Heat the milk in a saucepan until it begins to bubble and rise.
2 Remove the saucepan from the heat and stir in the vinegar or lemon juice.
3 Pour the milk into a bowl, cover with a cloth and leave to stand undisturbed for 4–12 hours, or overnight if more convenient.
4 Tip or ladle the curds into a muslin bag, or a piece of double muslin placed over a colander.
5 Tie up the muslin bag or cloth with string and hang it on a hook for the whey to drain into a bowl for 4 hours, or overnight.
6 If liked, keep the drained whey, which aids digestion, to add to soups and stews or cakes and puddings.
7 Place the cheese from the cloth in a bowl and mix in the seasoning. Store in a refrigerator. It keeps 2–3 days.

Of

ROOT, GREEN AND OTHER VEGETABLES

CONTAINING

NUMEROUS *Useful* FAMILY RECIPES

for GARDEN & WILD, FRESH & DRIED VEGETABLES & SALADS & other WHOLESOME PRODUCE

AND

A SELECTION of RECIPES from OTHER LANDS

AND WITH

DIRECTIONS *for* BASIC METHODS

for all kinds of Boiling, Steaming, Baking and Braising of Vegetables to Perfection

BAKED ONIONS
Countrywide

ONIONS have collected more than their fair share of superstitions through the ages. In 1665, when the Great Plague was raging through Britain, people were told that three or four onions left on the ground would absorb all infection in a neighbourhood, and sufferers were urged to apply poultices of butter, leaven, cloves, mallow and onions. At various times onions have been held to have the power to charm against snakes, foretell marriages and ward off witches.

Although their health-giving properties may have been exaggerated in the past, they are undoubtedly beneficial. In many parts of Britain today, onions are believed to be good for a cold, to help insomnia and to cure chilblains if rubbed raw with salt on the affected part.

Onions are the basic ingredient in many traditional recipes. Serve Baked Onions on their own or with grills, roast beef, lamb or chicken.

PREPARATION TIME: 5 MINUTES
COOKING TIME: 2–3 HOURS
PRE-HEAT THE OVEN TO 170°C (325°F)—GAS MARK 3

INGREDIENTS FOR FOUR

8 medium onions
Sea salt
Freshly ground black pepper
2 oz. (50 g.) butter
2 tablespoons chopped parsley

Wash the onions in their skins, removing as much grit as possible. Dry them well.

Line a baking tin with foil to prevent the onions sticking to the tin. Put in the onions and place in the pre-heated oven. Bake for 2–3 hours until tender when pierced with a skewer.

Sprinkle with salt and pepper and put a knob of butter on each. If you like, you can flavour the butter with cinnamon and Cayenne pepper.

Garnish with parsley and serve.

Onions baked in their skins and garnished with butter and parsley.

GLAZED CARROTS
Countrywide

THE sweet taste of the carrot caused it to be referred to as 'honey underground' in early Celtic literature, but it was not until the reign of Elizabeth I that it became a popular British vegetable.

Throughout the centuries, when sugar has been scarce or expensive, carrots have helped to replace it in puddings, pies and preserves. In this recipe, however, sugar is added. It is used to give carrots an appetising glaze. Serve them with roast beef, lamb, chicken, pork and game.

PREPARATION TIME: 10 MINUTES
COOKING TIME: 20–30 MINUTES

INGREDIENTS FOR FOUR TO SIX

1½ lb. (700 g.) carrots, peeled and sliced into 1 in. (2·5 cm.) rounds
¾ pint (450 ml.) chicken stock
2 tablespoons brown sugar
3 oz. (75 g.) butter, cut into small pieces
Freshly ground black pepper
Sea salt
2 tablespoons chopped parsley

Put the carrots in a saucepan with the stock, sugar and butter. Season with pepper. Cover the pan, bring to the boil, and simmer for about 20 minutes until the carrots are tender and the liquid has reduced to a glaze. If the liquid is not reducing fast enough, uncover towards the end of the cooking time and increase the heat under the pan.

Put the glazed carrots in a warmed serving dish. Add salt to taste and sprinkle with parsley.

BRAISED LEEKS
Wales

THE 'PORLEAC' or garden leek was one of the six members of the onion family known in England in pre-Norman days, while leeks and cabbages are the only two cultivated vegetables mentioned in the laws of Hywel Dda (*d.* 950), a Welsh prince of the 10th century.

The mildest of the onion family, the leek has always been appreciated by the perceptive cook for its flavour and adaptability.

PREPARATION TIME: 10 MINUTES
COOKING TIME: 40 MINUTES
PRE-HEAT THE OVEN TO
180°C (350°F)—GAS MARK 4

INGREDIENTS FOR FOUR

8 leeks
2 oz. (50 g.) butter, cut into pieces
½ pint (275/300 ml.) chicken stock
Sea salt
Freshly ground black pepper
1 tablespoon chopped parsley
Green peppercorns (optional)

Trim the base of the leeks and cut a cross in the white stem. Remove any withered or damaged leaves. Cut into the green part lengthwise and wash very thoroughly under cold running water, pulling the leaves apart to make sure you have removed all the grit.

Grease an ovenproof dish with a small amount of butter, and arrange the whole leeks in the dish.

Put the stock in a small saucepan and bring to the boil. Pour the hot stock over the leeks. Season with salt and pepper and add the butter. Cover, and bake in the pre-heated oven for 40 minutes. Remove the lid for the last 5 minutes of cooking.

Garnish with chopped parsley and green peppercorns, if liked.

Leeks are good with all kinds of meat and fish, and their mildness goes particularly well with rich stews.

Leeks braised gently in stock go well with a Sunday roast.

BEETROOT WITH PARSLEY BUTTER
Countrywide

THE ROMANS were familiar with beetroot, but it did not become popular in Britain until the 17th century. The herbalist Gerard, however, writing in 1587, mentions a Great Red Beet first given to him by 'Master Lete a merchant of London, who obtained seed from the Mediterranean regions'.

The most usual method of cooking beetroots is to boil them, but the flavour is much better if they are baked in the oven in their skins. Never cut or peel them before cooking, as this causes a loss of nutritional content as well as colour.

They have a high protein content, but remember that beetroots have more than twice the average number of calories to be found in other vegetables, so they are not for dedicated slimmers.

PREPARATION TIME: 15 MINUTES
COOKING TIME: 3 HOURS
PRE-HEAT THE OVEN TO
180°C (350°F)—GAS MARK 4

INGREDIENTS FOR SIX

6 medium, uncooked beetroots, scrubbed and dried

For parsley butter:

4 oz. (100/125 g.) unsalted butter
1½ tablespoons finely chopped parsley
Coarse salt
Freshly ground black pepper
Lemon juice

Place the beetroots in an ovenproof dish and bake in the pre-heated oven for 2½–3 hours.

Meanwhile, prepare the parsley butter.

Put the butter in a bowl and break it down well with a fork, working it until soft. Blend in the finely chopped parsley and add salt, pepper and lemon juice to taste. Mix thoroughly and set aside.

When the beetroots are cooked, peel them while they are hot (but not too hot) and slice them.

Arrange the slices on a warmed serving dish and dot with parsley butter. Serve immediately.

BRAISED CELERY
Countrywide

CELERY was first introduced into Britain in the 17th century as an Italian salad food—'the young shoots thereof they eat raw with oyl and pepper'.

However, English cooks soon developed it as a cooked vegetable, and today it is included in soups, sauces and savoury hot dishes, as well as salads.

If you make this recipe at a time of year when celery is expensive, use celery stalks rather than hearts. Scrape away the strings with a sharp knife, cut the stalks into short lengths of about 2½ in. (6·5 cm.), and do not blanch them.

PREPARATION TIME: 10 MINUTES
COOKING TIME: 1¼–1½ HOURS
PRE-HEAT THE OVEN TO 180°C (350°F)—GAS MARK 4

INGREDIENTS FOR SIX

- *6 celery hearts*
- *1 oz. (25 g.) butter*
- *1 tablespoon olive oil*
- *8 oz. (225 g.) carrots, peeled and sliced*
- *8 oz. (225 g.) onions, peeled and sliced*
- *½ pint (275/300 ml.) chicken stock*
- *Bouquet garni*
- *Sea salt*
- *Freshly ground black pepper*

Trim the celery hearts and blanch by plunging them into a bowl of boiling water for 2–3 minutes. Drain.

Melt the butter and oil in an ovenproof dish. Add the carrots and onions and fry gently for 10 minutes until tender. Arrange the celery hearts on top, and spoon some of the carrots and onions over the celery. Pour in the stock. Add the bouquet garni and season with salt and pepper. Cover the dish closely and bake in the pre-heated oven for 1–1¼ hours until the vegetables are tender. Remove the bouquet garni and serve with roast or grilled meat, fish or chicken.

BROAD BEANS AND BACON
Countrywide

THE STRONG FLAVOUR of bacon adds zest to the smooth blandness of broad beans in this dish, which was prepared as far back as medieval times, and known as 'beans and collops' in 17th-century England.

Increase the proportions of the ingredients if you wish to serve Broad Beans and Bacon as a dish on its own rather than as a side dish.

PREPARATION TIME: 15 MINUTES
COOKING TIME: 15 MINUTES

INGREDIENTS FOR FOUR TO SIX

- *1 oz. (25 g.) butter*
- *2 oz. (50 g.) bacon or gammon, diced and with rind removed*
- *1 small onion, peeled and finely chopped*
- *1½ lb. (700 g.) shelled broad beans*
- *¼ pint (150 ml.) chicken stock*
- *Freshly ground black pepper*
- *Sea salt*
- *2 tablespoons chopped parsley or 1 tablespoon each of chopped parsley and savory*

Melt the butter in a heavy frying pan. Add the bacon and onion and fry, without browning, for 5 minutes until the onion is soft. Add the broad beans and just enough stock to cover them. Bring to the boil, cover and simmer over a moderate heat for 10–15 minutes until the beans are cooked. There should be a small amount of liquid left in the pan with the beans; if there seems to be too much liquid, evaporate it by boiling very fast.

Season with pepper, and add salt if necessary—the bacon may have made the beans salty enough.

Place the beans and bacon in a warmed serving dish and sprinkle with the chopped parsley or parsley and savory.

BRAISED JERUSALEM ARTICHOKES
Countrywide

THE JERUSALEM ARTICHOKE was introduced into Europe from Canada in 1605 by French explorers, and soon became immensely popular. John Parkinson, in his *Theatre of Plants*, published 24 years later, notes that the artichoke 'has grown to be so common with us here in London that even the most vulgar begin to despise them, whereas when they were first received among us they were dainties for a Queen'.

The name 'Jerusalem' has aroused much discussion, but it is now generally accepted that it derives from the Italian word *Girasola*—a species of sunflower of the same family as the artichoke.

Jerusalem artichokes can be cooked like potatoes: mashed, sautéed in butter, sliced and baked *au gratin* or stewed whole in stock. They can be served in a rich white sauce or braised as below, their flavour sharpened with garlic and capers, and served with chicken, ham and game.

PREPARATION TIME: 15–20 MINUTES
COOKING TIME: 45 MINUTES

INGREDIENTS FOR FOUR

- *1 oz. (25 g.) butter*
- *1 tablespoon oil, preferably olive oil*
- *1 medium onion, peeled and sliced*
- *1 clove garlic, crushed (optional)*
- *1 tablespoon plain flour*
- *1 cup dry cider or white wine*
- *1½ lb. (700 g.) Jerusalem artichokes, peeled*
- *Sea salt*
- *Freshly ground black pepper*
- *1 tablespoon capers (optional)*
- *1 tablespoon chopped parsley*

Heat the butter and oil in a heavy saucepan. Add the onion and garlic, if used, and fry gently for 5 minutes until soft.

Stir in the flour and cook over a low heat for a few minutes, stirring to prevent it burning. Add the cider or wine and bring to the boil. Put in the artichokes and pour in enough water to just cover the vegetables. Season with salt and pepper. Cover the pan and simmer gently for about 45 minutes until cooked, adding more water if necessary. Cooking time will vary according to the size of the artichokes.

Sprinkle with capers and parsley, and serve.

BRAISED CHESTNUTS
Countrywide

HOW AN OLD JOKE came to be called a 'chestnut' is not known—but it may be because chestnuts have grown here since they were introduced by the Romans, and so have a venerable history in British cooking.

Braised Chestnuts are excellent with turkey, goose, pheasant and duck, as well as the more homely pork and sausage. They can also be combined with other vegetables, such as sprouts, onions, carrots and red cabbage.

PREPARATION TIME: 45 MINUTES
COOKING TIME: 45 MINUTES
PRE-HEAT THE OVEN TO 200°C (400°F)—GAS MARK 6

INGREDIENTS FOR FOUR

1 lb. (450 g.) chestnuts
2 oz. (50 g.) butter
1 onion, peeled and finely chopped
1 clove garlic, finely chopped (optional)
2 tablespoons port or Madeira
¾ pint (450 ml.) chicken stock
Sea salt
Freshly ground pepper
1 tablespoon chopped parsley

Using a sharp knife, slit the chestnuts at the narrow end. Put them in a roasting tin and place in the pre-heated oven for 10–15 minutes until the skins burst. Remove the shells and skins while still hot.

Alternatively, put the chestnuts in a saucepan, add water and bring to the boil. Cover and simmer gently for 15 minutes until the skins split. Then drain and peel.

Reduce the oven temperature to 180°C (350°F)—gas mark 4.

Melt the butter in a shallow, ovenproof casserole. Add the onion and garlic and fry gently for 5 minutes until soft. Add the chestnuts and stir so that they are coated with the butter. Pour in the port or Madeira and the stock.

Season with salt and pepper and bring to the boil. Cover the casserole, place it in the pre-heated oven and bake the chestnuts for 40 minutes. If, towards the end of the cooking time, there is too much liquid, remove the lid and let it reduce.

You can also cook this dish on top of the stove, by covering the casserole and leaving it to simmer for 45 minutes over a gentle heat, allowing it to reduce if there is too much liquid.

Sprinkle the chestnuts with parsley and serve.

As a variation, add chopped bacon or apple to the chestnuts.

A traditional spread—pheasant with Game Chips and Braised Chestnuts.

GAME CHIPS
Countrywide

THESE ARE THE MOST aristocratic of chips—cut very thinly indeed, and cooked to a crisp golden-brown. Like bread sauce, redcurrant jelly and watercress they are one of the customary accompaniments of game, but many people enjoy them with other roast meats.

PREPARATION TIME: 40 MINUTES
COOKING TIME: 10 MINUTES

INGREDIENTS FOR FOUR

1 lb. (450 g.) potatoes
Vegetable or peanut oil for deep-frying
Sea salt
Freshly ground black pepper

Peel the potatoes and slice them very thinly with a mandolin or cheese parer. Soak the slices in cold water for 30 minutes to remove excess starch. Drain well and pat dry on kitchen paper.

Put the oil in a deep pan and heat it to 200°C (400°F)—a cube of bread dropped in it should turn golden-brown in about 45 seconds.

Put half the potato slices into a frying basket and lower it carefully into the oil. Move the slices around so that they do not stick together. Remove them after about 5 minutes when they are golden-brown. Drain on paper towels. Keep them warm, uncovered, under a moderate grill while you cook the rest of the slices.

Sprinkle with salt and pepper.

CREAMED CABBAGE
Countrywide

THE ANGLO-SAXON WORD for a kitchen garden was *wyrt-tun*, meaning 'cabbage enclosure'. This hardy and serviceable vegetable has been a staple food in these islands for millennia, but the cabbage cooked by the Anglo-Saxons, a coarser form with less heart, was not the cabbage we know today. The modern variety, with its leaves densely packed in a large, tight head, is partly descended from a variety introduced to England from Holland in the 17th century, by Sir Anthony Ashley of Wimborne in Dorset. A cabbage carved in stone was placed at the foot of his tomb when he died in 1627.

Over the years, cabbage has become an everyday vegetable, often over-cooked and served with insufficient seasoning. The recipe which follows transforms it in flavour and appearance and is the perfect accompaniment to grilled meat.

PREPARATION TIME: 10 MINUTES
COOKING TIME: 15 MINUTES

INGREDIENTS FOR FOUR

2 oz. (50 g.) butter
1 lb. (450 g.) cabbage, coarsely chopped
1 clove garlic, finely chopped (optional)
Sea salt
Freshly ground black pepper
$\frac{1}{4}$ teaspoon freshly grated nutmeg
3 fl. oz. (90 ml.) double cream

Melt the butter in a heavy frying pan. Add the cabbage and the garlic. Fry gently, stirring frequently, for about 10 minutes, until the cabbage has softened a little but is still crunchy. Season with salt, pepper and nutmeg, and stir in the cream. Cook for 3–5 minutes, stirring. Remove from the heat and serve at once.

PARSNIPS WITH WALNUTS AND MADEIRA
Countrywide

THOMAS TUSSER (1524–80), the East Anglian farmer who was also a connoisseur of food, recommends parsnips as vegetables to be 'buttered' in the manner of the day. His contemporaries probably appreciated the saying 'Fine words butter no parsnips'—a just observation.

Young parsnips are very good simply boiled and buttered, but there are some more unusual ways of serving them.

The following recipe is excellent with a straightforward main course, such as grilled steak or chops. It can also be served with ham. The combined flavours of wine, cream and chopped walnuts give the parsnips unexpected character.

PREPARATION TIME: 15 MINUTES
COOKING TIME: 40 MINUTES
PRE-HEAT THE OVEN TO 190°C (375°F)—GAS MARK 5

INGREDIENTS FOR FOUR TO SIX

2 lb. (900 g.) parsnips, peeled
2 fl. oz. (50 ml.) dry Madeira
4 fl. oz. (100/125 ml.) double cream
$1\frac{1}{2}$ oz. (40 g.) butter
Sea salt
Freshly ground black pepper
2 oz. (50 g.) walnuts, chopped

If the parsnips are large, remove and discard the cores. Cut the parsnips into 1 in. (2·5 cm.) pieces.

Put the pieces in a vegetable steamer or wire colander, and place over a pan containing a few inches of water. Cover the pan tightly and

Madeira, chopped walnuts and cream give unexpected character to parsnips.

bring to the boil. Steam over gently bubbling water for 20 minutes until the parsnips are tender.

Put the parsnips into a bowl and add the Madeira, cream and 1 oz. (25 g.) of the butter. Season with salt and pepper, and mash all the ingredients well together.

Grease a baking dish with a little butter and put in the mashed parsnips. Dot with the rest of the butter and sprinkle the walnuts over the top. Put in the pre-heated oven and bake for 20 minutes.

CREAMED MUSHROOMS
Countrywide

THERE are 21 species of edible fungi in Britain. The best are those you pick yourself in the fields, and only two types are commonly available in the shops—small button mushrooms and large flat ones, which have more flavour.

Cook them soon after buying or picking, as mushrooms become limp quickly and lose their flavour.

Do not overcook or the texture and taste will be spoiled. Creamed Mushrooms can come to table as a savoury on toast, or with croûtons of fried bread; as a filling for omelettes, or under poached eggs on toast. They also go well with chicken, veal and sweetbreads.

PREPARATION TIME: 10 MINUTES
COOKING TIME: 10–15 MINUTES

INGREDIENTS FOR FOUR

1 tablespoon olive oil
2 oz. (50 g.) butter
1 lb. (450 g.) mushrooms, cleaned and sliced
2 tablespoons peeled and finely chopped shallots
¼ pint (150 ml.) double cream
Sea salt and freshly ground black pepper
2–3 tablespoons Madeira (optional)
1–2 tablespoons softened butter
¼ teaspoon freshly grated nutmeg

Heat the oil and butter in a heavy frying pan. Add the mushrooms and shallots. Cook over a moderate heat for about 3 minutes, stirring so that the vegetables do not stick to the bottom of the pan. Stir in the cream and salt and pepper. Cook for a further 5 minutes, stirring, until the sauce is reduced and thickened.

Add the Madeira, and bring to the boil for 1 minute.

Remove from the heat and stir in the softened butter. Add the nutmeg, check the seasoning and serve.

STEAMED NETTLES
Countrywide

AARON HILL (1685–1750) may have meant the following verse as a moral precept upon facing up to the difficulties of life; or it may have simply been intended as a warning to those who gathered nettles in order to cook them for the table:

'Tender-handed stroke a nettle
It will sting you for your pains;
Grasp it like a man of mettle
And it soft as silk remains.'

Nettles have been eaten as a vegetable for centuries—the Romans are said to have brought a specially favoured variety with them to Britain. Their flavour is reminiscent of spinach, and they are good served as a purée, or steamed and buttered as in this recipe.

It is wise to wear gloves when preparing the nettles. Pick young tender leaves only, and discard the stalks. Serve with lamb, chicken, fish and meat stews.

PREPARATION TIME: 10 MINUTES
COOKING TIME: 15 MINUTES

INGREDIENTS FOR FOUR

2 lb. (900 g.) young nettles
2 oz. (50 g.) unsalted butter
Sea salt
Freshly ground black pepper

Wearing rubber gloves, wash the nettles and discard the stalks.

Put the nettle leaves in a steamer or wire colander and place this in a pan above boiling water. Cover the pan with a tightly fitting lid and steam the nettles for about 10 minutes, or until tender.

Melt the butter gently in a saucepan. Add the cooked nettles and toss them until they are coated with butter. Season with salt and pepper.

You can also fry nettles in a little butter or margarine.

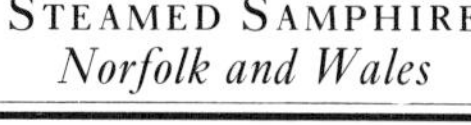

STEAMED SAMPHIRE
Norfolk and Wales

SAMPHIRE—also known as sea fennel and St Peter's cress—is a dark green, fleshy plant that grows along cliffs, rocky coasts and marshlands. The original spelling of the word, 'Sampier', came from the old French name for it—*herbe de St Pierre*.

The leaves were once widely used in salads and pickled in vinegar. It is included among the ingredients of a 1650 recipe with pickled cucumbers, vinegar, lemon, nutmeg and a little strong broth. The mixture was boiled, thickened, sweetened and served over meat on fried bread.

Steamed Samphire, served with melted butter, is delicious with lamb, mutton or fish.

PREPARATION TIME: 5 MINUTES
COOKING TIME: 15–20 MINUTES

INGREDIENTS FOR FOUR

1½ lb. (700 g.) samphire
4 oz. (100/125 g.) unsalted butter
Sea salt
Freshly ground black pepper
Squeeze of lemon juice

Wash the samphire thoroughly in plenty of cold water and trim off the coarse roots.

Put the samphire in a steamer and place the steamer in a pan above boiling water. Cover the pan with a tightly fitting lid and steam for 15–20 minutes or until tender.

Meanwhile, gently melt the butter in a small saucepan, season it with salt and pepper and squeeze in a little lemon juice to taste.

Arrange the samphire on a warmed serving dish and serve the butter separately in a warmed jug. Serve at once.

BOXTY PANCAKES
Ireland

BOXTY is an Irish potato dish, traditionally served in the northern counties on All Hallows Eve; there is Boxty bread, cooked in the oven on a greased baking sheet, and Boxty Pancakes—'Boxty on the griddle'. The name 'Boxty' came from the word *Bochty—boch* meaning 'poor' (that is, a poor-man's dish).

Most pancakes are made with a batter of eggs, milk and flour. But in this pancake, the Irish use potatoes and flour.

Fried to a crispy golden-brown on both sides—preferably in bacon fat—they have a flavour as delicious as the old rhyme claims:

'Butter on the one side
Gravy on the other,
Sure them that gave me Boxty
Were better than my mother.'

Serve them with chops, roasts, liver and bacon, and stews.

PREPARATION TIME: 10 MINUTES
COOKING TIME: 15 MINUTES

INGREDIENTS FOR FOUR

1 lb. (450 g.) potatoes, peeled
4 oz. (100/125 g.) self-raising flour
3–4 fl. oz. (90–125 ml.) milk
Sea salt
Freshly ground black pepper
2 oz. (50 g.) butter or bacon fat

Grate the potatoes and put them in a colander. Cover with paper towels and press down to squeeze out the surplus starch.

Sieve the flour into a mixing bowl and stir in the milk. Mix in the grated potatoes and season with salt and pepper.

Heat the butter or bacon fat in a heavy frying pan until it foams. When the foam begins to subside, drop in about 1 tablespoon of batter to make each Boxty. Cook the pancakes for 3–4 minutes, or until golden-brown, on each side. Remove the pancakes with a fish slice, and keep warm under a moderate grill while you cook the rest of the pancakes in the same way.

Sprinkle with salt and serve.

As a variation, the pancakes can be flavoured with caraway seeds, sage or chopped onions. Stir in the flavouring with the salt and pepper and mix well. For a delicious light supper, serve the pancakes on their own, covered with tomato sauce and a sprinkling of chopped ham.

CREAMED BUTTON ONIONS
Countrywide

WHEN THESE little onions are brought to the table bathed in creamy sauce, it is not difficult to believe that the word 'onion' comes from the Latin *unio*—originally meaning 'a large pearl'. They have a light, delicate flavour and are a delicious accompaniment to plain roast chicken or turkey, grilled chops, steak, or liver and bacon.

PREPARATION TIME: 20 MINUTES
COOKING TIME: 40 MINUTES

INGREDIENTS FOR SIX

2 lb. (900 g.) button onions
¼ pint (150 ml.) chicken stock or dry white wine
2 oz. (50 g.) softened butter
2 tablespoons plain flour
¾ pint (450 ml.) milk
¼ pint (150 ml.) double cream
Sea salt
Freshly ground black pepper
¼ teaspoon freshly grated nutmeg
1 tablespoon chopped parsley

Bring a large pan of water to the boil and drop in the onions. Boil them for a few minutes. Drain and, while still hot, slip off their skins.

Put the onions back in the clean pan and add the stock or wine. Cover and simmer for about 30 minutes.

Meanwhile, melt 1 oz. (25 g.) of the butter in a small saucepan and add the flour. Cook over a low heat for 2 minutes, stirring all the time, but do not allow to brown. Add the milk and cream and bring to the boil, still stirring. Season with salt and pepper and simmer, stirring continuously, until thickened. Check the seasoning.

Drain the onions, return them to the pan and pour the sauce over them. Place over a gentle heat and mix in the rest of the butter in small pieces.

Transfer to a warmed serving dish, sprinkle with nutmeg and parsley, and serve while still very hot.

SORREL PURÉE
West Country

'SORREL SHARPENS THE APPETITE, assuages heat, cools the liver, and strengthens the heart', declared the diarist John Evelyn in his *Acetaria*, published in 1699. The plant was variously recommended as a fried vegetable, for use in a sharp sauce for fish, in a spring soup, in salads and even as a purgative and a cure for toothache. Farm labourers chewed on its leaves to combat thirst.

The best variety is French sorrel, which Mary, Queen of Scots is said to have introduced into England. Its flavour is milder than other varieties. As sorrel leaves become older they often turn bitter. The tender young leaves have a lemony tang that makes them delicious as a purée. Serve with eggs, white fish, ham, veal or chicken.

PREPARATION TIME: 10 MINUTES
COOKING TIME: 10 MINUTES

INGREDIENTS FOR FOUR

1½ oz. (40 g.) butter
2 lb. (900 g.) sorrel, washed and chopped
¼ pint (150 ml.) double cream
2 eggs, beaten
Sea salt
Freshly ground black pepper
¼ teaspoon freshly grated nutmeg

Melt the butter in a heavy frying pan and add the chopped sorrel. Cover, and cook the sorrel in its own juices for 4 minutes until tender. Remove the lid and add the cream and beaten eggs. Season with salt and pepper. Cook, uncovered, over a low heat for 5 minutes, stirring frequently, until the mixture has thickened; do not allow to boil. Check the seasoning.

Place in a warmed serving dish and sprinkle with nutmeg.

Brussels Sprouts with Chestnuts
Devonshire

Sprouts were introduced into Britain from the Low Countries in the 16th century.

The smallest ones, with tight heads, make the best eating, and when cooked they should retain their bright colour and crisp texture.

This recipe, which combines them with half their weight in chestnuts, makes a particularly crisp, nutty dish to serve with pork, game, turkey, duck or goose.

Preparation Time: 30–40 minutes
Cooking Time: 25–30 minutes
Pre-heat the Oven to 200°C (400°F)—gas mark 6

Ingredients for Four to Six

8 oz. (225 g.) chestnuts
1 lb. (450 g.) Brussels sprouts
1½ oz. (40 g.) butter
¼ pint (150 ml.) chicken stock
Sea salt
Freshly ground black pepper

Using a sharp knife, slit the chestnuts at the narrow end. Put them in a roasting tin and place in the pre-heated oven for 10–15 minutes until the skins burst. Peel while still hot.

Alternatively, put the chestnuts in a saucepan, add water and bring to the boil. Cover and simmer for 5 minutes until the skins split. Remove from the water one at a time and peel while still hot.

Discard the outer leaves of the sprouts. Trim the bases and cut a cross in each base so that the sprouts will cook evenly.

Heat the butter in a heavy frying pan and add the chestnuts. Cook gently until the chestnuts are coated with the butter. Pour in the stock, cover and simmer for 20 minutes. Add the sprouts and more stock if necessary to just cover the vegetables. Season with salt and pepper. Cover again and cook for 10 minutes or until the sprouts are just tender.

Check the seasoning and serve.

Stuffed Tomatoes
Countrywide

When they first gained acceptance as a food in England, in the second half of the 18th century, tomatoes were usually cooked and pulped for soups, or made into a sharp pickle with vinegar, garlic and ginger.

Cooked tomatoes became popular a few decades later, and candied tomatoes and tomato jam—both of which sound a little strange to our ears—enjoyed a vogue for a time.

Stuffed Tomatoes form an easily prepared dish that can be served as a first course, an accompaniment to a main course or on its own.

Preparation Time: 10 minutes
Cooking Time: 20 minutes
Pre-heat the Oven to 180°C (350°F)—gas mark 4

Ingredients for Six

6 large tomatoes, washed
1 oz. (25 g.) butter
1 medium onion, peeled and chopped
4 oz. (100/125 g.) mushrooms, washed and chopped
4 oz. (100/125 g.) fresh breadcrumbs
2 tablespoons chopped basil or parsley
Sea salt
Freshly ground black pepper
2 tablespoons Parmesan cheese, grated
½ teaspoon paprika

Slice the tops off the tomatoes and put the tops to one side. Scoop out the pulp from the tomatoes with a spoon, taking care not to break the skins. Put the pulp into a mixing bowl and put the skins aside.

Melt the butter in a frying pan over a gentle heat. Add the onion and fry until soft and transparent. Add the mushrooms and cook for a few minutes.

Put the onion and mushrooms into the bowl with the tomato pulp and add the breadcrumbs and herbs. Season with salt and pepper and mix all the ingredients well together.

Put spoonfuls of the mixture into the tomato skins, sprinkle with cheese and paprika and replace the tops.

Stand the stuffed tomatoes in a greased ovenproof dish and bake in the pre-heated oven for 15–20 minutes. Serve hot.

Celery and Carrots in Cider
West Country

France seems to have been the place where cider originated—or at least its presence was first recorded there in the 6th century. Probably it was unknown here before the Normans brought it over in the years following the Conquest. The Anglo-Saxons would have preferred ale anyway.

When the great apple orchards of later centuries developed, farmers grew cider apples for their own consumption, extracting the juice with presses, using wild yeast for the ferment and storing the brew in oak casks. The leftover pulp, known as 'pomace', was used to feed the farmer's livestock and the cottager's pig.

It is a happy coincidence that cider improves the flavour of so many recipes. A strong, very dry cider is best with this dish of winter vegetables. Serve with ham.

Preparation Time: 10 minutes
Cooking Time: 55 minutes

Ingredients for Four to Six

1 small head of celery
1 pint (575/600 ml.) very dry cider
1 lb. (450 g.) carrots, peeled and cut into 2 in. (5 cm.) lengths
Sea salt
Freshly ground black pepper
1 tablespoon chopped parsley

Trim the base of the celery and remove any leaves. Divide the stalks, wash them well and cut them into 2 in. (5 cm.) lengths.

Pour the cider into a large saucepan and bring to the boil. Put in the carrots, cover and simmer for 15 minutes. Add the celery and season with salt and pepper. Re-cover the pan, bring the cider back to the boil and simmer for 30 minutes. Drain the vegetables, keeping the cooking liquid, and put them in a warmed serving dish. Place under a moderate grill to keep warm.

Put the reserved cooking liquid into a small saucepan and boil rapidly until it has reduced to 4 tablespoons.

Pour the liquid over the vegetables, sprinkle with parsley and serve at once.

Ingredients for Stewed Red Cabbage—the sweet-sour dish that goes so well with pork or duck.

PREPARATION TIME: 20–25 MINUTES
COOKING TIME: 2½–3 HOURS
PRE-HEAT THE OVEN TO 150°C (300°F)—GAS MARK 2

INGREDIENTS FOR SIX

1 oz. (25 g.) butter
2 medium onions, peeled and chopped
3 carrots, peeled and chopped
4 rashers of bacon, rinds removed, chopped
4 tart cooking apples, peeled and chopped
2 lb. (900 g.) red cabbage, finely chopped
1 clove garlic, finely chopped
Sea salt
Freshly ground black pepper
½ teaspoon freshly grated nutmeg
1 bay leaf
2 cloves
2 tablespoons port
2 tablespoons red wine vinegar

Melt the butter in an ovenproof dish. Add the onions, carrots and bacon and cook for 5 minutes until soft. Remove from the heat and add the apples, cabbage and garlic. Season with salt, pepper and nutmeg, and add the bay leaf and cloves. Mix all the ingredients well together. Stir in the port and the red wine vinegar.

Cover the dish and bake in the pre-heated oven for 2½–3 hours. Serve hot or cold, as you wish.

STEWED RED CABBAGE
Countrywide

APPLES, ONIONS AND SPICES, together with wine and vinegar, are traditional ingredients to cook with red cabbage. The long, slow cooking allows the flavours to be absorbed, and gives the spicy, sweet-sour taste for which it is renowned.

The addition of the wine helps both colour and flavour, and prevents the cabbage from turning blue. Port began to be introduced into English cooking in the 18th century, when it was consumed in vast quantities; any left over or of inferior quality was kept for use in the kitchen.

Red cabbage goes well with duck, goose, venison and pork, and is also good with ham and sausages. It can be served cold or re-heated with a little cooked bacon added to it.

SPINACH SOUFFLÉ
Countrywide

SPINACH REACHED EUROPE from Persia through the Arab countries in the Middle Ages. From its earliest days in Britain there seem to have been two opinions about its virtues. The herbalist William Turner, writing in 1568, commented: 'I know not wherefore it is good savinge to fill the belly.' But John Murrell, some 20 years later, thought well of it, and gave a recipe for a dish that is still a favourite today—Spinach Garnished with Eggs.

Those who grow it in the garden, know spinach at its best—bright-hued, fresh and tender. If possible, pick it only a few minutes before cooking, so that it retains all its delicate flavour. Serve Spinach Soufflé on its own for a light luncheon or with plain grilled meat or fish.

PREPARATION TIME: 40 MINUTES
COOKING TIME: 1 HOUR
PRE-HEAT THE OVEN TO 190°C (375°F)—GAS MARK 5

INGREDIENTS FOR FOUR

2½ oz. (65 g.) butter
4 shallots, peeled and finely chopped
1 lb. (450 g.) spinach, washed and very finely chopped
Sea salt
Freshly ground black pepper
2 tablespoons plain flour
¼ pint (150 ml.) milk, warmed
2 egg yolks, beaten
2 oz. (50 g.) Cheddar or Gruyère cheese, grated
¼ teaspoon Cayenne pepper
5 egg whites, whisked

Melt 1 oz. (25 g.) of the butter in a large frying pan. Put in the chopped shallots and cook until soft. Add the chopped spinach, cover the pan, and cook the spinach in its own juices for 3–5 minutes, until tender. Season with salt and pepper.

In a saucepan, melt 1 oz. (25 g.) of the butter over gentle heat and add the flour. Stir, with a wooden spoon, for a few minutes so that the flour cooks. Add the warm milk, stirring continuously. Bring to the boil, still stirring, and, when thickened, remove from the heat. Stir in the beaten egg yolks and the cooked spinach. Add the grated cheese and the Cayenne pepper. Check the seasoning, and carefully fold in the egg whites.

Grease a 1½ pint (850 ml.) soufflé dish with the rest of the butter. Pour the spinach mixture into the dish and place it in the centre of the pre-heated oven. Bake for 30–40 minutes until puffy and golden-brown on the outside, but still runny in the middle. Serve at once, since a soufflé does not stay puffy for very long.

TURNIPS WITH ORANGE SAUCE
Countrywide

FOR MANY, the turnip is a vegetable to be served plain boiled, with no sauce or garnish. In the Middle Ages it was eaten on penitential days, and the association of ideas no doubt endowed it with an aura of austerity, although it was considered to have good, health-giving properties. Elyot, in his *Castle of Helthe* (1539), wrote: 'Turnips being welle boyled in water and after with fatte fleshe norysheth moche.'

Later centuries have demanded flavour and texture from vegetables as well as nourishment. The arrival of oranges in Britain in the late Middle Ages opened up new possibilities in sauces and garnishes.

Turnip with Orange Sauce turns a somewhat bland vegetable into a creamy dish to serve with duck, pork or ham.

PREPARATION TIME: 10 MINUTES
COOKING TIME: 30 MINUTES

INGREDIENTS FOR FOUR TO SIX

Juice of 2 oranges
1½ lb. (700 g.) young turnips, peeled and quartered
½ pint (275/300 ml.) chicken stock
Sea salt
Freshly ground black pepper
Coarsely grated rind of 1 orange

Put the orange juice in a saucepan with the turnip quarters. Add enough chicken stock to just cover the turnips, and season with salt and pepper. Cover, and simmer gently for about 30 minutes or until tender.

Drain the turnips in a colander, reserving the liquid, and put them in a warmed serving dish.

Put the cooking liquid in a small saucepan and boil rapidly until reduced by half.

Sprinkle the grated orange rind over the turnips and pour over the sauce.

PARSNIP BALLS
Countrywide

BEFORE the introduction of the sweet potato to Britain in the mid-16th century, parsnips played something of the role that potatoes were to play in later years. They were traditionally served with roast beef, and many people ate them with salt fish on Ash Wednesday and other fast days.

In Elizabethan times parsnips formed a basis for sweet puddings, with honey and spices.

Parsnip Balls—crunchy on the outside, and soft inside—are delicious served hot with roast or grilled meat. Or cover with cheese sauce and brown under the grill for a light lunch.

PREPARATION TIME: 25 MINUTES
COOKING TIME: 20 MINUTES

INGREDIENTS FOR FOUR TO SIX

1½ lb. (700 g.) parsnips, peeled and cut into 1 in. (2·5 cm.) pieces
Sea salt
3 oz. (75 g.) butter
2 tablespoons double cream
Freshly ground black pepper
¼ teaspoon freshly grated nutmeg
½ egg, beaten
2 oz. (50 g.) dried breadcrumbs
Vegetable or peanut oil for deep-frying

Put the parsnips in a pan and cover with cold water. Add salt and cover the pan. Bring to the boil and cook for 15 minutes until tender. Drain thoroughly.

Melt the butter in a small saucepan, and add it with the cream to the parsnips. Season with salt, pepper and nutmeg, and mash well.

Allow to cool, then stir in the egg. Using your fingers, form the mixture into walnut-sized balls and roll them in breadcrumbs.

Put the oil in a deep pan and heat to 200°C (400°F). In a frying basket, place as many balls as will fit without touching. Lower the basket carefully into the hot oil and fry for 2–3 minutes until golden-brown. Repeat with more batches of the balls until they are all cooked.

Serve hot, if liked, sprinkled with lemon juice and chopped parsley.

CHAMP
Ireland

THE POTATO is to the Irish what pasta is to an Italian, and they have created many ways of adding variety to this basically simple dish. Champ is one of the best—warm and heartening on a cold winter's day.

Champ is also made in Scotland, where it is known as Stelk or Thump. Red Champ can be made with cooked beetroot.

You can use green peas, nettles, or a mixture of peas and onions with the potatoes, as an alternative to leeks when these are difficult to obtain or expensively out of season.

PREPARATION TIME: 10–15 MINUTES
COOKING TIME: 25 MINUTES

INGREDIENTS FOR FOUR TO SIX

1 lb. (450 g.) potatoes, peeled and cut into even-sized pieces
Sea salt
8 oz. (225 g.) leeks
¼ pint (150 ml.) milk
Freshly ground black pepper
2 oz. (50 g.) butter

Put the potatoes in a saucepan and cover with cold water. Add salt, cover the pan and bring to the boil. Cook for 20 minutes or until tender.

Trim the base of the leeks and remove any withered or damaged leaves. Cut into the green part lengthwise and wash well under cold running water, pulling the leaves about to make sure you have removed all the grit. Slice into 1 in. (2·5 cm.) pieces.

Put the leeks in a saucepan with just enough milk to cover them. Simmer for about 10 minutes until cooked. Drain, keeping back a little of the milk.

Mash the potatoes with this milk, add the leeks and season with salt and black pepper. Mix well together.

Serve with the butter separately—each person puts a lump of butter in the middle of his helping.

PEASE PUDDING
Countrywide

THE NURSERY RHYME has Pease Pudding finding favour whether served hot, cold or in a pot nine days old. It is, in fact, one of the few vegetable dishes that can taste good when warmed through a second time.

Pease Pudding probably developed as a result of the cooked peas sold from stalls in the reign of James I, when 'Hot Grey Peas and a suck of Bacon' was a common street cry. The bacon was tied to a string, and the stall-keeper held on to the other end.

This recipe gives three methods for cooking the pudding. Baking is perhaps the least well known; it creates a light, almost fluffy dish which is well worth trying.

Pease Pudding makes an excellent accompaniment to roast pork, and any left over can be fried the next day and served with cold pork, ham or sausages.

PREPARATION TIME: PEAS SOAKED OVERNIGHT
COOKING TIME: 1½–2 HOURS DEPENDING ON METHOD USED
PRE-HEAT THE OVEN TO 180°C (350°F)—GAS MARK 4 FOR OVEN METHOD

INGREDIENTS FOR SIX

1 lb. (450 g.) dried split peas
2 oz. (50 g.) butter
1 egg, beaten
2 tablespoons freshly chopped mint or 1 tablespoon dried mint
Sea salt
Freshly ground black pepper

Cover the peas with cold water and leave to soak overnight.

Next day, drain the peas and put them in a saucepan. Cover with fresh cold water, bring to the boil and simmer for 1 hour. Drain well and sieve or liquidise the peas.

Put the peas in a mixing bowl and add the butter, egg and mint. Season with salt and pepper and mix all the ingredients well together.

The pudding can be cooked in one of three ways.

To boil it, cut a piece of white cloth 15 in. (38 cm.) square. Put the pudding in the cloth and tie lightly. Bring a large pan of water to the boil, add the pudding and simmer for 1 hour until cooked.

To steam the pudding, grease a pudding basin with a little butter and spoon in the purée. Cover with foil or greaseproof paper. Stand the basin in a pan and pour in water so that it reaches about halfway up the basin. Cover the pan and bring the water to the boil. Simmer for 30–45 minutes until the pudding is firm.

To bake the pudding, grease an ovenproof dish with butter. Spoon in the mixture, cover and cook for 30 minutes in the pre-heated oven.

PAN HAGGERTY
Northumberland

PAN HAGGERTY is a favourite supper dish in the north-east of England, where onions and potatoes are the main ingredients of a number of recipes. The name was originally one word—Panhaggerty—meaning 'onions and potatoes'; it is given in a word book of the dialect of Winlayton, near Newcastle. There are many variations of the recipe. This one includes cheese as well as onions and is best served with grilled or roast meats.

PREPARATION TIME: 20 MINUTES
COOKING TIME: 20 MINUTES

INGREDIENTS FOR FOUR

1 lb. (450 g.) potatoes, peeled
2 oz. (50 g.) beef dripping, or butter
8 oz. (225 g.) onions, peeled and finely chopped
Sea salt
Freshly ground black pepper
4 oz. (100/125 g.) Cheddar cheese, grated

Grate the potatoes and put them in a colander. Cover them with paper towels or a plate and press down to squeeze out the surplus starch.

Melt half the butter or dripping in a frying pan, add the onions and fry over a low heat for 5 minutes until soft and transparent. Remove the onions from the pan.

Melt the remaining butter in the frying pan. Cover the pan with the grated potatoes, then spread the onions over the potatoes. Season with salt and pepper and sprinkle with the grated cheese. Cook very gently over a moderate heat for about 10 minutes, until the bottom browns.

Put a plate over the frying pan and invert the Pan Haggerty on to it.

Melt a little more butter in the pan and carefully slide the Pan Haggerty back into it to brown the other side. Cook for a further 10 minutes so that the cake is cooked right through and browned on both sides. Slide it on to a warmed plate and serve at once.

STEWED LENTILS
Countrywide

LENTILS are one of the oldest foods known to man—the 'mess of pottage' for which Esau sold his birthright is said to have been made with red lentils. In medieval Persia, a dish of lentils and spinach was prepared to heal the sick. They were popular with both the Greeks and the Egyptians, while the Romans, according to Pliny the Elder and other distinguished authors of the period, considered that a lentil diet was conducive to a calm and equable temperament.

Lentils require little preparation and supervision while cooking, and they readily absorb the flavours of the meat, herbs or vegetables with which they are cooked.

Serve delicate stewed lentils with smoked or salt pork, lamb, beef or game.

PREPARATION TIME: 10 MINUTES
COOKING TIME: 1 HOUR

INGREDIENTS FOR FOUR

8 oz. (225 g.) brown lentils
2 tablespoons olive oil
1 small onion, peeled and finely chopped
1 small carrot, peeled and chopped
2 cloves garlic, chopped
Sprig of fresh mint
Sea salt
Freshly ground black pepper
1 tablespoon chopped parsley
1 oz. (25 g.) softened butter

Carefully pick over the lentils, removing any stones and grit. Rinse thoroughly in cold water and drain.

Heat the oil in a large pan, add the onion, carrot and garlic and fry gently for a few minutes.

Add the lentils and cover generously with fresh cold water.

Add the mint and season with salt and pepper. Cover the pan, bring to the boil and simmer for 1 hour, after which time all the water should have been absorbed and the lentils should be tender.

Remove the pan from the heat and stir in the parsley and butter. Serve immediately.

STUFFED MARROW
Countrywide

THE CREAMY TEXTURE and delicate flavour of young marrow make it a favourite vegetable to cook on its own and serve with a white sauce. When it is older it can be stuffed with a variety of fillings, or steamed and served with a savoury tomato sauce.

Vegetable marrows were introduced into England in the 19th century, and at first used as a substitute for mango in chutneys, pickles and relishes. Later, they were accepted as a vegetable and fried, stuffed or mashed, or simply plain boiled or steamed.

Marrow stuffed with minced beef and herbs can be served with rice or potatoes as a main course. For a perfect summertime supper, add a crisp, green salad too.

PREPARATION TIME: 15 MINUTES
COOKING TIME: 1 HOUR 10 MINUTES
PRE-HEAT THE OVEN TO 180°C (350°F)—GAS MARK 4

INGREDIENTS FOR FOUR

1 medium marrow
2 oz. (50 g.) butter
1 medium onion, peeled and finely chopped
1 clove garlic, chopped
8 oz. (225 g.) minced beef
4 tomatoes, skinned and chopped
½ oz. (15 g.) fresh breadcrumbs
1 tablespoon chopped fresh basil or ½ tablespoon dried basil
2 tablespoons chopped parsley
1 egg, beaten
Sea salt
Freshly ground black pepper

Cut off the end of the marrow and scoop out the seeds with a spoon.

Melt half the butter in a frying pan, add the chopped onion and garlic and fry gently for 5 minutes until soft. Add the minced beef and brown the meat for a few minutes, stirring occasionally to prevent burning. Put the onion, garlic and meat in a mixing bowl. Add the chopped tomato flesh, breadcrumbs, basil, parsley and egg. Season with salt and pepper and mix all the ingredients well together.

Stuff the marrow with this mixture and replace the end. Place the marrow in a greased, ovenproof dish and dot with pieces of the remaining butter. Arrange a layer of aluminium foil loosely over the top, and bake in the oven for 1 hour or until tender.

MASHED CELERIAC AND POTATOES
Countrywide

ALTHOUGH introduced into this country from Europe over 200 years ago, celeriac has been largely neglected by British cooks. This is a pity, for this root vegetable is highly adaptable. It is delicious braised, fried, boiled, *au gratin*, as a purée, or in a salad. This recipe goes very well with game.

PREPARATION TIME: 20 MINUTES
COOKING TIME: 20 MINUTES

INGREDIENTS FOR SIX

1 lb. (450 g.) potatoes, peeled and cut into even-sized pieces
Sea salt
1½ lb. (700 g.) celeriac, peeled and cut into ½ in. (1·5 cm.) cubes
2 oz. (50 g.) butter
2 fl. oz. (50 ml.) double cream
Freshly ground black pepper

Put the potatoes in one saucepan and the celeriac in another. Cover each with cold water. Add salt, cover the pans and bring to the boil. Cook each vegetable for 20 minutes or until tender. Drain.

Purée the celeriac, either by passing it through a sieve or putting it through a blender.

Mash the potatoes with a fork. Add the puréed celeriac, butter and cream. Season with salt and pepper. Mash well together and serve.

COLCANNON
Ireland

IN IRELAND, Colcannon is generally eaten at Hallowe'en, whose tradition of fortune-telling is invoked by dropping a button, a silver coin, a ring, a thimble and a horseshoe into the mixture. Whoever finds the ring will marry within the year; the coin indicates riches and the horseshoe good fortune. The finder of the thimble or button will never marry.

Although it is not usual to fry Colcannon, it gives a beautiful crust. Serve with steaks, chops or sausages.

PREPARATION TIME: 20 MINUTES
COOKING TIME: 20 MINUTES

INGREDIENTS FOR FOUR TO SIX

1 lb. (450 g.) green cabbage or kale, shredded
1½ lb. (700 g.) hot, mashed potatoes
2 tablespoons grated onion or 2 spring onions, finely chopped
About 2 fl. oz. (50 ml.) milk
Salt and freshly ground pepper
2 oz. (50 g.) butter

Cook the cabbage until tender but still crisp, by steaming, or by cooking it gently in a saucepan with 1 tablespoon of water. Mix it into the potato with the onion and milk to make a smooth, firm mixture. Season.

Heat half the butter in a frying pan and add the mixture. Fry until the edges are crisp, dot with the rest of the butter and brown under the grill.

CAULIFLOWER WITH ANCHOVY SAUCE
Countrywide

A RECIPE of the 17th century, 'How to Butter a Colle Flowre', uses the same ingredients as we use today, but without the anchovies.

Cooking in milk keeps the cauliflower white and retains all vitamins in the sauce.

PREPARATION TIME: 10 MINUTES
COOKING TIME: 35 MINUTES

INGREDIENTS FOR FOUR

1 cauliflower
1 pint (575/600 ml.) milk
1¾ oz. (45 g.) tin anchovies
1 oz. (25 g.) butter
2 tablespoons plain flour
1 teaspoon tomato paste (optional)
Freshly ground black pepper
1–2 tablespoons capers

Remove the outer leaves of the cauliflower, trim the base and cut a cross in the white stem.

Put the cauliflower in a saucepan and pour in the milk. Cook over a gentle heat for 20 minutes, turn the cauliflower upside-down and cook for a further 5 minutes until cooked through but still firm.

Remove the cauliflower from the milk, put it in a warmed serving dish and place it under a low grill to keep warm. Use the milk in which the cauliflower has cooked for the sauce.

Pound the anchovies to a paste using a pestle and mortar or reduce them to a purée in a blender.

Melt the butter in a small saucepan over a gentle heat. Add the flour and cook, stirring with a wooden spoon, for a few minutes, without browning. Add the milk, bring to the boil, stirring, and simmer, stirring continuously, until thickened.

Add the pounded anchovies and the tomato paste to the sauce and stir well. Season with pepper to taste.

Pour the sauce over the cauliflower, sprinkle with capers, and serve at once.

Vary this recipe by adding 2 oz. (50 g.) grated Gruyère or Cheddar cheese instead of anchovies.

Cauliflower with Anchovy Sauce topped with capers. Serve alone or with fish or lamb.

RECIPES *from* OTHER LANDS

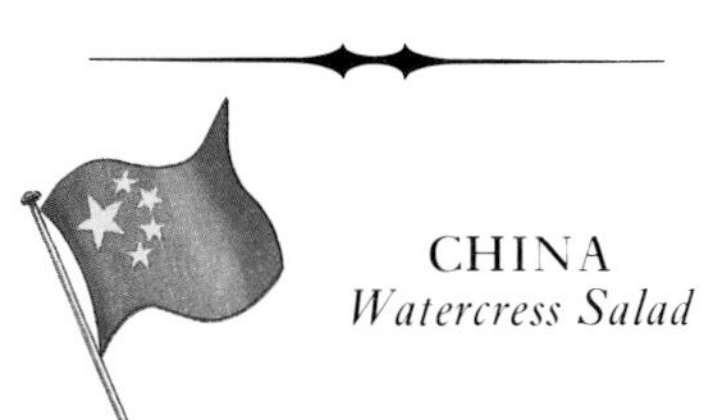

CHINA
Watercress Salad

In this adaptation of a Chinese recipe, water chestnuts and beansprouts add their delicate flavour and distinctive crispness to a tangy, Watercress Salad, which is very good with cold duck. You can use orange juice instead of lemon in the dressing, and garnish the duck with slices of orange.

Preparation Time: 15 minutes

Ingredients for Four to Six

2 bunches watercress
8 oz. (225 g.) fresh beansprouts
1 tin, 4 oz. (100/125 g.), water chestnuts, drained

For the dressing:

$1\frac{1}{2}$ tablespoons sesame seeds
2 fl. oz. (50 ml.) sesame or corn oil
4 tablespoons soy sauce
2 tablespoons lemon juice
$1\frac{1}{2}$ tablespoons grated onion
$\frac{1}{4}$ teaspoon granulated sugar
Freshly ground black pepper
Sea salt

Wash the watercress and beansprouts and pat dry with paper towels. Slice the water chestnuts. In a salad bowl, mix together the watercress, beansprouts and water chestnuts.

Toast the sesame seeds in a dry pan over a moderate heat. Put the seeds in a bowl and add the sesame oil, soy sauce, lemon juice, grated onion and sugar. Season with pepper and stir all the ingredients well together.

Pour the dressing over the salad and toss. Check the seasoning and add salt if necessary. Serve at once.

ITALY
Braised Fennel

Italy has so many distinct regional cuisines that it is not surprising to find 'finocchio', or Florentine fennel—the bulbous-stemmed vegetable with the slightly aniseed taste—cooked in so many different ways.

It is served raw dressed in oil and vinegar at the beginning of a meal, and is also sometimes eaten at the end of a meal, instead of fruit.

In Umbria, both the stalks and leaves of wild fennel are chopped up with garlic and used as a stuffing for suckling pig; the Sicilian serves it cooked in egg and breadcrumbs; a Venetian recipe gives risotto with fennel; pasta with fennel and pecorino cheese is a speciality of Calabria. Even the seeds—said in the England of Shakespeare's day to allay the pangs of hunger on fast days—are used in Italy today.

Although prized in Italy, fennel is still relatively little known in England. Choose fresh, white heads and serve this dish with fish, chicken, sausages or grilled meat.

Preparation Time: 5 minutes
Cooking Time: 50 minutes

Ingredients for Four

2 oz. (50 g.) butter
2 medium heads fennel, trimmed and cut into quarters
$\frac{1}{4}$ pint (150 ml.) chicken stock
1 tablespoon lemon juice
Sea salt
Freshly ground black pepper
2 tablespoons grated Parmesan cheese

Melt the butter in a heavy frying pan. Add the fennel and cook gently, stirring, until the fennel is coated with the butter. Pour in the stock and lemon juice. Season with salt and pepper, cover and simmer for 20–30 minutes until the liquid has evaporated and the fennel is tender. If the liquid is not reducing fast enough, remove the lid and increase the heat for the last 5 minutes of cooking.

When cooked, put the fennel in a serving dish and sprinkle it with the grated Parmesan cheese. Place under a hot grill for 5 minutes until the cheese has browned.

Alternatively, the fennel may be cooked, covered, for 40–50 minutes in an oven pre-heated to 170°C (325°F)—gas mark 3. Baste the fennel occasionally as it cooks. When cooked, remove it from the oven, sprinkle with Parmesan cheese and brown under a hot grill as above.

INDIA
Spiced Aubergines

The deep colour of the aubergine brought it under suspicion in the 16th century.

The herbalist John Gerard, in whose day it was known as the 'madde apple' or 'raging apple', commented in his *Herbal* (1597): 'Doubtless these apples have a mischievous qualitie, the use whereof is to bee utterly forsaken'—advice that his countrymen may have hearkened to, for the plant was rarely eaten here before this century.

As aubergines originally came from India, it is not surprising that some of the best recipes for them include spices which have become familiar to us in curries. Asafoetida is a gum resin, with a strong oniony odour, relished as a condiment in India and Iran, where it is used as a flavouring in cookery.

Serve this dish with grilled lamb or chicken.

Preparation Time: 45 minutes
Cooking Time: 35–40 minutes

Ingredients for Four to Six

2 aubergines, cut into $\frac{1}{2}$ in. (1·5 cm.) thick slices
Sea salt
6 tablespoons vegetable oil or ghee
2 tablespoons sesame seeds
Pinch of asafoetida (optional)
A piece of root ginger, about 1 in. (2·5 cm.), chopped
1 teaspoon paprika
$\frac{1}{4}$ teaspoon freshly ground black pepper
Juice of $1\frac{1}{2}$ lemons or 2 limes
2 tablespoons chopped fresh coriander or parsley

Put the aubergines in a colander and sprinkle them with salt. Leave them to stand for 40 minutes to remove some of the excess moisture. Dry with paper towels.

Heat 4 tablespoons of oil in a heavy frying pan and add the aubergines. Fry the slices quickly on both sides. Remove from the pan and set aside.

Heat the remaining 2 tablespoons of oil in the pan. Add the sesame seeds, asafoetida, ginger, paprika and black pepper and fry for 2–3 minutes.

Return the aubergines to the pan and stir in the lemon or lime juice. Cover and simmer over a very low heat for about 30 minutes.

Place the aubergines in a warmed serving dish and sprinkle them with the chopped coriander or parsley.

FRANCE
Ratatouille

COLOURFUL and richly flavoured, *Ratatouille* is a blend of vegetables and herbs that has in it the authentic taste of the South of France. Onions, aubergines, courgettes, peppers and tomatoes, all intermingle their flavours as they stew slowly in olive oil.

The name of the dish comes from two Provençal verbs, *ratouiller*, to soak or steep, and *tatouiller*, to soil or dirty. And the dish was probably first invented by frugal peasants as a way of using up vegetables which were not in perfect condition.

Two rules must be observed when making *Ratatouille*—always use olive oil and never add water. Serve it hot or cold with freshly baked bread as a first course and, if liked, top each portion with a fried egg. Or serve it as an accompaniment to roast or grilled meat or chicken.

PREPARATION TIME: 40 MINUTES
COOKING TIME: 1 HOUR

INGREDIENTS FOR SIX

- *2 large aubergines, cut into ½ in. (1·5 cm.) slices*
- *1 lb. (450 g.) courgettes, cut into ½ in. (1·5 cm.) slices*
- *Sea salt*
- *2 tablespoons olive oil*
- *8 oz. (225 g.) onions, peeled and sliced*
- *3 green peppers, de-seeded and sliced*
- *2 cloves garlic, finely chopped*
- *1 lb. (450 g.) tomatoes, skinned (see p. 198) and sliced*
- *1 tablespoon crushed coriander seeds*
- *Freshly ground black pepper*
- *1 tablespoon chopped basil*
- *1 tablespoon chopped parsley*

Put the aubergines and courgettes into a colander and sprinkle with salt. Leave them for 40 minutes so that the salt has time to draw out some of the excess moisture. Dry with paper towels.

Heat the oil in a large frying pan. Add the sliced onions and peppers, and cook for 5 minutes until the onions are soft and transparent. Add the aubergines, courgettes and garlic. Cover the pan and simmer for 10 minutes.

Add the tomatoes and coriander seeds. Season with salt and pepper. Cover again and cook for 45 minutes over a gentle heat, checking occasionally to make sure the vegetables are not sticking to the bottom of the pan.

Check the seasoning, sprinkle with basil and parsley, and serve.

ITALY
Broccoli Alla Parmigiana

BROCCOLI IS A VARIETY of cabbage which first came to Britain from Naples in the 17th century; in 1699 the diarist John Evelyn refers to 'the Broccoli from Naples'.

The word *Broccoli* means cabbage sprouts or flowers; but *Broccoletti*, meaning little branches, is the name by which the vegetable is sold on the colourful market stalls of Italy.

'Alla Parmigiana' means that the dish contains Parmesan. It also uses Mozzarella cheese, and a tomato sauce, fragrant with basil.

The dish makes a good first course to be followed by pasta; it can also be served as an accompaniment to grilled fish, meat or chicken.

PREPARATION TIME: 10 MINUTES
COOKING TIME: 55 MINUTES
PRE-HEAT THE OVEN TO 200°C (400°F)—GAS MARK 6

INGREDIENTS FOR FOUR

- *1 large head of broccoli*
- *2 tablespoons olive oil*
- *1 medium onion, finely chopped*
- *1 clove garlic, chopped*
- *4 tomatoes, skinned, or 1 small tin, 4 oz. (100/125 g.), Italian tomatoes*
- *1 tablespoon chopped fresh basil or ½ tablespoon dried basil*
- *Sea salt*
- *Freshly ground black pepper*
- *4 oz. (100/125 g.) Mozzarella cheese, finely sliced*
- *2 tablespoons grated Parmesan cheese*
- *1 tablespoon dried white breadcrumbs*

Wash the broccoli and break it into even-sized spears.

Put the spears in a steamer, and put the steamer in a pan above boiling water.

Cover the pan with a tightly fitting lid and steam for about 20 minutes until tender but still crunchy.

Heat the oil in a heavy frying pan, add the onion and garlic and fry gently for 5 minutes until soft. Add the tomatoes and basil and cook, stirring, until it forms a thick sauce, moistening with a little water if necessary. Season with salt and pepper.

Arrange the broccoli in an ovenproof dish and pour over the tomato sauce. Arrange slices of Mozzarella cheese on top. Sprinkle with the grated Parmesan cheese and then with the breadcrumbs.

Bake, uncovered, in the pre-heated oven for about 20 minutes until browned and bubbling. Serve hot in the same dish.

FRANCE
Pommes Gratin Dauphinois

THIS DISH, like the former heirs to the French throne, is named after the mountainous Dauphiné area of France that borders on Switzerland. Milk, butter and cream are the rich local ingredients that combine with potatoes in this classic dish.

When cooked, the potatoes are brown on top and the sauce has thickened and tastes of cheese, even though there is no cheese in it.

It goes well with grilled meat, roast beef, pork, lamb or chicken, and cold meats.

PREPARATION TIME: 15 MINUTES
COOKING TIME: 1 HOUR
PRE-HEAT THE OVEN TO 180°C (350°F)—GAS MARK 4

INGREDIENTS FOR FOUR

- *1½ oz. (40 g.) butter, cut into pieces*
- *1 clove garlic*
- *1 lb. (450 g.) potatoes, peeled and sliced very thinly*
- *Sea salt*
- *Freshly ground black pepper*
- *½ pint (275/300 ml.) double cream*

Grease an ovenproof dish with a little butter and rub it well with the clove of garlic. Arrange a layer of potato slices in the dish and season with salt and pepper. Add another layer, season, and continue in this way until all the potatoes are used up.

Pour over the cream until it comes to within ¾ in. (2 cm.) of the top of the potatoes. Dot the potatoes with butter. Place in the pre-heated oven and bake for 1 hour until the top is nicely browned. If necessary, turn up the heat for the last 10 minutes to brown completely. Serve hot.

ROOT, GREEN AND OTHER VEGETABLES

CENTURIES AGO, MANY WILD PLANTS, such as charlock, plantain, docks, mallow, nettles and the uncultivated natives of the onion family, were a part of our diet. They were usually added to a cereal-based pottage.

Roots such as wild turnip, parsnip and carrot were eaten in winter. When the Romans came to Britain, they brought many cultivated vegetables, including cabbage, lettuce, endive, beet and fennel. By the Middle Ages, peas and beans were being grown as field crops.

From Tudor times many new vegetables rose in popularity, among them cauliflowers, asparagus, artichokes and celery. Travellers and explorers introduced some, such as the potato and tomato, and contacts with Europe brought in others whose names declare their origin—Brussels sprouts and Savoys, for example.

The medieval suspicion of uncooked fruit, considered bad for health, did not seem to apply to vegetables and herbs. A 14th-century salad recipe mentions 'garden cresses, parsley, onions, leeks and fennel and red mint, all plucked smalle and mingled with oil, then vinegar laid on'. From Tudor times until the 18th century, most vegetables were boiled and served swimming in butter.

Vegetables

Freshness is all-important when you are buying vegetables. The flavour of vegetables is at its best when they are young and firm, and cooked as soon as possible after harvesting. Cellulose, which is the roughage or fibrous part of the vegetable, becomes coarser and more difficult to digest as the vegetable matures.

Roots and tubers should be crisp and fairly free from soil. Store them in a ventilated rack. Pre-packed, scrubbed root vegetables, while being easier to prepare, generally do not keep as well as those in the natural state.

Green vegetables rot quickly. Remove any rotting outside leaves that may affect the rest. Wrap in newspaper or a brown paper bag and store in a cool place or a refrigerator.

Leaf vegetables should be a good colour, crisp and fresh-looking. The rib of a large leaf should snap sharply when broken. Brussels sprouts should be compact and round. Cauliflowers should have a firm, compact and white head. Beans and peas should be a good, bright colour, with no yellowing, and the beans should snap crisply when broken in half.

PREPARING VEGETABLES

Trim or peel vegetables as economically as possible, removing coarse stalks and leaves, or any decayed parts. These outer leaves and parings, or trimmings, can all be cleaned and used to make a vegetable stock or sauce.

Wash and rinse vegetables thoroughly, particularly spinach and leeks. You may need to put some green vegetables, such as cabbage, in cold water with a little salt added to remove any small insects or slugs. Do not leave them in the water for more than a few minutes; long soaking will destroy mineral salts and vitamins, which are soluble in water.

You can, if necessary, scrub most root vegetables with a brush, especially if they are to be cooked with the skin on. Beetroot should never be scrubbed, however, as it tends to bleed and lose its colour if the skin is broken before cooking.

When you are peeling root vegetables and onions, peel away only a thin layer because the most nutritious part of the vegetable lies just under the skin. If the vegetables are young, just scrape off the thin skin lightly. Many vegetables can, in fact, be cooked in their skins. Mature root vegetables may develop woody patches. Cut these away before cooking.

When you peel potatoes, put them in water as soon as the skin is removed, or they will turn brown. Jerusalem artichokes also discolour very rapidly when peeled or scraped. To prevent this, place them immediately in cold water to which a few drops of lemon juice or vinegar have been added. Leave in the water until ready to cook.

Some vegetables, such as potatoes and small turnips, can be cooked whole. But you can shorten the cooking time for vegetables by cutting them up. Use a sharp kitchen knife and cut even-sized pieces that will all be cooked in the same length of time. Potatoes can be cut into halves or quarters, but other vegetables are usually cut into smaller pieces.

Slicing

Cut vegetables such as swedes crossways to get thick, round slices. These can be divided into strips. To slice some vegetables very thinly, use a mandolin slicer or cheese parer.

Dicing

Slice the vegetables and cut into strips, then cut these across into small cubes.

Chopping

Cut the vegetables finely or roughly, as required. Do not lift the point of the knife from the chopping board, but use it as a pivot as you raise the blade just above the vegetable and bring it down again. Keep your forefinger down the back of the blade to guide it.

Shredding
Use this method for large leaf vegetables such as cabbage. Quarter the vegetable first, then cut thin slivers from each quarter.

Grating
To grate vegetables, use the large hole of a cheese grater.

Skinning tomatoes
Bring a kettle of water to the boil. Put the tomatoes three or four at a time into a bowl and cover with boiling water. Remove the tomatoes one at a time and quickly peel off the skin while still hot.

Blanching
To blanch vegetables, put them in boiling water for 2–3 minutes. This will remove any acid flavour, preserve the colour of green vegetables or loosen skins. Cabbage leaves that are to be stuffed and rolled are blanched to make them more pliable.

Removing excess moisture
Some vegetables, such as aubergines and courgettes, contain a lot of moisture. It is best to remove this before sautéing or baking, or it will run out during cooking. Slice the vegetables, put them in a colander and sprinkle with salt. Cover with a plate and put a weight on it. Leave them for 30–40 minutes so that the salt has time to draw out some of the excess moisture. Dry well with paper towels. Take care not to add too much salt during cooking because of this earlier salting.

COOKING VEGETABLES

Vitamins A, B and, particularly, C are present in most vegetables. Vitamin C is, however, unstable and much of it can be lost with wrong storage and preparation. Prolonged soaking or cooking, or the addition of bicarbonate of soda, destroys Vitamin C. Bicarbonate of soda was often added to vegetables in the past to preserve their colour, but this loss of colour was almost always due to over-cooking.

When cooking vegetables, use sea salt to give a better flavour than refined cooking salt.

Boiling
Roots and tubers These include potatoes, carrots, turnips, parsnips, swedes, celeriac, beetroots, salsify, Jerusalem artichokes and the bulbous roots of onions, shallots and leeks.

Put the cleaned and prepared vegetables into a saucepan and add sufficient cold water to cover. For each ½ pint (275/300 ml.) of water add ½ teaspoon of salt. Cover the pan and bring the water to the boil. When boiling root vegetables with a close texture, such as carrots and parsnips, boil quickly and steadily. Those with tender, less-dense fibres, such as turnips and Jerusalem artichokes, should be simmered after bringing to the boil, as rapid boiling will cause them to break up. Boil the vegetables until they are tender but firm. One of the most common mistakes in British cooking in the past has been to overboil vegetables, at the expense of texture, flavour and nutritional value.
Green vegetables These include cabbages, kale, Brussels sprouts, cauliflowers, broccoli, spinach, and globe artichokes.

Use only a small amount of water for boiling green vegetables. About ¼ pint (150 ml.) of water to every 1 lb. (450 g.) of vegetables is sufficient.

Bring the salted water to the boil before adding the vegetables. If a large quantity is being cooked, add a handful at a time, so that the temperature of the water is not lowered much. Cover the pan and boil at a moderate heat until the vegetables are tender but firm.

Some vegetables, spinach in particular, cook in their own juices and do not need the addition of any water. Wash well in several lots of water to remove all soil or grit. Drain, salt very lightly and cook in a tightly covered saucepan over a gentle heat, shaking the pan from time to time until the juices run. Cook until just tender.

Drain the vegetables well and finish according to the recipe.

Steaming
The flavour and food value of vegetables is retained when they are steamed.

Prepare the vegetables and place them in a perforated vegetable steamer or wire colander, and fit this in a pan over rapidly boiling water. Make sure the water is not deep enough to reach the vegetables. Sprinkle with salt, allowing 1 teaspoon to each 1 lb. (450 g.) of vegetables. Cover the pan with a tightly fitting lid and steam until the vegetables are just tender. This will take at least 5 minutes longer than boiling.

Braising
Braising is a good cooking method, as it preserves most of the food value of the vegetable. Vegetables such as celery and lettuce are blanched first.

To braise, fry the prepared vegetables lightly in butter, or a mixture of butter and oil, in a heavy-based saucepan. The addition of oil will prevent the butter from burning. Then add ¼–½ pint (150–300 ml.) chicken stock for each 1 lb. (450 g.) of vegetables. Season with salt and pepper—lightly if the stock is already salted. Cover with a tightly fitting lid and simmer until tender. Lift the vegetables on to a warm serving dish. Reduce the juices in the pan by rapid boiling, or thicken them to make a sauce. Pour over the vegetables.

Alternatively, put the lightly fried vegetables in an ovenproof dish with the stock. Cover and cook in the oven, pre-heated to 180°C (350°F)—gas mark 4, until tender. Strain off the juices into a pan and reduce them by rapid boiling, or thicken them to make a sauce.

Roasting
This method is suitable for root vegetables such as potatoes, onions and parsnips. They are often roasted round a meat joint. They can also be roasted separately in an ovenproof dish in which you have heated enough dripping to make a ¼ in. (5 mm.) layer. Turn the vegetables about in the hot fat to coat them, then cook at 220°C (425°F)—gas mark 7, for ¾–1 hour.

If it is more convenient to have a shorter roasting time, boil the vegetables first for 5 minutes, then drain. Turn them in the hot fat to coat them. Roast at 220°C (425°F)—gas mark 7, for 30 minutes.

Baking
This cooking method is used mostly for potatoes. Choose vegetables of equal size and scrub well but do not peel. Prick the skins in several places, or they will burst during cooking. Place the prepared vegetables on a roasting rack or in an ovenproof dish, brush them with melted butter or oil and cook in an oven pre-heated to 200°C (400°F)—gas mark 6, until they feel tender when pricked with a fork or pinched between finger and thumb. The cooking time will depend on the size of the potatoes.

A metal skewer can be stuck into each potato to convey heat more quickly to the centre.

Grilling
This method is suitable for cooking mushrooms and tomatoes. Dot with butter or oil and cook under a medium-hot grill.

Frying
Shallow-frying or sautéing
Suitable vegetables for frying are courgettes, tomatoes, mushrooms, aubergines, onions and other tender vegetables. Halve tomatoes and slice other vegetables. In a heavy-based frying pan heat enough butter or oil to cover the base thinly. Add the vegetables and fry gently until tender and golden-brown, turning over from time to time during cooking. Salt lightly after cooking. Less tender vegetables must be pre-cooked or boiled for 5 minutes before shallow-frying.
Deep-frying For deep-frying chipped potatoes, see the recipe for Fish and Chips (p. 66). Many other vegetables can be deep-fried, usually coated with batter or egg and breadcrumbs. Use soft vegetables such as aubergines and courgettes. Cut them into ¼ in. (5 mm.) slices, sprinkle with salt and leave to stand for 1 hour. Drain and pat dry, then dust with flour and dip in batter or egg and breadcrumbs.

For the best results use refined peanut or vegetable oil for deep-frying. Heat about 3 in. (8 cm.) of oil in a deep, heavy-based pan to 190°C (375°F). Test the temperature first by dropping in a small cube of bread; it should become golden-brown in just under 1 minute.

Place some of the prepared vegetables in a wire basket and lower carefully into the hot fat. Cook until crisp and golden-brown. Keep these warm, and repeat until all the vegetables are cooked. Do not try to fry too much at once, or the oil temperature will drop and the vegetables will absorb some of the oil and become soggy instead of being sealed quickly and becoming crisp.
Stir-frying When vegetables are stir-fried they keep their texture and flavour. Chop the vegetables into small pieces of even size so that they will all be ready at the same time. Heat a thin layer of oil in a heavy frying pan until sizzling, and add the vegetables. Stir continuously with a wooden spoon or spatula and turn down the heat. The vegetables are done when their colour has brightened and they are still crunchy.

Serving
Serve vegetables as soon as possible after they are cooked. They can be served plain, tossed in butter, sprinkled with chopped parsley and other herbs, or coated with a sauce.

Making use of pulses
The more common pulses are peas (green and yellow), beans (haricot, butter and red), and lentils (green and yellow).

To prepare pulses pick over the seeds, discarding any black or discoloured ones, and wash the pulses under cold running water. Peas or beans should be placed in a large bowl and covered with cold water. Leave them to soak for several hours, and if possible overnight. Lentils can be cooked without soaking. Dried beans contain lectin, a poisonous chemical destroyed by rapid boiling. Soak the beans, drain and rinse them under running water, cover with fresh cold water, bring slowly to boil and keep boiling rapidly for 10 minutes.

To cook, drain the pulses and place in a saucepan. Cover with plenty of fresh cold water. Do not add salt at this stage as it makes the pulses hard. Bring to the boil and simmer gently until soft. Cooking time varies, depending on the type and age of the pulses, and can be anything from 30 minutes to 2 hours. About 15 minutes before the end of the cooking time add 1 teaspoon of salt for each 8 oz. (225 g.) of the vegetables. The cooking liquid can be set aside and used for making soups.

Rice and Pasta

Rice or pasta can supply the starchy part of a main course in place of potatoes, dumplings or pastry.

Rice
There are several kinds of rice: white polished rice, brown unpolished rice; wild rice. For savoury dishes, long-grain or patna rice is best. Basmati is the best-quality long-grain rice, and well worth buying. Round-grain rice is suitable for risottos and puddings, where the grains need to be very absorbent.

Cooking plain boiled rice
Allow 3–4 oz. (75–125 g.) of uncooked rice for each person. Put the rice in a fine sieve and wash well in plenty of cold running water. Drain and put in a pan. Pour in enough cold water to cover 1 in. (2·5 cm.) above the rice. Add salt to taste and cover the pan. Bring to the boil and simmer for 10–12 minutes until all the water has been absorbed. Remove the pan from the heat and leave, covered, for 10–12 minutes. The rice should be dry and fluffy.

Alternatively, measure out the rice in cups, and put into a sieve to wash under cold water. For each cup of rice allow 2 cups of water. One cup of uncooked rice is enough for two servings. Cook as above.

Pasta
The basis of pasta is flour from hard durum wheat, which grows particularly well in Italy. The flour is mixed with oil and water to a paste. Sometimes spinach purée and egg are added. The pasta is moulded into various shapes and dried before being sold. The commonest shapes are long threads (spaghetti), tubes (macaroni), and strips (noodles). It is also moulded into broad ribbons, short thin threads, butterflies, shells and several other fancy shapes.

Cooking pasta
Allow 3–4 oz. (75–125 g.) of uncooked pasta for each person. All pasta is boiled, but cooking times depend on size and freshness. Pasta should be just firm to the bite, or '*al dente*' as the Italians say.

For every 4 oz. (100/125 g.) of pasta use 2 pints (1·1 litres) of water and 2 level teaspoons of salt. Bring the water to the boil in a large saucepan, add the salt and put in the pasta. Do not break up the long strands of spaghetti, but hold them at one end and curl the strands gradually into the boiling water as they soften. Cook the pasta at a steady boil, uncovered, until just tender. Drain thoroughly in a colander and return to the pan with a large knob of butter or 1 tablespoon of oil. Season with salt and pepper, and toss the pasta until it is well coated with the butter or oil.

Of SAVOURY PIES, PUDDINGS AND PASTRIES

CONTAINING

NUMEROUS *Useful* FAMILY RECIPES

for MEAT & FISH PASTRIES & PUDDINGS, TARTS & FLANS

& all other SATISFYING DISHES

PAGES 202–213

AND

A SELECTION of RECIPES from OTHER LANDS

PAGES 214–215

AND WITH

DIRECTIONS *for* BASIC METHODS

for all kinds of Making, Raising, Moulding and Baking of Savoury Crusts to Perfection

PAGES 216–221

Fidget Pie
Shropshire

No one knows why this Shropshire speciality is called Fidget (or sometimes Fitchett) Pie. It was once a heartening farm supper dish to welcome the harvesters home from the fields. In lean times it was made with vegetables only; when times were better, with gammon; and for a special treat, lamb chops from the scrag end of the neck were put in, one for each person, in which case only half the amount of gammon was used. Its characteristic apple-onion-meat mixture (not unlike squab pie) harks back to the medieval way of combining sweet and savoury tastes, and suggests that it is a truly well-tried recipe.

Preparation Time: 30 minutes
Cooking Time: 1¼ hours
Pre-heat the Oven to 180°C (350°F)—gas mark 4

Ingredients for Four

- *1 lb. (450 g.) potatoes, peeled and thickly sliced*
- *12 oz. (350 g.) gammon, rind and fat removed, diced*
- *2 large onions, peeled and sliced*
- *3 large cooking apples, peeled, cored and thinly sliced*
- *2 teaspoons sugar*
- *½ teaspoon dried thyme*
- *Salt and pepper*
- *½ pint (275/300 ml.) stock (see pp. 33–34)*
- *8 oz. (225 g.) shortcrust pastry (see p. 217)*

Put a layer of sliced potatoes in the bottom of a 2 pint (1·1 litre) pie dish. Cover this with a layer of gammon, a layer of sliced onion, and then a layer of apple. Sprinkle well with sugar.

Repeat these layers until the pie dish is full, ending with a layer of gammon. Sprinkle with thyme, and season well. Pour in just enough stock to cover the filling.

Roll out the pastry to make a fairly thick pie crust, about ¼ in. (5 mm.). Cut out a lid and cover the top of the dish (see p. 221).

Bake the pie in the top of the pre-heated oven for about 20 minutes, until the pastry is brown. Then, transfer the pie to a lower shelf and cook for a further 55 minutes. If the top seems to be browning too much, cover the pastry with foil.

If you want to add lamb chops to the pie, arrange them on top of the first layer of potatoes before adding the other layers.

Liver and Onion Pie
Countrywide

The combination of liver with onions—which has almost the status of a national dish—is an old one. In medieval times, plenty of onions and pungent herbs were needed to disguise the taste of the liver, which tended to be somewhat rank in flavour since it was cooked together with the lung, spleen and gut. In this recipe the liver, cooked alone, is not sealed first by frying, and so is very tender with a rich gravy.

Preparation Time: 20 minutes
Cooking Time: 1 hour 20 minutes
Pre-heat the Oven to 200°C (400°F)—gas mark 6

Ingredients for Four to Six

- *2 oz. (50 g.) butter*
- *2 lb. (900 g.) onions, peeled and cut in rings*
- *1½ lb. (700 g.) ox or lamb's liver, cut in very thin slices*
- *1 oz. (25 g.) seasoned flour*
- *2 sprigs or ½ teaspoon chopped thyme*
- *1 sprig or ½ teaspoon chopped rosemary*
- *¾ pint (450 ml.) warmed brown stock (see pp. 33–34)*
- *Salt and pepper*
- *1 lb. (450 g.) shortcrust or rough puff pastry (see pp. 217, 218)*

Heat the butter in a frying pan and fry the onions in it over a low heat, until they are just transparent and beginning to brown. Lay half the onions in the bottom of a large pie dish.

Cut the liver into thin strips about 3 by 1 in. (8 by 2·5 cm.), discarding any skin or gristle. Turn the strips of liver in the seasoned flour. Place a layer of liver over the onions. Put in the sprigs of herbs, or sprinkle the chopped herbs over the top. Repeat the layers of onions and liver, ending with a layer of onions.

Pour on enough of the stock just to cover the top layer. Season well with salt and pepper. Roll out the pastry but keep it fairly thick, about ⅜ in. (1 cm.), and cut out a round large enough to fit the top of the pie dish. Put the lid on the pie (see p. 221), and bake near the top of the pre-heated oven for 20 minutes. Cover the top loosely with foil and then move the pie to a lower shelf and cook for a further 60 minutes.

Beef and Tomato Pie
Devon

The appetising mixture of meat with tomatoes is more characteristic of continental than English cookery, even though tomatoes made their first appearance here as long ago as the 16th century. The plant was grown for its ornamental value, and because it is related to deadly nightshade the fruit itself was long thought to be dangerous.

For this recipe, which comes from a farm in Devonshire, you need tomatoes which are firm and just ripe enough to blanch.

Preparation Time: 30 minutes
Cooking Time: 2 hours
Pre-heat the Oven to 180°C (350°F)—gas mark 4

Ingredients for Six

- *1½ lb. (700 g.) best stewing steak, cut in 1 in. (2·5 cm.) cubes*
- *2 oz. (50 g.) seasoned flour*
- *2 medium onions, peeled and sliced*
- *3 oz. (75 g.) butter*
- *2 lb. (900 g.) tomatoes*
- *1 teaspoon sugar*
- *Black pepper*
- *1 teaspoon dried basil (if possible)*
- *8 oz. (225 g.) shortcrust pastry (see p. 217)*

Remove all the fat and skin from the steak cubes and dip them in the seasoned flour. Fry the onions gently in 2 oz. (50 g.) of the butter until they are soft. Put the onions in the bottom of a very large pie dish. Add the rest of the butter to the pan and fry the beef in it.

When the beef is lightly browned, arrange it in the dish on top of the onion and add just enough water to cover the meat. Cover the top of the dish with foil and cook it in the pre-heated oven for 1½ hours.

Meanwhile, blanch and skin the tomatoes (see p. 198) and cut them in quarters, preserving all the juice. Sprinkle them with the sugar, black pepper and basil, if you are using it. Set aside the tomatoes, while you roll out the pastry.

When the meat has been cooking for 1½ hours, remove it from the oven. Place the tomatoes on top so that they form a cool layer on the hot meat—this stops the meat steaming the inside of the pastry and making it heavy.

Roll out the pastry fairly thinly, cut out a lid and put it on top of the pie dish (see p. 221). Bake the pie near the top of the oven, still at the same temperature, for 30 minutes, or until the crust is golden-brown.

STEAK AND KIDNEY PUDDING
Countrywide

CONSIDERING that this is one of England's most famous national dishes, it is surprising to discover that the recipe for it was first written down as late as 1840. In that year, Anne Cobbett, in her book *The English Housekeeper*, recommended adding kidney to a beefsteak pudding.

Steak pudding without the kidney was known to the 19th-century food writer Eliza Acton as 'John Bull's Pudding', a name with a sturdy, British sound. But the addition of kidney is a culinary masterstroke, as it makes the gravy juicy and pungent.

In Victorian times, oysters took the place of the mushrooms in this version. Before the oyster beds became depleted at the end of the last century, oysters were as cheap as mushrooms are today.

PREPARATION TIME: 20 MINUTES
COOKING TIME: 3 HOURS

INGREDIENTS FOR SIX TO EIGHT

$1\frac{1}{2}$ lb. (700 g.) rump steak
8 oz. (225 g.) ox kidney
$1\frac{1}{2}$ lb. (700 g.) suet crust pastry (see p. 219)
$1\frac{1}{2}$ oz. (40 g.) seasoned flour
$\frac{3}{4}$ pint (450 ml.) stock
8 oz. (225 g.) mushrooms

Trim the steak of all skin and fat and cut it into slices about $\frac{1}{4}$ in. (5 mm.) thick, 1 in. (2·5 cm.) wide and 3 in. (8 cm.) long. Flatten each slice by beating it with a rolling pin. Remove the skin and core from the kidney and dice it.

Line a large, well-greased pudding basin with the suet crust pastry (see p. 221), leaving a circle to form the lid.

Roll the pieces of steak in the seasoned flour and put a little kidney on each piece. Roll up all the pieces of steak and put half these little rolls into the lined basin. Pour in enough of the stock just to cover the meat rolls. Trim and wipe the mushrooms and put them on top of the layer of meat. Cover with the remaining meat rolls. Add half of the remaining stock, reserving the rest to add to the pudding later. Put on the lid, damping the top edge of the crust with a little cold water to make it stick. Cover the basin tightly with buttered foil or greaseproof paper, then put a saucer or small plate over the top.

Stand the basin in a large saucepan with enough water to come halfway up the sides of the bowl. Bring the water to the boil and steam the pudding for 3 hours.

Do not let the water go off the boil while the pudding is cooking, and add more boiling water from time to time to maintain the level.

When the pudding is cooked, bring the reserved stock to the boil in a small saucepan. Serve the pudding in the basin with a clean napkin or tea towel pinned round it. Before serving the pudding, make a small cut in the top and pour in a little of the reserved stock. Bring the rest of the stock to table in a jug and add it to the pudding basin after the first two or three helpings have been served so that the pudding stays moist.

Serve with mashed potatoes and peas or, on a cold winter's day, serve with buttered swedes.

Kidney rolled in thin slices of steak, with mushrooms and suet crust pastry, makes a special Steak and Kidney Pudding.

Forfar Bridies—little steak pies for a picnic or a snack.

FORFAR BRIDIES
Scotland

'GOLDEN-BROWN, DAPPLED BEAUTIES' is how these delicious little steak pies are described by Mrs F. Marian McNeill in her book *The Scots Kitchen,* published in 1929. They were invented by a Forfar baker, Mr Jolly, in the 1870s, and were called 'bridies' because they are the sort of simple, sustaining meal that a young wife could easily add to her repertoire. Like their near relation, the Cornish pasty, they can be eaten hot or cold and are a handy addition to the picnic basket. Or they can be served as a main course with potatoes and other vegetables.

PREPARATION TIME: 30 MINUTES
COOKING TIME: 1¼ HOURS
PRE-HEAT THE OVEN TO
220°C (425°F)—GAS MARK 7

INGREDIENTS FOR FOUR

1 lb. (450 g.) rump or best stewing steak
1 small onion, peeled and chopped
1 teaspoon salt
¼ teaspoon pepper
¼ teaspoon mustard powder
1 lb. (450 g.) shortcrust or flaky pastry (see pp. 217, 218)
3 oz. (75 g.) beef suet, shredded
1 egg, beaten

Cut the meat into narrow strips and then divide these into small pieces. Add the chopped onion. Season with the salt, pepper and mustard, and mix well.

Roll out the pastry to about ¼ in. (5 mm.) thick, and cut it into four rounds or ovals. Cover half of each piece of pastry with a quarter of the meat, keeping the filling ¼ in. (5 mm.) from the edge. Sprinkle each portion of meat with a quarter of the suet.

Dampen the edges of the pastry with a little cold water, and fold the tops over to make half-moon shapes. Crimp the edges together between your thumb and forefinger. Brush the top of each bridie with a little beaten egg, and make a small hole in the centre of each to let out the steam.

Bake the bridies in the pre-heated oven for 15 minutes. Then lower the oven heat to 180°C (350°F)—gas mark 4 and bake for a further hour.

MUTTON AND TURNIP PIE
Cornwall

ORIGINALLY, this pie, in which the subtle, radishy flavour of the turnips greatly enriches the mutton taste and reduces the fattiness, was designed on a far greater scale. It was meant to feed a hunting party at the end of a hard day's ride. You will find it useful if you have a large gathering of hungry people to cater for, as the ingredients can be doubled or trebled and cooked in a larger dish.

PREPARATION TIME: 20 MINUTES
COOKING TIME: 2 HOURS 35 MINUTES
PRE-HEAT THE OVEN TO
200°C (400°F)—GAS MARK 6

INGREDIENTS FOR FOUR TO SIX

2 lb. (900 g.) lean mutton or lamb, preferably top of leg
2 onions, peeled and quartered
1 lb. (450 g.) turnips, peeled and sliced
1 teaspoon dried rosemary
2 teaspoons chopped parsley
1 oz. (25 g.) butter
1 oz. (25 g.) flour
Salt and pepper
12 oz. (350 g.) rough puff pastry (see p. 218)

Cut the mutton into 1 in. (2·5 cm.) cubes, removing any skin, fat and gristle. Put the meat in a heavy-based saucepan with the onions, turnips and just enough water to cover. Bring to the boil and then cook over a low heat for 2 hours. Remove the meat and vegetables from the pan and allow to cool, reserving the liquid.

Arrange the mutton, onions and turnips in a large pie dish and sprinkle with the rosemary and parsley.

Heat the butter gently in a saucepan. Gradually stir in the flour, cook for a few minutes and then stir in the reserved liquid slowly. When it has thickened slightly, season it and pour enough of the liquid into the pie dish just to cover the meat.

Roll out the rough puff pastry and cut out a lid. When the pie dish has stopped steaming, cover the dish with the lid and decorate it with leaves cut from the trimmings (see p. 221).

Bake the pie in the pre-heated oven for 35 minutes. Serve very hot.

VEAL AND HAM PIE
Norfolk

A FRESH, HOME-MADE Veal and Ham Pie is so much more delicious than the factory-made version. The veal filling is quite solid when cold, so that you can easily eat the pie with your fingers; or serve it as a hot supper dish with vegetables. This recipe comes from Norfolk, and was used to make pies of gigantic proportions for hungry farm workers. The combination of veal with egg and ham goes back to the 17th century.

PREPARATION TIME: 20 MINUTES
COOKING TIME: 1 HOUR 25 MINUTES
PRE-HEAT THE OVEN TO 200°C (400°F)—GAS MARK 6

INGREDIENTS FOR FOUR

1 lb. (450 g.) fillet of veal or pie veal
1 large onion, peeled and stuck with 10 cloves
1 teaspoon chopped parsley
Grated rind of half a lemon
½ teaspoon chopped mixed herbs
Salt and pepper
4 oz. (100/125 g.) lean, home-cooked ham in thick slices
2 hard-boiled eggs, sliced
12 oz. (350 g.) rough puff or flaky pastry (see p. 218)

If you are using pie veal, trim it very carefully and remove all the skin and fat. Put the veal and the onion stuck with cloves in a saucepan with enough water just to cover the meat. Cook over a low heat for 40 minutes. Remove the meat and onion from the pan, reserving the stock.

When the veal is cold, cut it into very thin slices using a very sharp knife. Put a little parsley, grated lemon rind, chopped herbs, salt and pepper on each slice and roll the slice of meat up carefully. Put a layer of the veal rolls inside a 2 pint (1·1 litre) pie dish.

Cut the thick ham slices into short strips. Arrange a layer of ham strips and sliced egg on top of the veal rolls. Put another layer of veal rolls on top.

Reduce the stock by fast boiling to about half its original quantity, then season well and pour into the pie dish. Allow to cool. Roll out the pastry to about ¼ in. (5 mm.) thick, cut out a lid and cover the pie dish with it. Decorate with a rose and two leaves (see p. 221).

Bake the pie at the top of the pre-heated oven for 25 minutes or until the pastry is crisp and golden-brown. Cover the crust lightly with foil, move the pie to a lower shelf and cook for a further 10 minutes.

WELSH LAMB PIE
Wales

LAMB AND MUTTON PIES were an integral part of the old hiring and animal fairs that used to be held at various times of year throughout Wales. Some of the fairs were renowned for particular recipes; visitors to Templeton Fair in Pembrokeshire, for example, used to rejoice in the Katt pie, a confection of minced lamb or mutton with currants and brown sugar. This present pie of lamb and leeks was a traditional favourite at St Martin's Fair, held at Trevine, also in Pembrokeshire, and at several other gatherings up and down the Principality.

PREPARATION TIME: 30 MINUTES
COOKING TIME: 2 HOURS 25 MINUTES
COOLING TIME: 30 MINUTES
PRE-HEAT THE OVEN TO 180°C (350°F)—GAS MARK 4

INGREDIENTS FOR FOUR

8 lamb cutlets from the best end of the neck, or 1 lb. (450 g.) fillet end of a leg of lamb
1 oz. (25 g.) seasoned flour
½ teaspoon dried thyme
½ teaspoon dried rosemary
2 lamb's kidneys, skinned and cored
1 lb. (450 g.) leeks
1½ lb. (700 g.) small potatoes, peeled, cut in slices ½ in. (1·5 cm.) thick
Salt and pepper
1 pint (575/600 ml.) white or chicken stock (see pp. 33–34)
12 oz. (350 g.) shortcrust pastry (see p. 217)

Trim the cutlets, leaving the bone in. If using leg meat, remove all the skin, fat and bone, and cut it into 1 in. (2·5 cm.) cubes. Coat whichever meat you are using in the seasoned flour. Grease a large pie dish well, and put in the meat. Sprinkle it with the thyme and rosemary.

Cut each of the kidneys into four slices and dip them in the seasoned flour. Add the kidneys to the pie dish. Discard the outside leaves of the leeks, wash the leeks very carefully and cut them in slices 1 in. (2·5 cm.) long.

Pack a layer of leeks in the dish, and then a layer of sliced potatoes. Repeat the vegetable layers until the dish is full. Season well. Pour in the stock. Cover the top of the dish closely with foil and bake the pie on the lowest shelf of the pre-heated oven for about 1¾ hours.

Remove the dish from the oven and allow it to cool for a few minutes. Then stand in cold water until tepid before putting on the pastry lid—this will take about 30 minutes. Roll out the pastry to about ¼ in. (5 mm.) thick. Cut out a lid and cover the top of the dish with it (see p. 221). Return the pie to the top of the oven and bake for another 30–40 minutes. Serve hot with a green vegetable.

The filling for this pie may be cooked the day before you wish to eat it and the pastry lid added later.

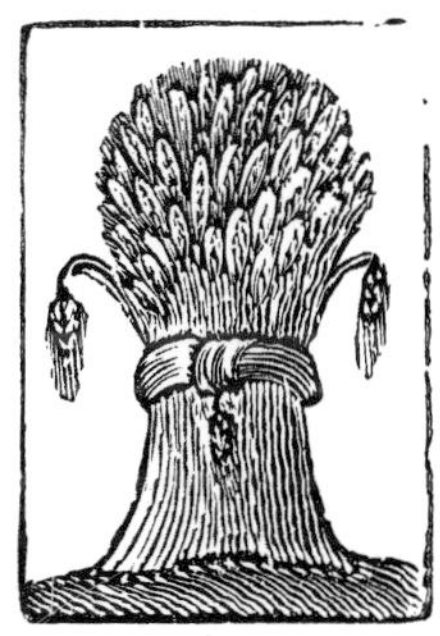

PIGEON PIE
Countrywide

THE TERM 'PIE' seems to have been derived from 'magpie'. Just as the bird collects assorted objects, so the dish gathers assorted ingredients. This pie, whose origins go back to the Middle Ages, illustrates the theory well, since it mingles all kinds of good things with the basic pigeons.

For many years it was the custom to serve the dish with four pigeon feet embedded in the crust. But in 1877, *Kettner's Book of the Table* noted that it was a custom 'to which many good people object, because they can see no use in it'.

PREPARATION TIME: 1 HOUR
COOKING TIME: 1 HOUR
PRE-HEAT THE OVEN TO 190°C (375°F)—GAS MARK 5

INGREDIENTS FOR FOUR

- *4 young pigeons, prepared by the butcher*
- *2 oz. (50 g.) mixed butter and oil*
- *8 oz. (225 g.) best rump steak, sliced thinly*
- *4 hard-boiled eggs, shelled*
- *½ pint (275/300 ml.) stock (game, chicken or white, see pp. 33–34)*
- *¼ teaspoon thyme*
- *1 oz. (25 g.) chopped parsley*
- *Salt and pepper*
- *8 oz. (225 g.) shortcrust pastry (see p. 217)*

Cut each pigeon in half lengthways.

Heat the butter and oil together in a frying pan and quickly brown the pigeons on both sides.

Line a pie dish with the thin slices of rump steak and arrange the halved pigeons on top. Cut each hard-boiled egg in two, and arrange the eight halves neatly between the pieces of pigeon. Heat the stock and pour it over the top, then sprinkle the dish with the thyme and parsley and season well.

Roll out the pastry to a thickness of no more than ¼ in. (5 mm.) and cover the pie dish with it (see p. 221).

Cover the top of the pie with greaseproof paper or kitchen foil, and bake it in the pre-heated oven for 1 hour. After 30 minutes, remove the greaseproof paper or foil.

DOUBLE CRUST PIE
Yorkshire

A COLD DAY'S WORK in the fields gives farmworkers a hefty appetite, but this Yorkshire farmhouse pie was created to take the edge off the keenest hunger—a good meaty filling and an inside crust of so-called 'huff' pastry, which turns into a kind of delicious dumpling.

PREPARATION TIME: 45 MINUTES
COOKING TIME: 2 HOURS
PRE-HEAT THE OVEN TO 180°C (350°F)—GAS MARK 4

INGREDIENTS FOR SIX TO EIGHT

- *½ oz. (15 g.) butter*
- *1 large onion, finely chopped*
- *¼ teaspoon garlic salt*
- *1 bay leaf*
- *1 lb. (450 g.) rump steak, trimmed and cut in 12 strips*
- *6 small chicken quarters*
- *Salt and pepper*
- *6 green bacon rashers, cut in very thin strips*
- *8 oz. (225 g.) mushrooms, quartered*
- *1½ pints (850 ml.) stock thickened with cornflour (see p. 163)*
- *12 oz. (350 g.) suet crust pastry (see p. 219)*
- *1 lb. (450 g.) shortcrust pastry (see p. 217)*

Grease a large pie dish with the butter. Put in the onion, garlic salt and bay leaf. Lay the 12 strips of steak on top. Arrange the chicken quarters on top of the steak. Season well. Pack in the bacon and mushrooms, and fill up the dish with half the thickened stock.

Cover the dish with a thin suet crust, about ¼ in. (5 mm.) thick. Press this down on to the meat and up against the sides of the dish, just below the rim. Cover the dish closely with foil, and bake the pie for 1½ hours in the pre-heated oven—this inside crust seals in all the flavour.

When the pie is ready, remove the foil, cut the suet crust into 12 squares and push them down among the chicken joints. Heat up the rest of the thickened stock until it is just warm, and pour it into the dish.

Roll out the shortcrust pastry to about ¼ in. (5 mm.) thick. Cut out a lid and put it on top of the pie dish (see p. 221). Return the pie to the oven and bake for 30–35 minutes near the top of the oven until the crust is golden-brown.

MELTON MOWBRAY PIE
Leicestershire

THE MOST FAMOUS of English pies was originally designed to satisfy the proverbial appetites of hunters in Leicestershire and the surrounding 'shires', or hunting counties. The earliest-known recipe for a pork pie dates from the 14th century, and advises you to 'flay your pig and cut him in pieces' and then to 'lay in your coffin good store of raisins and currants'.

Every household in the county had its own special recipe, but one unlikely ingredient was anchovy, which turned the filling a delicate pink. This pie makes a good tasty filler for picnic baskets and summer or winter buffets. Serve hot or cold.

PREPARATION TIME: 35 MINUTES
COOKING TIME: 4½ HOURS (INCLUDING MAKING THE STOCK)
PRE-HEAT THE OVEN TO 190°C (375°F)—GAS MARK 5

INGREDIENTS FOR FOUR

For the stock:

- *Pork or veal bones*
- *1 pint (575/600 ml.) water*
- *1 onion, peeled*
- *1 sage leaf*
- *1 bay leaf*
- *1 sprig marjoram*
- *1 sprig thyme*
- *Salt and pepper*

For the filling:

- *1 lb. (450 g.) pork from leg or shoulder (two-thirds lean and one-third fat)*
- *½ teaspoon salt*
- *¼ teaspoon pepper*
- *1 sage leaf, finely chopped*
- *A few drops anchovy essence (optional)*

For the crust:

- *1 lb. (450 g.) hot-water crust (see p. 219)*
- *A little milk*
- *1 egg, beaten*

First, make the stock. Put any bones from the pork, plus a few extra, to boil in the water with the onion, sage, bay leaf, marjoram, thyme, salt and pepper.

Boil for 2 hours to reduce the stock to little more than ½ pint (275/300 ml.). Let it cool, then skim off all the fat and taste it to check the seasoning. The stock should begin to jell as it cools.

Meanwhile, prepare the filling. Dice the pork in very small pieces, approximately ¼ in. (5 mm.) square.

Do not mince it, as the texture will not be the same. Remove any skin or gristle. Combine the pork, salt, pepper, sage and anchovy essence, if used.

Prepare the hot-water crust and raise the pastry in the following way, or as described under Hot-Water Crust Pastry on pp. 219–20.

Set aside one-third of the dough for the lid. Form the rest of the dough into a lump and put it inside a lightly greased cake tin or pie mould, about 7 in. (18 cm.) in diameter, with hinged sides and detachable base. Using your knuckles and the ball of your thumbs, work the dough up the sides of the mould or tin. When it is quite cool, bake it in the pre-heated oven for 20 minutes or until the pastry is set and beginning to brown.

Remove the pie case from the oven and carefully remove the tin or mould. Stand the pie case on a baking tray and put in the pork filling. Roll out the rest of the pastry to make a lid. Damp the top edges of the pie with a little milk, press on the lid and firmly crimp the edges all round to make a raised ridge, being careful not to break the pie case. Make a hole in the centre of the lid to let the steam out during cooking.

Lower the oven temperature to 180°C (350°F)—gas mark 4. Bake the pie for a further 1¾ hours, covering the top lightly with foil if it begins to brown too quickly.

To glaze the pie, remove it from the oven 10 minutes before it should be cooked, brush the top with beaten egg and return it to the oven.

When the pie is cooked, take it out of the oven and let it stand for 15 minutes. Meanwhile, re-heat the jellied stock until it has just melted. When it is fairly cool, but still liquid, pour as much stock as the pie will hold through the hole in the top of the crust, using a small funnel if you have one.

Kentish Chicken Pudding
Kent

As the old saying goes: 'They make puddings of everything in Kent and East Sussex.' And certainly they have been doing so since the 17th century, when the innovation of the pudding-cloth made it possible for the poor to have a hot, two-course meal by boiling the pudding and the meat together in the single family pot.

Kentish Chicken Pudding reflects the culinary history of the not so well off of the area. Pigs were killed and salted, after having gorged themselves on early-autumn windfalls; there was often an old boiling-fowl available, whose laying days were done; and by the mid-17th century, Kent's reputation for fruit-growing was already well established.

All three find their place in this fine, filling dish.

Preparation Time: 40 minutes
Cooking Time: 3 hours

Ingredients for Four to Six

- *1 boiling chicken, about 3 lb. (1·4 kg.), jointed*
- *Salt and pepper*
- *12 oz. (350 g.) suet crust pastry (see p. 219)*
- *8 oz. (225 g.) salt belly pork, chopped in ½ in. (1·5 cm.) cubes*
- *1 large onion, peeled and finely chopped*
- *3 medium cooking apples, peeled, cored and chopped*
- *1 tablespoon chopped parsley*
- *¼ teaspoon sugar*

For the sauce:

- *1 oz. (25 g.) butter*
- *1 oz. (25 g.) flour*
- *1 pint (575/600 ml.) hot chicken stock*
- *3 tablespoons chopped parsley*

Remove the skin and bones from the chicken and use to make the stock (see pp. 33–34). Cut the chicken flesh into neat pieces.

Roll out the suet pastry to about ½ in. (1·5 cm.) thick. Grease a 2½ pint (1·4 litre) basin and line the sides and bottom of it with the pastry, reserving enough to make the lid. Fill the basin to within 1 in. (2·5 cm.) of the top with the chicken, pork, onion, apples, parsley and sugar. Season to taste with salt and pepper.

Skim the fat from the chicken stock and add 2–3 tablespoons of it to the basin. Roll out the rest of the pastry and cover the pudding with it. Cover with buttered greaseproof paper and a clean cloth or foil, and tie down.

Put the basin into a saucepan with enough boiling water to come halfway up the basin. Cook gently for 2½–3 hours, adding more water to the pan if necessary to maintain the level.

Just before the pudding is ready, make the sauce. In a small saucepan, melt the butter, add the flour and cook for 1 minute. Gradually add the hot stock, stirring with a wooden spoon until the sauce thickens. Add the chopped parsley and serve the hot sauce with the pudding.

Melton Mowbray Pie—created for appetites sharpened on the hunting field.

STARGAZY PIE
Cornwall

STARGAZY PIE is one of those traditional dishes that many have heard of, but few people—outside Cornwall—have tasted. Originally it was made from pilchards, which are simply mature sardines. Shortly before the First World War, the vast shoals that arrived each year off the Cornish coast changed their migratory pattern and disappeared into the Atlantic. This caused great hardship to Cornish fishermen, who sold pilchards for smoking and canning, and for untold generations had obtained fish oil from them. A minor offshoot of this disaster was that the pie was made with herrings instead. Or you can make it with sardines.

Today, pilchards are once more available, though in much reduced numbers. Stargazy is so named because the fishes' heads protrude from the crust—a remarkable piece of culinary ingenuity. Though the heads are not eaten, the oil contained in them drains back into the fish during cooking. This oil would be lost if the heads were removed first.

PREPARATION TIME: 15 MINUTES
COOKING TIME: 45 MINUTES
PRE-HEAT THE OVEN TO 200°C (400°F)—GAS MARK 6

INGREDIENTS FOR SIX TO EIGHT

8 pilchards or 12 large sardines
Salt and pepper
1 large onion, peeled and chopped
2 heaped tablespoons chopped green herbs
8 rashers fat streaky bacon
¼ teaspoon saffron filaments (optional)
6 tablespoons milk
12 oz. (350 g.) shortcrust pastry (see p. 217)

Clean and bone the fish (see p. 74) and season the insides. Mix the onion and herbs together and put a little of this mixture inside each fish. Press the sides of the fish together. Cut the rind from the bacon and, if using sardines, cut the rashers in half.

If you are using it, bring the saffron to boiling point in the milk. Remove from the heat and leave to infuse, while you roll out half the pastry thinly.

Line a greased pie plate with the pastry. Scatter over any left-over onion mixture. Brush the pastry rim with a little saffron milk or plain milk. Lay the fish on the pastry, cut sides down, their heads lying on the pastry rim. Tuck the bacon between the fish and season.

Add any pastry scraps to the remaining half of the pastry. Roll it out rather more thickly than the bottom half. Cut out a circle the size of the pie plate and lay it over the pie, easing it back to expose the fish heads, and pressing it down firmly between the fish to seal the crusts together. Brush with milk or saffron milk.

Bake for about 15 minutes in the pre-heated oven or until the top is slightly golden. Lower the heat to 180°C (350°F)—gas mark 4 and cook for a further 30 minutes.

STEAK AND KIDNEY PIE
Countrywide

IN MEDIEVAL TIMES a meat pie of this kind would have been prepared on a mammoth scale, in order to feed a vast household. A thick 'coffin' of pastry made from flour, butter, broth and an egg or two was raised, and filled with a mixture of meats.

The modern Steak and Kidney Pie seems a slender dish in comparison, but to our palates much more delicious. Instead of a 'coffin', this recipe calls for a lid of light, rich puff pastry. You can omit the oysters, if

Preparing Stargazy Pie, with sardines, bacon and saffron milk.

you wish, and use mushrooms instead, but only rump steak will give the pie the right flavour.

PREPARATION TIME: 40 MINUTES
COOKING TIME: 2 HOURS 5 MINUTES
COOLING TIME: SEVERAL HOURS
PRE-HEAT THE OVEN TO
150°C (300°F)—GAS MARK 2

INGREDIENTS FOR FOUR

2 oz. (50 g.) butter
1 large onion, peeled and sliced
1 lb. (450 g.) rump steak, cut in 2 in. (5 cm.) cubes
2 tablespoons seasoned flour
12 oz. (350 g.) ox kidney
8 oz. (225 g.) mushrooms or 18 oysters, fresh or tinned
1 tablespoon flour
About ½ pint (275/300 ml.) brown stock (see pp. 33–34)
2 hard-boiled eggs (optional)
Salt and pepper
12 oz. (350 g.) puff pastry (see p. 219)
1 egg, beaten

Heat the butter in a frying pan and cook the onion in it until soft. Using a slotted spoon, transfer the onion to a warmed plate. Remove any fat from the cubes of rump steak and dip them in the seasoned flour. Then brown the cubes in the pan in which the onion was cooked, adding a little more butter, if necessary. Remove from the pan.

Chop the kidney quite thinly, remove all skin and fat and dip the kidney in the seasoned flour. Lightly brown it in the same pan as the steak.

Place a little kidney and a little onion on each piece of steak and arrange the steak in layers in a large pie dish. If you are adding mushrooms rather than oysters, slice the mushrooms thinly and lay some of the slices between the layers of meat.

Using a wooden spoon, stir the flour into the pan in which the meat and onion browned and add the stock. Cook together for a few minutes, stirring all the time, until the stock is slightly thickened. Pour just enough stock into the dish to almost cover the meat. Cover the dish closely with kitchen foil and cook in the preheated oven for 1½ hours, adding more stock during cooking if the meat becomes dry. Remove from the oven and allow to cool completely. This may well be done the day before you want to eat the pie.

Pre-heat the oven to 230°C (450°F)—gas mark 8. When the meat is cold, cut the hard-boiled eggs in quarters, if you are using them, and add them to the pie dish. If you have decided to use oysters instead of mushrooms, add these now. Use fresh oysters for preference, but canned oysters are delicious too.

Roll out the pastry to make a lid for the pie. Lay it over the filling, decorate the top (see p. 221) and glaze with the beaten egg. Bake in the preheated oven for 10 minutes. Reduce the heat to 180°C (350°F)—gas mark 4, and cook for a further 25 minutes or until the pastry is crisp and golden-brown.

Serve with creamed potatoes and carrots. If the filling is cooked the day before and the pastry ready to roll out, the pie can be finished off in very little time.

BEDFORDSHIRE CLANGERS
Bedfordshire

THE CLANGER was originally a long suet pudding filled with meat and vegetables at one end and fruit at the other—a complete two-course meal in its own edible lunch box. It is supposed to have been invented by resourceful lady hat-makers of Luton as a complete meal to be left on the hob for their husbands, while they themselves were at work.

This version retains the idea of the two courses, but uses shortcrust pastry instead of the original suet crust.

PREPARATION TIME: 30 MINUTES
COOKING TIME: 40 MINUTES
PRE-HEAT THE OVEN TO
220°C (425°F)—GAS MARK 7

INGREDIENTS FOR TWO CLANGERS

1 lb. (450 g.) shortcrust pastry (see p. 217)
1 egg, beaten
2 teaspoons granulated sugar

For the savoury filling:

1 small onion, peeled and chopped
1 tablespoon lard
8 oz. (225 g.) minced pork
1 teaspoon dried sage
1 cooking apple
2 oz. (50 g.) cooked peas
Salt and pepper

For the sweet filling:

2 eating apples
2 oz. (50 g.) dates, stoned and chopped
Grated rind of 1 orange
2 oz. (50 g.) sultanas
2 tablespoons caster sugar

Make the savoury filling first. Cook the chopped onion in the lard until it is soft and golden. Stir in the pork and sage and cook gently for 5 minutes, stirring often. Peel, core and chop the apple and add it to the pork mixture. Continue to cook for a further 5 minutes. Stir in the peas, season to taste and leave to cool.

Now make the sweet filling. Mix the peeled and chopped apples with the chopped dates, orange rind, sultanas and sugar.

Roll out the pastry to about ¼ in. (5 mm.) thick and cut out two circles 10 in. (25 cm.) in diameter. Using the trimmings, cut out two 5 in. (13 cm.) strips of pastry and stand one of these strips from the edge to the centre of each circle to form a wall. Make the strip stand firmly on each circle by brushing both edges with a little beaten egg and then pressing the bottom edge quite firmly on the circle. Brush the edges of the circles all the way round with beaten egg.

On one side of the pastry 'wall', put some of the savoury filling. On the other side, put some of the sweet filling. Fold the side of the circle that does not have the dividing strip along it right over to form a pasty shape. Press the centre lightly so that the dividing strip sticks to the top of the clanger. Pinch the edges firmly together. Brush each clanger with the rest of the beaten egg and sprinkle the sweet ends with sugar.

Bake the clangers in the pre-heated oven for 15 minutes. Lower the heat to 190°C (375°F)—gas mark 5, and bake for another 25 minutes.

LEEK PIE
Wales and Cornwall

THERE IS SOMETHING COMFORTING about the sight of a row of leeks sticking up through the snow; this useful pie, with its taste of greenness and freshness, is a pleasant meal for midwinter.

In the days when Lent was strictly observed, leeks were a valuable source of vitamins, lasting well into the spring. You can serve the pie in summer, too, accompanied by grilled or stuffed tomatoes.

PREPARATION TIME: 25 MINUTES
COOKING TIME: 30–40 MINUTES
PRE-HEAT THE OVEN TO
190°C (375°F)—GAS MARK 5

INGREDIENTS FOR FOUR

8 leeks, cut in 1 in. (2·5 cm.) pieces
1 oz. (25 g.) butter
4 oz. (100/125 g.) green or smoked bacon, chopped
About ¼ pint (150 ml.) stock (see pp. 33–34)
1 bay leaf
Salt and pepper
12 oz. (350 g.) shortcrust pastry (see p. 217)
1 egg, beaten

Wash the leeks thoroughly in several changes of water. Heat the butter in a frying pan, add the bacon pieces and fry gently for about 5 minutes until the fat runs. Add the leeks and cook together gently for a couple of minutes. Then pour in just enough stock to cover the leeks. Add the bay leaf, season and simmer for about 10–15 minutes. Tip most of the liquid from the pan. Set the filling aside to cool.

Grease a shallow pie dish, about 9 in. (23 cm.) in diameter, with butter. Roll out the pastry to about ¼ in. (5 mm.) thick and cut two circles to line and cover the dish (see p. 221). Line the pie dish with a pastry circle and put in the filling. Cover with the second circle. Make a hole in the top to allow the steam to escape. Press the edges down and brush the top with the beaten egg.

Bake in the centre of the pre-heated oven for 30–40 minutes.

CORNISH PASTIES
Cornwall

THEY SAY IN DEVONSHIRE that if the Devil crossed the Tamar—the river dividing Devon from Cornwall—the Cornish would make him into a pasty. Perhaps this is a reference to the 'horns' of the Cornish Pasty.

Certainly, its shape served a practical purpose in providing the working men of Cornwall with a perfect, portable lunch.

The pastry for a pasty used to be cut over a dinner plate, so it was quite a hefty size. It was the custom to mark one corner with an initial and claim the half-eaten pasty later.

PREPARATION TIME: 30 MINUTES
COOKING TIME: 40 MINUTES
PRE-HEAT THE OVEN TO
220°C (425°F)—GAS MARK 7

INGREDIENTS FOR FOUR PASTIES

1 lb. (450 g.) shortcrust pastry (see p. 217)
4 medium potatoes, peeled
1 medium onion, peeled and diced
4 oz. (100/125 g.) swede, peeled and diced
12 oz. (350 g.) chuck steak, diced
Salt and pepper
Parsley, roughly chopped (optional)
2 oz. (50 g.) butter
1 egg, beaten, for glazing

Roll out the pastry to about ¼ in. (5 mm.) thick and cut out four 6 in. (15 cm.) rounds.

Cut the potatoes by 'shripping' them—cutting them into very fine wafers by constantly turning them to 'shrip' off the corners. Put a few pieces of potato in the centre of each pastry round. Cover this with some diced onion and diced swede, and then some of the diced meat. If using parsley, add it now and dot with butter. Season well and cover the meat with some more potato slices to prevent it drying. Dampen the edges of the pastry and fold each round over to make a half-moon shape. Turn the edges round a little to make 'horns'.

Pinch and crimp the pastry edges into ridges to give a rope-like effect. Glaze with beaten egg and put the pasties on a greased baking sheet.

Bake in the pre-heated oven for 10 minutes. Lower the heat to 180°C (350°F)—gas mark 4, and continue cooking for 30 minutes.

The pasties are delicious hot or cold. They will stay warm for an hour or two if you wrap them up in a tea towel.

SMALL MUTTON PIES
Scotland

THERE ARE FEW DISHES so simple, so delectable or so absolutely Scottish as these small mutton pies. Once, they were sold by piemen on street corners to the cry of:

'One for a penny, four for a groat!'

They were praised by Dr Johnson, and favoured so highly by Queen Victoria and George V that they were served as appetisers at receptions in Balmoral Castle and Buckingham Palace—so that they are literally fit for a king. Perhaps they are at their best served piping hot, but they are also excellent cold for picnics.

PREPARATION TIME: 30 MINUTES
COOKING TIME: 30–40 MINUTES
PRE-HEAT THE OVEN TO
190°C (375°F)—GAS MARK 5

INGREDIENTS FOR SIX PIES

8 oz. (225 g.) hot-water crust pastry (see p. 219)
1 lb. (450 g.) lean lamb or mutton
1 teaspoon salt
¼ teaspoon pepper
¼ teaspoon nutmeg
6 tablespoons stock, gravy or water
1 egg yolk, beaten

Use one-third of the prepared pastry to make six lids for the pies, and divide the rest into six pieces. Mould these to make six small pie cases (see pp. 219–20).

Remove any skin and gristle from the mutton or lamb. Cut the meat into small pieces and season it with the salt, pepper and nutmeg. Fill the pie cases with the meat mixture and moisten each pie with 1 tablespoon of the stock, gravy or water.

Moisten the edges of the pastry lids with a little cold water, then place them on the pies, wet side down, pressing the edges firmly together. Trim the edges with a sharp knife. Make a small hole in the centre of each pie to allow steam to escape and brush the tops lightly with a little of the beaten egg yolk.

Bake the pies in the pre-heated oven for 30–40 minutes.

Serve them very hot with potatoes and broad beans or cold with a green salad.

Bacon and Egg Flan
Yorkshire

Bacon was once the only meat that a poor farm labourer could afford. He might eat a cold chunk of it for his midday meal in the fields, with an onion and bread. At harvest time a simple flan of bacon and egg could be made large enough to feed a whole family, and be taken out to them as they worked in the fields.

This recipe for a smaller family makes a good light lunch or supper dish.

Preparation Time: 15 minutes
Cooking Time: 30 minutes
Pre-heat the Oven to
190°C (375°F)—gas mark 5

Ingredients for Four

6 oz. (175 g.) shortcrust pastry (see p. 217)
6 oz. (175 g.) lean green bacon rashers, without rinds
2 eggs
Salt and pepper
¼ pint (150 ml.) creamy milk or single cream

Roll the pastry large enough to line a 7 in. (18 cm.) plain or fluted flan ring.

Cut two-thirds of the bacon rashers into strips, 2 in. (5 cm.) long, and line the pastry case with them. Chop the rest of the rashers finely and sprinkle them over the bacon strips.

Whisk the eggs with a generous shake of salt and pepper and then stir in the milk or cream. Pour the egg mixture over the bacon.

Bake the flan in the centre of the pre-heated oven for 30 minutes until the filling is set and golden-brown.

Serve the flan hot or cold with a salad. A little grated cheese may be sprinkled over the flan before baking it.

Bacon and Egg Flan, Mutton Pies and Cornish Pasties: an out-of-doors meal from three regions of Britain.

COCKLE AND CORN PIE
Wales

COCKLES have been a favourite fish food in Britain since Roman times, and over the centuries cockle-gardens were in operation along enclosed parts of the coast in both England and Wales.

In the 1880s, a writer on shellfish told how cockle-wives scraped for cockles, 'the scraper being made from an old reaping-hook'. Today, cockles are still gathered in the sand and mud and sold cleaned and cooked.

Their name comes from the Latin word for cockle: *conchylium.*

PREPARATION TIME: 20 MINUTES
COOKING TIME: 45 MINUTES
PRE-HEAT THE OVEN TO 200°C (400°F)—GAS MARK 6

INGREDIENTS FOR FOUR TO FIVE

- *2 eggs*
- *¼ pint (150 ml.) milk*
- *4 oz. (100/125 g.) coarse oatmeal*
- *1 lb. (450 g.) cockles*
- *6 oz. (175 g.) sweet-corn kernels, fresh, frozen or tinned*
- *1 medium onion, peeled and chopped*
- *3 tablespoons melted butter*
- *Salt and pepper*
- *1 teaspoon Worcestershire sauce (optional)*
- *8 oz. (225 g.) cheese pastry (see p. 218)*

Check the cockles for saltiness and rinse in cold water, if necessary. Beat the eggs and milk together in a pie dish, mix in the oatmeal and leave to stand for 10–15 minutes. Stir in the cockles, corn, onion, butter, salt and pepper and the Worcestershire sauce, if liked. Mix well.

Roll out the cheese pastry to about ¼ in. (5 mm.) thick and fix a pastry lid on to the pie dish (see p. 221). Bake the pie on the top shelf of the pre-heated oven for 10 minutes. Then reduce the heat to 180°C (350°F)—gas mark 4, and move the pie to a lower shelf. Cook for another 35 minutes, covering the crust loosely with foil if it begins to become too brown too quickly.

Serve with salad and brown bread.

If using frozen corn, be sure that it thaws properly first.

You may use plain shortcrust pastry or just a layer of grated cheese to cover the pie, but the cheese pastry goes particularly well with the cockle filling.

VEAL UNDER CRUST
Shropshire

THE NORMANS LOVED VEAL, and it was very popular in medieval cookery, usually baked in chunks with eggs, dried fruit and spices.

This unusual recipe from Shropshire dates back to those times, and was originally intended for a feast-day pie, containing 8 lb. of veal! It is expensive to make, but your guests will enjoy the delicate flavour of the meat enhanced by herbs, and with the faintest trace of medieval sweetness from the raisins.

PREPARATION TIME: 40 MINUTES
COOKING TIME: 1 HOUR 40 MINUTES
PRE-HEAT THE OVEN TO 200°C (400°F)—GAS MARK 6

INGREDIENTS FOR FOUR

- *1 lb. (450 g.) veal fillet or leg of veal, cut in 2 long flattish pieces*
- *1 oz. (25 g.) seasoned flour*
- *8 oz. (225 g.) sausagemeat*
- *2 oz. (50 g.) white breadcrumbs*
- *4 oz. (100/125 g.) mushrooms, finely sliced and lightly fried*
- *1 small onion, peeled and chopped*
- *½ teaspoon dried thyme*
- *½ teaspoon dried rosemary*
- *1 teaspoon finely chopped fresh parsley*
- *2 oz. (50 g.) butter*
- *4 rindless rashers green bacon*
- *12 raisins*
- *16 stoned green olives or 4 artichoke hearts, fresh or tinned*
- *About ¼ pint (150 ml.) chicken stock (see pp. 33–34) or ¼ pint (150 ml.) white wine*
- *12 oz. (350 g.) rough puff or shortcrust pastry (see pp. 218, 217)*

Remove any skin or gristle from the veal. Dip both slices all over in the seasoned flour and set aside.

Mix together in a bowl the sausagemeat, breadcrumbs, mushrooms, onion and herbs. Work them well together and divide the mixture in two. Shape each half into a large, flat cake about the same size as the veal fillets. Fry these cakes on both sides in the butter for about 20 minutes, until each side is a light golden-brown.

In a large pie dish, lay one of the forcemeat cakes. Lay a fillet of veal on top and then the second forcemeat cake. Cover with the second slice of veal. Cut the bacon rashers into ½ in. (1·5 cm.) strips and pack them around the meat. Add the raisins, olives or artichoke hearts. Pour enough chicken stock or white wine into the dish to just cover all the contents.

Roll out the pastry to about ¼ in. (5 mm.) thick, cut out a lid and put on top of the pie dish (see p. 221). Bake near the top of the pre-heated oven for 20 minutes. Reduce the heat to 180°C (350°F)—gas mark 4, move the pie to the lowest shelf and continue cooking for another hour. If the pastry begins to get too brown, cover the top lightly with a piece of foil.

To serve the pie, cut through the crust across the middle and turn one half of the crust back over the uncut section. Cut down through the veal with a sharp knife and lift out a portion of the filling with a serving spoon. Cut the turned back piece of crust in half and place one piece over the serving on the plate. Cut off the second half of the crust and lay it over the empty end of the dish while you serve the rest of the pie.

The pie is very rich and needs only a green salad to go with it.

A salad made of young raw spinach leaves, watercress and chicory gives a particularly good contrast in flavours.

SALMON IN PASTRY WITH HERB SAUCE
Countrywide

PREPARING SALMON in a pastry case is the medieval equivalent of cooking it in foil—a means of sealing in the essential oils, juices and flavours. But, as opposed to the modern method, you do get the pastry as well.

Salmon have had their social ups and downs. Under the feudal system, anyone who had a salmon weir paid dearly to his overlord in either service or kind. However, in the 16th century the fish became so plentiful that the apprentices of London, Perth and Newcastle revolted, demanding that their masters should not give them 'kippered' salmon more than three times a week.

This aspect of industrial relations no longer besets us, and the price of making this recipe is fairly steep. But it can turn a dinner into a banquet.

PREPARATION TIME: 20 MINUTES
COOKING TIME: 30 MINUTES
PRE-HEAT THE OVEN TO
220°C (425°F)—GAS MARK 7

INGREDIENTS FOR SIX

2 thick salmon fillets, about $2\frac{1}{2}$ lb. (1·1 kg.) in all
Salt and pepper
3 oz. (75 g.) butter
2 pieces ginger in syrup
1 generous tablespoon currants
8 oz. (225 g.) shortcrust pastry (see p. 217)
1 beaten egg to glaze

For the sauce:

2 oz. (50 g.) butter
2 shallots, peeled and chopped
1 tablespoon chopped parsley
2 teaspoons chopped chervil
2 teaspoons chopped tarragon
1 heaped teaspoon flour
$\frac{1}{2}$ pint (275/300 ml.) cream
Salt and pepper
1 teaspoon Dijon mustard
2 egg yolks
Lemon juice

Ask the fishmonger to skin and bone the fish, and season the fillets with salt and pepper. Mash the butter. Chop the ginger and fork it into the butter. Add the currants to the mixture and sandwich two-thirds of it between the salmon fillets. Spread the rest of the butter mixture on top.

Roll out the pastry to about $\frac{1}{4}$ in. (5 mm.) thick. Lift the salmon on to it and seal the edges of the pastry very firmly around the fish. Cut away any surplus pastry and carefully turn the fish parcel over on to a greased baking sheet, so that the seam is underneath. Slash the top of the pastry case in three places, to allow steam to escape. Make decorative shapes out of the pastry trimmings, and fix these decorations on top with the beaten egg. Brush the top with more beaten egg, and bake in the pre-heated oven for 30 minutes or until golden-brown.

Meanwhile, prepare the sauce as the fish is cooking. Melt the butter in a frying pan, add the shallots and the herbs, and cook over a very low flame until soft. Stir in the flour, all but 1 tablespoon of the cream, and the salt and pepper. Simmer, stirring all the time, for 10 minutes, then beat in the mustard. Stir the egg yolks into the remaining cream and beat this into the sauce. Continue to stir the sauce until it thickens slightly but do not let it boil. Correct the seasoning and add lemon juice to taste.

Serve the sauce separately.

Salmon in Pastry—the juices are sealed in, making the fish more tender, and the flavour is enhanced by a light herb sauce.

RECIPES *from* OTHER LANDS

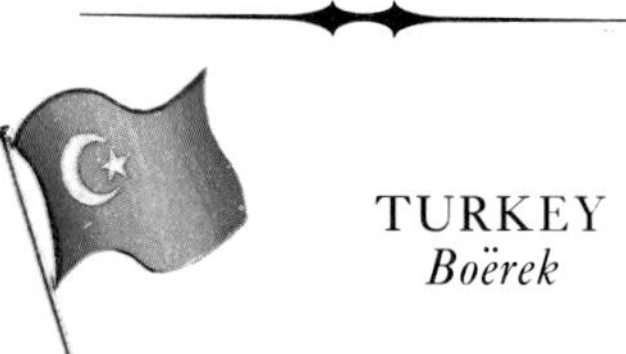

TURKEY
Boërek

AMONG the most mouth-watering of Middle-Eastern dishes are Boërek—a group of savoury pastries, which come in many shapes and sizes. There are numerous recipes for them. The savoury version is usually eaten before dinner, and the sweet version after it with coffee.

The outstanding feature of Boërek is their very thin pastry, and great care is needed in making it. However, the outcome is well worth the time and trouble spent. Remember to dust the pastry board with cornflour, or it will be very difficult to remove the almost transparent pastry from the board. They make a delicious first course or, filled with a mixture of nuts and honey, a good dessert.

PREPARATION TIME: ABOUT 3 HOURS (INCLUDING RESTING THE PASTRY)

COOKING TIME: 20–30 MINUTES

PRE-HEAT THE OVEN TO 190°C (375°F)—GAS MARK 5 (IF BAKING THE BOËREK)

INGREDIENTS FOR 40–45 BOËREK

For the pastry:

10 oz. (275 g.) plain flour
$\frac{1}{4}$ pint (150 ml.) water
$\frac{1}{4}$ oz. (7 g.) melted butter
$\frac{1}{2}$ teaspoon salt
1 oz. (25 g.) cornflour
1 oz. (25 g.) melted butter

For the savoury filling:

8 oz. (225 g.) cottage or cream cheese
1 oz. (25 g.) butter
1 or 2 tablespoons of milk to moisten, if necessary
2 tablespoons finely chopped parsley
A pinch of salt
1 egg, beaten

To make the pastry, mix the flour with the water, melted butter and salt and knead it lightly into a dough. Cover with a cloth and leave for 1–2 hours in a cool place. Divide the pastry into four pieces.

Dust a pastry board generously with cornflour to prevent the pastry sticking, and roll out each piece of pastry as nearly as possible paper-thin. Dust the rim of a large glass, about $2\frac{1}{2}$ in. (6·5 cm.) in diameter, with cornflour and cut the pastry into rounds with the rim of the glass.

To make the savoury filling, blend all the ingredients well together and bind with the beaten egg.

Brush each circle of pastry with melted butter and put 1 teaspoon of filling on each. Roll the pieces into the shape of a pencil or fold them over, pressing the edges together. Deep-fry in fairly hot oil, about 150°C (300°F), cooking four of the Boërek at a time, for 3–4 minutes each. Alternatively, put the Boërek on a greased baking sheet and bake in the pre-heated oven for about 30 minutes. Eat while still warm as a first course.

To make a sweet filling, mix together 4 oz. (100/125 g.) each of shelled, skinned and chopped walnuts, almonds and hazelnuts, 1 tablespoon of honey, $\frac{1}{2}$ teaspoon of powdered cinnamon, and $\frac{1}{2}$ teaspoon of caster sugar. Put a little of the mixture on each pastry round and either roll the Boërek up or fold them over. Cook as for savoury Boërek and eat while warm.

BOLIVIA
Empanadas de Carne (Meat Pasties)

AS IT IS NOT EXPORTED, beef is plentiful and not too expensive in Bolivia, and it forms the basis of *Empanadas de Carne*. What makes the pasties so typically South American, however, is the mixture of red and green peppers, raisins, and green chillies, with which they are stuffed.

The pasties are snack-sized and are delicious served with drinks. In general, *empanadas*—or individual pasties—are among the most versatile of Latin American foods. They can be filled with several kinds of meat or fish and contain various spicy titbits. For a party snack, the Empanadas can be made in advance and then deep-fried in very hot oil just before serving.

PREPARATION TIME: 45 MINUTES
COOKING TIME: 15 MINUTES

INGREDIENTS FOR 15 EMPANADAS

1 oz. (25 g.) butter and vegetable oil mixed
1 small onion, sliced
1 small green pepper, de-seeded and finely chopped
1 small red pepper, de-seeded and finely chopped
4 oz. (100/125 g.) beef, finely chopped
1 small green chilli, chopped, or a pinch of chilli powder
Salt and pepper
$\frac{1}{4}$ pint (150 ml.) beef stock
1 oz. (25 g.) raisins
1 teaspoon cornflour
Oil for deep-frying
8 oz. (225 g.) shortcrust pastry (see p. 217)
1 egg, beaten

To make the filling, heat the butter and oil together in a frying pan and cook the onion until soft. Add the red and green peppers and cook for 5 minutes more. Add the meat, the chilli or chilli powder, salt and pepper, stock and raisins. Bring to the boil, then simmer until the meat is cooked—about 20 minutes.

Mix the cornflour with 1 teaspoon of cold water and add it to the meat mixture. Stir constantly and well with a wooden spoon until the mixture thickens. Leave to cool.

Roll out the pastry very thinly to about $\frac{1}{16}$ in. (1·5 mm.). Flour the rim of a very wide cup and use it to cut out pastry rounds about $3\frac{1}{2}$–4 in. (9–10 cm.) in diameter. With a pastry brush, wet all around the edges of each pastry circle with beaten egg. Place a little filling in one half of each circle, turn over the other half and press the edges to completely seal them.

Heat the oil in a deep-fryer as if making Fish and Chips (see p. 67). Cook the Empanadas in batches until golden-brown—about 3–4 minutes, turning them over once. Serve hot.

RUSSIA
Fish Koulibiaka

KOULIBIAKA—which simply means a long pie made of rolled pastry—is a popular dish throughout most of Russia. Although fish is the best-known filling, Koulibiaka can alternatively be stuffed with meat and cabbage or other vegetables.

The fame of the dish spread to France in the 18th century, when Parisian chefs—who had been employed by the Russian nobility—took the recipe home with them. The fish used in Russia was salmon—and, on special occasions, sturgeon from the Caspian Sea. In Paris, where neither fish was readily available, they were replaced by turbot.

PREPARATION TIME: 40 MINUTES
COOKING TIME: ABOUT 1½ HOURS
PRE-HEAT THE OVEN TO
230°C (450°F)—GAS MARK 8

INGREDIENTS FOR SIX

1½ lb. (700 g.) puff pastry (see p. 219)
1½ lb. (700 g.) salmon or a mixture of salmon and firm white fish, such as halibut or turbot
2 oz. (50 g.) butter
1 large onion, sliced
2 oz. (50 g.) mushrooms, chopped
2 tablespoons chopped parsley
Salt and pepper
4 fl. oz. (100/125 ml.) Madeira or dry white wine
3 hard-boiled eggs, chopped
1 egg, beaten
2–4 oz. (50–125 g.) melted butter

For the cereal layers:

8 oz. (225 g.) buckwheat cooked with 2 oz. (50 g.) butter, or 8 oz. (225 g.) rice, cooked (see p. 199)

Divide the pastry in two pieces, one larger than the other, and roll out the smaller piece to form a rectangle about 12 by 7 in. (30 by 18 cm.). Lay this on a greased baking sheet.

Skin and bone the fish, and chop it into small pieces. In a frying pan, heat 2 oz. (50 g.) of butter and fry the onion in it for 10 minutes. Add the mushrooms and cook for 5 minutes more. Add the fish and the chopped parsley to the pan and continue to cook for 5 minutes. Season and stir in the Madeira or wine and simmer for a few more minutes. Drain off most of the liquid and leave the mixture to cool.

If you are using the buckwheat, put it in a saucepan with the butter and an equal volume of water. Cover and cook over a low heat for 15 minutes. When it is cooked, the grains should be separate, like rice. Let it cool for 15 minutes. If using rice, prepare it and cool for 15 minutes.

Wet the edges of the pastry on the baking sheet and spread it with a layer of the cooked and cooled buckwheat or rice. Add a sprinkling of chopped egg and a layer of the fish mixture. Repeat the layers, ending with cereal. The filling should be about 5 in. (13 cm.) deep. Make sure that the filling does not come right to the edges of the pastry. Roll out the larger piece of pastry and drape it over the filling. Pinch the sides together to seal them. Prick the surface a few times with a fork. Brush the top and edges with the beaten egg.

Bake the Koulibiaka in the pre-heated oven for 15 minutes. Turn the heat down to 150°C (300°F)—gas mark 2, and cook for 1 hour more.

Serve hot with melted butter and a green vegetable or salad.

RUSSIA
Piroshky

PIROSHKY, or 'little pies', have been a popular savoury in Russia for many centuries. They were probably made with dough until the time of Ivan the Terrible (1530–84), when Italian architects and designers came to repair and redecorate the Moscow Kremlin and introduced pastry to the court. Piroshky are normally stuffed with meat, but other fillings can be used.

PREPARATION TIME: 40 MINUTES
COOKING TIME: ABOUT 45 MINUTES
PRE-HEAT THE OVEN TO
230°C (450°F)—GAS MARK 8

INGREDIENTS FOR 15–25 PIROSHKY

For the pastry cases:

2½ oz. (65 g.) choux pastry (see p. 220)
1 egg, beaten

For the meat filling:

2 oz. (50 g.) butter
1 onion, sliced
8 oz. (225 g.) freshly minced beef
Salt and pepper
1 tablespoon chopped parsley

For the cabbage and egg filling:

8 oz. (225 g.) hard white cabbage, chopped
2 oz. (50 g.) butter
¼ pint (150 ml.) water
Salt
1 onion, sliced
1 hard-boiled egg, chopped
Pepper
1 tablespoon chopped parsley

To make the meat filling, heat the butter gently in a frying pan and cook the sliced onion in it for about 10 minutes, or until soft. Raise the heat and add the meat, stirring it well so that it browns on all sides. Season and cook for 2–3 minutes. Add the parsley and stir well. Leave to cool.

To make the cabbage and egg filling, put the cabbage in a saucepan with 1 oz. (25 g.) of the butter, the water and a pinch of salt. Cover and cook over a low heat until the water is absorbed and the cabbage is soft.

Meanwhile, lightly cook the onion in the rest of the butter for 10 minutes, until it is soft but not brown. Mix the cabbage and onion together, add the chopped egg, season, and add the parsley. Leave to cool.

To make choux pastry cases, take a spoon dipped in hot water and put blobs of the pastry on to a greased baking sheet. Glaze them with the beaten egg. Bake in the pre-heated oven for 15 minutes or until the pastry is beginning to brown. Leave the pastry shells to cool, then hollow out the centres and stuff them with one of the fillings. When ready to serve, re-heat the Piroshky in a hot oven for 5 minutes.

FRANCE
Tarte à l'Oignon

TARTE À L'OIGNON is said to have first been made in Alsace-Lorraine in the 16th century. As their popularity spread, and they came to be baked throughout France, grated cheese was added as a tasty extra.

PREPARATION TIME: 20 MINUTES
COOKING TIME: 55 MINUTES
PRE-HEAT THE OVEN TO
200°C (400°F)—GAS MARK 6

INGREDIENTS FOR FOUR TO SIX

4 oz. (100/125 g.) butter and cooking oil mixed
2 lb. (900 g.) onions, sliced very thinly
Salt and pepper
3 eggs, beaten
2 oz. (50 g.) grated cheese, preferably Gruyère
8 oz. (225 g.) shortcrust pastry (see p. 217)

Heat the butter and oil in a frying pan and cook the onions gently, with a lid on the pan, for about 30 minutes. Season and leave to cool. Add the eggs and grated cheese to the onion.

Grease a shallow baking tin, 12 in. (30 cm.) in diameter. Roll out the pastry to line the baking tin (see p. 220). Cover with the egg and onion mixture and spread it over the pastry.

Cook in the centre of the pre-heated oven for 20–25 minutes, until the top is golden. Serve hot or cold.

SAVOURY PIES, PUDDINGS AND PASTRIES

PIES WERE PROBABLY a development of the Roman idea of sealing meat inside a paste of oil and flour for cooking. The practice of shaping the pastry into thick walls developed in the Middle Ages. Early pie crusts were mainly containers for the filling, the pastry was not always eaten.

By late medieval times, pie-makers were common in towns, and people often took their own meat to the pie-maker to be baked in a pie for a small fee. Pies were sold in the streets by pie wives and pie men.

Small animals, birds, fish or pieces of meat in a pastry crust—sometimes moulded to the body shape—were called bakemeats. They were eaten hot or preserved for eating cold, clarified butter being poured in to exclude air. A true pie contained a mixture of ingredients, with sweets and savouries such as dried fruit and meat combined. By the 18th century, however, separate pies for sweets and savouries were more usual.

Savoury Pies and Tarts

A savoury pie is a dish of meat, fish or vegetables (or meat or fish with vegetables) covered with a pastry crust and baked in the oven. Some pies are completely enclosed in pastry—usually when the fillings are pork, veal, ham or game. A filling enclosed in suet pastry and steamed is usually known as a pudding—such as steak and kidney pudding.

A savoury tart or flan is a pastry case holding a meat, fish or vegetable filling and baked in the oven. It may have a pastry lid or cover, but if not it is known as an open tart.

Savoury pies, tarts and puddings make substantial dishes from a limited amount of filling, and the pastry covering helps to keep the filling moist and to retain its aroma.

Shortcrust pastry is mostly used for pie crusts, tart cases and meat rolls. Other types, such as flaky pastry, can be used, depending on the richness and texture required.

Assessing the amount of pastry

When a recipe states the amount of pastry needed, the quantity given is the amount of flour to be used. The actual amount of pastry will be roughly the total of flour and fat.

The pastry recipes given here use 8 oz. (225 g.) of flour. To make a greater amount of pastry, increase all ingredients in proportion. When doubling amounts, increase the salt to 1 level teaspoon.

Preparing savoury fillings

To prepare meat, trim off any gristle or excess fat and cut the meat into bite-size pieces. It can also be minced. For game pies, joint the meat and cut it into pieces of a suitable size. Game can be mixed with other meats.

For pies with liquid added to the meat, coat the meat in seasoned flour. To do this, put 1 tablespoon of flour and a good pinch of both salt and pepper into a polythene bag, add the pieces of meat and shake well. Tip the contents into the pie dish. The flour helps to thicken the liquid.

Prepare fish by cleaning and scaling (see p. 74), then cut it into bite-size pieces or chunks. Small fish can be left whole. Coat the fish with seasoned flour. If using a flavourless fish, add chopped parsley or other chopped herbs to the seasoned flour.

Vegetables used as a savoury filling should be cut into cubes of about 1 in. (2·5 cm.), as they need to cook in the same length of time as the pastry. A pie containing mainly vegetables needs seasoning well.

A Guide to Good Pastry-Making

HUFF paste was the name of the pastry used for centuries to wrap round food before it was baked. It is still used today for baking hams.

Very little is known of the quality of medieval pastry, for few recipes were written down before the 16th century. But, as it had to be moulded into 'raised' pies to contain fillings such as a partridge or a goose, it was probably a strong dough made from coarse wheaten or rye flour.

Small pies and pasties were often fried in lard rather than baked. By Elizabethan times, a rich butter pastry known as puff paste was in use. It was mixed with seven or eight eggs, rosewater and spices, and after baking was sugared and served on its own.

PASTRY AND ITS INGREDIENTS

Pastry is basically flour and fat mixed with water, or sometimes milk and water. Other ingredients are added as flavouring or to ensure rising.

The proportions of the basic ingredients and the method of mixing are crucial to the texture of the pastry. Flour contains a sticky, elastic substance called gluten, which holds the dough together. Different mixing methods are used to control the gluten and vary the pastry texture. The type and amount of fat determines the richness and flavour.

Another vital ingredient is air, introduced during mixing and rolling. When the pastry is heated, the air expands causing the pastry to rise and helping to make it light.

The ingredients

Flour Use soft, plain flour to make sure the pastry has a fine, short texture and only a small rise when heated. Strong flour, as used in bread, is not usually suitable because it is high in gluten and would make the pastry rise too much and be too elastic, but it can be used in puff pastry. Self-raising flour, which contains a raising agent, can be used in suet crust pastry.

Sieve the flour before use to make sure it is fresh, dry and free from lumps. If it has become damp, dry it in a warm place before using. Damp flour can make pastry heavy.

Baking powder is a chemical mixture (mainly sodium bicarbonate) that produces gas, and can be used with plain flour as a raising agent. It is needed only if the amount of fat used is less than half the amount of flour (although hot-water crust pastry needs no baking powder), or in suet crust pastry made with plain flour.

Pastry containing too much baking powder goes stale quickly and has a dry taste. If you use baking powder, do not leave the pastry to stand—mix it quickly and bake immediately, because the raising agent begins to work at once.

Fat Use fresh fat of good quality. If the fat is stale and has a slightly off flavour, this will be even more pronounced in the cooked pastry.

Butter, lard, good dripping, clarified fat, margarine, vegetable fat and suet can all be used. Butter on its own produces rich pastry, and unsalted butter is best for puff pastry. For economical, well-flavoured short pastry, use a mixture of lard and margarine, or margarine and one of the vegetable fats.

Always use good margarine in preference to cheap butter. Lard used on its own can give a flavour that many people find unacceptable, particularly if it is not of good quality. Suet, like lard, is an animal fat. You can buy it fresh from the butcher or ready shredded in packets. Packeted suet contains a preservative, but make sure it is dry, free-flowing and has no smell. Cooking oil can be used, but do not mix it with fat. Follow the recipe for quantities.

Salt A pinch of salt helps to develop the flavour of the pastry.

Lemon juice Flaky, puff and rough puff pastries are rich; adding lemon juice counteracts the richness.

Egg yolk Adding an egg yolk enriches pastry and gives a very short texture.

Hints for Pastry-Making

When mixing and rolling pastry, the aim is to introduce as much air as possible so that the pastry will rise well when heated. The colder the air, the more it will expand when heated during cooking.

Keep all utensils and ingredients as cool as possible, and wash your hands in cold water before you mix pastry. The only exception to this is when making hot-water crust pastry.

Mixing the dough

Sieve together the dry ingredients—flour, salt, and baking powder if used. This not only sifts out any lumps, but also ensures even distribution. If the baking powder is not well distributed, the pastry will rise unevenly.

Weigh out the correct amount of fat. Too much will make the pastry break easily; too little could make it hard and tough. Fat is added in various ways according to the type of pastry. Whichever method you use, the fat must be properly incorporated and distributed as evenly as possible. Otherwise, it will melt and run before it is absorbed into the flour during baking, giving tough, streaky pastry.

Mix in the water or other liquid with a broad-bladed knife, as a knife is cooler than hands. Use water fresh from the tap—it is cooler and more aerated than water that has been standing.

Measure the amount of water carefully and add it gradually, because too much will spoil the texture of the pastry. Some flours absorb more water than others, so it is difficult to give the exact amount in a recipe.

When the dough is properly mixed, it should be soft and elastic and leave the side of the bowl clean. Do not rub off any little pieces from your fingers into the pastry. This can result in rough spots and flecks when the pastry is rolled out.

Electric mixers can be used for mixing pastry. Carefully follow the maker's instructions on timing.

Rolling pastry

If time allows, leave the lump of pastry to rest in a cool place for 10–20 minutes before rolling it out (unless it contains baking powder), particularly in hot weather. Pastry that gets over-heated during handling will be tough.

Dredge the board and rolling pin with flour, but not the pastry. Too much flour rolled in can alter the ratio of flour to fat, particularly if you are making only a small quantity.

When rolling pastry, use short, quick, light strokes with even pressure from both hands. Always roll in a forward direction, and lift the pin between strokes. Stop rolling just short of the edges to ensure a uniform thickness and to avoid squeezing out air. Lift the pastry lightly at the edges to make sure it is not sticking to the board. If it is, very lightly dust beneath it with flour.

Do not handle pastry unless necessary. To move it, or lift it on to a dish, turn it over a floured rolling pin. Unroll it on to a freshly dredged surface or across the surface of the dish. The rolled side of the pastry is the smoothest, and should be used for the pie surface.

Storing uncooked pastry

Unless it contains baking powder, pastry can be stored after mixing until ready for use. If sealed in a polythene bag, it will keep in a refrigerator for up to 3 days, whether in a lump or rolled and shaped. It can also be deep-frozen for up to 3 months, but roll and shape it before freezing.

Shortcrust pastry, mixed to a crumb stage but with no liquid added, can be stored in a polythene bag or covered container in a refrigerator for up to 4 weeks. Use portions as required. It can also be deep-frozen and will keep for up to 6 months.

Shortcrust Pastry

Shortcrust pastry is made with 4 parts flour to 2 parts fat. It should have a crisp, short (melt-in-the-mouth) texture. This is achieved by rubbing the fat and flour together with the fingers to make a crumb-like mixture with an even distribution of fat-coated flour particles.

The pastry is usually baked at 190–220°C (375–425°F)—gas mark 5 to 7, depending on richness and size.

How to make shortcrust pastry

The quantity given is enough to line a 9 in. (23 cm.) flan ring, to line and cover a 7 in. (18 cm.) pie plate, or cover a 2 pint (1·1 litre) pie dish.

INGREDIENTS

8 oz. (225 g.) plain flour
½ teaspoon salt
2 oz. (50 g.) lard
2 oz. (50 g.) margarine
About 2 tablespoons cold water

1 Sieve the flour and salt into a bowl.
2 Cut the fat into ½ in. (1·5 cm.)

cubes and distribute evenly over the flour.

3 Rub the fat lightly into the flour with your fingertips, lifting up the mixture while rubbing to keep it as cool and airy as possible. Continue rubbing until the mixture resembles fine breadcrumbs.

4 Make a well in the centre of the mixture and add the water gradually while you stir it in with a knife. Use just enough water to produce a soft but not sticky dough.

5 Turn out the dough on to a floured surface and roll once only to the thickness required. The pastry will be heavy if you roll it too much.

Cheese pastry
You can make cheese pastry in the same way as shortcrust, but use all butter or all margarine. Add up to 4 oz. (100/125 g.) of dry, well-flavoured grated cheese to the crumb mixture before you add the liquid. Mix to a paste with half water and half beaten egg.

Sweet shortcrust pastry
Flans and tarts to serve cold are sometimes made with sweet, enriched shortcrust pastry that can be rolled out very thinly. The quantity given is sufficient for two 7 in. (18 cm.) flans.

INGREDIENTS

8 oz. (225 g.) plain flour
½ teaspoon salt
4 oz. (100/125 g.) butter
1 oz. (25 g.) caster sugar
2 egg yolks
1 tablespoon water

1 Prepare the flour and mix in the fat as for shortcrust pastry.

2 Add the sugar to the dry ingredients and mix it well in.

3 Beat the egg yolks together and mix in the cold water, then make a well in the centre of the flour and stir in the egg and water mixture with a knife to produce a soft dough.

4 Turn out the dough on to a floured board and knead gently until it is pliable and free from cracks. Roll out once to the required thickness.

FLAKY PASTRY

Flaky pastry is in thin, crisp layers with air in between. It is made with 4 parts flour to 3 parts fat, and is particularly suitable for pies to be served cold.

The flaky texture is achieved by kneading lightly then folding and rolling the dough in layers with dabs of fat between. The dabs of fat produce air pockets and help to separate the flakes.

When the pastry is baked at a high temperature, steam rises between the flaked layers and lifts them. Flaky pastry is usually baked at 220°C (425°F)—gas mark 7.

How to make flaky pastry
The quantity given is enough to cover a 1½–2 pint (850 ml.–1·1 litre) pie dish, or make 12 sausage rolls or 8 turnovers.

INGREDIENTS

8 oz. (225 g.) plain flour
½ teaspoon salt
6 oz. (175 g.) firm margarine or butter, or both mixed
1 teaspoon lemon juice
4 fl. oz. (100/125 ml.) cold water

1 Sieve the flour and salt into a bowl.

2 Divide the fat into four equal portions.

3 Take one portion of fat, cut it into small pieces and rub it into the flour with your fingertips, lifting up the mixture while rubbing to keep it as cool and airy as possible. Continue until the mixture resembles fine breadcrumbs.

4 Make a well in the centre of the mixture and add the lemon juice and just enough water to mix, with a knife, to a firm, elastic dough.

5 Turn out the dough on to a floured board and knead it until it is free from cracks.

6 Roll the dough into a strip three times as long as it is wide and about 1 in. (2·5 cm.) thick.

7 Take a second portion of the fat and, with a knife, flake it in even rows along two-thirds of the strip of pastry. Leave a clear strip about ¾ in. (2 cm.) wide at the edge. If the fat is too close to the edge, it will be squeezed out when you roll the pastry.

8 Fold one-third of the strip (the end with no butter) over to the middle. Then fold the other end (covered with butter) over that, so that the pastry is folded into three layers.

9 Turn the pastry round so that an open edge is towards you, then leave it to relax for 15–20 minutes in a cool place.

10 Press the open edges together with a rolling pin to enclose the air. Then make ridges in two or three places by pressing with the rolling pin. This distributes the air and stops it from collecting in one large bubble that is difficult not to break when rolling.

11 Roll out the pastry again to a strip three times as long as its width, then flake on the third portion of fat in the same way as the second. Fold, rest, seal and ridge as before.

12 Repeat the whole process using the fourth portion of fat. Then roll out to the thickness required.

ROUGH PUFF PASTRY

Rough puff pastry is similar to flaky pastry, but has larger flakes and is not as light. It is made with 4 parts flour to 3 parts fat. The texture is achieved by distributing the fat in lumps throughout the dough before folding and rolling in layers. It is usually baked at 220°C (425°F)—gas mark 7.

How to make rough puff pastry
The quantity given is enough to cover a 1½–2 pint (850 ml.–1·1 litre) pie dish, or to make 12 sausage rolls or 8 turnovers.

INGREDIENTS

8 oz. (225 g.) plain flour
½ teaspoon salt
6 oz. (175 g.) firm margarine or butter, or both mixed
4 fl. oz. (100/125 ml.) cold water
1 teaspoon lemon juice

1 Sieve the flour and salt into a mixing bowl.

2 Add the fat in one lump, cover it with flour then, with a knife, cut it into ½ in. (1·5 cm.) cubes—each about the size of a hazelnut.

3 Make a well in the centre of the mixture and add the lemon juice. Then stir in the water gradually with a knife, mixing lightly so you do not break down the fat. Continue until the mixture is a firm, elastic dough.

4 Turn out the pastry on to a floured board and press it into a lump, but do not knead it.

5 Roll the pastry lightly into a strip about three times as long as it is wide and about ¼ in. (5 mm.) thick.

6 Fold one-third of the length into the middle, then the other end over the top to form three layers.

7 Seal the open edges by pressing firmly with a rolling pin to enclose as much air as possible.

8 Turn the pastry so that a sealed edge is facing you, and make ridges in two or three places with a rolling pin. This distributes the air and stops it from collecting in a large bubble that

will be difficult not to break when rolling.
9 Roll the pastry into a strip again, but be careful not to roll beyond the top and bottom edges, as this will press out air.
10 Fold the pastry in three as before, then seal, turn and ridge again.
11 Roll out the pastry for a third time, then seal, turn and ridge again.
12 Roll out the pastry for a fourth time, then fold, seal, turn and ridge as before.
13 Roll out the pastry to the size and thickness required. Be very careful not to stretch it, as this will cause excessive shrinkage from the edge of the dish when baked.

Puff Pastry

Puff pastry is rich and very light, and is made with equal quantities of fat and flour. It is similar to flaky pastry but lighter and with more layers, and is used for vol-au-vent cases. Strong flour can be used instead of soft.

The texture is achieved by enveloping the fat in a lump in the dough, kneading to strengthen the gluten, then folding and rolling seven times to properly incorporate the fat and make the pastry light. Puff pastry is baked at a higher temperature than flaky and rough puff—usually 230°C (450°F)—gas mark 8.

It is worth buying puff pastry ready mixed and frozen, usually in 4 or 8 oz. (100/125 or 225 g.) packets. It is ready for rolling once thawed. Note that the amount of pastry specified in a recipe is based on the quantity of flour; you will need more than an 8 oz. (225 g.) packet for a recipe that specifies 8 oz. (225 g.) of puff pastry.

How to make puff pastry
The quantity given is enough for 2 large or 12 small vol-au-vent cases.

Ingredients

8 oz. (225 g.) flour
½ teaspoon salt
8 oz. (225 g.) unsalted butter or firm margarine
1 teaspoon lemon juice
Cold water to mix

1 Pat the fat into a square and put it in a cool place to get firm, but not hard. For best results, the fat should be as near as possible the same consistency as the mixed dough when the two are combined.
2 Sieve the flour and salt into a bowl.
3 Make a well in the centre of the flour and add the lemon juice. Then stir in with a knife enough water to form an elastic dough.
4 Turn out the dough on to a floured board and knead it gently for 5–10 minutes until it is smooth and does not stick to your fingers.
5 Roll out the pastry to a strip large enough to enclose the fat.
6 Place the fat in the middle of the pastry and fold the ends over it one at a time.
7 Flatten in one or two places with the rolling pin, then roll out evenly and lightly into a long strip, taking care that the fat does not break through. Do not roll beyond the top and bottom edges.
8 Fold one-third of the length into the middle and press it down gently, then fold the other end over to form three layers and press down gently. Do not seal the edges, as this could trap large air bubbles and cause the very light pastry to rise unevenly.
9 Leave the pastry to rest in a cool place for 15 minutes.
10 Place the pastry on the floured board so that an unsealed edge is towards you, then roll and fold again. Each rolling and folding is known as a turn, so this completes the second turn.
11 Repeat the rolling and folding twice more so that you have completed four turns, then leave the pastry to cool again for 10 minutes.
12 Roll and fold the pastry again three more times to give seven turns in all.
13 Roll out the pastry to the size and thickness required. Leave in a cool place for 10 minutes before baking.

Suet Crust Pastry

Suet crust pastry is similar to shortcrust in texture, but is tougher and more elastic. It is made with animal fat, using 2 parts flour to 1 part fat. Self-raising flour can be used, otherwise baking powder is needed to ensure rising.

The pastry is usually used for steamed puddings enclosing a filling, or baked or steamed roly-poly puddings. Sometimes it is made into a pie covering using overlapping scone-shaped pieces of dough.

How to make suet crust pastry
The quantity given is enough to line and cover a 1½ pint (850 ml.) basin or pie dish.

Ingredients

8 oz. (225 g.) plain flour
½ teaspoon salt
2 level teaspoons baking powder
4 oz. (100/125 g.) packet (shredded) or fresh suet
About 4 fl. oz. (100/125 ml.) cold water

1 Sieve the flour, salt and baking powder into a bowl.
2 If using fresh suet, remove the skin and dust with a little flour from the bowl to prevent stickiness when chopping.
3 Place the suet on a chopping board and chop with a long, sharp knife until it resembles breadcrumbs. You can grate the suet instead, but the pastry may not be so light or well flavoured.
4 Mix the chopped suet or the shredded packet suet into the flour.
5 Make a well in the centre of the mixture and gradually mix in the water with a knife until the dough is soft and will come away from the side of the bowl, leaving it clean.
6 Turn out the pastry on to a floured board and knead it gently until it is free from cracks.
7 Roll out once only to the size required and a thickness of about ¼ in. (5 mm.)—unless a different thickness is specified in the recipe.

Hot-Water Crust Pastry

Hot-water crust or 'raised' pastry is similar in texture to shortcrust, but the dough is stiff enough to be 'raised'—that is, to stand alone without the support of a dish. It is made with 3–4 parts flour to 1 part fat, and mixed with boiling liquid.

The pastry is usually used for pork, game, and veal and ham pies.

How to make hot-water crust pastry
The quantity given is enough for 2 small pies, each moulded round a 1 lb. (450 g.) jam jar.

Ingredients

8 oz. (225 g.) plain flour
½ teaspoon salt
2 oz. (50 g.) lard
About 4 fl. oz. (100/125 ml.) liquid (equal quantities of milk and water)

1 Prepare the filling before making the pastry.
2 Warm the pastry board, bowl, wooden spoon and mould you will be using.
3 Sieve the flour and salt into the

warmed bowl and make a well in the middle of the flour.
4 Put the fat and liquid into a saucepan, bring to the boil, then pour at once into the flour well.
5 Mix rapidly with a wooden spoon to a soft, elastic dough.
6 Turn out on to a floured board and knead until smooth. If the pastry is too dry, add a few drops of boiling water.
7 Cut off one-third of the pastry to make the lid, and keep it warm and moist by placing it in a container over a bowl of hot water while you are moulding the case.
8 Mould the pastry into the required shape while it is still warm, otherwise it will become too hard and difficult to handle. There are four ways of moulding:

Over a floured jar or tin.

Making a case by joining a strip for the side and two circles for the base and lid.

Moulding the shape with your hands.

Lining a special mould which has hinged sides and a detachable base.

9 Place a double strip of greaseproof paper, secured with a piece of string, round each moulded pie while filling and for the first 20 minutes of cooking. Make two holes in the lid to allow steam to escape.
10 After baking, allow the pie to cool before pouring in stock through a funnel inserted in the steam vents. Good stock forms a jelly as it cools.

Choux Pastry

Choux pastry is usually shaped through a forcing bag to make both sweet and savoury dishes, such as eclairs and cheese puffs. The pastry is very light and airy, and has a hollow centre cavity.

It is made with 2½ parts flour to 2 parts fat, and the texture is achieved by absorbing the flour into the melted fat. During cooking, choux pastry puffs up to about three times its original size.

How to make choux pastry
The quantity given is sufficient to make 16–18 chocolate eclairs or about 30 cheese puffs.

Ingredients

2½ oz. (65 g.) plain flour
2 oz. (50 g.) butter
¼ teaspoon salt
¼ pint (150 ml.) water
2 eggs

1 Sift the flour and salt on to a sheet of greaseproof paper.
2 Put the butter and water in a heavy-based pan and place over a low heat until the butter melts, then increase the heat and bring rapidly to the boil.
3 Remove the pan from the heat and pour in all the sifted flour, stirring quickly with a wooden spoon until the flour has been absorbed into the liquid.
4 Return the pan to gentle heat, then cook for 2–3 minutes until the mixture is smooth and comes away from the side of the saucepan.
5 Cool the mixture for a few minutes, then beat in the eggs gradually. The pastry must be firm enough for piping, but not too stiff.
6 If you are not going to use the pastry immediately, closely cover the saucepan with a sheet of moist greaseproof paper under the lid. This keeps the dough pliable.
7 Do not open the oven door while the pastry is cooking, otherwise it will be flat.
8 When the pastry is cooked, split each puff open and leave in the oven for 30–60 seconds to dry the inside of the pastry.

Shaping Pastry for Pies and Puddings

Early pies were known as pastry coffins, for the word coffin was originally applied to any box, basket or case. Large, decorative 'coffins' were made for feasts and banquets, sometimes with battlemented edges and brightly coloured fillings.

In great houses, some pies were made to provide entertainment—the filling might be a flock of birds that flew out when the pie was opened. The covered pastry shell was baked blind with a temporary filling of bran, and after baking the bran was removed and the birds put in through a hole in the bottom crust.

Lining a Shallow Dish or Flan Ring

1 Grease the dish or ring, using a pastry brush or a piece of greaseproof paper. Be particularly careful if using cheese pastry, which is likely to stick.
2 Roll out the pastry to the thickness required and a size large enough to allow for the depth as well as the width of the container, adding an extra ¼ in. (5 mm.) to allow for shrinkage during cooking.
3 Lift the pastry on a floured rolling pin and place it over the dish or ring.
4 Press it into the container gently with the fingertips to fit it to shape and to make sure there are no air bubbles trapped underneath.
5 To give a clean finish to the edges, roll the rolling pin across the top of the container, and the surplus bits of pastry will drop off.
6 If you need a lid, roll out the pastry to the same diameter as the dish. Fit as for covering a pie (see opposite).

Baking blind
A pastry case is baked blind—without a filling—if the filling needs little or no cooking or will be added later.
1 Prick the base of the pastry lining with a fork to let the air out.
2 Cover the base with a circle of greaseproof paper or foil, and put in a temporary filling of dried beans or dried rice to prevent the pastry rising.
3 Bake in the centre of an oven preheated to 190°C (375°F)—gas mark 5, for about 15 minutes.
4 When the pastry is cooked, take out the greaseproof or foil and the filling (which can be used again), and put the case back into the oven for 2–3 minutes to dry out.
5 Once the case is ready, proceed with the recipe.

Filling a Pie or Pudding

1 Fill the dish or case to the rim and distribute the filling evenly.
2 If the pie is to be covered, pile the filling up in the centre to support the lid. If there is not enough filling to make a pile in the centre, put an egg cup or pie funnel in the bottom of the dish, in the middle, to raise the filling.
3 If the filling has been partially cooked before the lid is put on, make sure it is quite cool before you cover it with pastry. If it is warm, the pastry will become heavy and sodden.

Covering a Pie

1 Roll out the pastry to the thickness required—usually no more than ¼ in. (5 mm.)—and a size roughly ¾ in. (2 cm.) larger all round than the top of the dish from rim to rim.
2 Invert the pie dish on to the pastry and cut away the spare pastry.
3 Roll these trimmings into a strip about 1 in. (2·5 cm.) wide.
4 Damp the rim of the dish with a pastry brush dipped in cold water and then shaken, then line the moistened rim with the pastry strip. This forms the base of a double rim that provides a good seal and lessens the risk of liquid boiling out of a pie.
5 Brush the pastry rim with water, lift the pastry lid on a floured rolling pin and lay it over the top of the dish. Gently press the two edges together.
6 Hold the pie dish in one hand and, with the other, trim off any excess pastry with a sharp knife. Hold the knife slightly towards the dish so that the trimmed edge slopes outwards from the rim. This allows for a little shrinkage during cooking.
7 Make two slits in the centre of the lid, over the pie funnel if there is one, to let steam escape.
8 Decorate and glaze the lid if desired (see below), then seal or 'knock up' the edge of the pastry with the back of a floured knife blade held horizontally. Tap all round the edges with a slight lifting movement.

Glazing a pie lid

1 To give the pie an attractive, shiny golden-brown finish, make a wash from a well-beaten egg or a small amount of beaten egg or egg yolk diluted with an equal amount of milk or water. A wash of milk can be used on its own, but it does not give such a rich colour.
2 Brush the wash over the lid of the pie, usually before you bake it. Any decorations can be stuck down with the glaze, and then also brushed over with the glaze.
3 Do not glaze pies that need long cooking, such as game pie, before baking. Wait until the pie is almost cooked, quickly remove it from the oven and brush on the glaze, then return it to complete cooking.

Decorating a pie lid

To flake the edge, flour the first finger of your left hand and press it down lightly on the pastry rim. Using the back of a floured knife blade, make a mark beside your finger. Mark in the same way all round, using finger and knife blade alternately. This gives a flaked appearance, and also opens the edges and helps the pastry to rise.

Alternatively, you can scallop the edges by drawing the back of a floured knife blade upwards and inwards across the edges of the rim. Do this at 1 in. (2·5 cm.) intervals, and at the same time press the pastry between the knife marks downwards and outwards with your thumb to form the scallop.

To make pastry leaves to decorate the lid, roll out the trimmings and divide them into strips about 1¼ in. (3 cm.) wide. Cut the strips diagonally about every 1½ in. (4 cm.) to produce diamond shapes, and use the back of a knife to imitate vein markings.

To make a rose, cut two circles about 1¼ in. (3 cm.) across from a strip of thinly rolled pastry. Roll another piece into a ball about ¼ in. (5 mm.) across. Put the circles one on top of the other and place the ball in the middle. Fold the circles almost over the ball, sealing lightly. Turn the pastry over and cut a cross in the centre of the ball with a sharp knife. Open out the two layers of segments and fold them back to form a rose.

Damp the decorations on the back with a wet pastry brush before placing them on the pie, or use the moist glaze to stick them. Do not cover the central steam vents with decorations.

Lining a Basin with Suet Pastry

1 Grease the inside of the basin, using a pastry brush or a piece of greaseproof paper.
2 Turn out the pastry on to a floured board; cut off one-third for the lid.
3 Roll the rest to a thickness of about ¼ in. (5 mm.) and about 1½ times the diameter of the basin.
4 Turn it over so that the rolled side will go against the basin side.
5 Fold it loosely in half and half again to form a triangle. Put the triangle point downwards into the basin and unfold it to line the side.
6 Press the pastry gently into position to flatten any creases and expel any trapped air. Bubbles of trapped air can make the pudding look pitted.
7 Trim any excess pastry from the basin rim with a sharp knife, and use the trimmings to patch any breaks or thin portions in the lining.
8 Add the filling to the rim and roll out the pastry lid to the same diameter as the top of the basin.
9 Damp the edge of the pastry with a pastry brush dipped in cold water and then shaken.
10 Place the lid over the filling and press the edges of the lid and lining together, turning them slightly inwards, to give a secure seal.
11 Instructions for covering the basin and steaming the pudding are on p. 259.

Tips for Cooking Pastry

Always pre-heat the oven before baking pastry. If you put it into a cool oven, the fat will melt and run out before it is absorbed into the flour. This will make the pastry tough, greasy and of poor texture.

Make sure the oven is at the correct setting and not too hot, otherwise the pastry surface will set too quickly and form a crust that prevents full expansion of steam and air. This makes the pastry hard and biscuit-like. Place the pie or flan dish on a baking tray before you put it in the oven. It is easier to get out when hot.

The top of the oven is normally the hottest part and the bottom the coolest part. It is usual to bake in the centre of the oven, but this varies according to the make of oven. Always follow the manufacturer's instructions for the baking position.

If you have to open and close the oven door during baking, do it very gently. If possible, avoid doing it before the pastry has set, because a rush of cold air may cause it to drop, particularly if the pastry is light. Puff pastry needs a very hot oven; do not put anything else in at the same time.

When baking pies, it may be necessary to bake at a high temperature initially to set the pastry, then move the pie to a cooler part of the oven or adjust the oven setting for longer, slower cooking of the filling. Follow the instructions in the recipe.

If the pastry starts to brown too quickly, wait until it has finished rising, then cover it with foil or a double sheet of greaseproof paper. When baking a large pie in a small oven (or a pie that needs long cooking, such as a game pie), once the pie has reached the desired colour put a stiff collar of cardboard or a double collar of foil round the dish and secure it with string. Lay the foil or greaseproof on top of the collar.

After cooking, leave the pudding or pie to cool slowly in a warm kitchen. If it cools too quickly in a draught or a cold room, it will be heavy.

Of HOT AND COLD SWEET PUDDINGS

CONTAINING

NUMEROUS *Useful* FAMILY RECIPES

for FRESH & DRIED FRUIT PUDDINGS & PIES, CREAMS & SAUCES

& all other SWEET DELIGHTES

PAGES 224–253

AND

A SELECTION of RECIPES from OTHER LANDS

PAGES 254–255

AND WITH

NOTES AND ADVICE

on all kinds of Boiling, Steaming, Baking and Making of Sweet Puddings to Perfection

PAGES 256–259

Parsnip Flan
Kent

The sweet-flavoured parsnip has at various times been added to sweet dishes, especially in the Tudor period when sugar was expensive. In the Middle Ages, both parsnips and water parsnips were dipped in batter and served as fritters.

This dish has a creamy taste and the consistency of lemon curd. In springtime it is traditionally decorated with sugared primroses.

Preparation Time: 20 minutes

Cooking Time: 20–30 minutes for the parsnips; 30–35 minutes for the flan

Pre-heat the Oven to 200°C (400°F)—gas mark 6

Ingredients for Four to Six

8 oz. (225 g.) shortcrust pastry (see p. 217)
1½ lb. (700 g.) parsnips, peeled and quartered
2 tablespoons thick honey
1 level teaspoon ground ginger
½ teaspoon ground mixed spice
¼ teaspoon grated nutmeg
2 egg yolks
Juice and grated rind of 2 lemons
Fresh garden primroses for decoration (optional)

Roll out the shortcrust pastry and line an 8–9 in. (20–23 cm.) pie plate or flan tin with it. Trim the edges and put to one side.

Boil the parsnips until soft—the time will depend on the age of the parsnips. (Remove the woody centre from old vegetables before cooking.) Drain well and mash thoroughly to a soft pulp. Add the honey, spices, egg yolks and grated rind and juice of the lemons. Mix well and spoon into the pastry case.

Cut the trimmings of pastry into thin strips and make a lattice pattern across the top of the flan. Bake in the pre-heated oven for 30–35 minutes until golden-brown.

Allow the flan to become quite cold, then, if desired, decorate with a fresh primrose at each cross of the lattice pattern. Serve with cream.

Creamy-sweet Parsnip Flan from the days when sugar was a luxury.

Junket
Devon and Cornwall

Junket is Norman in origin and gets its name from the little rush baskets, *jonquets*, in which it was made. Originally it was made of pure cream, curdled with rennet and flavoured with rosewater; it was eaten as a sweetmeat at the close of a meal. Nowadays we make it with milk.

Junket is delicious served with stewed fruit, or with apricot sauce or clotted cream.

Preparation Time: 5–10 minutes

Standing Time: 2–3 hours

Chilling Time: 1–2 hours

Ingredients for Four

2 pints (1·1 litres) milk
2 level tablespoons caster sugar
2 teaspoons rennet essence
A few drops of raspberry or almond essence, or 2 tablespoons brandy
¼ teaspoon grated nutmeg (optional)
1 oz. (25 g.) chopped walnuts (optional)

Put the milk and sugar together in a heavy-based saucepan. Heat gently for about 5 minutes, stirring until the sugar dissolves. Cool until the milk is lukewarm to the touch, stir in the rennet essence as directed on the bottle. Then stir in the raspberry or almond essence, or the brandy.

Pour the mixture into a shallow serving dish, or individual dishes, and cover with muslin to keep out dust. Leave to stand at room temperature for 2–3 hours, or until set. Then put in the refrigerator and chill for at least 1 hour.

Sprinkle with nutmeg and decorate with chopped walnuts, if liked. Serve with home-made clotted cream (see p. 252) and a sprinkling of caster sugar to taste.

BREAD AND BUTTER PUDDING
Countrywide

THERE ARE MANY VARIATIONS to this long-standing family favourite, but the secret of success lies in letting it stand for an hour before baking. This allows the bread to swell and absorb the liquid, creating a light crusty pudding.

PREPARATION TIME: 15 MINUTES
STANDING TIME: 1 HOUR
COOKING TIME: 30–40 MINUTES
PRE-HEAT THE OVEN TO 180°C (350°F)—GAS MARK 4

INGREDIENTS FOR FOUR

4 thin slices from a large loaf of day-old white bread, with crusts removed
2 oz. (50 g.) butter
3 oz. (75 g.) currants
2 eggs
1 egg yolk
½ pint (275/300 ml.) milk
Grated rind of ½ lemon
2 tablespoons brandy or rum (optional)
1 oz. (25 g.) granulated sugar
½ level teaspoon grated or ground nutmeg

Butter the slices of bread and cut each into four triangles. Grease a 1 pint (575/600 ml.) pie dish and arrange the bread in layers, sprinkling each with currants. Finish with a layer of bread, butter side up.

Beat the eggs, egg yolk and milk together and stir in the lemon rind, then add the brandy or rum, if used. Pour the liquid over the bread and leave to stand for 1 hour.

Sprinkle the top of the pudding with the sugar and nutmeg just before placing it near the top of the pre-heated oven. Bake for 30–40 minutes, by which time it should be well risen with a golden-brown crusty top.

Serve hot with lemon or brandy sauce (see pp. 252–3).

JAM ROLY-POLY
Countrywide

JAM ROLY-POLY is one of the gastronomic adventures of childhood; a sound, suety, satisfying pudding that may be boiled or baked. Most children prefer it baked, since the jam filling seems richer and more delicious that way.

PREPARATION TIME: 20 MINUTES
COOKING TIME: 40 MINUTES
PRE-HEAT THE OVEN TO 220°C (425°F)—GAS MARK 7

INGREDIENTS FOR FOUR TO SIX

6 oz. (175 g.) suet crust pastry (see p. 219)
6–8 oz. (175–225 g.) jam—black currant, plum, strawberry or raspberry

Roll out the prepared pastry to a rectangle 8 by 12 in. (20 by 30 cm.). Spread it thickly with jam to within 1 in. (2·5 cm.) of the edges. Damp the edges and roll up from the shortest side, pinching the ends to seal.

Place on a greased baking sheet with the join underneath, and bake in the pre-heated oven for 40 minutes until golden-brown. If the pudding browns too quickly, reduce the heat to 200°C (400°F)—gas mark 6. Serve hot with custard (see p. 252).

Jam Roly-Poly and Bread and Butter Pudding—childhood favourites that taste good even to a grown-up.

Desserts for special occasions—Port-Wine Jelly; creamy, almond-flavoured Blancmange and a handsomely decorated Trifle.

PORT-WINE JELLY
Countrywide

WINE OR REAL FRUIT JUICE restores a jelly to the refreshing sweet it used to be. But the small, moulded fruit jellies served at the 'banquet', or dessert, course in the 17th century, demanded laborious preparation.

Nowadays, powdered gelatine is the time-saving setting agent that replaces the original boiled calf's foot, hartshorn shavings or isinglass. But loaf sugar, which gave the dish its early sparkle, is no longer available. Use preserving sugar as a good replacement, and note that this jelly has extra flavour because half the port has not been subjected to heat.

PREPARATION TIME: 10 MINUTES
SETTING TIME: 2 HOURS

INGREDIENTS FOR FOUR TO SIX

½ oz. (13 g.) powdered gelatine
2 teaspoons lemon juice
1 pint (575/600 ml.) good port
4 oz. (100/125 g.) preserving sugar
¼ teaspoon grated nutmeg
¼ teaspoon powdered cinnamon

Soak the gelatine in the lemon juice and 2 tablespoons of the port for a few minutes, until swollen and soft. Stir the gelatine mixture into half the remaining port.

Add the sugar, nutmeg and cinnamon and stir constantly over gentle heat until almost, but not quite, boiling. Strain through a very fine sieve into a bowl and gently stir in the remaining port.

Rinse out individual moulds with cold water and pour in the mixture. Stand in a cool place to set.

Turn the jellies out on to dishes and serve with whipped cream and almond biscuits.

OLD ENGLISH TRIFLE
Suffolk

RICH CREAM DISHES were the delight of the 18th century. Among them was a frivolous confection of biscuits or cake, soaked in sack, topped with custard, or syllabub, and decorated with almonds, ratafia cakes, jelly or crystallised fruits and flowers. This was known as a Trifle.

The following updated version of a 1790 recipe brings you close to the dish's exciting origins. Fresh strawberries or sliced peaches can be used instead of jam.

PREPARATION TIME: 10 MINUTES
COOKING TIME: 25 MINUTES
SETTING TIME: OVERNIGHT

INGREDIENTS FOR EIGHT TO TEN

For the custard base:

4 oz. (100/125 g.) macaroons, or 8–10 sponge cakes each split in half
3 tablespoons brandy
¼ pint (150 ml.) white wine
3–4 tablespoons thin raspberry or strawberry jam
1 pint (575/600 ml.) single cream
2 eggs, beaten
2 egg yolks, beaten
1 oz. (25 g.) caster sugar

For the topping:

Everlasting syllabub and prepared shreds of orange or lemon rind (see right)
3 oz. (75 g.) blanched almonds

Arrange the macaroons or sponge cakes on the bottom of a large glass dish. Spoon over the brandy and as much of the wine as they will soak up. Then carefully spread the macaroons or sponge cakes with the jam.

Bring the cream almost to boiling point, and stir it well into the beaten eggs and egg yolks. Pour into the top of a double saucepan and set this over the bottom pan of hot water, taking care that the water does not touch it.

Keep the double saucepan simmering steadily and stir the custard constantly until it thickens (about 15–20 minutes). Remove from the heat and stir in the sugar until it dissolves.

Leave until almost cold before pouring over the macaroons or sponge cakes. Set in a cold place overnight.

Next day, spread the syllabub carefully over the trifle and chill for 2 hours. Just before serving, sprinkle the blanched almonds and shredded lemon or orange peel on top.

EVERLASTING SYLLABUB
Countrywide

TO THE ELIZABETHANS, the syllabub was a frothy drink made by milking directly from the cow into a cup of ale, wine or cider. But by the 18th century the name had come to be applied to a number of creamy whips, often thickened with a variety of fresh fruit juices.

One of the most popular was this Everlasting Syllabub, so called because it can be kept in the glass for several days. This confection of sweetened wine laced with brandy and whipped cream sharpened by the juice of a lemon or a Seville orange can be eaten as a pudding in its own right, or used as a topping for trifle (see Old English Trifle, left).

But remember to start preparations a day in advance, so that the wine and fruit flavours are fully blended.

PREPARATION TIME: 25–30 MINUTES
STANDING TIME: OVERNIGHT (8 HOURS)
CHILLING TIME: 2 HOURS

INGREDIENTS FOR SIX

¼ pint (150 ml.) sweet white wine, such as Sauterne
1 tablespoon medium-sweet sherry
2 tablespoons brandy
1 lemon or 1 Seville (bitter) orange (or a sweet orange if preferred)
2 oz. (50 g.) caster sugar
½ pint (275/300 ml.) double cream

Pour the wine, sherry and brandy into a large basin. Peel the lemon or orange, removing only the coloured part of the peel, and put half the peel aside. Squeeze the juice from the lemon or orange and add it to the wine, with the other half of the peel. Leave the mixture to stand overnight, then remove and discard the peel.

Boil the peel previously put aside in ¼ pint (150 ml.) of water, simmering for 2 minutes, to remove its bitter taste. Drain off the water, then cut the peel into shreds and keep it for decoration.

Stir the sugar into the wine mixture until it dissolves, then add the cream and whip with a hand whisk until the mixture forms soft peaks. Spoon it into six wine glasses.

Stand the finished syllabub in the refrigerator for 2 hours. Before serving, decorate each syllabub with peel shreds.

BLANCMANGE
Countrywide

BLANCMANGE (white food) began in the Middle Ages as a pottage of finely chopped chicken, rice and almond milk. The Elizabethans added rosewater, then revolutionised the dish by omitting the chicken and replacing it with thick cream, sugar and eggs.

In the early 19th century, different versions employed new imports such as arrowroot and flavoured cornflour. But by the middle of Victoria's reign, Blancmange had settled down to become the light and creamy pudding described here.

PREPARATION TIME: 20–30 MINUTES
INFUSING TIME: 1 HOUR
SETTING TIME: 4–5 HOURS

INGREDIENTS FOR FOUR

Thinly peeled rind of 1 lemon
½ pint (275/300 ml.) milk
¾ oz. (20 g.) powdered gelatine
2–3 oz. (50–75 g.) caster sugar
½ pint (275/300 ml.) single cream
2 oz. (50 g.) ground almonds
3 tablespoons brandy

Put the milk and lemon rind in a covered saucepan. Stand on very low heat for 1 hour, stirring occasionally. Strain off the milk and dissolve the gelatine in a little of it. Add the gelatine mixture to the rest of the milk and stir in the sugar until it dissolves.

Mix in the cream and ground almonds, and stir the mixture until it is almost cold. Stir in the brandy and pour into a wetted mould. Chill in a refrigerator until completely set before turning out.

Serve on its own, with apricot sauce (see p. 252), with stewed fruit or with cream.

NORFOLK MILLION PIE
Norfolk

'MILLION' IS THE OLD WORD for melon, pumpkin or, indeed, any kind of gourd vegetable. Though this dish is now made with marrow, its original ingredient was pumpkin.

This pie crossed the Atlantic to the New World with the Pilgrim Fathers, who came mostly from East Anglia; and Pumpkin Pie was served at the Thanksgiving dinner for their first harvest in the New World. Americans eat the pie at least once a year in honour of their founding fathers.

Although the pumpkin has gone out of fashion in England, its memory lives on in this old Norfolk recipe.

PREPARATION TIME: 25 MINUTES
COOKING TIME: 30 MINUTES
PRE-HEAT THE OVEN TO 200°C (400°F)—GAS MARK 6

INGREDIENTS FOR FOUR TO SIX

8 oz. (225 g.) shortcrust pastry (see p. 217)
1 lb. (450 g.) pumpkin or vegetable marrow, with peel, pith and seeds removed, cut into 1 in. (2·5 cm.) slices
½ pint (275/300 ml.) water
2 oz. (50 g.) apricot, plum or greengage jam
1 egg
1½ tablespoons brown sugar
1 teaspoon ground nutmeg
1 oz. (25 g.) currants or raisins

Boil the pumpkin or marrow pieces in the water, stirring occasionally to prevent sticking, until they are soft (about 10 minutes). Drain and cool.

Roll out the pastry and line an 8 in. (20 cm.) flan tin or pie plate with it. Trim the edges of the pastry and keep the trimmings. Spread the pastry case with a thin layer of jam.

Norfolk Million Pie became the Pumpkin Pie Americans serve on Thanksgiving Day.

Add the egg, sugar and most of the nutmeg to the cooled pumpkin or marrow and beat together with a fork or in a blender until smooth. Mix in the dried fruit, then spread the mixture in the pastry case on top of the jam. Sprinkle with the rest of the nutmeg and lay on a lattice of pastry strips cut from the pastry trimmings.

Bake in the pre-heated oven for 10–15 minutes, then lower the oven temperature to 180°C (350°F)—gas mark 4 and cook for a further 15 minutes until the pastry is golden-brown. Serve hot with thick cream, or cold on its own.

RHUBARB SOUFFLÉ
Countrywide

RHUBARB, a native plant of Tibet, reached British gardens in the 17th century, but was not generally used as a food for another 100 years. Its tender forced stems give us our first home-grown fruit of the year.

This frothy pink soufflé makes a luxury sweet from inexpensive ingredients. You can virtually prepare it before the meal; then whisk the egg whites again and blend them with the rhubarb between courses.

PREPARATION TIME: 50 MINUTES
COOKING TIME: 12 MINUTES
PRE-HEAT THE OVEN TO 200°C (400°F)—GAS MARK 6

INGREDIENTS FOR FOUR

1 lb. (450 g.) rhubarb, cut into 1 in. (2·5 cm.) pieces
2 tablespoons water
3 tablespoons caster sugar
Grated rind of ½ orange
2 egg whites
¼ teaspoon salt
Melted butter
Caster sugar for coating

Simmer the rhubarb pieces with the water in a covered pan for 15 minutes, or until tender. Stir in 2 tablespoons of the sugar and leave to cool. Strain off most of the liquid, then whisk the rhubarb and orange rind together.

Beat the egg whites with the salt until stiff but not dry. Stir in the remaining sugar and fold the mixture gently, half at a time, into the rhubarb.

Paint the inside of a 1½ pint (850 ml.) soufflé dish with the melted butter and coat it with caster sugar. Pour in the mixture and bake in the pre-heated oven for 12 minutes. Serve at once with cream.

FLUMMERY
Scotland

ALL HUSKED CEREALS, if soaked and boiled, will set to make a kind of jelly. Breadcrumbs will do the same, and a jelly made from them was formerly considered a treat for those of delicate digestion: in Mrs Gaskell's *Cranford*, 'a present of her bread jelly was the highest mark of favour dear Mrs Forrester could confer'.

In poor households, the soaked grain itself was included in the dish, which was like a cold milk porridge. But a true flummery consisted only of the strained liquid from the cereal, together with milk and flavourings, such as orange or lemon juice, roseflower or orangeflower water, and wine or brandy.

The traditional and ancient Scottish name for flummery is Sowans. A properly made flummery has a smooth jellied texture, a very white colour, and a delicious and distinctive flavour.

SOAKING TIME: 48 HOURS
PREPARATION TIME: 10 MINUTES
COOKING TIME: ABOUT 10 MINUTES
SETTING TIME: 1 HOUR

INGREDIENTS FOR SIX TO EIGHT

3 heaped tablespoons fine oatmeal, or 4 heaped tablespoons cracked wheat
Juice of 2 oranges
2 tablespoons caster sugar
¼ pint (150 ml.) cream
Finely grated rind of 2 oranges
4 tablespoons of honey, brandy or whisky
¼ pint (150 ml.) whipped cream

Soak the oatmeal or cracked wheat in enough cold water to keep it covered for 24 hours. Pour off the water, and cover the grain again with about 2 pints (1·1 litres) of fresh, cold water. Leave to stand for another 24 hours.

Stir well, and strain the liquid into a pan. Add the strained orange juice and the sugar and boil, stirring frequently, for about 10 minutes or until very thick. Allow to cool a little before stirring in the cream.

Pour into one large dish or into individual dishes, sprinkle with the grated orange rind and leave on one side until set.

To serve, top each dish with 2 teaspoons of honey, brandy or whisky, and 1 heaped teaspoon of whipped cream.

Flummery—a simply made delicacy which includes orange juice, whisky and cream.

BLACKCAP PUDDING
Countrywide

BATTER IS A VERY OLD WAY of combining milk, eggs and flour into a pudding which could then be fried or boiled.

In the Middle Ages, a batter spit on which dates, figs and apples were impaled was hung before the fire. As they roasted, they were basted with batter, which gradually formed a thick, crisp crust around them. The resultant cake was served sprinkled with spices and sugar.

For this descendant of the medieval puddings, the batter is steamed, and the dish derives its name from the black cap of currants that tops it when it is turned out.

PREPARATION TIME: 25 MINUTES
COOKING TIME: 1½ HOURS

INGREDIENTS FOR FOUR

4 oz. (100/125 g.) plain flour
¼ level teaspoon salt
1 large egg, beaten
½ pint (275/300 ml.) milk
2 oz. (50 g.) currants
2 oz. (50 g.) butter, melted

Sift the flour and salt into a mixing bowl, make a well in the centre and add the egg. Beat it into the flour and gradually add the milk, beating well to make a smooth batter. Cover and leave to stand until thickened (about 15 minutes or longer).

Sprinkle currants over the base of a greased 1 pint (575/600 ml.) basin and pour in the batter. Prepare the basin for steaming (see p. 259), cover the saucepan and boil steadily for 1½ hours, topping up with more boiling water as necessary.

Turn out the pudding on to a warmed serving plate and serve with the melted butter poured over.

PLUM CRUMBLE
Countrywide

PERHAPS THE CRUMBLE was considered too lowly to be awarded a place in standard cookery books, for though it has been a firm favourite in this country for many years the first recorded appearance of this crumbed pastry is in an American recipe of the 1940s. There, it is described as a 'crunch' which is used as a topping for a 'candy pie' containing apples or peaches.

Whatever its name or origin, the pastry can be given a richer flavour by using brown sugar and adding a pinch of nutmeg, cinnamon or ginger.

PREPARATION TIME: 10 MINUTES
COOKING TIME: 45 MINUTES
PRE-HEAT THE OVEN TO 180°C (350°F)—GAS MARK 4

INGREDIENTS FOR FOUR TO SIX

For the filling:
- *1½ lb. (700 g.) cooking plums*
- *6 oz. (175 g.) granulated sugar*
- *2 tablespoons water*

For the crumble:
- *6 oz. (175 g.) plain flour*
- *¼ teaspoon salt*
- *3 oz. (75 g.) butter*
- *3 oz. (75 g.) caster sugar*

Wash the plums and halve and stone them. Put them in layers in a 1½ pint (850 ml.) pie dish and sprinkle each layer with the granulated sugar. Then add the water.

Sift the flour and mix it with the salt in a large mixing bowl. Rub in the butter lightly with the fingertips until the mixture resembles fine breadcrumbs. Stir in the caster sugar and mix well.

Spread the flour mixture over the plums, covering them completely. Immediately place the pie dish in the pre-heated oven and cook for 45 minutes until the crumble is golden-brown.

Serve with fresh whipped cream or custard (see p. 252).

ORANGE WATER ICE
Countrywide

THE FIRST WATER ICES in England were created by Charles I's Italian chefs, as a surprise for His Majesty. Then, as now, the Italians made the best ices in the world.

Yet this same concoction of fruit-flavoured syrups and sugar, known to the French as 'sorbet' and to the Arabs as 'sherbet', had been in existence centuries before it appeared in Italy.

Water ices were an invention of the Chinese, and their recipes travelled down the caravan routes to India and Persia. The Venetian traveller Marco Polo brought them to Italy on his return from his epic journey to Cathay in 1295.

Use the present recipe as a light pudding to follow a weighty main course, or as a refreshing offering to be given to your friends on a hot summer's afternoon.

PREPARATION TIME: 1 HOUR
FREEZING TIME: 4–6 HOURS
TURN THE REFRIGERATOR TO ITS COLDEST SETTING 1 HOUR BEFORE FREEZING

INGREDIENTS FOR SIX
- *1 lemon*
- *1 small orange*
- *6 oz. (175 g.) sugar*
- *½ pint (275/300 ml.) water*
- *6 Jaffa oranges*
- *12 teaspoons Cointreau*
- *2 heaped tablespoons stiffly whipped egg white*

Pare off the rind of the lemon and the small orange as thinly as possible. Put the rind, sugar and water in a pan and heat slowly, stirring until the sugar has dissolved. Then boil this syrup briskly for 6–7 minutes.

Cut off and keep the tops of the Jaffa oranges and, without damaging the skins, scoop out the flesh into a bowl. Use a curved grapefruit knife or a spoon for this. Crush the flesh to extract the juice, and squeeze the juice from the lemon and small orange. Measure ½ pint (275/300 ml.) of the juice and mix it into the syrup.

Let the liquid cool, then pour it into a plastic container and put it to freeze. When it has become mushy, in 1–2 hours, stir to an even texture with a fork and fold in the whipped egg white. Put it back in the freezing compartment until it becomes mushy again, after a further 1–2 hours.

Meanwhile, swirl 2 teaspoons of Cointreau round the inside of each orange skin and put the skins in the refrigerator to chill.

Take the mushy ice-cream and fill the chilled orange skins with it, then replace the tops and finish freezing. About 30 minutes before serving, remove the orange ices from the ice compartment to another part of the refrigerator.

SNOWDON PUDDING
Wales

THIS WHITE-CAPPED pudding (known to the Welsh as *Pwdin Eryri*) was named in honour of the legend-haunted Yr Wyddfa—Snowdon—on whose summit, the highest in Wales, snow often lies until late spring.

PREPARATION TIME: 30 MINUTES
COOKING TIME: 3 HOURS FOR THE PUDDING; 15 MINUTES FOR THE SAUCE

INGREDIENTS FOR SIX TO EIGHT
- *4 oz. (100/125 g.) stoned raisins*
- *8 oz. (225 g.) shredded suet*
- *1½ oz. (40 g.) plain flour or cornflour*
- *6 oz. (175 g.) brown sugar*
- *8 oz. (225 g.) white breadcrumbs*
- *6 oz. (175 g.) lemon marmalade*
- *Grated rind of 2 lemons*
- *¼ teaspoon salt*
- *6 eggs, beaten*

For the sauce (Snow on the Mountain):
- *1½ oz. (40 g.) caster sugar*
- *Rind of ½ lemon, whole*
- *¼ pint (150 ml.) water*
- *1 oz. (25 g.) butter*
- *2 level teaspoons plain flour or cornflour*
- *4 fl. oz. (100/125 ml.) white wine*

Put aside about 1 tablespoon of the raisins, then mix the rest together with the suet, flour, brown sugar, breadcrumbs, marmalade, grated lemon rind and salt. Beat the eggs and stir into the mixture. Sprinkle the tablespoon of raisins over the bottom of a 3 pint (1·7 litre) greased basin and pour the pudding mixture on top of them.

Prepare the pudding for steaming (see p. 259), cover with a lid and boil for 3 hours, topping up with boiling water from time to time to maintain the level.

To make the sauce, boil the sugar and lemon rind in the ¼ pint (150 ml.) of water for about 15 minutes, then discard the rind and add the butter. Take the pan off the heat, and cool it for 10–15 minutes, then stir in the flour to make a smooth mixture. Work in the wine, return the pan to the stove and stir over a gentle heat until the sauce thickens

Serve the pudding piping hot. Pour over the sauce just before taking it to the table.

Summer Pudding
Countrywide

Strictly speaking, Summer Pudding is a way of using up excess bread. But the pudding is such a favourite that nowadays it may be necessary to set a few slices aside deliberately to let them go stale. A liberal sprinkling of fruit juice transforms the bread into a cover as rich as any pastry.

Most soft fruits can be used: raspberries, stoned cherries, blackberries, black currants, red currants, loganberries or bilberries, and preferably a mixture of two or three. But be sparing with blackberries and black currants—they can give the pudding too dark a colour, and dominate the flavour.

Remember to prepare Summer Pudding the day before it is needed.

Preparation Time: 30 minutes
Standing Time: 8 hours

Ingredients for Six

- *7–8 slices day-old bread from a large white loaf, with crusts removed*
- *2 lb. (900 g.) mixed soft fruit*
- *About 4 oz. (100/125 g.) caster sugar*

Prepare and wash the fruit and place in a heavy-based saucepan with the sugar, which should be added according to taste, taking into account the tartness of the fruit. Cook over a low heat until the sugar has dissolved and the juice begins to flow.

Line the base and side of a 1½ pint (850 ml.) pudding basin with just over two-thirds of the bread, making sure that the slices overlap slightly and fit tightly with no gaps for the fruit to fall through. Pack in the fruit and sugar mixture, adding just enough juice to soak the bread. Cover with the remaining slices of bread—cut to fit exactly—and sprinkle with a little juice. But do not saturate to the point that the bread is soggy, or it will not mould well enough for the pudding to stand on its own. Set aside the rest of the juice for later.

Cover the top of the pudding with a saucer, curved side down, that just fits inside the top of the basin. Place a 1 lb. (450 g.) weight, or a heavy tin or jar, on top of the saucer to compress the pudding. Leave to stand overnight in a refrigerator or cool place.

To turn out, remove the weight and saucer carefully and ease round the side of the pudding with a round-bladed knife. Then invert on to the serving plate.

Serve cut into wedges with single cream and the reserved juice.

Freshly picked garden fruits are perfect for Summer Pudding and Loganberry Mousse.

Loganberry Mousse
Countrywide

The loganberry, a hybrid between the raspberry and the American blackberry, was first raised by Judge Logan in California in 1881, and was introduced to Britain in 1897.

Despite its tartness, the fruit makes delicious sweet puddings. It mixes well with rhubarb and any of the soft fruits in season, and its richness of colour adds to the appeal of any dish. The mousse can also be made with raspberries, strawberries or blackberries. You can equally well use fresh or frozen fruit.

Preparation Time: about 25 minutes
Setting Time: 2–3 hours

Ingredients for Four to Six

- *¾ oz. (20 g.) powdered gelatine*
- *¼ pint (150 ml.) hot water*
- *1 lb. (450 g.) loganberries, fresh or frozen*
- *1 teaspoon lemon juice*
- *2 egg whites*
- *4 oz. (100/125 g.) caster sugar*
- *½ pint (275/300 ml.) double cream*
- *Whipped cream for decoration*

If you use frozen loganberries, make sure they are well thawed before use. Soak the gelatine in the water (see p. 257). Set aside a few of the loganberries for decoration, then stew the remainder gently in a saucepan for 10–15 minutes.

Sieve the loganberries and add the soaked gelatine and lemon juice. Heat gently again until the gelatine is dissolved. Whisk the egg whites to soft peaks. Mix the sieved loganberries, sugar, cream and egg whites, spoon the mixture into a bowl or individual glasses and leave to set.

Serve decorated with loganberries and whipped cream.

Whortleberry and Apple Pie, a favourite from the West Country, is served with clotted cream.

WHORTLEBERRY AND APPLE PIE
Devon

PICKING WILD WHORTLEBERRIES on Exmoor is a favourite Sunday pastime in Devon. As the berries are even smaller than black currants, and are often hidden under foliage, it takes some time to pick enough for a pie. That is why apples are added.

Whortleberries are also known as bilberries, blueberries, or, in Scotland, blaeberries. They have a distinct sweet-sharp flavour. If using cultivated berries, which have more juice than wild ones, cut down the amount of water used to 2 fl. oz. (50 ml.). A few mint leaves can be laid on the berries before you add the pastry.

PREPARATION TIME: 30 MINUTES
COOKING TIME: 35–40 MINUTES
PRE-HEAT THE OVEN TO 200°C (400°F)—GAS MARK 6

INGREDIENTS FOR SIX TO EIGHT

- *6 oz. (175 g.) shortcrust pastry (see p. 217)*
- *1½ lb. (700 g.) whortleberries*
- *4 fl. oz. (100/125 ml.) water*
- *8 oz. (225 g.) cooking apples*
- *4 oz. (100/125 g.) brown sugar*
- *1 egg white*
- *Caster sugar for sprinkling*

Peel, core and slice the apples, and place in a saucepan with the whortleberries, brown sugar and water. Bring to the boil and simmer for 3 minutes.

Place a pie funnel in the centre of a 2½ pint (1·4 litre) pie dish, pour in the fruit and leave to cool. Cut a strip of the shortcrust pastry about 1 in. (2·5 cm.) wide to line the lip of the dish and dampen with water, then cover with the remaining pastry. Make two slits in the pastry lid for the steam to escape. Brush the pie with the white of an egg and sprinkle with the caster sugar.

Bake on a baking sheet in the centre of the pre-heated oven for 35–40 minutes until golden-brown.

Serve the pie on its own or with clotted cream (see p. 252).

Butterscotch Tart
Scotland

The Scots, it is said, eat more sweets than any other nation on earth. Certainly, they eat more butterscotch. This confection, of brown sugar and butter boiled together, is believed to have originated in 1667 when an enterprising Scots merchant brought a cargo of West Indian sugar to the Clyde.

The venture was doubly successful: it provided Scotland with a favourite sweet, and laid the foundations of the great sugar-refining industry at Greenock.

The filling for this tart can also be used as a thick sauce to spoon over ice-cream or cooked apples. It stores well in a refrigerator.

Preparation Time: 45 minutes
Cooking Time: 55 minutes
Pre-heat the Oven to 190°C (375°F)—gas mark 5

Ingredients for Four

- *4 oz. (100/125 g.) shortcrust pastry (see p. 217)*
- *5 oz. (150 g.) soft, light brown sugar*
- *2 oz. (50 g.) plain flour, sifted*
- *4 tablespoons water*
- *¼ pint (150 ml.) milk*
- *2 oz. (50 g.) butter*
- *3–4 drops vanilla essence*
- *1 egg, separated*
- *1½ oz. (40 g.) caster sugar*

Roll out the pastry and line a 7 in. (18 cm.) flan dish with it. Bake blind (see p. 220) in the pre-heated oven for 15 minutes.

To make the butterscotch filling, mix the sugar and flour together in a small saucepan and blend with the water. Boil the milk in another saucepan and then pour it over the sugar and flour mixture. Add the butter and mix well, then cook slowly over a low heat, stirring hard with a wooden spoon, until thick. Remove the pan from the heat and add the vanilla essence and egg yolk, beating them well in.

To make the meringue topping, whip the egg white in a small bowl until it is stiff, then fold in the caster sugar.

Pour the butterscotch filling into the baked pastry case and cover with a layer of meringue. Place in the oven at 150°C (300°F)—gas mark 2 for about 30 minutes until the meringue is crisp and lightly browned.

Serve hot or cold with cream.

Golden Sponge
Countrywide

This delightful pudding pleases the eye and the hearty appetite today as much as it did in the 1880s, when golden syrup was first developed. The feather-light sponge has a toffee-coloured coating that streams with melted golden syrup.

For a change of flavour, replace the syrup with lemon curd, marmalade or any kind of jam.

Preparation Time: 20 minutes
Cooking Time: 2½ hours

Ingredients for Four to Six

- *3 oz. (75 g.) butter or margarine*
- *3 oz. (75 g.) sugar*
- *1 egg, beaten*
- *6 oz. (175 g.) self-raising flour, sifted*
- *¼ teaspoon salt*
- *Milk*
- *4–5 heaped tablespoons golden syrup*

Cream the butter and sugar until fluffy. Beat in the egg and fold in the flour and salt. Stir in enough milk to give the mixture a soft, dropping consistency.

Butter a 2 pint (1·1 litre) basin, and coat all the inside liberally with syrup. Spoon in the mixture and prepare the basin for steaming (see p. 259). Stand it in a 5 pint (2·8 litre) pan with enough boiling water to come halfway up the basin. Steam for at least 2½ hours, adding more boiling water to the pan as necessary to maintain the level.

Turn the pudding out on to a hot plate and serve at once with custard, cream, more melted syrup, or lemon sauce (see p. 252).

Fruit Fritters
Countrywide

'Fry them in faire grece or butter till they ben browne and yellowe. Then put them in disshes and strawe sugar on them y nough, and surve forthe.'

These directions for making fritters are still as valid as when they were written 500 years ago, the only difference lying in the adventurousness of the fillings. Nowadays, we marinate apples in cider, or provide an echo of faraway places with recipes such as this one, which employs bananas soaked in rum. Still more exotic, perhaps, is the suggestion of using pieces of pineapple drenched in Curaçao for a festive occasion.

Preparation Time: 25 minutes
Standing Time: 1 hour
Cooking Time: 15–20 minutes

Ingredients for Four to Six

- *3 large ripe bananas, peeled*
- *2 tablespoons sugar*
- *4 tablespoons rum*
- *1 teaspoon vanilla essence*
- *4 oz. (100/125 g.) plain flour*
- *1 teaspoon baking powder*
- *¼ teaspoon salt*
- *1 oz. (25 g.) melted butter*
- *6 fl. oz. (175 ml.) milk*
- *1 egg white, whisked until stiff*
- *Oil for frying*

Cut the bananas in half lengthwise, and cut each half in three or four pieces. Arrange the pieces in one layer in a shallow dish. Mix together the sugar, 3 tablespoons of the rum and the vanilla essence and pour over the bananas. Leave to soak for 1 hour, turning the fruit occasionally.

To prepare the batter, sift the flour, baking powder and salt into a large bowl. Stir in the melted butter and the remaining tablespoon of rum. Add the milk a little at a time, beating well after each addition until the batter is perfectly smooth. Leave to stand for 1 hour. Fold in the whisked egg white to give the batter the consistency of thick cream.

Dip the banana pieces into the batter a few at a time and allow to drain until only thinly coated. Pour a 2 in. (5 cm.) layer of oil into a deep pan and heat it to 190°C (375°F) (see p. 259). Fry the pieces four or five at a time until golden-brown. Drain on kitchen paper and keep hot until all are ready. Serve sprinkled with vanilla sugar.

BAKED CUSTARDS
Countrywide

SHOP-BOUGHT CUSTARD powder is a far cry from the rich, spicy dessert beloved of our forefathers. Nineteenth-century Sack Cream, for example, employed a dozen eggs, a pint of sack (modern equivalent, in this case, is medium-sweet sherry), three pints of cream and a half a pound of fine sugar; this was strewn with nutmeg or cinnamon, and served chilled, in custard cups.

Baked custard is best made with cream, but a mixture of cream and milk creates a good substitute. It is delicious served alone or with fresh raspberries and strawberries.

PREPARATION TIME: 10 MINUTES
COOKING TIME: 1 HOUR
PRE-HEAT THE OVEN TO 170°C (325°F)—GAS MARK 3

INGREDIENTS FOR FOUR TO SIX

1 pint (575/600 ml.) single cream, or ¾ pint (450 ml.) milk and ¼ pint (150 ml.) double cream
1 vanilla pod
4 eggs
2 oz. (50 g.) granulated sugar
½ level teaspoon grated or ground nutmeg (optional)

Gently heat the cream (or cream and milk) with the vanilla pod until it just reaches boiling point. Beat the eggs lightly with the sugar in a 2 pint (1·1 litre) bowl.

Remove the vanilla pod (it can be washed and wiped for use again) and pour the cream on to the eggs, whisking thoroughly. Strain the custard into a lightly buttered pie or soufflé dish and sprinkle it with the nutmeg, if used.

Stand the dish in a roasting tin with sufficient hot water to come well up the dish side. Bake for 1 hour.

Serve the custard hot or cold.

CREAM CARAMEL

Make a caramel by stirring 4 oz. (100/125 g.) granulated sugar with 2 tablespoons water in a heavy-based pan over gentle heat until the sugar has completely dissolved. Bring to the boil, then boil briskly without stirring until it is a golden caramel colour.

Do not butter the pie or soufflé dish, but pour in the caramel and tilt the dish until all the inside is coated. Hold the dish with thick oven gloves as it will become very hot. Pour in the custard and cook as above.

BURNT CREAM

Cook the custard in a flameproof dish and leave to cool and set. Sprinkle soft, light brown sugar thickly over it and put under a hot grill until the sugar caramellises and bubbles. Watch carefully to make sure that it does not burn. Serve chilled.

APPLE TANSY
Countrywide

TANSIES TAKE THEIR NAME from a bitter-flavoured, yellow-flowered herb, once prized for medicinal properties and used to flavour this dish.

By a curious reversal, the tansy dish had lost all its bitterness by the 16th century and had become a sweet-tasting omelette, containing not a trace of the herb, but flavoured with flowers. By the 17th century a tansy had come to be much what it is today—a creamy, fruit and egg purée.

PREPARATION TIME: 10 MINUTES
COOKING TIME: ABOUT 35 MINUTES

INGREDIENTS FOR FOUR

1 lb. (450 g.) dessert apples, peeled, cored and sliced
2 oz. (50 g.) butter
4 oz. (100/125 g.) caster sugar
¼ teaspoon ground cloves
Rosewater (optional)
4 eggs, separated
4 tablespoons double cream

Put the apples and butter in a shallow, flameproof 10 in. (25 cm.) dish. Cook over a gentle heat, crushing the apples with a wooden spoon and adding water if they threaten to burn, until the apples are pulpy. Alternatively, put them through a blender when cooked. Remove from the heat and stir in the cloves, rosewater if used, and half the sugar.

Beat the egg yolks with 1 oz. (25 g.) sugar and all the cream. Whisk the egg whites until stiff, but not dry, and fold them into the yolks.

Fold the egg mixture into the dish of apples and cook over low heat, stirring gently, until the tansy has set. Put the dish under a hot grill to brown the top. Sprinkle with sugar and serve at once with cream.

FEN COUNTRY APPLE CAKE
East Anglia

THE FLAT FENLAND, dominated by the massive bulk of Ely Cathedral, and with river embankments standing higher than the roads, was created about 200 years ago out of a wilderness of swamp.

Now among the most fertile of English farmlands, the black, peaty soil produces a wealth of fine vegetables, strawberries, plums and apples.

The recipe for this rich pudding was noted down in 1847 by Elizabeth Garden of Redisham Hall, Suffolk.

PREPARATION TIME: 40 MINUTES
COOKING TIME: 25 MINUTES
PRE-HEAT THE OVEN TO 220°C (425°F)—GAS MARK 7

INGREDIENTS FOR FOUR TO SIX

8 oz. (225 g.) shortcrust pastry *(see p. 217)*
1½ lb. (700 g.) cooking apples
Juice of ½ lemon
1 oz. (25 g.) butter
2 oz. (50 g.) granulated sugar
2 rounded tablespoons semolina
1 oz. (25 g.) currants
3 tablespoons black treacle
Beaten egg or milk to glaze

Peel, core and thinly slice the apples, and place them in a saucepan with the lemon juice and butter. Cover and simmer very gently for about 10 minutes until they form a soft purée. Stir in the sugar and semolina, bring slowly to the boil, then simmer for 5 minutes, stirring occasionally, until the mixture thickens. Leave until completely cold.

Divide the shortcrust pastry in two, and roll out one piece to line an 8 in. (20 cm.) pie dish. Spread with half the apple mixture to within ½ in. (1·5 cm.)

of the edge. Sprinkle with currants and let the treacle drop from a warmed spoon over the filling. Then top with the remaining apple mixture.

Roll out the other piece of pastry to form a lid. Dampen the rim of the pastry base and cover the apple mixture with the lid, pressing lightly to seal the edges. Make a slit in the lid, brush the pastry with a little beaten egg or milk, and bake for 25 minutes until golden.

Serve hot or cold with custard or lemon sauce (see p. 252).

BAKED PEARS IN CIDER
Countrywide

PEARS USED TO GROW in many country gardens; they were often 'wardens'—very large, hard cooking pears—and many puddings and preserves were devised to make good use of them.

They are traditionally cooked in a slow oven with cider or wine to soften and flavour them. This creates a colourful dish with a delicious syrup.

PREPARATION TIME: 10 MINUTES
COOKING TIME: UP TO 4 HOURS
PRE-HEAT THE OVEN TO
150°C (300°F)—GAS MARK 2

INGREDIENTS FOR SIX

- *6 cooking pears, or hard dessert pears*
- *4 oz. (100/125 g.) sugar*
- *½ pint (275/300 ml.) sweet cider*
- *½ pint (275/300 ml.) water*
- *Thinly pared rind of half a small lemon*
- *1 oz. (25 g.) blanched almonds, cut into slivers*

Peel the pears thinly, but leave the stems on. Stand them upright in a deep casserole and sprinkle with the sugar. Mix the cider and water, and pour round the pears. Add the lemon rind.

Cover and cook in the pre-heated oven until tender. A fork should enter easily without breaking the fruit. This may take up to 4 hours or longer.

Leave the pears to cool in the liquid before lifting them carefully into a shallow serving bowl. Arrange them close together and in an upright position.

Remove the lemon rind, and boil the liquid in a small saucepan until reduced by half. This makes a thick syrup. Press in the almond slivers evenly over the fruit. Pour on the syrup and chill well. Serve with thick cream.

LEMON PUDDING
Yorkshire

THE FIRST BRITONS who tasted lemons were probably Richard I's Crusaders, who spent the winter of 1191–2 among the orange and lemon groves of Jaffa. But it was not until 1289, when 15 lemons, seven oranges and 230 pomegranates were purchased from a Spanish captain for Queen Eleanor, wife of Edward I, that the fruits were seen, or at least remarked upon, in this country.

By the end of the Tudor period lemons were being imported in large numbers from the Mediterranean. In those days they were especially valued for their 'zest'—the aromatic oil obtained from the peel—which was used in perfumes and as a flavouring. The zest is used in this Yorkshire pudding. As it cooks, it separates to give a layer of fluffy sponge over a base of tangy lemon curd.

PREPARATION TIME: 25 MINUTES
COOKING TIME: 45 MINUTES
PRE-HEAT THE OVEN TO
170°C (325°F)—GAS MARK 3

INGREDIENTS FOR FOUR TO SIX

- *4 oz. (100/125 g.) sugar*
- *2 oz. (50 g.) butter or margarine*
- *1 tablespoon boiling water*
- *2 oz. (50 g.) plain flour*
- *Juice and grated rind of 1 large lemon*
- *2 eggs, separated*
- *8 fl. oz. (225 ml.) milk*

Cream the sugar and butter, adding the tablespoon of water to make the mixture workable. Stir in the flour, lemon juice and rind. Whisk the egg yolks in the milk and add, a little at a time, to the creamed mixture. Beat the egg whites until stiff, and fold them into the mixture.

Pour the pudding into a buttered 2 pint (1·1 litre) pie dish and stand it in a roasting tin half filled with warm water. Bake in the pre-heated oven for 45 minutes.

Serve hot on its own, or cold with a little cream.

QUEEN MARY'S TART
Scotland

THE QUEEN referred to in the title may be Mary of Guise, wife of James V of Scotland, or their daughter, Mary, Queen of Scots. Both did much to revolutionise, and even to create, the Scottish cuisine; for example, 'desserts' were first served at good Scottish tables during their reigns—a full 50 years before the word was used in England.

This simple tart was a favourite both with the Court at Holyroodhouse and in Little France, the hamlet established by the French attendants of both Mary of Guise and Mary, Queen of Scots just outside Edinburgh.

PREPARATION TIME: 15 MINUTES
COOKING TIME: 20 MINUTES
PRE-HEAT THE OVEN TO
220°C (425°F)—GAS MARK 7

INGREDIENTS FOR FOUR TO SIX

- *8 oz. (225 g.) puff pastry (see p. 219)*
- *2 tablespoons apricot jam*
- *2 oz. (50 g.) butter*
- *2 oz. (50 g.) sugar*
- *2 eggs, beaten*
- *2 oz. (50 g.) mixed peel*
- *1 tablespoon sultanas*

Roll out the puff pastry and line a 7 in. (18 cm.) flan dish with it. Spread evenly with the apricot jam. To make the filling, cream the butter and sugar and mix in the beaten eggs, peel and sultanas.

Pour the filling, thin and runny at this stage, into the pastry case. Bake in the pre-heated oven for 20 minutes, or until the filling is set and golden-brown on top.

Serve hot or cold with single cream or apricot sauce (see p. 252).

APPLE BAKESTONE CAKE
Wales

THE BAKESTONE must be the most ancient of all cooking utensils—simply a flat stone or slate heated in the fire, on which bannocks, flapjacks, drop scones and other breads could be baked. Its descendants are the griddle—an iron plate serving the same purpose—and the frying pan.

Any of these three implements can be employed when cooking this traditional cake, which may be eaten hot, cold or, perhaps best of all, just wrapped in paper and packed in a haversack in anticipation of a hungry moment in the open air. The Welsh name for the cake is *Teisen Afal ar y Planc*.

For additional flavour, the pastry is often made with bacon dripping instead of butter and lard.

PREPARATION TIME: 30 MINUTES
COOKING TIME: 20 MINUTES

INGREDIENTS FOR THREE OR FOUR

8 oz. (225 g.) shortcrust pastry (see p. 217)
12 oz. (350 g.) cooking apples
$\frac{1}{2}$ oz. (15 g.) butter
2 oz. (50 g.) soft brown sugar
$\frac{1}{4}$ teaspoon nutmeg

Peel, core and finely slice the apples. Put the butter into a saucepan and add the apples, sugar and nutmeg. Cover and stew gently, stirring frequently to prevent sticking, for about 10 minutes. The apples should still be fairly firm, not pulpy; they will cook a little more on the griddle.

Divide the pastry in two, and roll each piece into a round about 7 in. (18 cm.) across. Moisten the rim of one round and spread the apple on top to within about $\frac{1}{2}$ in. (1·5 cm.) of the edge. Place the other round on top and press the edges lightly together.

Brush the griddle or heavy frying pan with oil before heating. To test the heat, sprinkle a little flour on the surface. If it turns golden-brown in about a minute, the heat is sufficient.

Lift the cake on to the griddle using a large spatula or fish slice (not plastic), and cook for 10 minutes until golden-brown. Turn it carefully, holding it between two large spatulas or fish slices, and cook for another 10 minutes on the other side.

Dredge with sugar and serve on hot plates with cream, custard or caramel sauce (see pp. 252, 253).

Sussex Pond Pudding is named after its moat of lemony-buttery sauce.

SUSSEX POND PUDDING
Sussex

THE NAME of this suet pudding is derived from the moat of buttery sauce that surrounds it. The inclusion of a whole lemon adds a brilliant piquancy to the sugar and butter sauce. Make sure, when dividing the pudding, that all receive a small piece of lemon on their plate.

PREPARATION TIME: 25 MINUTES
COOKING TIME: $3\frac{1}{2}$ HOURS

INGREDIENTS FOR FOUR TO SIX

8 oz. (225 g.) suet crust pastry (see p. 219)
4 oz. (100/125 g.) butter, cut in small flakes
4 oz. (100/125 g.) Demerara sugar
1 large lemon, washed and pricked all over with a thin skewer

Roll out the suet crust pastry into a large circle on a floured board. With a sharp knife, cut out a quarter segment of the circle and keep this to use as a lid. Put the remaining pastry into a greased $1\frac{1}{2}$ pint (850 ml.) basin to line it. Damp the cuts and press to seal.

Pack half the butter flakes and half the sugar into the suet crust lining and set the whole lemon on top. Cover with the remaining flaked butter and sugar.

Roll out the reserved quarter of pastry into a circle. Damp it round the edge, put it on top of the pudding and press the edges to seal them.

Prepare the basin for steaming (see p. 259) and steam in a covered saucepan for $3\frac{1}{2}$ hours, adding more boiling water as necessary to maintain the level.

Turn the pudding out carefully on to a hot shallow dish and serve hot with custard, cream or lemon sauce (see p. 252).

TEWKESBURY SAUCER BATTER
Gloucestershire

SAUCERS, AS THE NAME IMPLIES, were used as receptacles for sauces long before they became associated with teacups; they also went through an intermediate stage, in some areas, as containers for small pies and puddings.

Saucer batters are native to the Welsh Marches and the fruit-growing districts of the West Midlands. Soft fruit is the customary filling, but occasionally a savoury batter filled with young vegetables is served as an accompaniment to meat.

A very hot oven is needed, so you will have to use ovenproof dishes.

PREPARATION TIME: 15–20 MINUTES
STANDING TIME: 30 MINUTES
COOKING TIME: 10–20 MINUTES
PRE-HEAT THE OVEN TO 230°C (450°F)—GAS MARK 8

INGREDIENTS FOR TWO TO FOUR

For the filling:

8 oz. (225 g.) soft fruit, such as raspberries or strawberries
2 oz. (50 g.) granulated sugar

For the batter:

4 oz. (100/125 g.) plain flour
$\frac{1}{4}$ teaspoon salt
1 egg, separated
$\frac{1}{2}$ pint (275/300 ml.) milk

Put the fruit in an ovenproof dish, sprinkle with the sugar and cover with the lid to start the juices running. Put to one side.

Mix the flour and salt together, beat in the egg yolk and milk and whip to a batter. Let it stand for 30 minutes.

Thoroughly grease two deep, ovenproof saucers or round 6 in. (15 cm.) pie dishes with butter. Whip the egg white until it is stiff and stands up in peaks, then fold it into the batter. Immediately pour half the batter into each greased saucer, and put the two saucers and the dish of fruit (still covered) in the pre-heated oven.

Cook until the batter comes away from the edges of the saucers—after about 10–20 minutes. Remove from the oven and slide the batter from one saucer, hollow side up, on to a warmed serving dish. Fill it with the hot fruit then cover with the inverted batter from the second saucer.

Sprinkle with caster sugar and serve hot.

Tewkesbury Saucer Batter dates back to the days before teacups.

TREACLE TART
Countrywide

TREACLE—THE SYRUP remaining after the sugar has been crystallised—became generally available in the 17th century with the establishment of sugar refineries in British ports to process West Indian sugar cane. The blackest treacle, or molasses, is that which has had the most sugar removed from it.

The idea for this crumb and syrup tart may have developed from the old method of making gingerbread (mixing breadcrumbs with honey and spice). Treacle was used in tarts until the late 1800s, when golden syrup—a refined, diluted type—became available.

PREPARATION TIME: 15 MINUTES
COOKING TIME: 25 MINUTES
PRE-HEAT THE OVEN TO 190°C (375°F)—GAS MARK 5

INGREDIENTS FOR FOUR TO SIX

8 oz. (225 g.) shortcrust pastry (see p. 217)
8 tablespoons golden syrup
2 tablespoons lemon juice
2 oz. (50 g.) fresh white breadcrumbs
$\frac{1}{4}$ teaspoon ground ginger

Roll out the pastry and line a greased 8 in. (20 cm.) shallow pie plate with it. Trim the edges and reserve the excess pastry. Mix the breadcrumbs and ginger together and sprinkle evenly over the pastry base.

Warm the syrup over a very low heat and stir in the lemon juice. Pour the mixture over the breadcrumbs. Decorate with a lattice pattern of strips cut from the rolled trimmings.

Bake in the pre-heated oven for 25 minutes. Serve hot or cold with cream.

ICED STRAWBERRY SOUFFLÉ
Countrywide

THE ELIZABETHANS loved strawberries, and grew them in large numbers in their well-stocked kitchen gardens. As a gardener of the 1580s observed:

'The gooseberry, raspberry and roses all three,
With strawberries under them truly agree.'

Yet their strawberries were small, more akin to the wild variety than the familiar garden type which was developed out of New World crosses about 150 years later. These new, large strawberries were a popular ingredient in the fruit fools that had a considerable vogue in the 18th century. Below is an updated version of one of them.

PREPARATION TIME: ABOUT 45 MINUTES
SETTING TIME: AT LEAST 1 HOUR

INGREDIENTS FOR FOUR TO SIX

3 level teaspoons powdered gelatine
4 tablespoons orange juice
2 oz. (50 g.) granulated sugar
8 oz. (225 g.) clean, hulled strawberries
¼ pint (150 ml.) double cream, lightly whipped
3 egg whites, whipped until stiff but not dry

Put the gelatine and orange juice in the top of a double saucepan over hot water, or in a cup standing in a pan of hot water. Set over a low heat and stir the gelatine constantly until it dissolves. Add the sugar and, as soon as it has dissolved, set the liquid aside to cool a little.

Meanwhile, press the strawberries into a large bowl through a nylon or aluminium sieve. Stir in the gelatine mixture and fold in the whipped cream.

Cover the bowl and put it in a refrigerator for about 10 minutes, so that the gelatine just begins to set. Fold in the whisked egg whites. Pile the soufflé high into a straight-sided soufflé dish, or into individual dishes if preferred. Put in the refrigerator to set for 1 hour or more.

QUEEN OF PUDDINGS
Countrywide

THIS LAYERED PUDDING of fresh breadcrumbs, thick jam and golden meringue wears its title easily, for there are many who profess it to be the most royal of puddings.

PREPARATION TIME: 30 MINUTES
COOKING TIME: 40 MINUTES
PRE-HEAT THE OVEN TO 180°C (350°F)—GAS MARK 4

INGREDIENTS FOR FOUR TO SIX

5 oz. (150 g.) fresh white breadcrumbs
1 oz. (25 g.) caster sugar
Grated rind of 1 lemon
1 pint (575/600 ml.) milk
2 oz. (50 g.) butter
4 large egg yolks
2 tablespoons raspberry or apricot jam

For the meringue:

4 large egg whites
4 oz. (100/125 g.) caster sugar

Put the breadcrumbs, sugar and lemon rind into a mixing bowl. Heat the milk and butter in a saucepan over a low heat until the butter has melted and the milk is lukewarm.

Pour the warm milk and butter mixture on to the breadcrumb mixture and leave to stand for 10 minutes. Beat in the egg yolks.

Grease a 2 pint (1·1 litre) pie dish and pour in the crumb mixture. Bake in the centre of the pre-heated oven for 30 minutes or until just firm on the top.

Warm the jam so that it spreads easily, and very gently spread it over the pudding without breaking the surface.

To make the meringue topping, whisk the egg whites until they form stiff peaks and, using a metal spoon, fold in the caster sugar. Pile the meringue over the pudding and return to the oven for a further 10 minutes, or until the meringue is lightly browned and crisp.

Serve hot with cream or apricot sauce (see p. 252).

STEAMED TREACLE PUDDING
Scotland

THE EMPEROR NERO'S Greek physician, Andromachus, made the first treacle. He called his potion of drugs steeped in honey *theriaca antidotos* (antidote to wild beasts). This was supposed to be a cure for poisons as well as animal bites and, as such, continued in high esteem until Tudor times. By then it was known as *triacle*, a name maintained by Tudor apothecaries, when they replaced the honey base with molasses.

Molasses, or treacle, became a favourite sweetener in the north of England and Scotland during the 18th century, though in the south, beset by Enclosures, few people could afford it. As a result, the people of the north gained a reputation for devising treacle recipes, such as this old Scottish favourite; if you prefer, you can use golden syrup instead.

PREPARATION TIME: 15 MINUTES
COOKING TIME: 2 HOURS

INGREDIENTS FOR FOUR TO SIX

8 oz. (225 g.) plain flour
3 oz. (75 g.) suet, shredded
2 oz. (50 g.) soft brown sugar
2 teaspoons ground ginger
¼ teaspoon salt
1 level teaspoon bicarbonate of soda
1 egg, beaten
2 oz. (50 g.) black treacle or golden syrup
2½ fl. oz. (75 ml.) milk

Mix the flour, suet, brown sugar, ginger, salt and bicarbonate of soda in a large bowl and add the beaten egg, treacle and milk. Stir the mixture to a soft consistency. Pour into a greased 2 pint (1·1 litre) basin, leaving 1½–2 in. (4–5 cm.) headspace for the pudding to rise.

Prepare the pudding for steaming (see p. 259) and boil steadily over a low heat for 2 hours, topping up with boiling water from time to time to maintain the level.

Turn out onto a warmed plate and serve with cream, custard or lemon sauce (see p. 252), or with warmed treacle mixed with a little whisky.

BAKEWELL PUDDING
Derbyshire

THE COMMERCIAL VERSION of this dish is a rather solid tart filled with almond-flavoured cake. In fact, in the earliest recipes the filling consisted of a layer of jam covered by a light almond cake.

According to legend, the pudding was created in error by a cook at the Rutland Arms, Bakewell, who misunderstood her mistress's instruction that she should add butter, eggs and sugar to the pastry for a jam tart. Instead, she spread the mixture on top of the jam. The guests found the pudding delicious. Jane Austen was possibly among those who enjoyed this pudding at the Bakewell inn.

PREPARATION TIME: 15 MINUTES
COOKING TIME: 25–30 MINUTES
PRE-HEAT THE OVEN TO 200°C (400°F)—GAS MARK 6

INGREDIENTS FOR FOUR

8 oz. (225 g.) flaky or 6 oz. (175 g.) shortcrust pastry (see pp. 218, 217)
2 heaped tablespoons strawberry jam
3 eggs
3 oz. (75 g.) caster sugar
4 oz. (100/125 g.) butter, melted
3 oz. (75 g.) ground almonds

Roll out the pastry to line an 8 in. (20 cm.) oval pie dish 2–3 in. (5–8 cm.) deep. Trim the pastry flush with the edge of the dish.

Warm the jam gently in a saucepan and spread evenly over the pastry base. Beat the eggs and sugar until creamy, then stir in the butter and almonds and pour over the jam.

Bake in the centre of the pre-heated oven for 25–30 minutes, or until the filling is set. Serve hot with cream.

MRS KENT'S LEMON PIE
Suffolk

MRS KENT was an Ipswich housewife of the 18th century. Her name lingers on because of her friend and neighbour, Elizabeth Hicks, who wrote down popular local recipes in a notebook which has survived to this day and makes fascinating reading for the modern housewife.

To achieve the right degree of creaminess in the lemon-custard filling for the pie, Mrs Kent advocated the use of loaf sugar and clarified butter. However, caster sugar and unsalted butter will serve equally well—and they are a great deal easier to obtain nowadays.

PREPARATION TIME: 30 MINUTES
COOKING TIME: 25 MINUTES
PRE-HEAT THE OVEN TO 200°C (400°F)—GAS MARK 6

INGREDIENTS FOR FOUR TO SIX

6 oz. (175 g.) shortcrust pastry (see p. 217)
1 tablespoon grated lemon rind
3 tablespoons lemon juice
4 oz. (100/125 g.) caster sugar
2 oz. (50 g.) unsalted butter
4 eggs, beaten

Roll out the shortcrust pastry to line a 7 in. (18 cm.) pie dish. For the filling, put the lemon rind, lemon juice, sugar and butter into a small saucepan and heat gently without stirring until the sugar has dissolved. Then leave the mixture on one side until it is quite cold.

Strain the beaten eggs and mix them into the cold lemon, sugar and butter mixture. Pour gently into the pastry case and bake in the pre-heated oven for 10 minutes, then at a lower heat—180°C (350°F)—gas mark 4—for 15 minutes.

The pie is equally good served when hot or when cold.

This classic Bakewell Pudding was first created by a cook's mistake.

SOUFFLÉ JAM OMELETTE
Countrywide

SWEET OMELETTES were very popular in manor houses in Edwardian times. The cook could make them while the family and guests were eating the previous course. Nowadays, for most of us, it is necessary to leave the table and make the omelette from the prepared ingredients; but it is well worth the 5 minutes it takes to make this light, foamy pudding.

PREPARATION TIME: 10 MINUTES
COOKING TIME: 5 MINUTES
HEAT THE GRILL TO VERY HOT BEFORE STARTING TO COOK

INGREDIENTS FOR FOUR TO SIX

4 egg yolks
1 oz. (25 g.) caster sugar
6 egg whites
¼ teaspoon salt
1 oz. (25 g.) butter
1 tablespoon jam, warmed

Beat the egg yolks and sugar together. Whisk the egg whites with the salt until they are stiff enough to stand up in peaks. This can be done before the meal.

Just before cooking, whisk the eggs quickly again and stir them lightly into the beaten yolks while the butter is melting in a very large omelette pan.

When the butter is very hot, pour in the mixture and cook for 3 minutes. Finish cooking the top by holding the pan under the hot grill for 2 minutes, until the omelette is well risen and golden.

Slide it on to foil sprinkled with sugar, spread it carefully with the warmed jam and fold it in half by folding over the foil. Slide the omelette from the foil on to a warm serving dish and serve at once.

Upside-Down Winter Pudding
Countrywide

GLISTENING RED CHERRIES nestling in a wheel of pears give a festive air to this Victorian pudding.

Perfectly turned out, the pudding reflects great credit on the cook, yet is easy to make. It gives further use for that plentiful supply of cooking pears which ripen in the winter months.

PREPARATION TIME: 25 MINUTES
COOKING TIME: 45 MINUTES
PRE-HEAT THE OVEN TO 180°C (350°F)—GAS MARK 4

INGREDIENTS FOR SIX
- *3 level tablespoons Demerara sugar*
- *3 pears, peeled, halved and cored*
- *6 glacé cherries, rinsed*
- *4 oz. (100/125 g.) lard*
- *4 oz. (100/125 g.) golden syrup*
- *4 oz. (100/125 g.) black treacle*
- *1 egg, beaten*
- *$\frac{1}{4}$ pint (150 ml.) milk, lukewarm*
- *1 level teaspoon bicarbonate of soda*
- *8 oz. (225 g.) plain flour*
- *1 level teaspoon ground cinnamon*
- *1 level teaspoon ground ginger*
- *3 oz. (75 g.) soft, light brown sugar*

Line the base and side of a deep, 8 in. (20 cm.), round cake tin with greaseproof paper, and brush over with melted butter. Sprinkle the base with the Demerara sugar.

In the cavity of each pear half, where the core has been removed, put a cherry. Place the pears cut side down on the sugar, radiating from the centre of the tin.

Put the lard, syrup and treacle in a small pan over a low heat until the lard has melted. Set to one side. Stir together the beaten egg, milk and bicarbonate of soda.

Sift the flour, cinnamon and ginger into a mixing bowl and stir in the soft brown sugar. Make a well in the centre and pour in the melted lard mixture and the egg mixture. Stir together and beat thoroughly. Then pour into the prepared cake tin.

Bake in the centre of the pre-heated oven for about 45 minutes, or until well risen and firm to the touch. Turn out the pudding on to a warm plate and peel away the paper.

Serve hot, cut in wedges, with cream, custard or lemon sauce (see p. 252).

Cherry Batter Pudding
Kent

AROUND TUNBRIDGE WELLS, they say, the best and sweetest black cherries in the world are grown. Many fruit farmers now offer you the chance to pick your own. Gather a basketful and eat as many as you like. Take the remainder home and use them to make this delicious pudding from the county of Kent.

PREPARATION TIME: 35 MINUTES
COOKING TIME: 1 HOUR

INGREDIENTS FOR FOUR TO SIX
- *1 lb. (450 g.) sweet black cherries*
- *4 oz. (100/125 g.) caster sugar*
- *8 oz. (225 g.) plain flour*
- *$\frac{1}{4}$ level teaspoon salt*
- *4 eggs, separated*
- *$\frac{1}{2}$ pint (275/300 ml.) milk*

Stone the cherries and place in a buttered $2\frac{1}{2}$ pint (1·4 litre) pudding basin. Sprinkle with half the sugar. Sift the flour and salt into a mixing bowl. Beat in the egg yolks and gradually beat in the milk to make a frothy batter. Leave in a cool place while you whip the whites until they stand in stiff peaks. Fold them into

Upside-Down Winter Pudding—golden pear halves set with cherries, turned out ready to serve.

the batter, using a metal spoon, and pile the mixture over the cherries.

Prepare the basin for steaming (see p. 259). Steam for 1 hour, adding boiling water as needed to maintain the level.

Turn out on to a hot plate and sprinkle with the remaining caster sugar. Serve hot with cream or custard (see p. 252).

As an alternative filling, use stoned apricots and mix 1 level teaspoon of ground cinnamon with the sugar before sprinkling it over the fruit.

CREMPOG
Wales

AUTHORITIES DIFFER as to whether 'Crempog' is the Welsh translation of the Anglo-Saxon 'crumpet', or vice-versa.

In any event, the Crempog has occupied an honoured niche in Welsh tradition for centuries. Well within living memory, it was the custom for children to parade through the streets on Shrove Tuesday singing a special Crempog song. Housewives rewarded their efforts with a Crempog liberally smeared with butter and black treacle.

Sadly, Crempog collecting has ceased, but they are still served in the home, and are especially appealing in the layer-cake version.

PREPARATION TIME: 15 MINUTES
STANDING TIME: 1 HOUR
COOKING TIME: 20 MINUTES

INGREDIENTS FOR FOUR

1 oz. (25 g.) butter
8 oz. (225 g.) plain flour
½ pint (275/300 ml.) buttermilk
1 egg, beaten
½ level teaspoon bicarbonate of soda
½ teaspoon lemon juice or vinegar

For the filling:
Jam, lemon juice and sugar, or fresh fruit such as blackberries, strawberries or raspberries

Rub the butter into the sifted flour, stir in the buttermilk and beat the mixture until smooth. Blend in the beaten egg and leave the stiff batter to stand for at least 1 hour.

Just before cooking, mix the bicarbonate of soda with the lemon juice or vinegar and beat thoroughly into the batter.

Lightly grease an 8 in. (20 cm.) frying pan with butter and heat it until the fat smokes. Put 3 tablespoons of batter in the pan and cook over a high heat for about 1 minute on each side.

As the pancakes are ready, pile them up on a hot plate, sandwiching the layers together with jam, fresh soft fruit, or lemon juice and sugar. Keep piping hot until serving time, then cut the pile into quarters and serve on hot plates.

ORANGE AND APPLE FLAN
Countrywide

THIS RECIPE is adapted from one found in a 17th-century manuscript. At that time oranges were still rare enough to be considered rather novel as a flavouring. The fruits had in fact been imported for over 500 years, though seldom in sufficient numbers to penetrate much beyond the major ports and centres.

The Seville orange was the first to arrive, in the 13th century, but from the 17th century it was gradually ousted by the Chinese sweet orange.

The Seville orange is most often used in marmalade, but it is also ideal in this flan, together with a Cox's Orange Pippin; but when Sevilles are out of season, sweet oranges will serve almost as well.

PREPARATION TIME: 35 MINUTES
RESTING TIME FOR THE PASTRY: SEVERAL HOURS OR OVERNIGHT
COOKING TIME: 20 MINUTES
PRE-HEAT THE OVEN TO 180°C (350°F)—GAS MARK 4

INGREDIENTS FOR FOUR TO SIX

For the sweet pastry base:
4 oz. (100/125 g.) plain flour
¼ teaspoon salt
2 oz. (50 g.) soft butter
2 oz. (50 g.) vanilla sugar
2 egg yolks

For the filling:
3 oz. (75 g.) caster sugar
3½ oz. (90 g.) butter
4 egg yolks
Finely grated zest of 1½ oranges, Seville or sweet
Grated flesh of 1 crisp dessert apple, preferably a Cox's Orange Pippin

To make the pastry, sift the flour and salt into a heap on a clean, cold working surface and make a well in the centre. Stir the egg yolks, butter and sugar together in a basin until roughly blended. Pour the mixture into the well in the flour and gradually draw in the flour to work up a soft sticky dough. Knead it lightly, wrap it in kitchen foil and leave to rest in a refrigerator for several hours. Remove 30 minutes before using.

Roll out the pastry thinly to line a 7 in. (18 cm.) metal flan case. Prepare the filling by creaming the sugar and butter together until light and fluffy. Add the egg yolks one at a time, beating well. Add the grated orange zest and beat until smooth.

Turn the filling into the flan case; cover with the grated apple. Bake until golden-brown. Serve warm or cold.

DARK RED FRUIT SALAD
Suffolk

THIS GEORGIAN recipe comes from a Suffolk manor house. An existing manuscript notebook says that fruit salads should always be made with fine-scented China tea added to the fruit. The results are excellent and far more refreshing than fruit salad with brandy or sherry added. Raspberries or loganberries should always be included to give a good colour to the juice; frozen ones also serve the purpose well.

PREPARATION TIME: 30 MINUTES
STANDING TIME: 1 HOUR OR MORE

INGREDIENTS FOR FOUR

2 lb. (900 g.) mixed dark cherries, dark grapes, sweet dark plums, raspberries or loganberries, strawberries and mulberries, made up as available
½ pint (275/300 ml.) jasmin, scented Earl Grey, or scented orange pekoe tea, made at 1½ times usual strength and left until quite cold
4 oz. (100/125 g.) caster sugar

Halve and stone the cherries, grapes and plums, and cut the plums in slices. Pile all the fruit in a large bowl and strain the cold tea over it.

Sprinkle on the sugar and leave to stand for at least 1 hour, but not overnight. Stir lightly from time to time so that the sugar penetrates everywhere and the juice becomes evenly red.

Spiced Peaches capture the golden memories of summer days.

SPICED PEACHES
Countrywide

GLOWING AMBER PEACHES in a brandied, spicy syrup make a very grand sweet to serve at a dinner party. Although we now think of peaches as an imported delicacy, they were introduced to English gardens by the Romans. By the 17th century, 22 different varieties were growing here.

This recipe is an adaptation of Hannah Glasse's 1747 recipe. It is quick and simple to prepare. Keep it for 3 days before serving; by then the syrup will have fully penetrated the fruit. If you want to keep it longer, double the amount of brandy.

PREPARATION TIME: 15 MINUTES
COOKING TIME: 15–20 MINUTES
STANDING TIME: 3 DAYS

INGREDIENTS FOR SIX

6 ripe peaches of about the same size
6 cloves
¾ pint (450 ml.) water
12 oz. (350 g.) granulated sugar
2 in. (5 cm.) piece of cinammon stick, or 1 level teaspoon ground cinnamon
¼ teaspoon ground mace
4 fl. oz. (100/125 ml.) brandy

Put the peaches in boiling water for 2 or 3 minutes. Drain and peel them carefully. Stick a clove in each.

Put the water, sugar, cinnamon and mace in a deep pan and bring to the boil, stirring until the sugar has dissolved. Put the peaches in this syrup and cook them gently for 15–20 minutes, making sure that they are completely covered by the syrup. The cooking ensures that they will not discolour in the jar.

Lift the peaches carefully into a wide-mouthed, screw-topped jar. Then remove the cinnamon stick from the syrup and stir in the brandy. Pour over the peaches and leave to cool before covering tightly. Stand in a cool place and keep for 3 days before using.

STEAMED ORANGE PUDDING
Countrywide

THE INVENTION of the pudding cloth in the early 17th century was a major event in the history of puddings. For now it was generally possible to boil a sweet pudding in a pot over the fire at the same time as the main course. Before this, animal-gut containers—neither convenient nor always available—had been used.

The first-known pudding boiled in a cloth was College Pudding, served to students at Cambridge University in 1617. After this, a whole range of British steamed puddings emerged, including this modern descendant now steamed in a basin rather than boiled in a cloth.

PREPARATION TIME: 25 MINUTES
COOKING TIME: 2 HOURS

INGREDIENTS FOR SIX TO EIGHT

4 oz. (100/125 g.) butter
4 oz. (100/125 g.) sugar
4 oz. (100/125 g.) self-raising flour
¼ teaspoon salt
½ teaspoon baking powder
2 eggs, beaten
1 oz. (25 g.) white breadcrumbs
2 tablespoons milk
Juice and grated rind of 1½ oranges

Cream the butter with the sugar. Sift the flour, salt and baking powder together, and add to the creamed mixture a little at a time alternately with the egg. Beat well after each addition. Stir in the breadcrumbs, milk, orange rind and juice, and beat well again.

Put the mixture in a buttered 2 pint (1·1 litre) basin, prepare it for steaming (see p. 259) and cook it for 2 hours, adding more boiling water to the saucepan as necessary to maintain the level.

Turn the pudding out on to a hot plate and serve at once with custard, cream or marmalade sauce (see p. 252).

For a variation, make the pudding with lemon rind and juice, instead of orange, and serve with lemon sauce (see p. 252).

Curd Cheesecake
Yorkshire

CHEESECAKE, in one form or another, must be one of the earliest of sweet puddings. The Countess of Leicester's account books for 1265 reveal that in that year her ladyship purchased a considerable amount of soft cheese for tarts. The cheese was pounded in a mortar with egg yolks, ginger, cinnamon and sugar to make a filling.

Later, this recipe gave way to a range of cheesecakes concocted from curds, custard, butter, almonds and, recently, crushed biscuits, some of which omitted cheese altogether—in spite of the name.

This Yorkshire version, however, employs sharp-tasting curd cheese. The cake, known as 'sweet pye', was traditionally eaten by Wolds shepherds to sustain them through sheep-shearing.

If curd cheese is not available, cottage cheese can be used, but it must be sieved and the result is less rich.

PREPARATION TIME: 30 MINUTES
COOKING TIME: 40 MINUTES
PRE-HEAT THE OVEN TO 190°C (375°F)—GAS MARK 5

INGREDIENTS FOR EIGHT

4 oz. (100/125 g.) shortcrust pastry (see p. 217)
8 oz. (225 g.) curd cheese or sieved cottage cheese
2 oz. (50 g.) caster sugar
2 eggs, beaten
Grated rind of ½ lemon
Juice of 1 lemon
2 teaspoons cornflour
2 tablespoons double cream
1 tablespoon melted butter

Roll out the pastry to line a 9 in. (23 cm.) loose-bottomed tin. Bake blind (see p. 220) in the pre-heated oven for 15 minutes. Remove the tin and turn down the oven to 180°C (350°F)—gas mark 4.

Blend the cheese with the sugar, beaten eggs, and lemon rind and juice.

Beat until smooth and then add the cornflour blended with the cream. Fold in the melted butter.

Pour into the pastry case and bake in the pre-heated oven for 30 minutes. Serve cold on its own.

To give a different flavour to the cheesecake, there are several variations to choose from. Just before putting the cheesecake in the oven, sprinkle over it 2 oz. (50 g.) of raisins that have been soaked for 10 minutes in hot water and then drained. The soaking will prevent them from burning during cooking.

For a cooked fruit topping, cover the cooled cheesecake with stoned, stewed damsons thickened with arrowroot. Decorate with toasted flaked almonds.

For a fresh-fruit topping, arrange hulled strawberries or raspberries on the cooled cheesecake. Brush over the fruit with a glaze made from 2 tablespoons of strawberry jam warmed with 1 teaspoon of fresh lemon juice until it has melted.

Ground almonds give a different texture and taste to the cheesecake. Add 4 oz. (100/125 g.) of ground almonds and an extra egg to the recipe, and use cream cheese instead of curd cheese. Cover the cheesecake with soured cream for the last 10 minutes of cooking time and decorate with a sprinkling of toasted chopped almonds just before serving.

Yorkshire Curd Cheesecake can be topped with fresh or cooked fruit.

APPLE PIE
Countrywide

'OF ALL THE DELICATES that Britons try
To please the palate and delight the eye,
Of all the sev'ral kinds of sumptuous fare,
There is none that can with apple pie compare.'

William King (1663–1712)

Apple pie in its various forms is a dish that has been with us for a very long time. The Elizabethans filled their tarts with a purée of apples, red wine, sugar, cinnamon and ginger. Later, cooks of the 17th and 18th centuries preferred pies made with apples, quinces, lemon zest, and candied peel.

For a modern pie, a mixture of cooking and eating apples gives the best results. You can add a handful of blackberries when they are in season.

PREPARATION TIME: 20 MINUTES
COOKING TIME: 40 MINUTES
PRE-HEAT THE OVEN TO 200°C (400°F)—GAS MARK 6

INGREDIENTS FOR SIX TO EIGHT

8 oz. (225 g.) shortcrust pastry (see p. 217)
1 lb. (450 g.) cooking apples
8 oz. (225 g.) crisp eating apples
4 oz. (100/125 g.) sugar
1 teaspoon grated lemon rind
2 cloves or ¼ teaspoon ground cinnamon or ginger
Caster sugar for sprinkling

Peel, core and slice the cooking and eating apples and mix them together. Mix the sugar, lemon rind and spice together. Using a 1½ pint (850 ml.) pie dish, with a pie funnel placed in the centre if desired, arrange the apples and the sugar mixture in layers. Finish with a layer of apples.

Cover with the rolled-out pastry and make a small hole in the centre to allow the steam to escape. Brush the top with cold water and sprinkle with a little caster sugar to give a crisp coating. Bake in the pre-heated oven for 20 minutes, then reduce the heat to 190°C (375°F)—gas mark 5 and bake for another 20 minutes until the apples are tender.

Serve warm with cream, custard or caramel sauce (see pp. 252, 253).

POOR KNIGHTS OF WINDSOR
Countrywide

BREAD SLICES flavoured with sugar and sherry, dipped in egg yolks and fried in butter make up the Poor Knights pudding. Introduced into England by the Normans, it was a favourite (without the spices) in medieval times under the name of 'payn pur-dew'—derived from the French *pain perdu* (lost bread), the bread being 'lost' in the batter.

The Poor Knights was an order of military pensioners founded by Edward III in 1349. They were given small apartments in Windsor. Why the dish is named after them is uncertain—perhaps because it was a good way for a person of small means to convert slightly stale bread into a rich pudding.

Clarified butter is best used for the frying, as it does not burn.

PREPARATION TIME: 10 MINUTES
COOKING TIME: ABOUT 10 MINUTES

INGREDIENTS FOR FOUR

8 slices white bread from a large, day-old loaf
8 tablespoons milk
1 oz. (25 g.) caster sugar
1 tablespoon medium-sweet sherry
2 egg yolks
4–5 oz. (100/150 g.) clarified (see p. 49) or unsalted butter
Caster sugar for sprinkling
¼ level teaspoon ground cinnamon

Remove the crusts from the bread and cut each slice in half. Pour 6 tablespoons of the milk into a shallow basin and stir in the caster sugar until dissolved, then add the sherry.

Dip the bread slices in this mixture until soaked right through, and then let them drain.

Beat the egg yolks and the remaining milk together, and dip the slices in the mixture.

Heat the clarified butter in a large frying pan and fry the slices quickly, turning once, until they are golden-brown. Pile the slices on a warmed serving plate and sprinkle them with caster sugar flavoured with cinnamon.

Serve with warm jam or with melted butter flavoured with sugar or sherry.

PANCAKES
Countrywide

PANCAKES have been with us since the Middle Ages at least, when they served as an accompaniment to many different dishes. Then, as now, they were particularly associated with Shrove Tuesday, when they provided a convenient means of using up eggs and other foods before the beginning of the Lenten fast.

Pancake races have existed almost as long as pancakes, and take place in many towns. The Pancake Race at Olney, Buckinghamshire, for example, has been run since 1445. It is open to local housewives, who, over a 415 yd course, must toss a pancake in a pan at least three times; the winner and runner-up receive a prayer book and a kiss from the verger.

Compared with the standard one-egg batter mixture, this recipe makes particularly light pancakes. Serve them with lemon or orange juice, or roll them with different fillings.

PREPARATION TIME: ABOUT 10 MINUTES
COOKING TIME: ABOUT 20 MINUTES

INGREDIENTS FOR EIGHT PANCAKES

3 oz. (75 g.) plain flour
¼ teaspoon salt
3 eggs
½ pint (275/300 ml.) milk
1 oz. (25 g.) melted butter
Lemon juice for sprinkling
Caster sugar for sprinkling

Sift the flour and salt into a large bowl, and whisk in the eggs one by one. Add the milk a little at a time, beating thoroughly until the batter is smooth and free from lumps. Just before cooking, stir in the cooled melted butter.

Use an 8 in. (20 cm.) frying pan, and for each pancake grease it lightly with butter or lard and heat until the fat smokes. Pour about 3 tablespoons of the batter into the centre of the pan, and quickly tilt the pan to and fro to spread the mixture evenly.

Cook over a high heat for about 1 minute, until the batter has just set and the edges are turning light brown and crisp. Toss the pancake, or turn it over carefully with a palette knife or spatula, and cook for about another minute until it is golden-brown underneath.

Coventry Godcakes—sugar-coated jam puffs, once a teatime treat for godchildren on their confirmation.

Turn out the pancake on to a hot plate and sprinkle the top with sugar and lemon juice. Fold the pancake in half and then in half again, and either serve at once or, if you prefer, put it aside to keep hot until the remainder of the batter has been cooked.

Serve hot with more sugar and lemon juice. To vary the recipe, spread a tablespoon of one of the following fillings across the middle of each pancake and roll up.

A thick, hot purée of any fruit in season, such as apples, gooseberries, plums or apricots. Alternatively, 8 oz. (225 g.) curd cheese mixed with 2 oz. (50 g.) chopped almonds and 1 tablespoon of sugar, and moistened with lemon juice.

Arrange in a well-buttered shallow ovenproof dish, dredge thickly with sugar and keep in the oven, pre-heated to 170°C (325°F)—gas mark 3, until serving time.

COVENTRY GODCAKES
Warwickshire

DURING THE 16TH CENTURY it was the custom in Coventry for godparents to give their godchildren cakes for good luck at the time of their confirmation. The cakes were usually triangular turnovers whose three points were said to represent the Holy Trinity. The size of the cake denoted the wealth of the giver, and each family tried to outdo the others.

PREPARATION TIME: 20 MINUTES
COOKING TIME: 12–15 MINUTES
PRE-HEAT THE OVEN TO 220°C (425°F)—GAS MARK 7

INGREDIENTS FOR 12 TURNOVERS

12 oz. (350 g.) puff or flaky pastry (see pp. 219, 218)
8 oz. (225 g.) mincemeat or jam
Beaten egg to seal and glaze
Granulated sugar

Cut the pastry into two equal pieces. Roll out each piece on a lightly floured board and trim to an oblong about 12 by 8 in. (30 by 20 cm.). Cut each oblong into six 4 in. (10 cm.) squares and cut each square diagonally to give two triangles. There will be 24 triangles in all.

Wet two baking sheets and arrange six triangles on each. Put a teaspoon of mincemeat or jam on the centre of these triangles. Brush the pastry edges lightly with beaten egg and cover with the remaining triangles. Press the edges together to seal.

Brush the lids with beaten egg and make three slits in each with a sharp knife. Dredge each turnover liberally with granulated sugar. Bake in the centre of the pre-heated oven for 12–15 minutes until golden-brown.

Serve warm with cream, brandy butter or rum butter (see p. 253).

SUNDAY RICE PUDDING
Caernarvonshire

IN THE POOR hill-farming community of North Wales, milk sales formed a major part of the family income. Milk puddings were therefore a rare treat—to be consumed on Sunday after Chapel. Sunday Rice Pudding (called in Welsh *Pwdin Reis Dydd Sul*) is much lighter than the traditional recipe.

PREPARATION TIME: 15 MINUTES
COOKING TIME: 2 HOURS
PRE-HEAT THE OVEN TO 170°C (325°F)—GAS MARK 3

INGREDIENTS FOR FOUR TO SIX

2 oz. (50 g.) short-grain rice
1 pint (575/600 ml.) milk
3 oz. (75 g.) caster sugar
½ oz. (15 g.) butter, cut into flakes
½ teaspoon grated nutmeg
2 eggs, separated

Boil the rice in just enough water to cover it—about ¼ pint (150 ml.)—for 5 minutes. Drain the rice if necessary and put it in a buttered 2 pint (1·1 litre) ovenproof dish. Stir in the milk and 2 oz. (50 g.) of the sugar. Dot with butter and sprinkle on half the nutmeg. Bake for about 1 hour.

Remove the dish from the oven, cool for 5 minutes, then beat the egg yolks lightly into the rice. Return to the oven for another 30 minutes.

Meanwhile, whisk the egg whites with the remaining 1 oz. (25 g.) of sugar until they are stiff but not dry.

Remove the pudding from the oven and let it cool for 5 minutes. Fold in the beaten egg whites and sprinkle with the remaining nutmeg. Return the dish to the oven for 15 minutes to set the egg whites.

Serve with apricot or marmalade sauce (see p. 252).

BAKED STUFFED APPLES
Yorkshire

BAKED APPLES have been a country favourite for centuries, but the banana stuffing is a fairly recent innovation. Although the first bunch of bananas reached this country in 1633—it was exhibited in the window of a London herbalist—the fruit was not widely available until the late 19th century.

Many other stuffings blend well with apples, and some alternatives are given below. The sherry syrup adds an elegant touch to them all.

PREPARATION TIME: 10 MINUTES
COOKING TIME: 1 HOUR
PRE-HEAT THE OVEN TO 180°C (350°F)—GAS MARK 4

INGREDIENTS FOR SIX

6 large cooking apples, preferably Bramleys
3 oz. (75 g.) caster sugar
1 oz. (25 g.) butter
4 fl. oz. (100/125 ml.) sherry

Fillings (one of the following):

2 large bananas, peeled and mashed
6 oz. (175 g.) dried apricots, chopped and mixed with clear honey
6 oz. (175 g.) mincemeat (see p. 352)
6 oz. (175 g.) dried dates, chopped with 3 oz. (75 g.) nuts, and the juice of a lemon
6 level tablespoons soft, light brown sugar mixed with 2 level teaspoons ground mace

Core the apples and score the skin round the middle of each. Stand them in a deep buttered dish. Fill the cavities with your chosen filling. Put a knob of butter on each apple and sprinkle thickly with sugar. Pour the sherry round the apples.

Bake in the pre-heated oven for 1 hour. Baste occasionally with syrup.

Serve hot or cold with cream.

Stuffed Apples with mixed fillings to bake in a sherry syrup.

BREAD PUDDING
Countrywide

IN NORFOLK, this comforting pudding is known as Nelson's Cake or Nelson's Slices, after the great sailor who was born in the rectory of Burnham Thorpe in that county in 1758. It also bears these names in Plymouth, which was a major British naval base during the Napoleonic Wars, as it is today.

No one knows when the pudding was invented, but it remains highly popular in many parts of the country, especially in the Midlands and East Anglia.

PREPARATION TIME: 25 MINUTES
COOKING TIME: 2½ HOURS
PRE-HEAT THE OVEN TO
150°C (300°F)—GAS MARK 2

INGREDIENTS FOR 12 SQUARES

8 thick slices day-old white bread
½ pint (275/300 ml.) milk
1 eating apple
12 oz. (350 g.) mixed dried fruit
2 oz. (50 g.) chopped mixed peel
3 tablespoons soft, dark brown sugar
2 tablespoons mature orange marmalade
1½ oz. (40 g.) self-raising flour
2 eggs, beaten
1 teaspoon lemon juice
1 level teaspoon ground cinnamon
2 level teaspoons ground mixed spice
4 oz. (100/125 g.) butter

Break the bread, including the crusts, into small pieces and place in a mixing bowl. Pour over the milk and leave to soak for 20 minutes until soft. Beat well with a fork to form a smooth, lump-free mixture.

Core and grate the apple, and add to the bread mixture with the dried fruit and mixed peel. Stir in the sugar, marmalade, flour, eggs, lemon juice, cinnamon and ground mixed spice.

Melt the butter and stir half into the bread mixture. Beat well, using a wooden spoon, and spread into a greased 11 by 8 in. (28 by 20 cm.) roasting tin. Pour the remaining butter in a thin stream evenly over the surface of the pudding. Bake in the pre-heated oven for 2 hours. Increase the oven temperature to 180°C (350°F)—gas mark 4 and bake for a further 30 minutes.

Cut the pudding into squares and serve hot with custard, marmalade sauce or lemon sauce (see p. 252). Alternatively, sprinkle liberally with granulated sugar, leave to cool and cut into squares to serve as cake.

APPLE CHARLOTTE
Countrywide

THE ORIGIN of the term 'Charlotte', whether applied to rhubarb or apple dishes, is a subject of some debate.

Fifteenth-century gourmets relished *charlets,* a dish composed of finely chopped flesh (*chair*) seethed in milk (*lait*). Devotees of Goethe assert that it is named after Charlotte, the heroine of his novel *Werther,* and culinary scholars contend that it is a misspelling of the Hebrew *schaleth*—a sweet, spiced purée of dried fruit covered by a crisp crust.

The instigator of the controversy may have been the great French chef Carème (1784–1833), who invented a dish consisting of a wall of sponge fingers enclosing a filling of cream. Unsure of Hebrew spelling, he called it Charlotte Russe. Since Charlotte was the name of Britain's queen at that time—as well as being that of the daughter of the Prince Regent—the title stuck.

But, arguments apart, the homely British charlotte of spiced apples or rhubarb encased in buttered bread still remains a staunch favourite with children.

PREPARATION TIME: 30 MINUTES
COOKING TIME: 20 MINUTES
PRE-HEAT THE OVEN TO
200°C (400°F)—GAS MARK 6

INGREDIENTS FOR FOUR TO SIX

1 lb. (450 g.) cooking apples
2 oz. (50 g.) butter
6 oz. (175 g.) sugar
2 tablespoons lemon juice
1 tablespoon grated lemon peel
1 level teaspoon ground mixed spice
8 thin bread slices, without crusts, from large loaf
4 oz. (100/125 g.) clarified butter for frying (see p. 49)
1 tablespoon caster sugar for sprinkling

Peel, core and slice the apples and put them into a pan with the butter, sugar, lemon juice, lemon peel and mixed spice. Simmer very gently for about 10 minutes until the apples are pulpy.

Cut each bread slice into three strips, and fry in clarified butter until golden and crisp. Line the bottom and sides of a greased 1½ pint (850 ml.) soufflé dish or charlotte mould with the bread slices, and put in the pulped apples. Cover with the remaining strips of bread and sprinkle with half the caster sugar.

Bake in the pre-heated oven for 20 minutes. Turn out on to a plate and sprinkle with the rest of the caster sugar.

Serve hot with single cream or caramel sauce (see p. 253).

PLUM SPONGE PUDDING
Countrywide

THIS INFINITELY ADAPTABLE family pudding is ideal for cooking in the oven at the same time as a main course. The filling can include any fruit in season—apples, rhubarb, gooseberries, blackberries or damsons as well as the plums used here.

PREPARATION TIME: 20 MINUTES
COOKING TIME: ABOUT 50 MINUTES
PRE-HEAT THE OVEN TO
180°C (350°F)—GAS MARK 4

INGREDIENTS FOR FOUR

2 oz. (50 g.) butter or margarine
2 oz. (50 g.) granulated sugar
3 oz. (75 g.) self-raising flour
1 egg, beaten
1 tablespoon water
1 lb. (450 g.) plums, washed, halved and stoned
3 oz. (75 g.) brown sugar

Cream the butter and granulated sugar until fluffy. Add the flour and egg alternately, a little at a time, beating well after each addition. Stir in the water.

Put the plums and brown sugar in alternate layers in a buttered 1½ pint (850 ml.) ovenproof basin. Cover with the sponge mixture and bake in the centre of the pre-heated oven for about 50 minutes, or until the top of the sponge is springy to the touch.

Serve hot with custard (see p. 252) or cream.

DEBDEN CHOCOLATE PUDDING
Essex

THIS RICH CHOCOLATE PUDDING, invented by a Debden housewife, is said to have taken the area by storm. It creates its own fudge sauce beneath a cake-like top, and can be further enriched with a topping of whipped cream or ice-cream.

PREPARATION TIME: 15 MINUTES
COOKING TIME: 1 HOUR
COOLING TIME: 1 HOUR
PRE-HEAT THE OVEN TO 170°C (325°F)—GAS MARK 3

INGREDIENTS FOR SIX TO EIGHT

4 oz. (100/125 g.) plain flour
2 teaspoons baking powder
¼ teaspoon salt
6 oz. (175 g.) granulated sugar
1 oz. (25 g.) plain chocolate, melted
2 tablespoons butter, melted
¼ pint (150 ml.) milk
2 oz. (50 g.) brown sugar
2 oz. (50 g.) caster sugar
3 tablespoons cocoa
6 fl. oz. (175 ml.) cold water

Sift together the flour, baking powder and salt into a bowl. Stir in the granulated sugar, melted chocolate and melted butter. Blend in the milk. Pour the mixture into a buttered 1½ pint (850 ml.) ovenproof dish. Sprinkle over the top the brown sugar, caster sugar and cocoa in separate layers. Pour over the cold water.

Bake in the pre-heated oven for 1 hour. A layer of chocolate-fudge sauce will form under the sponge topping as the pudding cooks. Let the pudding cool for an hour before serving, but do not chill. Serve with whipped cream or ice-cream.

BROWN BREAD ICE-CREAM
Countrywide

ICE-CREAM BECAME POPULAR in Britain during the middle of the 18th century—one result of the ice-houses that were then being built in the grounds of large country estates. The ice-houses were deep, brick-lined pits, roofed with brick and stonework domes. If the winter was cold enough, ice was made locally—taken from frozen lakes or man-made pools—but if not, ice was brought by road from the Lake District or from the Fens in wagons insulated with straw.

The first ice-cream was a fruit-flavoured cream, poured into a tin and kept in a bucket of ice. The following recipe was developed about 1770, and remained a firm favourite throughout the Victorian and Edwardian periods. The Victorians sprinkled it with crushed crystallised violets.

PREPARATION TIME: 40 MINUTES
FREEZING TIME: 3 HOURS

INGREDIENTS FOR SIX

6 oz. (175 g.) wholemeal breadcrumbs of coarse texture
½ pint (275/300 ml.) double cream
8 fl. oz. (225 ml.) single cream
4 oz. (100/125 g.) light, soft brown sugar
2 eggs, separated
1 tablespoon rum

Creamy textured Brown Bread Ice-Cream makes a perfect summer dessert.

Spread the breadcrumbs on a baking tray and put under a medium grill until crisp and lightly browned. Stir them about frequently and watch them carefully while they toast, to make sure that they do not become too brown.

Whip the double and single cream with the sugar, until the mixture holds a soft peak. Beat the egg yolks with the rum and stir into the cream. Fold in the breadcrumbs and pour the mixture into an ice tray or plastic container. Cover and freeze for 1 hour.

Whisk the egg whites until stiff. Scrape the half-frozen ice-cream into a chilled bowl and stir well until of an even texture. Fold in the egg whites, return to the container, cover and freeze for at least 2 hours.

Transfer from the freezer to a refrigerator shelf half an hour before serving. Serve with apricot or chocolate sauce (see p. 252).

GOOSEBERRY FOOL
Countrywide

ENGLAND'S ELABORATE and elegant cold sweets were famous throughout Europe in Tudor times. The sweet course at a great feast was then known as the 'banquet', and consisted of preserved fruits, jellies and tarts. Some noblemen built banqueting houses in their grounds in order to serve the 'banquet' privately to their guests after the main part of the meal had been eaten in the Great Hall.

On prosperous farms these dishes were less elaborately served and decorated, but the same cold sweets with cream, butter, eggs and fruit were made for special occasions.

PREPARATION TIME: 10 MINUTES
COOKING TIME: 20 MINUTES
COOLING TIME: 1–2 HOURS

INGREDIENTS FOR EIGHT

1¼ lb. (575 g.) green gooseberries, washed, topped and tailed
8 oz. (225 g.) caster sugar
3 eggs
¾ pint (450 ml.) milk
½ pint (275/300 ml.) double cream
Whipped cream to decorate
Mint leaves to decorate

Put the gooseberries to stew very gently in a covered pan with 6 oz. (175 g.) of the sugar for about 15 minutes, or until soft.

Meanwhile, beat the remaining sugar with the eggs in a 1½ pint (850 ml.) basin. Heat the milk to just below boiling point and pour slowly on to the eggs and sugar, stirring all the time.

Stand the basin in a pan of almost boiling water. Keep the water just under boiling point over a low heat, and stir constantly with a wooden spoon until the mixture thickens (about 5 minutes). Take the basin out of the hot water and leave the custard on one side until it has become cold.

Rub the cooked gooseberries through a fine sieve, or put them through a fine mill. Leave the purée until it has become quite cold.

Whip the cream until it just holds a peak. Fold the cold custard into the cold gooseberry purée and add the cream. Stir until all three are completely blended. Serve in a large glass bowl or in individual glasses. Decorate the fool liberally with whipped cream, and a fresh mint leaf for each serving.

For a richer fool, make it with 1¼ pints (725 ml.) of double cream instead of the cream and custard.

The lively flavour of fruit emphasises the smooth coolness of Gooseberry Fool.

CLOOTIE DUMPLING
Scotland

'CLOUT' IS BROAD SCOTS for 'cloth'; hence Clootie Dumpling was a dumpling boiled in a cloth. Nowadays a basin is more convenient, and is commonly used for such puddings. Clootie Dumpling is traditionally associated with Hogmanay—New Year—when First Footers, the first visitors to cross the threshold after midnight, are given a slice, together with a dram.

PREPARATION TIME: 20 MINUTES
COOKING TIME: 3 HOURS

INGREDIENTS FOR FOUR TO SIX

3 oz. (75 g.) self-raising flour
3 oz. (75 g.) white breadcrumbs
4 oz. (100/125 g.) suet, shredded
4 oz. (100/125 g.) caster sugar
2 oz. (50 g.) raisins
2 oz. (50 g.) currants
2 oz. (50 g.) sultanas
1 tablespoon marmalade
1 teaspoon mixed spice
1 tablespoon treacle
1 egg, beaten
¼ pint (150 ml.) milk

Mix all the ingredients together in a large bowl to form a dough. Spoon it into a greased 2 pint (1·1 litre) basin and prepare for steaming (see p. 259). Cover with a lid and steam for 3 hours, topping up with boiling water from time to time to maintain the level.

Serve hot with custard, brandy sauce, marmalade sauce or lemon sauce (see pp. 252, 253), or serve cold, cut in slices and sprinkled with caster sugar.

The cold slices are also good fried in butter and sprinkled with caster sugar.

MINCE PIES
Countrywide

SMALL PIES filled with spicy mincemeat and coated with sugar have been traditional Christmas fare for centuries. It was customary to eat one for each of the 12 days of Christmas, to ensure 12 happy months ahead.

Some early mince pies were oval to represent the crib in which Jesus was laid. The spices in the mincemeat symbolised the exotic gifts brought by the three kings.

You can make the pies with puff pastry instead of shortcrust, but since this tends to be fatty it is best to eat the pies hot from the oven. And, of course, they should be filled with your own home-made mincemeat.

PREPARATION TIME: 35 MINUTES
COOKING TIME: 20 MINUTES
PRE-HEAT THE OVEN TO 220°C (425°F)—GAS MARK 7

INGREDIENTS FOR 18 TO 20 PIES

12 oz (350 g.) shortcrust pastry or 1 lb. (450 g.) puff pastry (see pp. 217, 219)
1 lb. (450 g.) fruit mincemeat (see p. 352)
1 egg white
Caster sugar for sprinkling

Roll out the prepared pastry thinly and cut out 18–20 rounds, about 3 in. (8 cm.) across, for the pie bases. Line 2½ in. (6·5 cm.) wide patty tins with these, and fill to about half their depth with the mincemeat.

Cut out slightly smaller rounds for the pie covers. Dampen the rims of the pie bases with cold water and place the covers on top, pressing the edges together lightly to seal them. Make a small slit in the top of each pie, brush with the egg white and sprinkle with caster sugar.

Put the pies in the pre-heated oven and bake for about 20 minutes until light golden-brown. Remove from the oven and let them stand for 3–5 minutes before lifting them from the tins with a round-bladed knife. Put them on a wire rack to cool.

Serve with cream, brandy butter or rum butter (see p. 253).

CHRISTMAS PUDDING
Countrywide

ROBERT ARGYLLON, chef to William the Conqueror, was presented with the Manor of Addington in Surrey by his grateful sovereign, for the service of creating a 'Messe in an earthen pot in the kitchen of our Lord the King, on the day of his coronation'—Christmas Day, 1066. The 'Messe' was a meat stew called 'girout', a dish served at every coronation until that of George V, and offered by the holder of the Manor of Addington on bended knee.

Far-off girout is the ancestor of Christmas pudding, though it has gone through many changes since William's day. The Elizabethans added herbs and prunes to the meat and called it 'stewed broth', but as early as the mid-16th century the Christmas association returned, and the dish was known as Christmas broth, porridge or pottage. It was eaten not only at Christmas, but also on All Saints' Day and at New Year as well. Gradually, the meat was phased out, prunes and sultanas were substituted for plums, and the modern Christmas pudding evolved.

Christmas puddings need to mature, and are all the better for being prepared several weeks or even months in advance. Store them in a well-ventilated dry place, and steam a second time before serving.

This well-tried recipe makes three medium puddings, light-textured, dark and delicious.

PREPARATION TIME: 1 HOUR
FIRST COOKING TIME: 7 HOURS (2¾ HOURS IN A PRESSURE COOKER)
MATURING TIME: AT LEAST 6 WEEKS
SECOND COOKING TIME: 3 HOURS (30 MINUTES IN A PRESSURE COOKER)

INGREDIENTS FOR THREE 1½ LB. (700 G.) PUDDINGS

8 oz. (225 g.) self-raising flour
8 oz. (225 g.) shredded suet
8 oz. (225 g.) fresh white breadcrumbs
8 oz. (225 g.) currants
12 oz. (350 g.) sultanas
12 oz. (350 g.) raisins, stoned
8 oz. (225 g.) soft, dark brown sugar
1 level teaspoon salt
1–2 teaspoons ground mixed spice
4 oz. (100/125 g.) chopped mixed peel
4 oz. (100/125 g.) glacé cherries, rinsed and chopped
1 small carrot, peeled and grated
1 small apple, peeled and grated
6 eggs, beaten
Grated rind and juice of 1 orange
Grated rind and juice of 1 lemon
½ pint (275/300 ml.) old ale, stout or Guinness

Grease three 2 pint (1·1 litre) pudding basins. Mix the flour, suet, breadcrumbs, dried fruit and sugar together in a large bowl. Stir in the salt, mixed spice, mixed peel, glacé cherries, carrot and apple.

Mix together the eggs, orange and lemon juice and rind and the ale, and add to the dry ingredients to give a soft, dropping consistency. Add more ale if necessary.

Divide the mixture between the prepared basins, leaving 2 in. (5 cm.) headspace to allow for rising. Cover each basin for steaming and place each in a saucepan of boiling water (see p. 259). Cover with lids and steam for 7 hours. Top up with more boiling water as necessary to maintain the level.

Remove the basins from the pans and leave to cool. Re-cover with fresh greaseproof paper, foil or cloth and store in a cool, dry place for as long as possible.

Before serving, cover with fresh greaseproof paper, foil or cloth again and steam for another 3 hours. Remove the covering, invert the pudding on to a warmed serving plate and decorate with a sprig of holly.

For a festive presentation, heat a small wineglass of brandy in a small saucepan and at the last moment pour it over the pudding and set it alight. Serve with brandy sauce, or brandy or rum butter (see p. 253).

If using a pressure cooker, cook each pudding for 15 minutes without pressure (pre-steaming) then for a further 2½ hours at high pressure. Before serving, steam at high pressure for 30 minutes.

Traditional Christmas Pudding and Mince Pies, dark with fruit and rich with spices, partnered by Brandy Butter.

SWEET SAUCES

Until the late 18th century, the usual sauce for a sweet pudding was melted butter and sugar flavoured with rose-water, a sharp fruit juice, wine, or brandy or rum on special occasions. The variety of sauces we know now developed to accompany steamed suet puddings, which became so popular during the late 18th and 19th centuries.

CLOTTED CREAM
Devon and Cornwall

'CLOWTED CRAYME and nawe crayme put together, is eaten more for a sensuall apptyte than for any good nouryshment'—such was the severe verdict of a dietician of 1542. His words fell on deaf ears, however, for the Elizabethans continued to enjoy their clotted cream in the summer-time—both on its own and as an accompaniment to fruit dishes.

When making your own clotted cream, prepare it a day in advance and serve it with tea-time scones or Devonshire splits, or with whortle-berry and apple pie.

MAKING TIME: 50 MINUTES
STANDING TIME: 24 HOURS

INGREDIENTS FOR FOUR

3 pints (1·7 litres) milk
½ pint (275/300 ml.) cream

Mix the milk with the cream and pour into a wide saucepan. Cover with muslin to keep out dust, and leave to stand in a cool place, but not a refrigerator, for several hours until the cream has risen to the top.

Lift the pan very carefully to the stove so that the risen cream layer is not disturbed or broken up. Warm through on the lowest possible heat, on an asbestos mat if you like. Keep at this low heat for 45–50 minutes until the top of the cream is crinkled and golden-yellow.

Remove the pan from the stove, cover with the muslin and leave to stand for several hours or overnight in a cool place, but again, not a refrigerator. Then, using a slotted spoon, skim off the cream into a dish, allowing the milk to drain back into the pan. It can be used to make scones or pancakes.

CHOCOLATE SAUCE
Countrywide

POWDERED COCOA was first made in the Netherlands in 1828. It is today's improved version of the product that makes this dark, rich sauce so easy to prepare. Serve it hot or cold with ice-cream or sponge puddings. It keeps well in a refrigerator.

MAKING TIME: 30 MINUTES

INGREDIENTS FOR EIGHT TO TEN

6 oz. (175 g.) granulated sugar
¼ pint (150 ml.) water
2 oz. (50 g.) cocoa powder
1 tablespoon soft butter

Put the sugar and water in a saucepan over a low heat, and stir until the sugar dissolves. Bring to the boil and simmer for 1 minute. Take the pan off the heat and whisk in the cocoa powder until the sauce is smooth.

Leave to cool for 10–15 minutes, stirring from time to time. It will thicken as it cools. Whip in the butter to give the sauce a gloss.

APRICOT OR MARMALADE SAUCE
Countrywide

THE DELICATE, perfumed flavour of ripe apricots, captured in jam, comes through this simply made sauce. Serve it hot with milk puddings and cold with ice-cream or junket.

You can adapt the recipe to make Marmalade Sauce, full of the bitter-sweet taste that is far too good to confine to the breakfast table alone. Serve it hot with steamed sponges, suet puddings and milk puddings.

MAKING TIME: 10–15 MINUTES

INGREDIENTS FOR FOUR

2–3 rounded tablespoons apricot jam or marmalade
2 level tablespoons sugar
6 tablespoons white wine

Gently heat the jam or marmalade with the sugar and wine in a small saucepan for about 10 minutes, stirring from time to time to blend thoroughly. Rub through a sieve to rid the sauce of apricot skin or chunks of orange peel.

LEMON SAUCE
Countrywide

AS LONG AGO as the 2nd century lemons were prized for their health-giving properties, as well as for their flavour and fragrance. The Ancient Greek physician Galen recommended dried lemon peel as one of the best digestives for delicate constitutions.

England was slow to appreciate the medicinal value of lemons, but loved their flavour so much that they were used in almost every kind of dish. The Victorians and Edwardians used them in this sauce, which they served both hot and cold with puddings and plain cake. Today, it sharpens the flavour of steamed fruit puddings and sponge puddings.

MAKING TIME: 20 MINUTES

INGREDIENTS FOR FOUR TO SIX

4 oz. (100/125 g.) caster sugar
1 rounded tablespoon cornflour
¼ teaspoon salt
9 fl. oz. (250 ml.) water
Finely grated rind of 1 lemon
1 oz. (25 g.) butter, cut into small pieces
3 tablespoons lemon juice

Put the sugar, cornflour and salt in a saucepan and stir in the water a little at a time to make a smooth paste. Stir in the grated lemon rind and put the pan over a low heat.

Cook gently, stirring all the time, until the mixture simmers and thickens. Continue simmering for about a minute then remove from the heat. Beat in the butter pieces one at a time and stir in the lemon juice.

CUSTARD SAUCE
Countrywide

MILK AND EGGS were always to hand in the farmhouse kitchen, and it was quite natural for the farmer's wife to reach out and marry the two in warm, nourishing dishes.

From custards baked in pastry cases or in custard cups, evolved the pouring sauce that is the most popular and versatile companion to sweet puddings. Synthetic preparations cannot be compared with true custard, which is made from milk thickened with eggs.

Serve it with steamed or baked puddings, pies, tarts and stewed fruits.

MAKING TIME: 20 MINUTES

INGREDIENTS FOR SIX TO EIGHT

2 eggs
1 tablespoon vanilla sugar, or 1 tablespoon caster sugar and ½ teaspoon vanilla essence
1 pint (575/600 ml.) hot milk

Beat the eggs and sugar together in a 1½ pint (850 ml.) basin until well blended. Gradually stir in some of the hot milk, then strain the mixture into the rest of the hot milk.

Pour the mixture into the top of a double saucepan, and set over the bottom pan of simmering water.

Using a wooden spoon, stir the mixture constantly over a gentle heat until it thickens just enough to coat the back of the spoon. If vanilla essence is to be used, stir it into the thickened sauce.

Serve hot or cold. If serving cold, cover the custard and stir it occasionally as it cools to prevent skin from forming.

CARAMEL SAUCE
Countrywide

MOST PEOPLE assume that putting caramel syrup beneath baked custard to produce *crême caramel* is a French or Continental practice. But England has similar caramel-cream recipes dating from the 18th century.

Here the caramel syrup is the basis of a creamy sauce that is particularly good when chilled and served with ice-cream or apple dishes.

MAKING TIME: 1 HOUR

INGREDIENTS FOR FOUR

4 oz. (100/125 g.) white sugar
Boiling water
¼ pint (150 ml.) double cream

Put the sugar in a small saucepan. Add 2 tablespoons of the water and set the pan over a low heat, stirring until the sugar has completely dissolved. Bring the mixture to the boil, and boil it rapidly until it becomes a deep-golden colour. This will take 2–3 minutes.

Quickly remove the pan from the heat and pour in 2 fl. oz. (50 ml.) of boiling water. Put the pan over a low heat and dissolve the caramel mixture without allowing it to boil. This may take 15–20 minutes. When the caramel has dissolved, leave it to become cold before stirring it into the cream.

Whip to thicken the sauce slightly if you wish.

CUMBERLAND RUM BUTTER
Cumberland

ROMANTIC TALES of rum smuggling along the Cumberland coast play a part in the local history of rum butter. One woman, who took a broken cask of the illicit cargo rather than let it be wasted, found that it had dripped into the sugar and butter stored on her larder shelf. To such a happy accident, it is claimed, we owe this rich blend of rum and brown sugar with butter and spices.

In Cumberland, rum butter is traditionally served with oatcakes at christening parties, and with Christmas pudding. Extend its use by serving it also with warm mince pies, Coventry Godcakes and any steamed pudding containing dried fruits.

MAKING TIME: 15–20 MINUTES

INGREDIENTS FOR FOUR TO SIX

8 oz. (225 g.) soft unsalted butter
4 oz. (100/125 g.) soft, light brown sugar
¼ teaspoon freshly grated nutmeg
½ teaspoon lemon juice
3–4 tablespoons rum

Cream the butter until it is fluffy, then beat in the sugar, nutmeg and lemon juice.

Add the rum carefully drop by drop, beating in each drop thoroughly before adding the next so that the butter does not curdle.

BRANDY SAUCE
Countrywide

BRANDY WAS ONCE a less expensive drink than tea or coffee, and more easily obtained than a drink of clean, pure water.

Those days are long gone, and for us brandy is a precious ingredient to be used on special occasions. The flavour it gives to this sauce can make a party piece of a steamed sponge or suet pudding.

MAKING TIME: 25 MINUTES

INGREDIENTS FOR FOUR TO SIX

2 teaspoons cornflour
½ pint (275/300 ml.) milk
2 teaspoons caster sugar
2 egg yolks, beaten
4 tablespoons brandy

Mix the cornflour to a paste with 2 tablespoons of the milk. Heat the rest of the milk in a saucepan until it just reaches boiling point. Remove from the heat and stir in the cornflour paste. Bring to the boil, and boil for 5 minutes stirring constantly. Stir in the sugar and leave the sauce to cool for 5 minutes.

Stir in the beaten egg yolks and brandy. Put the pan over another pan of boiling water and stir continuously until the sauce thickens. Take great care that it does not boil, or it will curdle.

BRANDY BUTTER
Countrywide

BRANDY FIRST CAME into England in the 17th century, when it achieved instant popularity—and not just with those who drank it. Governments saw it as a profitable source of revenue through Customs duty, and little Cornish fishing ports saw it as a prime cargo to smuggle.

Throughout the country brandy butter became a traditional Christmas side dish to serve with Christmas pudding and warm mince pies. It is also ideal with steamed puddings. Serve it well chilled, either piled in a small dish or formed into small balls.

MAKING TIME: 10 MINUTES

INGREDIENTS FOR FOUR

4 oz. (100/125 g.) soft unsalted butter
2 tablespoons caster sugar
4 tablespoons brandy

Cream the butter and sugar together thoroughly until fluffy and pale. Work in the brandy, a few drops at a time, beating well after each addition, until completely absorbed.

RECIPES *from* OTHER LANDS

ITALY
Zabaglione

ITALIANS REGARD this hot golden froth, imbued with the distinctive flavour of Marsala, not only as a dessert but also as a restorative. The dish originated in Sicily, where the local grapes go to make the fortified Marsala wine. The dish gives a delightful lift to a simple meal.

PREPARATION TIME: ABOUT 10 MINUTES
COOKING TIME: 5 MINUTES

INGREDIENTS FOR FOUR

4 egg yolks
1 tablespoon caster sugar
6 tablespoons Marsala, warmed to blood heat

Put the egg yolks and sugar in the top of a small double saucepan and whisk them with a balloon whisk until they thicken enough to fall from the whisk in a broad ribbon.

Set the pan over the bottom half of the double saucepan, in which water is just simmering over a low heat. Make sure that the top pan does not touch the hot water, or crusty grains will form in the mixture.

Add the warm Marsala and whisk the mixture continuously over a low heat until it rises and forms a creamy foam that has noticeably thickened. Serve at once in warmed individual glasses with sponge finger biscuits.

For a cold Zabaglione, not quite authentic, but nevertheless delicious and good for keeping up to three days in a refrigerator, take the top pan from the double saucepan as soon as the mixture has thickened. Set it immediately in a large pan already half filled with ice cubes. Keep whisking vigorously until the Zabaglione is cold, then fold into it ¼ pint (150 ml.) of double cream, whipped thick but not stiff. Chill in a refrigerator until serving time.

This cream version can also be made with sweet white wine and used as a sauce with fresh strawberries, raspberries or sliced peaches.

FRANCE
Tarte aux Pommes

RESTING IN THE MEMORY of all who have travelled in France is a small, typical restaurant or *pâtisserie*, where there waits an open tart filled with carefully arranged wheels within wheels of finely sliced apples under a shining glaze.

The following version combines the incomparable taste and texture of the best English cooking apple with the characteristic crisp French filling.

PREPARATION TIME: 40 MINUTES
STANDING TIME: AT LEAST 2 HOURS
COOKING TIME: 30–35 MINUTES
PRE-HEAT THE OVEN TO 180°C (350°F)—GAS MARK 4

INGREDIENTS FOR SIX TO EIGHT

For the *pâte sucrée* (sweet pastry):
9 oz. (250 g.) plain flour
¼ teaspoon salt
3 oz. (75 g.) vanilla sugar
6 oz. (175 g.) soft butter
1 egg, beaten

For the filling:
1 lb. (450 g.) Bramley apples, peeled, cored and sliced
2 tablespoons sugar
1 tablespoon water
3–4 crisp dessert apples, peeled, cored and thinly sliced in crescents

For the glaze:
3 tablespoons apple jelly, apricot jam or honey with lemon juice

To make the pastry, sift the flour and salt into a heap on a cold working surface and make a well in the centre. Put the vanilla sugar, butter and egg together in the well and mix them to a paste with a knife or the hands. Gradually draw in the flour and work up a soft dough. Knead it lightly, then wrap it in greaseproof paper and chill in the refrigerator for 2 hours.

Meanwhile, cook the prepared Bramley apples gently with the sugar and water in a covered pan until they make a thick purée.

Roll out the pastry to line a 10 in. (25 cm.) flan ring. Prick the base in several places with a fork.

Spread the apple purée over the base, and on it arrange a circle of closely overlapped slices of dessert apple. One tip of each apple slice should touch the rim of the crust, and the other tip point towards the centre of the flan. Fill the centre of this circle with a smaller circle of slices radiating from the centre of the flan.

Bake the tart in the centre of the pre-heated oven for 30–35 minutes, until the crust is crisp and golden-brown and the apple slices soft. When the tart is cooked, remove it from the flan ring and stand it on a wire rack.

Brush the fruit over with the warm apple jelly. Or glaze with warmed, strained apricot jam, or honey melted with 2 teaspoons of lemon juice. Let the tart cool before serving.

If liked, serve with a bowl of lightly whipped cream.

USA
American Cheesecake

CURD CHEESECAKE in a pastry shell was well established in Britain in the 17th century, but its revived popularity owes a lot to American adaptations. The American Cheesecake has a biscuit crust, and is filled with cream cheese rather than curds.

For special occasions, top the filling with a compôte of cherries, crushed strawberries, blueberries, pineapple or apricots, or with chocolate curls or split almonds.

PREPARATION TIME: 50 MINUTES
SETTING TIME FOR THE CRUST: 2 HOURS
COOKING TIME: 1 HOUR
COOLING AND CHILLING TIME: AT LEAST 4 HOURS
PRE-HEAT THE OVEN TO 180°C (350°F)—GAS MARK 4

INGREDIENTS FOR SIX TO EIGHT

For the crust:
8 oz. (225 g.) wheatmeal or digestive biscuits
1 oz. (25 g.) caster sugar
4 oz. (100/125 g.) butter, melted

For the filling:
8 oz. (225 g.) cottage cheese and 8 oz. (225 g.) cream cheese, or 1 lb. (450 g.) cream cheese
4 oz. (100/125 g.) caster sugar
2 eggs, separated
¼ pint (150 ml.) sour cream
2 tablespoons plain flour
1 teaspoon vanilla essence
1 teaspoon grated lemon rind

For the topping:
1 lb. (450 g.) cooked, stoned black cherries in syrup
2 tablespoons cornflour
1 teaspoon lemon juice
Caster sugar (optional)

To prepare the crust, reduce the biscuits to crumbs in a liquidiser, or put them in a paper bag or between sheets of greaseproof paper and crush them into crumbs with a rolling pin. Put the crumbs in a bowl, mix in the sugar and gradually blend in the melted butter until it is absorbed by the crumbs. Spread the mixture over the base and sides of a well-greased 7–8 in. (18–20 cm.) flan dish, loose-bottomed cake tin or flan ring set on a baking tray. Use the back of a wooden spoon to press the crumbs into an even layer. Leave to set in the refrigerator for 2 hours.

For the filling, rub the cottage cheese, if used, through a coarse sieve into a bowl and blend it to a smooth consistency with the cream cheese, which should have been softened at room temperature. Beat in the sugar and the egg yolks, one at a time. Stir in the sour cream, flour, vanilla essence and lemon rind, and then beat thoroughly until the mixture is smooth and glossy. Whisk the egg whites until stiff but not dry, and fold them carefully into the cheese mixture, using a metal spoon.

Spoon the filling into the prepared pie crust and bake in the centre of the pre-heated oven for 1 hour. Leave to cool at room temperature.

For the topping, put the cherries in a pan with their juice; if necessary make this up with cold water to 6 fl. oz. (175 ml.). Use 2 tablespoons of the liquid to blend the cornflour to a smooth paste in a small basin. Add the lemon juice to the pan of cherries and bring to the boil over gentle heat. Stir in the cornflour paste and continue boiling for 5 minutes, stirring constantly until the mixture clears and thickens. Add sugar to taste.

Let the cherries cool slightly before spreading them over the top of the cheesecake. Chill in the refrigerator for at least 3 hours before serving.

USA or FRANCE

Baked Alaska or Omelette à la Norvégienne

The popularity of this pudding may be judged by the passion with which its invention is claimed by both France and America; gastronomes of the two countries have been disputing the point for well over a century, and there is no likelihood that either will ever drop their claim.

According to the Americans, its originator was New Englander Benjamin Thompson (1753–1814), a physicist so widely revered for his knowledge of gunpowder and cookery that he was knighted by George III, and created Count of Rumford, New Hampshire, by the Elector of Bavaria.

The French, on the other hand, date the dish from June 1866, when there was 'an exchange of civilities and information' between the cooks of the Chinese Mission and the master-chefs of Paris. On this occasion, it is believed, the confectionery chef of the Grand Hotel gained the secret of baking ice-cream in a light pastry from an oriental brother-craftsman.

Either way, we must be grateful. Few puddings are more delicious.

American desserts: Baked Alaska and Cheesecake topped with cherries.

Preparation Time: 20 minutes
Cooking Time: 3–5 minutes
Pre-heat the Oven to 240°C (475°F)—gas mark 9, or Pre-heat the Grill to very hot

Ingredients for Four to Six

- *1 sponge cake (see p. 278) prepared as deep sponge cake but in a tin 8 in. (20 cm.) in diameter*
- *1 tablespoon brandy or liqueur (optional)*
- *1–1½ pints (575–850 ml.) vanilla ice-cream*
- *4 egg whites*
- *¼ teaspoon cream of tartar*
- *3 oz. (75 g.) caster sugar*

Set the sponge cake on an ovenproof dish large enough to leave at least a 1 in. (2·5 cm.) clear margin all round. Sprinkle the brandy or liqueur, if used, over the sponge cake.

Shape the ice-cream into a domed circle on a piece of kitchen foil. It should be a little smaller than the sponge, so that about 1 in. (2·5 cm.) of the cake is left clear all round. Return the ice-cream to freeze while preparing the meringue.

Put the egg whites in a bowl and whisk until frothy. Add the cream of tartar and half the sugar, and continue whisking until the egg whites will stand in firm peaks. Finally fold in the remaining sugar.

Working quickly, arrange the moulded ice-cream on the sponge base and spread the meringue over the top and sides to form an even, airtight covering. Any left-over meringue can be quickly piped on in a decorative pattern.

Put the pudding in the pre-heated oven, just above the centre, or under the very hot grill. Cook it for 3–5 minutes so that the meringue is pale brown but the ice-cream is still firm. Serve at once, on its own or with whipped cream.

HOT AND COLD SWEET PUDDINGS

SWEETS AND SAVOURIES were served as part of the same course from medieval times until the 18th century—quince pie and almond cream alongside roast beef or stewed venison, for example. People took what they fancied from the selection of dishes.

At the Lord of the Manor's table, courses were often rounded off with a 'subtlety' made from marchpane (marzipan) —a highly adorned and gilded model, sometimes with written comments (subtleties) attached. After it had been paraded and admired it was broken up and eaten. The peasant's sweetmeat was more likely a bowl of curds and honey or, in season, wild strawberries and cream.

During the 16th century, the final sweetmeat selection developed into a final course, originally called the banquet and later known as dessert.

Pies, Tarts and Fruit in Syrup

HIGHLY spiced fruit boiled to a thick purée was a medieval and Elizabethan tartstuff, or filling, for raw fruit was considered bad for health. In the 14th-century *Canterbury Tales*, Chaucer tells of 'a fine dish of apples roasted in galingale syrup and strewn with sugar candy'.

Hard fruits such as pears were thoroughly baked in pies, or were simmered in syrup to make a 'compost' (or compote) for winter eating.

Sweet pies and tarts became more widely enjoyed from the 17th century. This was when sugar became easier to get and cheaper, and as a result the use of spices declined.

PIES AND TARTS

A pie is two pastry layers enclosing a filling—or a filling in a deep container covered by a pastry lid.

A tart or flan is a flat pastry case containing a filling. Most are open with no lid, but some have lids.

Pies and tarts are usually made with shortcrust pastry (see p. 217). Whatever type of pastry you use, success depends on the same basic techniques. These are mainly the same as for savoury pies and tarts (see p. 216), but the following techniques apply only to sweet pies and tarts.

Tips for making sweet pies and tarts
Hard fruit such as gooseberries or whole plums will take longer to cook than the pastry. Soften the fruit a little by cooking it gently for 5–6 minutes before filling the pie or tart.

Do not place a pastry lid on a hot pie filling. Allow the filling to cool first or the pastry will become soggy.

Do not leave a final layer of sugar on top of any pie or tart filling, mix it in with the fruit. Otherwise the pastry lid or decorations will become soggy.

Glaze a pie lid by brushing it with cold water or milk, and sprinkling with caster sugar before you put it in the oven.

If you want to give it a more sparkling finish, take the pastry from the oven when it is almost baked and brush the lid with lightly beaten egg white, then dredge with caster sugar. Give the pastry a few more minutes in the oven to set the egg.

For tarts or flans with a custard filling, brush the base well with egg white before you add the filling. This seals the pastry and stops the custard mixture leaking through.

FRUIT IN SYRUP

Fresh or dried fruit cooked in syrup and served cold—a compote—is a popular way of serving fruit. Sometimes the fruit is cooked in a mixture of syrup and alcohol.

Choose the best-quality fruit available.

Select fruit of the same size and ripeness, to give a good appearance.

Make a syrup of the sugar and water first, then gently poach the fruit in it. Because you do not have to stir in the sugar, the fruit is less likely to be broken up.

Use the quantities of sugar and water stated in the recipe. The average syrup comprises 8 oz. (225 g.) of sugar to 1 pint (575/600 ml.) of water. The cooking time depends on the ripeness of the fruit.

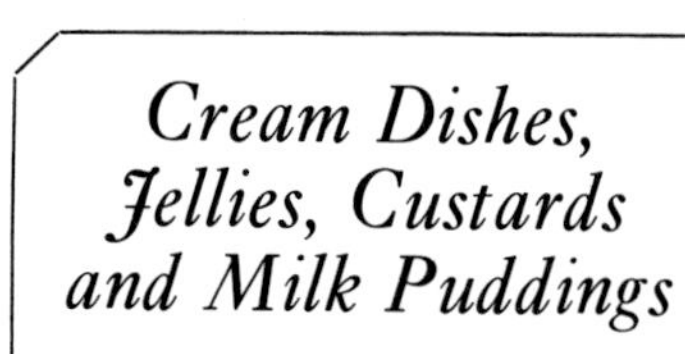

Cream Dishes, Jellies, Custards and Milk Puddings

MILK AND EGGS were the 'white meats' of medieval peasants. With a few sheep or goats or a cow on the common grazing land, they were able to enjoy a dish of curds, cream, buttermilk or junket.

From Tudor times, the increasing

enclosure of land led to the rise of country estates and wealthy farmers. Far more milk, butter and cream began to be produced, much of it sold to the towns. Rich cream dishes—such as whitepots, fools, flummeries, syllabubs, trifles—became popular among the better off.

Rosewater was commonly used to flavour creams, and also the sweet jellies stiffened with melted shavings of hartshorn (antler) or isinglass, that had developed from savoury jellies into a popular sweetmeat.

Thickening, setting and chilling
The main thickening and setting agents used in making cream dishes (such as fools, mousses and ice-creams), jellies and custards are cream, milk, eggs, gelatine and sugar in varying proportions.

Cream dishes and jellies—and sometimes custards and milk puddings—are set firm by chilling in a cool larder or refrigerator. Ice-creams and water ices (sorbets) are set by freezing.

CREAM DISHES AND JELLIES

Fools and ice-creams generally have equal quantities of whipped cream and custard combined with puréed fruit (in fools) or flavouring (in ice-creams). The more you increase the proportion of cream to custard, the richer the dish.

Water ices are sugar syrups flavoured with fruit juice, purée or other flavourings and sometimes thickened with egg whites.

Syllabubs are cream and sugar flavoured with wine, brandy or sherry. Trifles are similar, but in addition include jam and sponge cakes or macaroons. Mousses are flavoured cream mixtures thickened with eggs and stiffened with gelatine.

Flummeries are flavoured creams stiffened with gelatine or sometimes oatmeal.

Home-made clear jellies (as distinct from fruit-jelly preserves) consist of fruit juice, water, granulated sugar and gelatine. Jellies with milk or eggs and perhaps a little cream added are described as opaque.

Hints for using cream
Always use good, fresh cream—either double or whipping.

Never overwhip cream, it makes the final texture heavy. The cream is sufficiently whipped when it will remain in peaks lifted up with the whisk.

For fools, mousses and ice-creams, try to have the cream, custard and any fruit purée similar in consistency. If they are not, always add the thinner one to the thicker one.

For a cream mixture stiffened with gelatine, such as a mousse, add the dissolved gelatine while it is still lukewarm. If you add it too hot, the cream will not be so light in texture. If you add it too cold, it may stay in tiny lumps or specks.

How to dissolve gelatine
Gelatine is a natural substance that, when dissolved in hot liquid and added to other ingredients, cools to form a jelly. It is widely used as a setting agent and is available in powder or leaf form, although the powdered form is more common.

Six sheets of leaf gelatine equal 1 oz. (25 g.) of powdered gelatine. Both dissolve easily, but need careful handling to ensure good texture.

1 Use the correct proportions given in the instructions on the packet.
2 Wash leaf gelatine in cold water, soak it in cold water for 15–20 minutes until soft, then squeeze lightly to get rid of excess water.
3 Always add the powdered or leaf gelatine to the dissolvent liquid: do not pour the liquid on the gelatine.
4 Heat gently—overheating or boiling will produce a gummy, unusable mass. Gelatine dissolved in milk will curdle if it boils, because of the action of the acid used in refining.

Tips for making jellies
Jellies that will be left to set in a cool larder need slightly more gelatine than those to be set in a refrigerator. Increase the amount of gelatine by about one-third, or slightly reduce the quantity of liquid used.

When making milk jelly, ensure that the milk and syrup are both tepid before combining. If the temperatures are different, the milk may curdle.

Stir milk jelly occasionally until it starts to thicken, otherwise it will separate into thick and thin layers.

Eat jellies within 24 hours of making. They tend to toughen if kept too long, especially in a refrigerator.

Make sure that jelly for decoration is firm. Chop it evenly but not too small. If you chop it too small it will lose its sparkle.

Moulding and chilling
Aluminium, tin or tin-lined copper moulds give a sharper design and are more easily unmoulded than earthenware or china.

Rinse the mould or dish under the cold tap and shake off excess water before you fill it. This makes it easier to unmould the pudding.

Before pouring a mixture into a mould or dish, stir gently to make sure the ingredients are evenly distributed.

Do not over-refrigerate fools, jellies or other moulds; it detracts from their flavour. They generally take 2–3 hours to set in a refrigerator.

To unmould any chilled pudding, dip the mould up to the rim in hot water for 5–10 seconds. Rinse the serving plate under the cold tap for a moment, shake off any surplus water, then invert the mould on to the serving plate.

Give it a slight shake to free the mixture. The slightly moist serving plate allows you to slide the pudding to another position easily.

Making cream or water ices
The amount of sugar you use is crucial. Too little will leave the ice hard and tasteless, too much will prevent it setting.

If an ice-cream recipe recommends milk instead of cream, use evaporated milk as an alternative. It gives a creamier result.

Before adding a fruit purée as flavouring, strain it to remove any skin or seeds.

Freeze ices quickly to give them a good texture—slow freezing produces large crystals that are difficult to break up. Set the freezer or refrigerator freezing compartment at its maximum setting 1 hour before the mixture is ready for freezing.

Chill both the equipment and the ingredients you are using before you start.

Check progress from time to time during freezing. When the ice starts to thicken, stir the mixture from the edge of the container towards the middle to break up the ice crystals forming.

If the recipe recommends it, put the mixture into a bowl and beat it before returning it to the freezer.

Freezing time varies with different appliances, but is usually 6–8 hours in a refrigerator or about 4 hours in a freezer.

Before serving ices, move them from the freezer or refrigerator freezing compartment to a refrigerator shelf to soften. Move water ices 30 minutes before serving, ice-creams 1–1½ hours before.

Custards and Milk Puddings

Many hot and cold puddings are based on custard, which is a mixture of eggs and milk. Bread and butter pudding, for example, is a custard mixture with other ingredients.

Custard also makes a dish on its own—steamed, baked or used as a sauce. Custard sauce can be made with commercially prepared powder, which is simpler to use but does not give the same texture and flavour.

Milk puddings generally consist of milk, a cereal (such as semolina) and sometimes eggs and flavouring.

How to make good custard
Always use fresh eggs and milk. For a basic egg-custard sauce or a baked custard, use 2 egg yolks or 1 whole egg to 9 fl. oz. (250 ml.) of milk.

For a steamed egg custard, which has to support its own weight when turned out, use 3 whole eggs to 7 fl. oz. (200 ml.) of milk.

Cook custard mixtures with just enough heat to thicken them without curdling. Do not allow them to boil.

When making a baked custard, place the pie dish in a roasting tin containing enough cold water to come halfway up the side of the pie dish (an arrangement known as a bain-marie). This ensures slow, even cooking.

To make egg-custard sauce, heat the milk until it simmers, then pour a little on to the beaten eggs, stirring continuously. Strain the egg and milk mixture back into the pan with the rest of the milk, then add the chosen flavouring and sweeten to taste.

Hints for Beating Eggs

Eggs are beaten to increase their volume by drawing in air. Use them as soon as they are ready, before they lose their air.

When beating whole eggs by hand, break them into a bowl, not a cup, so that plenty of air can be taken in. Turn them over vigorously with upward movements of the fork, whisk or spoon. When whisking eggs, stand the bowl on a damp cloth to stop it sliding about.

To mix egg yolks and sugar, beat the eggs first, add the sugar, then continue beating until the mixture drops in broad ribbons.

Always strain beaten eggs through a sieve before adding them to a smooth-textured dish such as a fool or custard. This removes any 'threads', specks or small particles of shell.

When making meringues, never use fresh egg whites for whisking, they will not whisk to the necessary stiffness and volume. Use eggs that are at least 48 hours old.

To whisk egg whites, use a clean, dry bowl that is deep and rounded enough for the whisk to be in constant contact with the whites.

Add a pinch of salt to the whites—this makes them stiffen quicker and reduces whisking time. Whisking is completed when the whites can be raised into stiff peaks.

Folding in Use a metal spoon to fold beaten egg whites into a mixture. It will cause less air disturbance than a thicker, wooden spoon.

To fold in egg whites, pile them on top of the mixture and carefully draw part of the mixture from the bottom of the bowl over them, making sure they do not lose their air content. Continue doing this until all the whites are incorporated.

The best method of cooking is in a double saucepan with the outer saucepan half filled with gently boiling water and the custard mixture in the inner saucepan. As an alternative you can use a heatproof bowl fitted into the rim of a saucepan containing boiling water.

Stir the custard and heat until it thickens enough to just coat the back of a spoon. It always thickens a little on cooling.

Mild acids such as sherry or lemon juice should be added slowly at the end of the cooking time, to prevent curdling.

Tips for making milk puddings
Milk puddings are often thought of as nursery puddings, but a little cream or chopped fruit enriches them.

Use 2 oz. (50 g.) of cereal to 1 pint (575/600 ml.) of milk. When using ground rice or cornflour, mix the powder to a smooth paste with a little of the cold milk, heat the rest of the milk and pour on to the mixture, stir and then put in the pan for cooking.

Cook slowly and gently to produce a good, creamy texture. If the starchy contents are not thoroughly cooked, the pudding may be indigestible.

If adding eggs, wait until the pudding is thoroughly cooked, otherwise the heat needed for further cooking may curdle the eggs.

Let the pudding cool a little before you add the eggs, particularly if you are going to fold in stiffly whisked egg whites. Re-heat gently until the egg is cooked.

To give puddings a creamier texture, you can, if liked, use half fresh milk and half evaporated milk.

You can make milk puddings in shapes and moulds and turn them out on to a dish when cold and set (see Moulding and chilling, p. 257). The proportion of cereal to milk needs to be greater than for soft puddings.

Batters and Steamed Puddings

Ovals of apple dipped in a batter of egg yolks, flour and ale—the ancestor of our fruit fritters—were a popular dish in medieval times. So were 'trayne rostes'—strings of dried fruit threaded together, wound round a spit and basted with batter.

Early pancake batter was often made with water. Milk was thought to produce tough and sticky pancakes. But by the 18th century, recipes called for milk and even cream, and at the end of the 19th century *crêpes suzettes*, pancakes flamed in brandy, were introduced, probably from France.

The British boiled pudding had emerged by the early 17th century. It was discovered that fillings which had formerly been boiled in animal-gut containers could be boiled more conveniently in cloths.

Boiled puddings cooked in a pot over an open fire became a national dish. Varieties ranged from the fragile Quaking Pudding, mainly of cream and eggs, to the festive Figgy Pudding and the heavy, filling suet and dried-fruit puddings such as Plum Duff and Spotted Dog that helped to sustain the farmworker.

BATTERS

Batter is a mixture of flour, liquid (milk, water, oil or melted butter) and eggs. It can be baked, as in Tewkesbury Saucer Batter, fried in a thin film, as in Pancakes, used to coat fried food, as in Banana Fritters, or steamed, as in Cherry Batter Pudding.

How to make a basic batter

1 Sieve the flour to remove any lumps and incorporate air. Sieve any salt in the recipe along with the flour.

2 Make a well in the centre of the flour and break the egg into it. Pour a little of the liquid on to the egg and beat them together, gradually working in some of the flour.

3 Continue slowly working in the liquid and flour, beating to incorporate air and give a smooth, creamy texture. Aim to have about one-third of the liquid left by the time all the flour is worked in.

4 Before you work in the rest of the liquid, dispose of lumps by beating well with a wire whisk for a minute or two. Lumps are more difficult to get rid of once all the liquid is included. If you have no whisk or the lumps are persistent, sieve the mixture.

5 Work in the rest of the liquid, beating continuously. The final batter should have the consistency of single cream.

6 There is no need to leave the completed batter to rest. If it has to stand for any length of time, stir it before use.

Facts about batter

Thin, cream-like pancake batters include slightly more liquid than fritter batters, which must be thick enough to coat the food without running off.

Batter is lighter if plenty of cool air is taken into the mixture before cooking. This is done by sieving the flour and beating the mixture.

A little oil—usually about 2 teaspoons to 2 oz. (50 g.) of flour—in fritter batter gives it a crisp finish. Pour the oil into the flour well in place of the egg used in basic batter. Then start working in the liquid.

Whisked egg whites used in fritter batter give a lighter mixture. Fold them in evenly with a metal spoon once you have beaten the flour and liquid to a smooth cream.

Cooking with batter

If the cooking temperature is too low, batter will be heavy and 'damp'. Make sure the oven temperature is correct for the recipe before baking a batter in the oven. Keep steamed batter puddings at boiling point.

Deep frying Before frying batter in fat or oil, make sure the temperature is 190°C (375°F). To check, drop a cube of white bread in the fat—it should turn golden-brown in just under 60 seconds.

Shallow frying The fat or oil is hot enough when a slight haze rises from it. Before frying pancake batter, drain off any excess fat so that only a thin, smooth film remains to cover the pan. Pools of fat make the pancakes soggy.

STEAMED PUDDINGS

Today it is simpler to steam puddings in a covered basin than to boil them in a cloth. If you want to try the traditional method, tie the pudding in white sheeting or calico that has been scalded and floured to help seal it. But a characteristic of cloth-boiled puddings is their damp outer crust.

Steaming is particularly suitable for puddings made with suet pastry, they are lighter and more digestible than when cooked by other methods.

This applies to puddings with a suet-pastry lining enclosing a filling or to suet mixtures. Steamed sponge puddings have a more feathery texture than oven-baked sponge cakes.

Avoid using apples that are too juicy in a suet-crust filling. If using a dried-fruit filling, swell the fruit with boiling water, then drain, before filling the pudding.

Puddings are covered during steaming to prevent water splashes or steam entering the mixture and making it soggy.

Preparing the basin

1 Grease the inside of the basin, using a pastry brush or piece of crumpled greaseproof paper.

2 Line the basin with pastry if necessary (see p. 221), or place any topping such as jam, sugar, currants, at the bottom of the basin.

3 Fill sponge and suet mixtures to within ½ in. (1·5 cm.) of the top, batters about two-thirds full.

4 Cut out a square of greaseproof paper or aluminium foil for the basin cover, and grease one side with a brush, a piece of greaseproof paper or a flat-bladed knife.

5 Place the square greased side down over the top of the basin and make a 1 in. (2·5 cm.) pleat across the top to allow for expansion of the pudding.

6 Tie the covering down with fine string wound twice round the basin under the rim, then looped over the top as a handle.

Steaming

1 Puddings are best steamed in a two-tier steamer. Three-quarters fill the lower saucepan with boiling water and place the covered pudding basin in the top saucepan, which has a perforated base.

2 If you have no steamer, place the basin in a saucepan containing enough boiling water to come halfway up the side of the basin.

3 For both methods, the lid must be tight fitting and the water kept steadily at boiling point—with large bubbles agitating the surface. But do not let the water boil too violently, or the water level will go down very fast.

4 If the pudding is to be steamed for several hours—a Christmas pudding, for example—add 1 tablespoon of vinegar or lemon juice to the water to prevent discoloration of the pan.

5 Top up the saucepan with boiling water from time to time to maintain the level. Do not add cold water, as this will interrupt the boiling.

6 Follow the cooking time given in the recipe. There is no way of testing whether or not the pudding is cooked. If you use a pressure cooker, follow the maker's instructions.

7 Before turning out the cooked pudding, slide a round-bladed knife round the edge, against the basin side

8 To turn out, invert the pudding on to a warmed serving plate big enough to accommodate any sauce that may run down from the pudding crown.

Re-heating steamed puddings

Most steamed puddings, other than batter puddings, can be re-heated. To keep moist, add 1 tablespoon of milk to a jam or similar steamed sponge pudding, and 1 tablespoon of milk or golden syrup to a suet mixture or a suet-crust filling.

There is no need to cover the basin with greaseproof or foil. Steam in a steamer or over a saucepan of boiling water (with a plate or saucer covering the basin) for 20–30 minutes.

Alternatively, place the moistened pudding in a covered ovenproof dish and heat in the oven at 180°C (350°F)—gas mark 4 for about 30 minutes.

Suet and sponge mixtures can also be sliced and fried gently in a little butter, then served with a sprinkling of sugar or golden syrup.

BREADS, CAKES AND BISCUITS

CONTAINING

NUMEROUS *Useful* FAMILY RECIPES

for PLAIN & ENRICHED BREADS & CAKES, SCONES & BISCUITS

& all other TEATIME DELIGHTES

PAGES 262–292

AND

A SELECTION of RECIPES from OTHER LANDS

PAGES 293–294

AND WITH

DIRECTIONS *for* BASIC METHODS

for all kinds of Kneading, Rising, Mixing and Shaping of Baked Wares to Perfection

PAGES 295–301

OLD-FASHIONED HERB BREAD
Countrywide

HERBS HAVE BEEN USED to make food more palatable for 5,000 years and more. Stone Age men in Britain used charlock, white goosefoot, knotgrass, nettles and plantain to flavour a cooked mixture of cereals and weeds reaped with the grain.

But it was in Tudor times that herbs reached the height of their popularity. The poet and chronicler Thomas Tusser wrote in 1557 that no kitchen garden was complete unless it produced more than 40 different herbs.

This recipe is for a distinctly different loaf that is very light and open in texture. It makes an ideal accompaniment to cheese and pâté and is excellent with cold meats. The herbs can be varied to suit individual tastes. A mixture of green-dried marjoram and thyme is a good alternative to tarragon.

PREPARATION TIME: 15 MINUTES
RISING TIME: 30–35 MINUTES
COOKING TIME: 25–30 MINUTES
PRE-HEAT THE OVEN TO 180°C (350°F)—GAS MARK 4

INGREDIENTS FOR TWO SMALL LOAVES

1 large egg, beaten
8 fl. oz. (225 ml.) warm milk (see p. 296)
¾ oz. (20 g.) fresh yeast
1 tablespoon cooking oil
3 level teaspoons sugar
1 level teaspoon dried tarragon
12 oz. (350 g.) strong white flour
1½ level teaspoons salt
Fennel seed for sprinkling

Herb Bread—a light, open-textured loaf that goes well with cheese.

Combine the beaten egg with the warm milk and use 3 tablespoons of this liquid to mix the yeast to a smooth thin paste. Stir in the remaining egg and milk. Add the oil, sugar and tarragon.

Mix the flour and salt together and sieve three-quarters of it into the liquid ingredients. Beat well with a wooden spoon for 4–5 minutes to make a creamy, soft dough. Stir in the remaining flour and divide the mixture equally between two well-greased 1 lb. (450 g.) loaf tins. Long and narrow tins are best. Cover the tins with greased polythene and put in a warm place for the dough to rise for 30–35 minutes.

Sprinkle the top of the loaves with fennel seed and bake in the preheated oven for 25–30 minutes. If you prefer, put all the mixture into a long and narrow 2 lb. (900 g.) loaf tin, well greased, and bake for 35 minutes.

BATH BUNS
Countrywide

THE EXACT ORIGIN of the Bath Bun is not known, but there exists an early-17th-century recipe for Bath cake which has the same ingredients. Those who live in the city from which it takes its name claim that the genuine Bath Bun can be bought only there, and call those made outside, the 'London Bath Bun'.

Originally, Bath Buns were made without fruit, but with added spices. Caraway comfits—sugar-coated caraway seeds—were used as an ingredient, and to decorate the bun.

This present-day alternative looks like a rock cake and is one of the easiest of fermented buns to make.

PREPARATION TIME: 45 MINUTES
FERMENTING, RISING AND RESTING TIME: 2¼ HOURS
COOKING TIME: 10 MINUTES
PRE-HEAT THE OVEN TO 230°C (450°F)—GAS MARK 8

INGREDIENTS FOR 16 BUNS

For the ferment:

1 large egg, beaten
About ¼ pint (150 ml.) warm water (see p. 296)
2 rounded teaspoons sugar
¾ oz. (20 g.) fresh yeast
2 oz. (50 g.) strong white flour

For the dough:

10 oz. (275 g.) strong white flour
1 oz. (25 g.) granulated sugar
3 oz. (75 g.) softened butter
4 oz. (100/125 g.) sultanas

4 oz. (100/125 g.) roughly crushed lump sugar, or coffee crystals
1 oz. (25 g.) chopped, candied lemon peel
Finely grated rind of 1 lemon
A little beaten egg to glaze
Roughly crushed lump sugar, or coffee crystals for sprinkling

To prepare the ferment, stir the beaten egg and warm water together to make up 7½ fl. oz. (215 ml.) of liquid, comfortably warm to the touch. Dissolve the sugar in it and use 3 tablespoons of this liquid to mix the yeast to a smooth paste in a large bowl. Stir in the remaining liquid and whisk in the flour to make a smooth batter. Cover the bowl with polythene and put in a warm place to rise for 30 minutes.

To make the dough, sieve the flour on to a working surface or into a large mixing bowl and make a well in the centre. Put in the granulated sugar and pour on the ferment. Mix the sugar into the ferment until dissolved, then gradually draw in the flour and work the ingredients together to form a stiff dough.

Knead in (see p. 296) the soft butter a little at a time until the dough has a silky look. Shape it into a ball, put it in a warm, greased bowl, cover with a greased sheet of polythene and stand in a warm place for 1 hour, or until the dough has nearly trebled in bulk.

Turn the dough on to a working surface and put the sultanas, crushed lump sugar, candied peel and lemon rind on top. Knead them in until they are evenly distributed and the dough has a smooth texture. Cover it with polythene and leave for 5 minutes.

Divide the dough into 16 pieces by pulling and tearing, not cutting. Put the rough pieces, well spaced out, on a lightly buttered, warmed baking sheet, cover with the polythene and put to rise in a warm place for 15–20 minutes.

Brush the buns over lightly with beaten egg, sprinkle a little crushed lump sugar on top and put to rise, uncovered, for 20 minutes. Bake in the pre-heated oven for about 10 minutes, or until golden-brown.

Bara Brith, the 'speckled bread' of Wales, is rich with spices and fruit.

BARA BRITH
North Wales

IN WALES, cottage and farmhouse alike have been famed for many years for their sweet breads. Bara Brith—the name means 'speckled bread'—was originally made for special occasions such as Harvest, Easter and Christmas. A North Wales speciality, it has a rich, fruity mixture under a firm, nutty crust.

PREPARATION TIME: 20 MINUTES
RISING TIME: 1½ HOURS
COOKING TIME: 35 MINUTES
PRE-HEAT THE OVEN TO 180°C (350°F)—GAS MARK 4

INGREDIENTS FOR ONE LARGE LOAF
10 oz. (275 g.) strong white flour
1 level teaspoon salt
¾ oz. (20 g.) lard
1 oz. (25 g.) sugar
½ level teaspoon ground mixed spice
1 large egg, beaten
¼ pint (150 ml.) warm water (see p. 296)
¾ oz. (20 g.) fresh yeast
8 oz. (225 g.) currants
4 oz. (100/125 g.) sultanas
1 oz. (25 g.) chopped, mixed dried peel

Sieve the flour and salt on to a working surface or into a large mixing bowl. Rub in the lard and make a well in the centre. Mix the sugar and spice together and put into the well.

Combine the beaten egg with the warm water and use 3 tablespoons of it to mix the yeast to a smooth, thin paste, then stir in the rest of the liquid. Pour over the sugar in the well, mix vigorously to blend, then knead well (see p. 296) to make a smooth, elastic dough. Mix together the currants, sultanas and peel and knead lightly into the dough.

Mould the dough into a round or long shape, as you prefer, and put on a greased baking sheet or in a greased 2 lb. (900 g.) loaf tin. Cover with greased polythene and put in a gently warm place to rise for 1½ hours. Bake in the pre-heated oven for 35 minutes.

FARTHING BUNS
Countrywide

THE COPPER FARTHING was introduced into our coinage in 1613 during the reign of James I. The name farthing—from the Anglo-Saxon *feorthing*, or fourth part of something—had been given to earlier coins, but it was the copper farthing that gave the bun its name, for a farthing would buy one of the sweet buttery buns in Victorian times. The coin ceased to be legal tender in January 1961, but fortunately the bun is still with us.

PREPARATION TIME: 50 MINUTES

FERMENTING, RISING AND RESTING TIME: ABOUT 2 HOURS

COOKING TIME: 10 MINUTES

PRE-HEAT THE OVEN TO 220°C (425°F)—GAS MARK 7

INGREDIENTS FOR ABOUT 40 SMALL BUNS

For the ferment:

1 large egg, beaten
About 7½ fl. oz. (215 ml.) warm water (see p. 296)
1 oz. (25 g.) fresh yeast
4 oz. (100/125 g.) strong white flour
½ oz. (15 g.) sugar

For the dough:

14 oz. (400 g.) strong white flour
¼ teaspoon salt
3 oz. (75 g.) granulated sugar
2 oz. (50 g.) butter, soft but not oily
4 oz. (100/125 g.) mixed dried fruit
1½ oz. (40 g.) Demerara sugar
Melted butter for brushing over
Granulated sugar for sprinkling

To prepare the ferment, combine the beaten egg with enough warm water to make up ½ pint (275/300 ml.). Mix the yeast to a smooth paste in 3 tablespoons of the liquid. Add the rest of the liquid and whisk in the flour and sugar to make a smooth batter. Cover and put in a warm place for 30 minutes.

To make the dough, sieve the flour and salt on to a working surface or into a large mixing bowl. Make a well in the centre, put the granulated sugar in it and pour on the ferment. Stir until the sugar has dissolved, then gradually draw in the flour and mix vigorously to blend to a soft, sticky dough.

Knead (see p. 296) the soft butter into it thoroughly until the dough looks smooth and silky in texture. Mould it into a ball, put it in a warmed and lightly greased bowl, cover with greased polythene and put in a warm place to rise for 45 minutes.

Turn out the risen dough on to a working surface, knock out any air bubbles and knead in the dried fruit and Demerara sugar. Cover the dough with the greased polythene and leave it on the working surface to rest for 5 minutes.

Roll out the dough to a rectangle about ¼ in. (5 mm.) thick and brush melted butter over the surface, starting at one of the shorter ends of the rectangle and continuing over two-thirds of the sheet of dough. Fold the unbuttered third over the centre third of the dough, and the remaining third over these two. Cover the dough again and leave it to rest on the working surface for 10 minutes.

Roll out the dough again into a rectangle no more than ¼ in. (5 mm.) thick. Brush over all the surface with melted butter and sprinkle on granulated sugar. Cut the dough into pieces about 3 in. (8 cm.) long and 1 in. (2·5 cm.) wide.

Arrange the pieces ½ in. (1·5 cm.) apart on a greased baking sheet. Cover with greased polythene and put in a warm place to rise for 35 minutes. Bake in the pre-heated oven for about 10 minutes or until golden-brown.

WHOLEMEAL BREAD
Countrywide

MAN HAS BEEN MAKING BREAD for well over 8,000 years. By the Roman period, eating white bread carried social distinction, and the rougher, darker kinds were left for the poorer classes. 'In the 18th century,' writes the historian G. M. Trevelyan, 'Englishmen of all classes became so dainty as to insist on refined wheat bread . . . This new demand began in the town, but spread to the country, even to paupers.'

George III, who ate brown bread at his 1 o'clock dinner, was somewhat reproachfully given the title of 'Brown George' by some of his subjects.

It was not until the mid-19th century that doctors and dieticians started to value and recommend the natural bran that wholemeal flour retains.

PREPARATION TIME: 25 MINUTES

RISING TIME: 1 HOUR 35 MINUTES

COOKING TIME: 35–40 MINUTES

PRE-HEAT THE OVEN TO 235°C (460°F)—GAS MARK 8½

INGREDIENTS FOR ONE LARGE LOAF

1 lb. (450 g.) wholemeal flour
1 rounded teaspoon salt
¼ oz. (7 g.) lard
1 level teaspoon brown sugar
½ pint (275/300 ml.) warm water (see p. 296)
½ oz. (15 g.) fresh yeast
Wholemeal flour for sprinkling

Mix the flour and salt together on a working surface or in a large mixing bowl. Rub in the lard and make a well in the centre. Dissolve the sugar in the water and use 2 tablespoons of it to mix the yeast to a smooth paste. Add the rest of the water and pour into the well.

Mix vigorously to blend in the flour, then knead (see p. 296) for 5 minutes to make a smooth, elastic dough. Shape it into a ball and put in a warm, greased bowl. Cover with greased polythene and set in a warm place to rise for 1 hour.

Turn out the risen dough on to a working surface and knock out any air. Mould the dough into a ball and put it on a warmed and greased baking sheet. Cover with the polythene and put back to rise in a warm place for 35 minutes, cutting a cross in it ½ in. (1·5 cm.) deep with a sharp blade after 20 minutes.

Bake in the pre-heated oven for 35–40 minutes.

CRUSTY WHITE BREAD
Countrywide

THERE IS NO NEED to yearn for the yeasty aroma that used to float in the air round the village bakery. The domestic kitchen is the place for making crusty bread full of flavour. There, time can still be given for the yeast to ferment slowly and for the dough to cook thoroughly—ideals that many factory bakers have to forgo in order to increase output and cut costs.

Bake the bread in a tin or make it into one of the traditional British loaf shapes.

PREPARATION TIME: 35 MINUTES
RISING TIME: 3 HOURS 40 MINUTES
COOKING TIME: ABOUT 45 MINUTES
PRE-HEAT THE OVEN TO 225°C (435°F)—GAS MARK 7½

INGREDIENTS FOR TWO LOAVES

1¾ lb. (800 g.) strong white flour
2 level teaspoons salt
½ oz. (15 g.) lard
1 oz. (25 g.) fresh yeast
¾ pint (450 ml.) warm water (see p. 296)

Wholemeal and Crusty White Bread—perfect at teatime or breakfast.

Sieve the flour and salt on to a working surface or into a large mixing bowl, rub in the lard and make a well in the centre. Mix the yeast to a smooth paste with 1 tablespoon of the water, stir into the rest of the water and pour into the well. Draw in the flour gradually, mixing vigorously to blend well. Knead (see p. 296) for 5 minutes or more to make a stiff dough of an even, springy texture. Shape into a ball, place in a warm, greased bowl, cover with greased polythene and stand in a warm place to rise for 2 hours.

Turn out the dough on to a working surface and knock out the air bubbles. Knead again until smooth and springy, reshape into a ball, put back in the bowl, cover and put to rise again for 1 hour.

Divide the dough in half and mould each piece to fit a warmed and greased 2 lb. (900 g.) tin. Cover the tins with greased polythene and put in a warm place to rise for 40 minutes.

Bake in the pre-heated oven for about 45 minutes.

Instead of using the dough for tin loaves, you can use it to make two split tin loaves, two Coburgs, two Bloomers, or two Cottage Loaves (see p. 297).

Pikelets and Yorkshire Teacakes, crisp, hot and ready to smother with butter.

YORKSHIRE TEACAKES
Yorkshire and Lancashire

IN SPITE OF THE NAME, the Yorkshire teacake is also made in Lancashire where it is equally popular. Yorkshire teacakes are said to be direct descendants of manchet or 'hand-bread'—a medieval loaf in which fine flour was used, and the loaf shaped by hand and cooked without a tin.

There are two versions of the teacake—plain and fruited, the latter originally a Lenten speciality. Both are served split and buttered or toasted and buttered. The plain teacake is often given a savoury filling.

PREPARATION TIME: 35 MINUTES
RISING AND RESTING TIME: 1¾ HOURS
COOKING TIME: 10 MINUTES
PRE-HEAT THE OVEN TO 225°C (435°F)—GAS MARK 7½

INGREDIENTS FOR 10–12 TEACAKES
- *2 oz. (50 g.) currants*
- *2 oz. (50 g.) sultanas*
- *1 lb. (450 g.) strong white flour*
- *1 level teaspoon salt*
- *1½ oz. (40 g.) lard*
- *2 oz. (50 g.) sugar*
- *½ pint (275/300 ml.) warm milk (see p. 296)*
- *1 oz. (25 g.) fresh yeast*

Rinse the currants and sultanas with warm water, pat dry with kitchen paper and put in a warm place.

Sieve the flour and salt on to a working surface or into a large mixing bowl, rub in the lard and make a well in the centre.

Dissolve the sugar in the milk and use 3 tablespoons of the liquid to mix the yeast to a smooth paste. Stir in the rest of the milk and pour the liquid into the well. Mix vigorously to blend well, then knead (see p. 296) until the mixture forms a smooth, elastic dough. Work in the warm, slightly moist currants and sultanas. Shape the dough into a ball, put it into a warm, greased bowl, cover with greased polythene and set in a warm place to rise for 45 minutes.

Tip the dough on to a lightly floured working surface and knead for a few minutes to a smooth, even texture. Reshape it into a ball, cover again and put to rise for 15 minutes.

Divide the dough into 10–12 pieces each weighing about 3 oz. (75 g.). Shape each piece into a smooth ball. As the pieces are shaped, set them neatly to one side of the working surface under a sheet of greased polythene. Leave them to rest for about 5 minutes while you warm two lightly buttered baking sheets.

With a rolling pin, roll out the dough balls into 3½ in. (9 cm.) discs. Place them on the baking sheets about 1 in. (2·5 cm.) apart. Cover with greased polythene and set to rise in a warm place for 35–45 minutes. Bake in the pre-heated oven for about 10 minutes, or until golden-brown.

To make plain teacakes, which are popular for sandwiches, leave out the currants and sultanas and reduce the amount of sugar to ½ oz. (15 g.).

PIKELETS AND CRUMPETS
North Country

PIKELETS AND CRUMPETS are made basically from the same recipe. The word crumpet originally meant 'a twisted cake', from the Anglo-Saxon *crump* (to curl up). Crumpets are first recorded in 17th-century books where they are called 'crompid cake', meaning a griddle-baked cake so thin that it curled up. In Wales they are known as 'crempog'—pancakes or fritters.

Crumpets are baked on a griddle in

a metal ring and, because of the action of the heat from below on the yeast and raising agent, bubbles are formed quickly and burst at the surface, giving an uneven, pitted top. Pikelets are thinner, and are baked on a griddle without a ring to hold them.

PREPARATION TIME: 20 MINUTES
FERMENTING TIME: 30 MINUTES
COOKING TIME: ABOUT 40 MINUTES

INGREDIENTS FOR ABOUT 12 PIKELETS

8 oz. (225 g.) strong white flour
1 level teaspoon salt
½ oz. (15 g.) fresh yeast
¼ pint (150 ml.) warm milk (see p. 296)
¼ pint (150 ml.) warm water (see p. 296)
¼ teaspoon bicarbonate of soda
4 tablespoons cold water
1 egg white, lightly beaten

Sieve the flour and salt together into a large mixing bowl and mix in the yeast. Combine the warm milk and warm water and pour into the bowl. Beat vigorously for 5 minutes to make a smooth batter, then cover and put in a warm place for about 30 minutes or until the risen mixture starts to drop.

Dissolve the bicarbonate of soda in the cold water and beat it into the batter. Fold in the beaten egg white thoroughly to produce a batter the consistency of thick pouring cream.

To cook the pikelets, lightly grease a griddle, hot plate or heavy-based frying pan and heat until a drop of the batter sizzles immediately on contact. Put a full tablespoon of batter on to the hot surface and cook until the top of the pikelet is no longer wet. Turn over with a palette knife and cook until the other side is lightly browned. Continue until all the batter is used. Eat hot from the pan, or leave to cool then toast and butter.

To make crumpets, prepare the batter with 1 oz. (25 g.) more flour and cook on one side only, with the batter contained in a greased 3 in. (8 cm.) ring on the cooking surface. Serve toasted and buttered.

MUFFINS
Countrywide

MUFFINS reached the height of their popularity in this country in the last century, when the muffin man went round the streets with hot muffins in a tray upon his head. He rang a bell to let his customers know he was coming. Even in the 1930s the muffin man's bell was still heard.

Muffins are cooked on a griddle, on a hot plate or in a heavy frying pan, and turned over halfway with a broad-bladed knife. But a knife must never be used to split a muffin. The muffin should be carefully torn apart while still warm, spread thickly with butter and eaten immediately.

PREPARATION TIME: 35 MINUTES
RISING TIME: 1 HOUR 40 MINUTES
COOKING TIME: ABOUT 40 MINUTES

INGREDIENTS FOR 10 MUFFINS

10 oz. (275 g.) strong white flour
1 rounded teaspoon salt
½ level teaspoon sugar
7½–10 fl. oz. (215–300 ml.) warm water (see p. 296)
½ oz. (15 g.) fresh yeast
1 tablespoon olive oil

Sieve the flour and salt together into a heatproof basin and put in a warming drawer, or barely warm oven, until the flour is just warm to the touch.

Meanwhile, dissolve the sugar in 7½ fl. oz. (215 ml.) of the water and use 2 tablespoons of this liquid to mix the yeast to a smooth paste. Stir in the rest of the sugar and water mixture.

Tip the warm flour on to a working surface or into a large mixing bowl and make a well in the centre. Pour in the yeast mixture and the olive oil and mix vigorously to blend in the flour. Add more of the water, if necessary, to make a dough that is very soft but can just hold a shape. The softer the dough, the more difficult it is to handle, but the better are the muffins it makes. Knead (see p. 296) to a smooth, elastic dough, then shape into a ball and put in a warm, greased bowl. Cover with greased polythene and put to rise for 1 hour.

Turn out the risen dough on to a working surface and divide it into 10 equal pieces. Mould the pieces into balls and set them on a thickly floured board. Dust the tops well with flour, cover with polythene and put to rise in a warm place for 35–40 minutes.

Heat a griddle, hot plate or heavy-based frying pan, lightly oiled, and carefully lift on the dough pieces to cook three or four at a time. Cook over medium heat for 5–6 minutes, then turn over to cook for 6–7 minutes on the other side. The muffins will keep a better shape if they are held in by oiled 3½ in. (9 cm.) rings on the cooking surface.

SODA BREAD
Ireland

BAKING on a griddle or bakestone over the steady glow of a peat fire is said to have given the distinctive flavour to the original Irish Soda Bread. Many homes in Ireland still do some cooking in this way.

No yeast is used in this bread. Instead bicarbonate of soda, cream of tartar and buttermilk give the rise and flavour usually given by yeast. Buttermilk can be bought from large supermarkets and dairies. This recipe makes a bread that is good for eating fresh and a quick standby when bread or yeast are hard to get.

PREPARATION TIME: 20 MINUTES
COOKING TIME: 30 MINUTES
PRE-HEAT THE OVEN TO 230°C (450°F)—GAS MARK 8

INGREDIENTS FOR FOUR SMALL LOAVES

12 oz. (350 g.) wheatmeal flour
12 oz. (350 g.) plain white flour
1 level teaspoon salt
2 oz. (50 g.) lard
3 level teaspoons bicarbonate of soda
6 level teaspoons cream of tartar
2 level teaspoons sugar
1 pint (575/600 ml.) buttermilk

Mix together the wheatmeal flour, white flour and salt. Rub in the lard and then mix in the bicarbonate of soda, cream of tartar and sugar. Pour in the buttermilk and lightly work up a dough with the hands. Shape the dough gently into a ball and place it on a lightly greased baking sheet. Flatten it into a disc 1–1¼ in. (2·5–3 cm.) thick. Cut the disc into quarters and push them apart a little so that there is ¼–½ in. (5–15 mm.) between them. Dust them lightly with wheatmeal flour. Bake immediately in the pre-heated oven for 30 minutes.

Vary the proportions of brown and white flour as you wish, to give the bread a different colour and texture. Convert it into a fruited soda bread, if you like, by increasing the sugar to 2 oz. (50 g.) and mixing in a handful of sultanas or currants before adding the buttermilk. This fruited bread will need a lower cooking temperature, 220°C (425°F)—gas mark 7.

Liverpool Christmas Loaf
North Country

In the late 1920s and early 1930s, times were hard in many parts of the north. It was then that Christmas Loaf was first baked, as a substitute for Christmas cake. It still makes a good fruit loaf for special occasions.

The loaf was usually made a fortnight before Christmas; after a week, if it could be afforded, some ale would be poured over the cooked loaf to improve its texture.

Many housewives with no cookers relied upon the local baker to cook their cakes for a few pence, and it was a familiar sight to see the 'Mary Ellens'—poor housewives in black shawls and stockings, and with thick woollen skirts over their flannel petticoats—returning from the baker's with a delicious aroma arising from the newspaper-covered cake tins they carried in their arms.

Preparation Time: 40 minutes
Fermenting and Rising Time: $1\frac{1}{4}$ hours
Cooking Time: 35–40 minutes
Pre-heat the Oven to 190°C (375°F)—gas mark 5

Ingredients for Two Small Loaves

For the ferment:

1 large egg, beaten
About $2\frac{1}{2}$ fl. oz. (75 ml.) warm milk (see p. 296)
1 oz. (25 g.) sugar
$\frac{1}{2}$ oz. (15 g.) fresh yeast
2 oz. (50 g.) strong white flour

For the dough:

4 oz. (100/125 g.) lard or cooking fat
4 oz. (100/125 g.) soft brown sugar
1 tablespoon black treacle
1 large egg, beaten
8 oz. (225 g.) strong white flour
1 level teaspoon salt
2 level teaspoons baking powder
1 level teaspoon grated nutmeg
2 level teaspoons ground mixed spice
8 oz. (225 g.) currants
4 oz. (100/125 g.) sultanas
1 oz. (25 g.) mixed, chopped dried peel

To prepare the ferment, mix the beaten egg and warm milk together in a large bowl to give $\frac{1}{4}$ pint (150 ml.) of liquid. Whisk the sugar, yeast and flour into the liquid until thoroughly blended. Cover with polythene and put to rise in a warm place for 30 minutes.

To make the dough, cream the fat, sugar and treacle together with a wooden spoon in a large mixing bowl until light and fluffy. Beat the egg into the mixture, then sieve in the flour, salt, baking powder, nutmeg and mixed spice.

Mix together roughly, then pour in the ferment and mix well until the ingredients combine to make a smooth mixture. Work the currants, sultanas and peel into the mixture until evenly distributed.

Divide the dough in half, and shape each half to fit into a 1 lb. (450 g.) loaf tin, warmed and well greased. Cover the tins with greased polythene and put to rise in a warm place for 45 minutes. Bake in the pre-heated oven for 15 minutes at 190°C (375°F)—gas mark 5; then reduce the temperature to 170°C (325°F)—gas mark 3 for the remaining 20 to 25 minutes.

Milk Bread
Countrywide

Good cooks have always been adventurous. Even in the early days of bread-making they searched for ways of introducing ingredients that would give a change of flavour, appearance or texture. In the 1st century AD the Romans put anise and cumin beneath the bottom crust of their loaves for flavouring. In medieval times eggs, milk and butter added to dough produced the enriched breads which were the forerunners of cakes.

The art of making such breads was more highly developed in France than in England, but from the late 13th century, bakers in this country were making what they called 'French' bread or 'puffs'—a special milk bread containing butter and eggs.

Milk bread keeps well and is often shaped into decorative plaits or scrolls. But make at least one ordinary loaf, because milk bread makes superbly crisp and nutty toast.

Preparation Time: 30 minutes
Rising Time: 1 hour 35 minutes
Cooking Time: 30–35 minutes
Pre-heat the Oven to 220°C (425°F)—gas mark 7

Ingredients for One Loaf

1 lb. (450 g.) strong white flour
1 level teaspoon salt
1 level teaspoon sugar
$\frac{1}{2}$ pint (275/300 ml.) warm milk (see p. 296)
1 oz. (25 g.) fresh yeast
A little beaten egg and milk to glaze
Poppy seed for sprinkling (optional)

Sieve the flour and salt on to a working surface or into a large mixing bowl and make a well in the centre. Dissolve the sugar in the milk and use 3 tablespoons of the liquid to mix the yeast to a smooth, thin paste. Stir in the rest of the milk and pour the liquid into the well. Draw in the flour, mix thoroughly and then knead (see p. 296) to make a smooth, elastic dough. Shape into a ball, put into a warm, lightly greased bowl, cover with greased polythene and put in a warm place to rise for 45 minutes.

Turn out the risen dough on to the working surface and knock out all the air bubbles. Reshape the dough into a ball, put back in the bowl, cover again and put to rise for a further 15 minutes.

Since milk bread makes very good toast, bake it in or under a tin to give slices of a neat shape suitable for toasting. Grease and warm a 7 by 4 in. (18 by 10 cm.) loaf tin and shape the dough to fit it.

To bake the loaf in a tin, cover with greased polythene and put in a warm place to rise for a further 30–35 minutes. The loaf will have an attractive finish if, halfway through the rising in the tin, you brush it lightly with a mixture of egg and milk, or dust it with flour. You can also cut designs into the surface with a very sharp blade.

If you like, you can sprinkle poppy seed liberally on the loaf to give a deliciously nutty flavour. Bake in the pre-heated oven for 30–35 minutes.

To bake the loaf under a tin, put the dough into the tin in the normal way, allow it to rise in a warm place until it is just below the top of the tin, put a greased and warmed baking sheet over the tin, then carefully turn baking sheet and tin over together. Allow the dough to rise for another 5 minutes before baking. Bake with the baking sheet under the tin in the pre-heated oven for 30–35 minutes.

You can also use this dough to make a plaited or scroll loaf (see p. 297).

Milk breads moulded into shapes and sprinkled with poppy seeds to give a deliciously nutty flavour.

OATMEAL BREAD
Lancashire

A NUTTY TASTE and chewy texture are given to this bread by the oatmeal, an unusual ingredient in bread nowadays but formerly widely used throughout the country.

Medieval Scottish soldiers carried with them supplies of oatmeal and flat metal plates on which—with the addition of a little water—they could bake unleavened oatmeal bread. Scottish farmers stored their oatmeal in oak chests, and even humble crofts had an oak barrel for the grain.

The recipe given here has been adapted from that used for many years by a Lancashire family, for a loaf they called monastery bread.

PREPARATION TIME: 30 MINUTES
RISING TIME: 1¾ HOURS
COOKING TIME: 30–35 MINUTES
PRE-HEAT THE OVEN TO 235°C (460°F)—GAS MARK 8½

INGREDIENTS FOR TWO SMALL LOAVES
4 oz. (100/125 g.) fine oatmeal
12 oz. (350 g.) wheatmeal flour
4 oz. (100/125 g.) strong white flour
1 rounded teaspoon salt
1 rounded teaspoon brown sugar
¾ oz. (20 g.) fresh yeast
About 12 fl. oz. (350 ml.) warm water (see p. 296)
Fine oatmeal for coating

Mix together the oatmeal, wheatmeal flour, white flour and salt on a working surface or in a large mixing bowl. Make a well in the centre. Whisk together the sugar, yeast and about ½ pint (275/300 ml.) of the water and pour into the well. Draw in the flour gradually and mix well together, adding more of the water to work up a dough. Knead well (see p. 296), then shape into a ball and put in a warmed and greased bowl.

Cover with greased polythene and set in a warm place to rise for 45 minutes. Turn out the dough on to a working surface and knock out all the bubbles. Knead into a ball again, put back into the bowl, cover with the polythene and put back to rise for a further 15 minutes.

Turn out the dough on to the working surface and divide it into two equal pieces. Mould each to fit a warmed and greased 1 lb. (450 g.) loaf tin, and roll the pieces in oatmeal before putting them in the tins. Cover with the polythene, and put in a warm place to rise for 45 minutes. Bake in the pre-heated oven for 30–35 minutes.

DOUGHNUTS
Countrywide

'TWIXT optimist and pessimist
The difference is droll,
The optimist sees the doughnut
The pessimist the hole.'

These lines are attributed to the American poet McLandburgh Wilson, and indeed we are apt to think of doughnuts as American in origin, yet they were known in Europe long before they were first made in the United States. References to them can be found in the Isle of Wight in the 17th century.

In Baldock, Hertfordshire, Shrove Tuesday has been traditionally known as Doughnut Day, because mothers made doughnuts in great quantities for the children; and in neighbouring Bedfordshire also, doughnuts were eaten on Shrove Tuesday.

PREPARATION TIME: 20 MINUTES
RISING TIME: 2 HOURS
COOKING TIME: ABOUT 45 MINUTES

INGREDIENTS FOR 25–30 DOUGHNUTS
1 oz. (25 g.) fresh yeast
3 fl. oz. (90 ml.) warm water (see p. 296)
4 oz. (100/125 g.) sugar
2 oz. (50 g.) butter
5 fl. oz. (150 ml.) warm milk (see p. 296)
1 level teaspoon salt
1 egg, beaten
1 lb. (450 g.) plain flour
½ level teaspoon ground cinnamon
1 level teaspoon grated nutmeg
Oil for frying
Sugar for sprinkling

Mix the yeast to a smooth, thin paste in a large bowl with 3 tablespoons of the warm water. Stir in the remaining water. In a separate bowl stir the sugar and butter into the warm milk, add the salt, and combine with the yeast mixture. Stir in the beaten egg.

Sift the flour, cinnamon and nutmeg into the mixture and stir well to make a dough.

Turn it out on to a lightly floured working surface and knead until the dough is smooth and no longer sticks to the working surface. Put the dough into a buttered bowl, spread a little butter over it, cover and stand in a warm place to rise for 1 hour.

Knock any air bubbles out of the dough with the side of the hand, then roll it out to ¼ in. (5 mm.) thick. Cut it into fingers or stamp it out in rings or circles. Arrange, well spaced out, on individual pieces of lightly greased paper, on warmed baking sheets. Cover the doughnuts with greased polythene and stand in a warm place to rise again for 1 hour. Each doughnut can then be picked up on its paper and turned over into the oil, complete with its paper; this will quickly float off.

Deep-fry three or four doughnuts at a time in very hot oil (see p. 259). When they are golden-brown, after 5–7 minutes, lift out, drain well on kitchen paper and roll in sugar. Serve while still very fresh.

SELKIRK BANNOCKS
Scotland and the North

THE BANNOCK is a flat loaf about the size of a dinner-plate, and traditionally baked on a griddle. The name derives from the Latin *panicum* (bread). In the past, bannocks were often made for special occasions, for example the Bride's Bannock for May 1 and the Beltane Bannock baked on the first day of summer.

The Selkirk Bannock was first introduced in the mid-19th century by Robbie Douglas, who had a shop in Selkirk Market. He specified that it should be weighty, rounded on top, and contain half its weight in fruit.

PREPARATION TIME: 20 MINUTES
RISING TIME: 1¾ HOURS
COOKING TIME: ABOUT 20 MINUTES
PRE-HEAT THE OVEN TO 215°C (415°F)—GAS MARK 6½

INGREDIENTS FOR THREE BANNOCKS
1 lb. (450 g.) sultanas
1 lb. (450 g.) strong white flour
1 level teaspoon salt
3 oz. (75 g.) butter
3 oz. (75 g.) sugar
½ pint (275/300 ml.) warm milk (see p. 296)
1 oz. (25 g.) fresh yeast
A little beaten egg to glaze

Soak the sultanas for 30 minutes in sufficient hot water to cover, then drain them and pat dry between pieces of kitchen paper.

Meanwhile, sieve the flour and salt into a large mixing bowl, rub in the butter and make a well in the centre. Dissolve the sugar in the milk and use 3 tablespoons of this liquid to mix the yeast to a smooth paste. Stir in the remaining milk and pour into the well. Mix vigorously to blend, then knead (see p. 296) for 5 minutes or more to make a smooth, springy dough. Shape it into a ball, place in a warmed, lightly buttered bowl, cover with greased polythene and put in a warm place to rise for 30 minutes.

Gently knead in the sultanas without bursting them. When they are well distributed throughout the dough, shape it into a ball again, cover with greased polythene and stand in a warm place to rise for a further 15 minutes.

Divide the dough into three equal pieces, mould each into a smooth ball and place each on a warmed and lightly buttered baking sheet. Cover with greased polythene and put in a warm place to rise for 1 hour, flattening the balls with the hand and brushing lightly with beaten egg after the first 15 minutes. Bake in the pre-heated oven for about 20 minutes.

WALNUT BREAD
Countrywide

THE CUSTOM of adding sweet ingredients such as honey and dried fruits to the basic bread dough began in medieval times; but until near the end of the 18th century, bakers in this country were prohibited by law from making 'enriched breads' except for special occasions. Such a law may have been made at a time of poor harvests to ensure that all available flour went into plain bread, but the rich would still have fancy breads baked in their own ovens.

Nowadays, fruit loaves and tea breads are made all over the country, and practically every county has its own regional speciality. Many of them include walnuts, whose distinctive flavour and crispness combine well with dried fruits.

PREPARATION TIME: 50 MINUTES

FERMENTING, RISING AND RESTING TIME: 1 HOUR 40 MINUTES

COOKING TIME: 30 MINUTES

PRE-HEAT THE OVEN TO 190°C (375°F)—GAS MARK 5

INGREDIENTS FOR THREE SMALL LOAVES

For the ferment:

- *1 oz. (25 g.) fresh yeast*
- *2 level teaspoons sugar*
- *2 oz. (50 g.) strong white flour*
- *½ pint (275/300 ml.) warm milk (see p. 296)*

For the dough:

- *14 oz. (400 g.) strong white flour*
- *2 level teaspoons salt*
- *2 oz. (50 g.) butter*
- *1½ oz. (40 g.) sugar*
- *4 oz. (100/125 g.) shelled walnuts*
- *8 oz. (225 g.) sultanas (or currants, dried apricots, dates, glacé cherries, or a mixture of these)*
- *A little beaten egg to glaze*

To prepare the ferment, whisk the yeast, sugar and flour into the milk in a basin until they make a smooth batter. Cover with polythene and put in a warm place to rise for 20 minutes.

To make the dough, sieve the flour and salt on to a working surface or into a large mixing bowl, rub in the butter and make a well in the centre. Put the sugar in the well and pour on the ferment. Mix well together and knead (see p. 296) to a smooth, elastic dough. Shape into a ball, put in a greased, warm bowl, cover with greased polythene and put to rise in a warm place for 30 minutes.

Meanwhile, wash the walnuts in warm water, rubbing off as much of the skin as possible. Drain on kitchen paper and chop roughly. Wash the sultanas (or other chosen fruit) in hot water and spread on kitchen paper to drain.

Turn out the risen dough on to a working surface and knead the walnuts and sultanas into it until evenly distributed. Cover with greased polythene and leave to rest for 10–15 minutes.

Divide the dough into three equal pieces and mould each to fit a lightly greased, warmed 1 lb. (450 g.) loaf tin. Cover with greased polythene and put to rise in a warm place for 35 minutes, brushing lightly with beaten egg after 20 minutes. Bake in the pre-heated oven for 30 minutes.

CURRANT BREAD
Countrywide

THE BRITISH partiality for dried fruits has long been embodied in our cookery. The Venetian ambassador in London wrote home in 1610, when there was a possibility that Greece would reduce her export of currants, that 'the English population consumes a greater amount of this fruit than all the rest of the world'. The place of origin of the fruit was plain in the earlier name, raisins of Corinth. This was shortened to Corinths, which we now call currants.

PREPARATION TIME: 15 MINUTES

RISING AND RESTING TIME: 50–55 MINUTES

COOKING TIME: 25 MINUTES

PRE-HEAT THE OVEN TO 220°C (425°F)—GAS MARK 7

INGREDIENTS FOR TWO SMALL LOAVES

- *1 lb. (450 g.) strong white flour*
- *1 level teaspoon salt*
- *1½ oz. (40 g.) lard*
- *1 egg, beaten*
- *7½ fl. oz. (215 ml.) warm water (see p. 296)*
- *2 level teaspoons sugar*
- *¾ oz. (20 g.) fresh yeast*
- *5 oz. (150 g.) currants, washed, dried and slightly warm*
- *A little beaten egg and milk to glaze*

Sieve the flour and salt on to a working surface or into a large mixing bowl. Rub in the lard and make a well in the centre. Mix the beaten egg with the warm water and dissolve the sugar in the mixture. Use 3 tablespoons of it to mix the yeast to a smooth, thin paste, then stir in the rest of the liquid. Pour into the well and mix vigorously to blend, then knead (see p. 296) to make a smooth, silky-looking dough. Carefully work in the currants, trying not to break their skins. Shape the dough into a ball and set aside, covered with greased polythene, to rest for 10 minutes.

Lightly grease two 1 lb. (450 g.) loaf tins, preferably long and narrow in shape. Put the tins to warm slightly. Divide the rested dough into two equal pieces and mould to fit the tins. Place in the tins, cover with greased polythene and put in a warm place to rise for 40–45 minutes, brushing lightly after 20 minutes with the egg and milk.

Bake in the pre-heated oven for 25 minutes. If preferred, use all the dough to make one 2 lb. (900 g.) loaf. This will take 30 minutes to bake.

DEVONSHIRE SPLITS
West Country

THE DEVONSHIRE SPLIT, that essential item of the perfect Cream Tea which conjures up pictures of a summer afternoon, is a twin to the Cornish Split—it just depends on which side of the Tamar you are.

Traditionally, in the West Country both Devonshire and Cornish splits are filled with thick local cream and home-made strawberry jam. Treacle is sometimes used, and then the split is known as a 'Thunder and Lightning'.

PREPARATION TIME: 45 MINUTES

FERMENTING, RISING AND RESTING TIME: 2 HOURS

COOKING TIME: 10 MINUTES

PRE-HEAT THE OVEN TO 230°C (450°F)—GAS MARK 8

INGREDIENTS FOR 18 SPLITS

For the ferment:

1 large egg, beaten

About 7½ fl. oz. (215 ml.) warm water (see p. 296)

1 oz. (25 g.) fresh yeast

4 oz. (100/125 g.) strong white flour

½ oz. (15 g.) sugar

For the dough:

14 oz. (400 g.) strong white flour

¼ teaspoon salt

3 oz. (75 g.) sugar

2 oz. (50 g.) butter, soft but not oily

To make the ferment, mix together the beaten egg and enough warm water to give ½ pint (275/300 ml.) of liquid. Mix the yeast to a smooth paste in 3 tablespoons of the liquid. Add the rest of the liquid, and whisk in the flour and sugar to make a smooth batter. Cover and put in a warm place to rise for 30 minutes.

To make the dough, sieve the flour and salt on to a working surface or into a large mixing bowl and make a well in the centre. Put the sugar in the well and pour on the ferment. Stir to dissolve the sugar, then gradually draw in the flour and mix vigorously to make a soft, sticky dough.

Knead (see p. 296) the butter in well until the dough is smooth and silky. Shape into a ball, put in a warmed and greased bowl, cover with greased polythene and put to rise in a warm place for 45 minutes.

Turn out the risen dough on to a working surface, knock out any bubbles and divide it into 18 equal pieces. Mould them into balls, cover with the polythene, and leave on the working surface to rest for 5 minutes.

Roll out the balls to make 3 in. (8 cm.) discs. Brush any flour off the discs and fold them in half. Put them on a warmed and greased baking sheet, well spaced out. Cover with greased polythene and put in a warm place to rise for 40 minutes. Bake for 10 minutes in the pre-heated oven.

When the splits are cool, break them open, fill with jam and cream and dust with icing sugar to serve.

HOT CROSS BUNS
Countrywide

IT IS SAID that in medieval times, bakers marked all their loaves with a cross to ward off evil spirits and encourage the bread to rise. This practice was condemned as 'popish' during the 17th century and dropped. Only buns made on Good Friday continued to bear a cross, in token of the Crucifixion.

PREPARATION TIME: 40 MINUTES

FERMENTING, RISING AND RESTING TIME: 2¾ HOURS

COOKING TIME: 6–7 MINUTES

PRE-HEAT THE OVEN TO 240°C (475°F)—GAS MARK 9

INGREDIENTS FOR 12–13 BUNS

For the ferment:

1 large egg, beaten

About 7½ fl. oz. (215 ml.) warm water (see p. 296)

½ oz. (15 g.) fresh yeast

1 rounded teaspoon sugar

2 oz. (50 g.) strong white flour

For the dough:

4 oz. (100/125 g.) currants

1 oz. (25 g.) sultanas

1 oz. (25 g.) chopped, dried lemon peel

1 lb. (450 g.) strong white flour

1 level teaspoon salt

2–3 rounded teaspoons ground mixed spice

3 oz. (75 g.) lard

3 oz. (75 g.) sugar

Grated rind of 1 lemon

Golden syrup, heated, for glazing

Prepare the ferment by combining the beaten egg with enough warm water to give ½ pint (275/300 ml.) of liquid. Whisk in the yeast, sugar and flour, cover and put in a warm place for 30 minutes.

Before starting to mix the dough, rinse the currants, sultanas and chopped, dried lemon peel with hot water and spread on kitchen paper in a warm place to drain.

Sieve the flour, salt and spice into a large mixing bowl, rub in the lard and make a well in the centre. Put the sugar and grated lemon rind in the well and pour on the ferment. Gradually draw in the flour and mix vigorously, then knead (see p. 296) to a smooth, elastic dough.

Carefully work in the warm, moist currants, sultanas and lemon peel. Shape the dough into a ball, put it in a warm, greased bowl, cover with greased polythene and put to rise in a warm place for 1 hour.

Turn out the dough on to a working surface and knead to knock out any air bubbles and give the dough an even texture. Shape it into a ball again, put back into the bowl, cover and put back to rise for another 30 minutes.

Turn out the dough on to a working surface and divide into 3 oz. (75 g.) pieces. Shape them into balls and leave to rest for 5 minutes on the working surface covered with the polythene. Roll out the balls into 3 in. (8 cm.) discs and place on lightly greased baking sheets. Cut each disc into quarters, cutting right through the dough but leaving the quarters touching each other so that as the dough rises it has a well-marked cross on it.

Cover the buns with greased polythene and put in a warm place to rise for 40 minutes. Bake in the pre-heated oven for 6–7 minutes, and brush over the buns with hot golden syrup as soon as they are taken from the oven.

The cross on each bun can be made with shortcrust pastry to which water has been added until it is soft enough to pipe through a nozzle. Instead of cutting the discs of dough, pipe a cross of the pastry on to each immediately before baking.

LARDY CAKES
West Country

ESSENTIALLY A COUNTRY BREAD—it has been called 'the countryman's answer to a fruit cake'—this cake was once baked to celebrate the harvest. It probably originated in Wiltshire and Berkshire, where it is still always layered with a mixture of lard and sugar, in the traditional way. In other counties the cake has the fat mixed into the dough.

In the following recipe, the syrup of melted brown sugar, spice and lard is allowed to spread over the top of the cake when it is turned out of the tin, and gives it a glossy caramel-like topping.

PREPARATION TIME: 20 MINUTES
RISING AND RESTING TIME: 1 HOUR 20 MINUTES
COOKING TIME: 30 MINUTES
PRE-HEAT THE OVEN TO 200°C (400°F)—GAS MARK 6

INGREDIENTS FOR TWO LOAVES
1 lb. (450 g.) strong white flour
1 level teaspoon salt
1 oz. (25 g.) lard
2 oz. (50 g.) sugar
1 oz. (25 g.) fresh yeast
½ pint (275/300 ml.) warm milk (see p. 296)
8 oz. (225 g.) currants
4 oz. (100/125 g.) sultanas

For the filling:
4 oz. (100/125 g.) lard
4 oz. (100/125 g.) soft brown sugar
1 rounded teaspoon ground mixed spice

Sieve the flour and salt on to a working surface, or into a large mixing bowl. Rub in the lard and make a well in the centre of the mixture. Mix the sugar and yeast in a jug to a smooth, thin paste with 3 tablespoons of the warm milk. Stir in the rest of the milk and pour into the well. Mix vigorously to make a smooth dough. Shape into a ball and put in a large greased bowl. Cover with greased polythene and stand in a warm place to rise for 30 minutes.

Lightly knead the currants and sultanas into the dough, then let it rest, covered, for 10 minutes before rolling out into a long rectangle 18 by 6 in. (45·5 by 15 cm.).

Make the filling by mixing together the lard, brown sugar and ground mixed spice, and then spread it along two-thirds of the rolled dough. Fold the unspread one-third over the centre section and then the remaining spread section over these. Roll out the dough again to the same size as before. Roll it up from a short side like a Swiss roll. Cut the roll in half to give two rolled pieces 3 in. (8 cm.) long.

Stand each piece, cut end uppermost, in a well-greased round tin, 6 in. (15 cm.) across. Cover with greased polythene and stand in a warm place to rise for 40 minutes.

Bake in the pre-heated oven for 30 minutes. Turn out of the tins immediately to let the hot filling run over the loaves and form a glaze. It will be extremely hot, so hold the tin with a thick cloth and take care not to get burned.

For an alternative version of Lardy Cake, instead of rolling up the dough, fold it in three again after the second rolling out. Then roll out the folded dough to fit a greased, small roasting tin or put it on a lightly greased baking sheet.

Brush the top of the cake with beaten egg and sprinkle with sugar. Bake at 190°C (375°F)—gas mark 5 for 30–35 minutes. You may have to turn it round during baking to prevent the edges from browning too much. Cut this Lardy Cake into fingers while it is still warm.

Lardy Cake—a rich fruit loaf with a sweet spiced filling.

CHELSEA BUNS
London

IN the late 17th and early 18th centuries, all fashionable London came to the Chelsea Bun House in the Pimlico Road to eat the delicious buns, spicy, rich with fruit and crusty with sugar, hot from the oven of Mr Richard Hand.

Mr Richard Hand, who ran the Bun House with his family, always wore a dressing-gown and fez and was known as 'Captain Bun'. George III and Queen Charlotte were frequent visitors and would sit on the verandah munching buns, to the delight of the crowds.

The fame of the buns spread from town to country. The following well-tried recipe produces buns of a lightness that would arouse the admiration of Captain Bun himself.

With their characteristic square shape, spiced filling and sweet top, the buns make a tempting treat to enjoy with coffee or afternoon tea.

PREPARATION TIME: 45 MINUTES

FERMENTING AND RISING TIME: 1 HOUR 55 MINUTES

COOKING TIME: 12 MINUTES

PRE-HEAT THE OVEN TO 220°C (425°F)—GAS MARK 7

INGREDIENTS FOR 12 BUNS

For the ferment:

1 large egg, beaten
About 7½ fl. oz. (215 ml.) warm water (see p. 296)
1 oz. (25 g.) fresh yeast
4 oz. (100/125 g.) strong white flour
½ oz. (15 g.) sugar

For the dough:

14 oz. (400 g.) strong white flour
¼ teaspoon salt
3 oz. (75 g.) sugar
2 oz (50 g.) butter, softened
Melted butter for brushing over
Granulated sugar for sprinkling
Ground mixed spice or ground cinnamon for sprinkling
1–2 oz. (25–50 g.) sultanas
Caster sugar or glacé icing (see p. 301) for topping

Chelsea Buns—a treat concocted in Georgian times.

To make the ferment, mix together the beaten egg and enough warm water to give ½ pint (275/300 ml.) of liquid. Mix the yeast to a smooth paste with 3 tablespoons of the liquid. Add the remaining liquid and whisk in the flour and sugar to make a smooth batter. Cover and put in a warm place to rise for 30 minutes.

To make the dough, sieve the flour and salt on to a working surface or into a large mixing bowl and make a well in the centre. Put in the sugar and pour the ferment over it. Stir until the sugar has dissolved, then gradually draw in the flour and mix vigorously to make a soft dough.

Knead in (see p. 296) the softened butter thoroughly until the dough looks smooth and silky. Shape it into a ball, put it in a warm, greased bowl, cover with greased polythene and put in a warm place to rise for 45 minutes.

Turn out the risen dough on to a working surface and knock out any air bubbles. Roll out the dough to a rectangle about 9 by 12 in. (23 by 30 cm.). Brush over the dough with melted butter, leaving a ½ in. (1·5 cm.) strip uncoated along one shorter side. Brush this strip with water.

Sprinkle granulated sugar thinly over the butter, then dust lightly with mixed spice or cinnamon. Scatter the sultanas over the dough and roll it up from the buttered shorter edge, stretching it slightly while rolling so that the sugar and fruit is gripped tightly. Seal the roll by pressing the moistened edge down firmly on to it.

Brush the roll all over with melted butter, then cut into slices ¾ in. (2 cm.) thick, to give 12 pieces from the 9 in. (23 cm.) roll. Lay the pieces ½ in. (1·5 cm.) apart on a greased baking sheet, setting them with cut side uppermost. Cover with greased polythene and put to rise in a warm place for 40 minutes.

Bake in the pre-heated oven for 12 minutes. As the buns rise and are baked, they will spread together and become square. When they are baked, sprinkle immediately with caster sugar or spread with thin glacé icing made with water. Separate the buns when they are nearly cold.

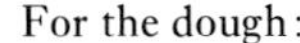

RYE BREAD
Countrywide

CENTURIES AGO, rye bread was eaten only by those who could not afford wheat flour. Today it has risen in the social scale and in cost. Its taste and nutritional value are as good as they were when Fynes Moryson, a 16th-century English traveller, observed that the husbandmen ate barley and rye bread 'and prefer it to white bread as abiding longer in the stomach and not so soon digested with their labour'.

Rye has a strong flavour, and even the smallest quantity will make a surprising difference to a loaf of bread. There is a wide variety of these breads, from the very dark pumpernickel, using only rye flour, to light rye bread which can be made from 4 parts of white flour to only 1 part of rye. The higher the proportion of rye flour used, the closer will be the texture of the bread.

PREPARATION TIME: 40 MINUTES
RISING TIME: 2 HOURS 10 MINUTES
COOKING TIME: 30–35 MINUTES
PRE-HEAT THE OVEN TO
220°C (425°F)—GAS MARK 7

INGREDIENTS FOR ONE LARGE LOAF AND ONE SMALL LOAF

14 oz. (400 g.) strong white flour
14 oz. (400 g.) rye flour or meal
$\frac{1}{2}$ oz. (15 g.) caraway seed
3 level teaspoons salt
$\frac{1}{2}$ oz. (15 g.) brown sugar
1 teaspoon black treacle
16 fl. oz. (475 ml.) warm water (see p. 296)
$\frac{3}{4}$ oz. (20 g.) fresh yeast
Rye flour for sprinkling

Mix the white flour, rye flour, caraway seed and salt together in a large mixing bowl and make a well in the centre. Mix the sugar, treacle and water together in a basin and whisk in the yeast until thoroughly blended. Pour into the well and gradually draw in the flour, mixing vigorously to make a soft, sticky dough. Put the dough in a warm, greased bowl, cover with greased polythene and stand in a warm place to rise for 1 hour.

Turn out the dough on to a working surface, knock out all the air bubbles from it, then knead it (see p. 296) to a smooth ball. Put it back in the bowl, cover again and put back to rise for a further 30 minutes.

Turn out the risen dough on to a working surface, cut off about one-third and mould this to fit a warmed and greased 1 lb. (450 g.) loaf tin. Knead and mould the remaining two-thirds into a fat baton like a heavy rolling pin and put it on a greased and warmed baking sheet. Cover the tin and the baking sheet with greased polythene and put in a warm place for 25 minutes for the dough to rise.

Using a very sharp blade, make a cut $\frac{1}{2}$ in. (1·5 cm.) deep from end to end of the tin loaf. Cut the baton loaf from side to side about $\frac{1}{4}$ in. (5 mm.) deep at intervals of about $\frac{3}{4}$ in. (2 cm.). Sprinkle a little rye flour on each loaf, cover again and put back to rise for 15 minutes. Bake in the preheated oven for 30–35 minutes.

For a lighter rye bread, leave out the caraway seed, replace the sugar and treacle by 1 oz. (25 g.) of honey, and use $1\frac{1}{4}$ lb. (575 g.) of strong white flour with 8 oz. (225 g.) of rye flour instead of equal quantities of each.

BUTTER BUNS
North Country

NOTHING MAKES BETTER USE of enriched dough than a batch of these golden buns. Under the crisp top are quadrant layers of light dough, its sweetness sharpened by a filling of home-made lemon curd.

To prevent the filling from being squeezed out as the buns rise, leave a narrow margin unbuttered round the edge of each disc of dough before you fold it over the curd.

PREPARATION TIME: 45 MINUTES
FERMENTING, AND RISING TIME: $1\frac{3}{4}$ HOURS
COOKING TIME: ABOUT 10 MINUTES
PRE-HEAT THE OVEN TO
220°C (425°F)—GAS MARK 7

INGREDIENTS FOR 20 BUNS

For the ferment:

1 large egg, beaten
About $7\frac{1}{2}$ fl. oz. (215 ml.) warm water (see p. 296)
1 oz. (25 g.) fresh yeast
4 oz. (100/125 g.) strong white flour
$\frac{1}{2}$ oz. (15 g.) sugar

For the dough:

14 oz. (400 g.) strong white flour
$\frac{1}{4}$ teaspoon salt
3 oz. (75 g.) sugar
2 oz. (50 g.) soft butter
2 oz. (50 g.) melted butter
Lemon curd for filling
A little beaten egg to glaze
Caster sugar for sprinkling

To prepare the ferment, combine the beaten egg with enough warm water to give $\frac{1}{2}$ pint (275/300 ml.) of liquid. Mix the yeast to a smooth paste in 3 tablespoons of the liquid. Add the remaining liquid and whisk in the flour and sugar. Cover and put in a warm place for 30 minutes.

To make the dough, sieve the flour and salt on to a working surface or into a large mixing bowl and make a well in the centre. Put the sugar in the well and pour on the ferment. Stir to dissolve the sugar then mix vigorously to make a soft, sticky dough.

Knead (see p. 296) the soft butter in well then mould the dough into a ball, put it in a warm, greased bowl, cover with greased polythene and put in a warm place to rise for 45 minutes.

Turn out the risen dough on to a working surface, knock out any bubbles and divide it into 20 equal pieces. Mould them into balls, cover them with the polythene and leave on the working surface to rest for 5 minutes.

Roll out each ball into a disc $\frac{1}{8}$ in. (3 mm.) thick, brush with melted butter almost to the edge and place $\frac{1}{2}$ teaspoon of lemon curd on the centre. Fold the disc in half, brush again with butter and fold again to make a quarter circle. Space out on greased baking sheets. Brush over with beaten egg and sprinkle with caster sugar. Put to rise uncovered in a warm place for 25–30 minutes. Bake in the preheated oven for about 10 minutes.

SALLY LUNN LOAF
Bath

THE NAME SALLY LUNN comes from the woman who first made this bread—a Bath pastrycook who owned a shop in Lilliput Alley in the 1780s. Her house is still to be seen in the city. The basement in which she mixed and baked her cakes rests on the foundation of a Roman building of about 2,000 years ago.

Sally Lunn sold her cakes mainly to the wealthy and fashionable who came to take the local waters. They were eaten in the Pump Room by its habitués.

This sweet bread should be eaten as soon as it is cool enough to cut with a very sharp knife. Spread it generously with butter.

PREPARATION TIME: 25 MINUTES
FERMENTING AND RISING TIME: $1\frac{1}{2}$ HOURS
COOKING TIME: 15 MINUTES
PRE-HEAT THE OVEN TO
230°C (450°F)—GAS MARK 8

INGREDIENTS FOR THREE SMALL LOAVES

For the ferment:

$\frac{3}{4}$ oz. (20 g.) fresh yeast
2 level teaspoons sugar
2 oz. (50 g.) strong white flour
$\frac{1}{4}$ pint (150 ml.) warm water (see p. 296)

For the dough:

10 oz. (275 g.) strong white flour
$1\frac{1}{2}$ oz. (40 g.) sugar
1 large egg, beaten
Finely grated rind of 1 lemon
2 oz. (50 g.) softened butter
A little beaten egg to glaze

For the ferment, mix the yeast, sugar and flour together in a warm basin and gradually stir in the water to make a smooth, thin paste. Cover with greased polythene and put in a warm place to rise for 20 minutes.

To make the dough, sieve the flour into a large mixing bowl, make a well in the centre and put in the sugar, beaten egg and lemon rind. Pour in the ferment, mix vigorously and knead (see p. 296) to make a smooth dough. Knead in the softened butter, shape the dough into a ball and put it in a warm, lightly buttered bowl. Cover with greased polythene and stand in a warm place to rise for 30 minutes.

Divide the risen dough into three equal pieces, mould each into a ball and put into warm, lightly buttered, round cake tins 5 in. (13 cm.) across. Cover with greased polythene and leave to rise in a warm place for 35–40 minutes, brushing the top with beaten egg after 20 minutes. Bake in the pre-heated oven for 15 minutes.

BROWN SCONE
Countrywide

TRADITIONALLY, scones were baked on a griddle. In *Kidnapped* (1886), Robert Louis Stevenson describes how his two on-the-run heroes 'lay on the bare top of a rock, like scones upon a girdle'. Today, however, we usually bake scones in the oven.

PREPARATION TIME: 15 MINUTES
COOKING TIME: 30 MINUTES
PRE-HEAT THE OVEN TO
190°C (375°F)—GAS MARK 5

INGREDIENTS FOR SIX TO EIGHT SEGMENTS

6 oz. (175 g.) wholemeal flour
2 oz. (50 g.) plain white flour
1 level teaspoon cream of tartar
$\frac{1}{2}$ level teaspoon bicarbonate of soda
$\frac{1}{2}$ teaspoon salt
1 oz. (25 g.) butter or margarine
About 7 fl. oz. (200 ml.) milk

Mix together the flours, cream of tartar, bicarbonate of soda and salt. Rub in the fat with the fingertips until the mixture looks like breadcrumbs. Gradually mix in enough milk to make a soft dough.

Place the dough on a greased baking tray and pat it into a large, round scone $\frac{1}{2}$ in. (1·5 cm.) thick, flatten slightly, then mark across into segments with the back of a knife. Bake in the pre-heated oven for about 30 minutes, giving the tin a quarter turn if necessary during this time to ensure that the scone cooks and browns evenly.

POTATO SCONES
Scotland and Lancashire

WITH TYPICAL THRIFTINESS, the Scots were among the first people in Britain to make Potato Scones. In a cookery book published in 1909, Lady Clark of Tillypronie pointed out that, in Scotland, potatoes were often used to make flour go further. The cakes also became a speciality in Lancashire, where the Irish influence was strong and most smallholders grew their own potatoes.

The scones are best eaten as fresh as possible, and should be kept warm in a tea towel until needed.

PREPARATION TIME: 15 MINUTES
COOKING TIME: ABOUT 20 MINUTES
PRE-HEAT THE OVEN TO
180°C (350°F)—GAS MARK 4

INGREDIENTS FOR SIX TO EIGHT SCONES

3 oz. (75 g.) self-raising flour
$\frac{1}{4}$ teaspoon salt
2 level teaspoons baking powder
1 oz. (25 g.) butter or margarine
3 oz. (75 g.) potatoes, freshly boiled and sieved

Sieve together the flour, salt and baking powder, and rub in the butter with the fingertips. Mix in the potatoes well. Roll out lightly to about $\frac{3}{4}$ in. (2 cm.) thick and cut into rounds about 2 in. (5 cm.) across. Place on a greased baking sheet and bake in the pre-heated oven for about 20 minutes or until golden-brown. Serve hot and buttered.

Cold, cooked potatoes can be sieved and used, but the dough will then need 1 tablespoon of milk added to bind it properly.

ANGLESEY CAKE
Wales

IN THE MIDDLE of the 18th century, when treacle was much cheaper to buy than refined sugar, it was often used to sweeten porridge and puddings. In Wales—and the island of Anglesey in particular—treacle was added to cakes to give them an appearance of richness.

Anglesey cakes, darkened with treacle, were often served at weddings in families too poor to afford wedding cake. Today, the cake survives as a moist, dark-brown delicacy—with the recipe, sometimes known as 'granny's recipe', being handed down from generation to generation.

Preparation Time: 20 minutes
Cooking Time: 50–60 minutes
Pre-heat the Oven to 180°C (350°F)—gas mark 4

Ingredients

4 oz. (100/125 g.) margarine, or 2 oz. (50 g.) margarine and 2 oz. (50 g.) pure lard
3 oz. (75 g.) soft brown sugar
1 egg
1 tablespoon black treacle
10 oz. (275 g.) self-raising flour
¼ teaspoon salt
1 teaspoon ground ginger
1 teaspoon ground mixed spice
½ teaspoon bicarbonate of soda
7 fl. oz. (200 ml.) milk
6 oz. (175 g.) mixed raisins and currants

Cream the fat and sugar together until pale and fluffy. Beat in the egg and mix in the treacle. Sieve together the flour, salt, ginger and mixed spice and stir them into the creamed mixture. Dissolve the bicarbonate of soda in the milk, add gradually to the mixture and stir thoroughly before adding the dried fruit. Spoon the mixture into a greased and lined 7–8 in. (18–20 cm.) cake tin and bake in the pre-heated oven for 50–60 minutes.

The cake is best if kept for 24 hours before cutting.

Filling Cakes
Ireland

Buttermilk, originally one of the principal ingredients of Filling Cakes, used to be a food for the Irish poor. In the 18th century, the Irish satirical writer Jonathan Swift stated that farmers and their families, who paid 'great rents', lived in 'filth and nastiness on buttermilk and potatoes'.

Buttermilk—the residue of butter-making—was sometimes called 'churn milk'. Used with bicarbonate of soda, it helped to lighten the dough. Today, however, most cooks prefer to make the cakes with ordinary dairy milk, which is easier to obtain.

Preparation Time: 20 minutes
Cooling Time for the Filling: about 45 minutes
Cooking Time: 20–25 minutes
Pre-heat the Oven to 180°C (350°F)—gas mark 4

Ingredients for 10–12 Cakes

10 oz. (275 g.) self-raising flour
2 oz. (50 g.) sugar
½ teaspoon bicarbonate of soda
½ teaspoon cream of tartar
3 oz. (75 g.) margarine
Milk or buttermilk for mixing
Milk for glazing

For the filling:

4 oz. (100/125 g.) sultanas
4 oz. (100/125 g.) currants
2 oz. (50 g.) sugar
½ teaspoon grated nutmeg or ground mixed spice
3 tablespoons water

To make the filling, place all the ingredients in a saucepan and bring to the boil. Simmer for 8–10 minutes, stirring occasionally. Remove the pan from the heat and allow the mixture to cool before being used.

To make the cakes, mix the flour and sugar together and add the bicarbonate of soda and cream of tartar, mixing well. Rub in the margarine with the fingertips until the mixture looks like breadcrumbs. Gradually mix in just enough milk to make a soft dough. Roll out into an oblong about 6 in. (15 cm.) wide and about ¼ in. (5 mm.) thick.

Spread the filling over it to within ¼ in. (5 mm.) of the edge. Roll up like a roly-poly, and use a floured knife to cut into ½ in. (1·5 cm.) slices. Place on a greased baking sheet, cut side up and spaced well apart, brush over with a little milk, and bake in the pre-heated oven for 20–25 minutes.

Cherry and Almond Cake
Countrywide

Fruit cakes were a great favourite on Victorian tea-tables, and none more so than the Cherry and Almond Cake. Cultivated sweet cherries—like almonds—came to Britain at the time of the Roman Conquest.

In the 13th century, cherry trees were planted in the royal gardens at Westminster. At that period, cherries were served to the wealthy at the beginning of a meal to 'open the stomach'. London street vendors sold cherries to the poor who ate them, according to a writer of the day, in order to 'poison hunger'.

Glacé cherries combined with almonds go to make a particularly pleasing cake. It will keep in an airtight tin for some four to six weeks, and is a fine alternative to Christmas cake for those who do not like their cakes to be too rich.

Preparation Time: 25 minutes
Cooking Time: 1½–2 hours
Pre-heat the Oven to 170°C (325°F)—gas mark 3

Ingredients

4 oz. (100/125 g.) margarine
4 oz. (100/125 g.) butter
8 oz. (225 g.) caster sugar
3 eggs
¼ teaspoon almond essence
4 oz. (100/125 g.) glacé cherries, rinsed and halved (see p. 299)
8 oz. (225 g.) plain flour
4 oz. (100/125 g.) ground almonds
1 level teaspoon baking powder
¼ teaspoon salt
1 tablespoon granulated sugar

Cream together the margarine, butter and caster sugar until fluffy. Beat the eggs and almond essence together and gradually beat into the creamed mixture. Stir in the cherries. Sieve the flour, ground almonds, baking powder and salt together and fold in.

Grease a cake tin 8 in. (20 cm.) in diameter and line it with a double layer of greaseproof paper. Spoon the mixture into the tin and smooth the top.

Sprinkle the cake with granulated sugar and bake in the centre of the pre-heated oven for 1½–2 hours.

Allow the cake to cool in the tin for 20 minutes before turning out to finish cooling on a wire rack.

Rich Chocolate Cake
Countrywide

Chocolate, as a beverage, took the British well-to-do by storm in the late 17th century—a direct result of our having captured Jamaica and its cocoa plantations from the Spaniards in 1655. The use of chocolate in baking, however, began somewhat later; probably the first chocolate cakes in this country were the puffs of the late 17th century—small, light confections of sugar and beaten eggs, flavoured with chocolate.

This present recipe is essentially, and richly, Victorian.

Preparation and Icing Time: 50 minutes
Cooking Time: 30–35 minutes
Pre-heat the Oven to 180°C (350°F)—gas mark 4

Ingredients

For the cake:
- *8 oz. (225 g.) plain flour*
- *2 level teaspoons baking powder*
- *½ level teaspoon bicarbonate of soda*
- *¼ teaspoon salt*
- *2 oz. (50 g.) cooking or plain chocolate*
- *8 fl. oz. (225 ml.) milk*
- *5 oz. (150 g.) butter*
- *10 oz. (275 g.) dark, soft brown sugar*
- *3 eggs*
- *1 tablespoon black treacle*
- *1 teaspoon vanilla essence*

For the fudge icing:
- *1 lb. (450 g.) granulated sugar*
- *¼ pint (150 ml.) milk*
- *4 oz. (100/125 g.) butter*
- *1 level tablespoon golden syrup*
- *1 heaped tablespoon cocoa*
- *2 oz. (50 g.) cooking or plain chocolate*

Mouth-watering dark Chocolate Cake layered with fudge icing.

To make the cake, sift together the flour, baking powder, bicarbonate of soda and salt. Put the chocolate with the milk in a small saucepan over a low heat and stir occasionally. When the chocolate has melted, remove the pan from the heat and allow the mixture to cool.

Cream the butter and sugar until fluffy. Beat in the eggs, one at a time, adding a little of the flour mixture alternately with each egg. Stir in the treacle and vanilla essence and fold in the remaining flour. Mix well, then gradually stir in the cooled chocolate and milk to make a thick batter.

Divide the mixture between three greased sandwich tins, 7 in. (18 cm.) in diameter, and bake in the pre-heated oven for 30–35 minutes. Turn out the cakes on to a cake rack and leave to cool.

To make the icing, put the sugar, milk, butter, syrup, cocoa and chocolate in a large, heavy-based pan. Heat gently, stirring, until the sugar has dissolved, then bring to the boil and cook to the soft-ball stage (see p. 317). Leave to cool for 10 minutes, then beat until it is thick enough to spread. Sandwich the cake layers together with the icing and spread it over the top and sides of the cake, swirling it with a knife. It sets fairly rapidly so work quickly.

This moist, rich cake will keep for a week in an airtight tin.

Sponge Sandwich
Countrywide

To those who want to diet and still have the occasional slice of cake, the answer would seem to be the fat-free Sponge Sandwich or cake. A 16th-century recipe for 'Diet Bread' resembles the sponge finger biscuit of today.

The secret of making a really successful sponge cake lies in the beating. In the days before the electric mixer, cooks were sometimes advised to 'beat for an hour'.

This recipe can be used for a sponge sandwich, a deep sponge cake which is often served with fruit compôte, or a Swiss Roll—but note the different cooking temperatures and times.

Preparation Time: 15 minutes
Cooking Time: 20 minutes
Pre-heat the Oven to 190°C (375°F)—gas mark 5

INGREDIENTS

3 oz. (75 g.) caster sugar
3 oz. (75 g.) plain flour
3 eggs, separated

Warm the sugar and flour in separate bowls in the pre-heated oven for 5 minutes. Meanwhile, whisk the egg whites in a large, dry bowl until stiff and standing in peaks. Whisk in the warmed sugar alternately with the egg yolks. Sieve the warmed flour and fold it gently into the mixture.

Grease two sandwich tins 6–7 in. (15–18 cm.) in diameter and line the bottoms with greaseproof paper. Sprinkle 1 teaspoon each of flour and caster sugar into each tin, shake until the sides are evenly coated, and tip out the excess.

Spread the mixture in the tins, dividing it as evenly as possible between the two. Bake just above the centre of the pre-heated oven for 20 minutes, or until the centre of each cake springs back if gently pressed. Cool on a wire cake rack before discarding the paper and sandwiching together with jam or lemon curd, and whipped cream.

To make one deep sponge cake, spread all the mixture in a greased, lined and floured cake tin 6–7 in. (15–18 cm.) in diameter and bake at 180°C (350°F)—gas mark 4, for 35–40 minutes. Turn out and cool on a rack.

To make a Swiss Roll, spread the mixture in a greased, lined and floured shallow tin about 12 by 8 in. (30 by 20 cm.). Bake in the pre-heated oven for 7–10 minutes. Turn out on to a sheet of greaseproof paper which has been sprinkled with sugar and laid on a damp tea towel. Trim the edges off the sponge and roll up inside the paper. Leave to cool then unroll the sponge, spread with jam, whipped cream or butter cream (see p. 301) and roll up again.

Sweet curd-cheese tartlets, dubbed 'Maids of Honour' by Henry VIII.

RICHMOND MAIDS OF HONOUR
Surrey

ONE DAY WHILE he was strolling through the grounds of Hampton Court, so one traditional story goes, Henry VIII encountered a group of Maids of Honour—which included Anne Boleyn, later to be the monarch's second wife. The Maids, attendants to the queen, were eating cakes. One was offered to Henry. He tasted it, declared that it was delicious, and demanded to know its name. At the time—the mid-1520s—the cakes had none, so Henry decided that they should be called 'Maids of Honour'.

The 'Maids' were the invention of the pastrycook to Catherine of Aragon, Henry's first wife, and for more than 200 years the recipe was a closely kept secret. Then, during the reign of George II, a local businessman named Burdekin wormed the secret out of one of the court ladies. He promptly set up shop in Richmond-on-Thames, and for generations the Burdekin family prospered by making and selling the cakes.

If you prefer a less rich cake, replace the traditional puff pastry with shortcrust pastry.

PREPARATION TIME: 15 MINUTES
COOKING TIME: 20–30 MINUTES
PRE-HEAT THE OVEN TO 190°C (375°F)—GAS MARK 5

INGREDIENTS FOR 16 CAKES

8 oz. (225 g.) puff pastry (see p. 219)
8 oz. (225 g.) curd or cottage cheese
3 oz. (75 g.) sugar
2 oz. (50 g.) currants
Grated rind of 1 lemon
½ oz. (15 g.) blanched almonds, chopped
1 egg, beaten
2 teaspoons brandy
½ oz. (15 g.) butter, melted

Rub the cheese through a fine sieve. Add the sugar, currants, lemon rind, chopped almonds, egg, brandy and butter and mix well to combine the ingredients thoroughly.

Roll out the pastry and cut it in rounds to line 16 greased patty tins. Half fill them with the curd mixture. Bake in the pre-heated oven for 20–30 minutes until golden-brown.

COCONUT CRISPS
Countrywide

PORTUGUESE MARINERS first brought coconuts from India to Europe soon after 1496. But travelling under their own sail, as it were, the light and buoyant nuts have sometimes been carried on the warm currents of the Gulf Stream from Central America to Scandinavia.

Today, coconut is often used in cakes and biscuits, and the quickly and easily made Coconut Crisps are a fine example.

PREPARATION TIME: 15 MINUTES
COOKING TIME: ABOUT 15 MINUTES
PRE-HEAT THE OVEN TO 190°C (375°F)—GAS MARK 5

INGREDIENTS FOR ABOUT 20 CRISPS
3 oz. (75 g.) lard
1 oz. (25 g.) margarine
3 oz. (75 g.) caster sugar
1 small egg, beaten
5 oz. (150 g.) self-raising flour
About 2 oz. (50 g.) desiccated coconut
2 teaspoons lemon juice
Glacé cherries, halved

Cream the lard, margarine and sugar together until light and fluffy. Beat in the egg, then fold in the flour and 1 oz. (25 g.) coconut. Add the lemon juice and mix well.

With floured hands, divide the mixture into walnut-sized balls, roll in the remaining coconut and place, with a little space round each ball, on a greased baking sheet. Press half a glacé cherry on top of each biscuit and bake in the pre-heated oven for about 15 minutes until golden-brown. Give the baking sheet a quarter turn if necessary after about 10 minutes to ensure that all the crisps brown evenly.

EASTER OR LENTEN BISCUITS
Countrywide

IN THE MIDDLE AGES, Easter or Lenten Biscuits were enjoyed by rich and poor alike. For the rich, the small glazed cakes helped to make Shrove Tuesday the last day of rich eating before fasting began. For the poor, they were a rare treat.

The recipe given here makes crisp biscuits with a sugar-coated top. Add a little ground mixed spice if you like; this is a traditional flavouring in some parts of the country.

PREPARATION TIME: 20 MINUTES
COOKING TIME: 15–20 MINUTES
PRE-HEAT THE OVEN TO 170°C (325°F)—GAS MARK 3

INGREDIENTS FOR ABOUT 24 BISCUITS
For the biscuits:
4 oz. (100/125 g.) butter or margarine
4 oz. (100/125 g.) caster sugar
1 egg yolk
8 oz. (225 g.) plain flour
2 oz. (50 g.) currants
1 oz. (25 g.) mixed chopped peel
Milk to mix
For the glaze:
1 egg white
Caster sugar

Cream the butter and sugar until fluffy. Beat in the egg yolk and fold in the flour, currants and peel, mixing well. Pour in a little milk at a time, mixing well until the mixture forms a fairly stiff dough. Roll out to about $\frac{1}{8}$ in. (3 mm.) thick and cut into 2 in. (5 cm.) rounds.

Arrange on a greased baking sheet and bake in the pre-heated oven for 15–20 minutes. After 10 minutes lift the sheet from the oven, brush the biscuits quickly with egg white and sprinkle with caster sugar. Return to the oven for 5–10 minutes more to finish baking. Put the biscuits on a wire rack to cool.

JERSEY WONDERS
Jersey

ORIGINALLY, Jersey Wonders—which come in various shapes, from knots to butterflies—were an Easter speciality. Today, they are specialities at fairs and festivals held on the island, as well as being on general sale.

The traditional recipes vary from parish to parish, but when it comes to cooking, the cakes are always deep-fried until golden-brown. Sometimes cooking brandy is added to the cakes, and some people like them served hot with a fruity sauce. They will keep well in a covered earthenware jar or an airtight tin.

PREPARATION TIME: 15 MINUTES
STANDING TIME: 20–30 MINUTES
COOKING TIME: 15–20 MINUTES

INGREDIENTS FOR 18–20 CAKES
12 oz. (350 g.) self-raising flour
4 oz. (100/125 g.) plain flour
4 oz. (100/125 g.) sugar
4 oz. (100/125 g.) butter
4 eggs, beaten
Lard or oil for deep-frying

Sieve together the self-raising flour and the plain flour and mix in the sugar. Rub in the butter with the fingertips until the mixture looks like breadcrumbs. Add the beaten eggs and mix thoroughly to bind the ingredients together. Knead well until the mixture forms a smooth but fairly stiff dough. Add a little extra flour if the dough is too soft. Divide it into about 18 balls and leave to stand for 20–30 minutes.

Roll out each ball into an oblong shape about $\frac{1}{4}$ in. (5 mm.) thick. Make a cut in the centre and tuck the two outside ends through the centre slit.

Deep-fry the cakes in two or three batches in hot lard or oil (see p. 259) until golden-brown. Lift them out, drain first on kitchen paper and then on a cake rack.

SIMNEL CAKE
Countrywide

MOTHERS whose daughters went into service in the late 1600s looked forward to the fourth Sunday in Lent. It was then that the girls came home bearing the proof of their cooking skills—a rich and delicious fruit cake enriched with almond paste and called a Simnel Cake.

Later, that Sunday became known as Mothering Sunday. Originally the cakes, richly fruited with currants, were decorated with 11 small paste balls, symbolising Christ's 11 faithful disciples. The cakes improved with keeping and were eaten at the end of the Lenten Fast, when they were sometimes known as Easter Cakes.

The name of the cake comes from the Latin word *simila*, meaning 'the very best wheat flour'.

PREPARATION TIME: 25 MINUTES
COOKING TIME: 1½–2 HOURS
PRE-HEAT THE OVEN TO
140°C (275°F)—GAS MARK 1

INGREDIENTS

For the cake:

4 oz. (100/125 g.) butter
4 oz. (100/125 g.) soft brown sugar
3 eggs, beaten
5 oz. (150 g.) plain flour
¼ teaspoon salt
½ teaspoon ground mixed spice (optional)
12 oz. (350 g.) mixed raisins, currants and sultanas
2 oz. (50 g.) chopped mixed peel
Grated rind of ½ lemon
A little apricot jam
A little beaten egg for glazing

For the almond paste:

4 oz. (100/125 g.) caster sugar
4 oz. (100/125 g.) ground almonds
1 egg, beaten
½ teaspoon almond essence

To make the almond paste, mix together the sugar and ground almonds, and add sufficient beaten egg to give a fairly soft consistency. Add the almond essence and knead for 1 minute until the paste is smooth and pliable. Roll out a third of the almond paste to make a circle 7 in. (18 cm.) in diameter. Reserve the remainder for topping the cooked cake.

To make the cake, cream the butter and sugar together until fluffy. Beat in the eggs, a little at a time. Sift the flour, salt and spice together and add to the mixture alternately with the dried fruit, peel and grated rind, mixing the ingredients well together.

Put half the mixture into a greased and lined 7 in. (18 cm.) cake tin. Smooth the top and cover with the circle of almond paste. Add the rest of the cake mixture and smooth the top, hollowing the centre slightly. Bake in the pre-heated oven for 1½–2 hours.

When the cake is cold, brush over the top with apricot jam. Form 11 small balls from the reserved almond paste and roll out the rest to cover the top of the cake. Lay it on the jam, set the balls round the edge and brush all the top with a very little beaten egg. Return the cake to the oven for about 10 minutes at 180°C (350°F)—gas mark 4, for the almond paste to brown.

If you like, you can decorate the centre of the cake with coloured marzipan Easter eggs.

This cake keeps well in a tin for 2 weeks or more.

Symbols of Easter: Simnel Cake with almond topping, deep-fried Jersey Wonders and sugar-coated Easter Biscuits.

RASPBERRY GRIDDLE SCONES
Wales

RASPBERRIES are a truly native fruit and the wild variety was eaten by the Bronze Age inhabitants of Britain. They were not recorded in Britain as a garden fruit until the 16th century—but they had probably been cultivated for some time before that.

It was the Welsh who first used raspberries in combination with griddle scones. The result was a favourite dish in medieval times, and it retains its popularity today—with a handful of strawberries as an equally delicious alternative ingredient.

Sour milk makes the scones lighter. If you have none, add a little vinegar to fresh milk until it curdles.

PREPARATION TIME: 10 MINUTES
COOKING TIME: 10 MINUTES

INGREDIENTS FOR 12 SCONES

- *4 oz. (100/125 g.) self-raising flour*
- *¼ teaspoon salt*
- *½ teaspoon baking powder or bicarbonate of soda*
- *1 egg, beaten*
- *About ½ pint (275/300 ml.) sour milk*
- *4–6 oz. (100–175 g.) raspberries*
- *Caster sugar for sprinkling*

Sift together the flour, salt and baking powder or bicarbonate of soda. Make a well in the centre and pour in the egg and half the milk. Beat well, adding more milk as necessary, to form a batter the consistency of thick cream. Stir in the fruit.

Heat a griddle or heavy-based frying pan and smear with a little butter or lard. Drop 3–4 separate tablespoons of the batter mixture on to it, spacing them out well to allow them to spread without running together. Cook for about 1½ minutes or until bubbles appear. Turn over and cook the second side a little, taking care not to burn the fruit.

Lift the scones on to a plate, using a palette knife or fish slice. Sprinkle them with sugar. Serve hot or cold.

SINGIN' HINNY
Tyneside

'HINNY' is a well-known Tyneside corruption of 'honey', and is used as a term of affection. The Singin' refers to the contented sound the cake makes as it cooks on a hot griddle or grid-iron.

In the 19th century the cake was a favourite with Geordie children, who ate it at birthday parties. It sometimes had hidden in it pearl buttons, small thimbles and threepenny pieces, and these were used to tell the youngsters' fortunes.

A boy who found a button in his piece of cake would be a bachelor for life. A girl who discovered a thimble was destined to be a thrifty housewife. And anyone getting a threepenny piece would be assured that they were going to grow up to be prosperous.

PREPARATION TIME: 20 MINUTES
COOKING TIME: 6–8 MINUTES
PRE-HEAT THE GRIDDLE, OR PRE-HEAT THE OVEN TO 190°C (375°F)—GAS MARK 5

INGREDIENTS

- *12 oz. (350 g.) self-raising flour*
- *2 oz. (50 g.) ground rice*
- *1 teaspoon salt*
- *2 oz. (50 g.) sugar*
- *2 teaspoons baking powder*
- *2 oz. (50 g.) lard*
- *3 oz. (75 g.) currants*
- *¼ pint (150 ml.) cream from the top of the milk, or half cream and half milk*

Raspberry Griddle Scones—a Welsh combination of soft fruit and light, crisp batter.

Mix together the flour, ground rice, salt, sugar and baking powder. Rub in the lard with the fingertips until the mixture resembles fine breadcrumbs, then mix in the currants. Make a well in the centre, pour in the liquid and mix to a soft dough.

Roll or pat out to about ¼ in. (5 mm.) thick. Prick all over with a fork and halve or quarter the circle if you like, to make turning over easier. Bake on a hot greased griddle or greased, heavy-based frying pan for 3–4 minutes on each side until well browned, using a fish slice for turning.

You can also bake Singin' Hinny for 10–15 minutes in a pre-heated oven on a greased baking sheet, but it is best when cooked on the traditional griddle. Serve it hot, split and buttered.

BANBURY CAKES
Oxfordshire

BANBURY in Oxfordshire is well known from the nursery rhyme:

'Ride a cock horse to Banbury Cross,
To see a fine lady upon a white horse.
With rings on her fingers and bells on her toes,
She shall have music wherever she goes.'

People visiting Banbury today will observe no music-accompanied lady on horseback. Nor will they see the original cross. However, they will find a replacement cross, and will doubtless sample the equally renowned Banbury Cakes.

The cakes were first made in the 16th century, and the spiced, currant pastry soon became a favourite with residents and travellers. The cock horse mentioned in the nursery rhyme refers to the fifth horse added to a coach-and-four on arduous journeys.

PREPARATION TIME: 20 MINUTES
COOKING TIME: 20–25 MINUTES
PRE-HEAT THE OVEN TO 200°C (400°F)—GAS MARK 6

INGREDIENTS FOR ABOUT 15 CAKES

12 oz. (350 g.) flaky pastry (see p. 218)
Egg white for brushing
Granulated sugar for sprinkling

For the filling:

4 oz. (100/125 g.) butter
8 oz. (225 g.) mixed peel, finely chopped
8 oz. (225 g.) currants
1 level teaspoon ground mixed spice
2 teaspoons lemon juice

To prepare the filling, cream the butter and mix in the peel, currants, spice and lemon juice.

Roll out the pastry to just under ¼ in. (5 mm.) thick and cut into rounds with a 3 in. (8 cm.) cutter. Put 1 heaped teaspoon of filling on each round and draw the edges up to cover the filling. Moisten the edges and pinch them together to make the cakes oval. Place on a greased baking sheet with the join underneath and make a slit in the top of each. Brush the tops with egg white and sprinkle with granulated sugar. Bake in the pre-heated oven for 20–25 minutes.

These cakes are best eaten within 24 hours, as are all flaky pastries. They can be freshened again by re-heating gently for 10 minutes.

FAIRY CAKES
Countrywide

FAIRIES MADE their literary début in the 14th century. Traditionally, these small, magical folk live in great luxury, happiness and freedom in woods and forests. Their chief pastimes are dancing and singing, and they are as airy as gossamer.

Appropriately, they gave their name to small, light Fairy Cakes. Topped with coloured icing they are the ideal choice for a children's tea party, and are best eaten within two or three days of baking.

PREPARATION TIME: 15 MINUTES
COOKING TIME: 7–10 MINUTES
PRE-HEAT THE OVEN TO 190°C (375°F)—GAS MARK 5

INGREDIENTS FOR 12 CAKES

2 oz. (50 g.) self-raising flour
2 oz. (50 g.) cornflour
1 level teaspoon baking powder
2 oz. (50 g.) butter
2 oz. (50 g.) sugar
1 egg, beaten
1–2 tablespoons milk
1 oz. (25 g.) currants

Sieve together the self-raising flour, cornflour and baking powder. Cream the butter and sugar until light and fluffy. Beat the egg into the creamed mixture alternately with the flour. Mix in sufficient milk to give a soft, dropping consistency.

Grease 12 shallow patty tins and put a few currants in the bottom of each. Spoon in the mixture, dividing it equally between the 12 tins. Bake in the pre-heated oven for 7–10 minutes. Remove from the tins and allow to cool on a wire rack.

When the cakes are completely cold you can decorate them with coloured glacé icing (see p. 301).

HONEY CAKE
Countrywide

HONEY CAKE was a much-served delicacy among the Ancient Greeks, who believed that honey—the earliest form of sweetening—contained life-promoting qualities. The philosopher and mathematician Pythagoras, who lived in the 6th century BC, recommended it to his followers as an aid to a long and healthy life.

Some 500 years later, Honey Cake was a popular delicacy among the Romans—sometimes with nuts and figs added. By the 18th century, the cake was much enjoyed throughout Britain—with the Scots using heather honey, and the Welsh their local honey and cinnamon. This moist cake sometimes sinks a little when the honey has a high water content, but this in no way spoils its flavour.

PREPARATION TIME: 20 MINUTES
COOKING TIME: 45–50 MINUTES
PRE-HEAT THE OVEN TO 180°C (350°F)—GAS MARK 4

INGREDIENTS

3 oz. (75 g.) butter
3 oz. (75 g.) sugar
2 eggs, beaten
4 oz. (100/125 g.) honey
8 oz. (225 g.) self-raising flour
1 teaspoon baking powder

Cream together the butter and sugar, and gradually beat in the eggs and honey. Add the sieved flour and baking powder, a little at a time, mixing well. Put into a greased and lined tin, 9 in. (23 cm.) in diameter or 8 in. (20 cm.) square, and bake in the pre-heated oven for 45–50 minutes.

The use of flavoured honeys, such as clover or heather, gives this cake a distinctive taste.

DUNDEE CAKE
Scotland

DESPITE ITS NAME, Dundee Cake is not a speciality of Dundee. Recipes for it throughout Scotland go back to the late 18th century. The cake is recognised by the almonds which decorate the top. Orange and lemon rind are essential ingredients; and rum, brandy or sherry can be added at the cook's discretion in place of some of the lemon or orange juice.

PREPARATION TIME: 20 MINUTES
COOKING TIME: $1\frac{3}{4}$–2 HOURS
PRE-HEAT THE OVEN TO 150°C (300°F)—GAS MARK 2

INGREDIENTS

- *6 oz. (175 g.) butter or margarine*
- *6 oz. (175 g.) soft brown sugar*
- *4 eggs*
- *8 oz. (225 g.) plain flour, sifted*
- *$\frac{1}{4}$ teaspoon salt*
- *1 oz. (25 g.) ground almonds*
- *6 oz. (175 g.) sultanas*
- *4 oz. (100/125 g.) currants*
- *2 oz. (50 g.) mixed chopped peel*
- *2 oz. (50 g.) glacé cherries, rinsed and chopped (see p. 299)*
- *Juice and grated rind of $\frac{1}{2}$ lemon*
- *Juice and grated rind of $\frac{1}{2}$ orange*
- *1 oz. (25 g.) whole almonds, blanched*

Cream the butter and sugar together until light and fluffy. Beat in the eggs, one at a time. Fold in the sifted flour and the salt and ground almonds and mix well. Stir in the sultanas, currants, peel, cherries, and the lemon and orange rind and juice.

Grease a cake tin 8–9 in. (20–23 cm.) in diameter and line it with a double layer of greaseproof paper. Spoon the mixture into the tin and smooth the top, hollowing the centre very slightly. Arrange the blanched almonds on top and bake in the pre-heated oven for $1\frac{3}{4}$–2 hours. Do not open the oven door during the first 30 minutes. If the cake is browning too much towards the end of cooking time, cover it lightly with a piece of greaseproof paper or foil.

Allow the cake to cool completely before wrapping in foil and storing in an airtight tin, where it will keep for many weeks.

A modern variation of this traditional recipe is to replace 2 oz. (50 g.) of the flour with powdered drinking chocolate.

SHORTBREAD
Scotland

ALTHOUGH SHORTBREAD is eaten all year round, in Scotland it is particularly associated with Hogmanay. Then, it is given to first-footers in return for the good luck they are said to bring to people's homes.

The melting, flat cake is unusual in that it contains no liquid. To keep its shape the shortbread relies on the adhesive power of the buttery flour particles, so use only the best flour, butter and sugar.

Traditionally, shortbread is presented at the table as a flat round cake and cut or broken into segments at table.

PREPARATION TIME: 15 MINUTES
COOKING TIME: 40–45 MINUTES
PRE-HEAT THE OVEN TO 180°C (350°F)—GAS MARK 4

INGREDIENTS FOR 8–10 SEGMENTS OR ABOUT 20 FINGERS

- *8 oz. (225 g.) butter*
- *$4\frac{1}{2}$ oz. (130 g.) caster sugar*
- *12 oz. (350 g.) plain flour*
- *Caster sugar for sprinkling*

Rub the butter and sugar together, then work in the flour lightly with the fingertips. Continue mixing it until the ingredients form a dough. Shape into a round $\frac{1}{2}$ in. (1·5 cm.) thick, or place inside a flan ring on a greased baking sheet. Prick all over with a fork, and mark across into segments.

Bake in the pre-heated oven for 40–45 minutes until light golden-brown. Allow the shortbread to cool a little before removing from the baking sheet. Dust with caster sugar and leave on a wire rack until cold.

Alternatively, pat the dough into an oblong about $\frac{1}{4}$ in. (5 mm.) thick and 3 in. (8 cm.) wide, and cut it into shortbread fingers. Space out well on a greased baking sheet and bake in the pre-heated oven for 20–25 minutes.

The shortbread will keep well if stored in an airtight tin.

SCONES
Countrywide

THE NAME 'SCONE' is believed to come from the Gaelic word *sgonn*, or 'large mouthful'.

Whether plain or fruited, scones have long been a tea-time favourite. Quickly made, they are ideal for serving to unexpected guests. Do not overcook them or their soft, light texture will be spoiled.

PREPARATION TIME: 15 MINUTES
COOKING TIME: 12–15 MINUTES
PRE-HEAT THE OVEN TO 190°C (375°F)—GAS MARK 5

INGREDIENTS FOR ABOUT 24 SCONES

- *4 oz. (100/125 g.) butter or margarine*
- *1 lb. (450 g.) self-raising flour*
- *$\frac{1}{4}$ teaspoon salt*
- *$\frac{1}{2}$ teaspoon bicarbonate of soda*
- *Milk to mix*

Rub the fat into the flour with the fingertips until the mixture looks like breadcrumbs. Add the salt and bicarbonate of soda. Mix in sufficient milk to make a soft dough.

Pat or roll out the dough lightly until it is about $\frac{1}{2}$ in. (1·5 cm.) thick, and cut into $1\frac{1}{2}$ in. (4 cm.) rounds. Bake in the pre-heated oven for 12–15 minutes.

You can make cheese scones by mixing in 2 oz. (50 g.) strong, grated Cheddar cheese and $\frac{1}{4}$ teaspoon dry mustard before the milk. Serve hot and buttered.

For another variation add 1–2 teaspoons of finely chopped chives to the basic recipe. These herb scones are best served, unbuttered, as an unusual accompaniment to a soup or a casserole.

You can sweeten plain scones by adding 1 tablespoon of sugar to the basic mixture before the milk. Serve with strawberry jam and whipped cream.

To make fruit scones, add 2 oz. (50 g.) sugar and 4 oz. (100/125 g.) sultanas to the basic mixture. You can add an egg with the milk to enrich the scones if you like.

Teatime in Scotland: Plain and Fruit Scones to spread with jam, Honey Cake, Dundee Cake and buttery Shortbread.

CORNISH FAIRINGS
Cornwall

DURING THE WEEK after Christmas, a well-patronised 'maid-hiring' fair was held in the market town of Launceston, in Cornwall. It was customary to eat or take home ginger-flavoured Cornish Fairings, one of a wide choice of sweet treats sold at the fair.

From late medieval times onward gingerbreads made with breadcrumbs were sold at fairs throughout the country. The crisp ginger biscuits were made rather later.

Cornish Fairings eventually included ginger biscuits sweetened with honey; richly coloured with saffron, liquorice, or sandalwood; and decorated with almonds, marzipan, icing, or gold leaf.

The original Cornish Fairings keep very well in an airtight tin, and have a most attractive cracked, deep golden-brown appearance.

PREPARATION TIME: 15 MINUTES
COOKING TIME: 10–12 MINUTES
PRE-HEAT THE OVEN TO 200°C (400°F)—GAS MARK 6

INGREDIENTS FOR ABOUT 18 BISCUITS

8 oz. (225 g.) plain flour
½ teaspoon salt
2 level teaspoons baking powder
2 level teaspoons bicarbonate of soda
2 level teaspoons ground mixed spice
3 level teaspoons ground ginger
1 level teaspoon cinnamon
4 oz. (100/125 g.) butter or margarine
4 oz. caster sugar
4 tablespoons golden syrup, gently heated

Sieve together the flour, salt, baking powder, bicarbonate of soda, spice, ginger and cinnamon. Rub in the fat with the fingertips until the mixture resembles breadcrumbs and add the sugar. Pour in the syrup and mix thoroughly to a fairly stiff consistency.

With floured hands, roll the mixture into walnut-sized balls. Place them on a greased baking sheet, well spaced out to allow room to spread. Bake in the pre-heated oven for 10–12 minutes, moving the sheet from the top to the bottom of the oven after 5–7 minutes or as soon as the biscuits start to brown. Leave the fairings to cool for a few minutes on the baking sheet before removing to a cake rack with a spatula or fish slice to stand until cooled completely.

OATCAKES
Scotland

ONE OF THE FIRST PEOPLE to hear of the defeat of 'Bonnie Prince Charlie' at the Battle of Culloden, in 1746, was an old woman living in a nearby cottage. Immediately, she took a small table, her griddle, and a bag of oatmeal down to the road. There, lighting a wood fire, she set about baking oatcakes, which she handed out to the Young Pretender's soldiers.

Today, oatcakes are still cooked on a griddle—but many people prefer to bake them in a moderate oven instead. To get the very best out of them, eat them with potted cheese. For a slightly sweeter oatcake, add two teaspoons of sugar to the dough.

PREPARATION TIME: 10 MINUTES
COOKING TIME: 20 MINUTES
PRE-HEAT THE OVEN TO 190°C (375°F)—GAS MARK 5

INGREDIENTS FOR FOUR OATCAKES

8 oz. (225 g.) fine oatmeal
½ teaspoon baking powder
¼ teaspoon salt
2 tablespoons melted butter or bacon fat
¼ pint (150 ml.) boiling water

Gingerbreads: plain and gilded fairings; and sandalwood, iced, marzipan and liquorice ginger biscuits.

Mix together the oatmeal, baking powder and salt. Add the melted butter or fat and the water, and stir well. Lightly knead the dough with hands coated with oatmeal, until it forms a smooth ball.

On a board well sprinkled with oatmeal, roll out the dough as thinly as possible into a round. Keep pinching the breaking edges together with your fingers. Cut the round into four pieces, and lift with a fish-slice on to a very large ungreased baking sheet.

Bake in the pre-heated oven for about 20 minutes, until pale fawn.

DIGESTION BISCUITS
Countrywide

AS THEIR NAME SUGGESTS, Digestion Biscuits were considered good for the stomach. Certainly the Victorians thought so, and the biscuits—made with oatmeal and wholemeal flour—were popular in many country households.

Digestion Biscuits were sometimes eaten as an alternative to bread. They are excellent with butter and cheese.

PREPARATION TIME: 15 MINUTES
COOKING TIME: 10–15 MINUTES
PRE-HEAT THE OVEN TO 190°C (375°F)—GAS MARK 5

INGREDIENTS FOR 12–14 BISCUITS

4 oz. (100/125 g.) medium oatmeal
4 oz. (100/125 g.) wholemeal flour
2 oz. (50 g.) caster sugar
¼ teaspoon salt
½ level teaspoon bicarbonate of soda
3 oz. (75 g.) butter or margarine
1 small egg, beaten

Mix together the oatmeal, flour, sugar, salt and bicarbonate of soda. Rub in the butter with the fingertips, then add the egg and mix well.

Place the dough on a working surface sprinkled with oatmeal. Roll out to about ½ in. (1·5 cm.) thick, and cut into 3 in. (8 cm.) rounds. Place on a greased baking sheet and bake in the pre-heated oven for 10–15 minutes.

Replace the wholemeal flour with plain flour if you prefer biscuits with less roughage.

PARKIN
Yorkshire

TRADITIONALLY, Yorkshire Parkin is eaten on Guy Fawkes' Night. The connection with the Gunpowder Plot conspirator is that he was a Yorkshire man—born in York in 1570. A dialect almanack published 300 years later recorded that: 'Th' children's all lukkin' forrad to th' plot an' parkin.'

This dark cake is sometimes eaten with a topping of stewed apple or accompanied by cheese. It is best kept in a box with a close-fitting lid. In Georgian times both parkin and gingerbread were stored in a special wooden container. Today, a tin will do.

PREPARATION TIME: 20 MINUTES
COOKING TIME: ABOUT 1 HOUR
PRE-HEAT THE OVEN TO 170°C (325°F)—GAS MARK 3

INGREDIENTS

4 oz. (100/125 g.) self-raising flour
1 teaspoon ground ginger
1 teaspoon bicarbonate of soda
¼ teaspoon salt
4 oz. (100/125 g.) pinhead or fine oatmeal
1 oz. (25 g.) chopped mixed peel (optional)
4 oz. (100/125 g.) black treacle
2 oz. (50 g.) sugar, white or brown
2 oz. (50 g.) butter or margarine
1 egg, beaten
About 2 tablespoons milk

Sift together in a bowl the flour, ginger, bicarbonate of soda and salt. Mix in the oatmeal, and peel if used.

Melt the treacle, sugar and butter in a small saucepan over a low heat. Stir in the egg with a wooden spoon, and pour the mixture over the dry ingredients. Mix well and add enough milk to make a soft, pouring consistency. Pour into a well-greased shallow tin 6 in. (15 cm.) square, and bake in the pre-heated oven for about 1 hour, until firm in the centre. When cool, cut into squares.

If you find black treacle is too strongly flavoured, replace half of it or all of it with golden syrup. The parkin will then be lighter in colour as well as in flavour.

SLY CAKES
Yorkshire and Northumberland

SOMETIMES known as 'Sally Sly Cakes', these are among our earliest party treats. The recipe dates from the beginning of the 16th century. The cakes probably got their name from their surprise element: for lying beneath their plain golden-brown tops is a rich filling of figs, raisins, currants and nuts.

PREPARATION TIME: 15 MINUTES
COOLING TIME: ABOUT 45 MINUTES
COOKING TIME: 25–30 MINUTES
PRE-HEAT THE OVEN TO 190°C (375°F)—GAS MARK 5

INGREDIENTS FOR 10 PIECES

8 oz. (225 g.) shortcrust pastry (see p. 217) with 2 oz. (50 g.) sugar added with the fat
A little milk to glaze

For the filling:

6 oz. (175 g.) dried figs, chopped
2 oz. (50 g.) raisins
2 oz. (50 g.) currants
2 oz. (50 g.) chopped walnuts
2 oz. (50 g.) sugar
4 tablespoons water

To make the filling, put the figs in a pan with the raisins, currants, walnuts and sugar. Add the water and simmer until the figs are tender and the water has been absorbed. Leave to cool.

Roll out half the pastry to line a greased, shallow oblong tin, about 9 by 4 in. (23 by 10 cm.). Spread on the filling and damp the rim of the pastry with water. Roll out the remaining pastry, lay it over the filling and pinch the edges together to seal. Brush with milk and bake in the pre-heated oven for 25–30 minutes, or until golden-brown. Sprinkle with sugar, if liked, and cut into squares when cool.

STRAWBERRY RING
Pembrokeshire

FORTUNATELY for families living in Pembrokeshire—now part of the county of Dyfed—strawberries grow near to the ground and so miss the full fury of the Atlantic winds. The coastal climate benefits strawberry plants, protecting them from the usual hazards of frost.

The fragrant fruits are shown to advantage against the fluffy cream filling in this party dish. Add the filling as late as possible to prevent the pastry from becoming too wet.

As an alternative to strawberries, you can use fresh or frozen raspberries in the filling. Some people like to sprinkle toasted almond flakes over the ring as a garnish.

PREPARATION TIME: 20 MINUTES
COOKING TIME: 30 MINUTES
PRE-HEAT THE OVEN TO
220°C (425°F)—GAS MARK 7

INGREDIENTS FOR SIX

2½ oz. (65 g.) choux pastry (see p. 220)
½ pint (275/300 ml.) double cream
3 tablespoons icing sugar, sifted
1 lb. (450 g.) fresh, hulled strawberries
Icing sugar for dusting

Spoon the pastry into a forcing bag fitted with a large plain nozzle. Pipe a ring about 1½ in. (4 cm.) wide and 8 in. (20 cm.) across on to a greased baking tray. Bake in the centre of the pre-heated oven for 30 minutes until golden-brown.

Allow the choux ring to cool on a wire rack. When cool, but not cold, split it in half horizontally with a sharp knife.

To make the filling, use a hand whisk and whip together the cream and icing sugar until light and fluffy. Spoon the cream into the bottom half of the ring.

Arrange the fruit on top and round the sides of the heaped-up cream. Place the choux-pastry lid on top gently, and dust over lightly with icing sugar.

Summer flavours: cream and plump fruit in a Strawberry Ring.

MADEIRA CAKE
Countrywide

MORNING CALLERS at well-to-do 19th-century households, both in town and in the country, were often given Madeira wine to drink and Madeira Cake to eat.

The wine has a rich and mysterious flavour, as it contains a small percentage of brandy to preserve it. Most of the Madeira shipped to England entered the country at Bristol, where the habit of taking it with the cake started.

As a social drink, Madeira was later replaced by sherry and port—although Madeira Cake continues to be served. It is well worth trying with its original partner. The cake itself is a true test of a cook's skill, since it must not be too dry. Use butter, not any other fat, when you make the cake, to give it the best flavour.

PREPARATION TIME: 20 MINUTES
COOKING TIME: 1½–1¾ HOURS
PRE-HEAT THE OVEN TO
170°C (325°F)—GAS MARK 3

INGREDIENTS

8 oz. (225 g.) self-raising flour
¼ teaspoon salt
6 oz. (175 g.) butter
6 oz. (175 g.) caster sugar
4 eggs
2 strips citron peel

Sieve the flour and salt together. Cream the butter and sugar until pale and fluffy. Beat in the eggs, one at a time, adding 1 tablespoon of the flour with each egg. Fold in the rest of the flour thoroughly and spoon the mixture into a greased and lined cake tin, 7 in. (18 cm.) in diameter. Bake in the pre-heated oven for about 1½–1¾ hours, reducing the heat to 150°C (300°F)—gas mark 2, after 1 hour.

Place the two strips of citron peel on top of the cake after it has been in the oven for 30 minutes.

Grated lemon rind may be added to the basic mixture to give the cake a tangy lemon flavour.

SEED CAKE
Countrywide

SEED CAKE is flavoured with caraway seeds, which are much lighter than the fruit usually added to cakes. For this reason, it was the first large rich cake to use eggs instead of yeast as its raising agent.

By the 18th century it had become a general tea-table favourite, and it remained so throughout Queen Victoria's reign. Its distinctive flavour marries well with tea—or even with a sweet wine.

PREPARATION TIME: 15 MINUTES
COOKING TIME: ABOUT 1 HOUR
PRE-HEAT THE OVEN TO 180°C (350°F)—GAS MARK 4

INGREDIENTS
- *4 oz. (100/125 g.) butter*
- *4 oz. (100/125 g.) caster sugar*
- *2 eggs, beaten*
- *6 oz. (175 g.) self-raising flour, sifted*
- *1 oz. (25 g.) mixed chopped peel*
- *1 heaped teaspoon caraway seeds*
- *1 tablespoon warm water*

Cream together the butter and sugar. Add the beaten egg, a little at a time, beating well. Stir in the flour, peel and caraway seeds. Mix well, then stir in the water. Spoon into a greased and lined cake tin 6–7 in. (15–18 cm.) in diameter, and smooth the top. If you like, sprinkle a few extra caraway seeds on top. Bake in the pre-heated oven for about 1 hour.

MACAROONS
Countrywide

AMONG THE THINGS the Romans brought to Britain were almonds, one of the basic ingredients of macaroons. The Romans, who believed that almonds had a sobering effect, ate them while drinking wine.

There is a traditional tale that 'macaroon' stems from the Greek word *makaria* (happy), and that the biscuits were introduced to Naples by the Greeks in the 10th century. Six-hundred years later, macaroons came to England from the Continent, where nuns served them with wine to visitors. Today, macaroons are still served with sherry and sweet wines.

PREPARATION TIME: 10 MINUTES
COOKING TIME: 25–30 MINUTES
PRE-HEAT THE OVEN TO 180°C (350°F)—GAS MARK 4

INGREDIENTS FOR 18–20 MACAROONS
- *4 oz. (100/125 g.) ground almonds*
- *8 oz. (225 g.) caster sugar*
- *1 oz. (25 g.) ground rice*
- *2 egg whites, stiffly whisked*
- *About 10 almonds, blanched, peeled and split*
- *Rice paper for lining baking sheets*

Use a metal spoon to fold the almonds, sugar and ground rice carefully into the egg whites.

Line one or two baking sheets with rice paper, and, using a teaspoon, spoon small heaps of the mixture on to the paper, well spaced out to allow room to spread. Put a split almond on top of each macaroon and bake in the pre-heated oven for 25–30 minutes. Cut the excess rice paper from the base of each macaroon, and leave them to cool on a wire rack.

You can use non-stick paper in place of the rice paper to line the baking sheets, and the macaroons will lift off it easily.

A Victorian morning, with almond Macaroons, caraway Seed Cake, Madeira Cake and the essential glass of Madeira wine.

CIDER CAKE
Herefordshire

WITH THE OPENING of what was to become the world's largest cider-making factory in Hereford in 1887, local cooks began to use the fermented drink in making spicy Cider Cake. To this day the cake—containing a generous measure of sweet or dry cider—is eaten all the year round, as well as at the annual cider festival which takes place in Hereford each June.

PREPARATION TIME: 15 MINUTES
COOKING TIME: 35–40 MINUTES
PRE-HEAT THE OVEN TO 180°C (350°F)—GAS MARK 4

INGREDIENTS

4 oz. (100/125 g.) butter or margarine
4 oz. (100/125 g.) sugar
2 eggs, beaten
8 oz. (225 g.) self-raising flour, sifted
1 teaspoon bicarbonate of soda
½ teaspoon grated nutmeg or powdered cinnamon
7 fl. oz. (200 ml.) cider
Caster sugar for sprinkling

Cream together the butter and sugar until fluffy and beat in the eggs. Fold in half the flour, the bicarbonate of soda and the nutmeg or cinnamon. Pour the cider into the mixture and mix thoroughly. Stir in the remaining flour. Pour the mixture into a greased shallow tin, about 8 by 5 in. (20 by 13 cm.), and bake in the pre-heated oven for 35–40 minutes. Cut into squares when cool and sprinkle with caster sugar.

VICTORIA SANDWICH
Countrywide

AFTER THE DEATH of her husband, Prince Albert, in 1861, Queen Victoria spent four months of every year in retreat at Osborne, her house on the Isle of Wight. It was left to her husband's former secretary, General Grey, to try to coax her out of retirement.

As well as suggesting that she reappear in public, he urged her to give tea-parties to which various friends, relatives and celebrities were invited. On these occasions, Victoria Sandwich cake was served.

The cake, named after the queen, was made of sponge and filled with various preserves or fruit. Its popularity spread throughout homes and farms, where it was usually filled with raspberry jam—although some people felt that lemon curd or apricot jam were just as good.

PREPARATION TIME: 15 MINUTES
COOKING TIME: 20–25 MINUTES
PRE-HEAT THE OVEN TO 190°C (375°F)—GAS MARK 5

INGREDIENTS

4 oz. (100/125 g.) butter or margarine
4 oz. (100/125 g.) caster sugar
2 eggs
4 oz. (100/125 g.) self-raising flour, sifted
A few drops vanilla essence or grated rind of 1 lemon

Cream together the butter and sugar until pale and fluffy. Beat in the eggs, one at a time, adding 1 teaspoon of the flour with the second. Fold in the rest of the flour and the flavouring. Divide the mixture equally between two greased sandwich tins, 6 in. (15 cm.) in diameter. Bake in the pre-heated oven for 20–25 minutes. Cool on a wire rack.

Sandwich the cakes together with the traditional filling of raspberry jam, or use apricot jam. For a fresh-tasting sponge, use lemon rind in the sponge and sandwich together with lemon curd.

GRASMERE GINGERBREAD
Lake District

ON A SATURDAY early in August the Grasmere rush-bearing ceremony is held—and specially baked gingerbread is handed out to the children taking part in the parade and church service.

Rush-bearing dates from the time when new rushes were strewn each year on the mud floors of churches. And today the children welcome the occasion for more than just the gingerbread. As well as receiving pieces of the crumbly, golden-brown cake, they are each given a coin to spend in the local Gingerbread Shop.

PREPARATION TIME: 15 MINUTES
COOKING TIME: 30 MINUTES
PRE-HEAT THE OVEN TO 170°C (325°F)—GAS MARK 3

INGREDIENTS FOR 16 SQUARES

8 oz. (225 g.) self-raising flour
3 oz. (75 g.) granulated sugar
1–2 teaspoons ground ginger, according to taste
¼ teaspoon salt
4 oz. (100/125 g.) margarine
2 teaspoons golden syrup
2 egg yolks, beaten
4 oz. (100/125 g.) mixed chopped peel

For the topping:
Egg white
2 tablespoons granulated sugar

Mix together in a basin the flour, sugar, ginger and salt. Melt the margarine and syrup in a small pan over a low heat. Draw the pan off the heat and stir in the egg yolks. Pour on to the dry ingredients and mix together thoroughly to combine the ingredients.

Grease an oblong tin, about 7 by 4 in. (18 by 10 cm.), and press half the soft mixture into it, using floured hands for easier handling. Sprinkle the peel over the mixture in the tin, and press the remaining mixture on top. Brush the top thickly with egg white and sprinkle with granulated sugar. Bake in the pre-heated oven for 30 minutes, giving the tin a quarter turn once during this time to cook the cake evenly. Cut into squares while cooling.

NUTTY NIBBLES
Countrywide

DESPITE THEIR NAME, Nutty Nibbles do not contain large quantities of nuts. The nuttiness refers to the taste and slightly rough consistency, provided by two of the ingredients—oats and desiccated coconut. A great favourite with adults and children alike, they are similar to the sweet biscuits made as far away as Tahiti and Samoa, where coconut is a home-grown ingredient.

PREPARATION TIME: 15 MINUTES
COOKING TIME: 15 MINUTES
PRE-HEAT THE OVEN TO 150°C (300°F)—GAS MARK 2

INGREDIENTS FOR 24 CAKES

6 oz. (175 g.) self-raising flour
4 oz. (100/125 g.) porridge oats
4 oz. (100/125 g.) desiccated coconut
4 oz. (100/125 g.) granulated sugar
$\frac{1}{2}$ teaspoon salt
1 level teaspoon bicarbonate of soda
4 oz. (100/125 g.) margarine
2 tablespoons golden syrup
2 tablespoons water
1 egg, beaten

Mix together the flour, oats, coconut, sugar, salt and bicarbonate of soda. Melt the margarine and syrup in a small saucepan with the water, over a low heat. Remove the pan from the heat and stir in the egg. Pour on to the dry ingredients and mix well. Using a spoon and fork, form the mixture into walnut-sized pieces and place them on a greased baking sheet, about 1$\frac{1}{2}$ in. (4 cm.) apart. Bake in the pre-heated oven for 15 minutes or until a very pale brown. Allow to cool for a few minutes before lifting from the sheet with a knife or fish slice to finish cooling on a wire rack. Store in an airtight tin or storage jar.

MOGGY
Yorkshire

IN ITS PRESENT FORM, this delicious, simple cake cannot be of any great age, since golden syrup was not invented until 1883. Before then it seems, it was probably made with black treacle and before that with honey. In one form or another, the recipe must be of considerable antiquity; at any rate, it is of sufficient age for the derivation of its name to have been long forgotten.

It makes a good surprise addition to the picnic hamper.

PREPARATION TIME: 25 MINUTES
COOKING TIME: 25–30 MINUTES
PRE-HEAT THE OVEN TO 170°C (325°F)—GAS MARK 3

INGREDIENTS FOR 12–16 SQUARES

12 oz. (350 g.) self-raising flour
$\frac{1}{2}$ teaspoon salt
1$\frac{1}{2}$ teaspoons baking powder
3 oz. (75 g.) lard
3 oz. (75 g.) margarine
4 oz. (100/125 g.) sugar
1 tablespoon golden syrup
About 3 fl. oz. (90 ml.) milk

Sieve together the flour, salt and baking powder. Mix in the lard and margarine by rubbing with the fingertips until the mixture looks like breadcrumbs. Add the sugar and golden syrup and mix well. Stir in sufficient milk to make a fairly stiff dough.

Roll out to about $\frac{1}{2}$ in. (1·5 cm.) thick, place on a large, greased baking sheet and bake in the pre-heated oven for 25–30 minutes, until golden-brown. Cut the cake into squares before it has quite cooled. It is at its best when freshly baked.

TOFFEE PIECES OR SQUARES
Countrywide

TOFFEE REACHED THE HEIGHT of its popularity in the late 1820s. Toffee-making clubs were formed up and down Britain. A chronicler of the time recorded that making toffee was 'very frequent amongst young persons'. Clearly, a sweet tooth was as common among young people then as now.

The word 'toffee' is of uncertain origin, but it sometimes used to be spelled 'toughy' because of its toughness. The main attributes of any kind of toffee are its rich flavour and 'chewiness', and Toffee Pieces or Squares are no exception, for the light sponge cake has a topping of nuts in a brown sugar meringue.

PREPARATION TIME: 15 MINUTES
COOKING TIME: 25–30 MINUTES
PRE-HEAT THE OVEN TO 170°C (325°F)—GAS MARK 3

INGREDIENTS FOR 12 SQUARES

4 oz. (100/125 g.) margarine
4 oz. (100/125 g.) caster sugar
1 egg
1 egg yolk
$\frac{1}{2}$ teaspoon vanilla essence
6 oz. (175 g.) self-raising flour
$\frac{1}{4}$ teaspoon salt

For the topping:

4 oz. (100/125 g.) mixed nuts, finely chopped
3 oz. (75 g.) soft brown sugar
1 egg white, stiffly beaten

Cream the margarine and sugar together. Beat the whole egg and the egg yolk together and beat into the creamed mixture. Mix in the vanilla essence and the sieved flour and salt. Spread the mixture in a greased oblong tin, about 9 by 7 in. (23 by 18 cm.). The mixture should be about $\frac{1}{2}$ in. (1·5 cm.) deep.

Sprinkle the chopped nuts over the mixture. Fold the brown sugar into the beaten egg white and spread this meringue over the nuts. Bake in the pre-heated oven for 25–30 minutes.

Cut into squares as it cools.

COLD TEA CAKE
Countrywide

THE HABIT of taking afternoon tea was popularised in Britain by Catherine of Braganza, Charles II's wife. It soon spread through all classes of society. Rich, spicy cakes were served on such occasions—or, in more modest homes, Cold Tea Cake, a treat that used up breakfast tea.

When you add the ingredients—including the essential cold tea—it does not matter if you use a breakfast cup or a teacup, so long as you use the same cup throughout.

Cold Tea Cake is very quick and easy to make, has an excellent flavour and texture, and keeps well.

PREPARATION TIME: 15 MINUTES
COOLING TIME: ABOUT 45 MINUTES
COOKING TIME: ABOUT 1 HOUR
PRE-HEAT THE OVEN TO 180°C (350°F)—GAS MARK 4

INGREDIENTS

1 cup cold tea
4 oz. (100/125 g.) margarine
1 cup mixed sultanas and currants
1 cup dates, chopped
1 cup brown sugar
2 cups self-raising flour, sifted
1 level teaspoon ground mixed spice (optional)
1 level teaspoon bicarbonate of soda

Put the tea, margarine, fruit and sugar in a large saucepan over a low heat and bring to the boil, stirring from time to time. Simmer for 3 minutes, then remove from the heat and allow to get cold.

Stir in the flour, spice and bicarbonate of soda, mixing thoroughly. Put in a greased and lined cake tin 8 in. (20 cm.) in diameter and bake in the pre-heated oven for about 1 hour.

Butter Biscuits
Countrywide

When farmers' wives in the 17th century made butter for salting and selling they kept a little back for their own use, to make crunchy Butter Biscuits. This recipe dates from that period.

The uncooked mixture freezes well if made into a roll and wrapped tightly in foil. Slices can then be cut off as required for baking these delicious rich biscuits.

Preparation Time: 20–25 minutes
Cooking Time: 15 minutes
Pre-heat the Oven to 190°C (375°F)—Gas Mark 5

Ingredients for about 30 Biscuits

8 oz. (225 g.) self-raising flour
$\frac{1}{4}$ teaspoon salt
$\frac{1}{2}$ level teaspoon baking powder
4 oz. (100/125 g.) butter
4 oz. (100/125 g.) sugar
4 oz. (100/125 g.) sultanas or seedless raisins
1 egg
2 tablespoons milk

Sift together the flour, salt and baking powder. Rub in the butter with the fingertips until the mixture looks like breadcrumbs. Stir in the sugar and fruit. Beat the egg and milk together. Add it to the mixture and mix to make a smooth dough. Roll out on a floured board to $\frac{1}{4}$ in. (5 mm.) thick and cut into 2 in. (5 cm.) rounds. Put on a greased baking sheet, leaving a good space round each biscuit. Bake in the pre-heated oven for 15 minutes until golden-brown. Turn round the baking sheet if necessary after 10 minutes to cook all the biscuits evenly. Allow to cool for 2 minutes before lifting off the sheet with a spatula and cooling on a wire rack.

Fat Rascals
Yorkshire

Visitors to moorland inns in Yorkshire are sometimes offered a Fat Rascal—a confection whose popularity is easy to understand, but whose name presents something of a problem. 'Fat' probably refers to the lard used in the cooking, and 'rascal' is a dialect word meaning 'a lean animal'. So a Fat Rascal would appear to be a contradiction in terms.

In the past, the cakes were made on a hot griddle. In some inns—where the cakes were cooked in the oven over a turf fire—they were simply called Turf Cakes.

Preparation Time: 10 minutes
Cooking Time: about 15 minutes
Pre-heat the Oven to 200°C (400°F)—Gas Mark 6

Ingredients for about 24 Rascals

8 oz. (225 g.) self-raising flour
$\frac{1}{4}$ teaspoon salt
4 oz. (100/125 g.) lard or vegetable fat
3 oz. (75 g.) sugar
2 oz. (50 g.) currants
1 oz. (25 g.) raisins or sultanas
1 egg, beaten, or 2 fl. oz. (50 ml.) water

Sieve the flour and salt together. Rub in the lard with the fingertips until the mixture resembles breadcrumbs, then stir in the sugar, currants, and raisins or sultanas. Add the beaten egg or water and mix well to make a soft dough.

Roll out to about $\frac{1}{2}$ in. (1·5 cm.) thick, cut into rounds about 2 in. (5 cm.) in diameter and place on a greased baking sheet. Bake in the pre-heated oven for about 15 minutes, or until golden-brown. You may need to give the baking sheet a quarter turn halfway through baking to prevent one edge of the cakes from burning.

Beaten egg makes richer 'rascals', but they were traditionally made with water.

Bosworth Jumbles
Countrywide

Jumbles were first written about in Elizabethan times, but one story goes that they were a speciality of Richard III's chef. The recipe for them is said, rather fancifully perhaps, to have been found on the battlefield at Bosworth where Richard was killed and his army routed by Henry Tudor's forces in 1485.

The name jumble comes from

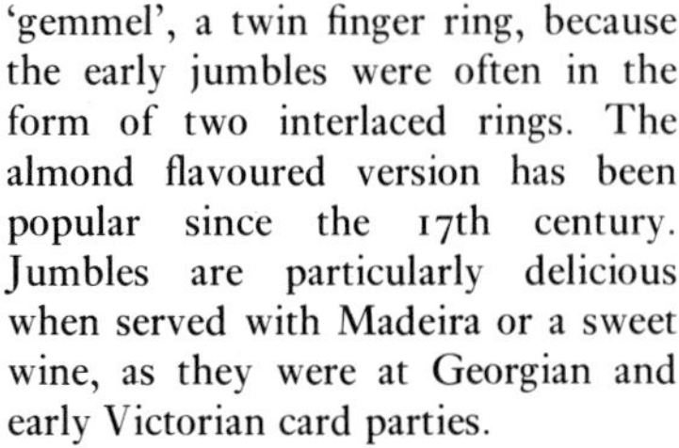

'gemmel', a twin finger ring, because the early jumbles were often in the form of two interlaced rings. The almond flavoured version has been popular since the 17th century. Jumbles are particularly delicious when served with Madeira or a sweet wine, as they were at Georgian and early Victorian card parties.

Preparation Time: 20 minutes
Cooking Time: 10 minutes
Pre-heat the Oven to 180°C (350°F)—Gas Mark 4

Ingredients for about 12 Jumbles

5 oz. (150 g.) self-raising flour
1 oz. (25 g.) rice flour
4 oz. (100/125 g.) caster sugar
4 oz. (100/125 g.) butter
$\frac{1}{2}$ egg, beaten
$\frac{1}{2}$ teaspoon almond essence

Mix the flours and sugar together, and rub in the butter with the fingertips until the mixture looks like breadcrumbs. Stir in the egg and almond essence, and knead for about 1 minute until the mixture forms a smooth dough.

Roll the dough out to form a panel about $\frac{1}{8}$ in. (3 mm.) thick and 4–5 in. (10–13 cm.) wide. Cut across the panel into $\frac{3}{4}$ in. (2 cm.) strips. With floured hands, tie some of these strips into loose, single knots. Form the others into rings.

Place the jumbles on a greased and floured baking sheet well spaced out so that they will not run together while baking. Bake in the pre-heated oven for about 10 minutes, giving the tin a quarter turn after 5–7 minutes if necessary so that all the jumbles bake evenly.

If you like, replace 1 oz. (25 g.) of flour with 1 oz. (25 g.) of ground almonds. This gives the jumbles a closer texture and a distinctive, nutty taste.

RECIPES

from OTHER LANDS

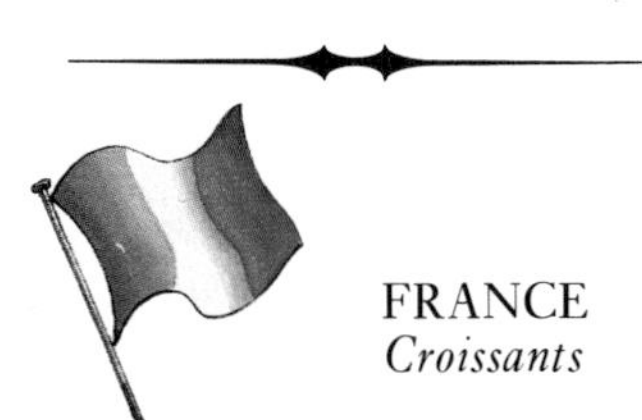

FRANCE
Croissants

TO MOST PEOPLE the croissant is as French as the Arc de Triomphe. But the Viennese, not the French, invented it when Vienna was attacked by the Turks in 1686. The invaders tunnelled their way under the walls and it was the all-night bakers who raised the alarm and so saved the day.

The Turks were repelled and the bakers asked to create a 'commemorative confection'. They devised a pastry-like bread shaped like the crescent emblem on the defeated enemy's flag. The roll's popularity spread to Italy and, in the 18th century, to France, where the French adopted the *croissant* as their own.

PREPARATION TIME: 45 MINUTES

RESTING AND RISING TIME: $1\frac{1}{4}$ HOURS

COOKING TIME: ABOUT 10 MINUTES

PRE-HEAT THE OVEN TO 235°C (460°F)—GAS MARK $8\frac{1}{2}$

INGREDIENTS FOR 12 CROISSANTS

1 lb. (450 g.) strong white flour
1 level teaspoon salt
1 oz. (25 g.) butter
1 large egg, beaten
$7\frac{1}{2}$ fl. oz. (215 ml.) warm water (see p. 296)
1 oz. (25 g.) fresh yeast
6 oz. (175 g.) butter, cut in pieces
A little beaten egg to glaze

Sieve the flour and salt into a large mixing bowl, rub in the 1 oz. (25 g.) butter and make a well in the centre. Mix together the egg and water, whisk in the yeast and pour into the well. Mix vigorously to blend well, then knead (see p. 296) to a smooth dough. Cover the bowl with polythene and put in a cold place for the dough to rest for 10 minutes.

Roll out the dough to a rectangle about 15 by 6 in. (38 by 15 cm.). Dot the butter pieces over two-thirds of it, starting from one short side. Fold the unbuttered third over the centre third, and the remaining third over these two.

Roll out the dough again to a rectangle the same size as before and fold in three in the same way as before, but without buttering. Wrap loosely in polythene and put in a refrigerator to rest for 10 minutes.

Repeat the rolling out and folding for a third time, wrap the dough again and put in a refrigerator to rest for 15 minutes.

Roll out the dough evenly to make a strip 24 by 8 in. (61 by 20 cm.) and $\frac{1}{8}$ in. (3 mm.) thick. Mark along one edge at 4 in. (10 cm.) intervals. Mark along the other long edge after 2 in. (5 cm.) and then at 4 in. (10 cm.) intervals. Cut across the strip from mark to mark to give 11 large triangles and a small one at each end; join these to make a twelfth triangle.

Roll up each triangle firmly from the short side to the pointed tip, then roll under the hand to make it slightly longer. Curve the rolls into crescents and place on a lightly greased baking sheet. Cover with greased polythene and put to rise in a warm place for 40 minutes, brushing lightly with beaten egg after 20 minutes.

Bake in the pre-heated oven for about 10 minutes. Bake lightly so that you can re-heat the croissants without fear of making them too brown.

FRANCE
Brioches

ONE OF THE DELIGHTS of a French breakfast is the brioche—crisp and golden on the outside, meltingly light and sweet in the mouth, it makes the ideal accompaniment to hot, fragrant coffee.

Brioches, now so firmly associated with France, were introduced there from Poland and Austria, through Alsace and Lorraine. The brioche dough made in Gisors and Gournay used to be acknowledged as especially good, probably because both were butter-making centres.

The home cook sometimes hesitates to try her hand at brioche dough, but it is certainly not difficult to make.

The recipe given here is equally suitable as a crust for pies and pâtés and for wrapping meats as it is for small or large loaves.

PREPARATION TIME: 40 MINUTES

RISING TIME: $2\frac{3}{4}$ HOURS

COOKING TIME: ABOUT 10 MINUTES

PRE-HEAT THE OVEN TO 235°C (460°F)—GAS MARK $8\frac{1}{2}$

INGREDIENTS FOR 18–20 SMALL BRIOCHES

1 oz. (25 g.) fresh yeast
2 rounded teaspoons sugar
6 tablespoons warm milk (see p. 296)
1 lb. (450 g.) strong white flour
2 level teaspoons salt
4 eggs, beaten
8 oz. (225 g.) butter, soft but not oily
A little beaten egg to glaze

Mix the yeast and sugar to a smooth paste with the milk. Sift the flour and salt together into a large mixing bowl, pour in the yeast mixture and the beaten eggs and beat vigorously with a wooden spoon. The dough will be soft and sticky at first, and should be beaten for 5 minutes or more until it is smooth, elastic and slightly shiny. Mix in the butter a little at a time until the dough is smooth and glossy. Shape it into a ball and put it into a warmed, lightly buttered bowl. Cover with greased polythene and stand in a warm place to rise for about 2 hours, or until it has trebled in bulk.

Tip the dough on to a lightly floured working surface and knock out all the air. Divide the dough into 20 pieces, each weighing about 2 oz. (50 g.). Mould each piece to fit a small fluted tin, warmed and lightly buttered. The dough should come about one-third of the way up the tin. Put the tins on a baking sheet, cover with greased polythene and stand in a warm place for about 45 minutes, or until the dough has risen to fill the tins. Brush over with beaten egg and bake in the pre-heated oven for about 10 minutes, or until golden-brown. Eat as soon as possible after baking.

You can divide the dough into four larger pieces if you prefer, and mould them to fit larger fluted tins or small loaf tins. Bake at 230°C (450°F)—gas mark 8 for 20–25 minutes.

For covering a pie, roll out the brioche dough instead of dividing it into pieces. Roll it to no more than $\frac{1}{4}$ in. (5 mm.) thick, fit it over the warm pie filling, brush it with beaten egg and stand in a warm place to rise for $\frac{3}{4}$–1 hour. Brush again with beaten egg and bake for about 15 minutes at 230°C (450°F)—gas mark 8.

Brioche dough can be made in advance and kept in the refrigerator for a day before use. When the air has been knocked out of the risen dough, shape it into a ball, place it in a buttered bowl, cover it and put it in the refrigerator.

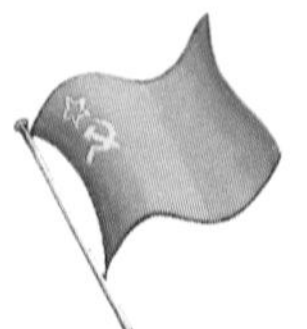

RUSSIA
Blini

BLINI—buckwheat pancakes—have been made in Russia for over 1,000 years.

In western Russia, during a spring festival called 'Mother-in-Law's Day', it was the custom for every young husband to go to his wife's mother's house to eat blini.

Apart from being presented with smoked salmon or caviare and soured cream as a stylish first course, they can be served for breakfast or tea spread with butter and jam.

PREPARATION TIME: 25 MINUTES
RISING TIME: 1½ HOURS
COOKING TIME: ABOUT 20 MINUTES

INGREDIENTS FOR 10–12 BLINI

- ¼ *teaspoon sugar*
- ½ *pint (275/300 ml.) warm milk* (*see p. 296*)
- ½ *oz. (15 g.) fresh yeast*
- *8 oz. (225 g.) buckwheat or wholewheat flour*
- *1 oz. (25 g.) butter, melted*
- *1 egg white, whisked stiff*

Dissolve the sugar in the warm milk and use 2 tablespoons of the liquid to mix the yeast to a smooth, thin paste in a large, warmed mixing bowl. Stir in the remaining milk. Add about two-thirds of the flour and whisk to make a smooth batter. Cover with greased polythene and stand in a warm place to rise for 1 hour.

Add the remaining flour and the butter to the batter and beat well. The mixture should have the consistency of thick cream; if it is too stiff add a little extra warm milk. Fold the egg white into the batter. Cover and put to rise again for 30 minutes.

Brush the inside of a large, heavy-based frying pan with oil and heat it until a slight haze comes from it. Cook three blini at a time, allowing a full tablespoon of batter for each one. Fry gently for about 2 minutes until the surface has just dried out and is a mass of small holes, then turn the blini over to brown the other sides gently for about 2 minutes.

Keep the cooked blini warm until serving time.

SPAIN
Sponge Cake

ON THE SOUTH ATLANTIC COAST of Spain, pine nuts are specially cultivated for culinary use. They are gathered in the winter, stored until summer, and then put in the sun to open. The delicately flavoured kernels are used in savoury dishes as well as in sweet dishes such as this cake.

PREPARATION TIME: 15 MINUTES
COOKING TIME: ABOUT 40 MINUTES
PRE-HEAT THE OVEN TO 180°C (350°F)—GAS MARK 4

INGREDIENTS

- *5 oz. (150 g.) butter or margarine*
- *Grated rind of 1 lemon*
- *5 oz. (150 g.) caster sugar*
- *8 oz. (225 g.) self-raising flour*
- ¼ *teaspoon salt*
- *3 eggs, beaten*
- *2 oz. (50 g.) pine kernels or almonds, blanched and flaked*
- *2 oz. (50 g.) rinsed and chopped glacé cherries*
- *12 sugar lumps, roughly crushed*

Cream together the butter, lemon rind and caster sugar until light and fluffy. Sift the flour and salt together and add little by little to the creamed mixture alternately with the egg, stirring well all the time.

Grease and line a cake tin 9 in. (23 cm.) in diameter. Spread the mixture evenly in the tin and sprinkle the top with the nuts and cherries. Scatter on the crushed sugar. Bake in the pre-heated oven for 35–40 minutes.

USA
Boston Brownies

BROWNIES are moist, chewy cakes found throughout the United States. Their name and recipe differs from area to area—but Boston Brownies are among the best.

Take care not to overcook brownies or they become dry and brittle.

PREPARATION TIME: 10 MINUTES
COOKING TIME: 25–30 MINUTES
PRE-HEAT THE OVEN TO 180°C (350°F)—GAS MARK 4

INGREDIENTS FOR 12–16 BROWNIES

- *2 oz. (50 g.) butter*
- *7 oz. (200 g.) soft brown sugar*
- *1 egg, beaten*
- *1 teaspoon vanilla essence*
- *4 oz. (100/125 g.) plain flour*
- ¼ *teaspoon salt*
- ½ *teaspoon baking powder*
- *4 oz. (100/125 g.) chopped dates or seedless raisins*

Melt the butter in a medium saucepan over a low heat. Add the sugar and stir well. Draw the pan off the heat and let the mixture cool for 1 minute, then add the egg and vanilla essence.

Sift the flour, salt and baking powder together and stir this into the butter mixture. Add the chopped dates or raisins and mix well.

Grease a tin 11 by 7 in. (28 by 18 cm.) and spread the mixture in it evenly. Bake in the pre-heated oven for 25–30 minutes, until a light crust has formed on the top. Cool in the tin for 15 minutes, cutting into squares after 5 minutes.

AUSTRALIA
Spiced Apple Cake

MOST OF THE FINEST Australian apples are grown in forest clearings in Tasmania, Victoria and Western Australia. Many of them are sent to processing plants for pulping, and the pulped fruit is then used in such agreeable dishes as this.

The raisins and sultanas which the cake also contains are home-grown in vineyards along the Murray River.

PREPARATION TIME: 10 MINUTES
COOKING TIME: 1 HOUR
PRE-HEAT THE OVEN TO 150°C (300°F)—GAS MARK 2

INGREDIENTS

- *4 oz. (100/125 g.) butter*
- *4 oz. (100/125 g.) sugar*
- *3 oz. (75 g.) sieved, cooked apple, unsweetened*
- *1 level teaspoon bicarbonate of soda*
- *6 oz. (175 g.) plain flour*
- ¼ *teaspoon grated nutmeg*
- ¼ *teaspoon ground cinnamon*
- *3 oz. (75 g.) seedless raisins or sultanas*

Cream the butter and sugar together well. Stir the bicarbonate of soda into the apple, then add to the creamed mixture. Sift the flour and spices together and add them to the mixture. Stir the raisins or sultanas in well.

Grease and line a cake tin 7 in. (18 cm.) in diameter. Put in the cake mixture, level the top, and bake in the pre-heated oven for 55–60 minutes.

DIRECTIONS FOR MAKING

BREADS, CAKES AND BISCUITS

BREAD HAS BEEN EATEN IN BRITAIN since before the Romans came, but it was very different from the bread we eat today. In the 1st-century-BC village found near Glastonbury, Somerset, remnants have been discovered of a kind of bread made from whole-grain wheat, barley, wild oats and a weed named chess, formed into small buns and baked on flat stones round the edge of the fire. These unleavened hearth cakes would certainly have had a rough, close texture and been hard to chew. By the Iron Age, leavened bread was being made and enriched breads were written about from Roman times. Cakes developed from enriched breads, but not until the 17th century did recipes appear for cakes as we know them. Biscuits came earlier—at first rusks and wheat paste dried and fried, but richer, more varied mixtures from Tudor times.

Breads

ONCE it was discovered that leavening gave bread a light and spongy texture, cereals were used much more for bread than for pottage, which had previously been their main use. Beer barm—the froth from fermenting beer—was used as leaven in Britain by the Iron Age Celts. They probably took the idea from the Celts in Spain and France, whose use of barm was recorded by the Romans.

It was the Romans who introduced into Britain an oven in which brushwood was burned before being raked out, leaving the oven hot enough for baking. Previously, bread was baked round the fire, uncovered at first but in later times covered by a clay pot or dome.

From medieval times, a bread oven became a fixture in large houses, manors and monasteries, but not in the homes of peasants or poorer people. They either continued to bake their bread as hearth cakes round their own fire, or took their dough to be baked in the oven of the local manor. They paid for the use of the oven with some of the bread they had baked. In some parts of the country, an iron cauldron with a lid was buried in burning fuel and hot ashes to act as an oven. Similar pots are still used occasionally in Eire for baking bread.

Many different cereals and mixtures have been used for bread. In the time of Elizabeth I, after a poor season, bakers were told to make their bread from rye, barley, peas and beans. From very early on, white bread was regarded as superior to brown. London's bakers even had separate guilds for those who baked white bread and those who baked brown, but the guilds were amalgamated in 1645, when there were few brown bread makers left.

The cereals used for bread were for centuries ground by hand in querns, or by windmills or watermills. The first steam-powered rollermill in Britain opened in Glasgow in 1872.

INGREDIENTS FOR BREAD-MAKING

Flour

Strong plain flour is the kind to use for bread-making. West European wheats have to be blended with grain imported from North America to produce strong flour. Because of this, strong flour is more expensive than ordinary flour. Strong flour has a high content of gluten, the substance which gives bread its volume and texture. Most good grocers and supermarkets now keep several white flours suitable for bread-making.

Wholemeal flour, as its name suggests, contains the whole grain, including the bran. Wheatmeal flour is similar, but has had some of the coarsest bran removed. Flours containing varying amounts of the bran are sold under similar names.

A brown flour used on its own to make bread will not give such a large volume or such a light texture as white flour. Mixed with an equal quantity of white flour, or even with more than half white flour, it gives a bread of good texture, colour and taste. The nutritional value is no greater than that of white flour alone.

Brown flours do not keep as well as white, especially after the bag has been opened, so it is best to buy only as much as you can use up quickly. Keep flour in the bag in which you buy it, remembering to mark it with the date of purchase. Keep it on a cool, dry shelf or put it, still in its bag, inside a stoneware jar or other special flour jar. Once the bag is opened, use up brown flour within 1 month and white within 3 months. Do not mix old and new flours together to store.

For bread-making, weigh out the flour you will need in advance, and put it in a large, warm mixing bowl in a warm place to come up to room temperature, or a little above.

Yeast

The raising agent used in bread is yeast. It is a living organism, *Saccharomyces cerevisiae*, consisting of a single cell and visible only under a microscope. Hundreds of thousands of these organisms are compressed together in the crumbly, putty-like block of greyish-cream yeast you buy from a baker.

Yeast feeds on carbohydrates—that is, starches and sugars. When it is mixed in dough and given the right conditions of warmth, moisture and food, it grows rapidly and gives off carbon dioxide, which permeates the dough, making it spongy in texture. It takes time for the yeast to carry out the process, which is called fermentation, and this is why the mixed dough is left to rise once or twice before baking. During fermentation, alcohols and acids are produced which help to develop the bread's flavour. The longer the fermentation time, the better will be the flavour.

It is not necessary to use up fresh yeast immediately. If you store it wrapped in a polythene bag or in a plastic box with a tightly fitting lid, and put it in a cool larder, it will keep for up to 5 days. In a refrigerator it will keep for up to 3 weeks. To store it in a freezer, measure it into the small amounts that your recipes call for, wrap each measured amount separately in foil and freeze for up to 3 months.

Dried yeast is now widely available from grocers, health-food shops, large supermarkets and chemists, but you must make sure that what you are buying is baker's yeast, not brewer's yeast or tonic yeast. Provided that it is kept in an airtight container and in a cool place, dried yeast will remain active for up to 6 months.

If you use dried yeast, follow the maker's directions for quantities carefully. Always check whether the amount given in your recipe refers to fresh yeast or dried.

The amount of yeast needed varies according to the type of dough being made. Brown bread and enriched breads need more yeast than white bread.

Both fresh and dried yeast need creaming with warm liquid before being added to the flour. Fresh yeast will cream easily in 2–3 tablespoons of the liquid. Dried yeast is best whisked with a fork into about ¼ pint (150 ml.) of the liquid and then left in a warm place for 10 minutes or until frothy.

Salt
The flavour in bread is developed partly by salt, but salt also slows down the fermentation process, and too much of it can kill the yeast. Do not exceed the amount of salt recommended in your recipe. Salt should never come into direct contact with yeast, as it withdraws all the yeast's natural moisture. This is why the salt is always mixed with the flour before it makes any contact with the yeast. The usual proportion of salt to give the right amount of flavour to bread is 2 level teaspoons to every 1 lb. (450 g.) of flour. Enriched breads and sweet buns do not need so much, so always follow the amounts given in your recipes.

Sugar
Traditionally, this was added to activate the yeast and was always creamed with the yeast. We now know that too much sugar can kill some of the yeast cells, and this gives the bread a more yeasty taste than most people like, so be careful not to exceed the amount recommended in your recipe. Some recipes now recommend that the yeast is creamed with liquid alone, and sugar is omitted completely.

Liquids—warm water or milk
The temperature of the liquid you use to mix dough is important. It should be 40°C (104°F), so that the mixed dough will be warm enough to start the yeast fermenting quickly. The liquid will feel gently warm to the touch but it is best to use a thermometer to test the temperature. Do not have the liquid warmer than 43°C (110°F) or it will start to kill the yeast.

Water, milk or a mixture of both are the liquids used in bread. The amount needed will vary depending on what kind of bread is being made and what kind of flour is being used. Enriched doughs, for example, are usually mixed to a softer consistency than ordinary bread dough.

Fat
Butter, margarine or lard rubbed into the flour in varying amounts enriches the dough, gives the bread a softer crumb and helps to keep the bread fresh.

Eggs
These are added to enriched doughs. They give a richer colour and flavour, increase the food value, add to the lightness and prolong the keeping time of the bread.

Fruit
When you are going to add dried fruits, such as sultanas or currants, to a dough, prepare them well in advance by covering them with boiling water and leaving them to stand in it for about 1 hour. Then drain the fruit well and spread it on kitchen paper in a warm place to dry a little. The fruit will not only be plumper and juicier, but will also be much less likely to burn during baking.

Mixing the Dough

Always work in a warm kitchen when you are using yeast. Make sure that the dry ingredients are at room temperature or a little above, the liquids warm to the touch, the mixing bowls warmed, and any baking tins and sheets warmed and lightly greased. Do not let any draughts of cold air reach the dough, especially when it starts to rise.

Basic method
To mix plain breads, sift the flour and salt together, rub in the fat and pour in the yeast mixture and any remaining liquid. Mix vigorously with a wooden spoon first and then with the hands until all the flour has been incorporated. This standard method is used with both fresh yeast and dried.

Ferment and dough method
This is a two-stage mixing process, rarely used by commercial bakers now but once widely used for high-quality enriched breads. Mix the yeast first with the combined liquids, some of the sugar and a little of the flour. Leave this mixture to ferment for up to 30 minutes. By the end of this time, the yeast has become very active, and at that stage the rest of the flour, and the enriching fat, sugar and fruit are added.

Kneading
This action develops the gluten in the flour. It changes the soft, sticky mixture into a firm and springy dough that will hold a shape.

To knead the dough, put it on a lightly floured working surface, hold it in place with one hand and, with the other, take hold of part of the edge, stretch it away from you and then fold it back to the centre and push it down with the ball of the hand or a fist. Turn the dough round a little and repeat the stretching, folding and pushing. Keep this up for 5–10 minutes. The dough will then have a smooth, silky feel, an even texture and a firmly elastic consistency.

The dough hook of an electric mixer will knead the dough quickly and thoroughly. Use it at a low speed, following the manufacturer's instructions.

Rising
When the dough has been kneaded to an even, springy texture, it must be

left to stand to give the yeast time to work. Cover the dough during rising, both to keep it warm and to prevent a hard skin from forming over it. Put the dough in a clean bowl and cover it with a sheet of lightly oiled polythene or a slightly dampened cloth or tea towel. If you like, you can put the dough inside an oiled polythene bag and fold the bag loosely, or you can put it in a lightly oiled plastic box with a lid on. Use a large container because the dough must rise until double in volume. When it is ready it will also spring back if pressed lightly with a floured finger.

The length of time it takes for the dough to reach this condition and size will vary, depending on the temperature of the place you put it to rise. It will take about 1 hour in a warm place such as an airing cupboard, in front of a fire, or on top of a boiler (with a towel under the bowl to prevent too much bottom heat). At room temperature it will take 2 hours. In a cool larder it will take 4–6 hours, and if you put it in a refrigerator it will take about 12 hours.

This is useful if you want to cook fresh rolls for breakfast or coffee-time the next day. Allow the dough to come to room temperature before shaping, proving and baking.

Storing surplus dough

If you have mixed and kneaded more dough than you want to bake on one day, store the surplus, unrisen and well wrapped in polythene, in a refrigerator for up to 2 days.

Unrisen dough can also be deep-frozen satisfactorily for 3 months but will deteriorate after that. Divide the dough into the quantities needed for individual loaves, pack each portion in an oiled polythene bag and seal. Use a bag of sufficient size to allow the dough to rise later. When the dough is needed, lift a bag from the freezer, unseal it and reseal it loosely, and put the bag of dough in a warm place to rise. You can allow the bag of dough to rise overnight in the refrigerator, or give it 3–4 hours at normal room temperature. Knock back, shape and prove in the usual way.

Knocking back

When the dough has risen it will have pockets of gas unevenly distributed through it, and it will have become soft. It has to be restored to an even, springy texture. Turn it out of its bowl or other container on to a clean working surface.

The dough will not be sticky now, so will need only a very little flour on the working surface, or even none at all. Too much flour on the dough at this stage could make streaks in the bread and on the crust.

Knock out the gas pockets from the dough with the side of your hand or with your fist, then knead it quickly until it is smooth and firmly elastic again.

SHAPING

The dough is now ready for shaping. You can bake it in a loaf tin, in a round earthenware pot or on a flat baking sheet.

Divide or weigh off the dough into the number of pieces you require, then cover them with oiled polythene or a dampened cloth and leave them to relax for 5 minutes. This will make them easier to shape.

As you mould the dough to the required shape, stretch and pull it to give a smooth, tight outer skin over the top and sides, with the ends being tucked in underneath.

If the loaf is to be baked in a tin or pot, mould it to an appropriate shape, fit it into the warmed and greased container and cover it for the final rising.

You can make various traditional shapes instead of a plain tin loaf.

Split tin loaf

When the shaped loaf has been rising in its tin for 25 minutes, make a cut ½ in. (1·5 cm.) deep from end to end along the centre of the loaf with a very sharp blade. Put the loaf back to rise for a further 15 minutes before baking.

Split Coburg loaf

Mould the dough into a smooth ball, put it on a warmed and greased baking sheet, cover it and put it to rise. After 20 minutes, cut a cross ½ in. (1·5 cm.) deep in the surface of the loaf with a very sharp blade. Put the loaf back to rise for a further 20 minutes before baking.

If you wish, mark the loaf with only one split across the middle instead of a cross; do this by pressing an oiled rolling pin almost down to the bottom of the loaf after 10 minutes of rising. Then push the two halves close together to continue rising for a further 30 minutes before baking.

Bloomer loaf

Mould the dough into a fat sausage shape, place it on a warm, greased baking sheet, cover it and put it to rise. After 25 minutes use a very sharp blade to make cuts diagonally along the loaf, ¼ in. (5 mm.) deep and 1½ in. (4 cm.) apart. Put the loaf back to rise for a further 15 minutes before baking.

Scroll loaf

Roll out the dough into a rectangle and fold it in half lengthways. Roll up from each end in opposite directions to form an S shape. Place it with the folded edge uppermost in a warmed and greased loaf tin, cover and put to rise for 30–35 minutes before baking.

Cottage loaf

Cut off one-third of the dough and shape both the larger and the smaller piece into a smooth ball. Slightly moisten the base of the smaller ball with water, and sit it on top of the larger ball on a warmed and greased baking sheet. Push the first two fingers of both hands together down from the centre of the top ball and into the bottom ball. This seals the two parts together. If you like, you can push the floured handle of a wooden spoon down through both balls. An old method was to push an elbow down into the loaf.

Cover the loaf and put it to rise for 40 minutes. Halfway through this time you can make small downward slits with a very sharp blade at 2 in. (5 cm.) intervals all round the side of the upper and lower parts of the loaf.

Plaited loaf

To make a three-strand plait, divide the dough into three equal pieces and roll each piece into a long sausage. Moisten one end of each strand with water and seal the three ends together. Plait the strands loosely, moisten the ends with water and press the ends firmly together to seal them in place.

To make a five-strand plait, divide the dough into five equal pieces and roll each into a long strand no more than ½ in. (1·5 cm.) thick. Moisten one end of each strand with water, stick all the moist ends together and spread the strands slightly apart, like the fingers on a hand. Think of the strands as numbered 1–5 from left to right and, each time a strand is moved, re-number it according to the position it then occupies, discarding the number it started with. Now lift strand 2 over 3, 5 over 2, and then 1 over 3. Repeat this sequence until you reach the ends of the strands. Moisten these very slightly with water and seal them together.

To make a seven-strand plait, divide the dough into seven equal pieces and roll them into long strands just over $\frac{1}{4}$ in. (5 mm.) thick. Lay the strands alongside each other and part them into two sections from the bottom of the strands to halfway up, with 4 strands on one side of the parting and 3 on the other. Take the outside strand of the section with 4, lift it over the others in its section and push it against the inside strand of the other section. Do the same with the outer strand on the opposite side, and repeat this sequence until you reach the ends of the strands. Moisten them slightly with water and seal together. Carefully turn over all the dough together and repeat the plaiting sequence with the other halves of the strands. Seal the ends together well.

Put a plaited loaf to rise for 30–35 minutes before baking.

Bridge rolls
Divide the dough into 1–1$\frac{1}{2}$ oz. (25–40 g.) pieces. Roll each piece under the slightly cupped palm of your hand to make a sausage shape with tapering ends. Place the rolls on a warmed and greased baking sheet and put them to rise until they have doubled in size before baking.

Rolls
Divide the dough into pieces weighing 1$\frac{1}{2}$–2 oz. (40–50 g.). Roll each piece under the cupped palm of your hand until it forms a smooth, round ball. Place the rolls on a warmed and greased baking sheet and put them to rise until they have doubled in size before baking.

Final rising or proving
Once the dough has been shaped, it must be left to rise again so that it will have a light, spongy texture. Cover it in the same way as for the first rising, so that a hard skin does not form over it. Put it in a warm place.

The dough needs to rise until it doubles in volume again. This will take 30–40 minutes.

If the bread is coated with a sticky glaze, such as beaten egg, part of the way through the final rising, leave it uncovered to finish rising, but make sure that it is in a warm place free of draughts.

Baking

Bread must always be put into a hot oven so that the heat will kill all the yeast. Bake at the temperature recommended in your recipe and in the hottest part of the oven. This will vary, depending on the type and make of oven. The manufacturer's handbook will tell you what part of your particular oven is right for bread.

During or at the end of the final rising, you can brush over the bread with one of several finishes to give the kind of crust you prefer.

For a soft crust, brush over the bread lightly with cooking oil or dust it over lightly with flour. To give a crisp crust, dissolve $\frac{1}{4}$ teaspoon of salt in 2 tablespoons of water and brush the bread over lightly with the mixture. Brushing over with a mixture of milk and sugar will give a rich brown crust, and a light glaze of beaten egg or egg white will give a shiny finish.

Poppy or sesame seeds sprinkled over white bread before it is baked will give it a crunchy coating, and cracked wheat sprinkled over brown bread will give the same effect.

Rolls will take 15–20 minutes to bake, 1 lb. (450 g.) loaves about 35 minutes, and 2 lb. (900 g.) loaves about 50 minutes. When the bread is ready, it will be well browned with its sides shrunken away from its container, and it will give a hollow sound if you tap it underneath with your knuckles.

If the underneath is not quite as crusty as you would like, invert the loaf in its tin for a final 5 minutes' baking.

Remove cooked bread from its tin or baking sheet immediately you take it out of the oven. Put it on a wire rack to cool so that air can circulate round it. If it is left in the tin, it will go soggy round the edges. The bread must be completely cold before it is put in a bread bin.

Cakes

The dividing line between bread and cake is hard to draw. Cakes now are distinguished by the large amount of sugar in them, by the high fat content which gives them a rich, melting texture, and by the fact that they are raised by eggs instead of yeast. They developed from the enriched breads that have been written about since Roman times.

Milk, honey, sugar, butter, egg yolks, spices, and currants and raisins were added to enrich bread dough. Recipes for cakes as we know them scarcely appear before the 17th century, but as oven baking became more widespread, the baking of richer mixtures became easier and more popular. By the end of the 17th century gingerbread was being made of flour, sugar, butter, eggs, black treacle, ginger, cinnamon and preserved fruits to produce a cake much as we would expect it to be today.

One of the earliest large cakes to be raised with eggs was seed cake, which became very popular during the 18th century. Early recipes still warned cooks not to leave the cake to rise, so the techniques of bread-making were clearly the instinctive ones. By the mid-18th century, fruit cakes raised solely by eggs had joined the cook's repertoire, and cake-making as we know it was established.

Ingredients for Cake-making

Flour
Soft household flour is the kind used in cakes. Most recipes now specify self-raising flour, but old recipes usually use plain flour mixed with some kind of raising agent. Use plain flour in fatless sponges, where the beaten eggs are the principal raising agent. Use it also in rich, heavily fruited cakes, which are close in texture rather than light and spongy.

Keep the flour in the bag in which you bought it, remembering to mark on it the date of purchase. Store the flour in a cool, dry cupboard or put it, still in its bag, in a stoneware jar or other special flour container.

Plain flour will keep unopened for 9 months in these conditions, and for 3 months once it has been opened. Self-raising flour will keep for 6 months unopened, and for 2 months opened.

Use up one batch of flour before you open the next, and do not mix new flour with old to store.

Fat
This can be butter, either salted or unsalted, margarine, lard or vegetable fat or oil. Sometimes a mixture of fats is used. Butter gives the best flavour, especially to a sponge without strong flavourings added, but many people prefer to use margarine for reasons of economy and health. Lard is used mainly in less rich cakes, well-flavoured with spices or other ingredients.

Remember to lift the fat out of the refrigerator or cold larder well before you want to use it. You will mix the cake much more quickly with fat that has softened at room temperature.

Sugar
If a recipe recommends caster sugar, try to use this whenever possible and do not be too ready to substitute granulated sugar for it. Granulated sugar is more difficult to cream thoroughly. It produces a cake of a coarser texture and can give a spotty appearance to the surface of the baked cake.

Eggs
These must be fresh to give the cake good flavour and lightness. Break an egg into a cup and add it to the mixture before you break open the next. This avoids all danger of adding a stale egg, either to your cake mixture or to the other eggs.

Make sure that you bring the eggs into the warm kitchen well before you make your cake. An egg that is much colder than the ingredients to which you add it will make the mixture curdle. Sometimes the cake mixture curdles when eggs are added too quickly. You can avoid this by beating 1 teaspoon of flour from the weighed ingredients into the mixture with each egg, or you can remedy curdling that has already occurred by stirring 1–2 teaspoons of flour from the weighed ingredients into the cake mixture.

Milk
Measure out milk carefully where a recipe gives an exact amount. Do not exceed the amount recommended, as too much milk can make a cake heavy. If you are short of milk, use a mixture of milk and water, which will give just as satisfactory a result.

Dried fruit
Currants, raisins and sultanas often need washing to make them clean enough to add to a cake. Weigh out the amount you need into a colander or sieve and pour plenty of boiling water through the fruit. Shake off as much water as you can, and dry the fruit well in kitchen paper or a tea towel. Leave it to become completely cold before adding it to the cake. Warm, wet fruit will produce a heavy cake.

Rinse and dry glacé cherries, crystallised fruit and candied peel in the same way to remove excess sugar. If the fruit is too sugary, it will sink to the bottom of the cake. Cherries are less likely to sink if you halve or quarter large ones and roll them in a very little flour before adding them to a cake mixture.

Raising agents
Self-raising flour has already had the required amount of raising agent added to it and distributed evenly throughout it. Raising agents that you add during mixing a cake include:
Air. This is the principal raising agent in a cake. It is introduced into the mixture by sieving the flour, by creaming the fat and sugar until light, and by beating in whole eggs or whisked egg whites. The air incorporated in the mixture expands during baking to give the cake an airy, spongy texture.
Baking powder. This must be measured exactly. Too much of it will make small cakes and biscuits dry. Too much in a large cake will give it a flat taste. Baking powder should be sifted thoroughly with the flour.
Cream of tartar and bicarbonate of soda. These must be mixed very thoroughly into the flour in the amounts specified in your recipe. It is usual to use 2 parts of cream of tartar to 1 part of bicarbonate of soda. Take care to keep to these proportions. Too much soda, in scones for example, gives a soapy taste and dark colour.
Buttermilk, or sour milk, with bicarbonate of soda. This is an old-fashioned raising combination that is rarely used today.
Vinegar, or lemon juice, mixed with bicarbonate of soda. This was an economical raising mixture used a great deal during the Second World War to replace eggs in a cake mixture.

Different types of Cake Mixture

Creamed mixtures
These are based on a mixture of equal quantities of fat and sugar. Use a wooden spoon to work the fat and sugar together until combined, then beat vigorously until the mixture becomes pale and fluffy. The beating is easier if the mixing bowl and the fat are at room temperature, but on no account allow the fat to become oily as this would produce a heavy cake. A hand-held or other electric mixer will cream the mixture quickly and thoroughly.

Eggs, flour and flavouring are added to the creamed mixture. The amounts vary according to whether the cake is a light sponge type with an open, airy texture, or a closer, more substantial cake, perhaps rich with fruit.

With some modern, soft fats, there is no need for a separate creaming stage. All the ingredients are put in a mixing bowl together and beaten until thoroughly combined. This quick and easy method is not suitable for all cakes, however, so use it only when it is recommended in your recipe.

Melted-fat mixtures
This method is used mostly for cakes containing syrup or treacle—gingerbread, for example. Heat the fat gently with the sweetening ingredients before adding it to the dry ingredients. Mix the fat and sweetening together thoroughly as they melt, and take care not to let the mixture come to the boil. Sift the flour and raising agent thoroughly together and combine them carefully with the melted ingredients to make sure that no lumps form in the mixture. The amount of fat used is generally half, or less than half, of the amount of flour.

Rubbed-in mixtures
This method is used for very plain mixtures, such as rock cakes and scones. The amount of fat used is half, or less than half, of the amount of flour. Sieve the flour, salt and raising agent together well before adding the fat. Then rub in the fat thoroughly with the fingertips until it is completely blended and the mixture resembles breadcrumbs. Mix in any other dry ingredients, such as sugar, spices or dried fruit, at this stage, and finally stir in enough liquid to bind the mixture together.

Whisked mixtures
Sponges are the cakes most commonly made by this method. A true sponge consists only of eggs, sugar and flour.

It depends for its light, spongy texture on the air beaten into the eggs. The eggs and sugar should be beaten together with a wire whisk until they form a pale, thick mixture. When the mixture is thick enough, a ribbon of mixture trailed from the whisk over the surface of the mixture in the bowl will lie there for a few seconds before sinking in. To speed up the whisking process place the mixing bowl over a pan of hot, but not boiling, water while you beat the mixture. You can use a hand-held or other electric mixer to whisk the mixture quickly.

When the eggs and sugar have been whisked enough, fold in the sifted flour gently with a metal spoon until incorporated completely. Beating or roughly mixing in the flour would drive out much of the air that the whisking has introduced and spoil the light, fluffy texture of the cake. Use a metal spoon to fold in the flour, because this cuts through the whisked mixture with the least disturbance.

Among other cakes based on a whisked mixture are meringues, macaroons and coconut pyramids. In these cakes the main ingredients are whisked egg whites and sugar.

BAKING CAKES

Always prepare the cake tins you need before starting to mix the cake. Many cake mixtures must be put in the oven as soon as they are mixed, and will be spoiled if they are kept waiting while a tin is lined.

If you are using non-stick baking ware, follow the manufacturer's instructions for preparing the tins.

Brush over other tins with a pastry brush dipped in cooking oil or rub them over lightly with a little butter, margarine or lard on a piece of greaseproof paper.

Rich cakes or delicate mixtures should be put into lined tins. For lining, use silicone paper, vegetable parchment, kitchen foil, or greaseproof paper rubbed over with oil or butter. This prevents burning or discoloration during cooking.

To line a square or oblong tin, cut a square or oblong sheet of paper large enough to cover the base of the tin and come up the sides to the rim. Make a cut from each corner of the paper towards the centre, and fit the paper into the tin, overlapping the cut edges at the corners.

To line a round tin, cut a circle of paper to fit the base and a long strip to go all round the side but slightly deeper than the tin. Make small cuts along the bottom edge of the strip so that when it is fitted into the tin, the cut edges lie neatly on the base of the tin. Lay the cut-out circle of paper over the base, covering the cut flap.

For any cake that requires long baking, such as a rich fruit cake, give extra protection by tying a double layer of thick brown paper round the outside of the tin, or fitting a double layer of brown paper between the tin and the lining paper. This prevents the formation of a dry, heavy crust during the long baking.

To give a crisp coating to sponge cakes, dredge the greased tin with 1 teaspoon of caster sugar mixed with 1 teaspoon of flour. Toss the mixture round the tin to coat all the greased surface, then tip out the surplus.

When the cake mixture is ready, pour it or scoop it into the prepared tin, or into paper baking cases if you are making small cakes. Smooth the top of the mixture and make a slight depression with the back of a spoon in the centre of a large cake. This will level out as the cake bakes; it prevents the cake from rising to a peak.

Small cakes are usually baked near the top of the oven, but place large cakes in the middle of the oven where they are less likely to brown too quickly. If a cake is browning too much before it is due out of the oven, place a square of greaseproof paper or kitchen foil lightly over it. This will prevent further browning.

Do not open the oven door unnecessarily while your cake is baking. An inrush of cold air can check the rising of the cake, or cause it to rise unevenly. If you have to open the oven, do it slowly and close the oven door gently afterwards.

To test whether small cakes or sponges are ready, press the centre very lightly with a fingertip. If the cake springs back after your touch, it is cooked.

To test whether a large, rich cake is ready, run a warmed, bright-metal skewer into the centre of the cake. If it comes out clean, the cake is cooked. Large, rich cakes also shrink from the sides of the tin when cooked.

Cooling and storing

When the cake is baked enough, lift the tin from the oven and leave the cake in it for 5–10 minutes. Then remove the cake from the tin and stand it on a cake rack in a draught-free place to cool completely. The paper used to line the tin should be left on until the cake is cold.

The one exception to these rules is a Swiss roll, which must be taken from the oven and immediately turned from its tin on to sugared paper laid on a damp tea towel. Peel away the paper that lined the baking tin, trim the edges off the sponge, and roll it up while it is still warm. When it is cold, unroll it, spread on the filling and roll it up again.

When your cake is cold, store it in a dry tin with an airtight lid. Large, rich cakes that need keeping to mature can be wrapped in kitchen foil before being put in a tin.

Tips to remember

1 Set out all the ingredients and utensils before you start mixing.
2 Prepare the cake tin before you start mixing.
3 Switch on the oven at the required temperature and arrange the shelves where you will need them.
4 Measure the ingredients accurately.
5 Do not beat a cake or mix it too much after you have added the flour, or the cake will be heavy.
6 Add fruit to a cake last if possible, dusted with a little of the weighed flour so that it does not form lumps.
7 When making a cake in sandwich tins, divide the mixture as equally as you can between the tins so the two parts will both be ready together.

Biscuits

BISCUITS have been made since Roman times, when cooks boiled wheat flour to a paste then let it dry out and cut it into pieces to fry and serve with honey. By medieval times, several other biscuits of this type were made; they were called simnels and cracknels.

Some of the earliest biscuits were what we would call rusks, being twice-cooked bread—hence their name, which comes from the French *bis cuit* (twice cooked). Biscuits of the Middle Ages were always cooked twice; the second cooking was to dry them out thoroughly. Richer types of biscuit were made from Tudor times. They were used as sweetmeats at feasts and banquets, and were served with wine. The practice of drying out continued until the 18th century, but after that many biscuits were developed, including sponge biscuits, lemon biscuits, drop biscuits and brandy snaps.

Making Biscuits

A true biscuit makes a decided snapping noise when it is broken in half. Many so-called biscuit recipes make a softer product, which is a cookie rather than a true biscuit.

Always use fresh ingredients to give your biscuits the best flavour. Biscuit dough is generally much firmer than that used for cakes—more the consistency of pastry. Biscuit doughs are made by rubbing-in, by creaming and by the melted-fat method.

Several biscuits, gingernuts for example, are shaped into small walnut-sized pieces with the hands. Others are stamped out with pastry cutters from a rolled-out sheet of dough. In hot weather, a biscuit mixture containing a high proportion of fat to flour may be too soft to handle easily. Wrap it in greaseproof paper and leave it in a cool larder or a refrigerator for 10–20 minutes to make it easier to roll out or shape. Roll the dough to an even thickness, and stamp out biscuits of equal size which will all bake in the same time.

Bake the biscuits in the centre of the oven, as this helps to give them even baking and colouring. If you want to bake two trays of biscuits at once, put one tray on the shelf above the other and, halfway through the baking time, change over the trays. You may also need to give each tray a quarter-turn if the biscuits at one side are browning faster than the rest.

When the biscuits are cooked, lift them from the oven but leave them on the baking tray to cool a little before moving them to a wire rack to cool completely. Do not put them away in a tin or box until they are cold.

Never store biscuits in the same tin as a cake. They will take up moisture from the cake and lose their crispness. Biscuits are never as crisp again as when they are freshly baked, but they will keep fairly well for a few days in a tin or box with a tightly fitting lid.

Icing

As well as giving an attractive finish, many icings are of practical use. On cakes they help to prevent drying out, and on rather bland sweet breads and biscuits they add extra flavour.

Tint them delicately with food colouring if you wish, and flavour them to taste with, for example, vanilla, coffee, chocolate or orange.

Butter Icing or Butter Cream

The recipe below makes enough of this uncooked icing to coat the top and sides of a 7 in. (18 cm.) cake.

INGREDIENTS

4 oz. (100/125 g.) butter, softened but not oily
8 oz. (225 g.) icing sugar, sifted
1 tablespoon milk
Flavouring

Beat the butter until pale, then gradually beat in the icing sugar until the mixture is fluffy. Add the milk, to make it easier to spread, and work in a little flavouring.

Frosting

This cooked icing sets quickly so use it as soon as it is mixed. It will cover the top and sides of an 8 in. (20 cm.) cake.

INGREDIENTS

1 lb. (450 g.) caster sugar
8 tablespoons water
¼ teaspoon cream of tartar
2 egg whites
Flavouring

Put the sugar and water in a heavy-based pan, and place the pan over a low heat. Allow the sugar to dissolve without stirring. Blend the cream of tartar with 1 teaspoon of water and add this to the sugar syrup.

Bring the mixture to the boil, and boil without stirring until it reaches 116°C (240°F) on a sugar thermometer or the soft-ball stage when tested in water (see p. 317). Just before the syrup is ready, whisk the egg whites until stiff in a large, heatproof bowl. Remove the syrup from the heat and allow the bubbles to subside. Pour the syrup in a thin stream into the egg whites, whisking all the time. Whisk until opaque, then mix in the flavouring.

Fudge Icing

Unsalted butter is best for this cooked icing. It will coat the top and sides of a 9 in. (23 cm.) cake.

INGREDIENTS

1 lb. (450 g.) caster sugar
½ pint (275/300 ml.) water
2 oz. (50 g.) butter
2 tablespoons golden syrup
Flavouring

Put all the ingredients in a saucepan and stir over a gentle heat without boiling until the sugar has completely dissolved.

Then bring the icing mixture to the boil, and boil it until it reaches 114°C (238°F) on a sugar thermometer or the soft-ball stage when tested in water (see p. 317). Remove the pan from the heat when it reaches this temperature and leave the mixture to cool. Add the flavouring and beat with a wooden spoon until thick. Use immediately.

Glacé Icing

This uncooked icing covers the top and sides of a 7 in. (18 cm.) cake, or about 15 fairy cakes.

INGREDIENTS

6 oz. (175 g.) icing sugar
1–2 tablespoons warm water, or other liquid such as lemon or orange juice
Flavouring

Sift the icing sugar into a bowl and add the water a little at a time, mixing until the icing is smooth and thick enough to coat the back of a spoon. Work in the flavouring.

Points to watch when icing

Do not ice a cake until it is cold, or the icing will melt and run off.

Brush off any loose crumbs.

Ideally, the surface to be iced should be flat. If it is a large cake, trim the top to level it, or turn the cake upside-down and ice the base.

For delicate-textured cakes, such as sponges, use icing of a very soft consistency that will spread without pulling lumps out of the cake.

If cakes or biscuits are to be sandwiched with a filling as well as iced, put the filling in first.

To coat a cake with soft icing, stand the cake on a wire rack with a large plate beneath the rack. Pour the icing over the cake and let it find its own level. As it trickles down the sides, spread it with a palette knife to cover the sides completely.

To coat a cake with butter icing, stand the cake on a flat board or large, upturned plate. Using a round-bladed knife, coat the sides first, spreading the icing evenly. Pile the rest of the icing on the cake and spread it to the edges. Mark a pattern on it with a fork, knife or confectioner's comb.

Of

MARZIPAN, TOFFEES AND OTHER SWEETMEATS

CONTAINING

NUMEROUS *Useful* FAMILY RECIPES

for PLAIN & DECORATED CREAMS & FONDANTS, CHOCOLATES & JUJUBES & other SWEET DELIGHTES

PAGES 304–313

AND

A SELECTION of RECIPES from OTHER LANDS

PAGES 314–315

AND WITH

NOTES AND ADVICE

on all kinds of Boiling, Shaping, Moulding and Testing of Sweetmeats to Perfection

PAGES 316–317

Rout Cakes—ornamental biscuits made of ground almonds or hazelnuts.

Rout Cakes
Countrywide

During the 18th and 19th centuries a rout meant a large gathering of people—not by any means a disorderly gathering as the term would suggest now. A favourite social event among the wealthier classes was the Rout Party, when a large assembly of people would gather for an evening reception. Their drink would be ratafia—brandy flavoured with almond or apricot kernels—or lemonade mixed with spirits. There would also be dishes laden with tiny ornamental biscuits made with almonds or hazelnuts. These were so much part of the occasion that they earned themselves the name of Rout Cakes. Nowadays, they often go by their French name, *petits fours*.

Preparation Time: 45 minutes
Cooking Time: 20 minutes
Pre-heat the Oven to 170°C (325°F)—gas mark 3

Ingredients for about 18 cakes
- *A sheet of rice paper*
- *1 egg white*
- *3 oz. (75 g.) ground almonds or ground hazelnuts*
- *1½ oz. (40 g.) caster sugar*
- *¼ teaspoon almond essence (if using ground almonds)*
- *A few glacé cherries*
- *A few strips of angelica*
- *A few split, blanched almonds*
- *A few pieces of crystallised ginger*

For the glaze:
- *2 teaspoons caster sugar*
- *1 tablespoon milk*
- *2 oz. (50 g.) plain chocolate (optional)*

Line a baking sheet with the rice paper. Whisk the egg white very stiffly and fold in the almonds or hazelnuts, and the sugar. Add the almond essence, if using ground almonds.

Spoon the mixture into a piping bag fitted with a ½ in. (1·5 cm.) star nozzle. Pipe about 18 small rings, fingers and circles on to the rice paper, leaving a little space round each cake. Decorate each shape with a piece of cherry, angelica, almond or ginger.

Bake the cakes on the middle shelf of the pre-heated oven for 15–20 minutes until lightly browned.

Make the glaze by dissolving the remaining sugar in the milk. Brush the cakes with this immediately after removing them from the oven, then lift each one on to a cooling rack.

When the cakes are quite cold, remove any excess rice paper from the edges. If you like, you can dip the ends of some of the finger-shaped cakes into melted chocolate and then leave it to harden.

Place the cakes in paper sweet cases. Arrange them in a colourful box with a transparent lid or add them to other candies to make an interesting assortment.

Marshmallows
Countrywide

The sweet-tasting root of the marshmallow plant used to be the main ingredient of this sweetmeat, but nowadays only the name survives in the recipe. Until the 18th century the plant was greatly esteemed for its medicinal properties, and a syrup of marshmallows was recommended to cure sore throats, hoarseness and all lung complaints. The first reference to marshmallow prepared as a sweetmeat instead of a medicine is in *Chambers's Journal* for 1884. This version is delicately flavoured with vanilla.

PREPARATION TIME: 45 MINUTES
COOLING AND DRYING TIME: 36 HOURS

INGREDIENTS TO YIELD
1¾ LB. (800 G.)

For the gelatine mixture:

1 oz. (25 g.) powdered gelatine
¼ pint (150 ml.) water
1 teaspoon vanilla essence

For the syrup:

1 lb. (450 g.) granulated sugar
7 fl. oz. (200 ml.) warm water
8 fl. oz. (225 ml.) liquid glucose
1 egg white

For the coating:

3 tablespoons cornflour
3 tablespoons sieved icing sugar

Place the water, gelatine and vanilla essence in a small bowl set over a saucepan of water. Heat it gently over a low heat to dissolve the gelatine, then take the pan off the heat. Leave the bowl on top of the pan to keep the mixture warm.

Dissolve the sugar in the warm water in a fairly large pan over a low heat, then gently stir in the glucose with a wooden spoon. Stop stirring and let the mixture boil to 118°C (245°F) (see p. 317). Remove the pan from the heat.

Pour the still-warm gelatine mixture into a heatproof mixing bowl rinsed out with water to stop the mixture sticking. Gradually trickle the sugar syrup into the gelatine mixture, whisking all the time. A balloon whisk gives the lightest mixture, but an electric mixer saves hard work.

When the mixture is well thickened, beat in the egg white little by little. The mixture will become thick, light and foamy.

Mix together the cornflour and icing sugar and sprinkle some of it over the base of an oiled 11 by 7 in. (28 by 18 cm.) tin. Pour the marshmallow into the tin and allow it to cool slowly, leaving it for 24 hours.

Dust a working surface and your fingers lightly with the coating mixture. Use a knife to lift a corner of the marshmallow, then pull it gently out of the tin on to the working area.

Using a hot, dry, sharp knife, cut the marshmallow into squares. Dip the cut sides in the coating mixture, and leave to dry for about 12 hours. Pack in layers in an airtight tin.

TREACLE TOFFEE
Yorkshire

TREACLE TOFFEE used to be sold at the market stalls all over the Midlands and the North of England until about 30 years ago. It was especially popular as the traditional treat to eat around the bonfire on Guy Fawkes night.

In Swaledale in Yorkshire they make a variety which goes by the name of Tom Trot. When the mixture is cooked enough to form threads in cold water it is poured into a buttered dish and then worked with the hands and pulled and twisted into long lengths, until the toffee is bright and clear.

An Irish treacle toffee goes by the evocative name of Peg's Leg, and is flavoured with the unlikely but interesting addition of peppermint and ginger.

PREPARATION TIME: 1¼ HOURS
SETTING TIME: 2 HOURS

INGREDIENTS TO YIELD
1½ LB. (700 G.)

2 tablespoons water
1 tablespoon white vinegar
4 oz. (100/125 g.) unsalted butter
1 lb. (450 g.) light, soft brown sugar
8 oz. (225 g.) black treacle

Place the water, vinegar and butter in a fairly large saucepan and heat them together gently until the butter has melted.

Stir in the sugar and the black treacle and follow the rules for sugar boiling (see p. 317). This does take time (about 20 minutes) but do not rush it.

When the sugar has dissolved, boil to 138°C (280°F). Remove the pan from the heat and allow the bubbles to subside a little. Pour the mixture into a well-oiled 7 in. (18 cm.) square sandwich tin.

When the toffee is beginning to set, mark it into squares with a knife. If you have the patience, go over the lines again from time to time, as the divisions tend to disappear, making it difficult to break the toffee into squares when it is cold. It is well worth while marking the toffee out more than once.

When the toffee has set hard, break it up into squares, wrap the sweets in Cellophane paper and keep them in an airtight tin.

PEPPERMINT CREAMS
Countrywide

THE SIGHT of a little china dish brimming with Peppermint Creams, somehow evokes a mood of quiet and homely comforts. Highly popular from Victorian times onwards, these little sweetmeats were always to be found on the dresser or sideboard waiting to be proffered to visitors.

With this same uncooked fondant mixture you can make a variety of creams, your own sugar mice, or a Neapolitan roll to coat with marzipan.

PREPARATION TIME: 30 MINUTES
DRYING TIME: 24 HOURS

INGREDIENTS TO YIELD
1 LB. (450 G.)

1 egg white
About 1 lb. (450 g.) icing sugar
A few drops of oil of peppermint or peppermint essence

Beat the egg white until it is frothy but not stiff. Sieve the icing sugar and stir enough of it into the egg white to form a fairly stiff mixture; the amount will depend on the size of the egg.

Add a few drops of peppermint oil or essence. Knead the mixture to a firm paste and then roll it out on a board lightly dusted with sieved icing sugar. Cut it out into rounds about ½ in. (1·5 cm.) across, or form the mixture into balls and flatten them with a fork.

Place the peppermint creams in a single layer on a sheet of vegetable parchment or waxed paper. Leave them in a warm place for 24 hours to dry before storing in an airtight tin. If liked, you can dip or half dip the dry creams in melted chocolate, either plain or milk.

To make sugar mice, prepare the mixture and divide it in half; colour one half pink. Divide each half into seven or eight equal pieces. Shape each piece into a thick oval, make one end pointed for the nose and pinch up two small pieces for the ears. Use currants or silver balls for the eyes and a piece of string for the tail. Leave the mice to dry for 24 hours.

ACID DROPS
Countrywide

THESE OLD ENGLISH FAVOURITES appear in several 18th-century cookery books. In *The Experienced English Housekeeper* (1769), Elizabeth Raffald describes the rather daunting procedure then involved: the lemons and the sugar had to be beaten for at least an hour, until they went 'white and bright'. When this result had been achieved, the cook had to 'drop them on to writing paper, and dry them before the fire or in the sun'.

PREPARATION TIME: 40 MINUTES
INGREDIENTS TO YIELD
8 OZ. (225 G.)

1 lb. (450 g.) granulated sugar
¼ teaspoon cream of tartar
4 fl. oz. (100/125 ml.) warm water
1 level teaspoon tartaric acid
A few drops of lemon essence

Place the sugar, the cream of tartar and the water in a fairly large, heavy saucepan. Place the pan over a low heat and dissolve the sugar slowly and carefully, brushing the sides of the pan down frequently (see rules for sugar boiling, p. 317). This mixture has less water in it than most other sweets, and so the sugar will take longer to dissolve.

When the sugar has completely dissolved, bring it to the boil, without stirring, until the mixture reaches 154°C (310°F). Remove the pan from the heat and plunge the base of the pan immediately into a bowl of cold water to prevent the syrup from continuing to cook and becoming too dark in colour.

Mix the tartaric acid with a little warm water and add it to the mixture with a few drops of the lemon essence. Stir well to mix in the lemon essence and leave the syrup to cool and thicken for a few minutes. Then, using a teaspoon lightly oiled with corn oil and working quickly, place small drops, in rounds, on to an oiled slab or oiled baking sheet.

Allow the acid drops to set completely then remove them from the slab and wrap each one in Cellophane. Pack them in tins or jars.

TOFFEE APPLES
Countrywide

FROM THE MIDDLE of the 17th century, sugar from the West Indies began to be imported in bulk. But this expensive commodity was used only by the more wealthy classes. The poorer, when they could afford it, used honey or treacle to satisfy their craving for sweetness. Nevertheless, even in medieval times, toffee apples were sold at fairs and markets. They were made of little windfall apples dipped in a sticky mixture of honey and beeswax.

PREPARATION TIME: 30 MINUTES
SETTING TIME: 15 MINUTES

INGREDIENTS TO YIELD
EIGHT TOFFEE APPLES

8 small eating apples
8 wooden skewers

For the toffee:

8 oz. (225 g.) soft brown sugar
1 oz. (25 g.) unsalted butter
1 tablespoon golden syrup
5 tablespoons water
1 teaspoon vinegar

Wash and dry the apples very thoroughly, making sure that any oiliness is removed. Remove the stalks and push a wooden skewer into the centre of each apple.

Place the sugar, butter, golden syrup, water and vinegar in a heavy-based, medium saucepan and heat the mixture gently, until the sugar has dissolved. Bring to the boil and cook fairly briskly until it reaches 143°C (290°F) (see p. 317), or until a drop of the mixture put into a bowl of cold water snaps cleanly.

Dip each apple into the toffee, twisting it round to coat it. Then dip each apple in a bowl of cold water to set the toffee. Stand the apples on a greased or non-stick tray.

When the toffee has set hard, wrap the apples in Cellophane or plastic film.

BARLEY SUGAR
Scotland

IN HIS POEM *John Barleycorn*, Robert Burns (1759–96) declared barley to be the 'King o' grain', and the Scots are justly proud of their bannocks of barley, their barley water and barley sugar.

A charming recipe from John Nott's *Cook's and Confectioner's Dictionary* (1723) explains how you must first boil the barley in water and then strain it through a hair sieve. This modern recipe uses tangy lemon zest and juice for the flavouring instead of barley.

PREPARATION TIME: 50 MINUTES
COOLING TIME: ABOUT 30 MINUTES
INGREDIENTS TO YIELD 12–14 STICKS OR ABOUT 1 LB. (450 G.)

1 lb. (450 g.) granulated sugar
6 lumps of sugar
1 lemon
7 fl. oz. (200 ml.) warm water

Place the granulated sugar in a large, heavy-based pan.

Rub the sugar lumps all over the lemon to absorb the lemon oil. Add these lumps to the sugar and add the warm water. Stir to melt the sugar lumps, then place the pan over a low heat until the sugar has completely dissolved. Brush the sides of the pan with a warm pastry brush to remove any undissolved sugar.

When the syrup is quite clear, bring it to the boil and heat to 132°C (270°F) (see p. 317). Remove the pan from the heat. Squeeze the juice from half the lemon and strain it into the pan, slowly stirring it into the syrup. Replace the pan on the heat and bring the temperature slowly up to 152°C (305°F). Remove the pan from the heat, allow the bubbles to subside and then pour the mixture on to a marble slab or enamel tray. Allow it to cool for about 2–3 minutes.

Using a sugar scraper (see p. 316), bring the mixture together into a neat, rectangular shape. Working very quickly, use scissors to cut the barley sugar into pieces ½ by 6 in. (1·5 by 15 cm.). Roll the pieces out to an even thickness or flatten them with your hands, then twist them. Place each twist on a sheet of non-stick paper or greaseproof. As the twists cool they will flatten a little, but it should be possible to twist them back while they are still pliable.

They will cool in about 30 minutes and should be put in an airtight container immediately, as they will become sticky if exposed to the air. Wrap them in different coloured Cellophane papers, as they will deteriorate if left unwrapped.

EVERTON TOFFEE
Lancashire

IN HER BOOK *Modern Cookery*, published in 1845, Eliza Acton gives a recipe for this traditional toffee. She stipulates that only 'very fresh' butter can be used, along with brown sugar of a 'moderate quality', and adds that the 'real Everton toffie is made with a much larger proportion of butter, but it is the less wholesome on that very account'.

Toffee-making is often among the first cooking experiences for children. It is the traditional testing time that most pleases them, that moment when, in the words of Eliza Acton, the toffee 'crackles when dropped into cold water, and snaps between the teeth without sticking'. You can use this method if you like, or use a sugar thermometer.

PREPARATION TIME: 50 MINUTES
SETTING TIME: $1\frac{1}{2}$ HOURS

INGREDIENTS TO YIELD
$1\frac{1}{4}$ LB. (575 G.)

1 lb. (450 g.) granulated sugar
$\frac{1}{4}$ pint (150 ml.) water
A pinch of cream of tartar
3 oz. (75 g.) unsalted butter

Place the sugar, the water and the cream of tartar in a fairly large saucepan. Heat gently to dissolve the sugar, then add the butter in small pieces and stir the mixture with a wooden spoon so that the butter melts.

When the butter has completely melted, bring the mixture to 152°C (305°F) without stirring it (see p. 317). Allow the bubbles to subside a little, then pour the toffee into a lightly oiled 7 in. (18 cm.) square sandwich tin. When the toffee has almost set, mark it out into square or oblong shapes with a sharp knife. Make sure that the indentations go right through to the bottom of the tin, as this will make it easier for the toffee to be broken into pieces.

When the toffee is hard, break it up as evenly as possible and wrap the sweets in Cellophane paper. Store them in an airtight tin or jar.

The wrapped and the ready: Acid Drops, Everton Toffee, Barley Sugar and Toffee Apples with Peppermint Cream mice.

WELSH TOFFEE
North Wales

EVEN AS LATE AS the first years of this century, the *Noson Gylflaith* (Toffee Evening) was an essential part of the Christmas and New Year celebrations in many areas of North Wales. Families would invite one another to supper and, at the conclusion of the meal, would gather round the fire to tell stories and make toffee. When the sweet had boiled sufficiently, it was poured on to the greased hearthstone to cool. Hosts and guests then buttered their hands and competed in 'pulling' the toffee while it was still warm. This was done with a twisting motion that involved more skill than might be supposed; but, if successful, it resulted in a beautiful, glassy, yellow-gold curl.

Two World Wars have swept away Toffee Evenings, but toffee-making remains as an absorbing and rewarding entertainment for an odd hour or two in winter.

PREPARATION TIME: 30 MINUTES
COOLING TIME: 1 HOUR

INGREDIENTS TO YIELD
1¾ LB. (800 G.)

4 oz. (100/125 g.) unsalted butter
1 lb. (450 g.) granulated sugar
2 tablespoons warm water
2 tablespoons white vinegar
4 tablespoons golden syrup, or 2 tablespoons each of syrup and treacle

Melt the butter in a fairly large pan, stir in the sugar and remove the pan from the heat.

Add the water, the vinegar and the syrup, or syrup and treacle. Stir over low heat until the sugar dissolves, taking care not to let the mixture boil. Then bring to boiling point. Boil steadily for about 15–20 minutes, or until a little of the toffee put into a bowl of cold water will snap. The temperature of the toffee at this point should be 152°C (305°F) (see p. 317).

Pour the toffee into a well-buttered rectangular tin, measuring 11 by 7 in. (28 by 18 cm.).

Leave the toffee to cool. As soon as it has begun to set, mark it out into squares. When the toffee is quite cold, break the squares up and wrap each one in Cellophane. Store the toffee in a jar or airtight tin.

COCONUT ICE
Countrywide

'THE SAID COCHOS hath a hard shell and a green huske over it, as hath our walnut ... within this hard shell is a white rine resembling in shewe very much even as any thing may do, to the white of an egg when it is hard boyled.'

In this way Sir Francis Drake described the coconut to the people of England. The tropical palm on which it grows is called *kalpa vriksha* in Sanskrit, meaning 'tree that gives all that is necessary for life'. Mrs Beeton describes its many uses in her *Household Management* (1861), while giving a recipe for Cocoa-nut Soup.

Since Drake's time the 'white rine' has been a popular addition to many spiced and sweet recipes. A slab of coconut ice is something few children can resist, and it is quick and easy to make.

PREPARATION TIME: 30 MINUTES
SETTING TIME: 2 HOURS

INGREDIENTS TO YIELD
2½ LB. (1·1 KG.)

¼ pint (150 ml.) water and ¼ pint (150 ml.) milk, or ½ pint (275/300 ml.) milk
2 lb. (900 g.) granulated sugar
1 oz. (25 g.) butter
8 oz. (225 g.) desiccated coconut
1 teaspoon vanilla essence
A few drops of red colouring or cochineal

Pour the water and milk, or the ½ pint (275/300 ml.) of milk, into a saucepan with the sugar and butter and heat it slowly until the sugar dissolves.

Bring to the boil and cook for 10 minutes, stirring occasionally until it reaches a temperature of 120°C (248°F) (see p. 317).

Meanwhile, oil an 8 in. (20 cm.) square, shallow tin. Remove the saucepan from the heat and add the coconut and vanilla essence.

Beat the mixture briskly with a wooden spoon until it is fairly thick and creamy. Then pour half the mixture into the oiled tin. Add the colouring quickly to the remaining half as the texture will soon change, making it difficult for the colour to spread evenly. Pour the pink mixture on top of the white and spread it evenly over the top.

Leave the coconut ice in a cool place until it is firm, and then cut it into narrow bars about 1½ in. (4 cm.) long. Store in an airtight tin.

LEMON PASTILLES
Countrywide

IN EARLY TUDOR TIMES pastilles were little aromatic tablets, 'kindes of mixtures of paste to perfume withal', that were burned in sick rooms to dispel evil humours. But by the end of the 17th century the word had more or less assumed its present meaning—that of flavoured lozenges of sugar paste that were sucked to sweeten the breath or bring ease to a sore throat. Early Georgian dandies used to carry pastilles scented with apricot, cinnamon or orange flowers in their waistcoat pockets as a shield against the social hazards of the day.

Lemon Pastilles were probably invented at about the same period. They are highly refreshing, and help to ward off the fatigue of driving.

PREPARATION TIME: 30 MINUTES
SETTING TIME: 12 HOURS

INGREDIENTS TO YIELD
1 LB. (450 G.)

1 pint (575/600 ml.) apple purée, unsweetened
12 oz. (350 g.) caster sugar
1½ oz. (40 g.) gelatine
2½ fl. oz. (75 ml.) cold water
1 tablespoon lemon juice or a few drops of lemon essence
A few drops of lemon colouring (optional)

For the coating:
2 teaspoons cornflour
2 teaspoons caster sugar

Place the apple purée and sugar in a small saucepan and cook over a low heat until really thick, stirring occasionally. Dissolve the gelatine in the water and add it to the apple mixture. Take the pan off the heat and add the lemon juice or lemon essence. Add the colouring, if liked. Mix well together with a wooden spoon and pour the mixture into a non-stick tin about 11 by 7 in. (28 by 18 cm.) and at least 1 in. (2·5 cm.) deep. Leave to set for about 12 hours.

When it has set, cut it into squares with a hot, dry knife and remove them from the tin. Mix the cornflour and sugar together. Roll each of the pastilles in this coating mixture and place each one in a paper sweet case.

HONEYCOMB
Sussex

AT THE BEGINNING of the last war, hundreds of children from south-east London were evacuated to Sussex. For many of them it was the first time they had seen the country-side, and also the first time they tasted this home-made sweetmeat, which even in rationing time could be an occasional luxury since the recipe calls for only half the amount of sugar usual in sweet-making.

The Honeycomb should be eaten as quickly as possible, because it soon becomes sticky when it is exposed to the air; with children in the house that should present no problem.

PREPARATION TIME: 30 MINUTES
SETTING TIME: 40 MINUTES

INGREDIENTS TO YIELD
12 OZ. (350 G.)

$\frac{1}{4}$ pint (150 ml.) cold water
1 tablespoon golden syrup
8 oz. (225 g.) granulated sugar
$\frac{1}{4}$ teaspoon cream of tartar
$\frac{1}{2}$ teaspoon bicarbonate of soda
1 teaspoon warm water

Put the cold water in a heavy-based saucepan. Add the golden syrup, sugar and cream of tartar. Place the pan over a low heat and stir with a wooden spoon until the sugar has dissolved and the ingredients are well blended. Raise the heat to bring the mixture to the boil, without stirring it. Continue to boil over a high heat until it reaches 154°C (310°F) (see p. 317).

Meanwhile, grease a 7 in. (18 cm.) square sandwich tin with butter. As soon as the syrup mixture reaches the required temperature, remove the saucepan from the heat. Quickly mix the bicarbonate of soda with the teaspoon of warm water and immediately add it to the syrup mixture, stirring gently.

Pour the mixture into the greased tin and leave the honeycomb in a cool place to set.

Mark the honeycomb into bars or squares just before it sets. Eat it without delay, as it soon softens and goes sticky.

EDINBURGH ROCK
Scotland

AS A YOUNG BOY Sandy Ferguson earned himself the nickname of Sweetie Sandy, because he enjoyed nothing so much as making sweets. In 1822 he turned his hobby into a profession when he left his home village of Doune in Perthshire and set up a sweet-making business in the heart of the city of Edinburgh.

There, soft sticks of rock in assorted pastel colours have been made according to his original recipe for over 150 years and packed in little tartan boxes for tourists to take away as souvenirs.

PREPARATION TIME: 45 MINUTES
SETTING TIME: 24 HOURS

INGREDIENTS FOR 16 SMALL
STICKS OF ROCK

1 lb. (450 g.) cube sugar
$\frac{1}{2}$ pint (275/300 ml.) cold water
$\frac{1}{4}$ teaspoon cream of tartar
A few drops of various flavourings and colourings, according to choice: raspberry or rose flavouring and pink colouring; peppermint flavouring and green colouring; ginger essence and fawn colouring; orange or tangerine flavouring and yellow colouring; lemon or vanilla flavouring without colouring

Put the sugar and water in a pan over a gentle heat and stir until the sugar has dissolved. Raise the heat and, when the mixture is nearly boiling, add the cream of tartar. Boil, without stirring, until the mixture reaches 121°C (250°F) in cold weather or 127°C (260°F) in hot weather. At this temperature a drop of the mixture will form a hard ball in cold water (see p. 317).

Remove the pan from the heat and divide the mixture between several heatproof containers, according to how many flavours you have chosen to use. Metal or Pyrex bowls are ideal, but plastic ones might melt. Add a few drops of flavouring to each batch of mixture, together with just enough of the appropriate colouring to give a delicate pastel shade. Mix together well.

Pour each batch of rock into a buttered candy bar (see p. 316) placed on a buttered marble slab. If you do not have candy bars, use a well-buttered foil container or flan tin for each batch.

The edges of the mixture will cool more quickly than the centres so, as the mixture cools, turn the edges and ends inwards with a buttered knife so that it cools more evenly.

When the pieces of rock have become cool enough to handle, dust them with icing sugar—this will reduce their shine.

Pick up each piece of rock and, without twisting, pull each one gently into a long sausage shape about $\frac{1}{2}$ in. (1·5 cm.) in diameter. This will take about 10–15 minutes, and the pieces will be completely dull. They should be firm enough to hold the shape but not too firm to pull.

Use scissors to cut the pieces into 4 in. (10 cm.) lengths. They will be round in section but rather ragged at the edges, unlike peppermint rock.

Arrange the pieces of rock on a baking tray and leave them in a warm room for at least 24 hours, until the sticks have become soft and powdery.

Store the pieces of rock in an airtight tin. Edinburgh Rock makes an attractive present arranged on small doilies inside fairly shallow, decorative tins.

MARZIPAN
Countrywide

MARZIPAN HAS a long and colourful history. It may have been first made in France by nuns during the Middle Ages, and served as a solid cake known as Saint Marc's *pain* (bread). Or it may have originated in Italy as *marzapane*, later anglicised to March-pane. Because it was soft and pliable, it was ideal material for the culinary fantasies of the Tudor and Stuart feasts, when it was served in decorative shapes with sweet wines, fruit tarts, marmalades, preserves and brightly coloured, elaborate jellies.

The Cook's and Confectioner's Dictionary (1723) gives instructions for the making of gilded marzipan, which it calls by its old English name of March-pane. You first ice it and bake it, and then garnish it with comfits. Then you 'Take Leaves of Gold, cut them into divers Forms, wash your March-pane over with Gum-water, and lay on your Leaf-gold'. The result was no doubt very pleasing to the eye, and small quantities of gold could not harm the digestion either.

PREPARATION TIME: 1 HOUR
SETTING TIME: 24 HOURS

INGREDIENTS TO YIELD
1½ LB. (700 G.)

12 oz. (350 g.) ground almonds
6 oz. (175 g.) icing sugar, sifted
6 oz. (175 g.) caster sugar
1½ teaspoons lemon juice
A few drops of almond essence
1 egg, lightly beaten
A few drops of red, green and yellow food colouring
A few dates, walnuts and glacé cherries
A few cloves
1 egg white
A little caster sugar

Put the ground almonds, icing sugar and caster sugar together in a mixing bowl. Add the lemon juice and the almond essence. Stir in enough of the beaten egg to make a fairly dry paste. Turn it on to a board lightly sprinkled with sieved icing sugar and knead it until it is smooth.

Divide the almond paste into four sections; leave one plain and colour the remaining three pieces red, green and yellow respectively by adding a few drops of colouring and kneading it into the paste with your hands. You can make sweets very quickly by placing a small piece of coloured paste in a stoned date, sandwiching a piece between two halves of a walnut, or partially enclosing a glacé cherry in the natural coloured paste, leaving a small piece of the cherry showing at the top.

Fruits and vegetables can be made by shaping paste as follows:

CAULIFLOWERS
Partially enclose a piece of natural paste, the size of a hazelnut, in green paste flattened to the size of a 10p piece. Mark the top with the point of a skewer to represent the flower, and press round the green 'leaves' with the side of the skewer.

ORANGES AND LEMONS
To obtain an orange paste, knead some of the red paste into some of the yellow. Shape the appropriate colour to resemble an orange or a lemon, and press a clove into one end for the stalk. Roll the sweet over a coarse grater to mark the surface.

STRAWBERRY
Shape a strawberry in red paste and pit the surface with the point of a cocktail stick. Make tiny leaves with green paste. Press four leaves into the end of the strawberry, using a cocktail stick.

Marzipan in 'divers forms'. This versatile sweetmeat brings out the artist in the cook.

BANANA

Shape a banana in yellow paste and trace thin brown lines on the sides with a metal skewer dipped in gravy browning.

MARZIPAN SANDWICHES

Roll out the various coloured pastes to equal oblongs, $\frac{1}{8}$ in. (3 mm.) thick. Brush each oblong, except for the one which will form the top layer, with a little egg white and put one on top of the other to make a three or four-tiered sandwich. Cover with greased paper and leave it for a day to set. Cut it with a sharp knife into squares, oblongs and diamonds. Roll the sweets in caster sugar.

JUJUBES
Countrywide

A PRICKLY TREE of the buckthorn family, with the unlikely name of the Zisyphus, is the bearer of a plum-like fruit with the even more unlikely name of the jujube.

In the early part of the 19th century the juice of this fruit was used to flavour little gelatine lozenges. Today a jujube is simply a fruit gum.

PREPARATION TIME: 30 MINUTES
SETTING TIME: 24 HOURS

INGREDIENTS TO YIELD
ABOUT $1\frac{1}{2}$ LB. (700 G.)

6 oz. (175 g.) dried apricots, soaked overnight, or 12 oz. (350 g.) fresh or frozen black currants
$\frac{1}{2}$ pint (275/300 ml.) water
1 lb. (450 g.) granulated sugar
2 oz. (50 g.) gelatine
$\frac{1}{4}$ pint (150 ml.) warm water
2 teaspoons lemon juice

For decoration:
A little caster sugar

Cook the apricots in $\frac{1}{2}$ pint (275/300 ml.) water until they are soft, then sieve or liquidise them. This will yield approximately $\frac{1}{2}$ pint (275/300 ml.) thick purée. If you use frozen black currants, cook them unthawed without water until they are soft, and sieve or liquidise them in the same way. Return the purée to the saucepan, add the granulated sugar and heat gently to dissolve.

Meanwhile, put the gelatine in a bowl containing $\frac{1}{4}$ pint (150 ml.) of warm water and place the bowl over a saucepan filled with boiling water. Place the pan over a low heat until the gelatine has dissolved (see p. 257). Stir the gelatine and then the lemon juice into the sugar syrup.

Rinse a 7 in. (18 cm.) square sandwich tin under the cold tap and strain the mixture into it. Leave to set overnight. Cut into squares with a hot knife and toss the jujubes in caster sugar.

Serve in paper sweet cases and eat fairly quickly, as they do not store well.

BUTTERSCOTCH
Scotland

UP TO THE BEGINNING of this century, the preparing of all varieties of candy was a big social occasion in the country districts of Scotland.

An old cottage cookery book declares that it was a 'regular adjunct to courting... It draws together all the lads and lasses round about for miles, and the fun and the daffing that go on during the boiling, clipping and cooling, both the lads and lasses declare, worth the money'. If that was the case, then many lovers must have wooed each other while making butterscotch.

PREPARATION TIME: 50 MINUTES
SETTING TIME: 30 MINUTES

INGREDIENTS TO YIELD
1 LB. (450 G.)

1 lb. (450 g.) granulated sugar
$\frac{1}{4}$ pint (150 ml.) hot water
$\frac{1}{4}$ teaspoon cream of tartar
3 oz. (75 g.) unsalted butter
$\frac{1}{4}$ teaspoon vanilla essence

Put the sugar and the water into a large, heavy-based saucepan. Dissolve the sugar, following the rules for sugar boiling (see p. 317).

Add the cream of tartar and boil to 116°C (240°F). Remove the pan from the heat and add the butter in small pieces. Return the pan to the heat and continue to boil to 138°C (280°F).

Remove the pan from the heat, stir in the vanilla essence and pour the mixture into a well-oiled shallow tin, 11 by 7 in. (28 by 18 cm.).

When the butterscotch has almost set, mark it into rectangles with a sharp knife. When it is cold, break the squares apart and wrap each piece in shiny metallic paper.

FAMILY FUDGE
Yorkshire

THIS FUDGE has been made for many years in the North Yorkshire village of Kirk Hammerton, a place which has long been well known for its home-made sweets. Family Fudge is easy to prepare and it makes an ideal contribution for a Christmas fair, or any other fund-raising activity.

PREPARATION TIME: 75 MINUTES
SETTING TIME: 3 HOURS

INGREDIENTS TO YIELD
2 LB. (900 G.)

2 lb. (900 g.) granulated sugar
8 oz. (225 g.) butter
1 large tin of evaporated milk
$\frac{1}{4}$ of the milk tin of cold water
$\frac{1}{4}$ teaspoon vanilla essence

Rinse out a 7 pint (4 litre) pan with cold water. Put in the sugar, butter, milk, water and vanilla essence. Set the pan over a low heat until the sugar has dissolved. Stir the mixture occasionally, and brush the sides of the pan with warm water from time to time. This is to make sure that sugar crystals do not form and drop into the mixture.

When the sugar has been dissolved, bring the mixture to the boil, and boil rapidly until it reaches the soft-ball stage or 114°C (238°F) (see p. 317).

Take the pan off the heat and allow the fudge to cool for 3 minutes, then beat it rapidly with a wooden spoon until the mixture thickens and feels rough.

Line an 8 in. (20 cm.) tin with waxed paper. Pour in the fudge and, when it is beginning to set, mark in squares with a knife. Cut the fudge into squares when cold, and store it in an airtight tin.

CHOCOLATE AND NUT FUDGE
Countrywide

IT WOULD SEEM that fudge, regarded as one of our most traditional sweets, is actually an import from America, and a fairly recent one at that. The earliest reference to it occurs in *The Inlander,* a now defunct Michigan magazine, which in 1896 carried an article on 'Fudges, kinds of chocolate bonbons'. However, if we did not invent the confection, we may have supplied the word. In the 18th century, to fudge meant to contrive in a bungling manner; perhaps the first chocolate fudge was the result of an attempt to make a bonbon recipe go further by adding milk and butter. Equally, 'Fadge', is an old word for a flat loaf or bannock, to which the uncut sweet bears a passing resemblance.

This fudge is a delight, and a wild success at children's parties.

PREPARATION TIME: 30 MINUTES
COOLING TIME: 1½ HOURS

INGREDIENTS TO YIELD
2 LB. (900 G.)

4 oz. (100/125 g.) unsalted butter
7 fl. oz. (200 ml.) milk
1½ oz. (40 g.) cocoa powder, sieved
1½ lb. (700 g.) granulated sugar
½ teaspoon vanilla essence
2 oz. (50 g.) chopped walnuts

Melt the butter in the milk in a large saucepan over a low heat. Mix in the sieved cocoa and the sugar. Heat gently to dissolve the sugar, bring to the boil and boil to 114°C (238°F) (see p. 317). Remove the pan from the heat, and beat until the mixture thickens but still has a gloss. Stir in the vanilla essence and the walnuts.

Pour the fudge into a greased 7 in. (18 cm.) square tin and leave to cool for about 1½ hours. When it is nearly cold, mark it out in squares with a sharp knife, and when cold remove it from the tin and cut it into squares.

Arrange the fudge squares in paper sweet cases and add to an assortment of candies in a pretty box.

FRUIT FONDANTS
Countrywide

THE NAME FONDANT is borrowed from French and literally means 'melting', an aptly descriptive title for these sweets that do melt in the mouth.

Flavoured with fruit essence, coloured in delicate shades, and dipped in chocolate if you like, fondants make the prettiest of all rewards for the home confectioner.

MAKING TIME: 1 HOUR
MATURING TIME: SEVERAL HOURS AT LEAST
SETTING TIME: 5 MINUTES

INGREDIENTS TO YIELD
ABOUT 1 LB. (450 G.)

1 lb. (450 g.) granulated sugar
¼ pint (150 ml.) warm water
1 fl. oz. (25 ml.) liquid glucose
A few drops each of: violet flavouring and mauve colouring; strawberry flavouring and red colouring; lemon flavouring and yellow colouring; orange flavouring and orange colouring
Stock syrup (see p. 317) for thinning if necessary
Fondant mat (see p. 316)

Put the sugar and water in a large, heavy-based saucepan. Stir gently, then put over a very low heat until the sugar has dissolved completely. Brush down the sides of the pan with a pastry brush dipped in warm water to remove all traces of sugar crystals.

Stir in the glucose and raise the heat to bring the mixture to the boil. Boil until it reaches 116°C (240°F) (see p. 317), then remove the pan from the heat. When the bubbles have died down, pour the mixture on to a marble slab or enamel tray.

Leave to cool a little, then, using a sugar scraper, scrape together in a figure-of-eight movement. Work as quickly as you can, as the mixture hardens rapidly. Remove any mixture that accumulates on the scraper, because this will harden first.

When the fondant becomes opaque, pick up walnut-sized pieces and knead them until soft and smooth. If they become lumpy, quick and thorough kneading will make them smooth again.

Put the pieces in an airtight container and leave to mature for several hours at least, and up to a few days if more convenient.

To finish making the Fruit Fondants, divide the matured pieces into four batches and work with one batch at a time. Put a batch in a small basin with a few drops each of the chosen flavouring and colouring. Set the basin over a pan of water and put over a gentle heat. As the mixture softens, beat with a wooden spoon to work in the flavouring and colouring thoroughly. If the mixture is too stiff to beat, add ¼ teaspoon of stock syrup. Be careful not to add too much, or the finished fondants will not harden properly. When a slight skin forms on the surface of the mixture, remove the pan from the heat.

Keep stirring the mixture well as you fill the fondant mat. Work with two spoons, using one to take mixture from the basin and the other to scrape it off into the mould on the mat. Fill the moulds as quickly as you can because the mixture will lose its characteristic texture if it becomes too hot or is overmixed. If a fondant mat is not available, roll small pieces of the mixture into balls and put them on a plate to set.

Work the remaining batches of fondant in the same way. Each batch should fill 8–10 moulds. The fondants will set in about 5 minutes, and will come out of the moulds easily if the mat is bent back a little. Trim round the base of each fondant to neaten it, if necessary. Dip some of the fondants in melted chocolate, if you like.

CHOCOLATES
Countrywide

IN 1655 THE BRITISH force sent out by Oliver Cromwell captured the island of Jamaica, and so the vast cocoa plantations established there by the Spaniards fell into British hands. By the following century, chocolate had established itself as a breakfast drink. There were also a few rather laborious recipes for making chocolate rolls by pounding the little beans into a powder, mixing them with sugar, cinnamon, vanilla and nutmeg, along with the exotic flavour of either musk or ambergris.

It was the French who first produced elegant chocolate confectionery, and by the mid-18th century it was being sold both in slabs and as little shaped dainties similar to the ones in this recipe.

PREPARATION TIME: 1½ HOURS
SETTING TIME: 30 MINUTES

INGREDIENTS TO YIELD
2 LB. (900 G.)

10 oz. (275 g.) plain chocolate
4 oz. (100/125 g.) marzipan (see p. 310)
4 oz. (100/125 g.) glacé cherries
2 oz. (50 g.) glacé pineapple
2 oz. (50 g.) crystallised ginger
4 oz. (100/125 g.) Brazil nuts
4 oz. (100/125 g.) fruit fondants (see p. 312)
4 oz. (100/125 g.) coconut ice (see p. 308)

Break up the chocolate and place it in a bowl over a saucepan of hot water set on a low heat. Stir the chocolate often with a wooden spoon until it melts, and then remove the pan from the heat.

Meanwhile, roll out the marzipan and cut it into pieces large enough to completely cover and seal each of the cherries. Cut the pineapple and coconut ice into cubes about ½ in. (1·5 cm.) square. Cut a strip off each piece of ginger to use for decorating the ginger chocolates.

Place some waxed paper on a cooling rack. Using two skewers—one in each hand to lift the chocolates—dip the pieces of ginger, nuts, fondants and coconut ice in turn into the melted chocolate.

Tap the skewers on the bowl edge to remove the excess chocolate. Put a piece of ginger on each of the ginger chocolates and place all the sweets on the rack for 30 minutes to harden.

Dip the cherries coated in marzipan and the pineapple cubes into the chocolate and place them on the cooling rack so that the chocolate drips down the sides and evenly coats and seals them.

When quite cold, place the sweets in paper cases and arrange in a chocolate box. If you prefer, you may coat some of the sweets in milk chocolate and some in plain.

Chocolate-coated nuts and fruits: home-made sweets with the professional look.

RECIPES

OTHER LANDS

SWITZERLAND
Canache or Noisette Cups

APART FROM BEING FRENCH for hazelnut, *noisette* has, in culinary terms, come to mean anything which has been given a hazelnut flavouring. Yet this confection is totally Swiss in origin; *canache* is a Swiss dialect for a baking technique in which a small sweet case is lined with chocolate, then filled—in this instance with a hazelnut mixture. Milk chocolate, an essential ingredient of this recipe, is also a Swiss creation. Its inventor, Daniel Peter, a candle-maker living near Lucerne, combined his own talents with those of his father-in-law, a chocolate manufacturer, to make the first slab of milk chocolate in 1876. Plain eating chocolate, incidentally, is a British invention, manufactured by Fry of Bristol in 1847.

These Canaches, packed in an ornamental box, make an admirable Christmas present. Laid in silver dishes, they are an elegant accompaniment to after-dinner coffee either alone or with other chocolates.

PREPARATION TIME: 1 HOUR 20 MINUTES
SETTING TIME: 2 HOURS 20 MINUTES

INGREDIENTS TO YIELD 36 SWEETS

6 oz. (175 g.) confectioner's milk chocolate
36 foil sweet cases

For the filling:

8 oz. (225 g.) plain chocolate
2 fl. oz. (50 ml.) double cream
½ oz. (15 g.) butter
2 oz. (50 g.) ground hazelnuts
2 tablespoons rum or brandy

For the decoration:

A few glacé cherries, cut into quarters
A few strips of angelica
A few hazelnuts, halved
A few edible silver balls

Break up the milk chocolate. Place it in a bowl set over a saucepan of hot water over a low heat. Stir the chocolate frequently until it has melted. Remove the pan from the heat and take the bowl off the pan.

Half fill about six of the foil cases with the melted chocolate, and roll the chocolate around the sides of the cases so that each case is coated fairly thickly. Add more chocolate if the coating is too thin. Continue coating the cases, six cases at a time, until they are all lined with chocolate. Towards the end, they will set more quickly as the chocolate will have cooled down. Chill the cases in the refrigerator for 5–10 minutes to completely set the chocolate.

Break up the plain chocolate and put it in a bowl over a pan of hot water set over a low heat. Stir it until it has just melted and remove the bowl from the heat. Stir the cream, butter, nuts and rum or brandy into the chocolate. Allow this mixture to cool for about 20–30 minutes, until it is fairly firm, then put it into a nylon piping bag fitted with a fluted vegetable nozzle. Pipe a little of the mixture into the centre of each chocolate cup.

Decorate each cup with a piece of cherry, angelica, half a hazelnut or a silver ball, and leave to cool for about 2 hours.

If liked, add the chocolate cups to an assortment of other chocolates and arrange them in a pretty box.

MEXICO
Peanut Brittle

PEANUTS, LIKE CHOCOLATE, vanilla, sweet corn, sweet potatoes, avocadoes, tomatoes and many other good things, are a legacy of the great civilisation of the Incas of South America.

Peanut Brittle, a simple concoction of nuts and sugar, is also Latin American in origin. There it is regarded as a food of the very poor, and is highly nutritious since it contains an almost perfect balance of protein, fat and sugar.

PREPARATION TIME: 45 MINUTES
SETTING TIME: 20 MINUTES

INGREDIENTS TO YIELD 6 OZ. (175 G.)

6 oz. (175 g.) fresh peanuts, skinned, chopped and toasted
8 oz. (225 g.) granulated sugar
4 oz. (100/125 g.) soft brown sugar
2 oz. (50 g.) golden syrup
2½ fl. oz. (75 ml.) hot water
1 oz. (25 g.) unsalted butter
A pinch of bicarbonate of soda

Put the chopped peanuts in a warm place, such as the top of the stove or an airing cupboard, until required.

Place the two sugars and the golden syrup in a fairly large, heavy saucepan with the hot water.

Follow the rules for sugar boiling, and boil to the hard-crack stage—154°C (310°F) (see p. 317). Remove the pan from the heat and stir in the butter, chopped peanuts and bicarbonate of soda.

Pour the mixture into a well-greased shallow tin, 10 by 6 in. (25 by 15 cm.) and leave to cool for 20 minutes. When the toffee is beginning to set, after about 10 minutes, mark it out into squares with a sharp knife. When it is quite cold, break up the squares and wrap each one in Cellophane. Store in a cool, dry place.

FRANCE
Rich Chocolate Truffles

TRUFFLES are those rare and highly prized little black fungi that grow around the roots of certain oak trees in southern France. These luxuriously rich sweets really do look rather similar, and hence their name.

PREPARATION TIME: 40 MINUTES
SETTING TIME: 1 HOUR

INGREDIENTS FOR 32 TRUFFLES

8 oz. (225 g.) plain dessert chocolate
3 oz. (75 g.) unsalted butter
2 oz. (50 g.) icing sugar, sieved
1 oz. (25 g.) powdered drinking chocolate or chocolate vermicelli

Break the chocolate into a bowl and stand it over a pan of very gently simmering water. After a few minutes, remove the pan from the heat, leaving the bowl on top to finish melting the chocolate.

Lift the bowl of melted chocolate off the saucepan of water. Add the butter to the chocolate and stir around the bowl to melt it. Stir in the icing sugar. Leave the mixture to cool for about 20 minutes, until firm.

When it is cool, make it into 32 balls and coat each one in the drinking chocolate or vermicelli. Leave to set for 1 hour.

SPAIN
Turrón de Castañas

ALL THE GRAND COUNTRY HOUSES of Spain, and many more-modest homesteads as well, had their own special recipes for making *turrón* or nougat. Traditionally it was prepared only at Christmas time, when the mistress of the house would present little packets of *turrón* to all the servants and tenants on her estate.

Nowadays you can buy it commercially, although it is at its best when made at home. A number of recipes use almonds instead of the chestnuts *(castañas)* included here.

It is worthwhile taking the time and trouble to prepare the *turrón* from fresh chestnuts, as the tinned variety do not give the sweet quite the same texture.

PREPARATION TIME: ABOUT 1 HOUR 40 MINUTES
COOLING TIME: 24 HOURS

INGREDIENTS TO YIELD 1 LB. (450 G.)

- *1 lb. (450 g.) chestnuts*
- *3 oz. (75 g.) unsalted butter*
- *3 oz. (75 g.) plain chocolate, grated*
- *3 oz. (75 g.) vanilla sugar or 3 oz. (75 g.) caster sugar, flavoured with ¼ teaspoon vanilla essence*

Wash the chestnuts, nick the skins and boil them, unpeeled, in a saucepan of water, until they are tender—about 1 hour. When they are cool enough to handle, peel them carefully removing both shell and skin.

Pass the chestnuts through a fine sieve and, while they are still warm, put them in a bowl with the butter, grated chocolate and vanilla sugar. Mix well with a wooden spoon.

Spread the mixture into a shallow baking tin or, better still, a cake tin with a removable base, as it will then be much easier to lift the nougat out when it is set. Smooth the top of the nougat and place it in a cool place for about 24 hours to set. After about 12 hours mark it out in bars, using a sharp knife.

When the nougat is quite cold, cut through the bars and wrap each piece of nougat in Cellophane or greaseproof paper. Keep refrigerated and eat within 1 week.

Turrón de Castañas—a chocolate-flavoured nougat from Spain.

SPAIN
Salted Almonds

ALMOND TREES are well adapted to survive the heat and dryness of the Mediterranean climate; they can be seen blossoming on the most austere patches of land.

The delicate sweetness of the nuts is in no way marred by salting, but is rather enhanced by the contrast of tastes.

PREPARATION TIME: 10 MINUTES
COOLING TIME: ABOUT 30 MINUTES

INGREDIENTS TO YIELD 8 OZ. (225 G.)

- *8 oz. (225 g.) blanched almonds (see p. 317)*
- *5–6 tablespoons olive oil or melted clarified butter (see p. 49)*
- *Salt*
- *Cayenne pepper (optional)*

Dry the blanched almonds well with a cloth. Heat the oil or butter in a small, heavy-based frying pan and fry the almonds—about two dozen at a time—until light golden-brown. Watch the pan closely and see that the almonds do not burn. Remove the almonds from the pan with a slotted spoon and drain them on sheets of crumpled kitchen paper.

Sprinkle a sheet of greaseproof paper with salt, and turn the nuts on to the salted paper while they are still warm. Sprinkle some more salt over the almonds and turn them over occasionally in the salt until they are quite cold. Store the Salted Almonds in glass screw-top jars.

To make devilled almonds, mix a few grains of Cayenne pepper with the salt before sprinkling the almonds with it.

ALL KINDS OF SWEETMEATS

ONE OF THE FIRST sweetmeats known to man was honey—fruits preserved in honey were enjoyed in Roman Britain. During the later Middle Ages primitive 'toffee apples', dipped in a mixture of cooked honey and beeswax were sold at fairs, along with gilded gingerbread men, or 'Fairings'.

The wealthy could buy twisted sticks of sugar candy, imported from the East on the spice ships and eaten as a cure for colds. Sugar was believed to be a medicine, and delicate children were encouraged to eat fancy sugars. In the 16th century, comfits were made by coating seeds, spices and fruits in a hard sugar syrup. Simple treacle sweetmeats were available in the 17th century and were probably sold by pedlars.

With the abolition of the sugar tax in 1846, sugar—already popular—became much cheaper, and this led to the appearance of a variety of new sweets.

Creams, Toffees and Chocolates

Sweets are fun to make, and are highly acceptable as presents. The cost of home-made sweets is very low compared to shop-bought ones, and the taste is often far superior.

Always take great care in the kitchen when making sweets. Never leave the pans of boiling sugar syrup unattended, particularly when young children are about.

Equipment for sweet-making
Large, heavy-based saucepans of steel, aluminium or tinned copper. Enamel pans will not withstand the high temperature needed in sugar boiling.

A sugar thermometer, which should be clearly marked and register up to 200°C (400°F). If you have no sugar thermometer, follow the water tests given opposite.

A marble slab is useful for shaping and cooling many sweets, particularly fondant, Edinburgh rock and barley sugar. If you have no marble slab, pour the mixture into a baking tin. Never pour syrup directly on to a laminated surface or wood, as it will stick to it.

Long-handled, flat-based wooden spatulas, which are better than metal for beating or stirring. Have two different sizes and use them only for sugar work.

Pastry brushes. Keep one brush exclusively for brushing down the sugar crystals from the pan and another for oiling tins.

A sugar scraper, although not essential, is ideal for fondant-making. You can use a plastic or metal spatula instead.

Candy bars to use for shaping sugar mixtures. You can use small loaf tins or foil baking cases instead.

Fondant mats, which are sheets of about 75 small moulds. They give a very professional finish to sweets such as fruit fondants. If you have no mat, spoon small amounts of the mixture on to a baking tray.

Kitchen scales to measure out the ingredients exactly.

Scissors. Some sweet mixtures, for example barley sugar and Edinburgh rock, have to be cut up with scissors.

Fine nylon or hair sieve for sieving icing sugar.

Waxed paper for lining and dividing boxes or containers of home-made sweets and chocolates. It can be bought in small packets from stationers and some chemists.

Rice paper. Edible paper for lining baking trays on which sticky mixtures such as nougat are placed.

INGREDIENTS

Sugar Weight for weight, all refined sugars are equally sweet. However, the finer the sugar, the faster it dissolves and the sweeter it seems.
GRANULATED SUGAR has a medium-sized, white sparkling crystal and is 99·9% pure sucrose. It is the most popular and widely used refined sugar, as well as the cheapest. It is used in many sweets, for example, butterscotch, marshmallows, coconut ice, fruit fondants and jujubes.
CASTER SUGAR dissolves more quickly than granulated sugar. In uncooked sweetmeats, such as marzipan, it gives a smoother texture.
ICING SUGAR is made by grinding sugar crystals to a fine powder. Because it has such a fine texture and dissolves rapidly, icing sugar is easily made into a smooth paste. It is used in uncooked peppermint-cream mixtures, in truffles, and for coating marshmallows and other sweets.
CUBE SUGAR is produced from granulated sugar, moistened and moulded into neat shapes. It is used in Edinburgh rock and barley sugar.
SOFT BROWN SUGARS are all finely grained refined sugars, but they range in colour from creamy-beige to dark brown. As well as sweetening a mixture, they give a rich flavour to such sweets as treacle toffee.
Golden syrups vary in flavour and colour according to the different refineries. They are made from the liquid left after refined sugar has been crystallised. They enrich the flavour of honeycomb and toffee apples.
Treacles are thinner, darker and less refined than syrups and have a flavour close to that of cane molasses. They are used for making some toffees and boiled sweets.

Vanilla sugar You can easily make your own by burying a whole vanilla pod in an airtight jar of caster sugar. Stir occasionally to move the pod around. The sugar will be ready for use after 1 week. Use it as required, and top up the jar as the sugar is used. The pod should last for months. Vanilla sugar gives a delicious flavour to simple fudge mixtures.
Liquid glucose This is less sweet than sugar. A glossy appearance is given to such sweets as nougat if some liquid glucose is added. It also keeps fondants in a soft, uncrystallised state.
Stock syrup Use very small amounts for moistening fondant mixtures that are too dry. Make a quantity to store in a well-stoppered bottle. Dissolve 4 oz. (100/125 g.) granulated sugar in 2½ fl. oz. (75 ml.) warm water as for sugar boiling. Boil to 105°C (220°F) then leave to cool before storing.
Fat When fat is needed in sweet-making, it is best to use unsalted butter. Use margarine only when the quantity of fat required is very small. Too large a quantity of margarine will separate from the toffee or other sweets. For greasing tins, use a salad oil such as sunflower or groundnut. Apply it with a pastry brush, for a thin overall film of oil.
Cream and milk If used, these must be fresh. Evaporated milk is sometimes used, but it may curdle if the cooking process is too long.
Cream of tartar or tartaric acid Some sweet recipes, such as Edinburgh rock, use this to reduce the tendency of sugar to recrystallise. Measure it carefully, according to the recipe, as too large a quantity can make sweets too soft and sticky.
Chocolate Both dark and milk chocolate are used in sweet-making. For very sweet fillings, such as fondant mixture, the less-sweet, dark chocolate gives an interesting contrast in taste.

Flavouring and colouring
Use good-quality flavourings and colourings and never tip them straight from the bottle, as they are very concentrated. Pour the flavouring or colouring on to a marked measuring spoon, or measure out the required number of drops by dipping a skewer into the bottle and shaking one drop at a time into the mixture.

Blanching nuts
Nuts are usually blanched and skinned before use in sweets and other dishes. For some recipes they are then roasted.

Place the nuts in a bowl, cover them with boiling water and allow to stand for a minute or two. Drain off the water; the skins will then slide or peel off easily. Almonds can be bought ready blanched. To roast nuts, spread the blanched nuts on a baking sheet or Swiss-roll tin. Place the tin in the oven, pre-heated to 180°C (350°F)—gas mark 4, until the nuts are golden-brown. This will take 5–10 minutes. Check after 5 minutes, as nuts can burn rapidly.

Rules for Sugar Boiling

1 Measure the sugar and water accurately. Excess water takes longer to boil off, which can be detrimental.
2 Heat the sugar and water gently and do not let the mixture boil until every grain of sugar has dissolved.
3 During the dissolving process, stir the mixture very carefully with a wooden spatula. Stir right to the bottom and corners of the pan, keeping the tip of the spatula under the liquid to avoid splashing.
4 Brush down the sides of the saucepan from time to time with a clean pastry brush dipped in warm water. This prevents crystals from forming on the side of the pan and dropping back into the mixture.
5 Never stir boiling syrup unless specifically directed to do so—as, for example, when milk is used.
6 It is essential to boil the sugar and water mixture on which most sweets are based to the temperature given in each individual recipe. If the temperature is too high, the mixture will burn, and if too low, it will not set properly when cooled. Measure the temperature with a sugar thermometer or, use the water tests described below.
7 If using a sugar thermometer, warm the bulb by dipping it in hot water before immersing it in the syrup. Hold the thermometer upright and make the reading at eye level.
8 When the correct temperature is reached, remove the pan from the heat immediately and place it on a damp cloth. This prevents any further cooking.
9 Take the thermometer out of the syrup and place it in a jug of hot water.

Water tests without a thermometer
If you have no sugar thermometer, use these water tests to assess the temperature.

Fill a small bowl with cold water. Remove the pan of sugar mixture from the heat, take ½ teaspoon of the mixture and drop into the water. Leave for 1 minute, and test between forefinger and thumb to see which of the following stages it has reached.
Thread At 110–114°C (230–238°F) the syrup in the water will form a fine thread between finger and thumb if they are pressed on it and then pulled apart.
Soft ball At 114–118°C (238–245°F) the syrup in the water will form a soft ball which can be squashed flat. As the temperature goes towards the higher end of this stage, the ball will become slightly firmer. This is the temperature for fondants and fudges.
Hard ball At 118–138°C (245–280°F) the syrup dropped into water forms a ball which holds its shape when pressed. This stage is for making caramels and marshmallows.
Small crack At 138–152°C (280–305°F) the syrup will separate into threads that will snap cleanly. This stage is used for toffee.
Hard crack At 152–163°C (305–325°F) the mixture dropped into cold water will form threads which are hard and brittle. This stage is used for hard toffees and rock.
Caramel At 174°C (345°F) the syrup becomes a golden colour and is used for praline and caramel sauce.

Tips for Making Sweets

Always collect everything required for the various processes before starting. Measure the ingredients accurately.

Make sure that there is no grease on kitchen scales or cooking utensils—this could spoil the sugar syrup.

If nuts are to be coated, warm them in a low oven for 10 minutes while the toffee is boiling. It will then stick to them more easily.

When finishing off sweets, mould or cut them in small, neat sizes. Make all sweets of one kind the same size.

Use Cellophane to wrap sweets such as toffees, toffee apples and nougat, which tend to go sticky when exposed to the air.

When packing sweets in boxes as gifts, use waxed paper to separate the layers and rows. Foil and paper cases make pretty, protective wrappings for some sweets, such as chocolates.

When packing boiled sweets in jars or tins, put a crumpled plug of waxed paper at the bottom and top to prevent the sweets from being tossed about and chipped in the jar.

LONDON
THE PROPERTY OF

Of

POSSETS, PUNCHES AND OTHER BEVERAGES

CONTAINING

NUMEROUS *Useful* FAMILY RECIPES

for HOT & COLD ALES & PUNCHES, WINES & SYRUPS & other STIMULATING DRINKS

PAGES 320–329

AND

A SELECTION of RECIPES from OTHER LANDS

PAGES 330–331

AND WITH

GUIDANCE ON BASIC METHODS

of Fermenting, Racking, Bottling and Corking of Liquid Refreshments to Perfection

PAGES 332–333

OATMEAL POSSET
Scotland

THROUGH THE CENTURIES, warm sustaining drinks have been widely used to relieve minor illnesses such as colds, to sustain travellers in wintry weather and as a soothing 'nightcap' for the poor sleeper. Possets, caudles and toddies all come in this classification. Possets and caudles are mentioned in literature from the 12th century onwards, toddies not before the 17th century.

A posset is a thickened milk drink curdled with either ale or wine; the thickener can be oatmeal, breadcrumbs or egg. During the medieval period it was drunk for breakfast or supper.

By the 18th century such mixtures had gone out of fashion in the south of England, but in the north, and especially in Scotland, they maintained their popularity.

On a winter's night, this posset makes a comforting bedtime drink.

PREPARATION TIME: 15 MINUTES
COOKING TIME: 5 MINUTES

INGREDIENTS FOR TWO

1 pint (575/600 ml.) milk
2 tablespoons oatmeal
¼ teaspoon salt
2 teaspoons sugar
¼ teaspoon grated nutmeg
1 tablespoon brandy

Put the milk in a 2 pint (1·1 litre) pan and sprinkle in the oatmeal and salt. Heat quickly, stirring, until nearly boiling. Remove from the heat and leave to stand for 10 minutes. Press the mixture through a sieve into a similar saucepan, add the sugar and nutmeg and re-heat nearly to boiling, stirring to prevent the mixture sticking to the pan. Remove from the heat, stir in the brandy and serve at once.

If nutmeg is not liked, some other spice such as ground mace, allspice or ginger may be substituted in the same quantity.

SLOE GIN
Countrywide

SLOES are the small plum-like fruits of the blackthorn tree, which is often used in hedging, its sharp, spiky branches forming a dense thicket. The small white flowers can be seen in late March or early April, and the sloes ripen in October.

Like black grapes sloes have a bluish-black colour and a soft bloom on their skins. They are far too astringent to eat, but when allowed to add their flavour to sweetened gin they make the most delicious fruit liqueur.

The almonds give their characteristic flavour to the clear red liquid, but are not essential.

You can also make this liqueur with damsons, which blend well with gin.

READY TO USE: AFTER 15 MONTHS

INGREDIENTS TO YIELD
1–1¼ PINTS (575–725 ML.)

12 oz. (350 g.) ripe sloes, wiped
6 oz. (175 g.) granulated sugar
8 almonds, blanched (optional)
1 pint (575/600 ml.) gin

Prick four holes in each sloe with a sharp-pronged fork or darning needle.

Put a layer of the sloes in a 2 pint (1·1 litre) preserving jar. Add a layer of sugar and continue putting in these layers until all the fruit and sugar are used up, ending with a layer of sugar.

Add the almonds to the jar and pour over the gin.

Place a rubber ring on top of the jar, cover with a lid and screw down tightly. Put the jar in a cool, dark place.

Shake the jar two or three times a week for 2–3 months, and then leave undisturbed for at least 6 months.

Strain the liquid through double muslin or filter paper several times until the gin is clear. Pour the gin through a funnel into a bottle. Cork securely and label.

Store for a further 6 months in a cool dark place before drinking. Serve in small liqueur glasses. The gin will keep for 2–3 years.

ATHOLL BROSE
Scotland

BROSE is ordinarily a broth, such as oatmeal boiled with milk or water. Atholl Brose is somewhat different, in that the liquid used includes whisky.

It is said that the mixture was first devised in the 16th century when it was used to trap a wild man of the woods, who was called Big Rory. This man had been robbing passers-by and making threats to the daughter of the Duke of Atholl. Whoever could capture him was promised her hand in marriage.

Many a man tried and failed, and then there came a youth who discovered that Big Rory drank every day at a certain well. The youth filled this well with a mixture of whisky, honey and water, and when the wild man came to drink he became so drunk that he fell into a stupor and was easily caught. Ever after, the drink was known as Atholl Brose.

The version of the recipe handed down by the Atholl family contains no cream, and one served under the same name in Edinburgh uses no oatmeal. The following version includes both.

PREPARATION TIME: 1¼ HOURS

INGREDIENTS FOR SIX TO EIGHT

4 oz. (100/125 g.) fine oatmeal
1 pint (575/600 ml.) cold water
2 tablespoons runny heather honey
¼ pint (150 ml.) whisky
¼ pint (150 ml.) double cream, whipped

Put the oatmeal and water into a mixing bowl. Mix together and leave to stand for 1 hour, then place in a fine strainer over a bowl. Using the back of a wooden spoon, press the mixture through the strainer until the oatmeal left in it is as dry as possible. Use the creamy liquid and discard the oatmeal.

Add the honey and whisky to the sieved liquid and stir well. Pour into small glasses or, if not required at once, bottle it.

Atholl Brose will keep for up to 2 months in a cool, dark place. Shake the bottle well before pouring.

Serve in small glasses, leaving room to float a heaped teaspoon of whipped cream on top.

WASSAIL
West Country

THE OLD CUSTOM of wassailing the trees, which was thought to make them bear more fruit, used to be practised by farming people in the

West of England. Robert Herrick describes it in *Hesperides* (1648):

'Wassaile the trees, that they
might beare
You many a plum and many a
peare;
For more or lesse fruits they will
bring,
As you do give them wassailing.'

For some, the ceremony was performed on Christmas Eve; for others, Twelfth Night was chosen. The ritual is so old that its origin is lost, although the word 'wassail' comes from the Old Norse *ves heill*, meaning 'Be in health'; to wassail was to drink a toast.

The Wassail Bowl was traditionally passed round to all the assembled family and guests, that they might all be united in drinking the sweet, hot liquid.

A Somerset variation, called Lambswool, combines the same ingredients with the pulp of baked apples.

PREPARATION TIME: 5 MINUTES
COOKING TIME: 35 MINUTES
PRE-HEAT THE OVEN TO
180°C (350°F)—GAS MARK 4

INGREDIENTS FOR EIGHT

3 small red apples
3 oz. (75 g.) soft brown sugar
2 pints (1·1 litres) brown ale
½ pint (275/300 ml.) dry sherry or dry white wine
¼ teaspoon ground cinnamon
¼ teaspoon grated nutmeg
¼ teaspoon ground ginger
Strip of lemon peel

Wassail—baked apples in hot brown ale, flavoured with spices and sugar.

Cut through the skin round the centre of the apples and put them in a 3 pint (1·7 litre) flameproof bowl. Add the brown sugar and 4 tablespoons of the ale. Cover the bowl and bake in the pre-heated oven for 20–30 minutes until the apples are tender. Remove the apples from the bowl and put on one side.

Put the rest of the ale and the sherry or wine into the bowl. Add the spices and lemon peel and simmer on top of the stove for 5 minutes. Add the apples and serve at once.

To make Lambswool, core 4 red apples and put them in a flameproof bowl with 3 tablespoons of water. Bake in the pre-heated oven for 15–20 minutes. Remove from the bowl and put on one side.

Put the ale, sherry or wine and sugar in the bowl. Add the spices and lemon peel and heat gently on top of the stove. Meanwhile, discard the skins and cores from the apples. Put the pulp in a small mixing bowl and mash with a wooden spoon.

Stir the apple pulp evenly into the liquid in the dish and heat for 5 minutes. Adjust the sweetening if necessary and serve hot.

THICK MULLED ALE
Yorkshire

PERHAPS it is because we no longer sit around open fires in the cold winter evenings that we have lost the habit of mulling (warming) ale. Indeed, the cone-shaped copper beer-warmers that used to be for ever at the ready beside the kitchen range are now antique curiosities.

During the Middle Ages all kinds of thickened mulled ales were popular as a breakfast drink, an evening night-cap, or even as a kind of alcoholic 'soup'. In a number of early recipes the ale was thickened with eggs and poured back and forth between pan and bowl until the right consistency had been reached.

In the south of England these mixtures tended to be relegated to the role of invalid food, but in the north they retained a wider popularity.

A drink such as this gave a man strength after the coldest journey; or, as one Wharfedale publican described her own mulled ale recipe to Dorothy Hartley (told in *Food in England*): 'it was wonderful if you'd bin drowned'.

PREPARATION TIME: 5 MINUTES
COOKING TIME: 10 MINUTES

INGREDIENTS FOR TWO

2 eggs
1 pint (575/600 ml.) light ale
3 teaspoons caster sugar
¼ teaspoon grated nutmeg
1 oz. (25 g.) butter, cut into pieces

Beat the eggs with 2 tablespoons of the ale in a large mixing bowl.

Pour the rest of the ale into a 2 pint (1·1 litre) saucepan. Heat gently, but do not boil. When hot, pour very carefully on to the eggs, beating all the time. Return the mixture to the pan, add the sugar and nutmeg and re-heat without boiling.

Remove from the heat, add the pieces of butter and stir until melted. Serve at once in warmed tankards.

Preparations for Dr Johnson's Punch—an inspired combination of wine, liqueur and spices to serve at Christmas.

DR JOHNSON'S PUNCH
Home Counties

ACCORDING to one theory, the name 'punch' is derived from *panch*, the Hindu word for 'five'. The drink was introduced to Britain by East India Company merchants in the 17th century. Some of the simplest recipes do contain five ingredients, but there are many variations.

This recipe is attributed to Dr Samuel Johnson, and although it may not cause the present-day imbiber to utter Johnsonian words of wisdom, it is a cheerful and heart-warming drink to serve at Christmas time.

Drink it hot in small glasses and top them up frequently.

PREPARATION TIME: 5 MINUTES
COOKING TIME: 40 MINUTES

INGREDIENTS FOR 25–30 GLASSES

1 orange
3 bottles Burgundy or other red wine
8 tablespoons granulated sugar
7 cloves
8 whole allspice
A 1 in. (2·5 cm.) piece of ginger
3 pints (1·7 litres) boiling water
6 fl. oz. (175 ml.) brandy
6 fl. oz. (175 ml.) Cointreau

A 10 pint (5·6 litre) saucepan is required for this quantity, and a preserving pan may be the only household vessel of suitable size. Otherwise, the recipe can be divided between two large saucepans.

Prick the whole orange in about 15 places with a clean skewer.

Pour the Burgundy into the pan

and add the sugar, cloves, allspice, ginger and the whole orange. Cover with the boiling water and simmer for 30–40 minutes.

Remove from the heat. Add the brandy and Cointreau immediately before serving, and mix them in with a few turns of the ladle. It is not necessary to strain out the spices, as it is easy to avoid scooping them up in the ladle. The orange will float on top of the punch.

COUNSELLOR'S CUP
Countrywide

CUPS were especially popular in the 19th century, when they were often prepared for large outdoor parties and picnics. The variations are endless and often extravagant. An 1869 book of recipes called *Cooling Cups*, by William Terrington, includes such extravaganzas as Claret Cup à la Lord Saltoun, and Balaklava Nectar Cup, which are very liberal with Champagne and liqueurs.

Counsellor's Cup is a restrained version, and the cost of preparation can be reduced by substituting wine for some of the brandy. For a thirst-quenching long drink—or for children—use lemonade instead of brandy. Serve hot or cold.

PREPARATION TIME: 10 MINUTES
COOKING TIME: 10 MINUTES

INGREDIENTS FOR SIX

4 oz. (100/125 g.) cube sugar
2–3 large oranges, washed and dried
1 pint (575/600 ml.) water
Juice of 1 large lemon, strained
½ pint (275/300 ml.) brandy

Rub the sugar cubes over the rinds of the oranges to absorb the oils, then put them in a 2 pint (1·1 litre) saucepan and add the water. Stir over a gentle heat to dissolve the sugar, then bring to the boil and boil for 2–3 minutes.

Put the lemon juice into a small mixing bowl. Squeeze the juice from the oranges, and strain into the bowl with the lemon juice to make up to ½ pint (275/300 ml.) in all.

Pour the lemon and orange juice into the pan containing the syrup and bring to the boil.

If the Cup is to be drunk hot, pour it into a warmed jug, stir in the brandy and serve at once.

To use cold, cover and cool the syrup. Keep in the refrigerator until required and add the brandy just before serving. Serve decorated with fine twists of orange peel. When making larger quantities, serve in a punch bowl with slices of apple, pear, banana and halved, seeded grapes floating on top.

MILK PUNCH
Cambridge

PUNCHES are often regarded as highly alcoholic, but in fact the alcohol is usually well diluted with water or, as in this recipe, with milk.

A variant of this punch was given by Eliza Acton in her book *Modern Cookery* (1845). She declares that 'at the University the lemon rind is usually omitted', although she does not approve of this idiosyncracy.

It is best to use an inexpensive brandy and dark rum for this recipe.

PREPARATION TIME: 10 MINUTES
COOKING TIME: 10 MINUTES

INGREDIENTS FOR THREE

1 pint (575/600 ml.) milk
12 sugar cubes or 2 oz. (50 g.) granulated white or brown sugar
Rind of ½ small lemon, thinly peeled, with all pith removed
1 egg yolk, beaten
2 tablespoons brandy
2–4 tablespoons dark rum

Put 1 tablespoon of cold milk on one side and pour the remainder into a 2 pint (1·1 litre) saucepan. Add the sugar and lemon rind. Simmer over a low heat for 10 minutes to extract the lemon flavour. Remove from the heat and discard the rind.

Put the beaten egg into a mixing bowl and add the tablespoon of cold milk. Whisk together and, still whisking, slowly add the brandy and rum to taste. Whisk this mixture into the heated milk until very frothy.

Serve at once in warmed mugs.

LOVING CUP
Countrywide

A LOVING CUP is supposed to be passed from hand to hand. In medieval days, all who were gathered together in a banqueting hall united in drinking this heady, sparkling mixture. However, in this age we usually prefer to ladle the Cup into individual glasses.

For composite drinks of this kind it is not necessary to use the best-quality wines; sparkling cider can be substituted for Champagne.

PREPARATION TIME: 20 MINUTES

INGREDIENTS TO YIELD 10 PINTS (5·6 LITRES)

1–1½ lb. (450–700 g.) granulated sugar, according to taste
2 pints (1·1 litres) water, warmed
2 bottles sherry
2 bottles Madeira
1 bottle port
1 bottle claret
Juice of 6 lemons
1 bottle Champagne or sparkling cider

Determine the amount of sugar to use from the sweetness of the wines and the palates of the tasters.

Put the sugar in a 3 pint (1·7 litre) saucepan and add the water. Stir over gentle heat to dissolve the sugar. Pour the syrup into a punch bowl and add the sherry, Madeira, port, claret and the lemon juice. Stir well and surround with crushed ice until required.

Just before serving, add the Champagne or sparkling cider.

For additional flavouring add ¼–½ teaspoon of any of the following during preparation: grated nutmeg, cinnamon or ginger, chopped fresh borage, verbena or mint, thinly peeled lemon or orange rind.

MEAD
Countrywide

MEAD, made from fermented honey, was the earliest of all alcoholic beverages. The Beaker People, who inhabited England from 2000 BC, drank it, or something like it. Later among the Celts and Saxons it was the drink of the warriors and noblemen, and a chieftain's bodyguard fought his battles in return for drinking his mead.

However, although beekeepers all over England continued making mead, it underwent a curious reversal of status. By the 18th century this drink, that had once been reserved for fighting men, was served as an occasional light refreshment for ladies making social calls.

The particular flower fragrance of the honey, combined with a sweet herb, gives a most delicate bouquet. Metheglin is the name given to mead flavoured with spices such as clove, ginger, cinnamon or caraway, and these must be added cautiously so as not to overpower the honey taste.

Ideally, use soft water when making mead and pure British honey, if possible. Avoid boiling the honey water for any length of time as this spoils the quality, and use mead yeast, if available.

Serve as an accompaniment to savoury or sweet dishes.

READY FOR USE: 4–6 MONTHS AFTER BOTTLING AT THE EARLIEST

INGREDIENTS TO YIELD
8 PINTS (4·5 LITRES)

2 oz. (50 g.) root ginger
Juice and thinly peeled rind of 2 lemons
8 pints (4·5 litres) water
3 lb. (1·4 kg.) light honey
1 oz. (25 g.) mead or baker's yeast

Bruise the root ginger by folding it in a clean cloth and hitting it with a hammer to release the flavour.

Tie the ginger and the lemon rind in a piece of muslin and put it in a 12 pint (6·8 litre) pan. Add the water and lemon juice and bring to the boil. Leave to cool to 50°C (122°F).

Meanwhile, stand the honey in a warm place to come to the same temperature.

Add the honey to the water and ginger, and mix together. Leave to cool to 21°C (70°F) and remove the ginger. Crumble the yeast lightly and add to the syrup.

Pour the liquid into an 8 pint (4·5 litre) fermentation jar, filling it three-quarters full, and fit an airlock. Leave until all fermentation has ceased, racking as necessary. See p. 333 for the full process. Leave for another 1–2 weeks before bottling and storing.

The mead can be used after 4–6 months, but it is best kept several years.

BLACKBERRY WINE
Countrywide

DESPITE the introduction of wine shortly before the Roman occupation, ale was the principal British drink for centuries. For medicinal reasons, it was frequently spiked with all kinds of berries, herbs and flowers. The addition of blackberry juice was considered particularly good for those with 'fretting and eating sores'.

Wine was not made from the juice of garden and hedgerow fruits until the late 17th century, when sugar became cheaper and more plentiful. Even then, only wealthy households could afford to do it. Blackberry Wine, with its rich, almost port-like flavour, was a very early favourite.

READY FOR USE: 6 MONTHS AFTER BOTTLING

INGREDIENTS TO YIELD
7–8 PINTS (4–4·5 LITRES)

1 stick cinnamon (optional)
Juice and thinly peeled rind of 2 lemons
8 pints (4·5 litres) cold water
3 lb. (1·4 kg.) granulated sugar
3 lb. (1·4 kg.) blackberries
½ oz. (15 g.) wine or baker's yeast

Put the cinnamon and lemon peel in the middle of a square of muslin. Tie the muslin into a bag, leaving a long piece of thread. Put the water and sugar in a 10 pint (5·6 litre) saucepan. Immerse the muslin bag in the liquid, hanging the thread over the side of the pan. Heat gently to dissolve the sugar, and simmer for 30 minutes. Remove the muslin bag and any scum formed on the top of the liquid.

Wash the blackberries and drain well, and then place them in a 12 pint (6·8 litre) bowl and mash with a wooden spoon. Pour the warm syrup over the berries and stir well.

Allow to cool to 21°C (70°F) and stir in the lemon juice. Sprinkle the yeast on top of the liquid. Cover the bowl with a clean cloth draped over a wire cake tray or two or three pieces of clean wood to prevent sagging. Secure with elastic and leave 2–3 days, stirring three times daily.

Strain the liquid into an 8 pint (4·5 litre) fermentation jar, filling to the bottom of the neck. Fit an airlock and leave until fermentation ceases, racking as necessary, then bottle and store. See p. 333 for the full process. Leave the wine for 6 months or longer before drinking.

BEETROOT WINE
Countrywide

BY THE LATE 18TH CENTURY, many better-off countryfolk had begun to make a wide variety of wines from garden and hedgerow fruits. All sorts of root vegetables were popular. In spite of their humble origins, wines made from parsnips, potatoes, turnips or, in this case, beetroot, taste very elegant and subtle, especially when stored for at least six months and preferably a year or two before drinking.

READY FOR USE:
6 MONTHS AFTER BOTTLING

INGREDIENTS TO YIELD
8 PINTS (4·5 LITRES)

3 lb. (1·4 kg.) uncooked beetroot
12 pints (6·8 litres) cold water
3 lb. (1·4 kg.) granulated sugar
6 cloves
3 unpeeled oranges, scrubbed and sliced
½ oz. (15 g.) wine or baker's yeast

Wash the beetroot well, but do not peel it. Cut into thin slices and put them into a very large saucepan. Add the water and bring to the boil. Simmer for 30–40 minutes until the beetroot is just tender.

Strain off the liquid into a 12 pint (6·8 litre) bowl and discard the beetroot. Put the liquid back into the saucepan and add the sugar, cloves and oranges. Heat gently, stirring to dissolve the sugar, then boil gently for 15 minutes.

Strain the liquid back into the bowl and let it cool to 21°C (70°F). Crumble the yeast lightly and sprinkle it into the liquid.

Cover the bowl with a clean cloth draped over a wire cake rack or two or three pieces of clean wood to prevent sagging, and secure with elastic. Leave 3 days, stirring daily.

Strain the liquid into an 8 pint (4·5 litre) fermentation jar, filling to the bottom of the neck. Fit an airlock and leave until fermentation ceases, racking as necessary, then bottle and store. See p. 333 for the full process. Leave the wine 6 months or longer before drinking.

PLUM WINE
Countrywide

PLUMS AND DAMSONS are a natural choice of fruit in wine-making. Until this century it was the small, hard damsons from little grey, twisted trees that were most common in old country orchard gardens. They have a spicy tang which makes for a very good wine flavour, although plum damsons, Victoria or purple plums can also be used to great effect in this sweet wine.

READY FOR USE:
6 MONTHS AFTER BOTTLING

INGREDIENTS TO YIELD
6–7 PINTS (3·4–4 LITRES)

3½ lb. (1·6 kg.) very ripe plums
8 pints (4·5 litres) boiling water
4 lb. (1·8 kg.) granulated sugar
¼ oz. (7 g.) wine or baker's yeast

Pick off all the stalks and leaves from the plums, and wash or wipe the fruit with a damp cloth.

Stone the plums and, using half the stones, crush or crack them by folding them in a clean cloth and hitting with a hammer.

Put the plums and stones in a 12 pint (6·8 litre) bowl and pour over the boiling water. Stir and mash the plums with a wooden spoon.

Cover the bowl with a clean cloth draped over a wire cake rack or two or three pieces of clean wood to prevent sagging, and secure with elastic. Leave, covered, for 10 days.

There will probably be a mould on top by this time. Remove this carefully; try not to break any off into the liquid.

Strain the liquid into an 8 pint (4·5 litre) saucepan. Add the sugar and heat gently, stirring to dissolve the sugar.

Leave to cool to 21°C (70°F), then strain the liquid into an 8 pint (4·5 litre) fermentation jar, filling it about three-quarters full. Crumble the yeast lightly and sprinkle into the liquid. Fit an airlock and leave until fermentation ceases, racking as necessary, then bottle and store. See p. 333 for the full process. Leave 6 months or longer before drinking.

POTATO WINE
Ireland

AN EARLY RECIPE for Potato Wine, or 'White Root' as it was called, tells how it must be mixed in a deep panshon—an earthenware bowl with sloping sides—and strained into a keg. Then, if left for many years, it resembles nothing so much as brandy—that is so long as the sugar used is true Demerara. But no matter how long you leave this wine to mature, it will never be transformed into that far more famous, potent and illegal Irish drink which goes by the name of 'poteen'.

READY FOR USE:
6 MONTHS AFTER BOTTLING

INGREDIENTS TO YIELD
8 PINTS (4·5 LITRES)

4 lb. (1·8 kg.) old potatoes
12 pints (6·8 litres) cold water
3 lb. (1·4 kg.) Demerara sugar
1 lemon and 1 orange, sliced
1 in. (2·5 cm.) root ginger
1 oz. (25 g.) wine or baker's yeast

Wash the potatoes well but do not peel them. Cut them into small pieces and put them into a very large pan. Add the cold water. If your pan is too small put in as much as you can and add the rest as the water evaporates. Bring to the boil, and boil the potatoes until soft but not mushy.

Strain off the liquid into a 12 pint (6·8 litre) bowl and add the sugar, lemon, orange and ginger. Stir until the sugar dissolves, then return to the pan and simmer for 30 minutes.

Leave to cool to 21°C (70°F), then strain the liquid into an 8 pint (4·5 litres) fermentation jar, filling it about three-quarters full. Crumble the yeast lightly and sprinkle into the liquid. Fit an airlock and leave until fermentation ceases, racking as necessary, then bottle and store. See p. 333 for the full process. Leave for 6 months or longer before drinking.

DANDELION WINE
Countrywide

MR MORTON SHAND, in his *Book of Food*, published in 1927, tells how an old lady offered him a glass of hock, assuring him it was genuine because she had made it from the hollyhocks that grew in her own garden. Doubtless the flavour was excellent, for many unlikely flowers can be transformed into the most pleasing and delicate wines.

Dandelion Wine needs six months to mature; flowers picked in April may make wine for Christmas.

Use only the petals from each dandelion head; discard the small green cup, or calix.

READY FOR USE:
6 MONTHS AFTER BOTTLING

INGREDIENTS TO YIELD
6–7 PINTS (3·4–4 LITRES)

4 pints (2·3 litres) dandelion petals
6 pints (3·4 litres) boiling water
3½ lb. (1·6 kg.) granulated sugar
Juice and thinly peeled rind of 1 lemon
Juice and thinly peeled rind of 1 orange
½ oz. (15 g.) wine or baker's yeast

Wash and drain the petals in a fine sieve. Put them in a 12 pint (6·8 litre) bowl and pour on the boiling water. Cover the bowl with a clean cloth draped over a wire cake rack or two or three pieces of clean wood to prevent sagging, and secure with elastic. Leave 3–4 days, stirring daily.

Strain the liquid into a very large saucepan and add the sugar and the lemon and orange peel. Heat gently and stir until the sugar is dissolved. Simmer for 30 minutes. Strain into the cleaned bowl and cool to 21°C (70°F). Stir the lemon and orange juice into the mixture.

Strain the liquid into an 8 pint (4·5 litre) fermentation jar, filling it about three-quarters full. Crumble the yeast lightly and sprinkle into the liquid. Fit an airlock and leave until fermentation ceases, racking as necessary, then bottle and store. See p. 333 for the full process. Leave for 6 months or longer before drinking.

CHERRY ALE
Kent

KENT is at the heart of the English cherry harvest, and it is therefore not surprising that it is famous for its Cherry Ale. It used to be sold in local public houses as the 'Best in England'.

All the 'spare cherries'—the ones the birds have pecked—can be used to make this ale. A few cracked stones will add a pleasing almond tang to the flavour and, since Kentish cherries are mainly whitehearts, a good handful of darker ones are added to give the ale a full-bodied colour.

Although most ales are ready to serve quite quickly, this one needs three years' storage to reach excellence and, if you can bear the suspense, nine years to reach perfection! If you like a drier ale, use less sugar.

READY FOR USE: 6 MONTHS AFTER BOTTLING

INGREDIENTS TO YIELD 7 PINTS (4 LITRES)

3 lb. (1·4 kg.) ripe cherries (cleaned, stalked and stoned)

4 pints (2·3 litres) boiling water

2 lb. (900 g.) granulated sugar

¼ oz. (7 g.) wine or baker's yeast

Put the fruit into a 7 pint (4 litre) bowl and crush thoroughly with a wooden spoon. To give an almond flavour, crush or crack the stones by folding them in a clean cloth and cracking with a hammer. If the kernels have a very marked almond flavour, crush only a few of them.

Pour the boiling water over the fruit and stones. Cover the bowl with a clean cloth draped over a wire cake rack or two or three pieces of clean wood to prevent sagging, and secure with elastic. Leave, covered, for 4 days, stirring well each day with a wooden spoon.

On the fifth day, scald a clean piece of butter muslin or old cotton sheet. Wring it out and strain the liquid through it into a large saucepan.

Add the sugar and cook over very gentle heat, stirring to dissolve the sugar. If you do not have a large enough saucepan, heat part of the liquid, dissolve all the sugar in it and then pour this back into the remainder of the liquid.

Leave to cool to 21°C (70°F), then pour the liquid into an 8 pint (4·5 litre) fermentation jar, filling it about three-quarters full. Crumble the yeast lightly and sprinkle into the jar. Fit an airlock and leave until fermentation ceases, racking as necessary. See p. 333 for the full process.

When fermentation has ceased, siphon off into strong bottles; beer bottles are ideal. Cork securely. Tie down the corks with string or fine wire, such as florist's wire, to prevent popping; but leave a little play on the tie to relieve pressure in the bottles. Label the bottles.

You can drink Cherry Ale 6 months after bottling, but it is best to keep it for 3 years.

NETTLE BEER
Countrywide

IN THE DAYS when country people knew and appreciated the value of all sorts of unlikely plants, nettles were highly esteemed, for they are strong in iron and Vitamin C.

Nettles were eaten as a vegetable, distilled as a medicine (good for asthma and rheumatism), and brewed as a light beer, which was traditionally offered to summer visitors.

The first brewing was made when the tender young shoots appeared in the spring, and then bunches of young nettles were hung up to dry, to be used later in the year.

READY FOR USE: 7 DAYS AFTER BOTTLING

INGREDIENTS TO YIELD 6–8 PINTS (3·4–4·5 LITRES)

2 lemons, scrubbed

2 lb. (900 g.) young nettle tops, washed and drained

8 pints (4·5 litres) water

1 lb. (450 g.) Demerara sugar

1 oz. (25 g.) cream of tartar

½ oz. (15 g.) wine or baker's yeast

Using a potato peeler, peel the rind very thinly from the lemons. Then squeeze out the lemon juice.

Put the nettles in a 12 pint (6·8 litre) pan, add the water and then bring to the boil. Boil steadily for 15 minutes. If you have not got a large enough pan, do two boilings in your largest pan. If much of the water has boiled off, replenish to make up to 8 pints (4·5 litres).

Put the lemon rind and juice, sugar and cream of tartar in a 12 pint (6·8 litre) bowl and strain in the boiling liquid. Stir briskly and leave to cool to 21°C (70°F).

In a small mixing bowl, cream the yeast with a little of the cooled liquid and stir it into the main bulk.

Cover the bowl with a clean cloth draped over a wire cake rack or two or three pieces of clean wood to prevent sagging, and secure with elastic. Leave in a temperature of about 21°C (70°F), for 3 days.

Strain the liquid and pour through a funnel into strong beer bottles. Close the bottles with corks. Tie down the corks with string or fine florist's wire, leaving a little play on the tie.

Store the bottles in a cool place. If fermentation is vigorous, release the wires slightly to relieve pressure in the bottles. The beer is ready to drink after 1 week.

As a variation, 1 oz. (25 g.) of bruised root ginger can be used instead of the 2 lemons. Another way of varying the flavour is to add 2 oz. (50 g.) of sarsaparilla or 8 oz. (225 g.) of malt extract, or both.

FRUIT VINEGARS
Midlands and East Anglia

ORIGINALLY, FRUIT VINEGAR was prepared as a sauce to serve with the plain steamed puddings that were once so popular in the Midlands and East Anglia.

However, it can also form the basis of a refreshing sherbet drink—you simply dilute it to taste with soda water—or it can make a hot drink to ease a cold or soothe a sore throat.

READY FOR USE: 2 WEEKS AFTER BOTTLING

INGREDIENTS

1 lb. (450 g.) ripe soft fruit, such as blackberries, raspberries or black currants

1 pint (575/600 ml.) wine vinegar

About 1 lb. (450 g.) white or brown sugar

Discard any mouldy berries and remove the leaves and stalks from the fruit.

Weigh the fruit before putting it in a large mixing bowl. Crush it with a wooden spoon or vegetable masher. Stir the vinegar into the fruit.

Cover the bowl with a clean cloth draped over a wire cake rack or two or three pieces of clean wood to prevent it from sagging into the bowl. Secure the cloth with elastic. Leave, covered, for 4–5 days, stirring once or twice daily.

Scald a clean cloth, wring it out and strain the fruit through it into a bowl.

Measure the juice into a saucepan and add 1 lb. (450 g.) of sugar for each pint (575/600 ml.) of juice. Heat gently, stirring until the sugar has dissolved, then bring to the boil and boil gently for 10 minutes.

Pour into clean, dry sauce bottles, filling to ½ in. (1·5 cm.) below the cap. Seal securely and label.

Store fruit vinegar for 2 weeks in a cool, dark place before using.

FRUIT SYRUPS
Countrywide

COMMERCIALLY prepared black-currant syrup is widely known, loved by children and valued for its high Vitamin C content. Fruit syrups can easily be made at home using fruits that are too soft and ripe for other preserving methods.

When preparing the syrup, keep the heating to the minimum to retain the fresh fruit flavour. Most fruits will give up their juices when treated by the method described below, but black currants and blackberries will need some water added to them.

With really ripe fruit the juice yield should be satisfactory, but juice yields can be improved by adding a pectin-destroying enzyme, available from stores stocking home wine-making equipment. Use ½ teaspoon to each 6 lb. (2·7 kg.) of fruit.

The freshness of ripe berries concentrated in a range of sweet fruit syrups.

READY FOR USE: AFTER 2–3 DAYS

INGREDIENTS

Any sound, ripe soft fruit, such as strawberries, raspberries, black currants or blackberries
Granulated sugar
See below for quantities

Wash the fruit if necessary, remove any leaves and stalks, place in a large heatproof bowl and crush it with a wooden spoon or vegetable masher.

If you are using black currants, add ½ pint (275/300 ml.) of water for each 1 lb. (450 g.) of fruit. For blackberries, add ½ pint (275/300 ml.) of water for each 6 lb. (2·7 kg.) of fruit.

Cover the bowl with a clean cloth draped over a wire cake rack or two or three pieces of clean wood to prevent sagging, and secure the cloth with elastic. Leave to stand for 2–3 days in a cool pantry or cupboard.

Bring a pan of water to the boil and place the bowl of fruit over the pan. Heat gently until the juice runs freely.

Scald a clean cloth, wring it out and strain the extract through into a measuring jug. Add sugar in the proportion of 12 oz. (350 g.) for each 1 pint (575/600 ml.) of juice. Stir in the sugar without heating, but if it is slow to dissolve pour into a saucepan and heat gently.

Pour the syrup through a funnel into sauce bottles. Screw the caps on tightly and label. Store in a refrigerator and use as required. It will keep for up to 6 weeks.

If you wish to store the bottles longer, they need to be sterilised in the same way as sauces (see p. 364). Label and store in a cool, dark place or a refrigerator for use as required.

Syrups can be deep-frozen in cartons; stir well when fully thawed.

Serve diluted to taste with iced water for a summer drink. To make a fruit cup use wine, cider or lemonade as the basic liquid. For a hot drink use 1 part syrup to 3–4 parts hot water, and add ground nutmeg and a dash of rum. To make a milk shake, allow 1 large tablespoon of syrup to ¼ pint (150 ml.) of milk. Add the syrup slowly to the milk while whisking.

To make blackberry cordial, take ½ pint (275/300 ml.) of blackberry syrup and add 2 tablespoons of water, 2 cloves and a pinch of nutmeg. Heat and then simmer gently with the lid on for about 10 minutes. Remove from the heat and add 1–2 tablespoons of rum or brandy. Pour into warm mugs. This amount serves two people.

ICED CHINA TEA
Countrywide

THE TEA PLANT was known in China from early times, but tea—the infusion of the leaves in hot water—goes back only to the 15th century. China tea is a refreshing drink at any time, but is particularly welcome in hot weather, when it is iced and laced with rum.

If desired, about two teaspoons of sugar can be added to the drink.

PREPARATION TIME: 1 HOUR

INGREDIENTS FOR THREE

3 teaspoons China tea
1 pint (575/600 ml.) boiling water
2–3 tablespoons dark rum
3 slices lemon
3 ice cubes
3 sprigs fresh mint

Put the tea in a jug and pour on the boiling water. Leave to stand for 10 minutes, then strain into another jug. When cool, place the jug in the refrigerator and leave until very cold.

Add the rum and stir well.

Place a slice of lemon and an ice cube in each of three glasses and pour in the tea. Garnish each glass with a sprig of mint.

BARLEY WATER
Countrywide

BARLEY WATER originated as a soothing drink for fever patients, but by the Middle Ages was seen as a refreshment for sick and healthy alike. The English, like the French, flavoured it with liquorice, but by the late 17th century tended to substitute lemon, a version still popular today. It makes a fine addition to a picnic.

PREPARATION TIME: 5 MINUTES
COOKING TIME: 20 MINUTES

INGREDIENTS FOR TWO

2 oz. (50 g.) pearl barley
1 pint (575/600 ml.) cold water
Strip of lemon rind
Juice of ½ lemon
1 level tablespoon sugar, to taste

Blanch the barley by placing it in a sieve and pouring boiling water over it. This cleans it and helps to keep the barley water a good, clear colour.

Place the clean barley, the water and the lemon rind in a covered pan and simmer for 20 minutes. Strain into a jug, add the lemon juice and sweeten to taste.

Keep the barley water in a cool place. Do not make large quantities at a time, as it should be drunk within 24 hours of making.

SPRUCE
Cornwall

IN SPITE OF ITS NAME, this old country recipe does not include the sap of the spruce tree among its ingredients. Spruce beer, which did, used to be drunk in spring during the 17th and 18th centuries to purify the blood.

This recipe is a simple variation of economical lemonade, with an added 'lift' provided by the ginger. It was an ideal daytime drink for farm workers.

PREPARATION TIME: 15 MINUTES

INGREDIENTS TO YIELD
7 PINTS (4 LITRES)

1 lemon, scrubbed
¾ lb. (350 g.) granulated sugar
1 pint (575/600 ml.) boiling water
6 pints (4 litres) very cold water
2 teaspoons tartaric acid
1–2 teaspoons ground ginger

Using a potato peeler, peel the rind thinly from the lemon in large pieces, and squeeze out the juice.

Put the sugar into a bowl and pour on the boiling water. Add the lemon juice and rind, the tartaric acid and the ginger. Stir to dissolve the sugar and leave until cold.

Remove the lemon rind, add the very cold water and serve.

OLD-FASHIONED LEMONADE
Countrywide

LEMONS must be the most universally used fruits in the preparation of drinks. Eliza Acton, in her 19th-century classic *Modern Cookery*, includes a simple recipe for 'an excellent portable lemonade'. It is in concentrated form to be dissolved in a glass of water for drinking. This recipe is similar, but partially diluted. The sugar is a preservative as well as a sweetener. Add an extra slice of lemon if it is too sweet for your taste.

Lemonade can be used to lace spirits, diluted with cold tea, served with young mint leaves or minted ice cubes, taken as a hot drink with a dash of whisky or an aspirin to ward off a cold, or simply diluted with iced water for a delicious and refreshing summer drink.

PREPARATION TIME: 5 MINUTES
COOKING TIME: 12 MINUTES

INGREDIENTS TO YIELD
2 PINTS (1·1 LITRES)

4 juicy lemons, scrubbed
1½ lb. (700 g.) granulated sugar
2 teaspoons citric acid
2 teaspoons tartaric acid
2 pints (1·1 litres) boiling water

Peel the lemons very thinly, using a potato peeler to remove only the coloured rind and no pith.

Squeeze the juice from the lemons into a large basin and add the sugar and the citric and tartaric acid.

Pour the boiling water into a 3 pint (1·7 litre) saucepan, add the lemon rind and boil together for 2 minutes. Remove from the heat, and strain the water over the lemon juice and sugar mixture. Stir to dissolve the sugar. Strain the lemonade, pour into clean lemonade or squash bottles and seal securely.

If stored in a cool place, this lemonade will keep for several weeks. To serve, dilute with hot or cold water to taste and add a half slice of lemon or orange or a twist of fine-cut peel to each glass.

GINGER BEER
Countrywide

MOST FARMS AND COUNTRY cottages had a batch of ginger beer on the brew all through the year, because its main ingredient is not dependent on a special season. The ginger-beer 'plants', or 'mothers' as they were sometimes called, consisted of a mixture of yeast, ginger and sugar, which provided the base for numerous batches of 'beer'. Such plants need careful tending, otherwise they tend to produce very strange flavours indeed, and as a result they are rare today. However, a good ginger beer can be made from scratch without the help of a 'mother', and it has the advantage of being ready to drink much more quickly than most fermented beverages.

Ginger beer used to be a popular drink among farmworkers, especially during harvest time, and it tastes good even when warmed by the sun.

READY FOR USE:
3 DAYS AFTER BOTTLING

INGREDIENTS TO YIELD
8 PINTS (4·5 LITRES)

1 oz. (25 g.) root ginger
1 lemon, scrubbed
1 lb. (450 g.) granulated sugar
1 oz. (25 g.) cream of tartar
8 pints (4·5 litres) boiling water
1 oz. (25 g.) wine or baker's yeast

Bruise the root ginger by folding it in a clean cloth and hitting it with a hammer to release the flavour.

Using a potato peeler, peel the rind very thinly from the lemon. Squeeze the juice from the lemon.

Put the ginger, sugar, cream of tartar and lemon rind into a 2 gallon (9 litre) light-coloured plastic bucket.

Pour on the boiling water—in two lots, if necessary. Add the lemon juice and stir well. Leave until the liquid has cooled to 21°C (70°F). Cream the yeast with a little water in a small mixing bowl and stir it into the liquid.

Cover the bowl with a clean cloth draped over a wire cake rack or two or three pieces of clean wood to prevent sagging. Secure the cloth with elastic, and leave in a warm place for 24 hours.

Skim off the froth and, without disturbing the sediment too much, use a jug to bale the 'beer' into strong beer bottles.

Alternatively, strain the 'beer' and pour it through a funnel into the bottles. Close the bottles with corks and tie the corks down with string or fine florist's wire, leaving a little play on the tie.

Store the bottles in a cool place and examine them frequently. If fermentation is vigorous, release the wires slightly to relieve the pressure in the bottles, until fermentation quietens down. The ginger beer is ready for drinking in 2–3 days.

Lemonade, Barley Water, Ginger Beer and Spruce—thirst-quenchers for a picnic in the fields.

RECIPES

from

OTHER LANDS

AUSTRIA
Glühwein

GLÜHWEIN, spiced and mulled, is, as the name translates, a wine with a glow—a warming draught that was quaffed by huntsmen and mountaineers after a chilly day on the Tyrol. Today, it is a favourite with skiers as a cosy and relaxing drink after a day on the slopes.

Austrian red wine is produced mostly for home consumption. Unlike the white, it is not of the finest quality, which is perhaps why so much of it, drawn from the barrel rather than the bottle, is converted into *Glühwein*. So when making it at home, you need not use the best wine.

PREPARATION TIME: 5 MINUTES
COOKING TIME: 15 MINUTES

INGREDIENTS FOR 6–8 GLASSES

- *½ pint (275/300 ml.) water*
- *4–6 cloves*
- *2 in. (5 cm.) piece of cinnamon stick*
- *2 in. (5 cm.) piece of lemon rind*
- *3 oz. (75 g.) caster sugar*
- *1 bottle red wine*

Put the water in a 2 pint (1·1 litre) saucepan. Add the cloves and cinnamon and simmer for 5 minutes. Put in the lemon rind and sugar, and heat gently, stirring to dissolve the sugar.

Pour in the bottle of wine and heat until the liquid starts to steam (it must not boil). Remove the spices and serve the wine as hot as possible in heatproof glasses or mugs.

JAMAICA
Jamaican Banger

RUM HAS BEEN BOTH A GLORY and a tragedy for the Caribbean islands. Bottled sunshine it may be, but it also provided the money for 17th and 18th-century slavers to buy Africans for the sugar plantations.

The English poet William Cowper (1731–1800) summed up the general British attitude towards the slaves:

'I pity them greatly, but must be mum,
For how could we do without sugar and rum?'

Every island and every bar in the Caribbean has its own rum-based cocktails. The islanders themselves, however, prefer drinks that permit the true flavour of the rum to emerge. This is one such recipe.

PREPARATION TIME: 5 MINUTES
COOKING TIME: 10 MINUTES

INGREDIENTS FOR THREE

- *1 egg yolk*
- *½ pint (275/300 ml.) milk*
- *2 oz. (50 g.) caster sugar*
- *½ pint (275/300 ml.) Jamaican rum*
- *3 tablespoons whipped double cream*

Beat the egg yolk and milk well together in a bowl. Place in a 2 pint (1·1 litre) saucepan and add the sugar. Heat gently, stirring to dissolve the sugar, then add the rum and heat again until hot but not boiling.

Pour into warmed mugs and, just before serving, add a tablespoon of whipped cream to each mug.

CANADA
Fruit Punch

IN A LAND LIKE CANADA, where fresh fruit and sunshine abound, Fruit Punch has long been one of the most popular summer drinks. Home-produced apples, along with oranges, bananas, peaches, cherries and grapes, make an ideal thirst-quencher for adults and children alike.

When making Fruit Punch in Britain, the best apples to use are the flavoursome Cox's Orange Pippins. You can lace it with gin or vodka.

PREPARATION TIME: 45 MINUTES
COOKING TIME: 10 MINUTES

INGREDIENTS FOR 10–12 SERVINGS

- *3 apples, peeled and sliced*
- *3 oranges, peeled and sliced*
- *2 bananas or peaches, peeled and sliced*
- *4 oz. (100/125 g.) grapes, halved and stoned*
- *4 oz. (100/125 g.) fresh or tinned cherries, stoned*
- *2 pints (1·1 litres) water*
- *1 lb. (450 g.) sugar*
- *Juice of 3 lemons*
- *Juice of 3 oranges*
- *1 pint (575/600 ml.) ginger ale*
- *½ pint (275/300 ml.) cold tea (without milk)*
- *1 pint (575/600 ml.) soda water*
- *12 ice cubes*

Put the apples and oranges, bananas or peaches, grapes and cherries in a 5 pint (2·8 litre) bowl.

Put the water in a 3 pint (1·7 litre) saucepan and add the sugar, lemon and orange juice. Heat gently until the sugar is dissolved, then boil for 5 minutes, stirring with a wooden spoon. Pour the syrup over the fruit in the bowl and leave until cool.

Just before the punch is required, add the ginger ale, cold tea, soda water and the ice cubes.

Serve in goblets, ladling a little fruit into each.

YUGOSLAVIA
Plum Brandy

IN WILDER TIMES, the crash of shattering glasses followed a round of *sljivovica*—Yugoslavia's plum brandy—in the coffee-houses where it is often served. Today, they enjoy the drink in quieter fashion. Dark 'Czar' cooking plums are best for this simple version of Yugoslavia's national drink.

PREPARATION TIME: 45 MINUTES
COOKING TIME: 20–30 MINUTES

INGREDIENTS FOR 2–3 PINTS (1·1–1·7 LITRES)

- *7 lb. (3·2 kg.) plums*
- *7 lb. (3·2 kg.) sugar*
- *Almond essence*
- *Brandy*

Wash and stalk the plums and place in a saucepan with the sugar. Cook slowly for 20–30 minutes until the fruit is pulpy. Pour the pulp into a sieve and drain into a large saucepan without pressing the fruit. (Use the pulp for fruit cheese or chutney).

Measure the drained liquid, and for each pint (575/600 ml.) add ½ teaspoon of almond essence and at least 2 tablespoons of brandy. Bottle and cork. It is ready for use after 1 week, or can be stored in a cool, dry place for up to 6 months.

Serve diluted to taste as a refreshing drink, or use in punch or cocktails or fresh fruit salad.

SPAIN
Sangria

WINE HAS BEEN PRODUCED in Spain since the 1st century BC, when the Romans established vineyards as far north as Rioja—the district that still yields the best of Iberian wines. Oranges and lemons came with the Moors, who arrived in Spain about 800 years later. Fruit and wine combine in Sangria which is pure Spain, both in concept and content. Even the name, which can also mean 'blood-letting', has echoes of the bull-ring.

However, the object of Sangria is not to rouse the blood, but to cool it in the heat of the Spanish summer, when it is drunk both as a cocktail and as an accompaniment to meals. Any fruits or liqueurs may be added to the wine, but generally the Spanish keep the drink simple.

PREPARATION TIME: 10 MINUTES

INGREDIENTS FOR 6 GLASSES

1 bottle red wine
2 fl. oz. (50 ml.) brandy
Juice of 2 lemons
Juice of 2 oranges
Caster sugar to taste
1 bottle soda water
6 ice cubes
2–3 slices of orange

Use a tall glass jug large enough to hold all the ingredients—about 2½ pints (1·4 litres) in capacity.

Pour the wine into the jug, and add the brandy, lemon and orange juice. Stir well, then, still stirring, add the sugar, 1 teaspoon at a time, to taste.

Keep the jug in a cool place and, just before serving, add the soda water and the ice cubes. Float the orange slices on top of the jug.

HOLLAND
Orange Gin

THE ORIGINS OF GIN lie in the medieval apothecary's art, when the juniper-flavoured corn spirit was distilled to provide a blood-cleansing medicine. 'Take one of these boluses (large pills)... washing it down with six spoonfuls of the best Holland's Geneva', ran the prescription in Henry Fielding's comedy of 1732, *The Mock Doctor*.

A century earlier, veterans of the Elizabethan wars in Holland had encountered the Dutch *genever*—from the French *genièvre* (Juniper)—as a popular pick-me-up. It stayed in favour to become a social drink, the name eventually shortened to gin.

Orange Gin is made by steeping orange peel in gin. Seville oranges are recommended, as their peel is particularly bitter and flavoursome. Ideally, use full-bodied Dutch gin, but the drier British and American gins are perfectly acceptable. If you use a litre bottle of gin, use an extra orange.

PREPARATION TIME: 20 MINUTES
READY FOR USE: AFTER 6–8 WEEKS

INGREDIENTS

3 Seville oranges
1 lemon
1 bottle gin
8 oz. (225 g.) sugar

Scrub the oranges and lemon, then peel the rind very thinly so that no white pith adheres to the rind.

Pour the gin into a 2 pint (1·1 litre) preserving jar. Add the orange and lemon rinds and the sugar. Place a rubber ring on top of the jar, cover with the lid and screw down tightly.

Shake daily for a week, then leave for 6–8 weeks. Strain, pour into a bottle and seal. Use as required.

Sangria—iced wine with brandy and fruits—provides cool refreshment on a hot summer's day.

COUNTRY WINES AND OTHER DRINKS

ALEHOUSES WERE WELL ESTABLISHED in Britain before the coming of the Normans in 1066, and ale (made from fermented grain) was the most common drink for centuries – ranging from strong, twice-brewed ales to medicinal ales made from herbs and weak 'small' ale for children.

Ale with hops added, which became known as beer, was introduced from Flanders in the 15th century. It kept longer than ale, and eventually overtook it in popularity. Home-brewing was common until the rise of the commercial breweries in the 19th century.

Wine was made from grapes in Roman Britain, and wine-making continued in the monasteries until they were dissolved in the early 16th century. Not until sugar became cheaper and more plentiful in the 17th century did country wines made from other fruits become popular.

TIPS, TOOLS AND MATERIALS

Many drinks are simple to make, with no special equipment needed. The exceptions are home-made wines and beers, and to a lesser extent fruit syrups and vinegars.

When heating ingredients for punches, possets or other drinks that include ale, wine, or spirits, never allow them to boil, or the alcohol will evaporate.

The equipment you may need

Punch bowl, usual capacity about 1 gallon (4·5 litres).

Large, heavy-based saucepan or preserving pan for heating wine, beer or punch ingredients, preferably of stainless steel or good-quality aluminium. Do not use iron, copper, lead or zinc saucepans or containers—they may react with the acid in the ingredients.

A 2 gallon (9 litre) bowl or good-quality, light-coloured plastic bucket for mixing and soaking ingredients. A bucket should have a close-fitting lid. If you use a bowl, you need a cloth or polythene sheet to cover it and a length of elastic to closely secure it; also some means of preventing the cloth from sagging.

Nylon or hair sieve.

Double layer of muslin cloth or a jelly bag for straining pulp.

Wine-maker's thermometer.

Funnel, about 5 in. (13 cm.) across.

Polythene tubing about $4\frac{1}{2}$ ft (1·4 m.) long and $\frac{1}{4}$ in. (5 mm.) in diameter for siphoning.

Two 1 gallon (4·5 litre) glass fermentation jars (demijohns).

An airlock that fits into the bung of the fermentation jar.

Sauce bottles with screw caps for storing fruit vinegars.

Wine and beer bottles. Use dark bottles for storing dark wines, as light causes the colour to fade.

Corks or plastic stoppers for wine or beer bottles. Always use new corks.

Sodium metabisulphite for sterilising wine-making equipment.

Sterilising equipment

All containers and bottles must be scrupulously clean. Sterilise them just before you are ready to use them.

Glass bottles and containers for fruit syrups and cordials can be sterilised by immersing in cold water and bringing to the boil, then removing and inverting to drain.

Corks and screw caps can be left in a pan of simmering water for 10–15 minutes before use. This also helps to soften corks, which makes them easier to drive well into the bottle.

The simplest way to sterilise wine-making equipment is to immerse it in a solution containing sulphite, which gives off purifying sulphur dioxide.

Sulphite (sodium metabisulphite) is obtainable from a chemist. Use as directed on the packet. Make sure all parts of the equipment are wetted. Leave bottles inverted to drain—do not dry with a cloth.

Choosing ingredients

Fruit, foliage, flowers and vegetables Always use fresh, good-quality material. Fruit for wines, syrups or juices should be sound and fully ripe. You can use frozen fruit. Pick all raw material on a dry day, if possible, because mould can grow rapidly on damp produce in a container. Make sure anything you gather has not been recently sprayed with a herbicide or insecticide.

Water Use drinking water.

Sugar White, granulated sugar is suitable for most drinks. Some recipes specify caster sugar as it is easier to blend with cold ingredients. Demerara sugar is used in some traditional wines, such as dandelion, to give a fuller flavour and colour.

Yeast is the fermenting agent in wine and beer-making. Wine yeast gives better results than baker's yeast. It is available, from a shop selling wine-maker's requisites, in tablet, powder or granular form. There are various strains, but an all-purpose type is available. Some types need to be activated in a starter bottle first. Active, granulated baker's yeast quickly begins vigorous fermentation and can produce good beer or wine. But it is slow to settle into a sediment making siphoning difficult. Yeast deposits in the finished drink make it cloudy and spoil the flavour.

Acid The acid balance must be correct for yeast to thrive. Most fruits have more than enough, and it is diluted in preparation. For flowers and vegetables, acid must be added to the ingredients. It is usually included in the recipe as citric acid, often in the form of orange or lemon juice and rind, or as tartaric acid.

Pectin-destroying enzyme Pectin, the substance in fruit that aids the setting of jam, makes fruit syrups and wines cloudy. This can be limited by a pectin-destroying enzyme, sold by chemists. Use about 1 teaspoon per gallon (4·5 litres).

Pectin-destroying enzyme added to wine ingredients helps to break down the fruit, as well as clear the wine. For high-pectin fruits, particularly (see p. 359), add it at least 24 hours before adding yeast.

Making Country Wines

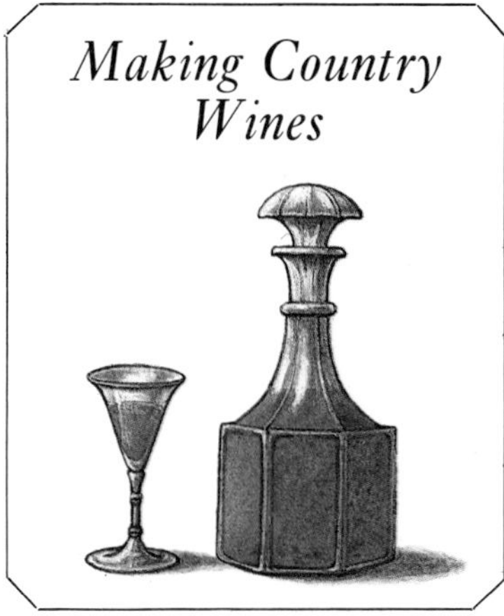

The wine and beer recipes included in this book are for simply made country wines. Results can vary considerably, but most well-made wines improve if kept a year or so.

The country ale or beer recipes are not true ales or beers because they do not contain malted grain. They may be named because of a similarity in taste or appearance to the true liquor.

Remember that it is illegal to sell home-made wine, ale, beer or cider.

How alcohol is formed

Yeast, the fermenting agent in wine and beer, is a tiny living cell that can reproduce about every three hours. It needs an acid environment, oxygen, warmth and food.

The yeast feeds on vegetable matter and sugar, and converts the sugar into alcohol and carbon dioxide in roughly equal parts. The bubbling during fermentation is the gas escaping.

Once the alcohol content reaches about 15%, the yeast dies or can no longer work, and fermentation ceases. The amount of sugar needed to achieve this amount of alcohol is 2½–3½ lb. per gallon (1·1–1·6 kg. per 4·5 litres). Any sugar left after fermentation sweetens the wine, so that about 2½ lb. (1·1 kg.) of sugar produces dry wine and 3½ lb. (1·6 kg.) sweet wine.

The Wine-Making Process

1 Extracting the flavour The simplest way is to place the raw material in a bowl or bucket, pour boiling water over it, break it up with a wooden spoon or vegetable masher, then leave it to soak for the number of days stated in the recipe, which varies according to the material.

Keep the vessel closely covered to keep out spoilage organisms, and stir once or twice a day. Vegetables are best boiled rather than soaked to extract juice and flavour.

2 Adding the sugar Sugar can be added as a syrup to the ingredients or added after they have been strained and squeezed through muslin to remove the pulp. After adding the sugar to the strained ingredients (known as the must), heat gently and stir until the sugar is dissolved.

3 Adding the yeast This is mostly added to the must once it has been cooled and strained into the fermentation jar. Sometimes it is added to ingredients left standing in a covered bowl for a few days before transfer to a fermentation jar.

4 Fermentation The best temperature for starting fermentation is about 21°C (70°F).

Fermentation is rapid at first while the yeast reproduces, but once all the oxygen is used up—after perhaps several days—and more air excluded, it cannot reproduce but continues working, so fermentation slows down. The best temperature for this secondary fermentation, which can take months, is 16–18°C (60–65°F); lower temperatures slow it down.

Unless the must is well covered during fermentation, wild yeast, bacteria or vinegar flies, attracted by the smell, may enter and spoil or sour the wine. A fermentation jar fitted with an airlock keeps out spoilage organisms and excludes air, yet allows gas to escape.

5 Racking As fermentation slows down, the yeast sinks to the bottom of the jar to form a sediment (the lees), and the wine gradually clears. If wine is left too long on the sediment it may affect the flavour; the clear wine should be siphoned to another fermentation bottle (this process is known as racking) and the sediment thrown out.

Some wine-makers siphon the wine from the sediment three or four times to ensure clear wine before bottling. Others bottle wine after only one racking. If you do this, fermentation may continue in the bottle, and escaping gas may blow off the corks. Tie corks down with two loops of florist's wire or string over them, loose enough for the corks to be pushed up to relieve pressure, otherwise the bottles may explode.

Very slow fermentation may continue for a long time. If fermentation seems to have finished, check by moving the wine to a warm temperature again—about 21°C (70°F). If it begins bubbling, fermentation is still not complete.

6 Storing and maturing Once fermentation has ceased, the wine cannot become any stronger but its flavour may improve with time. Most wines are best left 6–12 months.

When bottling, fill to allow about 1 in. (2·5 cm.) head space below a cork or stopper. Label clearly with the name and date of bottling.

Store in a cool, dark place—the ideal storage temperature is below 16°C (60°F). Store bottles with plastic stoppers upright, those with corks (but not tied-down corks) on their sides to keep the base of the cork moist and swollen. Check occasionally to make sure all corks are secure.

Using a fermentation jar

The most common type of airlock is a curved glass or plastic tube with a U-shaped piece between two bulbs. Fill between the bulbs with sulphite solution (see Sterilising equipment); this prevents air or bacteria entering, but allows gas to bubble out.

Strain the must through a funnel to fill the fermentation jar three-quarters full initially, so there is sufficient air for the first fermentation (unless this has been done in a covered bowl).

Moisten the straight end of the airlock to push it through the hole in the rubber bung, and fit the bung into the neck of the jar. Keep the sulphite topped up as necessary.

When racking wine must into a fermentation jar, fill to the bottom of the neck. There may not be sufficient must to do this, so top up with a sugar solution of similar strength to the original must. Fit the bung and airlock with the tube ¾ in. (2 cm.) above the liquid level.

How to siphon liquor

1 Remove the bung and airlock from the fermenting jar and insert one end of the siphoning tube (the blocked end with two side holes) into the wine must without disturbing the bottom sediment. Fix the tube in position at the neck with a peg and rubber band.

2 Place a clean, sterilised jar or bottle at a lower level than the full jar, but no more than 2 ft (60 cm.) lower.

3 Take the lower end of the plastic tube, hold it below the level of the full jar, and suck gently until the wine must begins to flow.

4 Squeeze the end of the tube between your thumb and forefinger and put it into the empty jar before releasing. Make sure no sediment reaches the clean jar.

Of JAMS, PICKLES AND OTHER PRESERVES

CONTAINING

NUMEROUS *Useful* FAMILY RECIPES

for MARMALADES & JELLIES, CHUTNEYS & RELISHES

& all other DELICIOUS CONSERVES

PAGES 336–355

AND

A SELECTION of RECIPES from OTHER LANDS

PAGES 356–357

AND WITH

DIRECTIONS *for* BASIC METHODS

for all kinds of Boiling, Testing, Potting and Storing of Preserves to Perfection

PAGES 358–365

Gooseberry and Elderflower Jam
Countrywide

A single head of elderflower drawn through any jam while cooking will leave a strongly scented memory of its passing. So when making this favourite country jam of high summer, be careful not to exceed the number of elderflower heads recommended in the recipe.

The colour of the jam will vary according to the variety and maturity of the fruit. For a green jam use slightly underripe fruit; this makes a good filling for a suet pudding, as the sharpness of the jam contrasts well with the suet pastry. A less sharp, yellower jam results from using dessert gooseberries, but they must not be overripe or the set and keeping quality of the jam will be impaired.

Preparation Time: 45 minutes
Cooking Time: 45 minutes
Pre-heat the Oven to 110°C (225°F)—gas mark ¼

Ingredients to Yield about 10 lb. (4·5 kg.)

4½ lb. (2 kg.) gooseberries
1½ pints (850 ml.) water
8–12 heads of elderflowers (optional)
6 lb. (2·7 kg.) sugar

Wash the gooseberries and top and tail them. Place in a large, heavy-based pan with the water. If using elderflowers, place in a muslin bag and add to the pan. Put the sugar in an ovenproof dish and place in the middle of the oven for 10–15 minutes to warm through.

Bring the fruit to the boil, then simmer for about 30 minutes until soft, stirring from time to time. Take the pan off the heat, remove the bag of elderflowers and squeeze it over the fruit, then discard.

Add the warmed sugar to the pan and stir until dissolved. Bring to the boil again and boil rapidly until setting point is reached—after about 15 minutes. Skim if necessary, then pot and seal (see p. 361).

High Dumpsy Dearie Jam
Worcestershire

No one knows why this delightfully fruity jam is called 'High Dumpsy Dearie'. The name was probably coined by a Worcestershire farmer's wife about 100 years ago, and since its very meaninglessness makes it memorable, the title has stuck ever since.

A thrifty way of using up odds and ends of fruit, this jam is especially good in baked roly-poly. If you have them, use juicy cooking apples such as the Bramley variety.

Preparation Time: 30 minutes
Cooking Time: 1 hour

Ingredients to Yield 7–8 lb. (3·2–3·6 kg.)

2 lb. (900 g.) cooking apples, peeled, cored and sliced
2 lb. (900 g.) pears, peeled, cored and sliced
2 lb. (900 g.) plums, stoned and halved
Water
Juice and grated rind of 1 lemon
Bruised root of dried ginger
4½ lb. (2 kg.) sugar

Place all the fruit in a large, heavy-based pan and add just enough water to cover the base. Simmer until the fruit is tender. This will take about 40–45 minutes.

Remove from the heat and add the sugar, stirring until dissolved. Add the juice and grated rind of the lemon, and the ginger root tied in a muslin bag. Bring to the boil and cook rapidly until the setting point of the jam is reached (see p. 360), after about 15 minutes. Then pot and seal the jam (see p. 361).

Blackcurrant Jam
Countrywide

An economical jam to make, since black currants are rich in pectin and provide an exceptionally high jam yield for each pound of fruit. This alone makes the trouble of stripping the currants from the stalks well worth while. There is an added bonus in the distinctive flavour, and in the rich, dark colour that admirably complements sponges and steamed puddings.

When picking or buying the black currants, make sure they are firm, ripe and a good, dark colour. Too many under-ripe currants will detract from the flavour and colour of the jam.

Preparation Time: 45 minutes
Cooking Time: 45 minutes
Pre-heat the Oven to 110°C (225°F)—gas mark ¼

Ingredients to Yield about 10 lb. (4·5 kg.)

4 lb. (1·8 kg.) black currants
3 pints (1·7 litres) water
6 lb. (2·7 kg.) sugar

Wash the black currants, removing stalks and any leaves. Place in a large, heavy-based pan and cover with the cold water. Bring to the boil and simmer for 30–35 minutes, until the fruit is tender. Stir occasionally as the pulp thickens. Meanwhile, put the sugar in an ovenproof bowl and place in the middle of the pre-heated oven to warm through for 10–15 minutes.

Remove the pan from the heat and stir in the warmed sugar until dissolved. Then boil again and cook rapidly until the setting point is reached (see p. 360). Skim if necessary, then pot and seal.

Marrow and Ginger Jam
Countrywide

People who remember the austere days of wartime and immediately after are likely to have an in-built resistance to any suggestion of marrow as an ingredient in jam.

In this case, at least, they should abandon memory, for this economical jam is very good indeed. Here, the marrow is no more than a vehicle for the lemon and the ginger—neither of which were likely to have figured in recipes of the utility years.

Marrows deepen in colour when stored, so jam made late in the season will be darker than any made earlier.

Preparation Time: 35 minutes
Cooking Time: about 1 hour

Ingredients to Yield 10–10½ lb. (4·5–4·7 kg.)

6 lb. (2·7 kg.) diced marrow flesh
Juice and grated rinds of 4 lemons
12 oz. (350 g.) crystallised ginger, chopped, or 3 oz. (75 g.) root of dried ginger, or 1 oz. (25 g.) ground ginger
6 lb. (2·7 kg.) sugar

Place the marrow flesh in a large, heavy-based pan and pour on a little cold water. Bring to the boil and simmer for about 20 minutes, until tender. Drain thoroughly and mash the flesh.

Return the marrow to the pan and add the grated rind and lemon juice. Add the crystallised ginger or ground ginger. If using root of dried ginger, place it in a muslin bag and bruise it thoroughly with a hammer before adding.

Bring to the boil, remove the pan from the heat and add the sugar, stirring until dissolved. Put the pan on the heat again and boil for about 20 minutes or until the jam is thick. If using root of dried ginger, remove it before potting. Pot and seal (see p. 361).

Raspberry, Blackcurrant, High Dumpsy Dearie and Marrow and Ginger—succulent jams made from choice summer fruits.

RASPBERRY JAM
Countrywide

THE CHIEF GLORY of Raspberry Jam lies in its bright red colour and its flavour of fine, fresh fruit. Be careful, therefore, not to overcook it, otherwise a brown, sticky concoction will result.

Neither water nor pectin are required in making this jam. Its colour and sharp-sweet taste make it particularly suitable as a filling for a sponge sandwich or Swiss roll. A raspberry jam tart covered with a layer of curd cheese would grace the most sophisticated dinner table.

Fruit freshly picked from the garden need not be washed, but shop-bought raspberries should be carefully picked over before use.

PREPARATION TIME: 45 MINUTES
COOKING TIME: 20 MINUTES
PRE-HEAT THE OVEN TO 110°C (225°F)—GAS MARK ¼

INGREDIENTS TO YIELD ABOUT 10 LB. (4·5 KG.)

6 lb. (2·7 kg.) sugar
6 lb. (2·7 kg.) raspberries

Put the sugar in an ovenproof bowl and place in the middle of the pre-heated oven for 10–15 minutes.

Carefully pick over the fruit and wash if necessary, draining well. Place in a large, heavy-based pan and simmer gently for about 10 minutes until the raspberries are tender and the juice is running.

Take the pan off the heat and stir in the warmed sugar until it is completely dissolved. This will take about 5 minutes.

Put the pan back on the heat, bring to the boil and cook rapidly for about 5 minutes, until the setting point is reached (see p. 360). Cool for 3 minutes, stir to distribute the fruit, then pot and seal.

Plum Rum Conserve
Essex

Plums are a good bulk ingredient for jam, and are greatly improved by the addition of dried fruit, nuts and rum.

Dark plums are best for this recipe which comes from Essex, the home of the dark Early Rivers plum. Alternatively, use a mixture of dark and light plums. There is a Surrey version which uses port instead of rum. The plums should be ripe and juicy, but not over-ripe.

This Plum Rum Conserve makes a delectable cake or tart filling.

Preparation Time: 30 minutes
Standing Time: 5 minutes
Cooking Time: 45 minutes

Ingredients to Yield about 5 lb. (2·3 kg.)

4 lb. (1·8 kg.) plums
6 oz. (175 g.) seedless raisins
½ pint (275/300 ml.) water
3 lb. (1·4 kg.) sugar
4 oz. (100/125 g.) almonds, blanched and finely chopped
4 tablespoons dark rum

Cut the plums in half, take out the stones and set them aside. Place the plums and the raisins in a large, heavy-based pan.

Put the stones, with the scraps of plum flesh still clinging, in a small pan. Pour the water over them and boil for 10 minutes. Strain this liquid over the fruit in the large pan.

Simmer the plums and raisins over a low heat for about 10 minutes, until the fruit is soft. Stir frequently to prevent burning. Remove the pan from the heat and stir in the sugar until dissolved. Bring to the boil again and cook rapidly for about 15 minutes, until the setting point is reached (see p. 360). Take the pan off the heat and add the finely chopped almonds and the rum. Leave to stand for 5 minutes.

Stir well, then pot and seal.

Strawberry Conserve
Countrywide

Whole strawberries drenched in syrup make this conserve, which is simpler to make than strawberry jam and provides an excellent filling for open tarts and flans.

Even the humble rice pudding is transformed by the addition of the conserve, which, like the jam, also combines superbly with freshly baked scones and clotted cream.

Choose strawberries of medium size. Avoid those sold at the end of the season as 'jam fruit'—they often vary widely in size and quality.

Preparation Time: 20 minutes
Standing Time: 3 days
Cooking Time: 20 minutes

Ingredients to Yield 6 lb. (2·7 kg.)

4 lb. (1·8 kg.) hulled strawberries
4 lb. (1·8 kg.) granulated sugar

Place the strawberries in a basin with alternate layers of sugar. Cover, and leave for 24 hours.

Next day, tip the contents of the basin into a large, heavy-based pan and bring to the boil, stirring occasionally. Boil for 5 minutes, then return the fruit and sugar mixture to the basin. Cover with a tea towel and leave for 48 hours.

Return the fruit to the pan, bring to the boil and cook for 10–15 minutes, until the setting point is reached (see p. 360).

Cool until a skin forms, then stir to distribute the fruit. Pot and seal (see p. 361).

This is a delicious, full-flavoured conserve. Because it does not set stiffly, it is not recommended for showing in competitions.

Strawberry Conserve—whole fruits in syrup—with clotted cream and scones.

Raspberry Preserve
Countrywide

This is a means of preserving both the whole fruits and their flavour for a limited period—from about four to six months—so providing superb fillings for tarts, cakes and sponges during the fruit-less months of the year.

A preserve does not set like a jam. The fruit rises, leaving the juice to set as a jelly underneath. When you want to use the preserve, simply open the jar and stir the contents well.

Preparation Time: 5 minutes
Heating Time: 25 minutes
Pre-heat the Oven to 110°C (225°F)—Gas Mark ¼

Ingredients to Yield about 8 lb. (3·6 kg.)

4 lb. (1·8 kg.) firm, dry raspberries
4 lb. (1·8 kg.) caster sugar

Do not wash the raspberries unless absolutely essential: some water will cling and the preserve will not set so well. Place the fruit in one ovenproof bowl and the sugar in another. Place both bowls in the pre-heated oven for 20 minutes, or until the juice has begun to ooze from the raspberries.

Remove both bowls from the oven and tip the sugar into the fruit. Stir well with a wooden spoon for 5 minutes, or until all the sugar has dissolved. Pot and seal (see p. 361).

Raspberry Preserve will keep for 4–6 months under correct storage conditions (see p. 361). It is not a true jam as the sugar and fruit are not boiled together, but an economical way of using fruit, with no waste.

All-the-Year-Round Jam
Countrywide

All-the-year-round Jam is so called because it is made from nuts and dried fruits, obtainable even in the depth of winter. It is also known as 'medicinal jam', because prunes are mildly laxative, and this is a good way of inducing a small child to take them without trouble.

In spite of the slightly chilling content of this title, the jam is delicious, and closely resembles the popular continental plum conserve.

Preparation Time: 20 minutes
Standing Time: 8 hours (overnight)
Cooking Time: 20 minutes

Ingredients to Yield about 3 lb. (1·4 kg.)

4 oz. (100/125 g.) whole almonds
1 lb. (450 g.) prunes
1 lb. (450 g.) seedless raisins
1 pint (575/600 ml.) water
1 lb. (450 g.) Demerara sugar

Blanch and chop the almonds and put them in a bowl with the prunes and raisins. Pour on the water and leave to soak overnight.

Next day, strain off the juice and put to one side. Remove the prune stones and chop the prunes and raisins. Place them with the strained juice and the almonds in a large, heavy-based pan and heat gently. Add the sugar, stirring continuously until it is dissolved.

Bring to the boil and cook rapidly, stirring from time to time, for about 20 minutes until setting point is reached (see p. 360). Pot and seal.

Strawberry Jam
Countrywide

The word 'jam' has been said to be derived from the cry '*J'aime!*' with which 18th-century children greeted the preserve on first tasting it.

True or not, the exclamation would certainly be appropriate to Strawberry Jam, perhaps the finest of them all, though in some ways the trickiest to make. This jam rarely sets stiffly, and overboiling will spoil the taste. Adding pectin (see p. 359) helps setting. The colour of the jam varies from light to dark red, depending on the variety of strawberry used.

Keep at least one pot to mingle with clotted cream as a filling for Devon splits, or mix 2 tablespoons with a block of vanilla ice-cream, refreeze for a short while, and serve with meringues and cream.

Preparation Time: 30 minutes
Cooking Time: 35–40 minutes
Pre-heat the Oven to 110°C (225°F)—Gas Mark ¼

Ingredients to Yield about 10 lb. (4·5 kg.)

6 lb. (2·7 kg.) strawberries
Juice of 2 lemons
6 lb. (2·7 kg.) sugar

Hull the strawberries and rinse if necessary. Place in a large, heavy-based pan with the lemon juice. Measure the sugar into an ovenproof dish and put in the middle of the oven to warm through for 10–15 minutes.

Cook the strawberries over a low heat for about 15 minutes, until the fruit is tender and the juices run. Take off the heat and add the warm sugar, stirring continuously until the sugar is dissolved.

Bring the fruit to the boil and cook rapidly for 15–20 minutes until the setting point is reached (see p. 360), stirring from time to time. Remove any scum.

Allow the jam to cool until a skin forms on the surface, then stir to distribute the fruit evenly. Pot and seal (see p. 361).

Dried Apricot Jam
Countrywide

Preserving fruit by drying has a long history. Since biblical times, grapes, figs and dates have been dried in the hot desert sands of Middle Eastern countries and exported.

It was in an attempt to emulate the sweet, sticky texture of these fruits that the English of the 18th century began to dry the more homely plums, gooseberries, quinces and eventually apricots that, with Elizabethan encouragement, had been established in the walled gardens of the south.

Apricot jam makes a good filling for tarts and flans, and is especially welcome with hot, fresh bread at breakfast time.

Preparation Time: 10 minutes
Soaking Time: 24–36 hours
Cooking Time: 1¼ hours

Ingredients to Yield about 10 lb. (4·5 kg.)

2 lb. (900 g.) dried apricots
6 pints (3·4 litres) water
Juice of 2 lemons
3 oz. (75 g.) almonds, blanched and shredded (optional)
6 lb. (2·7 kg.) sugar

Wash the apricots and soak them in the measured water for 24–36 hours. Tip the fruit and the water into a very large, heavy-based pan with the lemon juice. Bring to the boil, then simmer for 30 minutes, stirring occasionally.

Remove from the heat, add the almonds and sugar, and stir until the sugar dissolves. Return the pan to the heat and bring to the boil. Cook rapidly until the setting point is reached (see p. 360). Pot and seal.

The almonds are optional but give an attractive flavour.

Redcurrant Jelly
Countrywide

Red currants have a high pectin content, so any preserve made with them sets well.

This jelly is invaluable in the kitchen. It is the traditional accompaniment to hare and other game, and to mutton or lamb. A spoonful is often added to meat and game dishes to give a slight sharpness.

Redcurrant Jelly is also used to glaze fruit tarts and to fill tartlets. Spread a layer of Victoria sandwich with it, then spread lemon curd. The combination of flavours is delicious.

Preparation Time: about 50 minutes
Straining Time: about 2 hours
Cooking Time: 15 minutes

Ingredients to Yield about 3 lb. (1·4 kg.)

4 lb. (1·8 kg.) red currants
1 pint (575/600 ml.) water
Sugar

Wash the fruit and place in a large, heavy-based pan with the water. Bring to the boil and simmer for about 30 minutes until the fruit is soft, stirring and mashing the red currants with a wooden spoon from time to time. Strain through a scalded jelly bag for about 2 hours. Do not squeeze the bag, as this would make the jelly cloudy.

Heat the oven to 110°C (225°F)—gas mark ¼. Measure the strained juice and weigh out 1 lb. (450 g.) sugar for each pint (575/600 ml.). Put the sugar in an ovenproof dish and place in the middle of the oven to warm through for 10–15 minutes.

Pour the juice back into the pan and heat gently. Add the warmed sugar, stirring until dissolved. Bring to the boil and cook rapidly for 10–15 minutes until setting point (see p. 360) is reached. Skim if necessary, then pot and seal.

Quince Jelly
Countrywide

Quinces, the 'golden apples' that to the Ancient Greeks symbolised love and happiness, have been grown in southern England since Roman times. *Marmelada*, a Portuguese preserve made from quinces, evolved into our marmalade. A heavily spiced Tudor version of quince jelly was used as an accompaniment to meat or as a tart filling.

This modern recipe, with its sweet lemon fragrance, goes well with pork, venison and other strongly flavoured meats. It can also be served with apple pie or as a teatime spread.

Preparation Time: 1½–2 hours
Straining Time: about 4 hours
Cooking Time: 20 minutes

Ingredients to Yield 4–5 lb. (1·8–2·3 kg.)

4 lb. (1·8 kg.) quinces
Sugar
Juice of 2 lemons

Wash the quinces, chop them roughly and place in a large, heavy-based pan with enough water to just cover. Bring to the boil, and cover and simmer for 1–1½ hours until very soft.

Ladle the fruit and liquid into a scalded jelly bag and leave to strain for about 4 hours. Do not squeeze the bag, as this would make the jelly cloudy.

Heat the oven to 110°C (225°F)—gas mark ¼. Measure the strained juice and weigh out 1 lb. (450 g.) sugar for each pint (575/600 ml.). Place the sugar in an ovenproof dish in the middle of the oven to warm through for 10–15 minutes.

Warm the juice in the pan and add the lemon juice. Stir in the warmed sugar until dissolved. Bring the jelly to the boil and cook rapidly until the setting point (see p. 360) is reached, after about 10–15 minutes. Skim if necessary, pot and seal.

Quince Jelly adds its sweet lemon fragrance to a teatime spread.

Hedgerow Jelly
Countrywide

Whether you make this jelly with garden or hedgerow fruits, it glows with the warm richness of autumn—Autumn Jelly is an alternative name.

Perhaps the hedgerow version is more fun—seeking out and gathering the elderberries and blackberries, the sloes, rowan berries and wild rose hips can turn into a competitive family expedition.

Almost any mixture of berries can replace the blackberries or plums listed in the recipe, but the apples must remain. Their high pectin content is needed to set the fruit.

Preparation Time: about 1 hour
Straining Time: at least 4 hours
Cooking Time: 20–25 minutes

INGREDIENTS TO YIELD
ABOUT 4–5 LB. (1·8–2·3 KG.)

- *3 lb. (1·4 kg.) crab apples, windfall apples or cooking apples*
- *2 lb. (900 g.) blackberries or rowan berries*
- *2 lb. (900 g.) dark plums or damsons*
- *Juice of 1 lemon*
- *Sugar*

Wash the apples, and if you are using cooking apples chop them roughly. Wash and drain the blackberries or rowan berries. Wash and halve the plums or damsons. Put the fruit in a large, heavy-based pan with the lemon juice and add cold water to the level of the fruit.

Bring to the boil, then simmer gently until the fruit is tender and well broken down. Strain through a scalded jelly bag for at least 4 hours. Do not squeeze the bag.

Heat the oven to 110°C (225°F)—gas mark $\frac{1}{4}$. Measure the strained juice and weigh out 1 lb. (450 g.) sugar for each pint (575/600 ml.). Put the sugar in an ovenproof dish and place in the middle of the oven to warm through for 10–15 minutes.

Pour the juice back into the pan and heat gently. Add the warmed sugar, stirring until dissolved. Bring to the boil and cook rapidly until the setting point is reached (see p. 360). Skim, pot and seal.

BRAMBLE AND ROSE-HIP JELLY
Highlands

IN THE SCOTTISH HIGHLANDS the blackberry was called the 'blessed bramble', for its fruits were a joy in an area where fruit was rare. Its leaves soothed burns and bruises, and dye could be made from its fruit.

When rose-hips, the fruit of the wild rose, are combined with blackberries in a jelly, the result is a royal-purple confection, bitter-sweet in flavour, that combines equally well with buttered toast or oatcakes.

PREPARATION TIME: 1$\frac{1}{4}$ HOURS
STRAINING TIME: ABOUT 2 HOURS
COOKING TIME: 20 MINUTES

INGREDIENTS TO YIELD
ABOUT 5 LB. (2·3 KG.)

- *2 lb. (900 g.) blackberries*
- *2 lb. (900 g.) rose-hips*
- *Juice of 2 lemons*
- *2 pints (1·1 litres) water*
- *Sugar*

Wash the blackberries and simmer in 1 pint (575/600 ml.) of the water until they are soft. Wash the rose-hips and simmer in the remaining water until they form a soft pulp.

Ladle the fruit and liquid into a scalded jelly bag and strain for about 2 hours. Do not squeeze the bag or the jelly will be cloudy.

Heat the oven to 110°C (225°F)—gas mark $\frac{1}{4}$. Add the lemon juice to the strained liquid, measure it and weigh out 1 lb. (450 g.) sugar for each pint (575/600 ml.). Place the sugar in an ovenproof dish in the middle of the oven to warm for 10–15 minutes.

Warm the juice in a large, heavy-based pan over a low heat and stir in the warmed sugar until dissolved. Bring the jelly to the boil, and boil rapidly until it reaches setting point (see p. 360). Skim, pot and seal.

Wild rose-hips and the 'blessed bramble' of the Highland Scots, yield a bitter-sweet jelly for toast or oatcakes.

SPICED BRAMBLE JELLY
Countrywide

BECAUSE SATAN FELL into a bramble bush when he was cast out of Heaven on the first Michaelmas Day (September 29), he is said to wander the countryside each year on the anniversary, blasting blackberries with his breath or spitting on them.

It is therefore considered bad luck to pick them after that date. Certainly they become less juicy, their pips are more pronounced, and they lose much of their flavour once they have been touched by the first frosts.

Blackberries take a lot of picking, and it is best to set the children to the exacting task.

PREPARATION TIME: 45 MINUTES
STRAINING TIME: 2–3 HOURS
COOKING TIME: 25 MINUTES

INGREDIENTS TO YIELD 2–3 LB. (900 G.–1·4 KG.)

4 lb. (1·8 kg.) blackberries
4 medium cooking apples, cut in pieces, or juice of 2 lemons
2½ fl. oz. (75 ml.) water
Sugar
Ground mixed spice

Wash the blackberries, and apples if used. Put the berries in a large, heavy-based pan with the water and the apple pieces or lemon juice. Bring to the boil and simmer for 15–20 minutes, until tender. Strain through a jelly bag for 2–3 hours.

Heat the oven to 110°C (225°F)—gas mark ¼. Measure the strained juice and weigh out 1 lb. (450 g.) sugar and 1 level teaspoon of ground mixed spice for each pint (575/600 ml.). Put the sugar in an ovenproof dish and place in the middle of the oven for about 10–15 minutes to warm through.

Pour the juice back into the pan and heat gently. Add the warmed sugar and the mixed spice, stirring until dissolved. Bring to the boil and cook rapidly for 12–15 minutes, until the setting point is reached (see p. 360). Pot and seal.

FIVE-FRUIT JELLY
Countrywide

WHEN MAKING this delightfully unusual summer jelly, bear in mind the advice of the 16th-century jelly-maker: 'Out, fruit, go and gather, but not in the dew.'

Wait until the sun is high, and the fruit as dry as possible—soft fruit decays rapidly when damp. Pick it, too, when only just ripe. Over-ripe fruit has a low pectin content, making a set difficult to achieve.

This jelly is too good to spread on bread; use it instead as a filling for tarts. It is also worth buying preserving sugar, for this will give the jelly an extra sparkle.

PREPARATION TIME: 45 MINUTES
STRAINING TIME: 2–3 HOURS
COOKING TIME: ABOUT 30 MINUTES

INGREDIENTS TO YIELD ABOUT 2 LB. (900 G.)

8 oz. (225 g.) strawberries
8 oz. (225 g.) raspberries
8 oz. (225 g.) cherries
8 oz. (225 g.) red currants
8 oz. (225 g.) gooseberries
Sugar

Wash the fruit, but there is no need to remove hulls, stalks or stones. Put it in a large, heavy-based pan with enough cold water to cover. Bring to the boil, then simmer gently over a low heat for 30–40 minutes until all the fruits are soft.

Ladle the fruit and liquid into a scalded jelly bag and leave to strain for 2–3 hours. Do not squeeze the bag. Heat the oven to 110°C (225°F)—gas mark ¼. Measure the strained liquid and weigh out 1 lb. (450 g.) of sugar for each pint (575/600 ml.). Put the sugar in an ovenproof dish in the middle of the oven for 10–15 minutes.

Heat the juice in the cleaned pan and stir in the sugar until dissolved. Boil, and cook rapidly for 10–15 minutes, until the setting point is reached (see p. 360). Pot and seal.

MUSCAT JELLY
Countrywide

MUSCATS are the black and white grapes from which the sweetest French and Italian dessert wines are made. Charles Sorel, a French novelist, wrote of them with Gallic pride in 1655: 'That only one grain (of muscats) was enough to make all England to be perpetually drunk.'

But, long ago, the English discovered that the humble gooseberry, if flavoured with elderflower, so resembled the grape as to be almost indistinguishable. Hence, the combination has been used in jellies and country wines for 200 years and more.

This jelly, with its glowing and reddish colour, is good equally with lamb or as an accompaniment to scones, butter and cream.

PREPARATION TIME: 45 MINUTES
STRAINING TIME: AT LEAST 4 HOURS
COOKING TIME: 30–40 MINUTES

INGREDIENTS TO YIELD ABOUT 4–5 LB. (1·8–2·3 KG.)

6 lb. (2·7 kg.) gooseberries
Sugar
12 heads of elderflowers

Wash the gooseberries and place in a large, heavy-based pan with enough cold water to cover. Bring to the boil, then simmer until soft—which takes about 30 minutes—stirring from time to time. Ladle the contents of the pan into a scalded jelly bag and leave to strain for at least 4 hours.

Heat the oven to 110°C (225°F)—gas mark ¼. Measure the strained juice and weigh out 1 lb. (450 g.) sugar for each pint (575/600 ml.). Place the sugar in an ovenproof dish in the middle of the oven to warm through for 10–15 minutes. Put the elderflower heads in a muslin bag.

Heat the juice gently and add the warmed sugar, stirring constantly until dissolved. Bring to the boil and cook rapidly for 7 minutes, then plunge in the muslin bag containing the elderflower heads and cook for a further 3–5 minutes, until the setting point is reached. Take out the elderflowers, skim if necessary, and pot and seal (see p. 360).

HERB JELLIES
Countrywide

YOU CAN MAKE a whole range of herb jellies—sage, rosemary, marjoram, basil—as well as mint.

Follow the basic recipe, replacing mint with sprigs of your chosen herb.

Herb jellies go very well with meats of all kinds—the general principle being to serve the animal with a plant it ate, or a herb that is native to the same locality. Thus, lamb is served with mint or rosemary, venison with rowan, and so on. They complement salads superbly but, in fact, herb jellies are practically interchangeable.

PREPARATION TIME: ABOUT 30 MINUTES
STRAINING TIME: AT LEAST 4 HOURS
COOKING TIME: 30 MINUTES

INGREDIENTS TO YIELD
4–5 LB. (1·8–2·3 KG.)

6 lb. (2·7 kg.) green cooking apples
Juice of 3 lemons
12 sprigs of fresh mint
Sugar

Wash and cut up the apples and put them in a large, heavy-based pan with enough water to cover. Add the lemon juice and 8 sprigs of mint. Bring to the boil and simmer for about 20 minutes, until the fruit is soft. Strain through a jelly bag for at least 4 hours.

Heat the oven to 110°C (225°F)—gas mark $\frac{1}{4}$. Measure the strained juice and weigh out 1 lb. (450 g.) of sugar for each pint (575/600 ml.). Put the sugar in an ovenproof dish and place in the middle of the oven to warm through for 10–15 minutes.

Pour the juice back into the pan and heat gently. Add the warmed sugar, stirring until dissolved. Bring to the boil and add the finely chopped leaves of the remaining mint.

Cook rapidly for about 10–15 minutes until setting point is reached (see p. 360). Skim if necessary, leave to cool for 3 minutes, then stir so that the mint is evenly distributed before potting and sealing.

ROWAN JELLY
Scotland

THE ROWAN, OR MOUNTAIN ASH, native to the hillier parts of Britain, now provides a glorious blaze of green and scarlet in many suburban streets and gardens.

Crosses of rowan wood were once considered an infallible defence against witchcraft:

'Rowan tree or reed
Put witches to speed.'

A bunch of the berries tied round a cow's neck ensured a safe calving.

Rowan Jelly has a beautiful, deep red-amber colour, and its sharp, tart flavour goes well with venison, game or mutton. To get the best flavour, pick the berries when they are fully ripe and well coloured, but you may need to pick them as soon as they turn orange, before the trees are stripped by birds.

You can use windfall apples instead of the crab apples included in the recipe, but if you do, add the juice of a lemon.

PREPARATION TIME: 50 MINUTES
STRAINING TIME: AT LEAST 4 HOURS
COOKING TIME: 35 MINUTES

INGREDIENTS TO YIELD
ABOUT 3–4 LB. (1·4–1·8 KG.)

2 lb. (900 g.) rowan berries
2 lb. (900 g.) crab apples
3 pints (1·7 litres) water
Sugar

Wash and pick over the berries, removing stalks. Wash the whole crab apples, removing any bruised parts. Place the fruit in a heavy-based preserving pan and pour the water over it. Bring to the boil, cover the pan and simmer the fruit for about 20–25 minutes, until tender.

Strain the fruit through a scalded jelly bag, leaving to drip for at least 4 hours. Do not squeeze the bag, as this would make the jelly cloudy.

Heat the oven to 110°C (225°F)—gas mark $\frac{1}{4}$. Measure the strained juice and weigh out 1 lb. (450 g.) sugar for each pint (575/600 ml.). Put the sugar in an ovenproof dish and place in the middle of the oven to warm through for 10–15 minutes.

Warm the strained juice and stir in the warmed sugar until dissolved. Bring to the boil, and boil rapidly for about 10 minutes or until the setting point is reached (see p. 360). Skim the jelly if necessary, and then pot and seal it (see p. 361).

Jelly from the scarlet berries of the wild rowan tree. Its tartness counteracts the rich flavours of game.

DAMSON CHEESE
Countrywide

FRUIT CHEESE uses a large amount of fruit for a comparatively small yield, but there is no need to wait for a glut to make it. The pulp left from jelly-making serves just as well as whole fruit. Use strongly flavoured fruit such as damsons, plums, blackberries or apples.

Unlike a fruit curd, which has a limited keeping time because it contains eggs, fruit cheese is made for keeping. Curd is meant for spreading, but cheese is much firmer and is served in slices or wedges with chopped nuts and cream as a dessert, or with scones. Pot in a mould or small, straight-sided jars with wide mouths so that it can be turned out easily.

PREPARATION TIME: 30 MINUTES
COOKING TIME: $1\frac{1}{4}$ HOURS

INGREDIENTS TO YIELD
3–4 LB. (1·4–1·8 KG.)

6 lb. (2·7 kg.) damsons and $\frac{1}{2}$ pint (275/300 ml.) water, or damson pulp left from jelly-making
Sugar

If using whole damsons, wash and place in a large pan with the water. Bring to the boil, then cover and simmer very gently for about 30 minutes until tender. Pass the fruit pulp through a hair or nylon sieve and weigh it.

Put the weighed pulp (fresh or jelly) in the cleaned pan and add the sugar, allowing 1 lb. (450 g.) to each 1 lb. (450 g.) of pulp. Heat gently, stirring until all the sugar is dissolved, then cook gently for 45 minutes–1 hour, stirring frequently to prevent the cheese from burning or sticking.

The cheese is ready when it reaches a stiff consistency so that a wooden spoon drawn across it leaves a clear line. Pot and seal immediately (see p. 362). Leave to mature for at least 2 months.

ORANGE CHUTNEY
Countrywide

THIS IS a fairly powerful chutney, but provided you like its fiery, fruity flavour, there are few better accompaniments to duck, game or cold ham. Remove as much of the orange pith as possible; it can give the chutney a bitter taste.

PREPARATION TIME: 45 MINUTES–1 HOUR
COOKING TIME: ABOUT $2\frac{1}{2}$ HOURS

INGREDIENTS TO YIELD
ABOUT 7 LB. (3·2 KG.)

1 lb. (450 g.) onions, peeled and chopped
2 lb. (900 g.) cooking apples, peeled, cored and chopped
4 lb. (1·8 kg.) sweet oranges
1 lb. (450 g.) sultanas or seedless raisins
1 tablespoon salt
2 teaspoons ground ginger
1 teaspoon Cayenne pepper
3 pints (1·7 litres) vinegar
2 lb. (900 g.) sugar

Put the onions in a very large, heavy-based pan with a little water. Bring to the boil, then cook gently for about 10 minutes, until soft. Add the chopped apples and continue cooking for a further 15 minutes.

Meanwhile, thinly peel the oranges, discarding as much white pith as possible. Put the peel and the orange pulp through a mincer, catching the juice in a bowl.

Add the minced oranges, juice, dried fruit, salt, spices and half the vinegar to the pan with the onions and apples. Simmer for 1 hour, or until the peel is tender when tested with a knife.

Add the sugar and the rest of the vinegar, stirring until the sugar dissolves. Continue cooking until the mixture becomes thick, stirring from time to time. Pot and seal (see p. 364). Leave to mature for 4–6 weeks.

Vary the amount of Cayenne pepper according to taste.

Plump, tart damsons in a smooth fruit cheese. Serve as a dessert or with scones.

APPLE, DATE AND WALNUT CHUTNEY
Countrywide

CHUTNEYS ARE NOT SUPPOSED to have appeared in Europe before the 17th century, yet there is a medieval French recipe for a compote that sounds like a highly complicated version of this modern chutney. Among its less readily obtainable ingredients were grain of Paradise and red cedar. Another disadvantage was that it took five months to make.

This speedier recipe makes a sweet, nutty accompaniment to pork and ham, a bright topping for cocktail snacks and also a novel addition to cheese sandwiches of all kinds.

PREPARATION TIME: ABOUT 50 MINUTES
COOKING TIME: ABOUT $1\frac{1}{2}$–2 HOURS

INGREDIENTS TO YIELD
ABOUT 4 LB. (1·8 KG.)

- *1 lb. (450 g.) onions, peeled and chopped*
- *2 lb. (900 g.) cooking apples, peeled, cored and chopped*
- *$1\frac{1}{2}$ lb. (700 g.) dates, stoned and chopped*
- *3 oz. (75 g.) walnuts, chopped*
- *1 pint (575/600 ml.) vinegar*
- *1 teaspoon salt*
- *1 teaspoon ground ginger*
- *1 teaspoon Cayenne pepper*
- *8 oz. (225 g.) sugar*

Put the onions in a large, heavy-based pan with a little water. Bring to the boil and simmer until soft. Add the apples and continue cooking gently for 15–20 minutes. Put in the dates, walnuts, salt, spices and half the vinegar. Cook, stirring occasionally, until the mixture thickens.

Add the sugar and the rest of the vinegar, stirring until the sugar dissolves. Continue to simmer until the chutney becomes really thick. Stir occasionally. Pot and seal (see p. 364). Leave to mature for 2–3 weeks.

WINDFALL CHUTNEY
Kent

THIS IS A GOOD WAY of making the best of the gardening disaster of a chilly and exuberant early autumn. Windfall plums, pears and apples blend happily with the sharp-tasting green tomatoes to provide an ideal complement to either cold meats or strong farmhouse cheeses. Kent, a county of well-stocked gardens and strong south-easterlies, was the natural birthplace for this recipe.

PREPARATION TIME: ABOUT 1 HOUR
COOKING TIME: ABOUT $2\frac{1}{4}$ HOURS

INGREDIENTS TO YIELD
ABOUT 9–10 LB. (4·1–4·5 KG.)

- *$2\frac{1}{2}$ lb. (1·1 kg.) windfall apples, peeled and cored*
- *$2\frac{1}{2}$ lb. (1·1 kg.) windfall pears, peeled and cored*
- *$2\frac{1}{2}$ lb. (1·1 kg.) windfall plums, stoned*
- *2 lb. (900 g.) onions, peeled and chopped*
- *2 lb. (900 g.) green tomatoes, washed and quartered*
- *8 oz. (225 g.) mixed seedless raisins and sultanas*
- *1 lb. (450 g.) marrow flesh, cut in $\frac{1}{2}$ in. (1·5 cm.) cubes*
- *$1\frac{1}{2}$ pints (850 ml.) malt vinegar*
- *2 oz. (50 g.) whole mixed pickling spice, tied in a muslin bag*
- *8 oz. (225 g.) soft brown sugar*
- *2 oz. (50 g.) salt*

Cut away any bruised portions of the apples, pears and plums and chop the sound fruit into small chunks, about $\frac{1}{2}$ in. (1·5 cm.) across. Place the prepared fruit in a large, heavy-based pan with the chopped onions, quartered tomatoes, dried fruit and cubed marrow flesh.

Add half the vinegar, and the spices tied in a muslin bag. Bring to the boil, then simmer until tender and pulpy, stirring occasionally.

Put in the sugar, salt and the rest of the vinegar, stirring until the sugar dissolves. Continue cooking gently, stirring from time to time, until the chutney becomes thick. Remove the spices, pot and seal (see p. 364). Leave to mature for 4–6 weeks.

Windfall Chutney—a blend of autumn flavours to accompany meat or cheese.

GOOSEBERRY CHUTNEY
Countrywide

CHUTNEYS EVOLVED IN INDIA as a cooling or piquant accompaniment to curried dishes and, as such, were imported to this country some time during the 18th century.

As the years of the raj progressed, however, Imperial preference often dictated modifications in the traditional recipes. The sahibs who retired to England found ingenious replacements for the Indian ingredients.

This sweet-sharp chutney probably belongs to the second category.

PREPARATION TIME: 30–40 MINUTES
COOKING TIME: ABOUT $1\frac{1}{4}$ HOURS

INGREDIENTS TO YIELD ABOUT 4 LB. (1·8 KG.)

3 lb. (1·4 kg.) gooseberries, washed, topped and tailed
8 oz. (225 g.) onions, peeled and finely chopped
12 oz. (350 g.) seedless raisins or dates, chopped, or a mixture
1 tablespoon salt
1 tablespoon ground ginger
1 teaspoon ground mixed spices
1 pint (575/600 ml.) white vinegar
8 oz. (225 g.) sugar

Put the gooseberries and onions in a large, heavy-based pan with just enough water to prevent them burning as they cook. Bring to the boil, then simmer for about 20 minutes, until the fruit and onions become soft and pulpy, stirring occasionally.

Stir in the dried fruit, salt, spices and half the vinegar. Cook gently again for another 20 minutes or so, until the mixture thickens. Add the sugar and the rest of the vinegar, stirring until the sugar dissolves. Simmer gently for a further 20 minutes or more, stirring occasionally until thick. Pot and seal (see p. 364). Leave to mature for 2–4 weeks.

Gooseberry Chutney—a British country-garden version of an Indian side dish.

GREEN TOMATO CHUTNEY
Countrywide

THE TOMATO, a native of tropical America, made its European debut in the middle of the 16th century when, like many novel foods, it was erroneously hailed as an aphrodisiac—hence its early name of 'love apple' or '*pomme d'amour*'.

By the time this notion was abandoned, the tomato was widely grown in Europe and Britain. Our summers are not always sunny enough to permit the fruit to ripen, and this chutney is the best way of utilising green tomatoes.

It goes well with cold meats and cheeses, and can be served with or added to curries.

PREPARATION TIME: ABOUT 30 MINUTES
COOKING TIME: ABOUT 2 HOURS

INGREDIENTS TO YIELD ABOUT 6–7 LB. (2·7–3·2 KG.)

4 lb. (1·8 kg.) green tomatoes, washed and chopped
$1\frac{1}{2}$ lb. (700 g.) shallots or onions, peeled and chopped
1 lb. (450 g.) cooking apples, peeled, cored and chopped
1 pint (575/600 ml.) vinegar
8 red chillies
1 oz. (25 g.) dried root ginger
8 oz. (225 g.) seedless raisins or dates, chopped
2 teaspoons salt
1 lb. (450 g.) sugar

Put the chopped tomatoes, shallots or onions and the apples in a large, heavy-based pan with half the vinegar. Bring to the boil, then simmer gently for about 30 minutes until tender.

Tie the chillies and root ginger in a muslin bag, bruise with a hammer, and add to the pan with the raisins or chopped dates. Cook, stirring from time to time until the mixture thickens, after about 1 hour.

Add the salt, sugar and the rest of the vinegar, stirring well until the sugar dissolves. Continue cooking, pressing the bag of spices occasionally with a wooden spoon, until the mixture is thick. Remove the muslin bag before potting and sealing (see p. 364). Leave to mature for 6 weeks.

RED TOMATO CHUTNEY
Countrywide

IT SEEMS A PITY to turn sound, ripe red tomatoes into chutney, but if there is a glut in your garden, or they are especially cheap in the shops, capitalise on the bounty to make this extraordinarily versatile companion to fish, cheese and meats.

PREPARATION TIME: 30–40 MINUTES
COOKING TIME: 1½–2 HOURS

INGREDIENTS TO YIELD ABOUT 4 LB. (1·8 KG.)

6 lb. (2·7 kg.) ripe tomatoes, peeled and chopped
1 lb. (450 g.) onions, peeled and chopped
1 oz. (25 g.) salt
2 teaspoons paprika
¼ teaspoon Cayenne pepper
½ pint (275/300 ml.) spiced distilled or malt vinegar (see p. 363)
12 oz. (350 g.) white or brown sugar

Put the tomatoes and onions in a large, heavy-based pan. Bring to the boil, then simmer for 20–30 minutes until soft. Add the salt, spices and half the vinegar and cook gently for about 45 minutes more, or until thick.

Add the sugar and the rest of the vinegar, stirring until the sugar dissolves. Continue simmering until thick, stirring occasionally. Pot and seal (see p. 364). Leave to mature for 3–5 weeks.

MINT SAUCE
Countrywide

LIKE MANY aromatic herbs, garden mint was brought to this country by the Romans, and has held an honoured place in British cookery ever since.

Perfect with lamb, this recipe is designed to provide a sauce that will keep for four months or more.

An even longer-lasting version has the leaves chopped finely, put in a jar and covered with golden syrup. To use, take a spoonful of the mixture, stir with wine vinegar and serve. If you make enough, this method will provide you with fresh-tasting Mint Sauce until the new mint grows.

PREPARATION TIME: 5 MINUTES
COOKING TIME: ABOUT 15 MINUTES

INGREDIENTS TO YIELD ABOUT ½ PINT (275/300 ML.)

½ pint (275/300 ml.) distilled white vinegar
6 oz. (175 g.) sugar
3 oz. (75 g.) sprigs of mint, washed and drained

Put the vinegar with the sugar in a heavy-based pan. Bring to the boil slowly, stirring continuously until the sugar dissolves. Boil for 1 minute, then remove from the heat.

Strip the leaves from the washed and drained mint, chop them and add to the pan. Put the pan back on the heat and bring to the boil for about 1 minute more. Allow to cool before bottling (see p. 364).

PLUM SAUCE
Countrywide

A THICK, FRUITY SAUCE always goes well with cold meats or poultry, and plums are particularly useful for sauces because they have a sweet-sharp flavour which blends well with spices.

For this sauce, a mixture of plum varieties, including damsons, can be used, so it is a good way to use up windfalls or damaged fruit. Victoria or yellow plums give a golden-brown sauce, particularly if white vinegar is used instead of malt.

PREPARATION TIME: 15 MINUTES
COOKING TIME: 70 MINUTES

INGREDIENTS TO YIELD ABOUT 1½ PINTS (850 ML.)

2 lb. (900 g.) plums
8 oz. (225 g.) sugar
1 pint (575/600 ml.) malt vinegar
1 teaspoon salt
1 teaspoon ground ginger
½ teaspoon Cayenne pepper
8 cloves

Wash and dry the plums. Cut them up roughly and put into a large, heavy-based pan with the stones. Add the sugar, vinegar, salt, ginger, pepper and cloves. Stir well over a gentle heat until the sugar dissolves, then bring to the boil.

Reduce the heat and simmer for 30 minutes stirring occasionally. Then put the mixture through a sieve, rubbing well to make sure all the purée goes through. Wash the pan and return the fruit purée. Simmer for 40 minutes, stirring occasionally until the sauce takes on the consistency of whipping cream.

Bottle and seal the sauce (see p. 364), and keep for at least 1 month before using.

BENGAL SAUCE
Countrywide

ALMOST CERTAINLY, the original principal ingredient of Bengal Sauce would have been mangoes—apples do not appear in Indian cuisine. All the same, chutneys and sauces made from apples grown in Kashmir were much relished by the Britons of the raj, who used them as a refreshingly contrasting accompaniment to meats and curries.

PREPARATION TIME: 30 MINUTES
COOKING TIME: 1–1¼ HOURS

INGREDIENTS TO YIELD ABOUT 1½–2 PINTS (850 ML.–1·1 LITRES)

3 lb. (1·4 kg.) cooking apples, peeled, cored and sliced
8 oz. (225 g.) onions, peeled and sliced
1½ pints (850 ml.) malt vinegar
2 oz. (50 g.) garlic, peeled and finely chopped
1 lb. (450 g.) Demerara sugar
8 oz. (225 g.) seedless raisins
2 oz. (50 g.) ground ginger
1 oz. (25 g.) mustard seeds
6 dried red chillies

Put the sliced apples and onions in a large, heavy-based pan with the vinegar. Add the chopped garlic and all the other ingredients. Bring to the boil slowly, stirring continuously until the sugar dissolves. Then simmer gently for about 50 minutes, stirring occasionally until the mixture becomes thick.

Rub the mixture through a sieve into a large bowl, clean the pan and return the sauce to it. Put back on a low heat and continue cooking, stirring from time to time, until it takes on the consistency of whipping cream.

Bottle (see p. 364) and keep for 6–8 weeks before use.

SWEETCORN AND CABBAGE RELISH
Countrywide

SWEETCORN or maize was the prime food source that sustained the great empires of the Toltecs, the Mayas, the Aztecs and the Incas.

Columbus is credited with bringing the first sweetcorn seeds back to Europe, and its cultivation soon spread to the warm Mediterranean lands, then on to Asia and Africa. Varieties suitable for growing in Britain's uncertain climate have been developed only in the last 30 years, but maize has long been familiar on our breakfast tables—milled, flattened, roasted in giant ovens and then dried—in the form of cornflakes.

This relish is delicious eaten with cheese, any kind of cold meat or mixed into potato salad.

PREPARATION TIME: 20 MINUTES
COOKING TIME: 25 MINUTES

INGREDIENTS TO YIELD ABOUT 4 LB. (1·8 KG.)

- *5 ripe corn cobs*
- *1 small white or red cabbage*
- *2 medium onions*
- *1 pint (575/600 ml.) white vinegar*
- *4 oz. (100/125 g.) sugar*
- *2 teaspoons salt*
- *1 tablespoon dry mustard*
- *1 teaspoon turmeric*

Strip the husks and silk from the corn cobs. Boil for 5 minutes, then strip the corn from the cobs with a knife or a pointed teaspoon. Remove and discard the outer leaves from the cabbage, then core and shred it. Peel and chop the onions.

Heat the vinegar, sugar, salt and spices together in a large, heavy-based pan, stirring to dissolve the sugar. Bring to the boil and add the corn, cabbage and onion. Simmer for about 10 minutes, until the vegetables are just cooked but still crunchy.

Pot and seal the relish (see p. 363), and leave to mature for at least 8 weeks before using it.

TOMATO SAUCE
Countrywide

THIS IS THE BEST KNOWN of all our traditional sauces. Though it is true that the bottled variety frequently conceals a whole battery of culinary sins, well-made Tomato Sauce or ketchup is the finest of all complements to breakfast—that greatest of British meals.

Bacon, eggs, sausages and, in the north of England, black and white puddings too, all take on a new and benevolent glow in its sweet-sharp company at the beginning of the day.

PREPARATION TIME: 20 MINUTES
STANDING TIME: 2–3 HOURS
COOKING TIME: 45 MINUTES–1 HOUR

INGREDIENTS TO YIELD ABOUT $2\frac{1}{2}$ PINTS (1·4 LITRES)

- *1 teaspoon whole allspice*
- *2–3 in. (5–8 cm.) cinnamon stick*
- *3–4 blades mace*
- *1 pint (575/600 ml.) distilled white vinegar, or ½ pint (275/300 ml.) white vinegar and ½ pint (275/300 ml.) tarragon vinegar*
- *6 lb. (2·7 kg.) ripe tomatoes, washed and sliced*
- *1 oz. (25 g.) salt*
- *1 teaspoon paprika*
- *8 oz. (225 g.) sugar*

Tie the allspice, cinnamon stick and mace in a muslin bag and put in a pan with the vinegar. Bring to the boil, then remove from the heat, cover and leave to infuse for 2–3 hours.

Meanwhile, put the tomatoes in a large, heavy-based pan and simmer until pulpy. Rub the pulp through a sieve into a bowl, clean the pan and return the strained pulp to it.

Add the salt and paprika and cook gently, uncovered, stirring occasionally until thick. Add the sugar and the vinegar, stirring continuously until the sugar dissolves. Continue cooking slowly until the sauce takes on the consistency of whipping cream.

Pour into hot bottles, leaving about 1 in. (2·5 cm.) space at the top, and seal immediately. This sauce does not keep well unless sterilised (see p. 364). It can be used at once.

PICKLED EGGS
Countrywide

PICKLED EGGS have been traditional pub fare ever since some early-19th-century genius discovered that, like bread and cheese and cockles and mussels, they added a new dimension to a pint of ale. They are also excellent with mixed salad and cold meats.

Perhaps they are not as common now, but it is well worth pickling a dozen or so for their delicate, creamy flavour. Country people still pickle small, round bantam eggs. The longer you leave them in the jar, the better.

PREPARATION TIME: 5 MINUTES
COOKING TIME: 10–15 MINUTES

INGREDIENTS FOR TWELVE

- *12 fresh eggs*
- *Spiced malt or white vinegar (see p. 363)*
- *2 blades of mace*

Hard-boil the eggs for 10 minutes, giving them an occasional stir during the first few minutes to help centralise the yolks. Plunge them immediately into plenty of cold water to prevent a black ring forming round the yolks.

When the eggs are cool, shell them carefully and pack them loosely into clean glass or stone jars. Cover with cold spiced vinegar, adding the blades of mace.

Seal at once and keep for at least 3 weeks.

FRUIT VINEGAR
Countrywide

FRUIT VINEGARS, sweetened with honey or sugar, are not now so widely used as they were by the Victorians. This is a pity, for they are easy to make and quite delicious. Drunk neat and piping hot they are an excellent remedy for sore throats; diluted, 1 measure to 8 measures of water, and iced, they make a refreshing drink on a summer's day.

PREPARATION TIME: 15 MINUTES
STANDING TIME: 3–6 DAYS
COOKING TIME: 20 MINUTES

INGREDIENTS TO YIELD 2 PINTS (1·1 LITRES)

- *1 lb. (450 g.) blackberries, raspberries or black currants*
- *1 pint (575/600 ml.) wine or cider vinegar*
- *Sugar*

Wash the fruit, place it in a large china or earthenware bowl and pour the vinegar over it. Cover the bowl with a cloth and leave to stand in a cool place for 3–6 days, stirring occasionally.

Strain off and measure the liquid. Weigh out 1 lb. (450 g.) sugar for each pint (575/600 ml.). Pour the liquid into a large, heavy-based pan and heat gently. Add the sugar and stir until it has dissolved, then boil for 10 minutes. Pour into bottles and cork (see p. 364). Leave to mature for at least 2 weeks. Properly stored, it will keep for 6 months.

HERB VINEGAR
Countrywide

UNTIL HALF A CENTURY AGO, many country people fermented their own vinegars from cowslips, dandelions and rhubarb, leaving them to mature for a year or so in a cask before using.

Probably no one makes these pleasant, tangy vinegars nowadays, though their close relatives, herb vinegars, still remain firm favourites. Use them to give an extra lift to pickles, salad dressings and sauces.

It is, incidentally, a good idea to retain vinegars used for pickling when the pickle itself has been consumed. Onion and walnut vinegars can be used in some ketchups, and cucumber vinegar in salad dressings.

PREPARATION TIME: ABOUT 10 MINUTES

INGREDIENTS TO YIELD
1 PINT (575/600 ML.)

- *4–6 oz. (100–175 g.) freshly gathered tarragon, or sage, rosemary, mint, basil or other herb*
- *About 1 pint (575/600 ml.) white wine vinegar*

The subtle taste of herbs suspended in vinegar.

Pick the herbs just before they flower. Wash the leaves and the tender parts of the stalks, put them in a large jar, then bruise them with a wooden spoon.

Top up with wine vinegar, cover with a cloth and leave to steep for 2–3 weeks. If you use a clear glass jar, stand it in a dark cupboard to prevent colour loss.

Strain the vinegar through muslin. Place a fresh, washed sprig of the herb in the bottle, before bottling in the same way as sauces (see p. 365).

Leave the vinegar to mature for 2–4 weeks before use.

BREAD AND BUTTER PICKLE
Countrywide

EXCELLENT WITH HAM and other cold meats, this mild old country pickle gets its name from the custom of giving children a hunk of bread and butter or dripping, topped by a spoonful of the pickle, to munch on their way to school.

Virtually no cooking is required, so this pickle is remarkably easy to make. It is also a good way of using up misshapen, garden-grown cucumbers.

PREPARATION TIME: ABOUT 15 MINUTES
STANDING TIME: 3 HOURS
COOKING TIME: ABOUT 15 MINUTES

INGREDIENTS TO YIELD
ABOUT 4 LB. (1·8 KG.)

- *2½ lb. (1·1 kg.) cucumbers*
- *1 lb. (450 g.) onions, peeled and thinly sliced*
- *2 oz. (50 g.) salt*
- *1 pint (575/600 ml.) white vinegar*
- *6 oz. (175 g.) granulated sugar*
- *2 teaspoons mustard seeds*
- *3 cloves*
- *1 teaspoon turmeric*
- *2 teaspoons grated horseradish (optional)*

Wipe the cucumbers, but do not peel them. Cut them into slices $\frac{1}{8}$ in. (3 mm.) thick. Put them on a large plate with the sliced onions and sprinkle with the salt. Cover with another plate and leave for 3 hours.

Drain and rinse thoroughly and put in a large, heavy-based pan with the vinegar, sugar and spices. Heat gently, stirring occasionally until the sugar dissolves. Remove from the heat as soon as boiling point is reached. Pack the vegetables, spices and vinegar into hot jars, fill to the top and seal at once (see p. 363). Leave to mature for 6–8 weeks.

Spiced Crab Apples
Countrywide

LONG BEFORE crab-apple jelly was invented, medieval cooks created pickles and sauces from verjuice, a kind of vinegar made from crab apples. Vinegar itself, made from sour green grapes and mostly imported, gradually replaced the English product—at least in the homes of the rich—and verjuice came to be regarded as a poor, rustic substitute.

Yet as late as 1744, an East Anglian farmer wrote:

'It is much to be admir'd that we should give so great a price for Lemons and Limes and despise the Crab ... of which is made an Acid no less Pleasant and more Improvable, than what comes from any of them ...'

Spiced Crab Apples belong to the verjuice era, and were probably a forerunner of crab-apple jelly. Use these, too, to complement game and cold meats.

PREPARATION TIME: 15 MINUTES
COOKING TIME: ABOUT 1 HOUR

INGREDIENTS TO YIELD ABOUT 2 LB. (900 G.)

- *2 lb. (900 g.) sound crab apples*
- *¾ pint (450 ml.) malt vinegar*
- *1 lb. (450 g.) granulated or brown sugar*
- *8 cloves and 1 piece root ginger, tied in a muslin bag*
- *2 teaspoons ground allspice*
- *2 teaspoons ground cinnamon*

Wash the apples and remove the stalks, but do not peel or core them. Prick in a few places with a stainless-steel knitting needle or fork.

Put the vinegar in a large, heavy-based pan. Add the sugar and spices and place over a gentle heat, stirring the mixture until the sugar dissolves.

Bring the liquid to the boil and simmer for 5 minutes. Add the crab apples and simmer for about 6 minutes, until barely tender. Boiling too vigorously will make the fruit disintegrate.

Remove the apples carefully with a slotted spoon and put them gently in warm, sterilised jars. They should still be slightly firm.

Bring the liquid back to the boil, and boil steadily for about 30 minutes or until reduced by half. Leave it to cool for about 15 minutes, so that it will not cook the apples further when it is poured over them. Remove the bag of spices and pour the syrup carefully over the apples, filling the jars to the brim.

Cover and seal (see p. 363). Leave to mature for at least 8 weeks.

Piccalilli
Countrywide

A RECIPE of 1694 describes how 'To pickle-Lila, an Indian pickle'. But who or what Lila was, history does not relate.

An essential ingredient, mustard, was introduced to Britain by the Romans. They enjoyed it with pork, fish and vegetable dishes, and for centuries it was one of the cheapest spices available, since it was among the few that were home grown. During the Middle Ages, mustard seeds were ground, blanched and mixed with vinegar to make a pickle for turnips, and mustard sauce was made with honey, oil and vinegar.

Piccalilli, a good way of making use of end-of-season garden produce, goes well with cold meats. Use equal quantities of vegetables to make up the total amount.

PREPARATION TIME: 45 MINUTES
STANDING TIME: 24 HOURS
COOKING TIME: 15–20 MINUTES

INGREDIENTS TO YIELD ABOUT 6 LB. (2·7 KG.)

- *6 lb. (2·7 kg.) prepared vegetables: cucumber or gherkin and marrow in ½ in. (1·5 cm.) cubes; green beans, strung and in 1 in. (2·5 cm.) slices; small onions, peeled; small green tomatoes, sliced; cauliflower sprigs*
- *1 lb. (450 g.) cooking salt*
- *½ oz. (15 g.) turmeric*
- *1 oz. (25 g.) dry mustard*
- *1 oz. (25 g.) ground ginger*
- *6 oz. (175 g.) granulated sugar*
- *2 pints (1·1 litres) white vinegar*
- *1½ oz. (40 g.) plain flour or cornflour*

Spread the vegetables on a large dish and strew the salt over them. Put a plate on top, weight it, and leave for 24 hours. Next day, thoroughly drain, wash and rinse the vegetables.

Using a wooden spoon, stir the spices and sugar into most of the vinegar in a large pan. Heat gently, stirring until the sugar has dissolved. Add the prepared vegetables and simmer gently for 10–15 minutes, until the required texture is reached. The degree of crispness or tenderness depends on individual taste, but the vegetables must be whole, not mashed.

Blend the flour with the remaining vinegar and add to the pan. Bring to the boil, stirring carefully. Simmer for 2–3 minutes. Pot and seal (see p. 363). Leave for 6–8 weeks.

Pickled Onions
Countrywide

THE MOST POPULAR RELISH in Britain must be Pickled Onions. Not only are they eaten with cold meats, but they are an essential ingredient in the traditional ploughman's lunch of farmhouse cheese and crusty bread.

Small pickling onions can be grown or bought, but shallots may be used instead. If the onions are packed in cold vinegar, they will remain beautifully crisp during storage.

People with a sweet tooth can add 2 teaspoons of soft brown sugar to each jar of onions.

PREPARATION TIME: 1½–2 HOURS
SOAKING TIME: 36 HOURS

INGREDIENTS TO YIELD ABOUT 6 LB. (2·7 KG.)

- *6 lb. (2·7 kg.) pickling onions*
- *1 lb. (450 g.) cooking salt*
- *8 pints (4·5 litres) water*

For the second brining:

- *1 lb. (450 g.) cooking salt*
- *8 pints (4·5 litres) water*
- *2 pints (1·1 litres) spiced vinegar (see p. 363)*

Place the onions, unpeeled, in a brine made by dissolving the salt in the water. Cover with a plate, to keep the onions below the surface of the brine, and leave to soak for 12 hours.

Next day, drain the onions. Place them in a large bowl and scald them in boiling water for 1 minute. Drain, then top, tail and peel them.

Prepare a second solution of brine and leave the peeled onions to soak in it, covered by a plate, for a further 24 hours. Then remove the onions and drain thoroughly. Pot into clean bottles or jars, pour over cold, spiced vinegar and seal (see p. 363). Leave to mature for 6–8 weeks.

PICKLED RED CABBAGE
Countrywide

PICKLED CABBAGE has been eaten since the 18th century at least, when its sharp, near-lemony flavour led Captain Cook to believe, erroneously, that preserved cabbages fermented with juniper berries were a preventative for scurvy.

Pickled Red Cabbage is delicious with cold meats, sausages and English cheeses. It is best made in late autumn when the cabbages have been touched by a few early frosts; these help to enhance the characteristic texture. It will be ready for use after 1 week and the result will be crisp, bright red and sharp—unlike shop-bought pickles. It loses its crispness after 10–12 weeks' storage. This recipe may equally be used for white cabbage.

PREPARATION TIME: 30 MINUTES
STANDING TIME: 24 HOURS

INGREDIENTS TO YIELD
ABOUT 4–5 LB. (1·8–2·3 KG.)

1 red cabbage
4–6 oz. (100–175 g.) cooking salt
¾–1 pint (450–600 ml.) spiced malt or white vinegar (see p. 363)

Choose a good, firm cabbage of even colouring. Remove any discoloured leaves, cut into quarters and wash well. Cut away the tough inner stalk, and shred the cabbage. Place the cabbage and salt in layers in a basin, ending with a layer of salt. Leave for 24 hours.

Rinse thoroughly in cold water and drain well. Pack the cabbage loosely into jars, cover with cold, spiced vinegar and cover at once (see p. 363). Leave the pickle to mature for at least 1 week before using.

A trinity of crisp pickles—Onions, Red Cabbage and Piccalilli—goes well with sweet-cured ham.

MINCEMEAT
Countrywide

Originally, Mincemeat was made with minced meat—usually beef or tongue—mixed with dried fruit, highly spiced and preserved with brandy or another spirit. Today the meat is replaced by beef suet and the mixture contains apples.

Mincemeat is better if it matures for a week or two before use. It will remain fresh and juicy for up to six months if covered with a plastic top or screw-on lid to prevent it from drying out.

PREPARATION TIME: 45 MINUTES
STANDING TIME: 2–3 DAYS

INGREDIENTS TO YIELD 7 LB. (3·2 KG.)

- *1½ lb. (700 g.) cooking apples*
- *1 lb. (450 g.) seedless raisins*
- *1 lb. (450 g.) sultanas*
- *12 oz. (350 g.) currants*
- *8 oz. (225 g.) chopped candied peel*
- *1 lb. (450 g.) soft brown sugar*
- *1 lb. (450 g.) shredded suet, finely chopped*
- *2 oz. (50 g.) flaked or chopped almonds*
- *Juice and grated rinds of 2 lemons*
- *½ teaspoon ground mixed spice*
- *4 tablespoons brandy, whisky or rum*

Wash, peel and core the apples. Combine with the raisins, currants, sultanas and candied peel. Mince coarsely and place in a mixing bowl.

Add the sugar, suet, almonds, lemon juice and rind, and the spice. Mix thoroughly.

Cover the bowl with a tea towel and leave for 2–3 days. Stir the mixture well two or three times a day. Then add the spirit.

Pot and seal as jam (see p. 361).

Dried fruits, almonds and spices, laced with spirits, are the principal ingredients in a rich Mincemeat.

HODGKIN
Kent

Hodgkin is not a person, but a Kentish diminutive of 'hodge-podge', a 15th-century term for a mixture. And it takes all summer to mature as fruits are added—from June for strawberries until late September for autumn-fruiting raspberries.

After adding the last fruits, let the Hodgkin mature until Christmas. It is superb with cream, ice-cream or meringues, and the brandy can be served as a liqueur.

INGREDIENTS TO YIELD ABOUT 5 LB. (2·3 KG.)

- *1 lb. (450 g.) each strawberries, raspberries, pitted cherries, halved apricots and sliced peaches*
- *2½ lb. (1·1 kg.) granulated or caster sugar*
- *1 bottle of brandy*

Start the season with strawberries. Place 1 lb. (450 g.) clean, hulled fruit in a large stone jar. Add 8 oz. (225 g.) granulated or caster sugar. Pour in enough brandy to cover, and seal as jam (see p. 361).

As each fruit comes into season, add 1 lb. (450 g.) fruit, 8 oz. (225 g.) sugar and brandy to cover, stirring gently with a wooden spoon or spatula with each addition.

Finish in September. Cover with a tightly tied square of plastic skin or a tight-fitting lid. Leave to mature until Christmas.

APRICOT CURD
Countrywide

TUDOR GARDENERS THOUGHT of calling the apricot, rare in their day, 'the hasty peach tree', since the fruit resembled a peach, but ripened much earlier. Thinking better of it, they called it 'apricock' instead, a word derived from the Portuguese name, *albricoque*.

Like all fruit curds, this one has a shelf life of a couple of weeks at most, but will keep in the refrigerator for about 4 weeks. To avoid waste, plan its use in advance.

PREPARATION TIME: 10 MINUTES
SOAKING TIME: 24 HOURS
COOKING TIME: ABOUT 45 MINUTES

INGREDIENTS TO YIELD
ABOUT 2 LB. (900 G.)

6 oz. (175 g.) dried apricots
8 oz. (225 g.) caster sugar
2 oz. (50 g.) butter
Grated rind and juice of 1 lemon
2 eggs, beaten

Wash the apricots, cover with water and leave to soak for 24 hours. Tip into a pan, bring to the boil and simmer until tender; this takes about 30 minutes. Put through a coarse sieve or liquidiser.

Put the apricot pulp in the top of a double saucepan or in a large bowl over a pan of boiling water. Add the caster sugar and butter with the grated lemon rind and juice.

Cook over a low heat, stirring continuously until the sugar has dissolved. Remove from the heat and strain the beaten eggs into the pan or bowl. Return to a low heat and cook until the curd will coat the back of a spoon, stirring occasionally. Pot and seal (see p. 362).

Lemon Curd, a variation of 17th-century cheesecake, makes a smooth cake filling.

LEMON OR ORANGE CURD
Countrywide

LEMON CURD seems to be descended from the curd tarts of the early 17th century that were known as cheesecakes. Their fillings were composed of curds, eggs and spices.

Later in the century, as lemons became more widely available, the lemon cheesecake, filled with a mixture of pounded lemon peel, egg yolks, sugar and butter, came into vogue. Orange cheesecake was also made from the peel of Seville oranges, which was first boiled two or three times to reduce the bitter flavour.

But more than 200 years were to pass before it occurred to anyone that the filling might be delicious if spread on bread and butter.

PREPARATION TIME: 20 MINUTES
COOKING TIME: 30–40 MINUTES

INGREDIENTS TO YIELD
ABOUT $1\frac{1}{2}$–2 LB. (700–900 G.)

Juice and finely grated peel of 3 large or 4 medium lemons (or oranges)
8 oz. (225 g.) butter
1 lb. (450 g.) caster sugar
5 eggs, beaten

Place the juice and finely grated peel in the top of a double saucepan or in a bowl over a saucepan of boiling water. Add the butter and caster sugar and stir gently over a low heat until the sugar is completely dissolved.

Take the pan from the heat and strain in the beaten eggs.

Put back over a low heat and cook gently until the mixture coats the back of the spoon, stirring occasionally. Pot and seal (see p. 362).

This curd has a shelf life of 2 weeks but will keep for up to 1 month in the refrigerator.

Lemon Jelly Marmalade
Countrywide

For those who prefer a clear marmalade, the extra time taken in the making is well worth it. The light golden sparkling jelly, perhaps with a few pale shreds of peel hanging in it, reflects perfectly the clean sharp taste.

Preparation Time: 2–3 hours
Soaking Time: overnight (8 hours)
Straining Time: 2–3 hours
Cooking Time: 30 minutes

Ingredients to Yield
4–5 lb. (1·8–2·3 kg.)

3 lb. (1·4 kg.) lemons
5 pints (2·8 litres) water
Sugar

Scrub the lemons and pare off the rind as thinly as possible. Cut the rind into fine shreds with a sharp knife and tie in a muslin bag. Cut the rest of the fruit into chunks and put it in a large bowl with any juice, the water and the bag of rind. Leave to stand overnight.

Next day, tip the fruit, water and bag of rind into a large, heavy-based pan and bring to the boil. Simmer for 1½–2 hours, until the fruit is mushy and the rind tender. Remove and set aside the bag of rind, and pour the pulp into a jelly bag. Leave it to strain for 2–3 hours. Do not squeeze the bag, as this would make the jelly cloudy.

Measure the strained juice into the washed pan, put the bag of rind in it again and warm it over a low heat. Weigh out 1 lb. (450 g.) of sugar for each pint (575/600 ml.) of juice. Add it to the warm juice and stir until it has dissolved completely. Bring to the boil, and boil hard until setting point is reached. Remove the bag of rind from the pan and pot and seal the jelly at once or, if liked, allow to cool for 5–8 minutes and then stir in some of the shredded rind from the bag before potting and sealing (see p. 361).

Chunky Seville Orange Marmalade
Countrywide

This recipe, using a whole-fruit method, is recommended for frozen fruit. The first part of the cooking can be done much more quickly with a pressure cooker.

Preparation Time: 45 minutes–1 hour
Cooking Time: about 2½ hours (1 hour if using a pressure cooker)

Ingredients to Yield
about 10 lb. (4·5 kg.)

3 lb. (1·4 kg.) Seville oranges, scrubbed
5 pints (2·8 litres) boiling water
Juice of 2 lemons
6 lb. (2·7 kg.) sugar

Put the fruit and boiling water in a large pan with a lid, or in a flame-proof casserole, and simmer gently with the lid on for 2 hours.

If this preliminary cooking is done in a large pressure cooker, reduce the amount of water to 2½ pints (1·4 litres) and cook under high (15 lb.) pressure for 20 minutes. Allow the pressure cooker to cool at room temperature for 10 minutes before opening. This 10 minutes is a necessary part of the cooking time, and should not be reduced.

Lift the fruit from the pan, casserole or pressure cooker and, using a knife and fork or kitchen scissors, cut the fruit into ¼ in. (5 mm.) chunks. During the cutting, pick out the pips and return them to the cooking vessel.

Boil the liquid rapidly for 5 minutes, then strain it into a large, heavy-based pan. Add the cut fruit and the lemon juice. Stir in the sugar over gentle heat until it has completely dissolved. Boil hard until setting point is reached (see p. 360).

Remove any scum, allow the marmalade to cool for 5–8 minutes, and then stir well to distribute the fruit. Pot and seal (see p. 361).

To make a dark marmalade, use 3 lb. (1·4 kg.) of brown sugar with 3 lb. (1·4 kg.) of white sugar, or stir 1 tablespoon of black treacle into the finished marmalade just before potting.

Seville Orange Marmalade
Countrywide

January is the time to make this, the most traditional of marmalades, in the most traditional of ways—slicing carefully, simmering slowly and boiling fiercely, while the whole house fills with the distinctive bitter-sweet aroma of the fruit.

Unlike other bitter oranges, a true Seville has a very rough skin and has a beautiful, deep colour.

Preparation Time: 1–1½ hours
Cooking Time: about 2½ hours

Ingredients to Yield
about 10 lb. (4·5 kg.)

3 lb. (1·4 kg.) Seville oranges
5 pints (2·8 litres) water
Juice of 2 lemons
6 lb. (2·7 kg.) sugar

Scrub the oranges and cut them in half. Squeeze the juice and pips into a basin. Cut up the peel into thin strips or chunks, as preferred.

Put the cut peel, any soft pulp and the water in a large, heavy-based pan. Strain in the juice. Put the pips in a muslin bag and tie it to the pan handle so that it hangs well down in the water. Cook the fruit gently for 2 hours, or until the peel is tender.

Lift out the bag of pips and squeeze it between two spoons over the pan before discarding. Add the lemon juice and sugar, and stir until the sugar has completely dissolved.

Bring to the boil, and boil rapidly until setting point is reached. Remove any scum, cool for 5–8 minutes and then stir well to distribute the peel. Pot and seal (see p. 361).

Quick Ginger Marmalade
Countrywide

The ginger adds bite to both the texture and the flavour of this extremely labour-saving marmalade. It is another recipe to use at any time of year if the marmalade shelf is depleted.

Try spreading ginger marmalade on scones at teatime, or use it as a filling for a Victoria sandwich.

It also goes very well in a cheese-cake, or with cream cheese in brown-bread sandwiches.

Preparation Time: 20 minutes
Cooking Time: about 35 minutes

INGREDIENTS TO YIELD ABOUT 5 LB. (2·3 KG.)

2 lb. (900 g.) frozen unsweetened marmalade pulp, or 1 lb. 13 oz. (822 g.) canned unsweetened marmalade pulp
3 lb. (1·4 kg.) sugar
8 oz. (225 g.) preserved or crystallised ginger, cut into small pieces

Thaw the frozen pulp, if used. Put the pulp into a large saucepan and heat gently. Stir in the sugar until completely dissolved. Add the ginger and cook the mixture for about 20 minutes, or until it sets.

Leave to cool for 5–8 minutes, then stir to distribute the fruit before potting and sealing (see p. 361).

To give a richer colour and flavour, use a mixture of brown and white sugar.

ALL-THE-YEAR-ROUND MARMALADE
Countrywide

A FRESH FRUIT MARMALADE that can be made at any time of year is a bonus if you miss the short January season for Seville oranges, or if you have not made enough in January to carry you through the year. This marmalade has a good sharp flavour, provided that the lemons and grapefruit are not outweighed by the sweet oranges.

It is also very economical, ideal for breakfast toast or in a marmalade sauce to accompany a sweet pudding.

PREPARATION TIME: 1–1½ HOURS
COOKING TIME: ABOUT 2½ HOURS

INGREDIENTS TO YIELD ABOUT 10 LB. (4·5 KG.)

3 lb. (1·4 kg.) mixed lemons, grapefruit, sweet and bitter oranges, made up as available
5 pints (2·8 litres) water
6 lb. (2·7 kg.) sugar

Numerous fruits and a Victorian sugar cone for All-The-Year-Round Marmalade.

Scrub the fruit and cut in half. Squeeze out the juice and pips into a basin. Cut the peel into thin strips or chunks, as preferred.

Put the cut peel and any soft pulp into a large, heavy-based pan with the water. Strain in the juice. Put the pips in a muslin bag and tie this to the handle of the pan so that it hangs well down in the water. Cook gently for 2 hours, or until the peel is tender.

Lift out the bag of pips and squeeze it between two spoons over the pan before discarding. Add the sugar and stir until it dissolves.

Bring to the boil, and boil hard until setting point is reached. Remove any scum and leave to stand for 5–8 minutes, then stir well to distribute the peel. Pot and seal (see p. 361).

RECIPES *from* OTHER LANDS

GREECE
Grape Jelly

DIONYSUS, the Greek god of wine, was taught his trade by the satyr Silenus, who cultivated vineyards among the mountains of Thrace. From there, the young god carried the secrets of wine-making to the world.

Greek grapes, grown mostly in Attica and the Peloponnese, form the basis of this jelly. Spread on rolls at breakfast time, it makes a brilliant contrast to the many Greek honeys.

If possible, use seedless grapes, and choose them when they are greeny-yellow and ripe, but still firm.

PREPARATION TIME: ABOUT 45 MINUTES
STRAINING TIME: AT LEAST 4 HOURS
COOKING TIME: ABOUT 30 MINUTES

INGREDIENTS TO YIELD
ABOUT 2–3 LB. (900 G.–1·4 KG.)

4 lb. (1·8 kg.) ripe green grapes
$\frac{1}{2}$ pint (275/300 ml.) water
4 dessert or cooking apples, peeled, cored and sliced
1 dessertspoon lemon juice
Sugar

Wash and drain the grapes and put them in a large, heavy-based pan with the water. Crush them against the sides of the pan with a wooden spoon, then add the apples and lemon juice.

Bring to the boil, then simmer gently for about 30 minutes, stirring occasionally, until all the fruit is soft and broken down. Ladle the fruit and liquid into a scalded jelly bag and leave to strain for at least 4 hours. Do not squeeze the bag, as this would make the jelly cloudy.

Heat the oven to 110°C (225°F)—gas mark $\frac{1}{4}$. Measure the strained liquid and weigh out 1 lb. (450 g.) sugar for each pint (575/600 ml.). Put the sugar in an ovenproof dish in the middle of the oven to warm through for 10–15 minutes.

Heat the juice in the cleaned pan and add the sugar, stirring until dissolved. Bring to the boil and cook rapidly until the setting point is reached (see p. 360), about 10–15 minutes. Pot and seal.

CARIBBEAN
West Indian Pickle

FOR NEARLY THREE-THOUSAND miles, between Florida and Venezuela, the islands of the West Indies lie like emeralds thrown across the blue velvet of the Caribbean. Their cuisine reflects the extraordinary variety of people who have settled there, willingly or not, since Columbus first discovered the island chain in 1492. Carib Indians, African slaves, Dutch, Spanish, Portuguese, French and British settlers have all added to its rich variety. So has the fertility of the islands.

To the native sweet potatoes and pineapples, the colonists added breadfruit and citrus fruits, mangoes, rice, coffee and sugar cane. From there comes this mild, fruity sauce—a delicious complement to hot curries and cold meats.

To vary the recipe, substitute 1 teaspoon of ground cinnamon or ground, mixed spice for the ginger.

PREPARATION TIME: 20 MINUTES
COOKING TIME: ABOUT $1\frac{1}{2}$ HOURS

INGREDIENTS TO YIELD
ABOUT 3 LB. (1·4 KG.)

1 lb. (450 g.) mangoes, washed and sliced
12 oz. (350 g.) cooking apples, peeled, cored and sliced
6 oz. (175 g.) onions, peeled and chopped
1 pint (575/600 ml.) spiced vinegar (see p. 363)
1 lb. (450 g.) firm, ripe bananas
12 oz. (350 g.) soft brown sugar
1 teaspoon ground ginger
1 teaspoon salt

Place the sliced mangoes, apples and chopped onions in a large, heavy-based pan with half the vinegar. Bring to the boil, then simmer gently for about 30 minutes, until the onions are tender. Remove from the heat.

Add the sliced bananas, sugar, ginger, salt and the rest of the vinegar. Put back on a gentle heat, stirring continuously until the sugar dissolves. Simmer gently, stirring from time to time, for a further hour or until the pickle becomes thick. Pot and seal (see p. 363).

This pickle may be made with canned, drained mangoes. Simmer the apple and onion in half the vinegar for about 20 minutes before adding the mangoes. Cook for 10 minutes, then add the other ingredients. Leave to mature for 4–6 weeks.

USA
Apple Butter

PENNSYLVANIAN APPLE BUTTER was invented by Dutch settlers shortly after their arrival there in 1734. Their descendants still serve it at Thanksgiving, as part of the traditional commemorative feast.

The butter resembles an apple conserve made in this country in the 19th century, and considered 'extremely wholesome as supper for juveniles and for the aged'. But people of all ages can enjoy it, spread like jam on scones and toast.

PREPARATION TIME: 15 MINUTES
COOKING TIME: 1–$1\frac{1}{2}$ HOURS

INGREDIENTS TO YIELD
2–3 LB. (900 G.–1·4 KG.)

3 lb. (1·4 kg.) green cooking apples
1 pint (575/600 ml.) water
1 pint (575/600 ml.) medium-sweet cider
$\frac{1}{2}$ teaspoon ground cloves
$\frac{1}{2}$ teaspoon ground cinnamon
$\frac{1}{2}$ teaspoon ground nutmeg
Granulated or soft brown sugar

Wash and dry the apples but do not peel them. Cut them into large pieces, including the cores, and place them in a large, heavy-based pan with the water and the cider.

Bring to the boil and simmer until the fruit is soft, about 30–45 minutes. Rub through a sieve into a bowl and measure the apple pulp. Weigh out 12 oz. (350 g.) of sugar to each 1 lb. (450 g.) of pulp.

Return the pulp to the cleaned pan and simmer gently, stirring frequently, for 10 minutes. Add the spices and the sugar, stirring until it is dissolved. Keep simmering gently, stirring frequently, until the mixture is thick and creamy with no trace of surplus liquid. Pot and seal (see p. 362).

As an alternative, use equal quantities of cooking and eating apples. Add 1 tablespoon of chopped, crystallised ginger to the spices, or the grated rind of an orange or lemon.

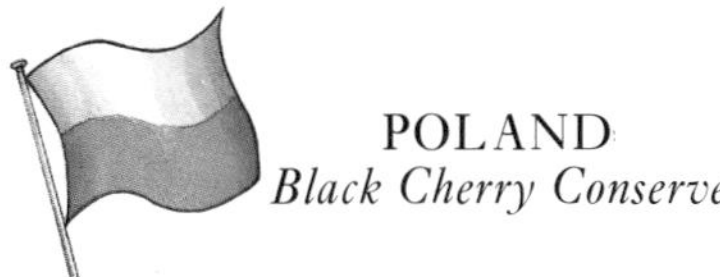

POLAND
Black Cherry Conserve

MORELLO CHERRIES, black and sour, play an important part in the traditional cuisines of central and eastern Europe. Admirably suited to the extremes of the continental climate, the fruits and their crushed kernels are distilled to make Kirsch, the powerful cherry liqueur of Austria and Switzerland. In Germany's Black Forest, *Kirschwasser* is a speciality, made from the pulp and crushed stones of the cherry, distilled and sweetened. So, too, is the rich Black Forest Cherry Cake, created from chocolate, cream and Morello cherries.

The Poles, who garnish wild duck with a sweet and sour cherry sauce, like the Swiss, spread the following conserve on hot, fresh rolls at breakfast time. Or they use it to fill flans and tartlets.

Make sure you use the small, sharp Morello variety: sweet black cherries are not suitable.

PREPARATION TIME: 30–40 MINUTES
COOKING TIME: 45–50 MINUTES

INGREDIENTS TO YIELD
ABOUT 4 LB. (1·8 KG.)

4 lb. (1·8 kg.) Morello cherries
$\frac{1}{4}$ pint (150 ml.) redcurrant juice or 8 oz. (225 g.) redcurrant jelly and juice of 1 lemon
4 lb. (1·8 kg.) sugar
2 tablespoons Kirsch, plum brandy or cherry brandy

Wash the cherries, drain well and pit them. Put the redcurrant juice, or jelly and lemon juice, with the sugar in a large, heavy-based pan and heat gently, stirring continuously until the sugar is dissolved.

Bring rapidly to the boil, then drop the cherries into the pan. Simmer for 10 minutes, stirring gently from time to time.

Remove the cherries from the pan with a slotted spoon and put them in a large bowl. Bring the syrup to the boil and cook rapidly for a further 15 minutes to reduce it.

Return the cherries to the pan and add the Kirsch or brandy. Simmer for a further 12–15 minutes, then remove the pan from the heat and leave to cool for a few minutes. Stir well to distribute the fruit, pot and seal (see p. 360). Unlike most jams, this does not set firmly.

Black Cherry Conserve—ripe, dark fruit blended with Kirsch or brandy.

AUSTRIA
Apple and Horseradish Sauce

ON THE WHOLE, the central Europeans are more imaginative in the use of apples than we are ourselves. They make apple soup, apples with herrings, apple and nut strudel with 'pastry so thin you can read your love letters through it', and the following sauce. Less fierily pungent than our own horseradish sauce, it is often suggested as an accompaniment to beef and fish in German, Austrian and Jewish cookery books.

If you are grating your own horseradish, try the old trick of holding a piece of bread in your mouth. The tears will still flow, but not so copiously.

PREPARATION TIME: 10 MINUTES
COOKING TIME: 10–15 MINUTES

INGREDIENTS TO YIELD
ABOUT $\frac{1}{2}$ PINT (275/300 ML.)

$\frac{1}{4}$ pint (150 ml.) cider vinegar
Juice of 1 lemon
1 heaped tablespoon sugar
$\frac{1}{4}$ teaspoon salt
2 medium cooking apples, peeled and cored
1 oz. (25 g.) grated horseradish

Put the vinegar, lemon juice, sugar and salt in a large pan. Bring to the boil, stirring until the sugar dissolves. Remove the pan from the heat and grate the apples into it.

Add the grated horseradish, put back on to a low heat and cook for 1 minute, stirring all the time. Allow to cool for a further 1 minute, then pot and seal (see p. 364).

The sauce is ready for use immediately, and will keep for 2–3 months.

Directions for Preparing, Potting and Storing

Jams, Pickles and Other Preserves

Until a few hundred years ago, people depended on preserved food to survive through the winter months. Most livestock was killed in the autumn, for there was little fodder available in winter, and the carcases were dried and salted to preserve them.

Preserving the plentiful fruits of summer for winter use was not widely practised until the 17th century, when sugar began to be more plentiful and cheaper. At about this time, too, there was an upsurge of interest in gardening; a wider range of vegetables began to be grown following introductions from Europe and the New World.

The stillroom was the workshop of the country household. Here the housewife prepared rosewater flavouring, perfumes, cosmetics and herbal medicines, and, in later centuries, jams, pickles and sauces.

Jam, Fruit Jelly and Marmalade

Bruised and crushed fruit boiled quickly in a sugar syrup appeared under the name jam—a slang word dating from Elizabethan times—in 18th-century cookery books. It had begun to take the place of the thick and paste-like tartstuffs of earlier days. Fruit juice boiled to a jelly with sugar was stored in pots and served in slices to garnish winter cream dishes.

The original marmalade was quince jelly, introduced from Portugal in the 14th century. It took its name from *marmelo*, the Portuguese word for 'quince'. Later, citrus fruits began to be used, particularly oranges. Until the 18th century at least, marmalade was a knife-cut conserve, solid enough to be eaten on its own or as an accompaniment to all kinds of dishes.

In the past, jam-making had to be undertaken during the short period when the fruit season was at its height. Today, with the use of a freezer to temporarily store fruit in prime condition, jam-making can be spread out conveniently for a longer period.

The equipment you need

A heavy-based preserving pan of good-quality aluminium or stainless steel, wide to allow for evaporation and deep enough to prevent the jam boiling over. The heavy base prevents burning. A lip for pouring may be useful.

Copper and brass pans are not suitable for making preserves, as the acid in the fruit reacts with the metal.

If you have no preserving pan, use a heavy-based 7–8 pint (4–4·5 litre) saucepan for making small quantities of jam.

Scales.

Nylon or hair sieves.

Wooden spoon for stirring. Buy a long-handled jam-making spoon, to reduce the risk of hot jam splashing your hands and arms.

Knives and peelers with stainless-steel blades, which do not discolour the fruit.

Heat-proof measuring jug.

Jam jars and covers. Ordinary jam jars can also be used for jellies, although some people prefer smaller jars that can be put on the table.

Jars vary considerably in size, so keep a selection of covers in stock. The types of cover generally available are circular transparent Cellophane tops, plastic skin that can be cut to the size you want and plastic-coated twist or screw tops. Twist or screw tops are the most expensive, but are useful if storage conditions are not ideal.

Both Cellophane tops and plastic skin are used with wax-coated discs to seal the surface of the jam. Tie the covers down with fine string, as rubber bands may perish during storage.

A wide-necked funnel for filling jam jars is useful but not essential.

Facts about Preserving

Preserving food is one of the best ways to make use of any surpluses or gluts of fruit or vegetables, whether home grown or bought. It also allows you to suit family tastes, and gives a wider range of choice than is available from commercial products.

When preserving food, the aim is to take it at the peak of its quality and nutritive value, and to keep it at that point. The main preserving agents used today are sugar, salt, vinegar and alcohol.

Methods of preserving include jam-making, pickling, drying, smoking and the more recent techniques of heat processing and freezing.

Successful preserving depends on using fresh food of the best quality available. Whether you use home-grown or bought food, process it as soon as possible after harvesting or buying. Choose fruits that are firmly ripe, and vegetables that are mature but not overblown or overripe.

Preservatives and preserving methods are not effective unless applied in the correct quantities and manner. Follow the instructions given exactly. Time spent on preparing preserves is wasted unless they are correctly packed and stored.

A sugar thermometer is useful for checking jam temperature to ascertain setting point, but it is not essential.

For making fruit jelly you will also need a jelly bag for straining the juice from the fruit. You can buy flannel jelly bags, with or without dripstands.

Alternatively, you can make your own bag from a square of white cotton or flannel, four to six layers of butter muslin, or a white cotton pillow case. For a home-made dripstand, tie each corner of the bag to the legs of an upturned stool and put a plastic or china bowl underneath to catch the juice. You can use an unchipped enamel bowl, but it may stain badly.

For making marmalade, a juice extractor is useful but not essential. The fruit can be minced in a mincing machine after the juice has been squeezed out, but the finished marmalade tends to have a paste-like texture. The slicing attachment on a mixer is useful for shredding peel.

Jam

Jam is crushed fruit boiled to a thick consistency and preserved by impregnation with sugar.

Pectin, a substance in fruit that reacts with acid when heated, is the jellying, or setting, agent. Fruits vary in their pectin and acid content.

Jam is made by first cooking the fruit to a pulp, then adding sugar and boiling until it is ready to set. For the best colour and flavour, simmer it slowly before adding the sugar and boil it rapidly afterwards. Underboiling causes jam to be runny, overboiling makes it sticky.

The amount of sugar used is crucial. Too little and the jam will ferment and be runny. Too much and the jam will crystallise and be dark and sticky.

The final yield from good, well-set jam should be about 10 lb. (4·5 kg.) for each 6 lb. (2·7 kg.) of sugar used. For example, a recipe using 4 lb. (1·8 kg.) of sugar should yield ($4 \times 10 \div 6$) lb.—that is, just under 7 lb. (3·2 kg.) of jam.

A guide to good jam-making

Good jam is bright in colour, well set but easy to spread, and has the true, distinct flavour of the fruit used.

1 Make fairly small quantities of jam at a time in case you do not like the flavour or get a poor result, which can mean wasted time and ingredients.

Never make more than 10 lb. (4·5 kg.) final weight at any time. The less time spent in cooking the jam, the better its colour and flavour.

2 Choose firmly ripe fresh fruit, picked dry. Do not use wet fruit, the water will account for some of its weight, and pound for pound it will have less pectin and acid than dry fruit. This may affect the set and flavour of the jam.

3 Prepare the fruit, removing stalks or any bruised portions, and wash if necessary. If you use cherries or damsons, either stone them or leave whole, but halve and stone plums, apricots, peaches and greengages.

4 Put the fruit in a large, heavy-based pan, with any acid required in the recipe. Do not overfill the pan, or the jam may spill over during boiling. It should be about one-third full of fruit.

5 Add water only if the recipe says so. Fruit in a deep pan will need less water than fruit in a shallow pan where evaporation is quicker.

Do not add water to soft, juicy fruits such as strawberries, raspberries and blackberries.

6 Bring the fruit to the boil, then simmer it gently to break down the skin and tissues and extract the pectin. Fruits with tough skins, such as plums, damsons and black currants, may need to simmer for 30–45 minutes to break down the skin.

7 Do not cover the pan unless the recipe says so. Evaporation of the water content is essential.

8 If you need to test the jam for its pectin content (see Pectin and Acid), do so before you add the sugar.

9 Use preserving sugar or granulated sugar—preserving sugar produces less scum. Do not use brown sugar, unless called for in the recipe, as it affects the flavour of the jam.

10 Carefully weigh out the amount of sugar to be added and warm it in a pre-heated oven at a temperature of

Pectin and Acid

When using a good jam recipe, it is rarely necessary to measure the pectin content of the fruit. If low-pectin fruits are included, they are normally blended with high-pectin fruits to achieve the right balance. Similarly, acid is usually included in the ingredients if low-acid fruits are used.

Fruits with a high pectin content are: black currants, red currants, cooking apples, damsons, quinces, gooseberries, some varieties of plums.

Fruits with a medium pectin content are: fresh apricots, early blackberries, greengages, loganberries and raspberries.

Fruits with a poor pectin content are: late blackberries, cherries, elderberries, pears, rhubarb, strawberries and medlars.

Fruits low in acid are: sweet apples, sweet cherries, quinces, late blackberries, bilberries (or whortleberries), strawberries, raspberries, peaches and pears.

Vegetables used in jam-making, such as marrow, are also low in acid.

The pectin test

Check the pectin content of the fruit after it has been simmered to a pulp but before you add the sugar.

1 Put 1 teaspoon of juice from the pan into a small glass jar and allow it to cool.

2 Add 1 tablespoon of methylated spirit to the cooled juice; shake well.

3 After 1 minute, a transparent clot should form:

If the clot is large and jelly-like, the pectin content is high. No extra pectin is needed.

If the clot is less firm and perhaps in two or three lumps, the pectin content is medium, but sufficient.

If there is no clot, or if there are a lot of very small ones, the pectin content is low. Extra pectin is needed.

Adding pectin

Pectin can be bought from a chemist or grocer. Add it according to the maker's instructions before returning the pan to the heat. Do not use too much pectin, it will spoil the flavour.

A simpler way of adding pectin to strawberry jam is to put in a grated cooking apple for each 1 lb. (450 g.) of strawberries. The apple does not affect the flavour.

Adding acid

Put in any acid included in the recipe before you start cooking the fruit.

As a guide, for each 2 lb. (900 g.) of fruit, one of the following acids is normally used in the quantity given:

Lemon juice, 1 tablespoon.

Citric or tartaric acid, ¼ level teaspoon.

Redcurrant or gooseberry juice, 2½ fl. oz. (75 ml.).

110°C (225°F)—gas mark ¼. This shortens the cooking time, as warm sugar dissolves quicker than cold.

Do not add the sugar too soon to damsons, plums, currants or gooseberries. Sugar toughens their skins, and no amount of boiling will soften them afterwards.

11 Add the sugar gradually, stirring continually until it has dissolved, then bring the jam to boiling point.

Do not let the jam boil before the sugar has dissolved. The set will be poor and the texture grainy.

12 If you are using granulated sugar, add a nut of butter or a few drops of glycerine during boiling. This cuts down the amount of scum.

13 After the jam has been boiling for a few minutes, remove the pan from the heat and test for setting point. Jam usually reaches setting point after boiling for 3–20 minutes, depending on the kind of fruit.

14 Remove any scum with a stainless-steel slotted or perforated spoon once the jam is finished. Do not remove during cooking, it is wasteful.

15 Cool the finished jam in the pan for 5–6 minutes before potting, to prevent the fruit rising—especially if making strawberry or cherry jam.

16 Before potting (see right), stir the jam gently to distribute the fruit.

17 Never leave the jam in the pan longer than necessary, as it may stain the metal.

Using frozen fruit in jam

Deep-frozen fruit is likely to have lost some of its original pectin content.

To compensate, use more fruit. Increase the quantity given in the recipe by 10%—for example, add an extra 8 oz. (225 g.) to 5 lb. (2·3 kg.).

Alternatively, use the amount of fruit given and decrease the sugar by 10%. For example, use 4½ lb. (2 kg.) of sugar instead of 5 lb. (2·3 kg.).

Some frozen fruits, such as strawberries, may darken a little during heating. The finished jam may not, therefore, be as bright in colour as that made from fresh fruit.

Do not attempt to make strawberry conserve (jam containing whole fruit) with frozen strawberries. The fruits will collapse.

Testing for Setting Point

There are three simple ways of testing whether jam has reached setting point—the flake test, the cold saucer test, and taking the temperature with a sugar thermometer. The first two methods are most commonly used.

Whichever test you use, remove the pan from the heat first, otherwise the jam may go past setting point and be overboiled.

The flake test

1 Dip a clean wooden spoon in the jam.

2 Remove it and hold it over the jam, twisting it round once or twice to cool the jam adhering.

3 Let the jam fall from the edge of the spoon. If the drops run together and form flakes that hang on the spoon edge for 15–30 seconds, the jam has reached setting point.

The cold saucer test

1 Chill a saucer in the refrigerator for 1 minute. This will speed up the cooling of the jam placed on it.

2 Put 1 teaspoon of jam on the saucer and let it cool for 1 minute.

3 Push the surface of the cooled jam with your fingertip. If the surface wrinkles, the jam has reached setting point.

The thermometer test

1 Stir the jam.

2 Dip the thermometer in hot water, then sink the bulb end in the jam.

3 If the temperature is 105°C (220°F) the jam has reached setting point.

Fruit Jelly

Fruit jelly is fruit juice boiled to a thick consistency and preserved by impregnation with sugar. It should have a clear, bright colour and true flavour. As for jam, the setting agent is the pectin in the fruit, which reacts with acid when heated. Because only the juice is used, fruit yields, pound for pound, less jelly than jam.

The removal of the skin, pulp and pips reduces the bulk and thus the flavour. Low-pectin fruits are not therefore suitable for jelly-making. So much pectin and acid would have to be added to ensure setting that the true flavour of the fruit would be lost.

The final yield can be estimated in the same way as for jam—about 10 lb. (4·5 kg.) for each 6 lb. (2·7 kg.) of sugar used. But the total quantity of sugar is not given in the recipe, as it depends on the quality and quantity of juice. It is generally apportioned according to the amount of juice produced—usually 1 lb. (450 g.) for every pint (575/600 ml.).

Points to note in jelly-making

Wild fruits such as blackberries, bilberries and rowan berries are commonly used in jelly-making. As the yield is low for the amount of fruit used, they help to keep down the cost. Damaged or bruised fruit, or windfalls, can be used as long as the unsound parts are cut away.

Crab apples make a jelly of delicious colour and flavour, but cooking-apple jelly is rather insipid. Cloves, lemon, ginger, or geranium leaves improve the flavour. Apple juice is a good base for herb jellies.

In general, fruit jelly is made in the same way as jam, except that the pulped fruit is strained and only the juice boiled with the sugar. Follow the guide given for jam-making, but take the following points into account.

1 There is no need to top and tail fruit such as gooseberries, or to peel apples. Remove any stalks and leaves. Cut large plums and apples into chunks to reduce cooking time.

2 Most fruits are best cooked in water—follow the amount given in the recipe. Tough-skinned fruits such as damsons need more water than soft fruits such as loganberries.

3 Gentle cooking to break down the fruit takes longer than for jam. The fruit must be thoroughly pulped to release the pectin and acid. Pulping may take 30 minutes to 1 hour, depending on skin toughness.

4 Before pouring the pulped fruit into the jelly bag to strain it, scald the bag with boiling water.

5 Allow the juice to drip through the bag into a large bowl for 2–4 hours or longer if needed. Follow the guidance in the recipe.

6 Never squeeze the jelly bag to hurry things up. If you do, the jelly will be cloudy because some of the fruit tissues will be forced into it.

7 Finish making the jelly within 24 hours of straining. Prolonged standing causes the juice to lose pectin and darken in colour. If you have to leave it for a time, cover the bowl with butter muslin or a tea towel.

8 If the juice is thick and sticky, it should set well. If it is thin and watery, simmer for 10–15 minutes to remove some of the excess water before you continue cooking.

If you are in doubt, use the pectin test to help you to decide the setting quality. Add pectin if necessary.

9 Measure the quantity of juice to determine how much sugar to use.

10 Bring the juice to the boil before you add the warmed sugar. Stir continually and do not let the juice re-boil while the sugar dissolves.

11 Jelly usually reaches setting point after 10–15 minutes' boiling. Reduce the boiling rate a little as setting point approaches, otherwise the finished jelly may be full of air bubbles.

12 Test for setting point. The flake or thermometer tests are the most reliable.

13 Once setting point is reached, take a large, stainless-steel spoon and dip it in boiling water, then shake well. With the pan off the heat, use the spoon to take the scum off the jelly—it will cling to the hot spoon.

14 To remove the last bits of scum, use a piece of greaseproof paper with torn edges. Draw it across the jelly surface to the side of the pan, where the scum will stick.

15 Pot the jelly immediately (see Potting). If you leave it too long it will start to set in the pan.

Marmalade

Marmalade, like jam, is jellied boiled fruit preserved by impregnation with sugar, but generally only citrus fruits—such as oranges, lemons, limes and grapefruit—are used. Thick marmalade mostly contains every part of the fruit but the pips. Jelly, or clear, marmalade—made from the juice of citrus fruits—can be left clear or contain shreds of the peel.

In citrus fruits, most of the pectin is in the pips and white inner skin, or pith. Despite their acidity, citrus fruits (except lemons) cannot produce enough acid to ensure setting, and more has to be added. This is because of the large yield of marmalade in relation to fruit size—it can be as much as three times the weight of the fruit.

The pith of bitter oranges becomes translucent when cooked, whereas the pith of sweet oranges, lemons and grapefruit remains opaque. This is why marmalade made with a mixture of citrus fruits looks cloudy although the flavour is unaffected.

The final yield can be estimated in the same way as for jam—6 lb. (2·7 kg.) of sugar yields about 10 lb. (4·5 kg.) of marmalade. But you need much less fruit than for a similar amount of jam. Jelly marmalade needs more fruit than thick marmalade to produce a given amount.

Points to note when making marmalade

Most marmalade is made from bitter oranges, distinguished by their rough outer skins. They are usually available in late December and January.

The methods for making thick marmalade and marmalade jelly are basically the same as for making jam and fruit jelly, but note the following points.

1 Choose firm fruit of good colour and heavy in relation to its size. Buy bitter oranges early in January, before they have been in the shops too long.

2 Use the fruit as soon as possible, or else freeze it for use at a later date.

3 Wash the fruit well before use and scrub if necessary. There is no need to soak it overnight to soften the peel.

4 The simplest way to prepare the fruit is to cut it in half and squeeze the juice and pips into a bowl, then shred the peel and put it in the pan with the water.

Next strain the juice into the pan, add the acid, and put the pips and tissue in a muslin bag tied to the pan handle. Hang well into the water.

5 If you cut away some of the thick pith when shredding the peel, put it in the muslin bag with the pips.

6 For jelly marmalade, put some of the shredded peel in a muslin bag and hang it in the pan during cooking. If you wish, stir this peel into the jelly when potting.

7 Because of their thick skins, citrus fruits need longer cooking and more water than fruits used in jam-making. Pulping generally takes 2–3 hours.

8 Make certain the peel is properly cooked. It should disintegrate when squeezed between finger and thumb.

9 Lift out the bag of pips between two spoons and squeeze it gently over the pan before you stir in the warmed sugar. For an Old English marmalade, replace half the white sugar with brown sugar. Alternatively, use white sugar and add 1 tablespoon of black treacle for every 1 lb. (450 g.) of marmalade in the given yield.

10 Marmalade usually reaches setting point after 15–20 minutes' boiling. Use the flake or cold saucer method to test for set.

11 Remove the scum as soon as possible after the marmalade reaches setting point, otherwise it tends to cling to the peel.

12 Cool for 5–10 minutes, then stir to distribute the fruit before potting (see below). This prevents the peel from rising in the jars.

Using frozen fruit in marmalade

You can freeze freshly bought citrus fruits for use at a later date. To freeze whole, scrub well, dry and pack in polythene bags. Alternatively, cut them up and cook to a pulp first, so that only the final boiling with sugar has to be done after thawing.

Always use extra fruit—one-eighth more than the recipe specifies—to offset pectin loss during freezing.

Potting, sealing and storing

Jam, fruit jelly and marmalade are potted and stored in the same way.

1 Thoroughly wash the jars in hot water and mild detergent, rinse and drain on a clean towel.

2 Warm the dry jars in the oven for a few minutes at a temperature of 110°C (225°F)—gas mark ¼. They can be placed in the pre-heated oven when you warm the sugar.

3 Fill the jars to the brim with the hot, finished jam, jelly or marmalade. It will shrink during cooling.

Tilt jelly jars while filling them, so that the jelly runs down the side—this prevents air bubbles forming. Once the jelly jar is filled, do not move or tilt it until the jelly has set.

4 If covering with Cellophane or plastic, put a wax disc on the jam surface after filling. This seal keeps the jam in good condition.

5 Seal the jars while the jam is hot—do not leave it to become lukewarm before sealing, as this encourages the growth of mould. You can put on Cellophane tops or tie down plastic skin tightly once the jam is cold and set and the jars are easier to handle.

6 If using plastic-coated twist or screw tops, put on as soon as a jar is filled. No wax disc is needed.

7 Label each sealed and covered jar with the contents and date.

8 Store in a dry, cool and dark place. Damp causes mould to grow on the surface, heat makes the contents shrink, and too much light may fade the colour. Most preserves will keep 6–12 months in good conditions.

Fruit Curd, Cheese and Butter

AMONG THE products of the country housewife's stillroom were the fruit cheeses and butters that were used as spreads, or served with cream and hazelnuts on festive occasions. Many types of fruit—apples, damsons, blackberries, gooseberries—were stored in pots in this way for winter and summer use. Orange or lemon curds began to be made at the end of the 17th century, originally as fillings for tarts.

Facts about fruit curd, cheese and butter

Fruit curd is pulped fruit (or in lemon curd, the lemon rind and juice) heated with sugar and thickened with eggs and butter to a spreading consistency.

It cannot be brought to boiling point with the sugar to arrest natural deterioration, because the eggs would curdle. It is not therefore strictly a preserve, and does not keep as long. Use it within 2 weeks of making, or 1 month if stored in a refrigerator.

Fruit cheese is finely pulped boiled fruit preserved by impregnation with sugar and cooked to a firm, solid consistency. Less sugar is used in proportion to the fruit than when making jam, but a large amount of fruit is needed for a small yield, so it is best made when you have a glut of fruit.

The most economical way is to make it with the pulp remaining after you have made fruit jelly.

Fruit cheese usually improves with keeping and should be left to mature for about 2 months. It will keep for about a year if stored in a cool, dry place.

Fruit butter is similar to fruit cheese, but is cooked to a creamy, spreading consistency. The proportion of sugar to fruit is less than in fruit cheese. Fruit butter will not keep long once it is opened.

MAKING FRUIT CURD

Lemon is the classic fruit curd, but oranges, apples and apricots all make fine-flavoured curds.

Most of your jam-making equipment can be used, but in addition you will need a double saucepan. If you do not have one, use a heat-proof bowl over a saucepan of hot water, with the rim on the saucepan edge.

Use eggs with deep-coloured yolks to give rich-looking curd.

Use butter with a mild flavour. Farmhouse or strongly flavoured butter will impair the delicate flavour of the curd.

Put the fruit pulp, butter and sugar into the top of the double saucepan and cook gently, stirring until the sugar dissolves.

Beat the eggs lightly—over-beating may produce bubbles in the curd.

Remove the saucepan from the heat and strain the eggs into the pan. This prevents threads or lumps of egg white getting into the curd.

Cook slowly and gently until the curd thickens and coats the back of a spoon, usually after 30–45 minutes.

Potting and sealing

Pot in the same way as jam (see p. 361), but use small jars so that the curd is not wasted. Fill right to the brim—curd shrinks more than jam, and thickens considerably as it cools.

Cover with wax discs and Cellophane tops. Do not use plastic tops or twist tops, as they will encourage mould.

MAKING FRUIT CHEESE AND BUTTER

Damsons, quinces, medlars and black currants are a few of the fruits that make good, well-flavoured fruit cheese and butter. Apples usually need extra flavouring—windfalls cooked in a mixture of cider and water with spices added make excellent fruit butter.

Fruit cheese can be served as a sweet dish, eaten with cheese or served as a cheese substitute. Fruit butter is tasty with scones or wholemeal bread and butter.

1 Wash and drain the fruit and cut into pieces if necessary.

2 Put it into a preserving pan with water just to the level of the fruit. Cook gently until it is soft and mushy.

3 Rub the mushy pulp through a nylon or hair sieve, then weigh it.

4 For cheese allow 1 lb. (450 g.) of sugar for each pound of pulp. For butter allow 8–12 oz. (225–350 g.) of sugar for each pound of pulp, depending on taste.

5 For fruit butter, cook the pulp gently for a few minutes before adding the sugar. Stir continuously until the sugar is dissolved.

Cooking time is usually 30–45 minutes. The butter is ready when it reaches a creamy consistency.

6 For fruit cheese, add the sugar to the pulp before cooking. Cook gently for 45 minutes to 1 hour, stirring continuously until the sugar has dissolved. Cheese needs constant watching, as it may burn.

Fruit cheese is ready when a wooden spoon drawn across the bottom of the pan leaves a clear line with no traces of liquid.

Potting and sealing

Pot fruit cheese into a warmed mould or jar from which it can be turned out whole for serving. Put a smear of glycerine on the inside of the jar so the cheese will turn out easily.

Seal jars with wax discs while still hot and cover with plastic skin or Cellophane covers when cool enough to handle.

Pot fruit butter into warm jars and place an airtight cover on each jar immediately. No wax disc is needed.

Pickles, Chutneys and Relishes

SALADS were the most popular way of eating vegetables in the 16th and 17th centuries. Many vegetables and flowers—mushrooms, cucumbers, beetroot, violets, primroses, borage, cowslips—were pickled for winter salads. Salad and meat garnishes were also pickled—barberries, nasturtium leaves, samphire (a cliff plant), and broom buds.

The word pickle is derived from the Germanic word *pekel* (brine), but vinegar—known since Celtic times—and verjuice—a kind of vinegar fermented from sour apples—were the main preservatives for vegetables.

In the 18th century, pickles increased in popularity as accompaniments to meat dishes. Following the development of trade with India, many Indian pickles and chutneys were introduced. Housewives copied them in their stillrooms, using melons, cucumbers, onions and peaches, for example, to simulate mango chutney.

Facts about pickles, chutneys and relishes

Pickles are vegetables or fruit preserved in spiced vinegar, with their shape, colour and texture retained as far as possible.

Some vegetables, such as onions and cauliflowers, need to be salted before being pickled; this is known as brining. It reduces the moisture content of the vegetable, and so ensures a crisp texture.

Most pickles are best left to mature for at least 6–8 weeks. Red cabbage can be eaten 1 week after pickling.

Chutneys are vegetables or fruit cooked to a smooth pulp and preserved in vinegar, salt and spices. They are often made from a blend of fruit and vegetables. There is no simple method of estimating the yield, which varies according to the ingredients. The yield stated in the recipe is the only guide.

Because the vegetables and fruit are not used whole, chutney can be made from damaged or bruised specimens, as long as unsound parts are cut away.

Relishes are vegetables or fruit preserved in vinegar, salt and spice, but the texture is different from chutney. The ingredients are coarsely chopped, not pulped.

Some relishes are cooked, some are made with raw ingredients. They are made, bottled and stored in the same ways as pickles and chutneys.

The equipment you need

A stainless-steel, aluminium or enamel saucepan. Do not use copper or brass pans, the vinegar will react with the metal and taint the preserve.

For chutney, use a heavy-based aluminium or stainless-steel saucepan.

Nylon or hair sieves.

Wooden spoons.

Stainless-steel knife.

Kitchen scales.

Measuring jug.

Jars with airtight screw tops or clip-on lids, preferably made of plastic or plastic-coated. If you use metal lids, fit a disc of ceresin paper (obtainable from most chemists) inside. This prevents the vinegar from corroding the metal. Clean jars in the same way as jam jars (see Potting, p. 361).

MAKING PICKLES

Pickles are simple to make and store. Many vegetables can be pickled cold and raw, or lightly cooked.

Sweet pickles are generally made from fruits such as peaches, damsons, crab apples, pears or blackberries, or sweet vegetables such as parsnips or marrows. They are cooked gently in a syrup of vinegar and sugar.

You can buy ready-spiced vinegar, but it is easy to make at home—you can then vary the spices to your taste. Malt vinegar can give pickles a better flavour. Cider vinegar can be used in fruit pickles.

1 Choose fresh young vegetables and firmly ripe fruits. Do not use any that are bruised or damaged.

2 Always use the best vinegar, which has an acetic acid content of at least 5%. Barrelled vinegar generally contains only about 4%.

3 Wash, drain and cut up the vegetables or fruit according to the instructions in the recipe.

4 Brine the vegetables if necessary (see Brining). Wash and drain well.

5 For sweet pickles, dissolve the sugar in the vinegar and cook the vegetables or fruit gently until just tender. Undercook a little rather than overcook, as they will go on softening in the hot vinegar.

6 Always pot hot and sweet pickles immediately. Never leave pickles standing in a saucepan for longer than necessary.

Potting and sealing

Use clean jars—warmed for cooked pickles—and fill to leave about 1 in. (2·5 cm.) headspace above the pickles. For raw pickles, drain off any water that collects at the bottom of the jar before adding vinegar.

Use cold spiced vinegar for raw pickles and hot spiced vinegar for cooked pickles. Cover the pickles with the vinegar to give a topping of at least ½ in. (1·5 cm.). Vinegar evaporates during storage, and any vegetables or fruit that become uncovered will discolour.

Cover and seal the jars at once. Tops must be airtight, or the vinegar will evaporate and the contents dry out.

Store in a cool, dark, dry place.

For fruit pickles, keep surplus sweetened vinegar in a jar so that you can top up as necessary. Some fruits absorb the vinegar as they mature.

Making your own spiced vinegar

1 At least 2 months before you intend to start pickling, buy vinegar in 2 pint (1·1 litre) bottles, or decant it into 2 pint (1·1 litre) containers.

2 Use whole spices whenever possible. Ground spices make the vinegar look cloudy and muddy.

3 To each 2 pints (1·1 litres) of vinegar, add 1 oz. (25 g.) of mixed pickling spice (obtainable from most supermarkets or grocers). Or add the following spice mixture:

¼ oz. (7 g.) cloves
¼ oz. (7 g.) mace
¼ oz. (7 g.) allspice
¼ oz. (7 g.) cinnamon
A few peppercorns
1 or 2 pieces dry root ginger.

4 Leave to steep for 6–8 weeks. The spices will gradually sink to the bottom of the bottle, so give the bottle a shake from time to time.

5 Strain to remove spices before use.

6 Alternatively, put the spices in a muslin bag and hang them in the vinegar to steep. You need not strain the vinegar before use.

Quick-spiced vinegar

If you want spiced vinegar for immediate use, make it as follows:

1 Put the vinegar and spices in a basin and place it in a pan of cold water. The water level should be halfway up the basin.

2 Cover the basin with a lid or plate and bring the water to the boil.

3 Take the saucepan from the heat and let it stand until the vinegar is cold.

4 Strain to remove spices before use.

Brining

There are two methods, soaking in salt solution or layering in dry salt for 12–24 hours. For both methods use coarse or block salt. Table salt may make the pickle cloudy.

To soak in brine, dissolve 8 oz. (225 g.) of salt in 4 pints (2·3 litres) of water and immerse the prepared vegetables in the solution. Put an upturned plate over the vegetables to keep them immersed.

For dry salting, spread a layer of the prepared vegetables on a large dish and sprinkle liberally with salt. Add other layers if necessary, sprinkling each with salt.

MAKING CHUTNEY

Good chutney should have a mellow flavour and a fairly smooth texture. Apples, gooseberries, plums, beetroot and red or green tomatoes are commonly used as bases for chutneys.

Chutney adds interest and flavour to many dishes—cold meats, curries, casseroles, bread and cheese snacks. You can alter the flavouring to suit your own taste, but keep to the proportions given in the recipe.

1 Make small amounts if using a new recipe, or if you are inexperienced. If the flavour is not to your taste, you can adjust it in the next batch.

2 Wash and prepare the vegetables and fruit as necessary. Cut them up as directed, or finely chop or mince them to ensure a smooth texture.

3 Soften onions and any other tough vegetables by cooking them gently in a little water in a covered pan.

4 Add the other ingredients as directed (the sugar is not usually added until cooking is nearly completed). Continue cooking with the lid off—evaporation is an essential part of cooking.

5 If you use plain vinegar rather than ready-spiced, add the spices to the fruit or vegetables. Put ground spices directly into the saucepan, tie whole spices to the pan handle in a muslin bag and hang well into the mixture.

6 Brown sugar is normally used to give a good flavour and dark, rich colour. But use white sugar if preferred, or if you want a light colour. White vinegar and white sugar help to keep the bright colour of red tomato chutney, for example.

7 Long, gentle simmering—up to 2 hours—gives the best results. To test when the chutney is ready, tilt the saucepan and draw a wooden spoon through the mixture. It should leave a clean path in the bottom of the pan, with no traces of liquid.

Potting and sealing

Pot into clean, warm jars while hot. Fill jars to within ½ in. (1·5 cm.) of the top and cover tightly with airtight lids. Use ceresin paper with metal lids (see The equipment you need, p. 363).

Store in a cool, dry, dark place. Leave to mature for 6–8 weeks or as recommended.

Check the bottles from time to time. If the chutney is shrinking, the cover is not airtight and the moisture is evaporating.

If loose liquid collects on the top of the chutney after a few weeks, it has not been cooked enough. Bring it to the boil again and cook gently until the liquid disappears.

Sauces, Ketchups and Flavoured Vinegars

IN WEALTHY medieval households, strong spicy sauces were eaten with practically everything. Often they were needed to hide the taste of salt meat and fish. Sauce preserves were made from vinegar, often spiced, and ingredients such as mushrooms, capers and flowers. Pickling liquid came to be used as a sauce base, and eventually was itself served as a sauce.

Other types of sauce preserves were introduced in the late 16th and early 17th centuries from the Far East—Soy sauce and anchovy ketchup, for example. They were used on East India Company trading ships on the long voyage home. Ketchup is thought to be derived from a Chinese word meaning the brine of pickled shellfish.

Herb and fruit vinegars were popular not only as dressings for salads or steamed puddings, but also as throat salves or cooling drinks.

Facts about sauces and ketchups

Sauce is liquidised fruit or vegetables with vinegar and spices added to flavour and preserve it.

Ketchup is usually the juice of two vegetables preserved and flavoured with vinegar and spices. It is normally more highly concentrated and seasoned, and thinner in consistency than sauce.

The equipment you need

In general, the equipment needed is the same as for Pickles, Chutneys and Relishes (see p. 363).

In place of jars use bottles with corks or screw tops. Clean and dry them in the same way as jam jars (see p. 361). Use new corks, and submerge them in boiling water for 10 minutes before use. This sterilises them and also softens them so that they are easy to insert.

Use plastic or plastic-coated screw tops to prevent corrosion by the vinegar. Plastic skins can be used, but must be tied down very tightly to make the bottle airtight.

MAKING SAUCES AND KETCHUPS

Like pickles, chutneys and relishes, sauces and ketchups are used as accompaniments or flavourings.

1 Use fresh, firm, sound fruit and vegetables.

2 Finely chop the ingredients to give quicker cooking.

3 Cook the fruit and vegetables to a soft pulp in an open pan to allow evaporation.

4 Sieve the pulped mixture.

5 Cook the mixture again if instructed in the recipe, adding any ingredients specified. The final consistency should be between that of single and double cream.

Bottling and sealing

Fill clean, dry, warm bottles to within 1 in. (2·5 cm.) of the top and seal immediately.

Sauces made from ingredients with a low acid content, such as ripe tomatoes and mushrooms, must be sterilised after bottling. This prevents fermentation during storage.

Store in the same way as jams.

Sterilised sauces and ketchups will keep for several months, and can be opened and re-opened during that time. Use unsterilised sauces and ketchups fairly quickly once opened.

Sterilising sauces and ketchups

1 Sterilise low-acid sauces and ketchups immediately after bottling.

2 If the bottles are sealed with corks, tie the corks down to prevent them blowing out.

3 If the bottles are sealed with screw caps, tighten them, then give a half turn back.

4 Use a deep saucepan, and make a false bottom of slatted wood, folded newspaper or straw.

5 Stand the prepared bottles on the

false bottom, making sure they do not touch each other or the sides. Use small pads of newspaper to keep them apart if necessary.

6 Add sufficient cold water to reach the bottom of the corks or screw tops.

7 Heat the water to 77°C (170°F). If you do not have a thermometer, heat slowly until tiny bubbles are rising continually from the bottom of the pan. This takes about 1 hour.

8 Keep the water at this temperature for about 30 minutes.

9 Remove the bottles from the pan and tighten the screw tops or push down the corks.

10 Rub a thin film of paraffin wax over each cork and bottle top to provide an airtight seal.

FLAVOURED VINEGARS

Flavoured vinegar has herbs, fruit or vegetables steeped in it for periods varying from several days to several weeks, according to the recipe. It is then strained and bottled.

Herb and vegetable vinegars can be used to flavour salads, cold meats, casseroles or grills. Vegetable vinegars are usually made from such distinctly flavoured vegetables as horseradish, cucumbers and celery.

Fruit vinegars are usually made from soft fruits such as raspberries. Use them as a flavouring in a sauce, or dilute them to make a hot drink.

Use wine vinegar for the best results. It is not as harsh as malt vinegar so will not mask the delicate flavours of the ingredients. Use fresh, firm, sound fruit and vegetables.

Bottling and storing

Bottle into clean, warm, dry bottles in the same way as sauces. There is no need to sterilise the bottles.

Store in a dark place to prevent loss of colour.

Drying Herbs

DRYING is the oldest method of preserving food. Meat, particularly bacon, was dried and salted in medieval Britain, and peas and beans were also dried as a winter standby. Many kinds of herb were dried and used extensively for seasoning food and drink and making medicines.

Methods of drying

Drying is most useful for storing herbs so that a supply is available to season cooked dishes throughout the winter until the following season.

For air-drying, use a warm, dry, airy place such as a rack over a boiler or cooker, or an airing cupboard.

Drying by artificial heat in an oven is usually more convenient. It can be carried out in a single operation, but it is more economical to use the residual heat after cooking. Drying by stages does not normally have any ill effect.

The equipment you need

Racks or trays on which to lay the herbs. You can make these at home by stretching muslin over wooden frames or cooling trays used in baking.

Containers for packing the dried herbs. Use opaque containers or store the herbs in a dark place. Light will cause their colours to fade.

An oven thermometer is useful for checking drying temperature, particularly if you are using the bottom oven of a solid-fuel cooker.

Gathering the herbs

1 Pick herbs for drying when they are in bud and just ready to flower—usually in May or June depending on the type. This is when they are at their peak and full of essential oils.

2 If possible, pick on a warm, dry day after the dew has dried but before the sun is hot. This is when the oil content is at its highest.

3 Pick one variety at a time, and do not pick more than you can dry in one batch. The herbs will deteriorate quickly if left lying around.

4 Avoid bruising the herbs during gathering, as the oils will be lost. Remove any dead or withered leaves.

Air-drying in bunches

1 Tie the herbs in small bunches and dip in boiling water for a few seconds. This helps to preserve the colour, as well as clean the herbs.

2 Shake each bunch to remove excess moisture and leave to dry on absorbent paper.

3 Wrap a piece of muslin loosely round each bunch as a protection against dust. Do not use plastic as it will encourage the growth of mould.

4 Hang bunches, leaves downwards, in a warm, dry, airy place such as an airing cupboard. Do not hang the herbs in strong sunlight.

5 Drying time depends on the temperature and ventilation. The herbs are dried when the leaves are brittle and the stems crack rather than bend—probably after 7–10 days.

Drying on trays

1 Dip the herbs in boiling water and dry, as for bunch-drying.

2 Strip the leaves off large-leaved herbs such as sage and mint.

3 Lay the leaves and sprigs well spaced out in a single layer and cover with a sheet of muslin.

4 When air-drying, turn the herbs frequently to ensure even drying. Drying time depends on temperature and ventilation, but will probably be 2–3 days in a warm, dry place.

5 For oven-drying, place the trays in a cool oven—temperature 45–55°C (110–130°F)—gas mark 0. Leave the door ajar $\frac{1}{2}$–1 in. (1·5–2·5 cm.).

Turn the herbs over after about 30 minutes to ensure even drying.

Dry the herbs until they are crisp, usually after about 1 hour.

Drying parsley

Parsley is such a useful herb that it is worth drying in large quantities.

1 For quick drying with good colour and flavour, blanch the parsley in boiling water, shake and pat dry.

2 Hang the stems over the bars of an oven shelf and heat for 1 minute at 200°C (400°F)—gas mark 6.

3 Turn the heat down to 130°C (250°F)—gas mark $\frac{1}{2}$ and continue drying for 15–30 minutes with the oven door open, watching carefully to prevent scorching.

4 Alternatively, tie the blanched parsley in bunches and hang in the oven at a temperature of 115°C (240°F)—gas mark $\frac{1}{2}$, for about 1 hour with the door ajar.

5 Switch off the heat and leave the parsley in the oven until crisp.

Crushing and storing herbs

1 Crush dried herbs with a rolling pin and remove any pieces of stalk.

2 Pack the flaked or powdered herbs in small, airtight containers.

3 Label with the contents and date.

4 Do not shake dried herbs direct from their containers into a cooking pot. The heat and steam may cause moulds to grow in the container.

PART THE THIRD

HEREIN it is hoped that several Delightes will bring Pleasure to the Mind, in the manner of Food and Drink taking pleasure to the Stomache and appeasement and Gratification to the appetite ❧

COUNTRY FAYRE

5,000 Years of Britain's Food

MANY of the foodstuffs we enjoy today we owe to the daring of our remote ancestors. For primitive man, eating could be as dangerous an activity as hunting. An eye-catching berry, or an aromatic mushroom might be nutritious or lethal.

Observing what other animals ate was not always an infallible guide to what the human digestion could take. With every new animal, fish or plant he ate, early man gambled with his life. If he lived, a new foodstuff became part of his diet; if he died, it was his survivors who gained the benefit, learning to distinguish between that which nourishes and that which kills.

In addition to our own abundance of native animals and plants—those that have reached these islands by themselves—a great many more have been brought from abroad. Foreign invaders, wandering merchants, returning explorers and horticulturists—all have helped to enrich our heritage of food. And it is the collective experience and knowledge of successive generations of cooks that have enhanced our appreciation of taste.

Before the Romans Came
(before AD 43)

The men who built Stonehenge would have recognised the taste—if not the appearance—of a quarter of the foods we eat today.

Primitive man ate root vegetables, seeds, fruits, nuts, berries and inshore seafood, including shellfish. Edible plants, fungi and herbs may also have been used to make soups.

Honey was probably taken from wild bees' nests, and salt may have been a seasoning and a preservative.

Towards the end of the Bronze Age (*c.* 2000–750 BC), barley was used for making unleavened bread, and by about 300 BC for brewing ale. The last Celtic settlers, who came during the 1st century BC, brought wine and vinegar to Britain, and may also have introduced the domestic chicken. During the New Stone Age (2700–2200 BC) wild cattle and pigs were indigenous; sheep and goats were introduced by settlers. Cows were used for their meat, as well as for milk, cheese and butter.

The native foods below were established here before Britain was separated from Europe during the last Ice Age, around 8000 BC.

Native foods
Bilberry
Black currant
Blackberry
Broad bean
Cabbage
Carrot
Chives
Crab apple
Cranberry
Damson
Elderberry
Fat hen
Gooseberry
Juniper
Laver
Leek
Marigold
Mushroom
Nettle
Parsnip
Raspberry
Rowan
Samphire
Sloe
Sorrel
Strawberry
Turnip
Walnut
Watercress
Wild rose

Imported foods
Plum (possibly)
Vinegar
Wine

Food Brought by the Romans
(AD 43–AD 410)

For the Romans, food was more than a means of survival—it was an aesthetic experience. When they invaded Britain in AD 43, the Romans brought with them a knowledge of food and its preparation embracing centuries of experience.

Among the first plants they brought were the cultivated varieties of various fruits and vegetables, such as apples and pears; cabbages and onions. They also brought herbs and spices. Pepper was the Roman cooks' favourite seasoning, closely followed by ginger. Cooking-soda and olive oil were also used.

The Romans introduced pheasants, rabbits and guinea fowl to Britain; but the last two species died out after the Romans left and were not reintroduced for several centuries. The climate was warm enough for a few vineyards in the south, such as Silchester; but most wine was imported from Italy, France and Spain.

Imported foods
Apple
Basil
Bay leaf
Cabbage
Carrot
Celery
Cherry
Chervil
Chickpea
Fennel
Garden mint
Garlic
Ginger
Guinea fowl
Leek
Lentil
Lettuce
Marjoram
Marrow (possibly)
Onion
Parsley
Parsnip
Pea
Pear
Pepper
Pheasant
Quince
Rabbit
Radish
Rosemary
Sage
Shallot
Sweet chestnut
Thyme
Turnip

Saxons, Normans and the Middle Ages
(*c.* 450–1500)

Throughout the early part of the period there was little international trade, and no new foodstuffs seemed to have reached Britain.

The Anglo-Saxons, with boats and fishing tackle advanced enough for deep-sea work, increased the range of fish they caught. Herrings, for example, were now common.

The new influence of British cooking was the beginning of the spice trade from Italy. Spices were essential to disguise doubtful flavours.

One of the most valued and costly of imports from the Levant was sugar—introduced through the Crusaders—available only to the wealthiest households.

During the 12th century, rabbits were reintroduced from France, soon escaping from captivity to breed in the wild. About the middle of the 14th century, cucumbers—which may have been a Roman import that died out after they had left—were reintroduced from India; and spinach was introduced from Persia.

Apple wine is mentioned in Saxon times, but seems not to have been widely in use until after the Conquest, when the Normans popularised cider-making.

Cultivated foods
Damson
Marigold
Mulberry
Pea
Peach
Plum
Strawberry
Walnut

Imported foods
Almond
Cinnamon
Clove
Cucumber
Currant
Date
Lemon
Mace
Nutmeg
Orange
Raisin
Rice
Saffron
Sesame
Spice
Sugar

THE AGE OF DISCOVERY (c. 1500 – 1600)

During the 16th century, as a by-product of exploration, several new foods came to Britain. Many were regarded as curiosities, and although introduced were not accepted into our diet until much later.

Cauliflower and asparagus were rarities until the 17th century, and beetroot, which was a variety of the earlier beet, until the 18th century—all three introduced from Italy.

The tomato was recognised as a relative of the deadly nightshade, and accordingly treated with suspicion. It only became widely available in this country from the 1880s.

Sir Francis Drake brought the potato to England from the Andes in about 1570, and Sir Walter Raleigh introduced it to Ireland—from a wrecked Armada vessel—in the 1580s. But it did not come into common use until the 18th century.

The French bean and the runner bean both came from France—the French bean introduced around 1596, and the runner bean soon after.

Two kinds of fowl were imported: the turkey from America, via Spain, and the guinea fowl from West Africa.

Imported foods
Apricot
Asparagus
Beetroot
French bean
Green pepper
Guinea fowl
Melon
Potato
Pumpkin
Quince
Runner bean
Tomato
Turkey

NEW FOODS UNDER THE STUARTS (1603 – 1714)

As a result of British colonisation in the tropics a new range of spices and flavourings became available, such as piccalilli and mushroom ketchup.

Bananas and pineapples also appeared at this time, but remained rarities until the 19th century when faster ships enabled them to be brought to this country without perishing. Another import was the Jerusalem artichoke—which originally came from Canada.

From the Low Countries came Brussels sprouts, and from Italy came broccoli and a new strain of rhubarb, a plant that had formerly only been used as a medicine. The new variety was used as a fruit, but it was not until the end of the 18th century that rhubarb gained popularity.

New types of wines and spirits emerged at this time: Madeira, port, gin and rum from the West Indies.

The most fundamental change in our drinking habits came about with the introduction, in the middle of the century, of tea, coffee and chocolate. Before these non-alcoholic beverages came within the financial reach of the common people, ale was the principal drink, and drunkenness the vice.

Imported foods
Allspice
Banana
Broccoli
Brussels sprouts
Chilli pepper
Cochineal
Jerusalem artichoke
Pistachio nuts
Rhubarb

New drinks
Chocolate
Coffee
Gin
Madeira
Port
Rum
Tea

THE GEORGIAN ERA (1715 – 1830)

Like their Roman predecessors, the Georgians—who heralded in an age of elegance and gracious living—nourished the pleasures of the table. And for the first half of the period, at least, it was a time of relative plenty for the working class.

Cayenne pepper was imported from India; the peanut from Brazil; and the coconut from the tropics. Both the peanut and the coconut had been known to Europeans for many centuries, but only as exotic rarities.

Curry powder is made up from many spices. Recipes for making it and the separate spices were imported from India during this period.

The importation of a Chilean strain of strawberry led to the hybridisation in 1806 of the strawberry that we know today.

The swede, as the name implies, came from Sweden, and was brought to Scotland in 1781–2. It was used as cattle fodder until the late 19th century. During the 1780s, Arthur Guinness began producing and distributing the Dublin porter—or stout—that still bears his name.

Mayonnaise sauce dates from this period. It is not known for certain whether it is named after the Battle of Mahon in Minorca; an Irish general; an old French word for the yolk of an egg; or the French town of Bayonne, where the recipe for the sauce is said to have originated.

Imported foods
Cayenne pepper
Coconut
Curry spices
Peanut
Strawberry
Swede

THE VICTORIAN DECADES (c. 1830 – 1900)

The age of industrialisation that transformed Britain affected the nation's diet in two ways: the invention of the steamship enabled food to be brought from abroad without spoiling; and factory methods heralded the use of processed foods, such as Tabasco sauce (1868), Bovril (1872), Golden Syrup (1883), and Marmite (1902).

Other 19th-century additions to our diet were butter beans, Brazil nuts, loganberries and cornflour.

India continued to provide Britain with spicy sauces and relishes such as chutney and Worcestershire sauce.

But the main feature of this period is the widespread availability of some foodstuffs, such as the tomato and the green pepper, that had previously been available only to a small and privileged section of society.

Imported foods
Brazil nut
Butter bean
Chutney
Cornflour
Loganberry

Since the turn of the century

The last 70 years have embraced two major wars and a social revolution—all of which have had their effect on our food and eating habits.

The need to ration food during the last war also revealed how a well-balanced diet contributed more to good health than quantity.

The post-war years ushered in considerable advances in preserving and processing food, with improved methods of freezing, canning, dehydration and packing.

Changing Mealtimes

Our eating and drinking habits, and customs of the table, have been a reflection of society for thousands of years. The story of this development includes mealtimes, changing from a time when primitive hunters ate as they made their kill, to the set times of our own generation.

During the Middle Ages, life on the land followed a regular rhythm of seed-sowing and harvest, work and worship, as season followed season.

For those who suffered extremes of poverty and were without work, there were no regular mealtimes—they ate whatever they could, whenever they could.

Breakfast

But the majority of the common people rose at dawn and broke their night's fast—hence breakfast—with the first meal of their day. They would usually have watery ale, curd cheese and bread or pottage made from the local grain. The grain would be rye or 'maslin'—a mixture of rye and wheat—in the south and east, but more usually barley or oats in the north and west.

The serfs who did compulsory 'boonwork' on their lord's land were, in most cases, given two further meals throughout the day: one around noon and another at vespers, that is, when church bells tolled across the fields calling the monks to evensong.

At Crawmarey in Oxfordshire—which was a manor of the Battle of Abbey—workers had wheaten bread, ale and cheese at midday, and bread, ale, pottage, meat or herrings and cheese in the evenings.

A MEAL FOR HARVESTERS *Farm workers' meals have always had to be taken when and where work allowed*

Manorial documents in Preston, Sussex, recorded in the second half of the 13th century that 'all who have oxen in the said ploughs shall come to the lord's manor for dinner, if they wish, and shall have one day meat and the next fish, and a fair amount of ale. And all who come to the harvest boonwork shall have one day at dinner, pottage, meat and cheese, and cheese at supper, and their fill of ale, and on the other (day) pottage, fish and cheese for dinner, and for supper their fill of ale and cheese'.

Pottage of meat or fish, roots, herbs and grain was the main dish at dinner for the vast majority of people throughout Britain from prehistoric times through and well beyond the Middle Ages. Andrew Boorde, a 16th-century physician, described it as 'the liquor in which flesh is sodden in, with putting-to of chopped herbs, and oatmeal and salt'. He added that pottage 'was not so much used in all Christendom as it is used in England'.

Along with bread, cheese and ale, pottage was popular at all levels of society. Simpler types of pottage, made from the local grain and water, were an alternative breakfast or a supper dish for the poor, but an extra dish for the well-to-do. The rich would sometimes thicken it even further with eggs.

Throughout most of the 18th century, the poor who worked on the land were still rising at dawn and going to bed at sunset, or soon after. Rush lights gave them their only illumination, and these were smoky and smelly. The well-to-do used candles for much of the century, but near the end of it oil lamps came into regular use and extended the length of the day. This, and fashion, were factors in changing mealtimes. Another factor was the growth of towns, which meant that those who had any business or profession spent longer at work and more time travelling to and from it.

By the end of the century, the upper and middle classes were getting up between seven and eight in the morning and taking a light breakfast at ten. They would have plain bread and butter with tea to drink rather than the fancy breads with chocolate or coffee, which had been the custom in the late 17th century. They ate a hearty dinner sometime between three and five in the afternoon.

In October 1770, James Woodeforde, a Norfolk parson, recorded in his diary: 'I gave them for dinner a fish of fine Tench which I had caught out of my brother's Pond in Pond Close this morning, Ham, and 3 fowls boiled, a Plumb pudding; a couple of Ducks roasted, a roasted neck of Pork, a Plumb Tart and an Apple Tart, Pears, Apples and Nutts after dinner; White wine and red, Beer and Cyder. Coffee and Tea in the evening at six o'clock. Hashed Fowl and Duck and Eggs and Potatoes etc. for supper. We did not dine till four o'clock—nor supped till ten.'

The origins of lunch

Dr Johnson's *Dictionary*, published in 1755, defined 'nunchion' as a 'piece of victuals eaten between meals', and 'lunch or luncheon' to be 'as much food as one's hand can hold'. However, neither the snack nor the word seem to have been fashionable until the turn of the century, when a midday snack was taken, to bridge the gap between breakfast and many people's increasingly later dinner time.

Throughout most of the 19th century, country people and the more traditionally

DINING IN THE GREAT HALL

THE MEDIEVAL peasant ate when and where he could, often in his draughty, smoke-filled hut. But retainers of a rich man dined with the master in his great hall. At one end of the hall—which was the principal room, with a big fire in the centre—was a raised dais, with tables for the master, his family and distinguished guests. The rest of the household sat at the lower level. The raised table was a permanent fixture; but the others were trestle tables, taken down after a meal.

Diners sat on one side of the tables only, so the servants could easily reach everybody. The master sat in the centre of the main table with the salt vessel in front of him. This was a large, ornate silver or gold-plated casket called a *nef*. Originally it was shaped like a ship and held the master's spoon, knife and napkin as well as salt. Later ones held only salt and were in the form of ships, castles or other imposing models.

The single cloth of earlier times became three. The top one almost reached the floor on one side of the table, perhaps to keep the dogs away.

Hashes, pottages and stews were eaten from bowls but slices of roast meat and small roast birds were placed on 'trenchers'—thick slices of bread. A hearty eater who used several trenchers became known as a good trencherman. The bread, soaked with meat juices, was eaten, given to the poor or tossed to the dogs. Towards the end of the Middle Ages, wooden trenchers were replacing bread slices.

Servants offer spits of meat and trenchers.

minded dined early in the afternoon, and did not take a midday snack; while the urban and more fashionable members of society ate luncheon and took a later dinner. Supper was taken more by the upper classes—especially if important guests were staying—generally about ten-thirty.

High tea and afternoon tea

The middle of the 19th century heralded a dramatic change in the country's eating habits. The Industrial Revolution, symbolised by the emergence of the machine and mass-produced goods, brought tens of thousands, who had formerly worked on the land, flocking to towns and cities to work in factories.

The working classes continued to have a modest breakfast, with dinner at midday; but they had a 'high tea' in the evening, about seven o'clock. This was either a stew or a boiled suet pudding with meat, that could be left on a low heat in the oven all day, during working hours, or a meal that could be cooked quickly on reaching home. This might be fried chops, bacon or kippers in the winter; or sliced cold meats, cheese and pickles in the summer—in either case followed by an apple tart or a milk pudding.

Afternoon tea was a more feminine and leisurely affair, introduced towards the end of the century. Initiated largely by women of the middle and upper classes, it was usually taken around five o'clock, between lunch and dinner.

Although delicate cups of Indian or China tea were served with thinly sliced savoury sandwiches followed by rich fruit cake, afternoon tea was primarily an opportunity for a few friends to gather and gossip.

The traditional English breakfast

The combination of ham and eggs for a meal is thought to have originated in the Middle Ages; but it was not until the Victorian era that bacon and eggs appeared on the breakfast tables of the gentry. It was one of many meat, ham, egg and fish dishes served at the large breakfast enjoyed by people who were going to be out all day with only a small midday snack. By 1887, bacon and egg was so popular that Mrs Beeton described it in her book, *Household Management*, as a 'national standard' dish.

By about 1880 the meal pattern of breakfast, luncheon and dinner had largely established itself among the middle and upper classes—a pattern that has more or less remained unchanged ever since.

Country people were not subjected to the same routines as town dwellers, but to the needs of crops, cattle and other livestock. For them, and for the working classes in towns as well, dinner continued to be the name given to the midday meal, which was the main meal of the day. The evening meal was high tea and a light supper might be taken at bedtime.

To some extent, the two systems still exist side by side in the north of England today. Those who eat high tea between five and six o'clock then have a further light supper of coffee, tea or cocoa, cakes, cheese and biscuits about nine.

KNIVES, FORKS AND SPOONS

AS RECENTLY as 300 years ago, the majority of people in Britain ate much of their food with their fingers. They used knives to cut their meat, and spoons for eating stews.

In bygone centuries, people who expected to be eating away from home carried their own knives with them. The sharp and pointed blade (1) was used to cut a piece of meat from a carcase, spear it and carry it to the mouth. It was Cardinal Richelieu who, in 1669, ordered the ends of dining-table knives to be rounded after a guest offended him by picking his teeth with his knife point. It was not long before the rounded knife (2) spread to fashionable society across the Channel. And once the folk in a grand house had stopped using knives to convey food to their mouths, artisans and cottagers followed suit.

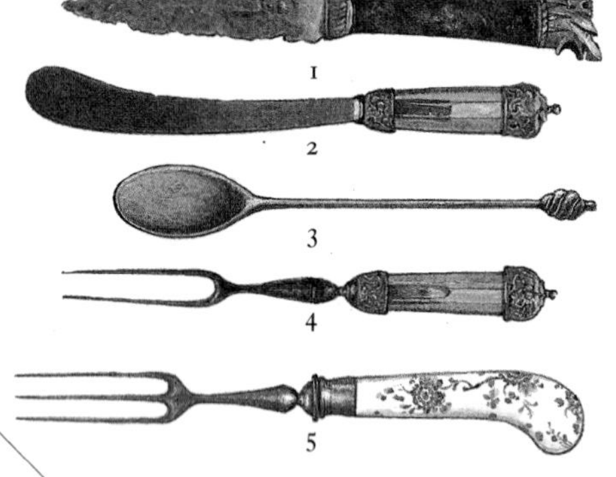

The Romans used two kinds of spoon: one for ladling chunks of meat from stews or soups; the other smaller, with a round bowl and pointed handle, used for eating eggs and shellfish. In medieval Britain, a spoon—like a knife—was a valuable possession. Spoons were made of wood, horn or pewter (3)—or silver for the rich.

It was not until the 18th century that the fork began to be accepted in general use in England. Forks existed in Roman Britain but were used to steady a joint while carving, or for serving—never for personal use when eating. Table forks, with two tines (4), probably reached England during the late 16th century, but were by no means common and were regarded by many as effeminate. In 1611, Tom Coryate, a traveller and writer, is said to have used a two-pronged fork he brought from the Continent.

After the Restoration, forks began to be more widely used; they were two-pronged. The three-pronged fork (5) was introduced during Queen Anne's reign (1702–14) and the four-pronged fork later that century. By about 1800 most wealthy households had complete sets of cutlery for guests as well as members of the family. But the practice of carrying 'travelling sets' of cutlery continued, until well into the 1800s.

THE PHILOSOPHY OF FOOD

JUST as many gourmets and gluttons have been moved to ecstasy by the delights of food, so philosophers and politicians, wits and pundits, have expressed finer feelings about the perils and pleasures of eating, drinking and cooking.

Centuries before the birth of Christ, people were pontificating about food. 'Abstain from beans,' advised Pythagoras. 'Wood-pigeons check and blunt the manly power,' warned Marcus Martial, the Latin poet and epigrammatist.

Food has even been a preoccupation of those on their death bed. If the attribution is true, the last words of William Pitt the Younger (1759–1806) before he died were: 'I think I could eat one of Bellamy's veal pies.'

Other thoughts expressed by historic personalities are as follows:

'Some people have a foolish way of not minding, or of pretending not to mind, what they eat. For my part, I mind my belly very studiously and very carefully; for I look upon it that he who does not mind his belly will hardly mind anything else.'
Dr Samuel Johnson (1709–84)

'Everything that is edible, and passes under the hands of the cook, is more or less changed, and assumes new forms. Hence the influence of that functionary is immense upon the happiness of a household.'
Isabella Beeton (1836–65)

'Digestion is the great secret of life.'
Rev. Sydney Smith (1771–1845)

Cookery '. . . means the knowledge of Medea and of Circe, and of Calypso, and Sheba.

It means knowledge of all herbs, and fruits, and balms and spices, and of all that is healing and sweet in grapes and savoury in meat.

It means carefulness, and inventiveness, watchfulness, willingness, and readiness of appliances.

It means the economy of your great-grandmother and the science of modern chemistry, and French art, and Arabian hospitality.

It means, in fine, that you are to see imperatively that everyone has something nice to eat.'
John Ruskin (1819–1900)

'The all-softening, overpowering knell, the tocsin of the soul—the dinner-bell.'
Lord Byron (1788–1824)

'After a good meal you can forgive anyone, even your own family.'
Oscar Wilde (1856–1900)

'There is no love sincerer than the love of food.'
Bernard Shaw (1856–1950)

'He was a bold man that first ate an oyster.'
Jonathan Swift (1667–1745)

'Domestic food is wholesome, though 'tis homely, And foreign dainties poisonous, though tasteful.'
Sir Walter Scott (1771–1832)

ADVICE FOR THE FARMER

IN 1573, THOMAS TUSSER, a writer on agriculture and a man of many other skills—farmer, musician, schoolmaster and poet—published *Five Hundreth Pointes of Good Husbandrie*.

The book gave month-by-month advice on the care of land, produce and cattle.

Among the 360 verses are the following:

FEBRUARY

Now thresh out thy barlie, for malt or for seed,
for breadcorne (if need be) to serve as shal need:
If worke for the thresher, ye mind for to have,
of wheat and of mestlin, unthreshed go save.

JUNE

The hop for his profit, I thus do exalt,
it strengtheneth drinke, and savoureth malt:
And being wel brued, long kept it wil last,
and drawing abide, if ye draw not too fast.

JULY

Not rent off but cut off, ripe bean with a knife,
for hindering stalke, or hir vegetive life,
So gather the lowest, and leaving the top,
shal teach thee a tricke, for to double thy crop.

SEPTEMBER

Fruit gathered too timelie, will tast of the wood,
will shrink and be bitter, and sildome prove good:
So fruit that is shaken, or beat off a tree,
with brusing in falling, soon faultie will be.

OCTOBER

Thy measeléd bacon hog, sow, or thy bore,
shut up for to heal, from infecting thy store:
Or kill it for bacon, or souse it to sell,
for Flemming that loves it so daintily well.

HERB GARDENS

Sources of Food Flavouring and Medicinal Plants

HERBS HAVE BEEN cultivated and used as food and for medicinal purposes since prehistoric times. Coriander seeds were found at a Bronze Age settlement in Kent and the Celts, who settled in Britain in 650 BC, had many herbal remedies.

The Romans brought herbs from the Mediterranean and grew them in their villa gardens, probably influencing the native population to do likewise.

Throughout the Middle Ages herbs continued to be cultivated by all classes—the rich and powerful owners of castles, fortified houses and monasteries, who had formally laid out gardens surrounded by stone walls; substantial cottagers who grew them in the 'croft', fenced-in land near the dwelling; and a peasant population who grew a few herbs beside their homes.

By the 1400s the herb garden had taken on a more regular pattern—rectangular, surrounded by a wall or a very thick hedge, and with the herbs grown on a bank of earth inside, after the style of the monastic garden. Part of the bank would be set aside as a 'herber'—a simple construction of poles over which grew roses and honeysuckle. Other small herb beds would be laid out in the centre of the garden leaving space to walk between, making the whole garden seem strictly utilitarian and formal.

In 1440 a manuscript—*The Feate of Gardening*—was written by Jon the Gardener. In his list of herb plants he mentions, among others, betony, groundsel, hollyhocks, horehound, saffron and wild strawberries. No herb garden was complete without violets, roses, marigolds, gillyflowers and elder.

In Tudor times sufficient herbs had to be grown to supply the household and fill a great variety of uses. Strong-

HERB GARDEN *A typical arrangement of herbs in the grounds of a 17th-century country house. The herbs are shown in their flowering stage.*

scented herbs were mixed with the reeds and rushes strewn on the floor to keep rooms smelling sweet.

The 'strewing' herbs most commonly used were germander, hyssop, pennyroyal, woodruff and rue. Meadowsweet was a particular favourite of Elizabeth I, and in the summer was laid on the floor of her private rooms.

Thyme, sage and rosemary were just a few of the herbs used to help in disguising the flavour of foods which had been kept overlong as well as for flavouring fresh foodstuffs. Meat and game were eaten in great quantity and, to vary the flavours and make the meats more digestible, garlic, marjoram and mugwort were added.

Wormwood and alecost were used in making ale, herb bennet and gillyflowers for flavouring wines, and other herbs to make tonic wines, teas, scents and cosmetics.

For general household purposes, mint, southernwood, lavender and others were employed as insect and moth repellents. Oils were obtained by crushing the seeds of herbs such as sweet cicely and used to polish wood floors and furniture.

In the 16th century, a new form of flower garden came into fashion. Lines of thyme, Dutch box, hyssop, germander and winter savory were all cultivated in a formal pattern of 'knots' or 'maze'—a fine example was the knot garden at Hampton Court. This style of garden was popular for many years.

In the gardens of the 16th-century manor-houses the herbs had a plot of their own, and were the responsibility of the lady of the house. She grew all the herbs she needed for the kitchen; for her teas, wines and cordials; for her ointments, cough syrups and other remedies; and for preparing the distilled waters, pomanders and scent bags.

Help and information for the housewife was provided by the great herbals of Turner, Gerard and Parkinson, and two books on gardening by Thomas Hyll—*The Proffitable Arte of Gardeninge* and *The Gardener's Labyrinth*. His books are a mixture of practical advice and astrology, typical of the period when astrology was at the height of its popularity. Hyll recommended that gardens should face the south-west, and cautioned his readers to sow seeds at the waxing of the moon and harvest them at the waning. He wrote that a hedge of briars round the garden would, within three years, 'defend out bouth thefe and beaste'. He also suggested planting a hedge of young elders, since superstition held that all herbs were protected by the spirit of the elder tree.

Until the 18th and 19th centuries herb gardens were cultivated on a wide scale, but because of the introduction of new plants and vegetables, discovered by the great explorers over the years, the form and content gradually changed. With new customs, new eating habits and major advances in medical knowledge, there was no longer a need for such a large range of herbs. Later, the Industrial Revolution hastened the decline of the herb garden.

During the 17th century the French selected a group of the best aromatic flavouring herbs from the Mediterranean—herbs fins—and developed the 'bouquet garni'. This selection was eventually adopted in England, since when there has been a steady reduction in the numbers of other herbs used.

Some herbs, for example ramson, have survived as fragrant plants in hedgerows and flower borders, while most gardens have a patch of mint, parsley, thyme or sage for flavouring food (see p. 165).

The herbs below are some of those shown in the 17th-century herb garden (left). The advice on how to use these herbs is from two 17th-century apothecaries, Nicolas Culpeper and William Salmon. Most of it is harmless, but those who took it all seriously may have put their health at risk.

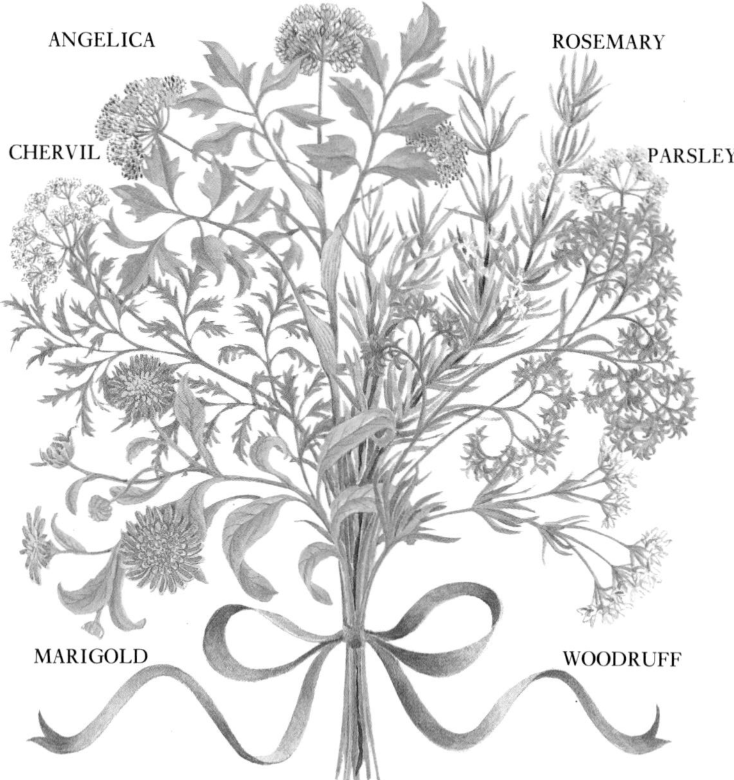

ANGELICA *Angelica archangelica*

'Dropt into the Eyes it clears them from Clouds, Films, Specks, Pearls, etc., and strengthens the Sight'

CHERVIL *Anthriscus cerefolium*

'The Essence being often taken it breeds Seed, and very much provokes Lust, and has restored some who have been Impotent'

MARIGOLD *Calendula officinalis*

'The juice of the Leaves used as a Gargarism in the Tooth-ach, it eases the Pain'

ROSEMARY *Rosmarinus officinalis*

'It causes Watchfulness and takes away Drowsiness and strengthens the Nerves powerfully'

PARSLEY *Petroselinum crispum*

'It eases the pain of the Stomach, resists and expels Poison and is good against the Bitings of Mad dogs and other Venomous Creatures'

WOODRUFF *Asperula odorata*

'Cheers the heart, makes men merry, helps melancholy and opens the stoppings of the liver'

FOOD *from the* WILD

Edible roots, plants, flowers and fungi, fruit and nuts, herbs and spices, seaweeds and shellfish—nature offers an abundance of these tasty foodstuffs growing wild throughout Britain.

WHEREVER YOU ARE in Britain's countryside, you are near a source of wild foods—in hedgerows and meadows, woodland and heathland, moorland and coastal regions. But this free produce, that includes fruit and nuts, flowers and fungi, herbs and seafood, can mean the difference between life and death for many animals, birds and insects. To preserve wildlife, therefore, gather over as large an area as possible.

Provided you do not damage land or property you may pick wild produce for your own use, except from nature reserves and land owned by the National Trust. But if you remove the plants, or attempt to sell the produce, you can be prosecuted for stealing. Remember, too, that all common land belongs to someone, and that while few owners will object to your making some selective picking, they are entitled to order you off their land for trespassing.

Avoid areas where chemical pesticides might have been used, and do not pick produce growing on the verges of major roads—it may have been contaminated by exhaust fumes.

Finally, be sure you know what you are picking to eat: some plants are deadly. Use a comprehensive field guide whenever you are in doubt.

But while caution is essential, an unreasonable suspicion of wild foods will rob you of a unique pleasure.

When to pick

Each food has not only its own habitat, but also its own season. Spring is the best time for leaves and

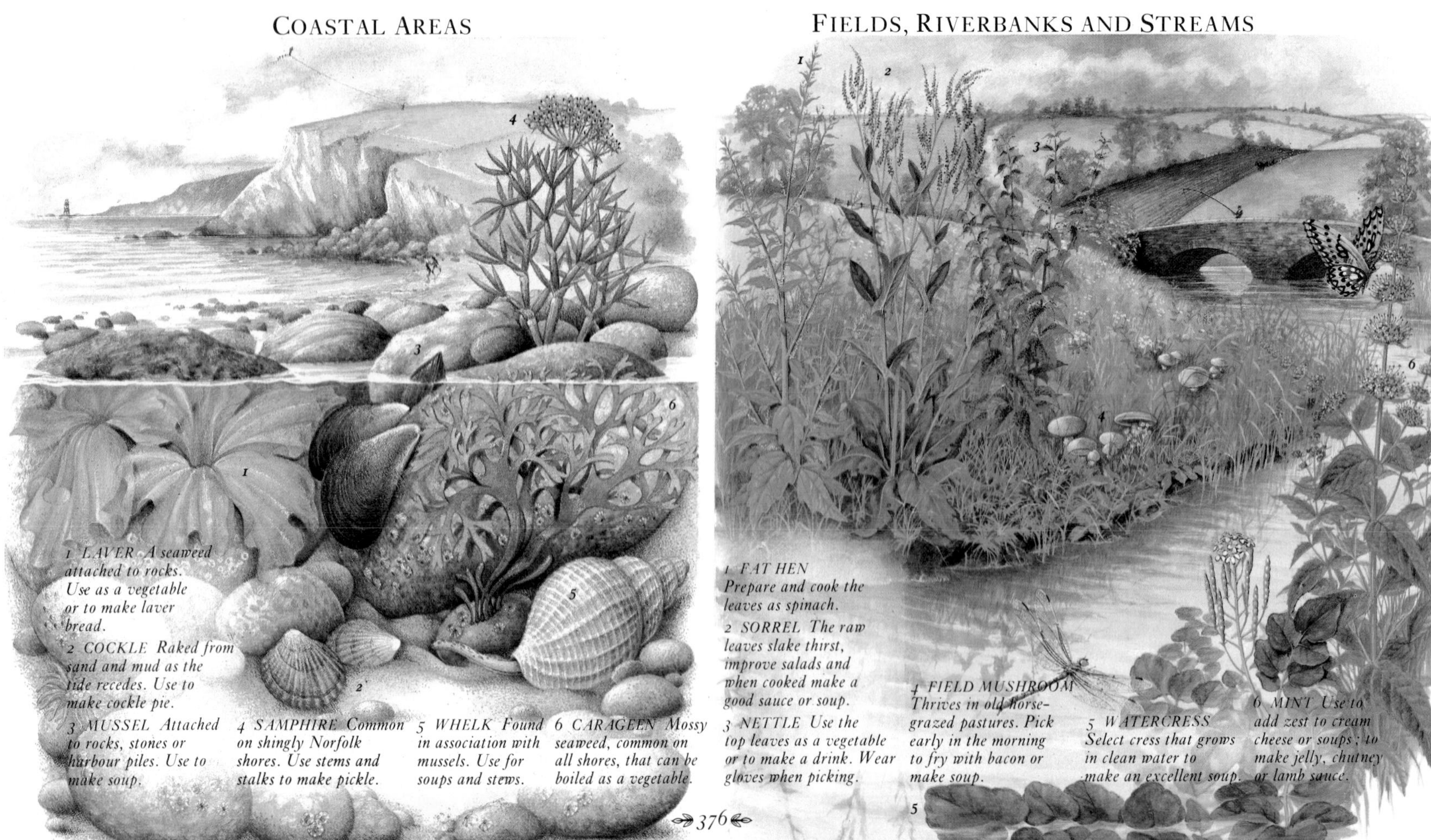

1 LAVER A seaweed attached to rocks. Use as a vegetable or to make laver bread.

2 COCKLE Raked from sand and mud as the tide recedes. Use to make cockle pie.

3 MUSSEL Attached to rocks, stones or harbour piles. Use to make soup.

4 SAMPHIRE Common on shingly Norfolk shores. Use stems and stalks to make pickle.

5 WHELK Found in association with mussels. Use for soups and stews.

6 CARAGEEN Mossy seaweed, common on all shores, that can be boiled as a vegetable.

1 FAT HEN Prepare and cook the leaves as spinach.

2 SORREL The raw leaves slake thirst, improve salads and when cooked make a good sauce or soup.

3 NETTLE Use the top leaves as a vegetable or to make a drink. Wear gloves when picking.

4 FIELD MUSHROOM Thrives in old horse-grazed pastures. Pick early in the morning to fry with bacon or make soup.

5 WATERCRESS Select cress that grows in clean water to make an excellent soup.

6 MINT Use to add zest to cream cheese or soups; to make jelly, chutney or lamb sauce.

seaweed; late spring and summer for flowers, herbs and molluscs; and autumn for berries, fungi and nuts. Winter is a lean time for wild foods, but a salad supply can be maintained if some dandelion roots are dug, planted in a box filled with earth and kept in a dark place. The roots will sprout pale, chicory-like leaves.

Where to look

The illustration below shows a selection of edible foods—there are more than 300 species in Britain—and the main habitats in which they can be found. Some plants, such as sorrel, are found in several habitats.

Molluscs and seaweed flourish on sandy, rocky beaches; samphire is found on the upper parts of the beach and on cliffs.

Avoid gathering shellfish during the warmer months of the year. When there is an R in the month roughly corresponds with the safe period. Take extra care with mussels: never gather them from habitats near human dwellings or where refuse or sewage are pumped into the sea, and gather only those which are still alive. If a mussel closes itself after being gently prised open a little, it is alive. If it opens easily or is already open, it is safer to discard it.

Finally, wash mussels thoroughly in clean water—outside and inside.

Most fungi can be found in woodland; but the field mushroom is common in pastures and meadows—particularly in areas where horses graze.

The best dandelions can usually be found on hedgebanks and roadsides. Blackberries and sloes are most commonly found in hedges. Scrubby woodland suits the elder and hazel, and mixed woodland the chestnut.

Water-loving plants, such as mint and watercress, grow by streams. Since cress absorbs much of the water it grows in, take care to avoid polluted water.

Rowan trees and thyme can be found on heathland, blue bilberry on any moor, heath or woodland except in the extreme south of England.

WOODLAND, HEDGEROWS AND ROADSIDES

HEATH AND MOORLAND

1 HAZEL The nuts are rich in protein, fats and minerals. Use in sweets.

2 SLOE When sweetened by a few frosts, the berries make a delicious wine.

3 BLACKBERRY Those which ripen in August are the sweetest. Eat them raw or use for jam or puddings.

4 DANDELION Young leaves for salads and the flowers for wine.

5 ELDER Young buds in salads; flowers in jam and berries for wine.

6 CHANTERELLE Best when apricot in colour. Cook in butter and parsley to preserve flavour.

7 WOOD MUSHROOM Make into a purée and use as a filling for an omelette, or as a sauce for chicken or veal.

8 SWEET CHESTNUT Eat raw at the end of a good summer, but better roasted. Use for sweets and stuffings.

1 ROWAN Jelly made from the berries goes well with venison and lamb.

2 BILBERRY (also known as whortleberry). Use the berries for puddings, jam or syrups.

3 THYME A herb to flavour soups, stews, stuffings and sauces. Thyme is thought to prevent bad dreams.

CALENDAR OF FEASTS AND FESTIVALS

Some of the many age-old customs still observed in the British Isles—occasions when food and drink are used to commemorate religious festivals, celebrate the blessings of a good harvest, or herald the beginning of a new season.

1st JANUARY

New Year's Day

COUNTRYWIDE

The Imperial Roman calendar, which was followed by all Christendom, was based on an average year of 365¼ days. This, over 1,000 years, produced an accumulative error—when compared with the true solar year—of eight added days. The calendar was reformed by Pope Gregory XIII in 1582, but his example, and that of most of Europe, was not followed in Britain until 1752. By then, we had to drop 11 days to conform, a change that wrought havoc with the placing of some of our most cherished festivals—particularly those occurring around Christmas.

Despite the change, we still wish each other a happy New Year on January 1, and feast upon boar's head—or more likely, roast pork, plums, and a cheering glass or two.

Roast pork *page 114*

Hogmanay

SCOTLAND

Traditionally, the fortunes of a Scottish household during the coming year are determined by the first person to cross the threshold after midnight on New Year's Eve. Preferably, this should be a dark man—who is not a member of the family—and he should bring with him bread, salt and coal: the symbols of life, hospitality and warmth. Only after these offerings have been placed on the table may he wish the family a happy Hogmanay—the first words he is permitted to utter.

In the past, the stranger brought a branch and some mistletoe: symbols of the new-born sun and the returning of spring. He thrust the wood on the fire and put the mistletoe on the mantelpiece, before breaking the silence to make his greeting.

The family then welcome the visitor and the New Year with a glass or two of whisky, Het Pint (a potent drink consisting of mulled ale, whisky and nutmeg) or Atholl Brose accompanied by some shortbread.

Atholl Brose *page 320*
Shortbread *page 284*

6th JANUARY

Twelfth Night

NORTH OF ENGLAND
WORCESTERSHIRE
HEREFORDSHIRE
GLOUCESTERSHIRE

Twelfth Night marks the end of the Christmas holidays, and is the time when all decorations must be removed if bad luck is to be avoided throughout the remainder of the year.

Traditionally, this was the most festive of all the Twelve Days; to some extent recalled by modern parties and dances held on this night, and by Twelfth Night feasts that still take place in different parts of the country.

A Twelfth Night cake, baked in honour of the Three Kings, is probably pagan in origin, and concealed a dried bean and a pea. The man to find the bean was King Bean; the woman to pick the pea was Queen of Misrule, setting the party pace for the evening. By tradition, if a woman finds the bean she chooses her king, and if a man finds the pea he picks his queen.

The Twelfth Night cake, a large flat cake of flour, sugar, honey, ginger, pepper, dried fruits and up to 18 eggs, was iced and decorated.

Some areas of the North of England celebrate the occasion with lobscouse—fried beef and vegetables—and ponsondie, a rich version of mulled ale, while farmers of the Western counties toast the next harvest in hot cider and plum cake.

Lobscouse *page 86*

First Monday after 6th JANUARY

Plough Monday

ENGLAND

Before the annual ploughing it was customary to drag the ploughs, gaily decorated with ribbons, through the village streets. The ceremony was generally followed by a play to ensure the fertility of the seed and the success of the harvest.

Today, the festival is somewhat modified. On Plough Monday, in a number of country churches, farmers and workers gather round the plough while the vicar blesses it, the men who will use it, and the work it will accomplish in the coming year.

Auld Handsel Monday

SCOTLAND

A handsel, originally, was any small coin given as a token that a bargain had been struck, and Auld Handsel Monday was the day on which apprentices, tradesmen and lamp-lighters were given their annual gratuities. Farmers, too, celebrated the occasion by giving their employees a breakfast of roast meat, whisky, bread and ale.

17th JANUARY

Old Twelfth Night Wassailing

SOMERSET, DEVON, CORNWALL

This is a Twelfth Night ceremony that refused to be budged from the pre-1752 calendar (see January 1) and is consequently held 11 days late. 'Wassail' comes from the Old English *'waes hail'*—more or less 'cheers'—and the Saxons celebrated Christmas and other festivals with a wassail bowl of hot ale spiked with honey, nutmeg and roasted apples.

Over the years the custom has become mingled with the equally ancient festival of blessing the apple trees, which is still enacted in the fruit-growing areas of the West Country. At dusk, villagers gather in the orchards, firing guns through the branches to drive away evil spirits and pouring cider on the roots. Cider-soaked bread is thrust into the forks of the trees as a thanks-offering, and the orchards are toasted with mugs of wassail and hot cider.

The trees are toasted with a traditional song, part of which goes:

'Here's to thee, old apple tree.
Whence thou mayst bud, and
whence thoust may blow.
Whence thou mayst bear apples
enow!'

Wassail *page 320*

25th JANUARY

Burns' Night

SCOTLAND AND ELSEWHERE

On this day in 1759, Scotland's national bard, Robert Burns, was born in Alloway.

For a century or more the Scots and their far-flung descendants have celebrated the anniversary with feasting and enthusiastic recitations from the poet's works, which custom decrees should include two or three verses of his renowned poem: *Address to a Haggis*.

The menu too must feature this dish, with its traditional accompaniment of bashed neeps (mashed swede) illuminated by the customary glass of malt whisky. Celebrants with hearty appetites may then proceed to Friar's Chicken Soup—chicken, veal, cream and seasoning—partan (crab) pie, collops, potted or roast game, mutton with rowan jelly and syllabub.

Collops *page 86*
Everlasting syllabub *page 227*
Haggis *page 105*
Partan pie *page 57*
Potted game *page 41*
Rowan jelly *page 343*

1st FEBRUARY

St Bride, or Brigid's, Day Candlemass Eve

SCOTTISH HIGHLANDS, IRELAND

In Christian tradition, St Bride or St Brigid was midwife to the Virgin, and in her honour, women who had borne children during the past year used to carry lighted candles round the church at Candlemass. But it may be that her cult long pre-dates Christianity.

Two-thousand years ago, Celtic women in labour prayed to Brigantia, the fertility goddess, whose Holy Day was also February 1—the first day of the old Celtic spring. As saint or goddess, St Bride (or St Brigid) is still remembered: in Ireland with decorations of plaited rushes and a meal of barm brack—a yeasty fruit loaf—and in the Highlands with the baking of the special St Bride's bannock.

Bannocks *page 270*

14th FEBRUARY

St Valentine's Day

St Valentine was a Bishop of Rome particularly renowned for his chastity; but since he was martyred on February 14, the eve of the Roman festival of Lupercalia when young people chose their sweethearts by lottery, he was swiftly adopted as the patron saint of lovers.

A certain element of chance still persists in the rituals of the day. Plum stones are counted off to the chant of 'He loves me, he loves me not', while a long apple peel thrown over the shoulder supposedly falls as the initial of one's beloved.

In some areas, the day is celebrated with a heart-shaped Valentine cake, which the girl presents to her sweetheart.

SHROVE TUESDAY

Pancake Tuesday Bannock Tuesday

Shrove Tuesday was the day when the faithful were shriven—that is, granted absolution after confession and penance—in preparation for the solemnities of Lent. It was also the last day on which foods proscribed by the Church—such as butter and eggs—might be consumed before the annual fast began.

Thoughts of Lenten austerity combined with the temporary food surplus made this a light-hearted day, in which sports and the making and eating of pancakes played a major part.

Pancake races are still run in many towns and villages; the one held at Olney, Bucks., so inspired visitors from Liberal, Kansas, that they instituted a sister race in their own town. There, the winner's prize of a kiss, which in Olney is bestowed by the verger, is donated instead by the British Consul.

Bannocks *page 270*
Pancakes *page 244*

1st MARCH

St David's Day

WALES

St David, or Dewi, patron saint of Wales, died on March 1, *c.* 600. St David's, Pembrokeshire which became a cathedral city, was probably founded by him.

His biographers credit him with many miracles, not least of which was his ability to subsist on a diet of leeks and water. This may be why the Welsh wear the plant on his day; another reason given is that it was worn as a badge of identity by the Welsh troops who defeated the Saxons at Heathfield in 633.

Whatever the reason, leek soup must figure in the traditional St David's Day dinner, to be followed by a main course of Welsh hill-fed lamb.

Cream of leek soup *page 26*

Fourth Sunday in LENT

Mothering Sunday Simnel Sunday

ENGLAND

On this day, until the 16th century at least, parishioners who normally attended chapels-of-ease in their outlying hamlets, would come instead to worship at the mother church of the parish.

By the 19th century, Mothering Sunday had evolved into a holiday on which apprentices and girls in service were given leave to visit their mothers. Traditionally, the offspring brought with them gifts of flowers and simnel cake and were regaled in exchange with frumenty—a treat, consisting of fermented wheat or barley with milk and eggs.

Simnel cake *page 280*

PALM SUNDAY

HEREFORDSHIRE

In an effort to promote better relations between the villages of Hentland, Sellack and King's Caple, near Ross-on-Wye, Lady Scudamore, an 18th-century land-owner, made provision in her will for the inhabitants of all three parishes to be provided in perpetuity with free cakes on Palm Sunday. Small individual Pax cakes, stamped with the slogan 'Peace and Good Neighbourhood' are still given out in Sellack Church at the end of the service on that day.

17th MARCH

St Patrick's Day

IRELAND

A telling point in St Patrick's conversion of the Irish was his use of the trefoil leaf of the shamrock to illustrate the Three-in-One doctrine of the Trinity. The shamrock has been celebrated as Ireland's national plant ever since.

The traditional dish for the day is St Patrick's Fishes. The story goes that the saint, tempted to eat meat in Lent, threw it into the sea, where it turned into fishes—a permissible substitute on days of fast. Nowadays, visitors are offered potato soup and boiled bacon and cabbage. Another favourite for the occasion is Dublin Coddle—oysters, potato cakes and Irish stew. With, of course, good Irish whiskey, stout and porter.

Last Thursday in MARCH

Oranges and Lemons

LONDON

At one time, the attendants of Clement's Inn of Court used to make an annual presentation of oranges and lemons to the residents—an act commemorated in the nursery rhyme and in St Clement Danes' famous peal of bells.

GOOD FRIDAY

COUNTRYWIDE

In Hebden Bridge, Luddenden and in several other places in Yorkshire, Pace Egg plays are performed in which the mummers celebrate the triumph of spring over winter. In St Bartholomew's churchyard in London's Smithfield, a very different ceremony used to be held. There, on Good Friday, 21 widows of the parish were given a small sum of money over the grave of an unknown 17th-century benefactor, together with a hot cross bun. Nowadays, only buns are handed out.

The cross on hot cross buns may be a relic of pre-Reformation days, when all bread was marked with a cross as a charm against evil spirits that might prevent the dough from rising. An alternative theory is that the quadrants formed by the cross symbolised the four seasons.

EASTER

COUNTRYWIDE

Easter may fall anywhere between March 22 and April 25, the date being determined by that of the Sunday following the first full moon after the Spring Equinox. This arrangement was settled by the Council of Nicea as long ago as AD 325, but many of the Easter customs pre-date Christianity.

The very name of the festival is that of Eostre, Saxon goddess of spring, whose feast day was the Spring Equinox. Eggs were sacred to her as the symbol of rebirth, and from this we get the Easter Egg and the custom of rolling hard-boiled, dyed eggs down hills, which still takes place in many parts of the country. The Easter Bunny is descended from the hare that the devotees of Eostre regarded as representing fertility and the spring regeneration of life.

Since time immemorial it has been customary to celebrate the end of Lent with a feast of roast lamb or veal, and egg custards and cream.

Custard sauce *page 252*

EASTER MONDAY

COUNTRYWIDE

This is a day of fairs and feasting; in Hallaton, Leicestershire, a Hare Pie Scramble (usually mutton or steak pies today) is held, in which the person who emerges from the scrum with the biggest piece is given a prize. This is followed by a 'Bottle-kicking' contest, in which a team of Hallaton stalwarts try to kick or carry a small cask over the parish boundary in the face of strong opposition by a team from nearby Medbourne.

Oranges and eggs are rolled down hillsides in various parts of the country, and in Epney, Gloucestershire, a fried elver-eating contest is held. There may be as many as 1,000 elvers to the pound; experts can consume that amount in under a minute.

Fried elvers *page 52*
Mutton pies *page 210*

1st MAY

COUNTRYWIDE

Political connotations apart, May Day was originally sacred to Flora, the Roman goddess of spring, and in Celtic lands to Beltane, the feast that marked the beginning of summer. Traces of both festivals still persist in England. The May Queen, with her crown of flowers, represents Flora, and the Maypole is Flora's Tree of Fertility. Beltane, on the other hand, is celebrated in Cornwall, Ireland, Wales and Scotland by the lighting of huge bonfires on hilltops.

In Scotland it was the custom to bake a Beltane bannock, which has nine knobs. Each knob represents a different danger that might beset the farm during the year. The knobs are torn off and flung over the crofter's shoulder as an offering to the deity.

Bannocks *page 270*

Wednesday before ASCENSION DAY

Blessing the Sea

HASTINGS, SUSSEX

The ceremony—held on the fortieth day after Easter—is a lingering vestige of the old Rogationtide, when clergy and congregation went in procession to bless the fruits of the earth. In Hastings, the rectors of All Saints' and St Clement's churches conduct a service from the RNLI lifeboat, asking for God's blessing on the coming fishing season, and on the fishermen themselves.

29th MAY

Founder's Day

ROYAL HOSPITAL, CHELSEA

This day is the birthday of Charles II, founder of the Royal Hospital. Since 1692 the Chelsea Pensioners have celebrated the occasion with an inspection by a distinguished soldier or member of the Royal Family. This is followed by a march past to the tune of *The Boys of the Old Brigade*, and the day is rounded off with a supper that includes plum pudding as a treat for the old soldiers.

SPRING BANK HOLIDAY

Cheese-rolling

BROCKWORTH, NR GLOUCESTER
IDE HILL, NR SEVENOAKS

Cheese-rolling was a traditional gesture made to establish common grazing rights.

At Cooper's Hill, Brockworth, where there is a 1 in 3 slope, young and sturdy competitors scramble down the hill pursuing a bouncing Gloucestershire cheese embellished with ribbons. The first down wins the cheese and the second and third, small sums of money. The starting point is marked by a flagstaff, as a reminder that the custom also represents the right of people to dance round the Maypole.

At Ide Hill, women and children pursue a cheese down the village green.

Last Sunday in JUNE

Alnwick Fair

NORTHUMBERLAND

The present fair, which lasts a week, is held by virtue of a charter granted to the de Vesseys, a local landowning family, in 1290. In fact, six previous charters had been granted even earlier. Following ancient custom, an ox is roasted whole in the market place, and large, soft scones known as singing hinnies are served hot from some of the stalls. The name of the scones was allegedly given by a Northumberland housewife who, being pestered by her children's nagging as to whether the scones were ready, cocked an ear to the sizzling note from the pan and replied: 'No, they're just singin', hinnies.'

Singin' hinny *page 282*

26th JUNE to 1st JULY

Mevagissey Feast Week

MEVAGISSEY, CORNWALL

During this week, honour is paid to St Peter when the children of the local Sunday schools are involved in sport and a church procession to the harbour—the rest of the week is devoted to carnival. In the past, saffron cakes and buns were traditional food.

First Sunday in JULY

Love Feast

ALPORT, DERBYSHIRE

Two miles down a footpath from the Ladybower Reservoir there is a lonely stone barn, in which, during the 18th century, Wesleyan services were held. At this time, Wesleyan Methodists were highly unpopular both with the Church of England and the Establishment in general; and, lacking churches in which to hold their services, held them instead in the open air, or in remote buildings such as this.

To remind the present generation of the difficulties of their forbears, a Love Feast and Methodist service takes place each July in the barn. Members of the congregation, which includes many visitors from overseas, testify to their faith, hymns are sung, and at the end of the service spiritual refreshment is supplemented with a slice of fruit cake and a sip of water from a Loving Cup, passed from hand to hand.

Late JULY

Blessing the Waters

REEVES BEACH, WHITSTABLE, KENT

A religious ceremony, which has been taking place for 150 years, is held on the foreshore to bless the fruits of the waters. The service is conducted by the Bishop of the Association of Men of Kent and Kentish Men, attended by a gathering immediately offshore of boats of local fishermen, sea cadets, sea scouts and visitors to Whitstable.

Last Monday in JULY

Swan Upping

RIVER THAMES

The Vintners' and Dyers' Companies have the ancient right, which they share with the Sovereign, of keeping a 'game of swans' on the Thames between London Bridge and Henley. During the last few days of July, the year's batch of cygnets is rounded up and marked—those claimed by the Vintners with a nick on each side of the bill, the Dyers' with a single nick—the royal swans are left unmarked.

At one time, all swans were the property of the Crown, until, in the 15th century, a few Livery Companies were granted the right to keep them as well.

Swan Upping concludes with the traditional banquet of roast cygnet.

Last Saturday in JULY

Apple Pie Fair

MARLDON, DEVON

Apple pies are sold and an Apple Pie Princess is crowned to commemorate the generosity of a 19th-century farmer, George Hill.

Each year, Hill gave windfalls from his orchards to his workers and donated an outsize apple pie, transported on a donkey cart, to the village fair. The ceremony is still commemorated by villagers.

Apple pie *page 244*

1st AUGUST

Lammas

COUNTRYWIDE

Traditionally, the first day of harvest. The word comes from the Old English *Hlafmaesse*—the Loaf Mass, at which bread made from the first corn of the harvest was eaten with due solemnity. The custom was continued in Scotland until well within living memory, with the baking of the special *Bonnach Lunastain* (Lammas bannock) for the occasion.

Saturday nearest 5th AUGUST

St Oswald's Day Rushbearing

GRASMERE, WESTMORLAND

This ceremony takes place in several towns and villages in the North of England, on various dates throughout the summer. Most likely it is a relic of the days when the stone floors of churches, and of many other buildings, were strewn with rushes, but it may also be connected with the cult of Flora, the Roman goddess of flowers.

Grasmere Rushbearing is particularly attractive. There, children dressed in their best and carrying 'bearings' of interwoven rushes and flowers, parade through the streets accompanied by the clergy and the local band. The children are later regaled with gingerbread from the Grasmere Gingerbread Shop—its recipe a closely guarded secret.

12th AUGUST

Grouse season opens

COUNTRYWIDE

Roast grouse *page 136*

AUGUST – SEPTEMBER

Oyster season opens

COLCHESTER

The oyster season opens with an inspection of the Colne Fishery by the Mayor of Colchester and civic dignitaries. The ancient proclamation of 1256, confirming that the fishing rights of the River Colne belong to the Corporation of the Borough of Colchester, is read out by the Town Clerk. A toast is drunk to the Queen in gin, and gingerbread is eaten.

The Mayor lowers the first trawl in Pyefleet Creek to bring up the first oysters, and the season is officially open.

Gingerbread *page 290*

24th AUGUST

St Bartholomew's Day

SANDWICH, KENT

St Bartholomew is the patron saint of bee-keepers, and at one time it was customary to harvest honey on his day. He was remembered until recently by the mead-makers of Cornwall, who used to bring their product—which is made from fermented honey—to be blessed in the church at Mount's Bay, near Penzance.

Bartholomew is also the patron saint of Sandwich, and in his honour a service is held at 11 a.m. at St Bartholomew's Hospital Chapel. After the service, Bartlemas biscuits impressed with the saint's seal are given out. A child wanting a share in the food must run round the chapel first to receive a Bartlemas biscuit and a traditional bun, such as a Chelsea bun.

The biscuits were originally distributed to the poor and wayfarers on pilgrimage to Canterbury. Today they are usually varnished and kept as mementoes.

Mead *page 324*
Chelsea buns *page 274*

Third Saturday in SEPTEMBER

Crab Fair

EGREMONT, CUMBERLAND

The fair, held annually since 1267 at the season when crab apples are ripe, was originally the day on which the Lord of the Manor received his share of each man's harvest. He, in return, rode through the crowd distributing largesse.

Crab Fair is the setting for the World Gurning Championship and the Pipe Smoking Competition. The winner of the first is the person who can pull the ugliest face while peering through a horsecollar, while, in the second, each competitor is given a clay pipe, a twist of black tobacco and a candle. The person who smokes the whole twist first is the winner.

Hedgerow jelly *page 340*

Wednesday before 20th SEPTEMBER

Ancient Chartered Fair

BARNSTAPLE, DEVON

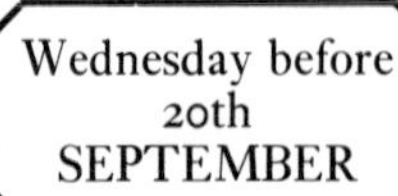

The three- or four-day fair was given its charter in the 10th century by Athelstan, grandson of Alfred the Great. It is one of the largest traditional gatherings of travelling fair people in England. The third day of the fair is devoted to cattle-dealing and general merrymaking. The proceedings are opened by the Senior Beadle, who provides a brew of spiced ale made according to an Elizabethan recipe, accompanied by toast, cheese, gingerbread and other old English confections.

Gingerbread *page 290*
Mulled ale *page 322*

29th SEPTEMBER

Michaelmas

COUNTRYWIDE

At Michaelmas, the year's third Quarter Day, it was customary to present your landlord with a goose fattened on the grain among the stubble, along with your quarterly rent. As the old rhyme has it, a tenant would bring his landlord:

At Christmas a capon,
At Michaelmas a goose
And somewhat else at New Year's tide
For feare their lease flie loose.

In England, Michaelmas goose was stuffed with herbs, quinces, pears, garlic and grapes, and served with a wine and spice sauce; in Wales, the bird was stuffed with potatoes.

Bannocks *page 270*
Yorkshire stuffed goose *page 127*

SEPTEMBER and OCTOBER

Harvest Home

COUNTRYWIDE

Harvest Home is a time of thanksgiving and relaxation that marks the end of the farming year; many of the customs attending it, traces of which still exist, long pre-date Christianity. It was thought, for example, that the Corn Spirit lived in the last stand to be cut, and since no worker wished to be the one to deprive the spirit of its home, each man stood back and all threw their sickles at the stand until it fell. Its corn was then woven into a corn-dolly, or kern-baby, a vaguely female shape that was given a place of honour at the Harvest Supper. Afterwards, the dolly was kept in the farmhouse, or church, to ensure a good harvest next year.

Nowadays, the Harvest Supper is simply a village feast; but within living memory the main traditional dish in England was frumenty—fermented wheat or barley with milk and eggs.

In Scotland, cream crowdies—oatmeal, cream and sugar—and ale crowdies—oatmeal, treacle, ale and whisky—were served.

Cold brisket of beef in cider *page 80*

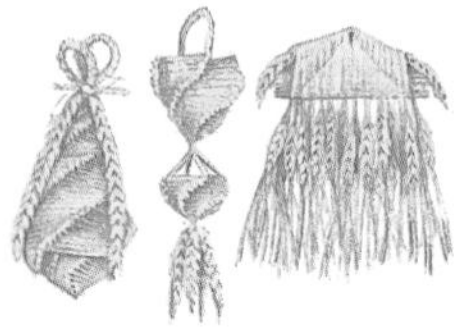

Last Friday in OCTOBER

Oyster Festival

COLCHESTER

Richard I granted the Colne Oyster Fisheries to the citizens of Colchester in perpetuity; the event is celebrated annually at a feast given by the Mayor and Aldermen at the Town Hall. There, the 500 or so invited guests are regaled with a gargantuan supper of gin, gingerbread and, of course, oysters.

Gingerbread *page 290*
Oyster loaf *page 55*

31st OCTOBER

Hallowe'en

NORTH OF ENGLAND, SCOTLAND, WALES, IRELAND

Hallowe'en, All Hallow's Eve, the Eve of All Saints' Day, is a direct descendant of the Celtic Samhain, the feast of the New Year. It was a night, the Celts believed, when all natural laws were suspended; ghosts, witches and goblins walked the night, and bonfires were lit on hilltops to encourage the sun to return the following year.

It is a night of celebration and divination, when girls see their future husbands' faces in the mirror, or try to discover his initial by throwing apple peel over their shoulders and studying the shape in which it falls. In the Highlands, girls used to eat salt herrings before going to bed; their future spouses would appear in their dreams and offer them a drink.

Throughout the British Isles traditional games are still played and traditional foods eaten.

In Ireland, apple dumplings and pies, and potato cakes or scones are eaten instead. Colcannon is a dish having charms in it, foretelling marriage, bachelorhood or luck to the recipients. In Scotland, special bannocks are baked, while in Wales, farmers offer ale and seed cake to visitors in celebration of the harvest.

Apple pie *page 244*
Bannocks *page 270*
Colcannon *page 194*
Potato scones *page 276*
Seed cake *page 289*

11th NOVEMBER

Martinmas

SCOTLAND

Nowadays, this is chiefly known as the Day of Remembrance for the dead of both World Wars; but it is also the feast day of St Martin of Tours, patron of horsemen and all domestic animals.

In Scotland, Martinmas was the first day of the farmworkers' annual holiday, and therefore a day of celebration. Each farmer would slaughter an ox and distribute meat, haggis and black and white puddings among the labourers—probably the only day in the year on which the men and their families would taste beef.

30th NOVEMBER

St Andrew's Day

SCOTLAND

St Andrew, brother of St Peter and one of the Twelve Apostles, had no connection with either Scotland or Russia in his lifetime, yet he is patron saint of both. Traditionally, Scotland celebrates St Andrew's feast day with haggis and whisky, cock-a-leekie soup, collops, venison and ptarmigan.

Cock-a-leekie soup *page 28*
Collops *page 86*
Haggis *page 105*
Venison *page 130*

24th DECEMBER

Christmas Eve

COUNTRYWIDE

On Christmas Eve, in parts of the Midlands, Dumb Cakes—made from wheatmeal and barley flour—used to be made by girls working alone and in silence. On the stroke of midnight, hopefully, the spirit of their future husbands would appear, and turn the cakes.

In Scotland, thin oatcakes known as farls were baked in honour of the Virgin's safe delivery. Each farl had a deeply-indented cross, and one was given to each member of the family. If the cakes were kept intact until the evening of Christmas Day, then good fortune was assured for the coming year.

25th DECEMBER

Christmas Day

COUNTRYWIDE

The birth of Christ is, by early Christian tradition, celebrated on this day. His true birth date is unknown. Many of the time-honoured rites associated with Christmas were in fact adopted from much earlier festivals, usually associated with the Winter Solstice, that took place on or about the same date.

The candle-lit Christmas tree comes from the Norse Yule, festival of fire and light. Mistletoe was sacred to the Druids, while the Forces' custom of officers and senior NCOs serving the other ranks on Christmas morning is a direct descendant of the Roman Saturnalia, in which masters and slaves changed places for a day. But whatever the derivations, it is a time for thanksgiving and charity.

Dr Johnson's Punch *page 322*
Boiled beef in Ale *page 86*
Christmas pudding *page 250*
Mince pies *page 250*
Yorkshire stuffed goose *page 127*
Roast turkey *page 124*
Brawn *page 42*

26th DECEMBER

Boxing Day

COUNTRYWIDE

The name may be derived from the medieval custom of placing alms boxes in churches during the weeks leading up to Christmas. The boxes were opened on Christmas Day, and their contents distributed to the poor on the following morning.

Alternatively, it may come from the later practice of servants and apprentices being permitted to collect monetary gifts from their master and his customers during the Christmas festivities. These were collected in a Christmas box, a name that has been transferred to the annual gratuities given to the postman, the milkman and to others who have rendered service during the year.

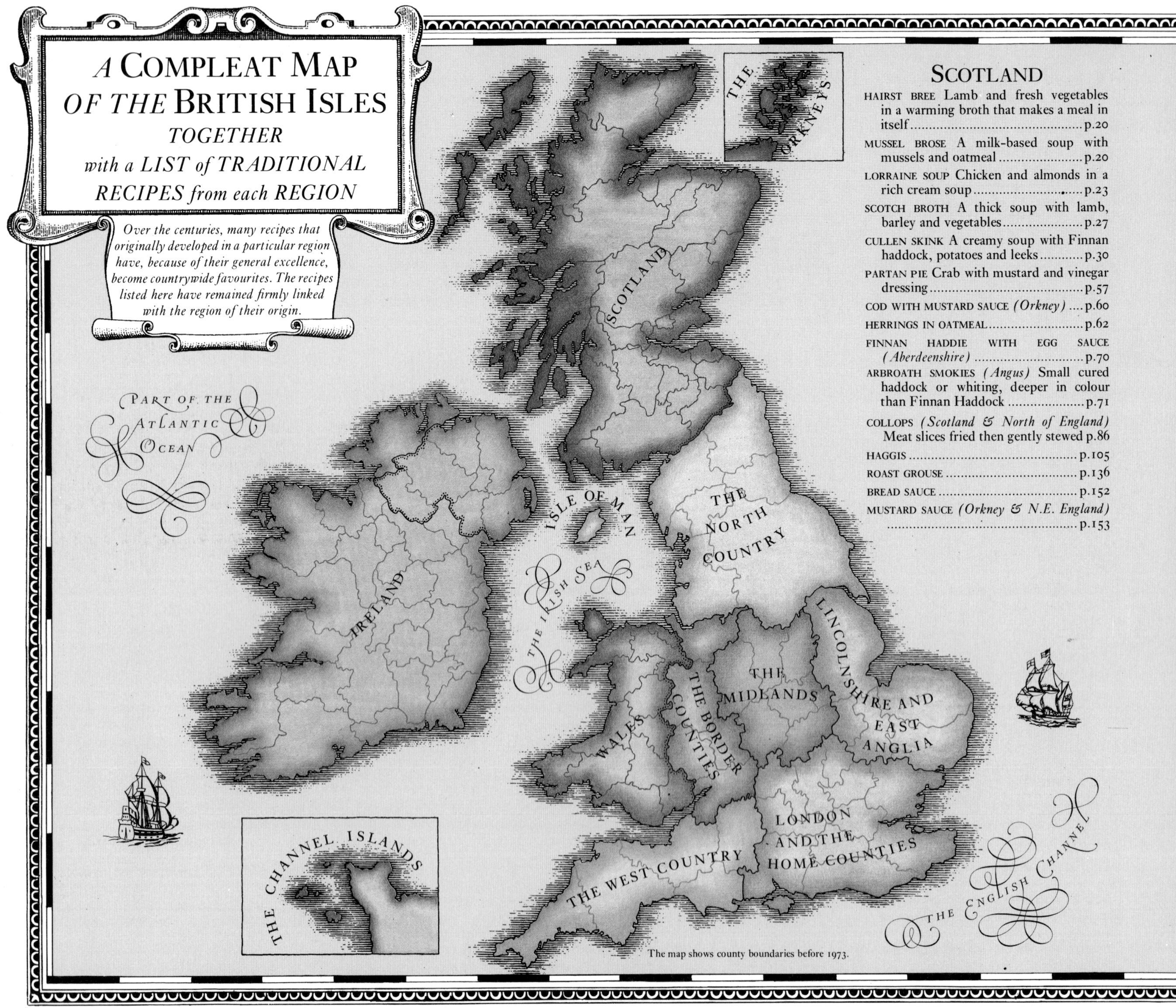

The map shows county boundaries before 1973.

ENGLAND

THE NORTH COUNTRY

THE MIDLANDS

THE BORDER COUNTIES

LINCOLNSHIRE AND EAST ANGLIA

continued overleaf

LONDON AND THE HOME COUNTIES

THE WEST COUNTRY

WALES

IRELAND

ISLE OF MAN

CHANNEL ISLANDS

PART THE FOURTH
GENERAL REFERENCE

A Dictionary of Cooking Terms

AL DENTE The cooked texture of pasta, firm to the bite.

ASPIC A clear jelly made from the cooked juices of meat or fish, used to mould or garnish savoury dishes.

AU GRATIN A method of finishing a cooked dish by covering it with sauce or breadcrumbs or both, and browning under the grill or in the oven.

BAIN-MARIE A shallow pan of cold or tepid water with a smaller pan placed in the water. Used to cook or keep hot sauces, baked custards or egg dishes without the over-heating that makes them curdle.

BAKE BLIND To bake a pastry case without its filling (see p. 220).

BARD To cover lean meat, game or poultry with strips of pork fat or fat bacon during cooking to prevent drying out.

BASTE To ladle hot fat or liquid over food during cooking.

BIND To work a liquid, egg or melted fat into a dry mixture to hold it together.

BLANCH To steep food in boiling water in order to soften, clean or whiten it, to remove strong flavours, or to make the skin easier to peel.

BLOOD HEAT A temperature of 37°C (98·4°F). Food at this heat feels lukewarm to the fingertip.

BOUQUET GARNI A small bunch of herbs (usually thyme, parsley, marjoram and a bay leaf) used to flavour soups and stews. It is tied with cotton or put in a muslin bag and removed before serving.

BRAISE To cook meat or vegetables slowly in steam in a covered pot with a little water or stock.

CARRAGEEN A nutritious edible seaweed, also known as Irish moss, found along Ireland's rocky Atlantic coast. It is used as a vegetable or to set jellies.

CASSEROLE An ovenproof cooking vessel with a lid; also the stew cooked in it.

CLARIFIED FAT Butter, or other fat that has been heated and strained to remove impurities or sediment (see p. 49).

CONSOMMÉ A clear soup.

CORAL Orange shellfish roe.

CREAMING Working together a mixture such as fat and sugar with a wooden spoon until light and fluffy, like whipped cream.

CROÛTES Slices or fingers of fried or toasted bread, used as a base for serving savoury mixtures or as a garnish.

CROÛTONS Small cubes of fried bread used to garnish soups and dishes served with a sauce.

CURD The semi-solid part of curdled milk. But lemon curd is lemon rind and juice cooked with sugar, eggs and butter to a spreading consistency. See p. 362.

CURDLE To separate milk into solid and liquid by heating and adding acid or rennet. It is the first stage in cheese-making. Milk, some sauces, soups, egg dishes and cream mixtures separate into solid and liquid because of overheating or the action of acid.

CURE To preserve meat or fish by drying, salting or smoking.

DEEP FRY To fry food by immersing in hot fat or oil.

DEVIL To prepare meat, poultry or fish with sharp, hot seasonings before grilling or roasting.

DOUBLE BOILER OR SAUCEPAN A two-part saucepan with a top pan fitted into a lower one that holds simmering water. Used for slow, gentle cooking.

DREDGE To sift flour or sugar evenly over food.

DRIPPING Fat extracted from meat during roasting, or from animal fat rendered down.

ESCALOPE (or Scallop) A thin slice of meat, usually veal, often fried in breadcrumbs.

FAGGOT A small savoury cake made from pork offal, onion and bread, usually baked. Also another name for a bouquet garni.

FINES HERBES Finely chopped mixed herbs.

FISH KETTLE An oval or oblong pan with a lid and an inner detachable grid for poaching fish.

FOLD IN To incorporate ingredients such as flour or whisked egg whites into a mixture without letting air escape. Use a metal spoon to cut through the mixture, slide it along the bottom of the bowl, then lift and turn the mixture over the ingredients to be folded in. Continue until all are incorporated.

FOOL A cold sweet dish made from whipped cream or custard, or both, and fruit purée.

FORCEMEAT Stuffing for meat, fish or vegetables (see p. 164).

FORCING BAG A funnel-shaped cotton or nylon bag with a nozzle through which creamy mixtures can be piped into designs.

FRICASSEE A white stew.

GALANTINE A mixture of cooked meats or poultry set in their own jelly and served cold.

GLAZE To brush liquid over food to give it a glossy appearance. Use a meat glaze (see p. 34) for meat, and egg and/or milk for bread and pastry (see p. 221).

GREEN BACON Bacon that has been cured in brine only. It does not keep as well as bacon that has been further cured by smoking.

GRIDDLE A flat metal plate for baking bread or cakes over a fire or on top of a stove; also known as a girdle.

HULL To remove the green stalk and cup (calix) from fruits such as strawberries, or the pods from peas or broad beans.

KNEADED BUTTER Softened butter mixed with flour, used to thicken soups, stocks or sauces (see p. 163).

LARDING Threading small strips of fat (lardons) into the surface of lean meat to prevent it drying out during roasting (see p. 145). It is done with a larding needle, which has a clip at one end. Anchovies can sometimes be used as lardons.

LIAISON A thickener for sauces and soups (see p. 35).

LIGHTS The lungs from an animal carcase, sold as offal.

MANDOLIN A vegetable slicer with an adjustable blade.

MARINATE To steep meat or fish in a seasoned liquid (marinade) to flavour or tenderise it.

MARSALA A sweet Italian wine drunk as an apéritif or used in cooking.

MASK To cover food with sauce.

MERINGUE Whisked egg white mixed with sugar and baked as a pie topping or small confection.

MORNAY A cheese sauce used to coat fish, egg or vegetable dishes.

MOUSSE A cream dish lightened with beaten egg whites, stiffened with gelatine and given a sweet or savoury flavouring.

MULL To heat and also spice or flavour ale and wine.

PARBOIL To partially cook food by boiling, usually to preserve it or keep it moist, before completing cooking by another method.

PATTY TIN A moulded tin for baking a batch of small cakes.

PECTIN A substance in fruit that causes the pulp to set (see p. 359).

PIE FUNNEL A funnel used to support a pastry lid.

PLUCK An offal mixture (see p. 113).

POACH To cook food in liquid kept just below boiling point.

POT-ROAST To cook food in steam, raised on a rack above a small amount of liquid in a covered pot.

POTTAGE A thick stew cooked in a pot over an open fire, a staple British food for centuries.

PURÉE Raw or cooked food crushed to a very smooth texture through a sieve or in an electric blender.

RAMEKIN A small baking vessel, usually earthenware or china, for cooking individual savoury dishes.

REDUCE To thicken, concentrate the flavour, or lessen the quantity of a stock or sauce by boiling rapidly to evaporate some of its water content.

RENDER To extract the fat from raw meat trimmings by slow heating.

RENNET A substance from the stomach lining of a calf, used to curdle milk in cheese-making.

ROAST To cook meat by direct heat from a fire or by radiant heat in an oven (see p. 114).

ROE The eggs from a female fish (hard roe), or the reproductive glands of a male fish (soft roe).

ROUX Fat and flour cooked together over a gentle heat, used as a sauce thickener (see p. 162).

SADDLE The undivided loin from a meat carcase.

SALTPETRE A chemical (potassium nitrate) used in very small amounts as a preservative in curing meat.

SAUTÉ To fry food rapidly in a small amount of fat until evenly browned, shaking the pan to toss and turn the contents.

SCORE To make shallow cuts on the surface of food so that heat can penetrate during cooking.

SEA SALT Strong-flavoured salt from evaporated sea water, used in cooking.

SEASONED FLOUR Flour with salt and pepper mixed in, used to dust meat and fish before frying or stewing.

SIMMER To keep liquid just below boiling point, with only faint ripples showing on the surface.

SOUFFLÉ A baked sweet or savoury dish thickened with egg yolks and with whipped egg whites folded in just before cooking.

SOUSE To cover food—generally fish—with a mixture of vinegar, spices and water, and usually to cook it in the mixture.

STOCK Liquid that has absorbed the flavour of the fish, meat or vegetables cooked in it.

STRONG FLOUR Flour made from hard wheat that forms a strong elastic dough. Used mainly in bread-making.

SUET Dry, firm fat surrounding the loins and kidneys in beef or mutton.

THICKENING A preparation such as flour and butter, egg yolk or cream used to thicken and bind sauces and soups (see p. 35).

TRUSS To tie and skewer the legs and wings of poultry or game before roasting.

VANILLA SUGAR Sugar given a vanilla flavour (see p. 317).

VOL-AU-VENT A puff-pastry case, with a lid, that can be given a savoury filling after cooking.

WHEY The liquid part of curdled milk (see Curd).

ZEST The outer rind of citrus fruits, containing characteristic flavouring oils. To obtain the flavour, grate or pare the rind thinly, avoiding the pith.

INDEX

Where a number appears in bold, the recipe has an illustration.

A

B

C

D

G

H

I

J

K

L

M

N

O

P

Q

R

S

T

U V

W

Y

Z

Printed and bound in Great Britain by
BPCC Hazells Ltd
Member of BPCC Ltd

40.132.4